DATE DUE

DEMCO 38-296

A Hebrew Christian looks at ROMANS

A Hebrew looks at

Christian

ROMANS

10189

Sanford C. Mills

DUNHAM PUBLISHING COMPANY
GRAND RAPIDS, MICHIGAN 49506

A HEBREW CHRISTIAN LOOKS AT ROMANS

Dedicated to the Memory of
MILDRED M. MILLS
who accepted the Lord at the same time as the
author, and with love and unselfish devotion
worked with him in his ministry throughout
the years of their married life until her Lord
called her home in 1963. She never counted
the cost, but gave of herself unstintingly and
tirelessly to further the cause of Christ.

ACKNOWLEDGMENTS

It is with gratitude in my heart and praise upon my lips that I thank God for leading me to write this commentary on Paul's Epistle to the Romans. The work connected with it has taken three years of persistent research and study, three of the most rewarding years of my life. One result of this labor for the Lord has been a deepened conviction of my belief in the verbal, inerrant, and God-breathed inspiration of the Scriptures, in all the cardinal doctrines of our Christian faith, in the premillennial return of the Saviour and the pre-Tribulation rapture of all blood-bought believers in the Lord Jesus Christ.

I am greatly indebted to a number of friends for their untiring help in making this book possible: to the Rev. Noel P. Irwin, A.B., ThM., D.D., Pastor, Calvary Baptist Church of South Bend, Indiana, for his counsel and advice of differences of interpretation among the many gifted exegetes of Scripture and for his careful scrutiny of the entire work as to my wording and emphasis; to Mrs. Jack (Shirley) Burrell, of South Bend, Indiana, for her secretarial assistance and the hundreds of hours spent in typing the original manuscript; and to Mr. Roland Cole, former editorial assistant to the late Joseph Hoffman Cohn, General Secretary of the American Board of Missions to the Jews for many years (and son of the founder, Leopold Cohn) for the preparation of the manuscript for the printer and the compilation of the indexes to scriptural references. Without the help of these friends the publication of this work would have been delayed for months, perhaps for years.

We have used the American Standard Version (1901) as the basic text for our commentary, feeling that it best reflects the original languages.

This book, therefore, is sent forth with the prayer that it may draw the reader closer to God and the Saviour. May the Holy Spirit challenge every Christian, Gentile and Jew, who reads it and inspire in them an increased zeal in witnessing to Israel and expanding the work of Jewish missions.

SANFORD C. MILLS

New York, 1968

FOREWORD

"Of making books there is no end," and many have been written on the book of Romans. However, to my knowledge, this is the only one written by a Hebrew Christian.

The author, Dr. Sanford Mills, is especially well qualified for this task. Brought up in an Orthodox Jewish home, attending rabbinical schools; reading Biblical Hebrew fluently, having access to the ancient writings, such as the Talmud and Targum; and understanding the idioms of the Hebrew language, enable him to project himself into the thinking of the Apostle, whom God, the Holy Spirit, used to give us this wonderful Book. However, his book is not a collection of quotations of various authors and expositors, yet there are over 2,000 biblical references. This perspective of the background of Romans enables the reader to approach it from a different angle and to experience its atmosphere as well as to comprehend its teaching.

It has been my happy privilege to check the manuscript as it was written. The Scripture quotations are from the American Revised Version, and Nestle's Revised Text of the Greek New Testament was the basis of research. However, many other versions were compared in order to arrive at the most accurate teaching of the Apostle.

No doctrine taught in the book of Romans has been overlooked. The sinful condition of the world has been pointed out, placing the blame on Jews and Gentiles alike, thus making the preaching of the Gospel imperative to both Jews and Gentiles.

The doctrine of Justification has been fully covered, placing the work of Justification on the Godhead, where it properly belongs and putting man completely at the mercy of God to justify him.

The doctrine of Sanctification has been so intertwined with the doctrine of dedication that no reader of this book can escape the challenge of dedication as he is consistently brought face to face with his responsibility to God and man.

The doctrine of Believer's Baptism has been fully expounded and substantiated by the writings of the ancient and contemporary scholars of various denominations.

The two-fold nature of the believer has been clearly explained in treatment of chapter 7, closing with the victorious note that every believer has the assurance of victory over sin in Christ Jesus.

The familiar and important eighth chapter, dealing with the indwelling of the Holy Spirit has been carefully and minutely discussed, causing one to ascend into the heavenlies as he revels in its great truths assuring one of his eternal position in Christ which will evoke his hearty amen.

For years it has been the general consensus of expositors that the ninth, tenth and eleventh chapters form a great parenthesis, but this author has uniquely brought a new, and I believe proper, viewpoint to light by showing them to be *pivotal* rather than *parenthetical.* He shows them to be proof chapters of the preceding portions and foundational chapters for the closing four chapters of the book.

The Sovereignty of God has been Scripturally developed and substantiated. God must and does act independently of man and Dr. Mills explains this clearly. In the tenth chapter, man's responsibility in view of this Sovereignty of God has been elucidated. Though man has consistently failed in his responsibility to God, the eleventh chapter so carefully dealt with, clearly reveals that God's will for Israel must be fulfilled.

Every facet of Christian activity and behavior in the light of the doctrines of the previous portions, and God's actions on man's behalf, is carefully considered in chapters 12 through 16, so that the theoretical and practical are linked inseparably together in the plan of God and should be in the activity of man.

There is much vacillation and disputation in relation to the program of eschatology even in fundamental circles. One need never wonder concerning the position of the author of this book. I have been associated with Dr. Mills for more than twenty years and have found him to be a Christian gentleman, a firm believer in the pre-millennial, pre-tribulation rapture position of interpretation and one whose constant study and tireless research makes him an able expositor of the Word of God. In every chapter of the book these prophetic doctrines come up for treatment and many proof texts are presented. Although he is a Baptist, his writing is biblical and not biased. He has not skipped the difficult portion or evaded any teaching of the book.

While the scholarly approach of this commentary on the Epistle to the Romans makes it a valuable book for the student of The Word, yet its language and style make its teaching easily within the grasp of those who will revel in its blessed truths, simply from the devotional standpoint; and since it is the only verse-by-verse exposition by a Hebrew Christian, it is a valuable contribution to Jewish evangelism.

While there are more than 2,000 biblical quotations, yet this book is fresh exegesis and not merely an anthology, clarifying the position of the Jew in the program of the church and the perspective view of eschatology. One can expect this, since the writer is a Hebrew Christian. One reads the book and feels the heartbeat of a contemporary Hebrew Christian as he utters the ancient cry, "my heart's desire and prayer to God for Israel is, that they might be saved." I predict its wide acceptance and profitable ministry.

REV. NOEL P. IRWIN, A.B., Th.M., D.D.
Pastor, Calvary Baptist Church
South Bend, Indiana

INTRODUCTION

The *Letter to the Romans* was written by the Apostle Paul, who was a Hebrew Christian. It is therefore very fitting that a Hebrew Christian should write a commentary on this pivotal book of the New Testament Scriptures. Dr. Sanford Mills is eminently qualified to undertake this task.

Dr. Mills was born and reared in an orthodox Jewish home, and as a young man he accepted the Lord Jesus Christ as his Messiah. After his conversion he had to face the same questions which the Apostle Paul had to face after his conversion. Many of these questions were answered by the Holy Spirit through Paul in the *Letter to the Romans*.

Although *Romans* is essentially a book of doctrine, it is also a book that is vibrant with life. The Church at Rome was probably started by Jewish believers who found the Lord in Jerusalem on the Day of Pentecost (Acts 2:41). Hebrew Christians and Gentile Christians attended this church. Undoubtedly there were unbelieving Hebrews, as well as unbelieving Gentiles, who would read this letter. The questions which would naturally be asked by an Orthodox Jew, living at Rome during the first century, regarding the Gospel of the Lord Jesus Christ are exactly the same questions which a concerned religious Jew asks in the twentieth century.

As the apostle's ministry was largely one among the Gentiles, so Dr. Mills' ministry has been; but, also as Paul, wherever he has gone, he has always ministered to and won many Jews to the Lord Jesus Christ. It has been a joy to work together with Dr. Mills and to consider him a dear friend in the Lord.

We believe that this exposition will not only enlighten the reader's understanding of the Scriptures, it will also stimulate him to a further study and proclamation of that faith which staggers not "at the promise of God through unbelief; but was strong in faith, giving glory to God" (Romans 4:20 KJV).

DANIEL FUCHS
Secretary of the American Board of Missions to the Jews, Inc.
Editor of *The Chosen People* Magazine

CONTENTS

Acknowledgements

Foreword

Introduction

A Hebrew Christian
looks
at ROMANS

A HEBREW CHRISTIAN
LOOKS AT ROMANS

1

THE EPISTLE TO THE ROMANS was written approximately A.D. 60 by the Apostle Paul. Paul had nothing to do with the beginning and establishment of this church. The church at Rome was already a going institution. Its testimony was widespread. Church historians agree that the church at Rome was started by a person who, in the course of his travels, had stopped at the house of Cornelius and there heard the Gospel. Coming to Rome, he founded the church and its testimony was established. In writing this Epistle, Paul is seeking to impart some tremendous truths to this church. At the outset he introduces himself in the first two verses of chapter 1, as follows:

Verses 1 and 2: (1) Paul, a servant of Jesus Christ, called to be an apostle, separated unto the gospel of God, (2) which he promised afore through his prophets in the holy scriptures . . . .

Why did the Apostle use the name of Paul instead of Saul? The opinion of many is that Paul was the "converted" form of the name, Saul. This is not true. Any Jew of Orthodox background knows that the Jew has two names, one of which was given to him in the synagogue on the first Saturday succeeding his circumcision. This makes him a full member in the Congregation of Israel, and he is given a name by which he is known in the synagogue. Officially, a son born into a Jewish home does not become a member of the Congregation of Israel until he is circumcised. After his circumcision he becomes a child of the "Covenant," is given a name, and is then a member of the synagogue with his father. He is not a member of Israel until he assumes responsibility for sins, and that does not occur until

15

his "Bar Mitzvah," when he becomes a "Son of the Law." The name given him as a member of the synagogue is not the same which he uses in the world.

To give a personal illustration, the writer's given name in the synagogue is Sholom, which means peace. So the name Sanford, beginnning with the first letter of that Hebrew word Sholom, was given to him.

Paul, therefore, here addresses himself to the world and to the church at Rome, which was comprised of a number of Gentiles and a sprinkling of Jews. The Edict of the Roman Emperor had ordered the Jews to be expelled from the Seven Hills of Rome. However, the Edict had not yet been put in force, and no doubt there were a number of Jews in the Roman church.

Paul introduces himself as "a servant of Jesus Christ." He was not a servant in the modern sense, that is, one who was free to choose his employer, his kind of work, and to receive pay for it. The term used here is more accurately translated, "bondslave." In the Scriptures we have two types of slaves: One is a person who has encumbered himself with debts. Unable to pay, he is placed on the auction block and auctioned off to the highest bidder for a term of six years. The price which the highest bidder pays for the slave is divided among the slave's creditors. This should satisfy the debt and the debtors. He is to serve six years and be freed the seventh: "If thou buy a Hebrew servant, six years he shall serve: and in the seventh he shall go out free for nothing" (Exodus 21:2). The second type is one who during his six-year term of service as a slave has been lovingly treated by his master and generously provided for, and at the end of his term of service wishes to continue as a slave. He then becomes a bondslave forever. His master takes him to the doorpost of the store-house and bores through the lobe of his right ear with an awl. When the ear is healed the hole should be large enough to be visible from the front and back of the slave's head. Thereafter, such a slave can never again be sold to another master. For the rest of the slave's earthly life he is the "servant" or the "bondslave" of his master. He is owned, "lock, stock and barrel" for he has given himself completely to his master. He has no will of his own, no wish of his own, no whim of his own, nor has he a plan of his own, a purpose of his own, or a prerogative of his own. He has lost himself completely in the service of his master, and must serve him unceasingly.

Paul says in Romans 1:1 that he is "a servant" (or bondslave) of Jesus Christ. Why does Paul introduce himself as "a servant

of Jesus Christ?" Because on the Damascus Road, when the Lord
Jesus Christ appeared to Paul in a vision, he cried out, "Who
art thou, Lord"? (Acts 9:5). Paul called our Saviour, *Lord!* and
thereby sold himself to Jesus Christ, who, from that moment, became his Lord and his Saviour. Paul sold himself for life! Of his
own volition, of his own choosing, without any outside coercion
or compulsion, he accepted the Lord and thereby literally sold
himself to Jesus Christ. The price paid was the most colossal
price that could be conceived even by God Himself. It was the
price of the "precious blood of Jesus Christ," the Son of God.

You ask then, what has this to do with us? We, too, like Paul,
have become "bondslaves" of Jesus Christ. We, like Paul, have
been bought! ". . . knowing that ye were redeemed, not with
corruptible things, with silver or gold," says Peter in I Peter 1:
18, 19, ". . . but with precious blood . . . of Christ." So it is
with us, having had the same experience as Paul, without outside
influence, with no one standing over us holding a club in his
hands, saying, "Believe, or else!" Of our own choice, voluntarily,
and without compulsion, we accepted the Lord Jesus Christ and
became His "bondslaves."

Paul goes on to say that he is a *commissioned* apostle. Notice
carefully that in the 1901 American Standard Version the words
"to be" in verse 1 are in italics, and, therefore, are not in the
Greek. Preferably the phrase should read, "called an apostle."
Such was the high office of Paul, this great bondslave in the
service of God. It was a rare commission to have been a chosen
witness of the resurrection of the Saviour as many of the early
saints were. Paul, however, *spoke* to the Lord Jesus Christ after
His *ascension.*

Three times in the New Testament we have the record that
certain people saw the Lord Jesus Christ after His *ascension.*
The first was Stephen. He was being stoned to death, and, looking
up into heaven, he said he saw the Lord standing at the right
hand of the Father. Stephen became a beautiful type of the
Church. The next person who saw the Lord Jesus Christ after
His *ascension* is the apostle Paul. He says that he is as, "of one
born out of due time," by which he becomes a type of converted
Israel. Bear in mind that Paul was the Apostle to the Gentiles.
This was his unique ministry. With the exception of Peter, and
the conversion of Cornelius, the Gentiles did not hear the Gospel
until after Paul was converted. Neither will we have world-wide
revival until Israel is brought back into fellowship with God. The
converted Jewish nation will become God's emissaries, and will

carry the message of God to the four corners of the world, "For the earth shall be filled with the knowledge of the glory of Jehovah, as the waters cover the sea" (Habakkuk 2:14). The third time that we have a record of the Lord being seen after His resurrection and ascension is recorded in the book of Revelation (19:11) where John sees Him riding on "a white horse," coming to judge the Gentile nations.

Here then are three aspects of the second coming of Christ: First, the Rapture of the Church before the tribulation period. Second, Israel in "the time of Jacob's trouble," in her extremity, hears the voice of God, looks to heaven, and with the psalmist of old accepts Him and says, "Blessed be he that cometh in the name of the Lord" (Psalm 118:26; Matthew 23:39). Third, John sees Him coming in judgment to the nations to introduce the Davidic Kingdom.

Paul is God's bondslave, God's messenger, God's Apostle. He is Christ's witness because he saw Christ and spoke to Him. Paul is the chosen vessel. His commission is given in Acts 9:15, "But the Lord said unto him, Go thy way: for he is a chosen vessel unto me, to bear my name before the Gentiles and kings, and the children of Israel." We must realize there is no such thing, basically and fundamentally, as a ministry to the Gentiles alone. This is where the Church has failed so signally in evangelizing the Jew. Paul never lost sight of this. Paul constantly and continuously, whenever he came into a city, preached the Gospel to the people of Israel! Thus he was separated to the service of God, for he himself says he is "separated unto the gospel of God" (verse 1). He is above and apart from all rules, regulations, laws, and precepts of men, and separated unto the Gospel. Nothing must hinder this commission or calling! This message *is* the Gospel, it *is* the good tidings. It is the announcement of Jesus Christ, the Son of God, the Saviour of men in whom God is reconciling the world unto Himself. Thus Paul introduces himself as "separated."

Let us think of the three phases of Paul's separation. (1) ". . . who separated me, even from my mother's womb" (Galatians 1:15). This separation at birth is not a new concept of the New Testament. It is an Old Testament reality; see Jeremiah 1:4, 5. (2) ". . . he is a chosen vessel unto me" (Acts 9:15). This separation at Paul's conversion does not limit his ministry to the Gentiles. It is far broader in its scope; it is to preach to "the Gentiles and kings, and the children of Israel." (3) ". . . Separate unto me Barnabas and Saul (Paul)" (Acts 13:2).

The autonomy of the "local church" is clearly shown here. And it is done by the Holy Spirit Himself. Let us not lose sight of this important truth.

We have lost sight of this autonomy of the local church in much of our thinking. So engrossed are we with the thought of "carrying out a program," "joining a campaign," or "merging into a movement," that the autonomy of the local church has escaped us. In this New Testament age God has chosen to have the message of the Gospel of Jesus Christ carried on by the local church. The *local church* sends out its missionaries! Paul clearly says in verse 1 that he is "separated unto the gospel." But to be separated *unto* something you must be separated *from* something. In other words, if we say that we are Christians, then we must be *separated* from the world. Let us always remember that the name "Christian" is not given to the Christian as a sort of compliment. Originally, the writer believes, it was probably given in ridicule. ". . . the disciples were called 'Christians' first in Antioch" (Acts 11:26). When a person calls himself a Christian he must realize that he is separated *from* the world *unto* God. For instance, if one lives in New York and leaves New York to go to Philadelphia, one is separated from New York *unto* Philadelphia. One cannot be separated just into midair. One must be separated *from* something *to* something. Paul says that he is "separated unto the gospel of God." The Gospel is the message of God, and it is God-given. We cannot deviate one iota from the gospel message. The moment we preach anything else we are immediately out of God's will. Preaching the Gospel is not the same as passing laws to elevate mankind or improve society. We cannot have a changed community, we cannot have a righteous community merely by passing good laws. A righteous community can become a righteous community only by righteous individuals who are a part of it. The message of the Gospel of Jesus Christ is to individuals. We must carry the redeeming message of God to a sin-cursed and dying world.

Paul so carefully states, "I determined not to know anything among you, save Jesus Christ, and him crucified" (I Corinthians 2:2). Again he says, ". . . for woe is unto me, if I preach not the gospel" (I Corinthians 9:16). Now what *is* the Gospel of Jesus Christ? Rather than to state what the Gospel is in our own words, let us look at I Corinthians 15:3, 4, "For I delivered unto you first of all that which I also received: that Christ died for our sins according to the scriptures; and that he was buried; and that he hath been raised on the third day according to the scriptures." Let us bear in mind the words, "according to the scriptures," for Paul says in Romans 1:2, ". . . which he promised afore through his prophets in the holy scriptures."

One criticism leveled against Christianity is that it was Paul who introduced Christianity to the world. The Jews say that the Christianity preached by Paul was not the same as that which was preached by Jesus Christ. Paul, we are told, was the one who changed the message and spread Christianity throughout the world, and that Paul's preaching was foreign to the preaching of Christ. But Paul nullifies this statement, for he says, ". . . according to the scriptures," and it was "promised afore through his prophets."

Now think in these terms for a moment: Remember that the Gospel is not a New Testament revelation. The Church *is* a New Testament revelation. The Gospel was preached and was established even as far back as the Garden of Eden, as recorded in Genesis 3:15. A careful study of the eleventh chapter of the Epistle to the Hebrews will show this to be true. In John 8:56, the Lord Jesus said to the Jews, "Your father Abraham rejoiced to see my day." What is the difference, basically and fundamentally, between Jacob who on his dying bed said, "I have waited for thy salvation, O Lord" (Genesis 49:18), and us who are born-again believers, when we sing, "Thank You Lord for saving my soul"? Jacob in the seventeenth century B.C. and we today are still talking of the same Christ. We are still talking of the same Person, the same program, the same plan, the same hope.

Is the story of a Saviour being born in Bethlehem (Matthew 2:1) a New Testament revelation only? It is not. In Micah 5:2 there is also the Christmas story: "But thou, Bethelehem Ephrathah, which art little to be among the thousands of Judah, out of thee shall one come forth unto me that is to be ruler in Israel; whose goings forth are from of old, from everlasting." So we see that it is not a New Testament revelation only, but an Old Testament revelation as well. Moreover, the New Testament record of our Lord's entry into Jerusalem in Matthew 21:5, on the day which is now known as Palm Sunday, is also found in the Old Testament: "Rejoice greatly, O daughter of Zion; shout, O daughter of Jerusalem: behold, thy king cometh unto thee; he is just, and having salvation; lowly, and riding upon an ass, even upon a colt the foal of an ass" (Zechariah 9:9). Here is the triumphal entry into Jerusalem! Here is Palm Sunday!

Is the story of the crucifixion found only in the New Testament? In Psalm 22, we read: "My God, My God, why hast thou forsaken me?" (v. 1); ". . . all my bones are out of joint" (v. 14); ". . . my tongue cleaveth to my jaws" (v. 15); ". . . they pierced my hands and my feet" (v. 16). Is not this the crucifixion? The fact is, Psalm 22 makes no sense whatsoever unless it is placed, so to speak, at the foot of the cross. These references to Christ in the Old Testament are prophetic. The Lord Jesus Christ "was despised, and rejected of men," as is recorded in Isaiah 53:3; and again in verse 6, "All we like sheep have gone astray; we have turned every one to his own way; and the Lord hath laid on him the iniquity of us all." The Old Testament is full of promises of a coming Messiah who is to rule and reign and who will speak in parables.

The flyleaf of the Talmud, which is the Jewish commentary on the Old Testament, opens with the words, "All the prophets prophesied not, but for the days of the Messiah." (*Sanhedrin* 99a). It is also recorded in Sanhedrin 98b, "The world was not created but only for the Messiah." It is of great interest to read in the Book of Acts (17:28), ". . . for in him we live, and move, and have our being . . ." (or our existence). What is this but an elaboration of these two Talmudic passages?

The Gospel is not new. Basically and fundamentally the Gospel is Jewish, Jewish in origin, Jewish in its message, ". . . for salvation is from the Jews" (John 4:22). It is *not* from the Gentiles. Paul says in the Epistle to the Ephesians (2:1) that they "were dead through your trespasses and sins"; that they were at that time without hope, and "without God in the world" (2:12). Therefore, the Saviour came into the world, born to Israel. It was a national birth (Luke 2:11), but a universal salvation that was wrought on the cross (John 1:29), and this Gospel must be adhered to by all, even the Jews. Since it was given to the prophets by God, it is divine revelation, and it is recorded in God's Book by the Holy Spirit. Consequently, the Lord Himself made this charge and accusation against the people of Israel, "For if ye believed Moses, ye would believe me; for he wrote of me" (John 5:46). Hence, God's Word *is* the Holy Scriptures. These Scriptures speak of a Holy God. They must be our final authority, the only authority.

This is why Paul tells Timothy to "preach the word" (II Timothy 4:2). When we begin to deviate from the Word of God, when we begin to question it, we are on dangerous ground. Scripture is either all of God, or it is not of God at all.

Scripture is God's revelation to us. It is truth which we must accept.

In Scripture there are many things that we are unable to explain. In these days we hear a number of questions raised about the Word of God. These questions and doubts are among the signs of the closing of the age. The Word of God must always be the final authority. We cannot, we must not, question it. We might not be able to explain every "jot and tittle" of the Law and the prophets, but the Word of God is something that we must adhere to because it must always be "thus saith the Lord." We cannot, we must not, question the Word of God, because when we begin to question the Word of God we begin to question God Himself. God has given to us a perfect revelation. Remember that the Gospel must be adhered to even by the Jews. This revelation is universal! It is for the entire world. "Hear ye the Word of the Lord" must be the message of the Church. This Gospel reveals to us a perfect Saviour; a perfect salvation with an eternal plan. Therefore, we cannot question the Word of God in any sense or under any circumstance. We must accept it by faith, and "faith cometh by hearing, and hearing by the word of God" (Romans 10:17 KJV).

Verse 3: . . . concerning his Son, who was born of the seed of David according to the flesh . . .

". . . concerning his Son." *This is the Gospel.* The second verse was written to show that the Gospel of God was not new, but was "promised afore through his prophets in the holy scriptures." And surely, by now, we realize that this was done with the Jew in mind. Although Paul was the Apostle to the Gentiles, God called him as a witness to the Jews. Such passages as Isaiah 53, and the others that we have dealt with, show us that the Gospel is not new. Romans 1 deals with the entire Gospel, our Lord's death, His burial, and His resurrection. Having proved this point Paul now picks up the thought that he first referred to in verse 1 in which he referred to himself as being "separated unto the gospel of God." This Gospel of God is concerning His Son. The Gospel of God — the entire Gospel — is contained in the knowledge of Jesus Christ so that whoever departs one step from Him departs from the Gospel.

The Gospel is contained in the words that the Lord Himself used, "And I, if I be lifted up from the earth, will draw all men unto myself" (John 12:32). The Saviour sets before us in this text the real object of our faith. The words, "concerning his

Son," place emphasis upon the one important thing. This *One* is not an ordinary person! This *One* is not just a mere human being! This *One* was not conceived through an earthly father! This *One* is *God's eternal Son!* For the first and only time in the history of mankind God is incarnate in human form. God had spoken to Adam, to Noah, to Abraham, to Isaac, and to Jacob, through angels and the prophets, and He had spoken even "mouth to mouth" with some of His prophets. But in the Gospel God has "spoken unto us in his Son," as recorded in the Epistle to the Hebrews (1:2). This Son was not conceived in the ordinary manner, but He was conceived of the Holy Spirit. This Son is perfect; He is omnipotent, omniscient, and omnipresent. This Son is "the seed of the woman" of Genesis 3:15. It was not the seed of the man, for sin came into the world by Adam (Romans 5:12). There was no sin in the Son, namely, Christ. He is the "Alpha and the Omega" of the Gospel. He is "the Way," "the Truth," and "the Life." He is *LIFE,* and God proved it by the resurrection. He is the "Head of the body," the Church, and gives life to it. He is the "Root" which renders the branches fruitful.

This is our reason for stating that "our life is hid with Christ in God." "We have been planted together with Him"; "buried with him by baptism into death." This is the true picture of baptism — the old nature buried in the waters of baptism and rising again "a new creature" in Christ Jesus. This is beautiful typology, portraying the believer as alive unto God as we are brought out of the waters of baptism. The Gospel transforms a person from immaturity to maturity. God expects this of us, going to greater heights for God. We *must!* Hebrews 6:1 (KJV) reads, "Therefore leaving (this in the Greek is in the past tense, *having left*) the principles of the doctrine of Christ, let us go on unto perfection; not laying again the foundation of repentance from dead works." God expects us to go on. We should go on to the full growth. We must mature — we must grow! We cannot remain spiritual babes. If we do, we become spiritual misfits, and in the final analysis we become stumbling blocks. This is a challenge for holy living. We must manifest that holy life even "in your body" (I Corinthians 6:20).

Let us take a closer look at verse 3, ". . . who was born of the seed of David," or, as it is in the King James Version, ". . . which was made of the seed of David according to the flesh," that is, according to His human nature. This does not denote corruption, but, rather, points to another nature, the nature of Deity.

Our Lord is the "son of David" and He is the "Son of God."
The word that is translated "was made," can be more accurately
translated "became." It is the same word used in the Gospel of
John, 1:14, "the Word was made flesh, and dwelt among us." It
is again used in Galatians 4:4, "But when the fulness of time was
come, God sent forth his Son, made of a woman." The verb
made in the Greek is so constructed as to mean the taking on of
a "new condition," that is, made flesh. This proves conclusively
that Christ was pre-existent with the Father. When born into
this world He took on a new nature. To use a more concrete
example, a clearer example: We wear shoes made of calfskin.
We can truthfully say, "These shoes were made of a calf's
skin, but now they are shoes" — showing a new nature or a new
condition.

When the Roman Catholic Church announces that "Mary is
the mother of God," the statement is as far from the truth as
the east is from the west. It is a complete misstatement of
Scripture. What Mary mothered was not God! What Mary
mothered was a body for God to indwell. In the "fulness of
time," when that embryo was fully developed, it was brought
forth as the eternal Christ incarnate. Never lose sight of this
fact. Do not be misled by any false Romish doctrine. The flesh
is not God; it is merely the tabernacle in which God dwells.
This verse (3) tells us of our Lord's humanity — "concerning
his Son, who was born of the seed of David according to the
flesh" (ASV). What Paul had in mind evidently in verse 3 is,
perhaps, an elaboration of Isaiah 9:6 (ASV), "For unto us a
child is born, unto us a son is given; and the government shall
be upon his shoulder: and his name shall be called Wonderful,
Counsellor, Mighty God, Everlasting Father, Prince of Peace."
Do we not see here that the prophet Isaiah is saying what Paul
is also saying; namely, that "a child is born" and a "son is given"
in the flesh, and that this one born in the flesh is "The mighty
God" (KJV)?

A book which this writer has been reading for some time is
a Targum on the interpretation of the book of Isaiah. Tradition-
ally, the authorship of this Targum is assigned to a man called
Johnathan ben Uzziel, the disciple of Hillel. It is interesting to
read how this Targum interprets Isaiah 9:6. It reads thus: "The
prophet saith to the House of David, a child has been born to us,
a Son has been given to us, and He has taken the law upon
Himself to keep it, and His name has been called from old,
Wonderful Counselor, Mighty God, He who lives forever; the

anointed one (or the Messiah), in whose days, peace shall increase upon us."

This quotation from the Targum looks back to a coming in past time, and not forward to a future coming. Israel is now looking back to what has become historic, this "child" *has been* born to us, a "Son" *has been* given to us. And this is the meaning of verse 6 in Isaiah 9 in Hebrew, but how sad it is that Israel has not accepted it!

Verse 3, and the foregoing comment upon it, proves the humanity of the Saviour. This is the eternal Christ "becoming" flesh. This is the Word which "became flesh," as John says in 1:14 (ASV) ". . . (and we beheld his glory, glory as of the only begotten from the Father), full of grace and truth."

Verse 4: . . . who was declared to be the Son of God with power, according to the spirit of holiness, by the resurrection from the dead; even Jesus Christ our Lord . . . .

This fourth verse is most interesting: ". . . who was declared (or declared *to be*) the Son of God." The phrase ". . . even Jesus Christ our Lord," is not in the King James Version. But let us look at this phrase more carefully. The third verse in the King James Version reads, "Concerning his Son Jesus Christ our Lord, *which was made* of the seed of David according to the flesh . . .". The American Standard Version reads, ". . . concerning his Son, *who was born* of the seed of David according to the flesh . . .". Notice that Paul does not say that the Son of God "became" but that He was *made* (KJV) or *born* (ASV); and the fourth verse in both Versions reads, "*declared* to be the Son of God with power." The Greek word which is translated "declared," could be translated, "defined" or "demonstrated." The expression, "the Son of God," definitely implies Deity. As in the third verse, so in the fourth verse, Paul is careful to establish once and for all the *Deity* of Jesus Christ. Having established this fact he moves on, as the prophet Isaiah moves on, in calling this child that was born, and this Son that was given, The mighty God (KJV). These words, "The mighty God," are used to describe Jehovah Himself. Moreover, the Rabbis also say that these words refer to the Messiah. He was designated to be the "Son of God," and this expression, "The Son of God," definitely means Deity.

Philippians 2:6 (ASV) reads: "Who, existing in the form of God, counted not the being on an equality with God a thing to be grasped, but emptied himself, taking the form of a servant, being made in the likeness of men; and being found in fashion as a man, he humbled himself, becoming obedient even unto death, yea, the death of the cross." Notice the expression, "existing in the form of God." People have asked me, "Do you believe that Jesus Christ is like God?" I reply, "No, I don't believe He is *like* God." Amazed they ask, "What do you mean, He is not like God?" To which I always answer emphatically, "In every sense of the word He is not *like* God, He *is* God! To repeat, He *is* God!"

Similar references to God as "God Almighty": and "The mighty God" are found throughout the Bible. In Exodus 3:14, God Almighty is speaking to Moses. Moses wants to know what he shall say to the children of Israel when they ask him who sent him, and what name he shall use. God answers Moses, "Tell them, I AM THAT I AM, hath sent thee." The literal translation of this phrase is, "I will be that I will be, hath sent thee." It is in the future tense. How beautifully this is confirmed in John 8:24. When the Saviour faces Israel He says, "Except ye believe that I am." Interestingly enough, the Greek translation of the Old Testament called the Septuagint has the same thought in it as the original Hebrew. Jesus Christ is not only the I AM, but He is the "I WAS," the "I WILL BE," the eternal one.

In Matthew 16:15 the Saviour asks His disciples, "But who say ye that I am" (ASV). Simon Peter replies, "Thou art the Christ." This states His person and His office. But Simon Peter doesn't finish there; he adds, "the Son of the living God." When Simon Peter makes this statement he is stating our Lord's nature. "The living God," is His nature, and, "Thou art the Christ," is His person and office. So Jesus is called God's own Son, the "only begotten Son of God." Christ is God's "own Son" because He is His Son by nature and not by adoption. Only Christ could have said, "I and my Father are one." The Jews fully understood that Jesus claimed co-equality and unity with God. That is why they accused Him of blasphemy in John 10:33.

The resurrection proved the unique sonship of Jesus Christ, and forever sealed the truth that every believer will be raised from the dead. It was the full accomplishment of the resurrection which, more than anything else, declared Him to be the Son of God. The literal sense of the Greek words, "the resurrection *from* the dead," would, perhaps, be better translated, "the resurrection *of* the dead." The thought is that Christ *is* the resurrection of the dead! He Himself said so at the grave of Lazarus. He said, "I am the resurrection and the life." If He *is* "the resurrection" — and you may be sure He *is* — then His own resurrection is a foregone conclusion, isn't it? Didn't He so state in John 2:19, "Destroy this temple, and in three days I will raise it up"? The resurrection, then, was the "power" of Christ. It was the "resurrection *of* the dead."

You ask, *"When was* the resurrection *of* the dead; when did *that* take place?"* This writer has his own conviction on this question. Too many times we read the Scriptures superficially. Remember the passage in Hebrews 11 where the author of the Epistle defines the meaning of faith, and refers to many Old Testament saints who displayed their faith; and where he states at the end of the chapter, ". . . God having provided some better thing concerning us, that apart from us they should not be made perfect" (Hebrews 11:40).

This writer believes that the resurrection of the saints took place after the resurrection of the Saviour. In reading the Word of God we have to read it a little more carefully. Matthew 27:51-53 reads this way, "And behold, the veil of the temple was rent in two from the top to the bottom; and the earth did quake; and the rocks were rent; and the tombs were opened; and many bodies of the saints that had fallen asleep were raised; and coming forth out of the tombs *after his resurrection* they entered into the holy city and appeared unto many" (ASV). Notice verse 53, "after his resurrection." This "resurrection of the dead" did not take place *before* the resurrection of the Saviour. The verse reads, "and coming forth out of the tombs after his resurrection (that is, Christ's resurrection) they entered into the holy city and appeared unto many." Only those saints who had been recently buried, and who had people in Jerusalem who knew them, appeared unto them in Jerusalem, as it says, ". . . they entered into the holy city and appeared unto many." Verses 52 and 53 are undoubtedly parenthetical. They brush aside the curtain of history and give us a glimpse of what happened after Christ's resurrection. This, to the present writer, seals the fact that like them we, too, shall be raised from the dead. What a marvelous comfort this is!

The "resurrection OF the dead" was the "power" of Christ. The phrase ". . . according to the spirit of holiness," in Romans 1:4, does not, in any sense of the word, point to the Third Person of the Trinity, the Holy Spirit. It is the spirit of Christ Himself. This whole fourth verse is endeavoring to do one thing, and one thing alone, and that is to prove conclusively and positively the Deity of the Lord Jesus Christ. As in the third verse, Paul proves the humanity of our Lord, so now, in the fourth verse, he is proving His Deity. This "spirit of holiness" is the "spirit" of Christ Himself which is spoken of, as distinguished from His flesh, and is Christ's attribute as the second Person of the Trinity. Remember, He is God the Son as much as God the Father and God the Holy Spirit. There is no less power and no less holiness in Christ than there is in God the Father or in God the Holy Spirit. (Don't ask here for an explanation of the Trinity; it is not within the scope of this present study.) To state that "the spirit of holiness" is Christ's attribute as the Second Person of the Trinity, is only saying that He is God.

The King James Version of Romans 1:4 does not have the next phrase, "even Jesus Christ our Lord," which appears only in the American Standard Version. This phrase is an extremely important statement. The Greek word for Lord is *qurion* and is the key to the whole phrase. This word *qurion* in the Septuagint version of the Old Testament stands for or takes three different Hebrew words; namely, Lord, God, and Jehovah, and translates them by the one word *qurion*. Actually, verse 4 of Romans 1 is saying, "who was declared to be the son of God with power, according to the spirit of holiness, by the resurrection of the dead; even Jesus Christ our Lord, God, Jehovah." In other words, Jesus Christ is God, who is Jehovah.

In evangelical circles when believers are invited to become Christians, we quote Romans 10:9, 10 (KJV), "If thou shalt confess with thy mouth the Lord Jesus, and shalt believe in thine heart that God hath raised him from the dead, thou shalt be saved. For with the heart man believeth unto righteousness; and with the mouth confession is made unto salvation." Looking at these words more closely and a little more carefully in the American Standard Version we find they read, "If thou shalt confess with thy mouth Jesus as Lord." This is the key. Basically, we do not confess the Lord Jesus Christ as "Saviour," we confess Him as LORD, Jehovah. If we were to paraphrase what the Apostle Paul is saying in Romans 10:9, 10, it would read as follows: "If thou shalt confess with thy mouth what your heart already believes, that Jesus Christ is Lord, or Jehovah, and that Jehovah or God has raised Him from the dead, thou shalt be saved. For with the heart man believeth unto righteousness; and with the mouth confession is made (that which the heart already believes) unto salvation." You see, the confession is that Jesus Christ is Lord.

Remember what happened on the road to Damascus when Paul, with papers in hand, was going forth to persecute and arrest the believers in Jesus Christ? He was going to destroy them

if it were in his power to do so. Walking along that road he was
suddenly confronted by a terrific light, a blinding light, and because of it he fell to the earth. It amazed him. Out of this blinding light came a Voice saying, "Saul, Saul, why persecutest thou
me?" (Acts 9:4). Paul said, "Who art thou, Lord?" The Voice replied, "I am Jesus whom thou persecutest." Paul, a Pharisaic Jew,
knew of a certainty, having been taught all his life that there
would be only one Voice out of heaven, that that Voice could
come from no One else but the Lord God Almighty Himself.
What Paul actually said was, "Who art thou, Jehovah?" Without
qualification, without any correction, the Lord Jesus Christ replied, "I am Jesus whom thou persecutest." Paul accepted Jesus
Christ as his Lord, as his Master, and as his Owner. This is
merely the elaboration of what Paul says in Romans 1:1, "Paul, a
servant (or bondslave) of Jesus Christ." He has been bought by
God Almighty as His eternal bondservant! And Paul said, "Lord,
what wilt thou have me to do? And the Lord said unto him,
Arise, and go." When God speaks to us, we must obey. We must
realize that when we are speaking to God we are not speaking
to a human being. Let us stop referring to the Lord Jesus
Christ merely as "Jesus." He is Jesus Christ our Lord. Let us
stop addressing God by the familiar personal pronoun "you" as if
He were a human being like ourselves. The King James Version
and the American Standard Version use "thou" when addressing
God, and "you" when speaking to man. In Jewish and German
there is a different word used when speaking to someone of our
own age and social stratum. When addressing someone older, or
someone in a higher social stratum, the word "thou," is used, or
its equivalent in Jewish or German. There is something respectful,
even exalted, about the word "thou," which implies reverence
when addressing Deity, and respect when addressing men.
Thus, when Moses came into the presence of God, he was so
overwhelmed by the holiness of God that he exclaimed, "If I
have found favor in thy sight!"

Let us realize that when we accept the Lord Jesus Christ
and His finished work on the cross, we have been washed in His
blood, we have been made whiter than snow; and that when we
accept His resurrection *from* the dead, and *of* the dead, it gives
us that great assurance which is expressed in His own words,
"Because I live, ye shall live also" (John 14:19), and, also, in the
words of Philip to Nathanael, "We have found him, of whom
Moses in the law, and the prophets did write" (John 1:45). At
His second coming we shall see Him in His full glory, in His full

power. "Wherefore God hath also highly exalted him, and given him a name which is above every name: that at the name of Jesus every knee should bow . . . and that every tongue should confess." Confess what? Confess that Jesus is Lord God Almighty to the glory of God the Father. Have we done that? Unless we have — unless we have accepted Him as God Almighty dying on the cross for our sins, without spot, without blemish, without sin — we are in jeopardy of being separated eternally from God Almighty. This, in a nutshell, is the Gospel of Jesus Christ. This is the "Gospel of God" "concerning His Son." It centers about His Son! It is the elaboration of His Son! This is the fulness of the revelation of the godhead, the complete revelation! Therefore, "God, who at sundry times and in divers manners spake in time past unto the fathers by the prophets, hath in these last days spoken unto us by his Son" (Hebrews 1:1, 2, KJV). This is the finality of it. Now redemption has been wrought. This is the meaning — the full meaning — of the words, "It is finished." In reality they actually mean, "It is accomplished."

What is accomplished? Salvation. Everything that God had sent His Son to do. Therefore, at the close of His ministry, even before His death, lifting up His eyes to Almighty God, His Father in heaven, He said, "I have glorified thee on the earth . . . (now) glorify thou me with thine own self with the glory which I had with thee before the world was" (John 17:4, 5 KJV). He had accomplished everything that God had sent Him to do. He redeemed all of creation; and all this has been done for you and for me who are believers in Jesus Christ, and for all others who will accept Him.

Verses 5 and 6: (5) . . . through whom we received grace and apostleship, unto obedience of faith among all the nations (Gentiles), for his name's sake; (6) . . . among whom are ye also, called to be Jesus Christ's . . . .

Thus, in these two verses, Paul goes on to say that we are our Lord's possession.

Verse 7: . . . to all that are in Rome, beloved of God, called to be saints: Grace to you and peace from God our Father and the Lord Jesus Christ.

Certainly not one of us in the flesh looks saintly. No matter what we think of ourselves, when we have accepted Jesus Christ **as** Lord, we are saved and sanctified, and in God's sight glorified, inasmuch as we are waiting for the hour of glorification that will come. For we are God's loved ones, called, divinely summoned, or, as the Greek word means, set apart. Thus a saint is a sinner who has placed his faith in Christ, who has been set apart by the Holy Spirit of God, set apart from sin to holiness. Romans 1:7 definitely calls for separation, something that God demands of us. It is a command. We must live holy lives because we have been delivered from the power of Satan by the Spirit of Almighty God Himself.

We have been taken out of the first Adam, which was of sin and death, into the last Adam, which is Jesus Christ, to live a life of separation and one that will portray and mirror the holiness and sanctity of a Christian life. This is the true meaning of the word "saint." A separated life! This is God's name for His followers. The word "Christian" denotes them to be Christ's ones. "The disciples were called Christians first in Antioch" (Acts 11:26). Whether this name was given to them by the world or by God has been argued. Be that as it may, we are to live as Christ's ones. The world will never know anything of Jesus Christ apart from our testimony. We are the ones who are to go into the world not only to preach but also to portray the Christian life. Thus the admonition in verse 7, "to all that are in Rome, beloved of God, called to be saints. . . ."

Verse 8: First, I thank my God through Jesus Christ for you all, that your faith is proclaimed throughout the whole world.

This verse speaks of the faith of the church at Rome. It is strange that one can read this verse and fail to contrast it with the condition of the church of Rome today. What a contrast! It is a truer picture of the failure of Christian testimony than anything else that could be named, because if Christians had continued in the "faith which was once delivered unto the saints" and contended for it, the apostolic faith would not have become corrupted by Romish doctrine. Nothing portrays this departure from the truth more strikingly than comparing the church *of* Rome in its present condition with the church *at* Rome at the time when Paul said that the believers' faith was "proclaimed throughout the whole world." This shows us the extent of the departure from the Word of God which followed apostolic Christianity. How can anyone, with this condition before him, speak of the "progress" which Christianity has made in these nineteen centuries? Nor is the corruption of the church *of* Rome an isolated instance. A similar charge can be brought against many so-called Christian churches today. Numbers have departed from the truth. Not many years after the early Christians had passed from the picture, several of the ancient cities in which good strong churches had been established in the first century with a living testimony of a living Christ, were overrun by either Mohammedanism, apostasy, ritualism, false cultism, demonism, or superstition. This fact alone should teach us that there has been a "progress of darkness" in many areas. Men speak of the "development of Christianity," but if we were to analyze the progress of so-called Christianity in the areas mentioned we would see clearly that it is a progression of evil and not of good — a progression of darkness, not light. What a challenge it is to us who are true believers in the Lord Jesus Christ, when Paul says to us, "your faith is proclaimed (or testified to, or spoken of) throughout the whole world!"

Verses 9, 10, 11: (9) For God is my witness, whom I serve in my spirit in the gospel of his Son, how unceasingly I make mention of you, always in my prayers (10) making request, if by any means now at length I may be prospered by the will of God to come unto you. (11) For I long to see you, that I may impart unto you some spiritual gift, to the end ye may be established....

Notice Paul says that he prays for the church at Rome "unceasingly." How can *we* pray unceasingly when we are working at a desk, no matter what kind of work it is? You see, we must realize that when we accept Jesus Christ, God's Son, as our Lord and Saviour, we should no longer say, as we many times do, "Lord, we come into Thy presence." We must realize that from the moment we accept the Lord as our Saviour, from the time we have made that public profession and have become truly converted, from that moment on, the Saviour never leaves us. We are never out of His presence. He is always beside us. He is not looking over our shoulder, but rather, as Paul says, "he is not far from each one of us: for in him we live, and move, and have our being" (Acts 17:27, 28). We can always talk to Him, under all circumstances. He is always there! No wonder Paul says that he prays "unceasingly" for the church at Rome and that he might be prospered by the will of God to ". . . impart unto you some spiritual gift, to the end ye may be established" (v. 11).

We wonder what spiritual gifts some pastors impart to their churches when they give a book review, or when they tell stories, or "cunningly devised fables," or present anything but the

Gospel of the Lord Jesus Christ? Paul's desire was to come to the church at Rome that he might enrich the church with the knowledge of the truth which they had accepted. He wanted to impart to them some "spiritual gift" to the end that they "may be established." What a crying need this is in our churches today! Christians are anything but "established." We are "carried about with every wind of doctrine" (Ephesians 4:14) and every "ism." Often as I have visited fundamental churches, pastors have confided in me some of their problems, among them the one having to do with "good" members of their congregations who have "gone off" on some tangent and joined an "ism." One reason for this "falling away" on the part of church members is our failure to establish our people in the faith. We do not root them and ground them in the truth of the Word of God. Because of this failure on our part they are snatched up by these carnal isms and sects, which glorify the flesh rather than the spirit. Paul says in this Epistle that he wants to come to them, that he may impart unto them "some spiritual gift, to the end ye may be established" in the faith. How needful this is!

Verse 12: . . . that is, that I with you may be comforted in you (or among you), each of us by the other's faith, both yours and mine.

In other words, at no time can any true minister of the Word of God stand before his people and teach and preach to them without being just as greatly comforted and established in the faith as they.

Verse 13 needs no elaboration.

Verse 14: I am debtor both to Greeks and to Barbarians, both to the wise and to the foolish.

We know that when Rome overran the Grecian Empire and subdued it she did not destroy the Grecian civilization, but grafted it into the language and culture of Rome. Greek was taught in the schools and spoken by the intelligentsia. So Paul says that he is "debtor both to Greeks and to Barbarians" and then elaborates upon this statement by adding ". . . both to the wise and to the foolish."

We must realize that the Gospel knows no bounds as to race, creed or social stratum. Just because a man happens to be a leader in society, in politics, or a profession, does not mean that he is not in need of the Gospel. No matter what stratum of society one moves in, no matter whether one is "down and out" or "up and in," so to speak, every one without the Gospel is lost and hell-bound in the sight of God. This is the reason we are debtors to all men. Paul is saying in effect that he is "debtor" to the aristocracy and "debtor" to the proletariat — the uneducated, the uncivilized, the unilluminated. Today we are more concerned over the person who has gone to the depths of sin, who has debased and debauched his life, and has spent most of his time in this world's "tents of wickedness" (Psalm 84:10), than we are concerned over the merely inoffensive and law-abiding sinner. When a social outcast accepts Christ as Lord and Saviour, we are inclined to exult over him. There is a tendency today in evangelistic work to feel that success in winning souls for Christ is achieved more readily when the evangelist has been an "ex" something — an ex-drunkard, an ex-gambler, an ex-rapist, an ex-prostitute, and that there is something about hearing converted sinners of this kind describe their former lives of sin that will help the unsaved to become saved. Far be it from this writer to minimize the work of our rescue missions and their efforts to save the souls of society's castaways. The aristocrat with his "gold ring and fine clothing" (James 2:2) can be just as sinful and immoral as any derelict. There can be just as great immorality in high society as in the so-called "lower levels" of life. People who know nothing about society often have greater ethics than our socialites. Paul makes no distinction — "I am debtor both to Greeks and to Barbarians, both to the wise and to the foolish" (v. 14), because all are lost.

Verse 15: So, as much as in me is, I am ready to preach the gospel to you also that are in Rome.

Thus writes the Apostle with all the power and conviction he can muster in his own heart and soul. The church at Rome was an established church, yet Paul says that he is ready to preach the Gospel to its members. The Gospel which Paul is ready to preach is the redeeming love of God and that Paul is coming "to establish" the church at Rome! That is, he is coming to give the church greater truths so that they may be wise in their understanding and be instructed in this "calling" of being a Christian. By instructing and by teaching them the Word of God and the truth of God they will be able to withstand "the wiles of the devil," and their souls will be encouraged, their hearts will be quickened.

The method that Paul is using is the question-and-answer

method. The Epistle to the Romans contains a great many questions and answers. Let us look at some of them: Romans 3:1 — "What advantage then hath the Jew? or what is the profit of circumcision?" Romans 3:5 — "But if our unrighteousness commendeth the righteousness of God, what shall we say? Is God unrighteous who visiteth with wrath?" Romans 3:9 — "What then? are we better than they? No, in no wise." Romans 3:29 — "Is God the God of Jews only? is he not the God of Gentiles also?" Romans 3:31 — "Do we then make the law of none effect through faith?" Romans 4:1-3 — "What then shall we say that Abraham, our forefather, hath found according to the flesh? For if Abraham were justified by works, he hath whereof to glory; but not toward God. For what saith the scripture?" Romans 7:7 — "What shall we say then? Is the law sin? God forbid." Romans 7:13 — "Did then that which is good become death unto me? God forbid."

We see that the Gospel is more than preaching "the redeeming love of God." The child of God must be firmly established in the faith to enable him to refute false doctrines and false accusations against the Word of God. To be able to say with Paul, "O man, who art thou that repliest against God?" (9:20), we must conclude that it is not simply a question of receiving the truth but we must be fortified against falsehood.

Verse 16: For I am not ashamed of the gospel (of Christ): for it is the power of God unto salvation to every one that believeth; to the Jew first, and also to the Greek.

The words, "the power of God," are significant. Remember, Rome, while it was a city, was also an empire where power was the keynote. Rome was then the headquarters of the greatest power in the world. But it was only human power. As victors the Romans overran the vanquished. Their power was everywhere predominant. In Romans 1:16 Paul is contrasting the power of Rome with the power of God. The power of Rome had as its goal, destruction, debauchery, the degradation of the vanquished. On the other hand, the power of God has as its goal, salvation, separation, transformation and translation. The power of the Gospel will deliver a sinner from sin, from trials, from tribulation, from torments, from hell, and from failure and tears. The Gospel in the final analysis, is God's offer of escape from all these evils.

The word for "power" in the Greek means omnipotent power — strength, energy, authority. It is so used in Matthew 26:64,

Luke 22:69 and Mark 14:62. It also means miraculous power, and is so used in Mark 5:30, Luke 1:35, and in many other places. The word is also translated "miracle" in Matthew 11: 20, 21, and elsewhere.

The Gospel's power is not demonstrated by argument, but rather by what it does. It brings salvation. Paul's life is a testimony and a proof of that when he says, "I am not ashamed of the gospel of Christ." He realizes what the Gospel was doing for him. The Greek word for "ashamed" does not mean guilt or dishonor, or a feeling for guilty conduct which would cause one to blush because of shame. Blushing in today's society is a "lost art" for either embarrassment or shame. Worldly people don't "blush" any more when confronted with their own sinful or evil acts. They merely get angry. What Paul means to say here is that he is not "confused" by the Gospel. It was not in his nature to be. The Gospel transformed his life. It changed him from a persecutor of the innocent into a seeker of lost souls. The Gospel made him realize exactly who he was and what he ought to be. In spite of all his former self-righteousness, all of his devotion, dedication and consecration to God as a Pharisaic Jew, he now realized that he had been actually working against God. This transformation which the Gospel wrought in Paul was revealed in his life. It changed the man into a new creature. It changed his whole life, his thoughts, his manners, his actions. This is what the Gospel should do for all of us.

The "power" of the Gospel can be likened to dynamite, as some scholars translate it. What does dynamite do? Dynamite, when it is let loose in its full power, will level a mountain. It will crush rocks. The "power" of the Gospel will transform a human being in like manner, and make of him a believer with power to transform other human beings into believers. The Gospel has all of God's omnipotence behind it. The Greek word for "power" puts the stress more on the source than on the process. The Gospel as a force in the spiritual realm has a power of like nature with some of the forces of nature, such as lightning, a tornado, a hurricane, an earthquake. Such is the sense in which "power" is used in I Corinthians 1:18, "For the word of the cross is to them that perish foolishness; but unto us who are saved it is the *power* of God." Again in I Corinthians 4:20, the word is similarly used, "For the kingdom of God is not in word, but in *power.*" Paul goes on to say that the Gospel "is the power of God unto salvation to every one that believeth." It is only to the believer that the Gospel becomes that *power.*

We have examined the greater portion of Romans 1:16. Now look at the last phrase of the verse, ". . . to the Jew first, and also to the Greek." This epistle to the church at Rome was written to an established church. The so-called "church age" had been in existence for 25 years. Paul's proclamation in this letter that the Gospel was "to the Jew first, and also to the Greek," was, we believe, without qualification and is just as applicable today as it was in Paul's time. It will not do merely to state that Paul had preached the Gospel to the Jews and then rejected them since they rejected him at Corinth because he said to them, "from henceforth I will go to the Gentiles" (Acts 18:6). It is true that he did say this to the Jews at Corinth, but let us follow Paul as he goes to the next city, and the next city: inevitably and invariably he goes to the Jews. We believe that Paul's phrase, "to the Jew first, and also to the Greek," has a different application than most of us realize. Otherwise, why put this phrase about the Jew being first, directly after the phrase about the Gospel being the power of God unto salvation unto every one that believeth, a phrase that carries so much force and such tremendous weight in the New Testament? Probably, the explanation is to be found in the fact that Paul, being a Jew, made these statements to the Gentiles, since he said, "I am debtor both to Greeks and to Barbarians." The Gospel needs to be preached to these people. Paul, the Jew, before his conversion, said in his own heart, "Why to me? After all, we Jews have the Word of God; we are the recipients of the truth; we have given to the world a law; we have no problems such as the Gentiles have." Even today the Jew boasts in his pride and says, "If you were to gather together all the Jewish inmates of all the penal institutions of this country, any medium-size auditorium would be ample to hold them all." The Jew boasts that his people are not affiliated with crime and its "syndicates." And as for alcoholism, it is the exception among Jews. Seldom do we hear of a Jewish alcoholic. Visitors to skid row, with all its squalor and filth, seldom report the presence of Jews there. The Jew is more apt to comment, "The Gospel needs to be preached to the Gentiles. Look at the lives they lead! After all, they are pagan, they are heathen, they don't know Jehovah as God. As for me needing the Gospel, no! certainly not! I'm above it!"

And there's the rub. Nevertheless, Paul says, "Not so; the Jew may have all he claims, but his boast is his biggest weakness. He relies upon the flesh. The Jew with all his abilities, with all his pride, with all his conceit, with all his self-righteousness, needs the Gospel as much and even more than the Gentiles and Barbarians, many of whom worship nothing, or believe in some form of superstition. The Gospel *must* be preached to the Jew first. He needs it more than anyone else because he claims to possess the truth, because he thinks he knows so much and because he boasts so much. And because he claims all these things for himself he is outside of God. So you see that actually, basically and fundamentally, he needs the Gospel much more than the Gentile. The Gospel *must* be 'to the Jew first.'"

But the sad part of it is this, that many sincere Christians who do not believe that the Gospel is "to the Jew first," do not believe that the Gospel is to the Jew at all! And our Lord said, "Go ye into all the world, and preach the gospel to every creature" (Mark 16:15), and no one can deny that the Jew is a creature. Later in this letter of Paul to the church at Rome we will find these words, "For all have sinned, and fall short of the glory of God" (3:23), and "There is none righteous, no, not one" (3:10), and "There is none that seeketh after God" (3:11). The Jew *must* be reached and the Gospel "*is* the power of God unto salvation to every one that believeth; to the Jew first, and also to the Greek."

Verse 17: For therein is revealed a righteousness of God from faith unto faith: as it is written, But the righteous shall live by faith.

Or as the King James Version has it, "The just shall live by faith." The "righteousness" must be according to God's standards. It is not what I think, or what you think, but rather what the Word of God *says*. It must be God's concept of righteousness. We must bear in mind that this is "a righteousness" which has been *bestowed* upon us by the Holy Spirit. God, the Holy Spirit, puts the believer into a state of righteousness which is akin to God's righteousness. I John 3:2 reads, "Beloved, now are we children of God, and it is not yet made manifest what we shall be." God's righteousness and His salvation are often joined together in Scripture, as for example in Psalm 24:5, "He shall receive a blessing from Jehovah, and righteousness from the God of his salvation"; and Psalm 98:2, "Jehovah hath made known his salvation: his righteousness hath he openly showed in the sight of the nations (or heathen)"; and again in Isaiah 45:21-25:

> Declare ye, and bring it forth; yea, let them take counsel together: who hath showed this from ancient time? who hath declared it of old?

have not I, Jehovah? and there is no God else besides me, a just
God and a Saviour; there is none besides me. Look unto me, and
be saved, all the ends of the earth; for I am God, and there is none
else. By myself have I sworn, the word is gone forth from my mouth
in righteousness, and shall not return, that unto me every knee shall
bow, every tongue shall swear. Only in Jehovah, it is said of me,
is righteousness and strength: even to him shall men come; and all
they that were incensed against him shall be put to shame. In
Jehovah shall all the seed of Israel be justified, and shall glory. Again
in Isaiah 46:13, I bring near my righteousness, it shall not be far
off, and my salvation shall not tarry; and I will place salvation in
Zion for Israel my glory. And again in Isaiah 51:5, 6, My righteousness is near, my salvation is gone forth, and mine arms shall
judge the people; the isles shall wait for me, and on mine arm shall
they trust. Lift up your eyes to the heavens, and look upon the
earth beneath; for the heavens shall vanish away like smoke, and the
earth shall wax old like a garment; and they that dwell therein shall
die in like manner: but my salvation shall be for ever, and my righteousness shall not be abolished.

Now these are the words of God Almighty Himself, and where
there is one, the other follows, righteousness — salvation. And
of necessity, the reverse is true. This is further proof of what
Paul claims in Romans 1:2, "Which he promised afore through
his prophets in the holy scriptures." The combination of Romans 3:26, "For the showing, I say, of his righteousness at this
present season: that he might himself be just, and the justifier of
him that hath faith in Jesus," with Romans 8:30, "and whom he
fore-ordained, them he also called: and whom he called, them
he also justified: and whom he justified, them he also glorified."

Dr. Sanday, in his book on Romans, paraphrases Romans 1:16
this way: "Even there in the imperial city itself, I am not ashamed
of my message, repellent and humiliating as some of its features
may seem, for it is the mighty agency, set in motion by God
Himself, and sweeping on with it toward the haven of Messianic
security every believer. First in order of precedence, the Jew
and after him the Gentile." Then Dr. Sanday paraphrases verse
17: "Do you ask how this agency works and then of what it
consists? It is a revelation of the righteousness of God, manifested in a new method by which righteousness is acquired by
man. A method, the secret of which is 'faith' or ardent loyalty
to Jesus as Messiah and Lord. Which 'faith' is every day both
widening its circles and deepening its hold. It was such an attitude as this which the prophet Habakkuk meant when in view of
the desolating Chaldean invasion, he wrote (a paraphrase of

Habakkuk 2:4): 'The righteous man shall save his life by his faith or loyalty to Jehovah,' while his proud observers perished."

Verse 18: For the wrath of God is revealed from heaven against all ungodliness and unrighteousness of men, who hinder the truth in unrighteousness . . . .

Because God is righteous, He loathes unrighteousness. He reveals His wrath toward it. He loves good and hates evil, an example of which we have in the Old Testament when God, in Malachi, says of Jacob and Esau, "I loved Jacob; but Esau I hated" (1:2, 3). Paul repeats this again in Romans 9:13. The life of Jacob will reveal his struggle for righteousness, for the love of God, the patience of God, and the guidance of God, while Esau's life was the very antithesis of this. The two, love and hate, are irreconcilable in the sight of God. God will establish His righteous kingdom only after He destroys the unrighteousness of Satan's kingdom. Let us not minimize the fact that "the times of the Gentiles" are the times in which Satan has his sway. The word "Gentiles" in the Hebrew is the same word that is translated "nations." Likewise, the Greek word that is translated "nations" stands also for "heathen" and "Gentiles." So you see, "the times of the Gentiles" are the times when heathenism is prevalent, when unrighteousness is rampant, and when, to paraphrase the poet, "Righteousness is forever on the scaffold, and sin forever on the throne." This is an inescapable reality. You cannot mix the two. This is the call to separation for all of us who have named the name of Jesus Christ as Lord and Saviour. Righteousness must separate itself from sinfulness. Co-existence of the two is not possible.

The thought of the "wrath of God" is also Jewish or Old Testament. Let us look at a series of texts: Leviticus 10:1, 2: "And Nadab and Abihu, the sons of Aaron, took each of them his censer, and put fire therein, and laid incense thereon, and offered strange fire before the Lord, which he had not commanded them. And there came forth fire from before the Lord and devoured them, and they died before the Lord." Numbers 16:32, 33: "And the earth opened its mouth, and swallowed them up, and their households, and all the men that appertained unto Korah, and all their goods. So they, and all that appertained to them, went down alive into the grave: and the earth closed upon them, and they perished from among the assembly." In Numbers 16:46, we see what Moses said to Aaron, "And Moses said unto Aaron, Take thy censer, and put fire therein from off the altar, and lay incense thereon, and carry it quickly unto the congregation, and make atonement for them: for there is wrath gone out from the Lord."

"The wrath of God" is poured out upon the Gentiles for the persecutions of the people of Israel and is fully explained in Jeremiah 50:11-18; and Ezekiel 36:5. In prophecy the "wrath of God" is "the day of the Lord." Here are just a few passages to consider: Isaiah 2:10-22; Jeremiah 30:7, 8; Joel 3; Obadiah 8; and Zephaniah 3:8.

Verse 19 is really the conclusion of verse 18.

Verse 20: For the invisible things of him since the creation of the world are clearly seen, being perceived through the things that are made, even his everlasting power and divinity; that they may be without excuse . . . .

Let us consider the words, "that they may be without excuse." The Greek translation and the sense is that they may be inexcusable.

"God's sovereignty in dealing with man is not the question here. Rather, it is man's inexcusableness in holding back the truth by unrighteousness. God has not done this for this express purpose even though it has so turned out. He did not put forth the knowledge of Himself to deprive sinful man of all excuse but that man might know Him. By forgetting Him the human race deprived itself of all excuse" (quoted from the writings of Saint John Chrysostom, A.D. 407).

Verse 21: . . . because that, knowing God, they glorified him not as God, neither gave thanks; but became vain in their reasonings, and their senseless heart was darkened.

The word "because" in this verse introduces the reason why they were "without excuse" (verse 20), namely, they did not glorify Him as God. How tragic this is! In Paul's day even as in ours, the world goes on as though there were no God in existence. The grave is the end, and that this life is all the heaven and hell there is, or, as Solomon put it in Ecclesiastes 8:15, "to eat, and to drink, and to be joyful," which is repeated in Isaiah 22:13 and in I Corinthians 15:32, with this added, "for tomorrow we die." People do not today, and people did not in Paul's day, glorify God as God in their religion. They have deposed God from His place as Creator. In our lives we are ungrateful for His gifts which He has so lavishly bestowed upon us. We become "vain," translated from a Greek word which can also be translated, devoid of success, futile. We become vain in our imaginations. The elaboration of the Greek word for "imagination" (KJV) is not only imagination but also vain in life and its purpose, its thoughts, its cogitations, its reasonings (ASV), its disputations and contentions. We become devoid of scruples.

Could we have a better picture than this of the world we are living in today? We have here an illustration of the fact that history repeats itself. The people of whom Paul wrote not only became vain in their imaginations (KJV) (reasonings ASV), but they became fools; and the Greek word for "fools" can also be translated unintelligent, dull. They became reckless, perverse, heathenish, so that in the final analysis, "their senseless heart was darkened." The King James Version reads, "And their *foolish* heart was darkened." The heart is considered to be the seat of the feelings, the moral choice. Paul says in Romans 10:10, "For with the heart man believeth unto righteousness." Here we begin to see why the foolish or senseless heart of this people was darkened.

Verse 22: Professing themselves to be wise, they became fools.

The word here translated "professing," is not only accurately translated but can also be translated pretending, or asserting. It means being the opposite, or "fools." Since people who pretend or assert themselves to be wise, and are not, they are the opposite of what they profess or pretend to be. The philosopher Aristotle explains the word "wise" as referring to "excellence in its highest form," such as striving after the best ends, using the best means, being expert, skilled in letters, cultivated, learned. This is something which the people Paul referred to thought they were. And many people of whom we read today are doing the very same thing. There are men who profess, who pretend, who assert, that if it were not for them the world would disintegrate. They allege themselves to be the repository of all the truth and wisdom in the world. What Job said to his comforters millenniums ago could be repeated to the wiseacres of today: "No doubt but ye are the people, and wisdom shall die with you" (12:2). And the tragic fact is that Paul's own people, the Jews, became fools. They, like the wiseacres of today, when they thought they were smart, were actually fools in the sight of God. The Greek word which is translated "became fools," is the identical word from which we get our English word "moron." In other words, these so-called wise ones who think that they possess all the wisdom, who think they have the answer to everything, are morons in the sight of God. Isn't this exactly what Paul says to the church at Corinth?

> . . . but unto them that are called, both Jews and Greeks, Christ the power of God, and the wisdom of God. Because the foolishness of God is wiser than men; and the weakness of God is stronger than men. For behold your calling, brethren, that not many wise after the flesh, not many mighty, not many noble, are called: but God chose the foolish things of the world, that he might put to shame them that are wise; and God chose the weak things of the world that he might put to shame the things that are strong; and the base things of the world, and the things that are despised, did God choose, yea and the things that are not, that he might bring to nought the things that are: that no flesh should glory before God (I Corinthians 1:24-29).

Why was all this said to the church at Corinth? Verse 30, next following, is the answer: "But of him are ye in Christ Jesus, who was made unto us wisdom from God, and righteousness and sanctification, redemption." So all such, who profess themselves to be wise, who profess themselves to be geniuses, are, in the sight of God, nothing more and nothing less than spiritual morons.

Verse 23: . . . and changed the glory of the incorruptible God for the likeness of an image of corruptible man, and of birds, and four-footed beasts, and creeping things.

They changed the "incorruptible" and became corruptible. God versus man — what a contrast! Puny, insignificant man is here described as trying to make himself as God.

The tendency by our youth to lionize popular entertainers and actors, is evidenced by the infectious follies and outbursts of violence that occur from time to time throughout the world, not only among the young but also among adult populations. When it does not result in the destruction of life and property, it goes in the opposite direction toward the kind of adulation that borders on worship. In these outbreaks of lawlessness and human passion, we can see how people can change the incorruptible for the corruptible, by changing God for man. What tragic contrast! What a pity! We are, in this case, worshiping material things, the flesh rather than the spirit and God. We are placing so much emphasis on material things, that the spiritual has lost its power and importance in our life today.

Verse 24: **Wherefore God gave them up in the lusts of their hearts unto uncleanness, that their bodies should be dishonored among themselves . . . .**

These are tragic words, condemning words, which have been ringing in our ears ever since Paul wrote them and are still ringing at this very moment. We begin, in this section of the first chapter of Romans to see the degrading paths in which the Gentiles have walked through past millenniums. Notice how often the words, "God gave them up," occur in verses 24, 26, and 28. In verse 24, "God gave them up in the lusts of their hearts." In verse 26, "God gave them up unto vile passions." In verse 28, "God gave them up unto a reprobate mind." In other words, God gave them up because they did not approve of having God in their knowledge, or they refused to have God in their knowledge. Bear in mind that Paul is saying all this of the Gentile civilizations. He is painting a very dismal picture of despicable, deplorable and depraved Gentile civilizations. There are words in the verses just quoted that appear not more than once or twice in the New Testament. To realize to the fullest extent the immorality and godlessness of the Gentile world in Paul's day, we have only to read a second time from Romans 1:18 to 2:16, to see the Gentile world in all of its heathenism, debauchery and sinfulness. In the sight of God this world's civilization is revolting and nauseating. One almost dreads to dwell on these things realizing, as one must, that we are seeing history repeating itself in the life of today. The so-called wheel of progress does not seem to turn when men forsake God.

The only other place where similar words appear in the New Testament is in II Timothy 3:1-13: "But know this that in the last days grievous times shall come," and there follows a description of conditions which will prevail in the last days and are even now beginning to be enacted. We are today seeing such sin, such immorality, that one shudders to think of children growing up in such a civilization. The so-called wheel of progress has indeed turned but in the wrong direction. The Gentile world of Romans 1:23-32 is with us again today.

Look more closely at verse 24: "Wherefore God gave them up in the lusts of their hearts unto uncleanness, that their bodies should be dishonored among themselves . . .". As the Gentiles, in ages past, deserted God, God in turn deserted them, not even sending them prophets. This too is Talmudic. In Pirqe Aboth, chapter 4, verse 2, we find, "Wherefore God also gave them up."

Again, in the Talmud of Shabbath, 104a, "Every fulfillment of
duty is rewarded by another, and every transgression is punished
by another." In Webber's "Book on Theology," page 66, are
these words, "Whosoever strives to keep himself pure receives
the power to do so; and whosoever will be impure, to him it
(the door of vice) is thrown open." The Jews held that the
heathen (Gentiles) because of their rejection of the law were
wholly abandoned by God and that the Holy Spirit was withdrawn from them.

The Jew in dispersion with the Law of Moses in his hand,
could not but rebel against the heathen vices which he found
among the Gentiles. He looked upon the heathen as given over
to the sins of the flesh and to have become as brute beasts. (This
too is a quotation from the same book (Webber's "Book on Theology"), pages 58, 67 and 68. The whole world would seem to
be in the grasp of Satan and is being subjected to all the evils
connected with him. The apostle John writes in I John 5:19,
confirming the reality of this, "We know that we are of God,
and the whole world lieth in the evil one." Surely we must be in
the closing days of this age. The conditions presented in Romans
1 are very clear and convincing.

**Verse 25: . . . for that they exchanged the truth of God for a lie,
and worshipped and served the creature rather than the Creator,
who is blessed for ever. Amen.**

This verse tells why God gave up the Gentiles. The King
James Version reads, "Who changed the truth of God into a
lie." It is impossible to change truth. Truth is truth no matter
what one may do to it. A person may *exchange* truth for a lie,
but one cannot *change truth into a lie*. It is better and more accurate to read, "they exchanged the truth of God for a lie."
Why and how they did it then follows: ". . . and worshipped
and served the creature rather than the Creator."

This not only gives us a graphic picture of what happened in
the ages past among the Gentiles, and the underlying factor of
God's drastic actions in verse 24, it also gives us a clear picture
of what is happening in the world today. We worship and serve
creatures. We make gods out of people. We have literally worshiped at the altar of humanity rather than at the altar of Deity.
Even so far as the Gospel is concerned, we have tried to humanize the Saviour instead of deifying His personality. In evangelical circles we speak of Him as Jesus only, His human name. We
humanize Him in other aspects, we bring Him down to the level

of humanity. Our eyes, instead of looking heavenward, are looking earthward. We are worshiping and serving the creature rather than the Creator. We are serving the flesh rather than God: and it doesn't matter where we are, in church at worship, or in the home. This 25th verse makes us realize how close we must be to that inevitable hour when God shall call a halt to all of this. The Lord Jesus Christ will return for His Church. Then the horror and devastation of the Tribulation will begin. All because man, who was created for the one purpose of worshiping and fellowshiping with God, has so degraded and debased himself, his mind, his morals, his concepts of Deity, that he has turned his eyes away from God and has focused them on himself. It makes no difference whether this is done in the practice of Christian Science, Jehovah's Witnesses, or within any of the historic denominations. Men are more concerned with the human hierarchy than with the hierarchy of God. We men are more interested in the human program than in God's plan of salvation. This is the charge against us in verse 25, "for that they exchanged the truth of God for a lie, and worshipped and served the creature." This is the charge laid at our feet in this twentieth century. Paul closes the verse with this comment, "who is blessed for ever. Amen." This is a doxology, many of which occur in Jewish writings and the Talmud.

Verses 26 and 27: (26) For this cause God gave them up unto vile passions: for their women changed the natural use into that which is against nature: (27) and likewise also the men, leaving the natural use of the woman, burned in their lust one toward another, men with men working unseemliness, and receiving in themselves that recompense of their error which was due.

Or, the term which is translated "vile passions," is in the Greek, "passions of dishonor." We see here the steady retrogression of civilization as it veers from the worship of God and begins to glorify, to satisfy and magnify the flesh. What a revolting picture this is! Verses 26 and 27 should be taken together for they portray the debased condition and the wickedness and degradation of humanity. This is perversion in its lowest aspect, "men, leaving the natural use of the woman" and "men with men working unseemliness." How shocking and degrading! Yet is it so shocking when we realize our spiritual bankruptcy? We see this happening even in the twentieth century in the high circles of society and politics. Men in the highest places, men of intelligence, of learning, of authority, are being exposed as guilty of these practices. Yet we probably ought not to be surprised, for were not the philosophers of ancient days just as immoral? History tells us that Aristotle, Plato and Socrates, men of brilliant minds, men of more than ordinary intelligence, were amoral. Not immoral, but *amoral,* that is, neither moral nor immoral, but with no moral standards. All of them, we are told, were sexual perverts. It was Aristotle who molded the life of Alexander the Great, who at the age of 32 died, a chronic alcoholic; and Aristotle himself who lived in the palace with Alexander the Great was his companion in voluptuousness and moral abandonment. These "passions of dishonor" and misuse and abuse are prevalent today in our society.

The conditions I have just described are by-products of a civilization in which the hearts of its citizens have turned away from God. Is it any wonder that the character of such a civilization has become debased?

Our children are taught things in schools that negate the story of creation in Genesis. Teachers minimize God in the classroom. We ought not to wonder at the inevitable result, for when we do away with God, we do away with all moral restraint. For us there is nothing left to do but "eat, drink, and be merry; for tomorrow we die." We hear the statement made many times that "tomorrow never comes." The other day I heard a man speak on the subject, "Tomorrow Does Come." It was a revelation to me, for tomorrow *does* indeed come. Inevitably, invariably, in every one of our lives, tomorrow will come just as surely as today came. Tomorrow will come when our sin will find us out. Tomorrow will come when we will face death, with its stark reality and finality. Tomorrow will come when we shall stand in the presence of the Lord Jesus Christ. The words of Paul are eternally true, "Every knee shall bow . . . and every tongue shall confess" the Lord (Philippians 2:10, 11). It will not matter where we are, whether we are in heaven, on earth, or under the earth in sheol. Paul says "every tongue should confess that Jesus Christ is Lord (Jehovah incarnate in the flesh as God Almighty) to the glory of God the Father." Tomorrow does come. Tomorrow will come in every one of our lives. We cast our bread on the waters and tomorrow it returns. It is either a glad day or a sad day, but the reaping is sure, and for those who sin, the result is certain. They will be "receiving in themselves that recompense of their error which was due" (Romans 1:27). In other words they will get exactly what is coming to them. God, in the final analysis, "gave them up." What a horrible epitaph to read of any civilization, "God gave them up!" Was there anything else for God to do? They turned their backs on Him, they rejected Him, they abused Him. There was no alternative!

The burden of every evangelical message should be to point the sinner to the necessity of repentance. Civilization, as a whole, must make an about-face. It is either Christ or chaos. Mind you, civilization is not what the world needs. Civilization has brought us to the present brink of self-destruction, and has brought us to a hybrid doctrine called "New-Evangelicalism." The dictionary defines a hybrid as an offspring of two species — a tame sow and a wild boar. "New-Evangelicalism" is neither new nor evangelical. The devil cannot destroy the Gospel but he is destroying the vessels that are supposed to carry it. Scripture knows nothing of an evangelized *community*, but it does speak of a transformed *individual*, a converted *individual* and a born-again *individual*. Even the Lord Jesus Christ didn't perform the miracle of converting a community. All He could gather together, after an intensive three and a half years of labor, was a group of 120 individuals. Are we more powerful, more capable, more efficient, more effective than the Lord of Glory? Away with this new stuff! ". . . except ye repent, ye shall all in like manner perish" (Luke 13:3), is still the message for today. "Except ye be converted . . . ye shall not enter into the kingdom of heaven" (Matthew 18:3). This is what the world needs today, not civilization. It is either Christ or chaos! The "way of the Cross" is the message. What can wash away my sin? Nothing but the blood of Jesus. This is the evangelical message.

Verse 28: And even as they refused to have God in their knowledge, God gave them up unto a reprobate mind, to do those things which are not fitting....

For the third time Paul records the fact that "God gave them (the Gentiles) up." First, in verse 24, "God gave them up in the lusts of their hearts," resulting in the worship of the creature rather than the Creator. The second time, verse 26, "God gave them up into vile passions," resulting in immorality and lustful indulgences into which the world plunged. For the third time in verse 28, "they refused to have God in their knowledge," or in their minds. Another translation states, "that they did not approve of having God in their knowledge," or "they did not approve of acknowledging God." This refusal to acknowledge God resulted in His giving the Gentiles up to a reprobate mind. There is, in the

Greek, a play on words, which can be expressed this way: "because they reprobated the knowledge of God, God gave them over
to a reprobate mind"; or, "as they thought fit, they cast out the ac-
knowledgement of God; God gave them over to an outcast mind."
That is, God withdrew from the Gentile world at that time. His
grace left them to the evil which they had chosen. This was their
own choice. We talk of progress, but when we read these words,
we realize it is an old story. Twice in the Book of Job, which
Bible historians tell us is the oldest book of the Old Testament,
in 21:14 and 22:15-17, this is the charge — that they refused to
acknowledge God. This is back in the Old Testament. It is
also Jewish.

**Verses 29-32: (29) . . . being filled with all unrighteousness,
wickedness, covetousness, maliciousness; full of envy, murder,
strife, deceit, malignity; whisperers, (30) backbiters, hateful to
God, insolent, haughty, boastful, inventors of evil things, disobedient to parents, (31) without understanding, covenant-break-
ers, without natural affection, unmerciful: (32) who, knowing the
ordinance of God, that they that practise such things are worthy
of death, not only do the same, but also consent with them that
practise them.**

Let us take a closer look at verses 28 to 32 and consider them
as one unit. The fact that the Gentile world "refused to have
God in their knowledge" (v. 28) resulted in the conditions described in the preceding verses (vss. 18-27).

It seems to this writer, that when we read these words we
begin to see a horrible picture of the world we live in. These
words describe a world filled with unrighteousness, wickedness
and envy. There is deceit and murder, people without natural
affection, who are actually haters of God and hateful to God,
disobedient to parents, without understanding, breakers of truce
and the covenants. These sins are worthy of death. In the final
analysis the people referred to even rejoice in doing these things.
The words that appear here in verses 18-32 appear only twice
in the New Testament, here and in II Timothy 3:1-9 wherein
Paul writes "In the last days" these same things are to come to
pass. The same conditions which caused God to give the Gentile
world over to a reprobate mind are to be repeated in the last
days. II Timothy 3:1 begins with the words, "But know this,
that in the last days grievous times shall come," or as the King
James Version states, ". . . perilous times shall come." Paul says
men today are going to do the very same thing which they did

in ancient times. These things are upon us. We have literally thrown God out of our schools. The Supreme Court of the United States says, in effect, that it is wrong to pray to God, and that it is wrong for a teacher to take any portion of the Scripture, Old or New Testaments, any version, Protestant, Catholic or Jewish, and read it in the classroom. This writer wouldn't argue too much over this order of the Supreme Court if it stopped where it ended, but it doesn't. If it is wrong for a teacher in a classroom to teach anything at all about God then, surely, it must be just as wrong and just as illegal to teach a child against God, or to teach anything in the classroom that would discredit the Bible. If it is wrong to read it, it is equally wrong to discredit it.

Similarly, we talk of the theory of evolution which at best is only a theory, inasmuch as an unproven statement is not a fact. In reading Romans 1:18-32 we find that the same things which are happening before our eyes today are to happen in the latter days, as seen in II Timothy 3:1-9. How near must be our Lord's coming! We, seemingly, have already cast aside every restraint of God. Men have become amoral, and when left in that state are uncontrollable creatures. When God gives men over to a reprobate mind they are filled with unrighteousness and their generation becomes wicked and covetous and filled with maliciousness and envy in every pathway of life. This is the condition of the Gentile world today.

The human mind, without God, could do only one thing; namely, invent evil. Because the Gentiles did not acknowledge God they became disobedient to parents; they became non-social, without natural affection; and mercy as a human attribute was non-existent. They not only committed the same sins over and over again, but they actually took pleasure in them. The conditions mentioned in Romans 1:18-32 are the very ones now appearing in our newspapers and periodicals. In our cities it is dangerous to go out at night, and one never knows when a law-breaker will walk into one's home. It is almost necessary to put prison bars on our windows to discourage prowlers. People are being killed in public, in sight of other people, and no one has the courage to intervene. An event recently occurred in Dayton, Ohio, in which a woman lost control of her automobile, and after it landed in a body of water, she battled her way out of it and got on the roof. Not being able to swim she screamed for help. A crowd of fifty people standing a few yards away did nothing to help her, but merely stood and watched as she fell into the muddy water and drowned. This was in Dayton, Ohio, not in the jungles.

This public and individual lethargy on the part of people is one aspect of our godlessness, the result of refusing "to acknowledge God." The steps of our "falling away" are progressive, leading us to deeper and greater sin. Such occurrences we can expect in the world, and events similar to these were happening in the days of the apostle Paul "when God gave the Gentile world up" — a world with no enlightenment. Remember that the conditions referred to in Romans 1:18-32 were prevalent during a time when there was no "revelation," no written Word of God. The Bible, God's Word, had not been printed even in the original languages. Today, in Bible times, we are able to know God's revelation and what He requires of us. Even in our churches there is a tremendous "falling away." Although hundreds and thousands of people attend Sunday morning services in our churches only a small percentage of these same churches hold services on Sunday evening. Like the great majority of church members throughout so-called Christendom, many of us who profess to be followers of Christ have a "form of godliness" but are denying "the power thereof" (II Timothy 3:5). The sad part of it is that this "falling away" is even reaching the pulpit.

Among fundamental believers the thought of having a divorced man as a minister was unheard of. According to New Testament standards, the pastor of a church had to be a man whose character was above reproach. Only such a one was qualified to stand in God's pulpit and preach the Gospel. The pulpit of a Christ-believing church was a sacred place. How sad it is to see Christian ministers, who should be persons of unblemished personal life, marrying couples who have been previously divorced, and ministers seeking divorces for themselves. There is a tremendous "falling away" in every avenue of our church work and life. The "apostasy" has crept in. We speak of progress, but where is it? Because we have beautiful church buildings? We are adding every inducement in the form of modern conveniences for the people of God to come to worship, but it is of no avail. This writer is told that churches in Europe do not even have pews. People come and stand to listen to the sermon. We, in the United States, have padded seats, comfortably-heated buildings in the wintertime, and excellently ventilated and air-conditioned buildings in the summertime. We have gone from sermons to "sermonettes." Today we are told that a sermon must not be more than fifteen or twenty minutes in duration, as if that were all we want of God! I am speaking of fundamental churches where the "Word of God" is proclaimed, or supposed to be. The proclamation of the Gospel should be not only in word, but in deed as well. We speak of the *imminent* return of Christ, but if we actually believe in our Lord's return, where are the multitudes of believers on Sunday nights? Where are they during an evangelistic campaign? Where are they on prayer-meeting nights? This "falling away" among Christians has reached the place where it is difficult to tell the difference between a child of God and a child of the world. In this life we want the comforts of the world rather than the presence of God. Large numbers of us are without "spiritual understanding," and, like worldlings, without "natural affection." We know that we shall have to stand in the presence of God and give an accounting "for the deeds we have done in the flesh," yet we go on living as though the return of Christ, even though we believe it to be "imminent," will never happen in our lifetime. We have lost all sense of consecration, dedication and devotion to God. The world, as a Scotsman of old once said, has not become more churchly, but rather the church has become more worldly.

Kenneth S. Wuest, the Greek Bible scholar, in his English New Testament (an expanded translation), printed by the Wm. B. Eerdmans Pub. Co., translates verses 28 through 32 this way:

> And even after putting God to the test for the purpose of approving Him, should He meet these specifications, and finding that He did not, they disapproved of holding Him in their full and precise knowledge, God gave them up to a mind that would not meet the test for that which a mind was meant, to practice those things, which are not becoming or befitting; being filled with every unrighteousness, pernicious evil, avarice, malice, full of envy, murder, wrangling, guile, malicious craftiness; secret slanderers, backbiters; hateful to God, insolent, haughty; swaggerers, inventors of evil things; disobedient to parents, stupid, faithless, without natural affection, merciless; such are those who, knowing the judgment of God that these who practice such things are worthy of death, not only habitually do the same things but also take pleasure in those who practice them.

The foregoing is a simple but accurate description of our civilization in this twentieth century, and is a succinct statement of what we have accomplished as an enlightened, civilized, free and so-called Christian society — a fitting epitaph for our epoch as it draws to a close. It is not a picture of progression, but of retrogression. Bear in mind that Paul describes in Romans 1:18-32 a civilization over 3400 years old, yet this description applies to us today. The Word of God is as modern as tomorrow. It is as up-to-date as any newscast on any given day or night of the present time.

2

WHEREAS Romans 1 is addressed to the Gentile world as a whole, in all ages, at all times, under all circumstances, Romans 2:1-16 is addressed to the individual Gentile:

Verse 1: Wherefore thou art without excuse, O man, whosoever thou art that judgest: for wherein thou judgest another, thou condemnest thyself; for thou that judgest dost practise the same things.

The expression, "without excuse," is translated from a Greek word meaning, without a defense, without an apology, to talk oneself out of a charge. Thus Paul addresses each one of us even today.

Some years ago an outstanding Bible teacher and Christian, Dr. H. A. Ironside, made the following remark: "When you point a finger of accusation at another person, three of your fingers are pointing backwards at yourself." This is good exegesis of Romans 2:1, and good homiletics, as well. The verse actually states that the man who judges another is guilty of the same thing, ". . . for wherein thou judgest another, thou condemnest thyself; for thou that judgest dost practise the same things."

How many of us who call ourselves Christians would have to confess that as a rule our lives are no different from the lives of those who live in the world? So many Christians talk of a "separated life" but fail to show evidences of it. Peter's protestation of his faith in Jesus, "Though I should die with thee, yet will I not deny thee" (Matthew 26:35), proved his faith to be non-existent when in the palace of the high priest he cried, "I know not the man" (Matthew 26:74). Could this ever happen to us? So often neither our lives nor our speech give any evidence of the fact that we have been born again or "washed in the blood of Jesus Christ." The very same thing

that we are accusing the world of doing, we, ourselves, who are
followers of Jesus Christ, are doing. In other words, our lives
bear out the testimony of our lips, whether for good or evil.
We ought to be as epistles, "known and read of all men" (II
Corinthians 3:2). Surely, the world ought to be able to read
in our lives that we have been with Jesus Christ, and that we
have "died unto the world." The words of Romans 2:1 condemn
all men who judge others for committing sins which they themselves are guilty of and in so doing they condemn themselves.

**Verse 2: And we know that the judgment of God is according
to truth against them that practise such things.**

The King James Version states it this way, "But we are sure
(or positive) that the judgment of God is according to truth
against them which commit such things." The Greek word
which is translated "sure" in the King James Version, means to
know for a fact by external testimony that the judgment of God
is true.

**Verse 3: And reckonest thou this, O man, who judgest them
that practise such things, and doest the same, that thou shalt
escape the judgment of God?**

The King James Version reads, "And *thinkest* thou this, O
man," in which the word "thinkest" loses the full meaning of
the word "reckonest" in the American Standard Version. Reckoning is not merely knowing, it is "counting" or "figuring up."
What verse 3 actually means is this, "And reckonest thou this,
O man, who judgest and practices those things, that the ones
who do those same things are going to escape the judgment
of God?" This is not only an admonition to the unregenerate,
it ought also to stir our conscience as believers to this truth. In
the presence of Him who is the truth we shall not escape that
judgment. Every man's works shall be tried by fire, as Paul
writes in (I Corinthians 3:13): ". . . each man's work shall be
made manifest: for the day shall declare it, because it is revealed
in fire; and the fire itself shall prove each man's work of what
sort it is" (or, and each man's work of what sort it is, the fire
shall prove it). This is an elaboration of Romans 2:3.

**Verse 4: Or despisest thou the riches of his goodness and for-
bearance and longsuffering, not knowing that the goodness of God
leadeth thee to repentance?**

Paul in this verse goes on to make accusation against the individual Gentile. Certainly the love, the compassion, the tender-heartedness of God, the pleadings of God, the cross in its every aspect, ought to prove to every individual that he is a sinner. The goodness of God should lead each and every one of us to repentance.

Verse 5: . . . but after thy hardness and impenitent heart treasurest up for thyself wrath in the day of wrath and revelation of the righteous judgment of God . . . ;

Because they hardened their hearts and did not repent, they were treasuring up (laying up little by little) and accumulating a storehouse of wrath for themselves. The righteous judgment of God is impartial. God does not judge a person by outward advantages, by form, by birth, by stratum of life and society, by mental ability, skill, religious exercises, or even by baptism. He judges only by the heart, "for with the heart man believeth unto righteousness" (Romans 10:10). This is the seed and the secret of faith. There are many, no doubt, who have a head knowledge and who give mental assent to the verities of the Gospel, and that is the extent of their faith. It is a mental status, not a heartfelt conviction and repentance.

Verse 6: . . . who will render to every man according to his works . . . :

This statement does not nullify the doctrine of salvation by grace, as some have thought. This portion of Scripture may create a lot of controversy but, nevertheless, let us brush aside our preconceived ideas, and let Scripture make the decision for us.

The paraphrase of James 2:17 is, "Faith without works is dead." Faith without the accompaniment of works is not faith and does not result in salvation unto eternal life. Faith without works is as dead as works without faith.

In chemistry the two component parts of water are expressed by the symbols H_2O. In order to have water, one must have the proper ingredients or elements. So it is with the faith that results in eternal life. We must have faith *and works*, which is pleasing to God. One must follow the other. If this is not done, then there is no true faith and the results are disastrous. The Scriptures state that "without faith it is impossible to be well-pleasing unto him" (Hebrews 11:6), and "Whatsoever is not of faith is sin" (Romans 14:23). We must realize that faith is the prerequisite for salvation and eternal life in the sight of God. Implicit faith in Jesus Christ who died for us on the cross will always result and manifest itself in good works. Works is always the ambition, the outgrowth, the result, the very genius of true faith.

Verses 7 through 10: We shall deal with these four verses as a unit. This portion has caused many Bible teachers and expositors embarrassment; therefore, it is often skipped. However, it sets forth a profound truth, and covers a great deal of Scripture, as many truths are crammed into these four verses.

Verse 7: . . . to them that by patience in well-doing seek for glory and honor and incorruption, eternal life . . . . :

This verse deals with individuals who are endeavoring to please God in every facet of life, knowing that the ultimate result is eternal life which they have received as "the free gift of God" (Romans 6:23). We must remember that our salvation is in three phases, i.e., we were saved from the *penalty* of sin; we are now, daily, being saved from the *power* of sin; and we shall finally be saved from the *presence* of sin when we are brought into the presence of God.

Just what is a Christian in Scripture? He is a person who has been born again. He is one who has been baptized scripturally after he has accepted Christ as Lord and Saviour. He is one who has been separated from worldly habits and lusts. He is one who has been living and witnessing daily for his Lord. He is one who, in whatever phase of life he finds himself, serves the Lord as an act of worship. (For "is serving," notice the Greek word *service* in Romans 12:1, "spiritual" service.) This is the definition and the requirement of one who calls himself a Christian. The command is to be *transformed*, and the result is that "the world has been crucified unto me, and I unto the world" (Galatians 6:14). A person becomes a Christian "through faith" (Ephesians 2:8, 9). He then becomes a "new creature in Christ" (II Corinthians 5:17), or, as the Greek has it, "a new creation," which results in good works in Christ, as in Ephesians 2:10, "For we are his workmanship, created in Christ Jesus for good works, which God afore prepared that we should walk in them."

One must not use just one part of a Scripture text to present the truth, but the complete text if one wishes to present the *whole* truth, as in Ephesians 2:8-10.

This is the kind of Christian set forth in our proclamation of the Gospel in this, the New Testament church age, and is in complete harmony with Paul's approach to the gospel ministry as set forth in Romans; and is precisely why he concludes in verse 10 with the phrase "to the Jew first, and also the Greek" (Gentile). It also confirms what Paul has stated earlier in this Epistle, i. e., 1:16.

Verse 8, 9, 10: (8) . . . but unto them that are factious, and obey not the truth, but obey unrighteousness, shall be wrath and indignation, (9) tribulation and anguish, upon every soul of man that worketh evil, of the Jew first, and also of the Greek; (10) but glory and honor and peace to every man that worketh good, to the Jew first, and also to the Greek . . . :

The persons referred to in verses 8 and 9 are the factious and disobedient ones; and the words "factious" and "obey not," could be translated contentious, or feuding, as applied to those who do not obey the truth.

What is the "truth" in Scripture? Is it not the Lord Jesus Christ Himself, as He says in John 14:6, "I am the way, and the *truth* and the life"? The "factious" ones who "obey not" the truth and who are continually rejecting and scorning it, are those who will receive "wrath and indignation." "Wrath" as it is translated from the Greek can mean vengeance or punishment; "indignation" can mean pressure, or compression, or affliction, or distressing circumstances, or trials. "Tribulation and anguish" follow "wrath and indignation," and all are to be in this life and in the hereafter as described in II Thessalonians 1:7-9. But notice again in Romans 2:9, it is "of the Jew first, and also of the Greek" (Gentile). Oh, the accuracy and the clarity of the Bible if we would only believe it! We who believe in the premillennial return of our Saviour and in the pre-tribulation rapture of the Church, should shout the truth of Romans 2:7-10 from the rooftops. Is not God's wrath going to be poured out on "the Jew first?" Is not the tribulation period "the time of Jacob's trouble?" (Jeremiah 30:7). Is not this to take place first, after which God will pour His wrath upon the Gentile nations? This is the chronological order in God's Word. Compare Isaiah 62 with Isaiah 63:1-6; Joel 3:1 with Joel 3:2; Zechariah 12:2-8 with Romans 2:9, and Matthew 25:31-46. Any true servant of God will admit that this is an earthly judgment, that "these my brethren" in Matthew 25:31-46 are the Jews, and that these "my brethren" have been restored. They have gone through the "indignation" and are now the mute witnesses of this judgment. They are the "evidence," the ones who have been ministered unto, or, if you please, who have not been ministered unto. How neglectful we have been in not expounding Scripture accurately and chronologically! This is the truth of the verses (Romans 2:7-10) we have just finished. In this dispensation of Grace the Gospel is to go to the "Jew first and also to the Greek" (Gentile).

At this time, in this age of Grace, it is needless to quibble over whether the Gospel is to "the Jew first" or "to the Jew last." The sad thing about this question is that, as a rule, people who do not believe in the Jew first, do not believe in the Jew at all. They believe and declare that this is the "Gentile Church Age" and that God in this dispensation of Grace is calling the people for His name from among the Gentiles.

To accept this post-millennial theory of the "Gentile Church Age" is to reject the entire truth of the epistle to the Ephesians. In that epistle we have the content of the true Church, the Body of Christ, not the local church. As previously stated, hydrogen and oxygen are the two component parts of water; and, likewise, the two component parts of the Church, which the epistle to the Ephesians states are the "twain" (2:15 KJV); or "two" (ASV), are nothing more than the repentant Jew and the repentant Gentile. Accepting the completed work of the cross as the basis of our faith — as the *foundation* of our faith — when these two come to God, this "twain" makes up the Church. The middle wall of partition (Ephesians 2:14) between the Jew and the Gentile has been broken down. But, this writer regrets to say, there are many in fundamental circles who have built this wall up higher than it was before. They tell us that the Jew is "done with" for this age! How sad to neglect so great a truth and so great a blessing! The "lostness" of the Jew in this age is just as great, just as pitiful, just as punishable as the "lostness" of the native in the jungles of Africa, in the degradation and poverty of the native of India or the illiteracy of the native of South America.

"All have sinned" and are lost, Jew and Gentile alike. Those who want to be saved must accept the work of the cross and the risen Saviour as the basis and foundation of faith in order to attain eternal life. If the writer, who is Jewish, had to wait for some of the readers of these pages to present the Gospel to him, he would still be lost in the ceremonialism of Judaism. With the apostle Paul of old, the writer pleads, "I beseech you therefore, brethren, by the mercies of God, to present your bodies a living sacrifice" (Romans 12:1), that even the Jew may see in us "him whom to know aright is life eternal." It doesn't matter in what denomination we find ourselves, or in what fellowship we may be working. The writer has been in Bible conferences where foreign and domestic missions have been presented, and hundreds have been challenged to enter the gospel ministry, and to support missionaries, but where missions to the Jews were never mentioned. And all the time, standing on the sidelines is the Jew, without the Gospel of Jesus Christ because the middle wall of partition has not been broken down. "How doth the love of God" abide in you when you see the need of the Jew and do nothing about it?

Verse 11: . . . for there is no respect of persons with God.

The words here translated, "respect of persons," are in the Greek made up of two words, one of which means face, countenance, person, individual, personal presence, or appearance; and the other means, to take, to take up, to assume, to put on, to admit, or to give reception to. Both these words, used together in the Greek can be translated, to give a gracious reception to a petitioner, or, to show partiality or give unfair judgment.

In the New Testament the expression, "respect of persons," is used at times in a bad sense. See Ephesians 6:9; Colossians 3:25; James 2:1. This idea of "respect of persons" is Jewish in background. It is based on Deuteronomy 10:17, which is the source for the "respect of persons" thought. In the Talmud, in Pirqe Aboth 4:31, there occurs this, "He is about to judge with whom there is no iniquity nor forgetfulness, nor respect of persons, nor taking of a bribe." In other words, the thought here is that God is not partial. God cannot give a corrupt judgment. God cannot take a reward or be bought off with a price.

At this point the following story, or Jewish legend, will enable us to understand Deuteronomy 10:17 better:

"Yochannan Ben Van Zakki, the Rabbinical scholar, was visited one morning by his disciples (or his student body). He had failed to appear in the classroom. When his students came in they found him on his bed in a dying condition with tears rolling down his cheeks. A student said to him, 'Rabbi, why weepest thou?' He replied, 'I am about to come into the presence of the King of kings, blessed be His name. If I were to come into the presence of an earthly king, whose favor could be bought with a price, whose wrath could be eased, who is on the throne today and in the grave tomorrow; even if I were to come into the presence of this kind of a king, it would be with fear and trembling. But I am about to come into the presence of the King of kings, blessed be His name, whose throne is eternal, whose favor cannot be bought with a price. He has set before me one path leading to Gan Edin (which in Judaism means heaven) and another to Gehennan. Which path I am to tread I know not. If I am to come into the presence of this kind of a King, should I not weep?"

The title of this Jewish Rabbi is the "Pillar of Right, The Mighty Hammer in Israel." The thought in Romans 2:11 is that God never gives a corrupt judgment. His judgments are righteous. They are just. They are without partiality.

Verse 12: For as many as have sinned without the law shall also perish without the law: and as many as have sinned under the law shall be judged by the law . . . ;

We must realize that no one today is without the law. To the Jews, "the Law was given through Moses"; to the Gentiles, God has written the substance of it on their hearts. Both are without excuse.

Verse 13: . . . for not the hearers of the law are just before God, but the doers of the law shall be justified . . . ;

This verse, interestingly enough, is based on the writings of Judaism; namely, Pirqe Aboth 1:18, and are the sayings of Gamaliel's son, who was a classmate of Paul. Bear in mind, there is a difference between works of the law which we do in order to try to justify ourselves before God, and after we have been justified by our faith, we show our works. We who have faith, heed the law, is the argument here. We shall elaborate on this as we examine succeeding verses.

Verse 14: . . . for when Gentiles that have not the law, do by nature the things of the law, these, not having the law, are the law unto themselves . . . ;

The Talmud recognizes no merit in the good deeds of the heathen (Gentiles), unless such good deeds are accompanied by a definite wish for admission to the privileges of Judaism. Even if a Gentile were to keep the whole Law, it would avail him nothing without circumcision. Debarim Rabba I reads, "If he prays to Jehovah, his prayer is not heard." Peskita, 156a says, "If he commits sin and repents, that too does not help him"; and Peskita 12b continues, "Even for his alms he gets no credit." It is interesting to note that in Jewish writings, Jewish

Law, and Jewish thinking, circumcision is the most important thing. In fact, the Rabbis even believe that if a male child dies before he is circumcised, circumcision must be performed on the child's dead body. In a book called, *The Code of Jewish Law,* by Hyman E. Goldin (Hebrew Publishing Co., N.Y., 1961), are these words, "An infant who dies before circumcision, whether within the eight days or thereafter, must be circumcised at the grave, in order to remove the fore-skin which is a disgrace to him, but no benedictions should be pronounced over this circumcision. He should be given a name to perpetuate his memory, and that mercy may be shown him from heaven to be included in the resurrection of the dead, and that he may then have sufficient understanding to recognize his father and his mother. If he was buried without circumcision and they became aware of it immediately, when there is no likelihood that the body has already begun to decompose, the grave should be opened and the circumcision should be performed. But if they became aware of it only after some days, the grave should not be opened" (Chapter 163, p. 44, Law 7 under Circumcision).

Thus we see the great importance that Judaism places on circumcision. From this Jewish custom and circumcising the dead, infant baptism originated, as did also the last rites over the dead in the Roman Catholic Church. This writer would like to have the Rabbis show us where in the Old Testament it is commanded to circumcise a dead body, and to have our Roman Catholic friends show us where the Bible tells us why we must sprinkle an infant, dead or alive. However, we can understand now the importance that Judaism places on circumcision.

It is frightening to realize how far people can get away from God, but we can at least understand why in the sight of the Jew the Gentiles are so lost. The Gentile, in the Jewish mind, does not stand a chance of being righteous in the sight of God. If circumcision is one of the prerequisites for righteousness in Judaism, then of course the Gentile is irretrievably lost. In Romans 2:14 there is a different kind of argument. We must recognize too that although "the Gentiles that have not the law" they must have had a law operating for them. There must have been another law of God operative before the Law given at Mount Sinai. How else would Joseph have known that it would have been wrong for him "to do this great wickedness and sin against God" with Potiphar's wife (Genesis 39:9)? How would Abraham, Isaac and Jacob have known of the tithe? Basically, these examples may not be the Law as such but they are God's requirements of man. So today, even though we are under grace, that does not eliminate the law, "For we know that the law is spiritual: but I am carnal, sold under sin" (Romans 7:14).

Verse 15: . . . in that they show the work of the law written in their hearts, their conscience bearing witness therewith, and their thoughts one with another accusing or else excusing them . . . ;

In verse 14 it is stated that even though "Gentiles that have not the law" which was written on stone, they have a "law unto themselves" which is "written in their hearts" and consciences. Paul states just that in verse 15, "they show the work of the law." That this must be the case is obvious from a casual reading of Genesis 37:8-20, describing the treatment of Joseph by his brethren. As a man reflects within himself, as a person cogitates on the good or evil of his own acts, it becomes a sort of mental soliloquy which causes him to wonder was it right or wrong?

Verse 16: . . . in the day when God shall judge the secrets of men, according to my gospel, by Jesus Christ.

This writer believes the word "day" in this passage refers to the time when the Lord returns to the earth at the close of the Tribulation (Matthew 24:21, 27). Was not Paul's gospel the setting forth of the first and second coming of Christ? How can any minister claim that he is preaching the Gospel if in his preaching he does not tell of the two comings of the Lord, namely, one for salvation and the other for judgment? We must emphasize both. The first coming tells us how to be saved, the second is the motive for Christian living. ". . . all be made manifest before the judgment seat of Christ; . . ." (II Corinthians 5:10). Nothing will inspire and purify a Christian's life more than the realization of the imminent return of the Lord Jesus Christ. Is not this the thought expressed in I John 3:3, "and every one that hath this hope set on him purifieth himself, even as he is pure"? The Greek word for "pure" means perfect, chaste and clean, as well as pure.

Fundamentalism is at times accused by some people of preaching a negative Gospel. The New Evangelicalism (and one wonders how new this hybrid is) claims that the Gospel is not negative but positive. If the Gospel is only positive, a good portion of the Scriptures would have to be discarded. We can become so broad in our thinking that we become flat. The old, worn-out cliche is that we must be "all things to all men"

(I Corinthians 9:22). The people who like to make this statement become nothing to anyone. The context is Paul's vindication of his ministry in reaching the lost. As the Christian life is set forth in the New Testament, it would seem to have a negative ring to it — "be not conformed or fashioned" (Romans 12:2); "not unequally yoked with unbelievers" (in worship) (II Corinthians 6:14); "touch no unclean thing" (Isaiah 52:11) which refers to the Gentile's possession of sacrificial meats (II Corinthians 6:17). Even though this is concerned with worship, this writer believes that the implications reach many facets of the Christian's life. We Christians are challenged to be dead to the world; to be guided and energized by the Holy Spirit; to be epistles read of all men. We have to be different. What is this but a negative attitude in the sight of the world? The Psalmist of old caught the truth of God when he said what could be expressed in modern language, "Walk not, stand not, lest you wind up in an ungodly crowd" (Psalm 1:1). Who will deny that the Ten Commandments are a negative approach? Just a casual look at Exodus 20:3: "Thou shalt have no other"; verse 4: "Thou shalt not make"; verse 5: Thou shalt not bow down"; verse 7: "Thou shalt not take"; verse 10: "Thou shalt not do any work"; verse 13: "Thou shalt not kill"; and so on to verse 17, "Thou shalt not covet." All this is negative. Since when have the Ten Commandments been abrogated or nullified? They are, in fact, reiterated in Romans 13:9. The only affimative commandment is Exodus 20:12, "Honor thy father and thy mother."

God's ancient standards have never been lowered under the dispensation of Grace; in fact, grace is the motive for keeping them as guidelines for Christian living. Since when have not these "Thou shalt nots" been practiced under grace? Grace is no license for the practice of sin. Is not this the thought that Paul expresses in the ordinance of the Lord's table (I Corinthians 11:26), in which the partaker is admonished to "examine himself" (verse 28)? Would not this examination result in leading one to purify his life? Surely, we must rethink the scriptural position of Grace, not man's position or concept of grace. Grace demands all the believer's life.

In I Peter 1:16, the Apostle says, in the King James Version, "Be ye holy; for I am holy," which, in the American Standard Version reads, "Ye shall be holy; for I am holy" This is an order. a command, and it comes from none other than the Lord God **Almighty**. The words are quoted from Leviticus 11:44, in which the same God who says "be ye holy for I am holy," says to you and to me today "Except ye repent, ye shall all likewise perish" (Luke 13:5). We must mend our ways. Our lives must be different. We must separate from worldly habits, from worldly practices. We must return to the principle of being holy even as God, Himself, has commanded us to be.

In V. 16 Paul says, "God shall judge the secrets of men, according to my gospel, by Jesus Christ." This judgment will include both Jew and Gentile. Paul has been showing the depravity of the Gentile mind, heart, morals, and conscience. This is the tenor of the first two and a half chapters of the book of Romans. The Gentile has been the one who has been scolded, berated and judged. Now from here on to the end of Chapter 2 and the first few verses of Chapter 3, Paul turns to his own flesh and blood, the people of Israel.

Verse 17: But if thou bearest the name of a Jew, and restest upon the law, and gloriest in God ... ,

This verse is based on Jeremiah 8:8 and 9:24. From Romans 2:17 to 3:13 Paul is talking directly to the Jew and what he says is based on the Old Testament. He begins with strong words, some of them very cutting, but they are words of correction and not of criticism. He is no less severe with the sins of the Jews than he was with the sins of the Gentiles. The punishment fits the crime regardless and irrespective of whether Jew or Gentile is the one in view. Since the Jews know the truth and do not follow it, the crime becomes greater and the threatened punishment more severe. Paul directs his accusations, his harsh words, his castigating statements, to the Jew.

"Behold, thou art called a Jew" (King James Version), or better, "assuming thou art a Jew," or "embrace the name of a Jew." Resting upon the law and glorying in God, constitute the value which is attached to the name Jew. However, it is one thing to be called something, and another really to be something. After all, a uniform does not make a soldier; a gun does not make a marksman; a scalpel in a man's hand does not make him a surgeon; a stethoscope in the ears of a person does not mean that he is in the medical profession; even as a cross on the lapel does not mean that one is a Christian, or a six-pointed star of David, signify the wearer to be a Jew. If a person uses the title of "Jew" he had better make sure that all the requirements connected with that word or title are met in his life. The Jew in his pride does not realize his sin; in fact, his pride *is* his sin.

Verse 18: . . . and knowest his will, and approvest the things that are excellent, being instructed out of the law . . . ,

The things that a Jew approves as "excellent" might not be "excellent" according to God's revealed Word. What difference does it make in a man's faith in God if the fork with which he is eating meat falls into a pot of soup made with milk? If he throws away the pot of soup, does it make him a better Jew? Does God look at his stomach, or does God look into his heart? In which way are these things "excellent"? None. They are not God's commandment, but rabbinical concoctions, the traditions of men which have always been the downfall of Israel. "In those days there was no king in Israel: every man did that which was right in his own eyes" (Judges 17:6). The weightier things of God are brushed aside for the insignificant things of the Rabbis, with disastrous consequences for Israel. This is what our Lord meant when He said to the Jews of His day, "Ye blind guides that strain out the gnat and swallow the camel" (Matthew 23:24). The claim of the Jew that he is instructed out of Law is a sham. The Proverb (16:25) which states "There is a way which seemeth right unto a man, but the end thereof are the ways of death," really gets to the heart of the Jew and his faith.

Verse 19: . . . and art confident that thou thyself art a guide of the blind, a light of them that are in darkness . . . ,

Oh, this confidence of the Jew in the flesh! Jeremiah made the same scathing accusation against Israel when he found out that Israel's confidence was in the flesh (17:5): ". . . cursed is the man that trusteth in man" (or puts his confidence in man). The next charge in verse 19 is ". . . a light of them that are in darkness." Some of the outstanding Rabbis in Judaism are given such illustrious titles as the "Lamp of Light" in the Zohar; the "Holy Lamp" in the Babylonian Talmud, Bercatol, Folio 28:2; and the "Lamp of Israel" in the Babylonian Talmud, Cetubot, Folio 28:2. But what dim lights these men were! The true light is God's Word. The Psalmist caught the full significance of it in Psalm 119:105, "Thy word is a lamp unto my feet, and a light unto my path." Oh, how Israel has stumbled across the years, decades, centuries, millenniums! The New Testament says of their leaders, "They are blind guides. And if the blind guide the blind, both shall fall into a pit" (Matthew 15:14). What a tremendous pit! The Gentiles substituted philosophy for God's Word, and when the Jews left God's Word, they left the truth.

Consequently, both embraced a lie. God's word, "Thy word is a lamp unto my feet . . . " was to have been the guiding light of Israel. When our Saviour walked the streets of Jerusalem in His flesh, He said, "I am the light of the world." Not only is He the Light of Israel, but He is also the Light of the whole world. "In him was life; and the life was the light of men" (John 1:4; 8:12; and 12:46).

In the Talmud, Ba Kama, Folio 52a, we find this: "When a shepherd is angry with the sheep, he blinds the leader; that is, when God determines to punish the Israelites, He gives them unworthy rulers." What a commentary! Two thousand years of pilgrimage have led Israel to disaster. God's purpose for Israel was and still is, that they guide and lead the Gentiles to the truth of God (Micah 4:1-5; Isaiah 2:2-4). This is God's plan for Israel, and we may rest assured that God's will will be done. The final goal for Israel is to bring salvation to the entire world. "Salvation is from the Jews" (John 4:22). But how far Israel has wandered from this truth!

The Psalmist in 3:8 writes, "Salvation belongeth unto Jehovah . . ." and Isaiah says in 43:11, "I, even I, am Jehovah, and besides me there is no saviour;" and also in 46:13, "I bring near my righteousness, it shall not be far off, and my salvation shall not tarry; and I will place salvation in Zion for Israel my glory." But the classic verse in Scripture, which summarizes all that is contained in the verses just quoted, is the brief but powerful utterance of Jonah (2:9) from the belly of the great fish which God created to swallow him, "Salvation is of Jehovah" (the Lord). For the Jew must realize that salvation is in the God of Israel, not in the writings of the Rabbis. It is useless to run away from God. Where can one run from God that God cannot find him? When a person deals with the Omnipotent, Omnipresent and Omniscient God, where can he run to hide from Him? Psalm 139:7-12 has this wonderful answer: "Whither shall I flee from thy presence? If I ascend up into heaven, thou art there: If I make my bed in Sheol, behold, thou art there. If I take the wings of the morning and dwell in the uttermost parts of the sea (as Jonah did); even there shall thy hand lead me, and thy right hand shall hold me . . . Even the darkness hideth not from thee," even as God found Jonah in the fish.

With God there is neither light nor darkness. It is impossible to hide from God, and Jonah realized it. He reached his extremity before making the honest confession, "Salvation is of the Lord." Israel slowly but surely is reaching this position and she, too, will

cry to God, "Blessed be he that cometh in the name of the Lord"
(or Jehovah) (Psalm 118:26). There is salvation in no other
name. The Saviour saw Israel's blindness when He looked over
Jerusalem, which is to be the center of peace and of righteousness, but has become a den of iniquity. He wept over the city
and said, "O Jerusalem, Jerusalem, that killeth the prophets, and
stoneth them that were sent unto her! . . ." (Matthew 23:37).
Words of pity and great sorrow. However, they do not close in a
minor key. They close in triumph! Jesus said, "Behold, your
house is left unto you desolate . . . till ye shall say, Blessed is he
that cometh in the name of the Lord." Israel's depravity as a nation is not final or fatal.

**Verse 20: . . . a corrector of the foolish, a teacher of babes, hav-
ing in the law the form of knowledge and of the truth . . . ;**

Instead of "corrector" (ASV) it is "instructor" (KJV) which in
the Greek means, educator, trainer, nurturer, chastiser. Education without God is the most dangerous thing in the world, because a godless individual has no fear of God. He lives only unto
himself and for today. The Jew claims to be an instructor, or
corrector. An instructor or corrector of whom? The Greek word
for "foolish" and "babes" means unwise, simple, ignorant and
unenlightened. It is used in a religious sense in this text as
"teacher of babes" (ASV). In Judaism this phrase would read,
"teacher of sucklings." The great Jewish teachers, who were
great only in their own eyes, and who taught the unlearned,
needed light and instruction themselves, even as our Lord had to
say to Nicodemus, "Art thou the teacher of Israel and under-
standest not these things?" (John 3:10).

Previously, on page 60, we spoke of Rabbi Yochannan Ben Zakki
who had such magnificent titles, yet when he reached the darkest hour of his life he found himself, even as did Nicodemus,
uneducated, unenlightened, untrained, and as unilluminated as
any heathen in the jungles of Africa. He didn't know where to
go, even though he was supposed to be a teacher of babes. The
terms "babes" or "sucklings" referred in Judaism, to Gentiles who
became proselytes. Paul uses this word to describe one who is
immature (Galatians 4:1; I Corinthians 3:1; Hebrews 5:13).

V. 20: "having in the law the form of knowledge and of the
truth," that is, the outer form and outline, not the inner meaning,
because "The fear of Jehovah is the beginning of wisdom" (Psalm
111:10 and Proverbs 1:7). Judaism's concept of "wisdom" was
only a form, a rough sketch, an outline. Paul realizes this fully as

he writes to young Timothy (II Timothy 3:5) that evil men in the
last days will be holding a "form of godliness but (as) having
denied the power thereof." The power is the Gospel. God has
no omnipotence apart from the Gospel, because it is only in the
Gospel and through the Gospel and by the Gospel that God's
salvation is operative. Israel does not know this; therefore, she
does not have the knowledge which she claims. The word in
the Greek which is translated "wisdom," means not only wisdom
and knowledge, but also to know in a complete and settled manner, and to ascertain by examination and experience. This experience comes only by being born anew: "Except one be born
anew, he cannot see the kingdom of God" (John 3:3), let alone
enter it. These words have to be written in indelible characters on
the self-righteous mind of the Jew, as well as on the depraved
mind of the Gentile. The way of the cross leads home for both
Jew and Gentile. It is impossible to come to God except by the
Gospel and by the new birth. This isn't a question of should I or
shouldn't I, or, to use a common expression, there are no "ands,
ifs or buts" about it. We do not go to heaven on our geneaologies,
our righteousnesses or by our associations. We go to heaven only
because we have been born again. Unless we have been born
again, hell is our final destiny. "There is a way which seemeth
right unto a man; but the end thereof are the ways of death,"
Solomon wrote in Proverbs 14:12.

The Gospel was, the Gospel is, and always will be, the power
of God unto salvation. This plan, this program, is eternal, unalterable and unwavering. It has the sanction of God Almighty in the words of His prophets and the apostles, "Thus
saith the Lord." The Gospel is the power of God through Jesus
Christ, His virgin birth, His holy life, His death on the cross, His
resurrection and His coming again. This is the Gospel. Believe it
and go to heaven; reject it and you are at this moment in the
suburbs of eternal hell.

**Verse 21: . . . thou therefore that teachest another, teachest
thou not thyself? thou that preachest a man should not steal, dost
thou steal?**

Paul is continuing his analysis of the meaning of the name
Jew and the responsibilities of a person who is a Jew. This is
also a continuation of the damaging charges the Apostle is making
against the Jews. He speaks out of his heart's experience. Who
among the Jews could accuse Paul of not knowing what he is

talking about? After all, he was reared and nurtured among Jews.

It is one thing for a person to know the Law in its every letter, but it is all the more damaging for that person not to obey the Law. This is exactly the charge that James makes when he says, "To him therefore that knoweth to do good, and doeth it not, to him it is sin" (James 4:17); and what Peter says, "For it were better for them not to have known the way of righteousness, than, after knowing it, to turn back from the holy commandment delivered unto them" (II Peter 2:21). This is exactly what Paul is saying here in verse 21. The person who teaches others ought to know and practice that which he is teaching. Should not this apply to Israel of all the people in the world? Israel alone, as a nation, was the recipient of the Word of God. They had it in the beginning and have it today. They boast of it; they exult in it. The Jewish people make this prayer, "Thou hast chosen us from all nations, Thou hast exalted us above every tongue, Thou hast sanctified us by thy law." These are tremendous claims and responsibilities, and people who claim them must live up to them; in other words, inasmuch as the Law was given to the Jews, they should practice it. If they are the chosen people of God, and they are, then by all means they ought to live as such in order that their position and experience as God's chosen people will be apparent to the people around them. It is God's will that they be in complete fellowship with Him, but this has not been the case. Had Israel been true to her calling, she would not be scattered to the four corners of the world as she is today. She would not be under the domination of a Gentile world, dispersed, scattered and lost among the nations.

Israel should be God's emissaries. If Israel boasts in the Law, then there is every right to expect, as Paul says here, that she should not fail to practice obedience to the Law. The words of verse 21 form a damaging statement. The word "teach" can also be translated, proclaim. This word has the suggestion of command. Even though the Jews were demanding that others observe the Law, they did the very opposite. It is the old, old adage, "Don't do as I do, do as I say." Then, too, when Paul asks in verse 21, "dost thou steal?" he is not referring to the eighth commandment only, but to all ten commandments as one composite whole. Breaking any one of the ten commandments entails the same penalty as breaking another. One commandment broken is as though all ten were broken. The Jewish penalty for breaking any one or all of the commandments was the same — stoning.

In God's sight, to tell a lie is just as great a sin as to kill. This is something for all of us to think about. To covet is just as wrong as to steal. The Jew boasts of possessing the Law, glories in it, and claims to have a thorough knowledge of it, yet he fails to realize the fact that though he abhors murder (and who doesn't?) the breaking of the Sabbath, in God's sight, is just as great a sin as murder.

Americans were appalled along with a good part of the civilized world because of an incident which occurred in the city of Stanleyville, Congo, South Africa, in November 1964, when a group of nuns, missionaries and American consular officers was ruthlessly massacred by a bloodthirsty tribe of Congolese rebels called the Simbas. Among those selected for torture was an important Congolese official thought to have much power. His liver was cut out from his body while he was still alive. Pieces were snatched up by the savages and devoured eagerly, believing this would give them power.

This writer tells this story, shocking as it is, to point out to Israel that the revolting murder of that Congolese official was no greater in God's sight than the breaking of the Sabbath. This is no exaggerated or fictitious comparison. The breaking of one commandment is like breaking all ten of them.

Verse 22: . . . thou that sayest a man should not commit adultery, dost thou commit adultery? thou that abhorrest idols, dost thou rob temples? . . . .

This verse is merely a continuation of heaping charges upon charges, a familiar habit of speech among the Jews. Adultery was a sin practiced by the Gentiles. The history of ancient Corinth is filled with stories of vice, immorality and debauchery unfit for Christians to read. Even animals do not become so degraded. The sin of ancient Ephesus, with its temple of Diana (Acts 19:24-28), and the worship of idols, is also referred to by Paul in verse 22, ". . . thou that abhorrest idols, dost thou rob temples? . . ." The statue of "Diana of the Ephesians" represented a heathen goddess having one hundred breasts, evidently symbolizing the reproductive powers of nature. Yet Diana was an object of worship to the degraded minds of the heathen. From the context of verse 22, we see that Paul is painting a picture in which he is implying that the people of Israel were no better than the heathen.

V. 22: ". . . thou that abhorrest idols, dost thou rob temples? . . ." The Greek word for "abhorrest" means to loathe, or to detest. Vincent, in his *Word Studies of the New Testament,* says of this word, "The verb abhor means originally to turn away from the thing on account of the stench." This is what God and Israel think of idols. If we leaf through the pages of the books of Kings and Chronicles, and even the book of Exodus, we find idol worship in Israel. Aaron even states that the creation of the golden calf was, in itself, a miracle. In Exodus 32:4, we see the truth. God took nine hundred years from the time that He brought Israel out of the Land of Egypt until they came out of the Babylonian dispersion to rid Israel of polytheism and idols and turn all their attention to Him. From the Babylonian dispersion to this day Israel has not worshiped idols. This thought of abhorring idols and robbing temples Paul is taking from Deuteronomy 7:25, 26. In the Old Testament text it is shown that even the gold and silver that overlaid these idols were detested by God and should have been detested by Israel. The charge in Romans 2:22, this writer believes is this: The Gentiles by worshiping idols were robbing God of the worship and honor due Him. The Jews in Paul's day were rightfully accusing the Gentiles of this sin. Yet the Jews themselves were guilty of the same thing. In the Greek, robbing temples is committing sacrilege. In either case, the sense of this text and the charge that Paul makes is that the sin of the Jews in God's sight is the same as the sin of the Gentiles.

Verse 23 . . . thou who gloriest in the law, through thy transgression of the law dishonorest thou God?

Here again we have the things that the Jew as a nation and as a person glories in. There are thirteen things that the Jew glories in: (1) That he is a man of praise; (2) that he is a man of thanksgiving; (3) that his trust is in the Law; (4) that his boast is God; (5) that he notes God's will; (6) that he approves the things that are excellent; (7) that he is a leader of the blind; (8) that he is a light for those who are in darkness; (9) that he is an instructor of the ignorant; (10) that he is a teacher of babes; (11) that he is a man who directs others; (12) that he is a man who preaches against theft, adultery and idolatry; and (13) that, finally, he is a man who glories in the commandments of God. What a beautiful portrait of the perfect man, in God's sight! But the tragedy of it is that the opposite is the true picture of the individual Jew. How much like the Gentile the Jew has become! Truly they are the same. Only the names — Jew and Gentile — are different. As human beings they are identical. Why are the Jew and the Gentile alike? Who taught the Jew all he knows? Whence did he learn these things? Did he not learn them from mingling with the Gentiles? For example, where did the Jew learn to eat garlic? From the Egyptians (Numbers 11:5). Where did the Jew, as a people, learn of a golden calf? In Egypt (Exodus 32:2-4). Where did the Jew learn to worship idols in groves upon mountain tops? From the Gentiles (Deuteronomy 16:21, 22; I Kings 18:19), from whom the Jews refused to separate themselves.

The problem of the Jew is his propensity to learn too easily from others, especially those things forbidden by his Law. So then, the sins of both Jew and Gentile are ungodliness, intemperance and unrighteousness. These three words cover every facet of sin of which any human being is guilty in the sight of God. The attributes of the real man of God are found in Paul's Epistle to Titus (2:12), that "denying ungodliness and worldly lusts, we should live soberly and righteously and godly in this present world."

Verse 24: For the name of God is blasphemed among the Gentiles because of you, even as it is written.

This is the accusation Paul makes against the Jew, that the Jew is the cause of God's name being blasphemed among the Gentiles. Can this mean that every time a Gentile takes the name of God in vain it is because the Jew has neglected to live as a Jew? This is the same charge found in the Old Testament in Ezekiel 36:20 where God accuses Israel of profaning His holy name when they came among the Gentiles. The Gentiles said, "These are the people of Jehovah, and are gone forth out of his land." Had Israel not sinned they would have remained in the land. A series of blessings was to come upon Israel if they accepted the condition laid down by God in Deuteronomy 28: 1, 2, "If thou shalt hearken diligently unto the voice of Jehovah thy God," but if they did not accept God's condition, a long list of curses would come upon them, enumerated in verses 16-68. Every time the Gentile takes the name of God in vain it is blasphemy. Every time a Gentile takes the name of the Saviour in vain that, too, can be laid at the feet of Israel. These are the charges, these are the words, these are the accusations of Romans 2:24.

Verse 25: For circumcision indeed profiteth, if thou be a doer of the law: but if thou be a transgressor of the law, thy circumcision is become uncircumcision.

Here Paul strikes at the foundation of Judaism, circumcision. He brings the most honorable thing in Judaism to the forefront. This is the most sacred thing, the most sacred practice, as we mentioned earlier, and showed the important place of circumcision in Judaism. The greatest insult in Judaism is to call a man an uncircumcised one. Circumcision makes the Jew. It is a sign of the covenant people. He becomes an heir of the promises of God. He gains the right to the Kingdom of God. It gives him a share in the world to come. It makes him a child of God. In the prayers which the Jew makes he says, "All Israel has a share in the world to come." All Israel shares by circumcision. There is a legend that God at some future time will send His angel to remove the marks of circumcision from the wicked. The very thing that Israel claims as the basis for justification — circumcision — then proves to be the basis for condemnation. What Paul says here is this: If circumcision, as the Jews claim, gives them all this, then circumcision "indeed profiteth." It is the keeping of the Law. But if "thou be a transgressor of the law, thy circumcision is become no circumcision," and is, in the final analysis, condemnation. Thus, by not keeping the law, "circumcision is become uncircumcision."

Verses 26 and 27: (26) If therefore the uncircumcision keep the ordinances of the law, shall not his uncircumcision be reckoned for circumcision? (27) and shall not the uncircumcision which is by nature, if it fulfil the law, judge thee, who with the letter and circumcision art a transgressor of the law?

Here is the whole question: If circumcision accomplishes so much for the one who is circumcised and keeps the Law, shall not the one who is not circumcised but keeps the Law, gain the same privilege by thus keeping the Law (the tense of the Greek is a continuing action) as the one who has been circumcised? If the breaking of the Law renders one to be as though he were not circumcised, then the keeping of the Law should render one as though he were circumcised. It must be that circumcision is subordinate to the keeping of the Law itself. The whole argument is Jewish thinking, and is in keeping with the Old Testament; in fact, these two verses in Romans 2:25, 26, summarize God's argument with Israel in the Old Testament (Deuteronomy 10:16; Jeremiah 4:4 and 9:25). In Jeremiah 9:25, 26, God places the Jew under the same condemnation as He does the Edomites, the children of Ammon, and the Moabites. As these nations were uncircumcised, so was all the house of Israel uncircumcised in heart; therefore, circumcision in the flesh and circumcision in the heart are on the same level. This was precisely the accusation that Stephen made in the presence of Israel as he was about to be stoned to death (Acts 7:51) — "Ye stiffnecked and uncircumcised in heart and ears, ye do always resist the Holy Spirit," the will and wish of God.

Verses 28 and 29: (28) For he is not a Jew who is one outwardly; neither is that circumcision which is outward in the flesh: (29) but he is a Jew who is one inwardly; and circumcision is that of the heart, in the spirit not in the letter; whose praise is not of men, but of God.

By taking the first part of verse 28 only and the first part only of verse 29, Paul's meaning becomes crystal clear, "For he is not a Jew who is one outwardly . . . but he is a Jew who is one inwardly." We must not forget that from Romans 2:17 to 3:2 of this Epistle, Paul is talking to the Jews, not to the Gentiles. There is no such thing as a Gentile becoming a spiritual Jew when he becomes a Christian. A Jew who becomes a Christian, a believer in the Lord Jesus Christ, is a COMPLETED JEW. In Christ, in the light of the New Testament, there is neither Jew nor Gentile (Galatians 3:28), we are one. Here, in these verses, the Apostle is pushing the Jews into a corner to make them see that in the sight of God their position is the same as that of the Gentiles. The name Jew carries along with it many privileges if the individual Jew will assume his responsibilities, but merely to boast of being a Jew is meaningless. In God's sight it is a burst soap bubble. The Jews are depraved and lost, the same as the Gentiles. The Jew is just as much in need of the Gospel in his "lostness" as the Gentile is. Verses 28 and 29, it seems to me, are a continuation of Romans 1:16, "to the Jew first," because of what the Jew is and has, as Paul later explains in Romans 9:4, 5. Because of what the Jew is, and ought to be spiritually, he is all the more in need of the Gospel. Due to his background, he should be in complete fellowship with God. But he is not! His position in the world, his condition in the light of the Gospel, places him in the same depraved position as any pagan or heathen.

3

Verse 1: What advantage then hath the Jew? or what is the profit of circumcision?

From the preceding verses in Chapter 2, it is clear that the circumcised Jew is just as lost as the uncircumcised Gentile. This is a very humiliating conclusion for a Jew to accept, especially since it comes from the lips of a highly-trained and educated Pharisee like Paul. What good can there be in Jews claiming that "we have Abraham to our father" (Luke 3:8)? How meaningless is the phrase in the Jewish prayerbook, "All Israel has a share in the world to come." How meaningless, too, are the words in the prayer, "Thou hast chosen us from among all peoples." Is there any advantage then in being a Jew? There should be, because the word Jew comes from the Hebrew word *Yehudah,* a word which means "praise unto Jehovah."

How can this be reconciled with Romans 2:24 in which Paul says that God's name is blasphemed among the Gentiles because of the Jew? In other words, Paul blames the Jews because the Gentiles blaspheme God! Paul then returns to the subject of circumcision and asks, "What is the profit of circumcision?" (v. 1). His argument at this point is based on certain verses in the book of Ecclesiastes; namely, 1:3, "What profit hath man?"; 6:8, "For what advantage hath the wise?"; and 6:11, "What is man the better?" The Jew is well acquainted with these questions. Therefore Paul asks, "What advantage then hath the Jew?" We must realize that Paul is quoting from the Septuagint version of the Old Testament and uses the same Greek word for "advantage" in Ecclesiastes as the Septuagint does, which means over and above, extraordinary, more, greater or pre-eminent. Vincent, in his *Word Studies of the New Testament,* translates "advantage" to mean surplus or prerogative, which would give Romans 3:1, the sense of "What prerogative (or surplus) then hath the Jew?"

Throughout this Epistle, Paul is relentlessly pushing the Jews into a corner. These are body blows to Judaism. The Jews are embarrassed when Paul continues with the rest of the question, "What is the profit of circumcision?" The Greek word translated "profit" means also advantage, benefit or gain. For the Jew there is none. But the Jew can retort, Did not the Saviour say, "Salvation is from the Jews"? (John 4:22). True, salvation can come only through the Jews. According to the Old Testament the Saviour had to be of the tribe of Judah of the lineage of David.

A prominent radio preacher has written a book trying to disprove the fact that the Saviour was a Jew. It is a shocking thing to realize that a preacher who claims to be an ardent believer in the Word of God and its inspiration, and believes the fundamentals of the Christian faith, tries to nullify the fact that the Saviour was Jewish. If the Saviour was not Jewish, the statement in John 4:22, "Salvation is from the Jews," could not be true. If Christ was not Jewish, then He could not be the promised Messiah of Israel. The Scriptures contain abundant proof that our Lord is Jewish, of the House of David and Jesse and the tribe of Judah. How sad it is to reflect that the Jews, through whom God willed to bring salvation to all men, Jew and Gentile alike, should be the ones to reject it! They have rejected the means, the way and the truth of salvation. What tragedy! By rejecting all this, they have doomed themselves to an eternal hell and separation from God.

It may be too early in the Epistle to the Romans to discuss this, but here it ought to be clearly stated as it is in Romans 11:8, that "God gave them (Israel) a spirit of blindness, eyes that they should not see, and ears that they should not hear, unto this very day." Bear in mind that Paul said, "God gave them," not the Pharisees, not the Sadducees, not the scribes, not traditionalism, but that "God gave them a spirit of blindness." Paul also stated that it has lasted unto this very day. Why? Why has all this been done? For one reason only: "They are enemies (of the Gospel) for your sake," (meaning the sake of the Gentiles) (Romans 11:28). We see here the plan and program of God and His sovereignty, which are being dealt with in this chapter. There are many things we do not understand about God's ways simply because they are as high above man as the heavens are above the earth.

Verse 2: Much every way: first of all, that they were intrusted with the oracles of God.

There is much advantage in being a Jew, Paul is saying, because, "first of all, that they were intrusted with the oracles of God." We must bear in mind that every promise of God, and every word of God, and all revelation from Genesis 1 to Revelation 22, has come to us through the Jews. It must be conceded that *they are* "intrusted with the oracles of God." The Old Testament, together with the oracles, is in the New revealed. The Bible is a Jewish book that reveals a Jewish God, the God of Israel; and a Jewish Saviour, Jesus Christ, of the seed of David; and in which is also revealed a Jewish salvation and a Jewish throne, the Throne of David; in a Jewish capital, Jerusalem, with a Jewish message (Isaiah 2:3; Micah 4:1, 2); through Jewish messengers (Isaiah 61:6; Zechariah 8:23). All this is summarized in Romans 9:4, ". . . who are Israelites; whose is the adoption, and the glory, and the covenants . . ." or the Oracles of God. This word "oracle" is used only four times in the New Testament, Romans 3:2; Hebrews 5:12; I Peter 4:11; and Acts 7:38 (ASV) where it is translated "living oracles." Let us not lose sight of the fact that the Old Testament clearly states that the Jew has an advantage (Deuteronomy 4:7, 8), "For what great nation is there, that hath a god so nigh unto them, as Jehovah our God is whensoever we call upon him?" There are also the great promises of Psalm 147:19, 20, "He showeth his word unto Jacob, his statutes and his ordinances unto Israel." God has never dealt with any other nation in this way. Verse 20 (Psalm 147) ends with these words, "Praise ye Jehovah," or Hallelujah! This could never be said of the Gentiles for they never possessed such a God.

If the final judgment of God upon a man, or a race, is based on character or a "form of godliness," then the Gentile is just as good without the Law as the Jew is with Law. We shall discuss this subject further when we come to chapters 9, 10, and 11 (Romans). From all that has been said so far, we must conclude that the Jew does have an advantage, for "that they (the Jews) were intrusted with the oracles of God."

Verse 3: For what if some were without faith? shall their want of faith make of none effect the faithfulness of God?

Paul asks "For what if some were without faith?" or, "if some did not believe?" Just because some of the Jews did not believe, this did not nullify the covenant relation which God had with Israel, for it was only some that did not believe, not all. The relationship was on a national basis with the children of Israel, which term in the Hebrew entails sonship. Under Jewish law, no parent can disown a son, nor can a parent make a will and disinherit a son. The parent must always include his son, if any, and bequeath a portion of his estate to him. God has this kind of a relationship with Israel (Exodus 4:22). As a nation they have a place of service (Exodus 19:5, 6; Isaiah 61:6). This is a relationship that cannot be broken because God's covenant-keeping power is everlasting. If God were to break a covenant, then the whole structure of God's economy would collapse and God's Word would be meaningless. We must differentiate at this point between national rejection and individual election. Some were without faith, not all. The covenant that God made in the Old Testament with Israel was a national covenant, made with Israel as a nation, and is not to be confused with the new covenant that God makes with the believer in the New Testament. We must keep in mind the fact that the new covenant is *not* with Israel as a nation but with the individual Jew (and Gentile as well) as a person. See I John 5:12, and note the singular personal pronoun *he*: "*He* that hath the Son hath the life; *he* that hath not the Son of God hath not the life." In the present dispensation of Grace, when the individual Jew becomes a believer in the Lord Jesus Christ as his Messiah and Saviour, he at once possesses the new covenant. At the end of this age, when Israel as a nation accepts the Lord Jesus Christ as Messiah and Lord, the new covenant will then become Israel's national possession.

The argument in verse 3 is very strong. It continues, ". . . shall their want of faith make of none effect the faithfulness of God?" The faithlessness of Israel does not and did not destroy, or make of none effect, the faithfulness of God. Nothing can alter God's faithfulness. The Greek word for "faith" is a strong word, it is the guarantee of God Himself. In the New Testament the word faith is used to mean faith in God and in Christ. (See Acts 6:7 and Jude 3.) Thanks be to God, the "some" in verse 3 who were without faith, implies that there were some with faith. God always has had a remnant. God has never been left powerless and without a witness on this earth. When God led the faithless Israelites out of Egypt, two remained faithful, Joshua and Caleb (Numbers 14). Again, when Elijah thought he was the only one left who remained faithful, God had left for Himself, "seven thousand men, who have not bowed the knee to Baal" (Romans 11:4). In this day God has a remnant according to the election of grace. God's word, God's promises, God's covenants, cannot be broken. In the midst of a changing world, God remains changeless. In the midst of a faithless world, He remains faithful.

In the midst of a distrustful world, He remains trustworthy. In the midst of a mutable world, He remains immutable. "For I, Jehovah, change not; therefore ye, O sons of Jacob, are not consumed" (Malachi 3:6). "Jesus Christ is the same yesterday and today and for ever" (Hebrews 13:8). "For ever, O Jehovah, thy word is settled in heaven" (Psalm 119:89). We have an eternal God, an eternal Saviour, an eternal salvation, an eternal plan, an eternal hope, an eternal destiny. This cannot be altered even though "some (of Israel) were without faith." God has always kept His word and His covenants, as recorded in Deuteronomy 7:9; Jeremiah 31:35-37; Hebrews 6:17, 18; James 1:17. To the Jewish nation God has promised eternal existence as we see in I Chronicles 17:22; Isaiah 43:1; 44:7. A more literal translation of Isaiah 44:7 in the ASV reads, "And who, as I, shall call, and shall declare it, and set it in order for me, since I established the ancient people? and the things that are coming, and that shall come to pass, let them declare." The word translated "ancient," should be translated _eternal_.

So we see that God's promises to Israel are eternal. To us, Jewish and Gentile believers in the Lord Jesus Christ, it is the same God who gives us the same kind of promises. The Saviour says of His sheep, that is, those who believe on Him, "I give unto them eternal life; and they shall never perish" (John 10:28). Of course, we must make certain that we _are_ His sheep. He says in the preceding verse, "My sheep hear my voice." We must, come what may, make our individual choice. "Choose you this day whom ye will serve" (Joshua 24:15). Surely, in the world we live in today we need some stability, some assurance. Those of us who have accepted Christ as Lord and Saviour, have built our house upon a Rock and it shall never fall (Matthew 7:24, 25).

Verse 4: God forbid: yea, let God be found true, but every man a liar; as it is written, That thou mightest be justified in thy words, and mightest prevail when thou comest into judgment.

We come now to one of Paul's favorite exclamations, "God forbid!" Though in the Greek this is the strongest phrase to express the negative, in Paul's mind it is a Hebrew word which carries with it the thought of blasphemy. In other words, to question God's faithfulness, or even to hint at such an impossible fault in God's nature, is tantamount to calling God a liar. How terrible this thought must have been to a Jew like Paul! The expression, "God forbid!" is equivalent to expressions like, Unthinkable! Impossible! Perish the thought! In exclaiming, "God forbid!" Paul is quoting the Septuagint — "yea, let God be found true, but every man a liar." The Greek word for "true" means not only true but also worthy of all credit, sincerity, veracity, trustworthiness. You see, in God, there can be no "shadow that is cast by turning" (James 1:17). God is the only one who has always been true, as James states. The thought here is this: Let anyone put God on trial, test Him, try Him, question Him, and God will be found true, but every man a liar. This sin of lying attributed to man is the very antithesis — the very opposite — of the nature of God. God can be trusted and found true in all His dealings; man, when put to the test, will do anything to serve his own purpose. For man, the end justifies the means, no matter what the means may be. For God it has been, it is and always will be, Truth. That is why the incarnate God, Jesus Christ, could say, "I am the truth."

The completion of verse 4 is a quotation from Psalm 51:4, "That thou mightest be justified in thy words, and mightest prevail when thou comest into judgment." Another translation of this statement is, "That thou mayest be justified in these sayings of thine and will overcome when thou art judged." This is the meaning of Paul's thought. The result of the Psalmist's sin (in Psalm 54:1) is that God is pronounced righteous in His sentence, and free from blame in His judging. Paul applies this as if God Himself were put on trial and declared guiltless in respect to the promises which He has fulfilled, though man refuses to believe in that fulfillment.

To summarize verse 4. Man, in his final attempt to disprove God, puts God on trial and discovers when the verdict is given that he has only proved God to be true and man a liar. Mankind in their disobedience and defiance of God have always questioned and tried to disprove and to discredit God, and have always failed. But they relentlessly continue to pursue this hopeless task. The question arises, How long will man continue in his depraved condition to fight an Omnipotent, Omnipresent, Omniscient God? Since man will not give up in this hopeless task, energized by Satan, God must call a halt.

When God does call a halt to this foolish battle of man in his sin against a righteous God, the end will be most terrible. The awfulness of God's judgment against rebellious humanity is almost beyond human comprehension. We have glimpses of it in Joel 3:2, and also in verses 9 thru 17, when the world nations finally face God in their last rebellion. Depraved humanity has

always resisted God. Psalm 2 gives us an exact description of the
end time. What is the thought in the early portion of Psalm 2,
but that man is rebellious against the restraint of God, and that
he is always scheming to break that restraint. This is the object
of man's rebellion, and one might well call it the coming "world
revolution." God's answer to this is, "He that sitteth in the
heavens will laugh" (Psalm 2:4). Out of this verse, I am sure,
there came into being the well-known adage, 'Man proposes, but
God disposes." (This expression occurs in the *Imitation of
Christ,* by Thomas A Kempis, 1380-1471.) There is a similar
expression in Judaism which rhymes in Yiddish but loses the
rhyme in English, thus, "a man plans, and God laughs."

Man is here today and in the grave tomorrow. In the light of
an Omnipotent God, man's plans are worthless. In spite of man's
rebellion against God, the Almighty still extends His hands of
love, His hands of mercy. Psalm 2 closes with the words, "Kiss
the son, lest he be angry." When the Lord Jesus Christ saw the
lost condition of His people, Israel, He said, "Come unto me, all
ye that labor and are heavy laden, and I will give you rest"
(Matthew 11:28). Rest from sin! Rest from privation! Rest from
persecution! God's eternal rest such as the world cannot understand. But how sad is the answer to that invitation when His
people rejected Him and He said to them, "Ye will not come unto
me, that ye may have life" (John 5:40). Unregenerate man in the
final test is still defiant even in the presence of God Himself.

**Verse 5: But if our unrighteousness commendeth the righteous-
ness of God, what shall we say? Is God unrighteous who visiteth
with wrath? (I speak after the manner of men).**

Thus Paul continues the argument concerning the failure of
some of the Jews, as in verses 1-3. He borrows the expression,
"What shall we say?" or "What is there to say?" from Pharisaic
Judaism. This is a direct quote from passages in the Talmud.
If man's sin (David's in particular) so demonstrates and glorifies
God's righteousness, is God unrighteous in taking vengeance on
man, not only by punishing him here but also in the hereafter?
You ask, what is meant by the "here and hereafter"? We have the
story in the New Testament of the rich man and Lazarus (Luke
16:19-31), which provides an answer. The rich man in the hereafter, in his sin, was being punished. The whole argument — is
God unrighteous who visiteth with wrath? — is the argument
that an unbelieving Jew would present. It is not Paul's own argument. Paul states, "I speak after the manner of men." This is

Jewish thinking. Paul is quoting a Jewish idiom, "according to the language of the children of men." The whole discussion is Jewish in its concept and style. A careful scrutiny of the text reveals this. The Greek word for "commend" in the KJV is "commendeth" in the ASV, and both are in the present tense. The word means, to recommend, or is recommended for, or to place in a striking point of view, or to show forth and render illustrious. This is exactly the effect that David's sin had on David's mind and life. When David realized all that he had done to Uriah and Bathsheba, he cried out to God for mercy and said, in Psalm 51:4, "Against thee, and thee only, have I sinned." No matter what punishment God would inflict upon David, the "righteousness of God" would be gloriously portrayed. God's punishment, no matter how severe, would be just and righteous, but it was the grace of God that spared David. This is exactly what Paul states in I Corinthians 15:10, "But by the grace of God I am what I am"; and in Proverbs 3:34, "Surely he scoffeth at the scoffers; but he giveth grace unto the lowly." This is the same as James writes in 4:6, "But he giveth more grace. Wherefore the scripture saith, God resisteth the proud, but giveth grace to the humble."

What a marvelous portrayal of God's righteousness is the grace of God in the finished work of the cross! But for the grace of God and His mercy all mankind would be doomed. David writes in Psalm 32:1, 2, "Blessed is he whose transgression is forgiven, whose sin is covered. Blessed is the man unto whom the Lord imputeth not iniquity." Luke records in 18:9-14, the story of the Pharisee and the Publican as they stood and prayed. The Publican said, "God, be thou merciful to me a sinner." The literal translation of this sentence is, "God be thou mercy seated." The whole scene in this incident happened before the cross. Today this prayer does not need to be made. We do not need to plead, "God be thou mercy seated." God did that 1900 years ago. The writer of the book of Hebrews said, ". . . when he had made purification of sins, (he) sat down on the right hand of the Majesty on high" (1:3d). This has been accomplished. Blessed is the man who putteth his trust in the Son of God, and "whose sin is covered."

This is the old, old story of the cross. If we do not accept the Gospel of the grace of God in which "is revealed a righteousness of God," then God takes vengeance. The American Standard Version reads, "Who visiteth with wrath" (Romans 3:5). The Greek word for "visiteth" means to bring upon, or to inflict vengeance, anger, indignation, wrath or punishment. The whole phrase means, "Who inflicts punishment." This is a re-statement of Genesis 18:25, "shall not the Judge of all the earth do right?" The context of that portion of Scripture has to do with Abraham's argument with God because of the sin and debauchery of Sodom and Gomorrah. The answer that God gives Abraham is that if he could find only ten righteous persons in Sodom, He (God) would spare the city. You see, it is always the grace of God. It does not matter whether the sinner finds himself in the book of Genesis or in the gospel of John. There has always been one plan of salvation. God has never saved a soul in any other way than by the grace of God.

The cross is at the center when sin is in question. The way of the cross leads home. Sin can be covered only by a blood sacrifice. It doesn't matter whether we look at it in the book of Leviticus or in the epistle to the Hebrews. The book of Leviticus points to the epistle to the Hebrews. In Leviticus it is the blood of an animal sacrifice; in Hebrews it is the Blood of the Perfect Lamb of God. "Apart from shedding of blood there is no remission" (Hebrews 9:22). Why? Because Moses said, "the life of the flesh is in the blood" (Leviticus 17:11), and it has been given upon the altar to make an atonement for the sinning soul. The grace of God spoke to men then. The grace of God speaks to men today. There again we have the reality of an immutable God. God never changes. He doesn't have to! He knows the end before He comes to the beginning. The provision is made and has been made. Surely in the light of this fact it must be self-evident from the Apostle John's clear statement in the Revelation that the Lamb of God was slain even before the foundation of the world (13:8 KJV).

Verse 6: God forbid: for then how shall God judge the world?

The words "to judge" mean to make distinction between, to separate, to call to account, to bring to trial, to sentence, to pass judgment. This writer feels that the thought of "to judge" is expressed fully in the judgment of the Gentile nations in Matthew 25:31-46. Romans 3:6 answers the question of Romans 3:5. Is the vengeance of God just? Paul uses the rabbinical method of answering a question with a question. How else can God judge and punish the world for its sin? It must be remembered that these words of Paul are addressed to the Jews. The fact of God judging the world permeates the Old Testament and Jewish theology. (Genesis 18:25; Isaiah 63; Ezekiel 38-39; Joel 3.) Such

being the case, Paul says, "God forbid." This is not the place
to discuss this phrase, beyond what we have already written on
Romans 3:4. We will take it up in Romans chapter 11. It must
be that even "the wrath of man shall praise thee," as the Psalmist
states in 76:10. Even the very thought of God being capable of
injustice causes Paul to exclaim, "God forbid!" the meaning of
which could be, Abominable! Unthinkable! Perish the thought!
Such a thought even smacks of blasphemy! "Shall not the Judge
of all the earth do right?" (Genesis 18:25). Every lost sinner will
be an eternal monument to the Justice of God.

**Verse 7: But if the truth of God through my lie abounded unto
his glory, why am I also still judged as a sinner? ...**

The antithesis of a truth is a lie. Nothing illustrates and reveals
the truth more than a lie; nothing is more contrary to God's
nature and righteousness than a lie. It is of the devil, for the
devil is the father of lies (John 8:44). He introduced lying into
the world (Genesis 3). Paul does not imply in verse 7 that he,
a saved man, lies. He says in verse 5, "I speak after the manner
of men," meaning an unsaved man. How sad to be unsaved!
Would to God all of us as saved, blood-bought people, could say
with the English martyr, John Bradford, burned as a heretic in
1555, "But for the grace of God there goes John Bradford," whenever he saw a criminal on the way to execution (I John 1:6-10).
Don't forget, Paul is still addressing himself to Jews. If by
Israel's unfaithfulness to the covenants, occasion should be given
to God to reveal His truthfulness, His glory, and His honor, why
should Paul condemn Israel's unfaithfulness? How can an act,
which promotes the glory of God, be regarded as evil? The
reasoning is wrong. It is only because Jehovah is the Sovereign
God of creation, that He can transform the sinful action of His
people to His glory. Even though His people become faithless,
He must remain faithful. God always completes that which He
has begun or promised. Philippians 1:6; Romans 8:30; 11:29.

**Verse 8: ... and why not (as we are slanderously reported,
and as some affirm that we say), Let us do evil, that good may
come? whose condemnation is just.**

In the Greek the sentence which is translated, "as we are
slanderously reported," carries the thought, as we are blasphemed.
The whole argument, this writer believes, stems from the teaching
of the sovereignty of God. The Pharisaic Jew should know that
it is wrong to do evil that good may come, for the sovereignty of

God is one of his beliefs or dogmas. Salvation is by grace. It must be! Otherwise mankind would be doomed in the sight of a holy God. Paul, because of this statement, has been accused of "antinomianism," a false doctrine which holds that faith, alone, not obedience to the moral law, is necessary for salvation (*Webster's New World Dictionary*). Because Paul said that righteousness is not obtained through legal works, it is the gift of God, or imputed righteousness, he might have been justly accused of saying, "therefore it does not matter what man does — let us sin!" This inference he repudiates; see Romans 6:1, 15. "For by grace have ye been saved through faith . . . for good works" (Ephesians 2:8-10). Since each one of us is a "new creature," or "creation," we are the "workmanship" of God (Ephesians 2:10 Sinaitic Codex Greek Text). Again, it is the same old story. Jehovah is sovereign and He, alone, can make "the wrath of man to praise Him" (Psalm 76:10).

Verse 9: What then? are we better than they? No, in no wise: for we before laid to the charge both of Jews and Greeks, that they are all under sin . . . ,

Do we Jews excel in God's estimation? Do we have the pre-eminence? The oracles of God of which the Jews were the recipients taught them better, but did not make them better. If a person who has an illness goes to a doctor and gets a prescription which the doctor tells him will cure his illness, it does not mean that because the person has the prescription he is going to be cured. The prescription must be filled, and it must be taken according to directions. Having a prescription does not cure an illness. Taking the medicine and letting it do its work accomplishes its purpose. And so it is with Israel. They were the recipients of the law, the oracles of God, but their possession did not make them any better. Rabbis have taught Israel differently. They have taught Israel that they have a choice place or a choice position. They say that, "all Israel has a share in the world to come." If this were true, how does it come to pass that Israel is the tail and not the head of the nations and must wait until the Lord Himself will make the change? Deuteronomy 28:13 says, "And Jehovah will make thee the head, and not the tail; and thou shalt be above only, and thou shalt not be beneath; if thou shalt hearken unto the commandments of Jehovah thy God which I command thee this day." So we see that Israel is depraved just the same as the Gentiles. She does not have that choice position which the Rabbis have taught she would have.

This Rabbinical wishful thinking of the Jew is contrary to the testimony of the Scriptures. Compare Psalms 5:9; 10:7; 14:2-4; 140:3; Ecclesiastes 7:20; and Isaiah 59:7, 8. These are the verses that Paul proceeds to develop in Romans 3:10-18. Compare Romans 3:18 and Psalm 36:1, the summary of Paul's argument.

The Jews had God's preference. They had a number of advantages. But they are not better than the Gentiles. Paul is breaking down the self-righteousness of the Jew to show that in God's sight both Jew and Gentile are guilty of sin and are depraved. They both need the Gospel.

Verses 10-18: (10) . . . as it is written, There is none righteous, no, not one; (11) There is none that understandeth, There is none that seeketh after God; (12) They have all turned aside, they are together become unprofitable; There is none that doeth good, no, not so much as one: (13) Their throat is an open sepulchre; With their tongues they have used deceit: The poison of asps is under their lips: (14) Whose mouth is full of cursing and bitterness: (15) Their feet are swift to shed blood; (16) Destruction and misery are in their ways; (17) And the way of peace have they not known: (18) There is no fear of God before their eyes.

These nine verses paint for us a clear picture of what mankind is like in God's sight. This picture of man is the very opposite of man in his own sight. A careful look at these verses should cause anyone guilty of such sins to plead for forgiveness. This is the summary of these accusations against man: There is none righteous; none doing good. Man's tongue is deceitful; his lips are poisonous; his feet and his pathway are bloody and destructive; his mind devoid of peace and without the fear of God.

What a graphic picture of man in this twentieth century! No artist, no matter how gifted, could paint a more accurate picture than is here painted of the depraved, debauched, desecrated, deceitful and desperately sinful and dying world in which we are living today! What is there left of man? Paul analyzes all of man's members. He speaks of his tongue, his lips, his mouth, his feet and of his eyes. What is left? There is no necessity for speaking of the heart because the Old Testament says, "the heart is deceitful above all things . . . and who can know it?" (Jeremiah 17:9). It is "out of the abundance of the heart the mouth speaketh." Man's head might tell him better, but it is out of the heart that sin evolves; it is out of the heart that man praises God. This is the analysis that Paul makes of Israel, and brings her down as a nation, with all her pride, with all her conceit of righteousness, and all her conceit of being the chosen people of God, which she is. Paul brings her down to the level of the depraved heathen! "For all have sinned, and fall short of the glory of God" (Romans 3:23); and ". . . with the heart man believeth unto righteousness" (Romans 10:10).

Verse 19: Now we know that what things soever the law saith, it speaketh to them that are under the law; that every mouth may be stopped, and all the world may be brought under the judgment of God . . . :

Or, as the King James Version has it, ". . . may become guilty." Paul is proving in verses 10 through 18, what he has stated in verses 4 through 9, i.e., God's sovereign powers in overruling man's unrighteousness and bringing man's salvation out of his sinfulness. Man was created for God's glory and fellowship. Man has failed throughout all the ages, with no exception, regardless and irrespective of every provision God has made for his redemption. But because man has failed, does not mean that God has abandoned him. God's will must be done "on earth as it is in heaven," no matter how long it takes to bring man to his senses. It took God approximately 900 years to bring Israel out of idolatry, from the Exodus in Egypt to the deliverance out of the Babylonian Dispersion. When Israel came out of Babylon, she became a monotheistic nation and left the polytheistic practices of the heathen Gentiles. It is now 2,500 years that God has been trying to bring Israel to her senses, and nearly 2,000 years to accept the Lord Jesus Christ as her promised Messiah.

How much longer it will take to restore Israel to complete fellowship with God, we do not know. It is much later than many of us think. God is not short-sighted, but rather He is long-suffering. When the "fulness of the Gentiles" has run its course, God will bring Israel to her repentance, and she will accept and confess Jesus Christ as her promised Messiah whom she rejected 2,000 years ago. This will surely come to pass. Zechariah 12:10 tells us of the time when Israel will reach her extremity. She will then look to God and accept Jesus Christ as her Messiah, which will not take place until the Spirit of God falls upon "the house of David." In this present dispensation of the Church of Christ, God has placed upon Israel "the spirit of blindness," so that the Gentiles, "who were once aliens from the commonwealth of Israel," might be brought into that grand and glorious relationship of becoming the children of God, redeemed through the blood of Jesus Christ. Thus God, in this present time, is working with mankind to bring man into the relationship of fellowship with Himself. Ever since man fell in the Garden of Eden, God has been working with him to restore him to Himself, as our Lord has said, "The Son of man came to seek and to save that which was lost" (Luke 19:10). All creation must and will be brought back to God (Romans 8). The foundation of that return or redemption has been laid with mortar mixed with the blood of Christ.

The completed work of Christ was fully accomplished when the Saviour said, "It is finished." An amplified translation of that declaration is, "It is accomplished." What is meant by this, "It is accomplished"? Christ, in His work on the cross, accomplished everything that God sent Him to do; i.e., to redeem mankind, both Jew and Gentile, and to redeem creation. At the present time, ". . . we know that the whole creation groaneth and travaileth in pain together until now" (Romans 8:22). We (believers) too "groan within ourselves, waiting for our adoption, to wit, the redemption of our body" (8:23). All must wait until Israel is restored to her proper place. In the meantime, the Lord Jesus Christ and His accomplished work, is the message that must be carried to the entire world. This message will convert the entire world. But it will not be brought to pass through the Church of Christ, but rather through Israel. Israel is to be the messenger to the entire world, which is definitely stated in such passages as Micah 4:1-5; Zechariah 8:23; Isaiah 61:6. The message to the world is Isaiah 11:10; 2:2-4; 51:4, 5; and the goal is Romans 8:20-23. We see then that God is bringing mankind to the goal of redemption. Since man is incapable of redeeming himself, and is constantly rebelling against God, God is proving His sovereignty by bringing the world under the judgment of God. The Greek work for "world," means the world order. The word "guilty" (KJV) means under legal process, under judicial sentence, liable to penalty, all answerable to God. "Guilty" is in the dative case, meaning answerable to or owing to. The world has offended God and owes God satisfaction. This is the meaning of verse 19.

Verse 20: . . . because by the works of the law shall no flesh be justified in his sight; for through the law cometh the knowledge of sin.

Or, as it is in the King James Version, "Therefore by the *deeds* of the law." The Law opens man's eyes to sin, but cannot remove it; as in Romans 7:7, ". . . for I had not known coveting, except

the law had said, Thou shalt not covet." Galatians 3:24 also says
". . . the law is become our tutor to bring us unto Christ. . . ."
Since the law is perfect (Psalm 19:7), man in his sinful state and
in his imperfection, cannot fulfill the perfect Law. Christ, who is
the perfect man, fulfilled it. He became "the end of the law unto
righteousness to every one that believeth" (Romans 10:4). Here
the final nail of the sovereignty of God is driven: Man's righteousness must be *imputed righteousness*. See Galatians 3:6, "It was
reckoned (imputed) unto him for righteousness." Salvation is by
grace and "not by works done in righteousness, which we did
ourselves" (Titus 3:5; Ephesians 2:8, 9).

The purpose of the Law was, and is today, to bring Jew and
Gentile to the realization that both are sinners. For by the Law
is the knowledge of sin. The Greek word for "knowledge" means
full knowledge; to make a thing a subject for observation; to arrive
at knowledge from preliminaries; to acknowledge; to admit.
"The law of Jehovah is perfect, restoring the soul" (Psalm 19:7);
coming to the knowledge of a thing, i.e., sin; to have one's character discerned and acknowledged. Scripture does just that.
"Surely there is not a righteous man upon earth" (Ecclesiastes
7:20); and, "Enter not into judgment with thy servant; for in thy
sight no man living is righteous" (Psalm 143:2). In justifying
man, God does *all*. Man receiving it, contributes nothing. This
is a truth appearing on every page of the Scriptures. It should
be emphasized that God in His plan and program of salvation
never presented two ways of salvation; i.e., by the Law in the Old
Testament, by grace in the New Testament. The Law "was added
because of transgressions" (Galatians 3:19). If by the Law man
could be saved, then Christ's death on the cross was unneces-
sary, ". . . for if righteousness is through the law, then Christ
died for nought" (Galatians 2:21). The word "wherefore" (3:
19) in the King James Version means because, on account of.
Because of what has been said before, the truth is that "by the
works of the law shall no flesh be justified" (Romans 3:20).
The Law was never given for the purpose of making man just
before God, but rather to show man his inability to keep the
Law and cause him to cry out, "Abba, Father" (Romans 8:15).
We must realize that in the sight of a holy God, sinful man
cannot be justified by his (man's) own ability. Psalm 143:2;
Acts 13:39; Galatians 2:16; 3:11. The Law is like a mirror, showing each of us that we are sinners by nature, and proving to each
of us our inability to extricate ourselves from sin. Salvation must
be *imputed righteousness* by the working of the Holy Spirit. The

Law is pure, holy and perfect. Man is defiled, sinful and imperfect. These hindering attributes of man, make it impossible for him to keep the Law of God. Man is incapable of keeping the laws of his own human government, let alone trying to keep God's Law. The prophet Daniel fully realized this when he said, "O Lord, righteousness belongeth unto thee" (Daniel 9:7).

Summarizing our discussion, let us use the words of Paul in Romans 3:19, ". . . every mouth may be stopped" in the sight of a Holy God. It was and still is the purpose of God to show to man only one way of justification. This is the way of the cross, which is, even today, "unto Jews a stumbling block, and unto Gentiles foolishness," and they are both perishing. But to us who are the saved ones, it is "the power of God and the wisdom of God unto salvation."

Verse 21: But now apart from the law a righteousness of God hath been manifested, being witnessed by the law and the prophets...;

Having thoroughly analyzed the doctrine of sin and the depravity of man, of Jew and Gentile alike, the righteousness of God, and the sovereignty of God, Paul is now developing the doctrine of justification.

The Law shows man what righteousness is. It also shows him that sin is the separating factor between man and God. The entire preceding portion of this Epistle has been correcting man's concept of himself. Paul, guided by the Holy Spirit, is not trying to be critical or vindictive. God is using this "soldier of the cross" as a pen to show that God's greatest attribute is Love. This verse (21) in the King James Version reads, "But now the righteousness of God without the law." The Greek word translated "without" means apart from, alien from, independent from. Righteousness has to be achieved "apart from the law." Since the Law could not, did not, and does not, make a man righteous, something else must do it, and it must be independent of the Law. "But now" it is revealed. The "righteousness of God hath been manifested." In the Greek, the word translated "is" in the King James Version is translated "hath been" in the ASV. It is the perfect indicative passive. Thus the rest of the verse reads ". . . being witnessed by the law and the prophets." God has been revealing this all along. The Scriptures have always shown God's righteousness. This is nothing new. The entire Old Testament, phrase upon phrase, line upon line, verse upon verse, chapter upon chapter has been doing nothing else but portraying to man the righteousness of God and the sinfulness of man. Justification by faith is a doctrine as old as eternity. No one has ever been justified in God's sight apart from the grace of God through faith. The stupidity of saying that there are two ways of salvation in the Scriptures must surely be obnoxious in God's sight. Just a casual look at Hebrews 11 would contradict the theory that there are two ways of salvation. Hebrew 11:2 (KJV) says, "For by it (faith) the elders obtained a good report"; verse 4, "By faith Abel"; "By faith Enoch"; verse 7, "By faith Noah"; verse 8, "By faith Abraham"; verse 9, "By faith . . . Isaac and Jacob"; verse 11, "Through faith also Sara"; verse 20, "By faith Isaac blessed Jacob"; verse 22, "By faith, Joseph"; verses 23 to 29, "By faith Moses"; verse 30, "By faith, the walls of Jericho"; verse 31, "By faith Rahab"; verses 32 to 40, "By faith Gideon, Barak, Samson, Jephtha, David, Samuel, and the prophets." Is this not sufficient evidence to prove that the doctrine of justification by faith is eternal? Paul is not introducing anything new. It is Judaism that has departed from God and not Paul. It is rabbinic interpretation, or rather rabbinic distortion, in explaining away these truths of God's Word that has so befuddled and beguiled the mind of Israel. Judaism and its blind leaders of the blind have caused both of them to fall into the ditch.

The verb for "hath been manifested" in verse 21 (ASV) means to cause to appear, to bring to light, to be visible, to make known. It is interesting, to say the least, that the verb form of this term "hath been manifested" is regularly used for the: (1) Incarnation of our Lord, i.e., manifested in the flesh (I Timothy 3:16; II Timothy 1:10; I Peter 1:20; I John 3:5, 8). (2) Atonement is manifested (Hebrews 9:26). (3) The risen Christ is manifested (Mark 16:12, 14; John 21:14). (4) Manifested to the saints (I Peter 5:4; I John 2:28).

Paul continues to state that the doctrine of justification by faith is a continuing thing. He says that it is "being witnessed." It is by no means new. This doctrine "hath been manifested" and is now "being witnessed" to. Paul is merely elaborating on it, and explaining it, and showing the development which was foreseen and provided for (Romans 1:2; 9:25-33; 10:16-21; 11:1-10, 26-29; 15:8-12; 16:26).

The Bible is a progressive revelation. "God, having of old time spoken unto the fathers in the prophets . . . hath at the end of these days spoken unto us in his Son" (Hebrews 1:1). The doctrine of sin, the righteousness of God, justification by faith, retribution for sin, sanctification, atonement — all are gradually

unfolded in the Scriptures. It begins in the Garden of Eden and
continues through the New Testament just as it did through the
Old Testament, and in the fulness of time it was completed in
the crucifixion. Now that revelation is complete, "God . . . hath
at the end of these days spoken unto us in his Son." Here is the
great tragedy. We speak much *about* the Son. There is a great
deal of preaching *about* the cross. There is much preaching
about the Saviour. There is much preaching *about* peace. There
is a lot of preaching *about* everything. The only preaching that
should come from the Christian pulpit (the kind of preaching we
must return to, and the sooner, the better) is the plan of salvation. We must preach the cross of Jesus Christ. We must preach
His first coming for salvation. We must preach His second coming
for judgment, for condemnation, for devastation, for destruction,
for the decimation of the world. The idea of preaching anything
and everything from the pulpit is foolishness. These are "the
last days." If the writer of the Epistle to the Hebrews was so
convinced that God hath spoken to us at the end of these days
in His Son, we must return to the old, old story, "the way of the
cross leads home." Nothing can wash us from our sin except the
blood of Jesus Christ. We are not redeemed with corruptible
things, such as silver and gold, and good works, and everything
else, but only with the precious blood of Jesus Christ. The sooner
we return to this primitive Christianity, the better. Unless we do,
we shall have chaos. "Choose you this day whom you will serve"
(Joshua 24:15). The time to choose may be running out.

**Verse 22: . . . even the righteousness of God through faith in
Jesus Christ unto all them that believe; for there is no distinction . . . ;**

The "righteousness" here does not refer to the attribute of God
i.e., God's righteousness. The thought expresses here how *man
can be made* righteous in the sight of God, which righteousness
comes through faith in Jesus Christ. Such righteousness will be
finally and completely established in the fulness of time when it
shall last forever (Isaiah 51:6), which is by faith in Jesus Christ.
What is meant here is that "faith in Jesus Christ" is the means
through which the sinner receives "the righteousness of God."
The sinner, realizing his own unrighteousness and guilt, commits
himself to Christ, whom he accepts as his Lord. Bear in mind,
this righteousness is only "unto all them that believe." This is
the crux of the whole thing, belief from the heart, not from the
head. The thought that "unto all them that believe" is elab-

orated on in just one verse, Philippians 3:9. We must believe.
We must place our implicit trust in Christ.

Paul goes on to say, "for there is no distinction" in God's sight
in believers, in no stratum of life or society, Jew or Gentile, bond
or free, male or female, rich or poor, proud or humble, "For all
have sinned" (verse 23). "All" means the depravity of all men.
If one is to be saved at all, it must be by complete surrender of
self to Jesus Christ as Lord. It must be by faith, since faith is
the instrument which God uses to apply "His righteousness."
Notice that this is to "all." It must be set before "all." The
Great Commission is, "Go ye into all the world and preach the
gospel to the whole creation" (Mark 16:15; Luke 24:47).

Now let us look at the phrase, ". . . unto all them that believe."
Those who believe are said to be "in Christ." The believer is
clothed with Christ, since he is in Christ (Isaiah 61:10). It is with
"the white garments" of Revelation 3:18. It is "fine linen, bright
and pure: for the fine linen is the righteous acts of the saints"
(Revelation 19:8). Paul tells us that Christ was made unto us
righteousness. He has covered our sins (Psalm 32:1). The writer
believes that the phrase, "unto all them that believe," means what
it says, and that it is not that the flesh has been made righteous,
but that the soul of the believer is made righteous. At our conversion the flesh has not been changed, but we have received a
new nature, the Holy Spirit then indwells the believer and he
then receives the power to fight the evil nature (the flesh) which
he received through his natural birth. The soul and the spirit
are converted and still dwell within this flesh, which is "at
enmity" with the spirit nature. Hence, the warfare within the
life of the believer. Since the flesh is sin and must die, and God
cannot look upon sin, the accomplishment of the cross has clothed
us and covered us — or imputed to us — God's righteousness. Remember this is only done "unto all them that believe."

**Verse 23: . . . for all have sinned, and fall short of the glory of
God . . . ;**

This has been fully established in all that has been said in
this Epistle up to now. It is not how deep in sin a person goes that
separates him from God. It is merely one sin that is sufficient.
How many lies does one have to tell to be a liar? How many
persons does one have to kill to be a murderer and to "fall short
of the glory of God"? The Rabbis held that Adam by the fall,
lost six things: (1) The Glory; (2) Life (immortality); (3)
his stature (which was above that of his descendants); (4)

the fruit of the field; (5) the fruits of the trees; and (6) The light (by which the world was created and which was withdrawn from it and reserved for the righteous in the world to come).

The Rabbis explained that "the Glory" was the reflection from the Divine Glory which, before the fall, brightened Adam's face. Is it possible that this "glory" which fell from Adam's face after he sinned was that same brightness, that same glory, which brightened the face of Moses when·he had been in the presence of God and returned to the children of Israel? His face so shone that he had to cover it. Just a thought, but interesting enough to ponder over.

Verse 24: . . . being justified freely by his grace through the redemption that is in Christ Jesus . . . ;

"Being justified" is in the present tense. Since "all have sinned" implies that all have missed the mark, and that all of us right now are sinners, who among us would say that he has not sinned? What man is there in the world with any consciousness of a Holy, Righteous God, that would not readily confess that he is a sinner? So all of us need to be justified, inasmuch as the Apostle has stated that everyone of us is incapable of meeting God face to face because of being a sinner. Habakkuk 1:13 says, "Thou that art of purer eyes than to behold evil, and that canst not look on perverseness." We realize that righteousness, or being justified, must be accomplished by God. The word for justified in the New Testament, to quote another commentator, means that the work of the cross is so complete in God's sight, that each sinner is brought into the presence of God just-as-if-he-had-never-sinned. This surely must be accomplished by God. God did accomplish it and does accomplish it for each one who comes to Him, even today. He does it freely. The Greek word for "freely" means gratuitously — undeservedly. It is a free gift. It is not merited by our own deeds or abilities, upon which we have no claim. The motivating factor in all this is the love of God. "For God so loved the world, that he gave his only begotten Son" (John 3:16). We must not forget that God did this for us at a tremendous cost, the blood of His own Son. What a price! Paul states in I Corinthians 6:19, 20, ". . . ye are not your own; for ye were bought with a price," and repeats it in I Corinthians 7:23. This price was the most colossal, the most stupendous price for even God Himself to pay. To each and every one of us who accepts this price it is free, but this doesn't mean that it is worth nothing. It is worth everything! It purchases all that we are and have. The gift of salvation is free, it is the free gift of God. The requirements and the demands of the upkeep of this free gift requires our all. "Take up thy cross and follow me" is the invitation of the Saviour: "He that findeth his life shall lose it; and he that loseth his life for my sake shall find it" (Matthew 10:39). This is something each of us should bear in mind, that the cross of Christ and the cost of this cross to God demands that we daily live a holy life in the light of that cross. We are to be constantly aware of the fact that even while we are in the midst of a sinful world, we are in the presence of a Holy God.

V. 24: "Through the redemption." This noun in the Greek is in the genitive singular, and its construction shows that this redemption is the possession of the Saviour. Apart from Him, our redemption is unattainable. This is what is meant by the genitive singular; it belongs to the Saviour. In Him *is* redemption. This is why the Gospel must and should be preached. And by the Gospel the writer does not believe that it means anything short of the death, burial, resurrection and imminent return of the Saviour. This is the need today and it is just as great a need as it was in Paul's day. Paul said to the Corinthian church, "I determined not to know anything among you, save Jesus Christ, and him crucified" (I Corinthians 2:2). The preaching of any other gospel is strongly condemned by Paul in Galatians 1:8, 9.

The Greek word translated "redemption" is made up of two words which together mean ransom paid, deliverance procured by payment of a ransom, or simply deliverance with the idea of ransom excluded. (See: Romans 3:24; 8:23; I Corinthians 1:30; Ephesians 1:7, 14; 4:30; and Hebrews 9:15.) The thought in this word is that *Christ is the price* that has been paid. Without that price, redemption cannot be attained. This is the true meaning of the second half of the Greek word. "It is not Christ's death that is the price but, rather, it is Christ Himself that is the price" (Vincent's *Word Studies in the New Testament*), the ransom that God paid for us (Matthew 20:28; Mark 10:45; I Timothy 2:6.) Many passages in the New Testament bear out the thought that the believer is bought with a price. The Greek word for "redemption" has also the thought of loosing, i.e., to set free; to unfasten; to set at liberty. There is much more that can be said about this word. The reader can, if he so wishes, pursue the research of the word and the phrase. It is pregnant with sermonic material.

When we look at the Saviour and His cross, we see the high

price that God had to pay for our redemption. This high price portrays the depth of sin to which mankind has descended. The extreme height shows the lowest depth. The depravity of man is fully shown in the first chapter of Romans. This is the biblical doctrine of sin. When one reads that chapter he almost, if he is a saved person, feels that he has walked in the degradation of sin and needs a spiritual bath. God does not look on mankind with contempt, but rather with compassion. It is the redeeming love of God that is presented here. God's hands of mercy are extended to a lost world. God's invitation is to all the world regardless of race, creed or color. "Whosoever will, let him take the water of life freely" (Revelation 22:17 KJV). No matter how guilty a sinner may be, no matter how despicable a sinner has become, God still invites him and offers not only pardon but justification as well. The Saviour bore not only our punishment but also our guilt. "The Lord hath laid upon him the iniquity of us all" (Isaiah 53:6). This is the thought of Romans 3:24.

Verse 25: . . . whom God set forth to be a propitiation, through faith, in his blood, to show his righteousness because of the passing over of the sins done aforetime, in the forbearance of God . . . ;

The Greek word which is here translated "set forth" means, to set or to place before, propose publicly. In Romans 1:13 and Ephesians 1:9 the same word is translated "purposed." The word is made up of two Greek words. The first word means, before, in front, or in advance. The second word means, to set, to place, to lay, to deposit, to lay down, to allocate, to assign, or to appoint. The number (25) of this verse breaks the continuity of the thought. The death of Christ is a visible manifestation of the righteousness of God. The redemption that is in Christ (verse 24) is set forth; whom God has purposed; whom God hath set forth publicly; so that all may see. The veil of the temple was rent in two and the earthly "holy of holies" has been nullified. Now, in Christ we have a better holy of holies to which we can come at all times. The mercy-seat in the holy of holies was approached only once a year and then only by the High Priest. But here in verse 25 God hath set forth publicly Jesus Christ to be a propitiation. The word "propitiation" as it is constructed in verse 25 appears only twice in the New Testament, Romans 3:25 and I John 2:2. In the Septuagint Old Testament the cover of the Ark of the Covenant became the mercy-seat (Exodus 25:22; Leviticus 16:2, 15). As in the Old Testament, so here in the New Testament, it is carried over with the same thought in mind.

God spoke to Moses giving him instructions in how to build the Tabernacle and the mercy-seat. This was the place where peace would be made by the High Priest on the Day of Atonement. Reconciliation was brought here on the Day of Atonement. Paul states in II Corinthians 5:19 that Christ has become the eternal mercy-seat; i.e., "God was in Christ reconciling the world unto himself." This is what the Publican was asking God to do for him when he prayed, "God, be thou merciful (mercy-seated) to me a sinner" (Luke 18:13). The mercy-seat could be approached only with blood. So God has made peace through the blood of His (Christ's) cross (Colossians 1:20). The cover of the Ark of the Covenant became the mercy-seat only after the blood was sprinkled on it by the High Priest. Paul is careful to show that that has been fully accomplished for those who have put their faith and trust in the efficacy of the blood of Jesus Christ. The cross is the central theme of God's Word. As Moses wrote, "for it is the blood that maketh an atonement for your souls" (Leviticus 17:11 KJV), so it is today. By trusting in the propitiatory work of Christ, Jew and Gentile will find themselves fully justified from sin which the Law of Moses did not accomplish. It always has been and always will be that "apart from the shedding of blood there is no remission" (Hebrews 9:22). It is so used in the following texts: Romans 5:9; Ephesians 1:7; Colossians 1:20; Hebrews 9:12; 13:12; I Peter 1:19; and many others.

Another writer puts Romans 3:25 this way, "Whom God hath fore-appointed as a mercy-seat through faith in His blood." Why does he speak of Jesus as being "fore-appointed?" What does "fore-appointed" mean? It means that before Jesus appeared in the world, before He died, before His blood was shed, God had fore-appointed Him as a mercy-seat, and on this mercy-seat of His own Son had dealt with hundreds of thousands of souls. Otherwise, how could Abraham or Isaac or Jacob have been justified? Yes, or Moses or David; or anyone else? Were not myriads justified before Christ came? Now, this could not have been possible unless Christ had been fore-appointed as a mercy-seat. No one can be saved unless he knows God on the mercy-seat; it is the only appointed way of salvation. When we meet Him thus, we will never have to meet our Lord on the judgment-seat.

We read of the great white throne (Revelation 20:11) before which, by and by, the dead will stand to be judged according to their works. That is a judgment-seat, but no believer will be placed before that great white throne to be judged. "He that heareth my word, and believeth him that sent me, hath eternal

life, and cometh not into judgment" (John 5:24). Why will he
not meet God on the judgment-seat of His holiness? Why will
he not be placed there to be confronted by "the books" (Revelation 20:12)? Because he has previously known God on the
mercy-seat.

The mercy-seat is the place where God acts in the power of
propitiation. Propitiation is the exact meaning of mercy-seat, and
it is important to remember this, because the word mercy-seat is
not to be confused with God's mercy even toward a lost world.
Is not God merciful continually? Does He not extend His mercies
from day to day to every sinner on this earth? What sinner is
there in the world who has not received mercies from God
continually? Now if believers were recipients of mercies only
from God, they might all be lost in the end because the act of
receiving God's mercies from time to time does not imply an
eternal and enduring redemption. Therefore, the mercy-seat
means God's gift of eternal mercy secured through atonement,
or mercy bestowed upon believers by a propitiated, a placated
God. Thus God is represented as sitting on the mercy-seat where
He has received the propitiatory sacrifice that covers over all the
guilt, all the sin, so that the believer's guilt is not imputed because the propitiating or atoning blood that has been offered has
covered it all. That is the thought of the mercy-seat, and that
is the relation in which it stands to believers only, not to the
world, but only to those who have drawn nigh through faith in
Jesus. This relation to the mercy-seat becomes a covering and
enduring relation because the blood offered by our Great High
Priest always retains its efficacy; it has been once offered to perfect forever them who draw nigh to God thereby.

How indeed could it be otherwise if God undertakes from that
mercy-seat to view the believer as covered by the blood of Jesus?
When God undertakes so to view a believer, does not the precious
blood of our Lord necessarily secure all blessing? Only think of
what is implied in this! It has not only the effect of putting
away sin, but the preciousness of that blood always attaches itself to those who are under it. "They become precious in God's
sight according to the preciousness of the blood through which
He views them; and that is something far more than the oblitera-
tion of sin." (*Lectures on Romans*, pages 40-42, B. W. Newton,
published by C. M. Tucker, 1918.)

V. 25: ". . . to show his righteousness because of the passing
over of the sins done aforetime. . .". The Greek word for "show"
(ASV) or "declare" (KJV) also means to point out, to manifest

publicly just what is the righteousness that God expects of man. The righteousness here is not the attribute of God, but the plan by which God justifies sinners (look back at Romans 1:17), "for the remission of sins" (KJV) "the passing over of the sins" (ASV). This expression, "passing over," appears nowhere else in the New Testament, and is not used in the Septuagint Old Testament. It means passing by or letting pass. The thought is expressed in Micah 7:18; the term does not mean forgiveness or remission. What it does mean is that God was passing over or over-looking as in Acts 17:30. Forgiveness is the work of grace. By the sins "that are passed" are not meant the sins before a person is converted, but the sins of the Old Testament sinners. The writer is fully aware of the fact that there is disagreement over this interpretation.

Some believe that what is meant here is the sins of the believer. The writer does not believe that. He believes that this speaks of the sins of Old Testament saints before the Incarnation; otherwise, how else could Hebrews 11 be understood? We must remember that there was a cleansing of sinners in the Old Testament just the same as there is a cleansing for sinners in this present Church age. Leviticus 16:30 states that the people of Israel were "cleansed" from all their sin. This was done from year to year. The difference between that dispensation and our dispensation is that Old Testament sinners had to wait a whole year in faith believing that it would be accomplished by the High Priest on the Day of Atonement. We, thank the Lord, do not have to wait that long. The Apostle John states that, "If we confess our sins, he is faithful and righteous to forgive us our sins, and to cleanse us from all unrighteousness" (I John 1:9). The Apostle John also says, ". . . if we walk in the light, as he is in the light, we have fellowship one with another, and the blood of Jesus his Son cleanseth us from all sin" (I John 1:7). The only condition in the New Testament is "if we confess our sins," or "if we walk in the light." There is a tremendous amount of preaching on these two statements. The word "if" introduces so many truths, and confronts the believers with so many challenges, that the messages which can be preached on such texts are innumerable.

V. 25 ". . . in the forbearance of God," (ASV); or ". . . through the forbearance of God" (KJV). God waited until the fulness of time, i.e., the birth of the Saviour, His death, His burial, and His resurrection, to execute judgment. This is precisely what took place when Moses and Elijah faced the transfigured Lord and "spake of his decease" (Luke 9:30, 31). The bill had to be paid! Sins had to be paid for. The cross fully paid it, completely satisfied God, and established the sinner, in the sight of God, just as-if-he-had-never-sinned.

Verse 26: . . . for the showing, I say, of his righteousness at this present season: that he might himself be just, and the justifier of him that hath faith in Jesus.

For the second time in two verses (25, 26) the Apostle states that God, "for the showing" (ASV), "to declare (KJV), his righteousness." We must not lose sight of the fact that God is constantly "showing . . . his righteousness." This is always in the forefront when God deals with sin and sinful men. God's standards are at the highest level, and He never lowers them. His sovereignty is based on His righteousness; His justice is based on His Law of atoning sacrifice (Leviticus 17:11 KJV), "for it is the blood that maketh atonement for your souls." If sinners do not accept this sacrifice, they must bear the consequences of their guilt; namely, punishment and judgment. God is "showing" His remedy for sin, and does it because of His bountiful love (John 3:16; Psalm 32:1, 2a).

V. 26: The expression, ". . . for the showing . . . of his righteousness . . ." in this verse, is for the present time. It is for this Church age. God is reaching the point of a fuller revelation (Hebrews 12:1, 2; Galatians 4:4). The question of sins that are past and the sins of the present and future are now being met. The cross is central. The cross is the true mercy-seat and the completed propitiation. The righteousness of God is now being presented to the whole world. In the Old Testament, God spoke to Israel. Now He is showing His righteousness to all that believe, since salvation is for all.

V. 26: ". . . that he might himself be just, and the justifier of him that hath faith in Jesus." The "just and the justifier" are stated thus by Vincent in his *Words and Their Meaning in the New Testament,* "righteous and making believers righteous. This is a continuous action. God keeps on 'making believers righteous.'" The efficacy of the propitiatory work of Christ is continuous. The Gospel is still "the power of God unto salvation," even as it was on Pentecost (Acts 2). The difficulty is not with God, but with us who are failing to declare it. Yet God continues to do it on the merits of the cross. Our text in verse 26 states that God is "the justifier of him that hath faith in Jesus." The fact or reality of being "just" or the "justifier" in the presence of

God is based on having "faith in Jesus." The only ground of justification is faith in Jesus. This is what God is constantly endeavoring to show forth. Or, according to Hodge, "He whom God is just
in justifying, is the man who relies on Jesus as the propitiatory
sacrifice."

The program of the Old Testament is carried forward in the
New Testament. How could it be otherwise, since God is immutable (James 1:17; Malachi 3:6; Hebrews 13:8)? In Jewish
theology substitutionary atonement was always taught, the guilt
of the sinner being laid on the head of the animal or bird offered as the sacrifice. So it is even today in Orthodox Judaism.
The Day of Atonement is one time when the Jew offers a sacrifice. He does this in the following manner: each male member of
the family takes a rooster and each female member takes a
hen. The rooster or hen is then waved over their heads in a
circular fashion, accompanied by the following words: "This is
my atonement, this is my sacrifice. This chicken goes to its death
while I go to a long and peaceful life" (meaning life eternal).
If a chicken is not used, money may be used instead, with the
following words: "This is my atonement, this is my sacrifice.
This money goes to charity while I go to a long and peaceful life."
Also, on the Day of Atonement, the Orthodox Jew prays, and fasts
all day. As he prays he says, "Wouldst thou count the fat that I
have lost this day through fasting as an acceptable sacrifice in
thy sight." So, we see, substitutionary atonement is not foreign
to Judaism. It is based, or supposedly so, on the Old Testament. This is precisely what Paul is showing here in the verse
before us. He constantly asserts that men are justified through
the blood of Christ (Ephesians 1:7; Colossians 1:20).

**Verse 27: Where then is the glorying? It is excluded. By what
manner of law? of works? Nay: but by a law of faith.**

"Where then is the glorying?" or, as it is in the King James
Version, "Where is the boasting then?" According to Hodge, the
Greek word which is translated "boasting" in this verse is used to
express the idea of self-gratulation with or without sufficient reason. To continue: "It is excluded." "Excluded" is in the third
person, singular, indicative past, and means it is shut out once
for all time by one decisive act. It is forever excluded. The
word "excluded" means to shut out, to exclude, to shut off, to
leave no place for, to eliminate. "By what manner of law?" The
Greek word for "law" means a rule, a standard. It may be
translated, system. The word "law" to the ancient mind means a

constituted order of things. The question asked by this phrase in verse 27 is, "under what kind of a system is this result obtained?" Paul's answer, "By a law of faith," means under a system the essence of which is faith.

The fact that Law is brought into this question means that the Apostle is speaking directly to the Jews. But the implication of his words is not only to Jews but also to sinners in general before God. The Jews know (so they believe) the workings of the Law. They boast in the Law. They glory in the Law. They are the possessors of the Law. They claim to keep the Law and circumcision which gives them the right to the kingdom of God. But Paul refutes this claim. He says that there is only one divine Law under which a person can secure possession of hereditary property, i.e., the kingdom. This Law demands faith, trust, obedience, confidence. This is precisely what God has always required of Israel, as a people, as individuals. See Psalm 37:3, 5; 40:3; 62:8; 115:9-15; Proverbs 3:5; Isaiah 26:4. But Israel has always refused to obey God. God has been pleading with Israel ever since He brought them out of Egypt, and He is still pleading. See His loving invitations in Isaiah 1:18, 19, "Come now, and let us reason together"; and Matthew 11:28-30, "Come unto me, all ye that labor"; and Matthew 23:37-39, "O Jerusalem, Jerusalem, that killeth the prophets." God's invitation is still open to the people of Israel, even in this dispensation of Grace. The Gospel is to "all," and this word "all" includes the people of Israel.

There is no such thing as a Gentile church, as some maintain, and we shall not develop the argument against it here. Such an idea is a monstrosity in theology and has been created as a by-product of false doctrine, and is emphatically rejected by all who accept the pre-millennial return of our Lord, as we do. In this present dispensation of Grace, God is just as concerned about the salvation of the individual Jew as He is about the individual Gentile.

Verse 27 concludes: "Nay: but by a law of faith." Faith is the system of law that has always been operative in the lives of people, and all such people have always been blessed of God. This has been, and still is, God's requirement in all ages. Faith was required of Adam and Eve, of Enoch, of Abraham, of Isaac and Jacob, and of Israel, in the Old Testament; and also of all people in the New Testament. God's plan and program of salvation has never changed. It has always been the same. "Without faith it is impossible to please him" (Hebrews 11:6 KJV). And all that come unto God must come by faith in Jesus Christ.

See II Samuel 22:3, 4; Psalm 18:2; 30:31; 91:2-4; 118:8; 125:1; I Timothy 4:10; Ephesians 1:12.

This is exactly what Paul is establishing in Romans 3:27. Here is the summary of the doctrine of salvation by faith. Man's boastings are nullified and God is magnified and glorified. Mankind is incapable in its sinful condition of meeting the requirements of a sinless Holy God. Man cannot work out his own salvation by a system of law or works. He must rely upon God. If "all have sinned," and we have, where is there room for boastings? Of what can man boast? Of sin? Of degradation? Of immorality? Of pride?

Verse 28: We reckon therefore that a man is justified by faith apart from the works of the law.

For the second time in this chapter Paul arrives at a conclusion. In verse 20 his conclusion is, ". . . by the works of the law shall no flesh be justified . . .". In verse 28, he concludes, or reckons, ". . . that a man is justified by faith apart from the works of the law." "We conclude" (KJV) or "we reckon" (ASV). The Greek word means to tell, to declare, to explain, to announce. It is more clearly expressed by the words, "is declared righteous." The Greek word for "man" means any man. "Without the deeds of the law" (KJV), or "Apart from the works of the law" (ASV). The Greek word for "without" (KJV) means more than just without. It carries the thought of separate from and independent of. It means apart from (ASV), distinct from, without the presence of, without the agency of.

The whole phrase, "apart from the works of the law," needs clarification. We must guard ourselves against antinomianism, a sect which holds that faith alone, not obedience to the moral law, is necessary for salvation (*Webster's New World Dictionary*). This phrase, "apart from the works of the law," does not contradict James 2:14, which nullifies works as the ground or foundation for justification (Titus 3:5). The result of justification is always good works; otherwise faith is a dead faith. God gives us a living faith. Paul stresses a faith that portrays its life in works as we see in Romans 2:7; II Corinthians 9:8; Ephesians 2:10; I Timothy 6:18.

We must bear in mind, as we study Romans 3:28, that there is a difference between the "foundation" of something and the "result" of something. The foundation of justification is always faith, and that faith is in Jesus Christ which results in justification. Good works will always be seen in the life of one who has been justified by faith. It will be obvious by what he says, by what he does, by how he lives. It will be visible. It will intrigue the lost sinner as he will see something in the believer's life that will be a mark of difference from that of the unregenerate sinner. The fact that we have been "born again" must evidence itself by works that will substantiate that new birth. There must be a holy walk in each and every one of us, regardless and irrespective of our position in life or our position in the church. There are no two standards, one for the pulpit and one for the pew; or one for the male and one for the female. Christ must be exemplified. God must be glorified in every believer who claims Jesus Christ as his Lord and his Saviour.

Verse 29: Or is God the God of Jews only? is he not the God of Gentiles also? Yea, of Gentiles also . . . :

The Abrahamic covenant would contradict Paul's answer, "Yea, of Gentiles also," as the last part of Genesis 12:3 makes very clear, ". . . and in thee shall all the families of the earth be blessed." This of necessity, includes the Gentile. That Jehovah is the God of the Gentiles as well as of the Jews has always been in the plan and program of God. Moses is not the only one who writes of it. The prophets speak of it as well, as seen in Isaiah 11:10; 42:1, 6; 49:6; 60:3; Jeremiah 16:19; Malachi 1:11. In the plan and program of God, the Gentiles were not to be excluded. "For the earth shall be full of the knowledge of the Lord (Gentiles included) as the waters cover the sea" (Isaiah 11:9; Habakkuk 2:14).

In this age "God is calling out a people for His Name" from both Jews and Gentiles. We repeat, there is no such monstrosity as a "Jewish Christian Church" or a "Gentile Christian Church." This is post-millennial theology. Scofield's notes on Romans 11:25 are based on this thinking. The Church is comprised of the saved Jew and the saved Gentile. These two have become *one* in Christ. It is only in Christ that the middle wall of partition has been broken down. If this were not so, the Epistle to the Ephesians would be meaningless. "All have sinned," and the Gospel is "to all the world." The Great Commission (Mark 16:15) is just that. How neglectful the Church has been of the Great Commission! We have gone to the far reaches of the world by boat, plane and car, through deserts, over mountains, and have crossed rivers to reach the lost. This is commendable. But, we have neglected the unsaved at our back doors. We love the Chinese in China and Formosa, and the Africans in Africa, but we have shown little love for the people at our own back doors. To this group we must add the Jews. We all believe that the Jews are lost, but what are we doing for them today? We talk of the Jews in prophecy. We speak of the Tribulation Period as a time of Jacob's trouble. We elaborate upon the atrocities that the Jews will suffer, and of the handful, the remnant, that will be saved. This is good. But how terrible it is when we realize that we have done and are doing so little for the Jews in the missionary program of many of our churches. The Gospel is to *all*.

Verse 30: . . . if so be that God is one, and he shall justify the circumcision by faith, and the uncircumcision through faith.

Or, as the King James Version has it, "Seeing it is one God . . ." Another translation is, "Since indeed one God." There is only *one* God, and He is the God of Creation, the God of Redemption, who has supplied mankind with *one* Redeemer who is the only "mediator between God and men, the man Jesus Christ" (I Timothy 2:5 KJV). ". . . and he shall justify the circumcision by faith, and the uncircumcision through faith." Why the change in prepositions, "by faith — through faith"? The "by" for the Jew expresses the agent or the principle of justification. The agent or the principle is Law. "The law of Jehovah is perfect, restoring the soul" (Psalm 19:7). The Jew had only to accept the Law as *by* faith and not *by* works of the Law (Romans 3:20). The Gentile is not in such an advantageous position. Paul states in Romans 2:14 ". . . for when Gentiles that have not the law." The Gentile must obtain it *through* faith, i.e., his faith in the Gospel which is now revealed to him.

It is interesting, to say the least, that Paul has not wavered one bit from his God-given premise of Romans 1:16. There he states that the Gospel is "to the Jew first." He reiterates it here by saying that God "shall justify the circumcision by faith, and the uncircumcision through faith." Is this not saying again "to the Jew first"? Is not this doctrine of justification dispensational, too? How inconsistent can we get? Why do we say we believe the Bible, and then deny it by our actions? How sad! Usually the person who will not accept the fact, "to the Jew first," will not take it to the Jew at all. This has been the experience of this writer for over twenty-five years.

Verse 31: Do we then make the law of none effect through faith? God forbid: nay, we establish the law.

The Apostle is asking, "Do we destroy the Law through faith?" Is the Law nullified and destroyed because of what has been said; namely, that faith is the justifying factor in the sight of God? This is more thoroughly elaborated upon in Galatians 2: 16. The answer is that the Law was never given as a means of justification. It was given to convict man of sin. Faith establishes the whole principle and purpose of the Law. The Law was given to reveal God's holiness and man's sinfulness; in fact, sin was shown to be sin when the Law was given. This the Law does for every sinner who comes to Christ. The Law brings the sinner to Christ (Galatians 3:24). The Law becomes our tutor or schoolmaster unto Jesus Christ.

Faith as a justifying means is not a New Testament revelation exclusively. It is not a new doctrine that Paul introduces. Faith as the means of justification is the very backbone of the Old Testament, and is the substance of salvation in both Testaments. The cross is the center of salvation in the Old Testament as well as in the New Testament. There is complete harmony between Law and Faith. Paul shows the uselessness of works without faith. James shows the uselessness of faith without works. The problem with the Jew is that he does not practice faith. Even though God performed miracles in Egypt, Israel did not trust God at the Red Sea. After crossing the Red Sea by a miracle of God, the Israelites did not believe that God would sustain them in the wilderness. They constantly murmured in their wilderness journey even though God provided them with manna, water, and "a cloud by day, and a pillar of fire by night." They distrusted the words of Moses every step of the way in spite of the fact that God commanded them to believe Moses forever, as recorded in Exodus 19:9. Joshua inherited the difficulties of Moses. At the end of their 40-year journey all but two of the adult men, Joshua and Caleb, had died and never saw the Promised Land.

And so down through the centuries Israel refused to believe God, His Word, His Prophets and His Promises. When the Saviour came, they refused to believe Him, and what Moses had prophesied concerning Him, for our Lord said to the Jews of His day, "For if ye believed Moses ye would believe me; for he wrote of me" (John 5:46, 47). This condition prevailed at the time of Paul and is still true today. Israel does not harken unto the word of the Lord!

How tragic it would be for a pilot not to follow the instructions of his navigator; for a traveler not to look at a map; or for an orchestra leader to disregard his score. Israel has not followed the instructions of Jehovah, and how tragic have been the consequences! They do not know the Book! Is it any wonder that Hosea wrote these fateful words, "My people are destroyed for lack of knowledge" (4:6)? What a graphic picture this is of Israel even in this 20th century!

4

Verse 1: **What then shall we say that Abraham, our forefather, hath found according to the flesh?**

In this chapter the Apostle begins to discuss the consequences of the last clause of chapter 3, verse 31, "we establish the law," which is based on the questions and answers of verses 27 and 28 of Chapter 3. He brings in the example of Abraham, who was the progenitor of Israel, and who was called a Hebrew from the Hebrew verb *eber*, to "cross over" a stream. Abraham was a Gentile who became the first Hebrew. He was, so to speak, the one who stood at the crossroads when God "gave up" the Gentiles, "Wherefore God gave them up" (Romans 1:24-28), and a "new people" began, namely, Israel.

This writer believes that since Paul addresses Abraham as "our forefather (or our grandfather or ancestor) according to the flesh" (literal Greek translation), this is addressed primarily to the Jews who claim Abraham as their "father" (Matthew 3:9; John 8:39). Since the Jews make this claim, Paul brings into his argument the questions of Law, Works and Faith. These are pertinent words in Jewish theology and thinking.

Before we proceed further with this text it must be stated that this discussion is not directed to the Jews alone. In a very real sense Abraham is also the father of the household of faith, namely, believing Christians. "What then shall we say" or, to quote the literal Greek, "What therefore shall we say," or, to re-quote the whole verse, "What therefore shall we say that Abraham our forefather (as in the Sinaitic, Vatican and Alexandrine texts) hath found according to the flesh?" Circumcision is not included here as part of the question. Verse 2 speaks of works in the plural. Moreover, circumcision is not a work but a seal of the Abrahamic covenant. What Paul is seeking to bring out by this question may be stated thus: "Not *what* Abraham got by his righteousness, but *how* Abraham got his righteousness, by faith

109

or by works?" Faith was the cause, the means, the principle by which God reckoned him to be righteous. The Apostle proceeds to show that Abraham was justified in the sight of God even before his circumcision.

There is no need to bring the Law or its ramifications into question with regard to Abraham. The Law was still over 400 years away, and Genesis 15:6 ("And he believed in Jehovah; and he reckoned it to him for righteousness,") tells us the means by which Abraham was reckoned righteous in the sight of Jehovah. Jewish thinking cannot reconcile this with its concept of righteousness by the works of the Law. In fact, Genesis 15:6 contradicts Jewish thinking, Jewish theology, and even Jewish prayers, as, for example, in the following, "Prayer, charity and fasting overcometh the evil deeds" (Jewish Prayer Book, Musaph Prayers of the Day of Atonement). Paul and the Scriptures not only contradict the Jewish concept of righteousness by the works of the Law, but flatly deny it. Genesis 15:6 is of the Lord and not of man. Righteousness is by faith and not of works, and this is the Biblical reality of *imputed righteousness in both Testaments.* You see, the fact still remains that "justification is of the Lord," "righteousness is of the Lord," and "salvation is of the Lord." It could not be otherwise or man could attain righteousness and salvation by himself. We must realize that God is Sovereign, that God is sinless, and that God is the only One who can take a sinful man, change and transform him, and bring him into God's own presence just as if he had never sinned. See Isaiah 61:10. What advantage did Abraham derive from the flesh? See John 6:63, "the flesh profiteth nothing." Of course, the same question can be asked of the Jews today. The history of Abraham and Israel is an obvious answer to the question implied in verse 2.

Verse 2: For if Abraham was justified by works, he hath whereof to glory; but not toward God.

The question asked by the first part of this verse is whether Abraham could boast of justification by works in the sight of men. His father was an idol maker and, no doubt, was a wealthy man, probably well known and prominent. Many people must have brought sacrifices to the gods that Abraham's father created and displayed. Undoubtedly, his house was filled with all sorts of such idols. Yet, in the midst of all this heathenism, Abraham remained pure. In history Abraham is called an iconoclast, a term composed of two Greek words, *eikon,* an image, and *klaein,* to break. Why was Abraham called an iconoclast? Because he was an idol smasher!

There is a Jewish legend that Abraham's father, Terah, had to go on a trip and left Abraham in charge of the business. While Terah was gone, Abraham broke all the idols save one. Alongside this one idol he placed a club. When Terah returned, he was shocked by the sight of the broken idols and inquired of Abraham as to what had happened. Abraham replied that the idol with the club broke all the other idols. Terah thereupon scolded Abraham, since this was a very unlikely story. After all, the idols couldn't move! "Abraham," Terah cried, "what are you talking about? What kind of a story are you telling me?" It is because of this legend that Abraham has been called an iconoclast. But Abraham found Jehovah, the one true God, and when he was 99 years old, God spoke to him while his name was still Abram, father of elevation, and changed his name to Abraham, father of a multitude, made a covenant (Genesis 17:9) and sealed it with the rite of circumcision.

Abraham could also boast of the fact that he found God! After a long quest, when he was an old man, his prayers were answered. He found God!

This may sound difficult to believe, but don't scoff! How many times have we heard stories that were more far-fetched than this? Do we not hear people tell of dreams, of visions, of hearing God speak to them? We hear all kinds of questionable stories. In Christian circles this is commonplace. And we hear much boasting as well, the kind of boasting mentioned in Romans 3:27 (see my comments on this verse). Do not our ears ring with these stories? There is not a gathering of evangelicals in which weird tales are not heard.

But Abraham had a "goody" (an unusually good story) to tell! He could boast of being reared in the midst of heathenism, and that, finally, after 75 years he had found God! Can you not hear the shouts of "Praise the Lord," "Amen," and "Hallelujah"? Truly Abraham could boast in the presence of men.

Now let us look at the last phrase of Romans 4, verse 2, ". . . but not toward God." Toward God, or before God (ASV), Abraham could claim no merits. He had nothing "whereof to glory." He did not come to God! God came to him! God did it all! Abraham possessed no righteousness in God's sight. The years of his life before God came to him, were wasted years. There was, to be sure, unrighteousness on the part of Abraham. He told lies. He told them even after he was called by God and justified. See Genesis 12:13; 20:1-11. Because of this unrighteousness on Abraham's part, he could not boast in the presence of God who knew Abraham's every act and thought throughout his entire life. God in His love, in His mercy, and in His compassion, called Abraham. God "justified" him and "imputed righteousness" unto him, as He does to every believer today, and as He will continue to do throughout all ages. Salvation has always been "of the Lord." It must be. No person can extricate himself from sin. Abraham had no boast before God. Neither have we.

Verse 3: For what saith the scripture? And Abraham believed God, and it was reckoned unto him for righteousness.

The Greek word for "believe" carries far greater meaning than just the English word believe. It means to give credence to, or to commit to the charge or power of, to place confidence in. *The Greek Lexicon* by Thayer gives the meaning of the Greek word to be, "a condition full of joyful trust that Jesus is the Messiah, the divine Author of eternal salvation in the Kingdom of God, joined with obedience to Christ."

Abraham believed God implicitly, he gave complete credence to God's promises, and placed absolute confidence in God's promise to bring to pass what God said He would do. Because of this kind of faith, God bestowed upon Abraham that full justification which even such a faith as Abraham's never apprehended. Paul proves this by saying, "For what saith the scripture?" He disregards what man says, and bases his decision upon Scripture. In this case, it is Genesis 15:6.

It must always be the Scripture that is the final authority. It must always be, "Thus saith the Lord." When God speaks, doubt is removed, and suppositions and theories are brushed aside. "Never mind what you think," Paul is saying; "I appeal to Scripture." When Abraham was one hundred years old God promised him a son who would be born of Sarah, his wife, who was ninety years old (Genesis 18:11). Then Abraham realized that God would have to do for him what he, Abraham, could not do for himself. Abraham was childless all his married life. Sarah had now reached the state in life when it was absolutely impossible for her to bear children. Because Abraham completely trusted God to bring to fruition His promises, God exceeded Abraham's expectation, as we see in Genesis 15:5. God not only gave him a seed, a land, a blessing, but also reckoned (or counted, KJV) Abraham righteous. This is nothing else but imputed righteousness. God did it all! "Abraham rejoiced to see my day; and he saw it, and was glad" (John 8:56). The word "seed" in the Greek, although a collective noun, is in the singular form and means seed one; the plural form of this collective noun is "seeds," as both forms are described in Galatians 3:16, "Now to Abraham were the promises spoken, and to his seed. He saith not, And to seeds, as of many; but as of one." Here the discussion concerns the difference between "seeds many" and "seeds one." Thus we see that God promised Abraham far more than Abraham ever thought he would receive.

Notice, "it was reckoned unto him for righteousness." God did not make Abraham righteous, He merely clothed him with God's righteousness. This old nature — this Adamic nature — must be done away with, just as our earthly tabernacle, this corruptible flesh and blood, must put on incorruption, when we who are the Lord's body, the Church, are caught up to be with Christ in the air. See I Corinthians 15:51-54. Thus our earthly bodies will be changed to heavenly bodies. See Romans 8:13; Colossians 3:3, 10; 2 Corinthians 5:17. When this is done, the old nature dies. This is what God did for Abraham. This is what God still does for every believer today. Actually, the righteousness with which we are clothed belongs to Christ. Only when we are in Christ can we be clothed with His righteousness. The believer is in Christ; he is covered with Christ. The result is that the Father sees us in Christ, covered with the righteousness which Christ Himself possesses. It is not our possession, it is not something we have accomplished. We have not been and are not *filled* with God's righteousness. We are merely *clothed* with His righteousness, as sin is imputed to every man the moment he is born because of what Adam did in the Garden of Eden. Therefore, righteousness is imputed to every man the moment he is "born again" (Romans 5:12-17). This is the full meaning of the Hebrew and the Greek word that is translated "imputed" or "reckoned." All the above is summarized in Romans 5:19. Bear in mind, that faith is the principle which God has been pleased to designate as the condition on which a person is treated as righteous. We are said to be saved by or through faith, but never on account of our faith or on the ground of our faith. See Romans 3:25, "Through faith in His blood."

Verse 4: Now to him that worketh, the reward is not reckoned as of grace, but as of debt.

The Greek word for "worketh" means to work, to act, to labor, to trade, to do business, and to gain by one's labor. The Apostle is speaking about works as a means of attaining righteousness, which is not possible. A person who works for wages gets his reward, wages or remuneration. To him who is obedient, or performs a stipulated work for pay, the recompense is not regarded as a gratuity, gift or present, but as payment for value received. The Greek word for "reward" is actually not reward in the full meaning of reward, but rather wages. It is something earned as a result of working; it is money paid for work. This word "reward" is always used with the meaning of remuneration in one sense or another, for work or service rendered. When an employed person fulfills his end of the bargain, it is expected that his employer will pay him in full. It is a debt, and the employee has earned it. The word for "debt" means to owe, to be indebted, to be obligated, or to deserve that which is legally due. This denotes obligation. If a person can work out his own salvation, then it is no longer true that "salvation is of the Lord." Works have never saved a man. Salvation has always been a "gift of God." The wages of sin have never been reduced. It is still death. In like manner, salvation has never been something that a person could earn. It has always been a gift of God to undeserving sinners. God gives eternal life to every believer through Jesus Christ our Lord. It is of grace, i.e., unmerited favor.

Verse 5: But to him that worketh not, but believeth on him that justifieth the ungodly, his faith is reckoned for righteousness.

This verse might be put in other words as, for example, "Whosoever does not depend on his work for justification, his faith is counted, or reckoned, for righteousness." This again is "imputed righteousness." The present writer has dealt with this term, imputed righteousness, in verse 3. What should be emphasized here again is this: "The righteousness of Christ is not transferred to them who believe so as to become personally theirs; it is not infused into them, making them personally meritorious, for then they could not be spoken of as ungodly; but rather it is that Christ died in their stead and the benefits of His death are so reckoned or imputed as to make the believer righteous in God's sight" (Barnes, *Notes on Romans*).

This verse can also apply to Abraham as to one who "worketh not" but "believeth." The Greek word for "ungodly" means impious, wicked. The Apostle is preparing the setting for verse 6, where he speaks of David's invoked blessing on the man whose transgression is forgiven.

Verse 6: Even as David also pronounceth blessing upon the man, unto whom God reckoneth righteousness apart from works . . . ,

Having fully discussed Abraham's faith, his justification, his imputed righteousness, on the basis of grace, the Apostle now proceeds to show that even under the Law, the program of salvation and justification, with all that it entails, and with all its ramifications, is the same.

There is no Law, not even a whisper of Law, in Genesis. Abraham's imputed righteousness, Paul states, was all based on Abraham's faith in the promised Messiah of Israel, and on His, the Messiah's, own words, in John's Gospel, "Abraham rejoiced to see my day" (8:56). The "love of God" for the sinner is the same in Genesis, in Deuteronomy, in the Psalms, in the Prophets; and in the New Testament it is the same love, the same seeking. In Genesis 3:9, God sought Adam, calling unto him, "Where art thou?" In Genesis 7:1, God spoke to Noah and said, "Come thou . . . into the ark." In Genesis 12:1 God said to Abram, "Get thee out of . . . thy father's house." In Exodus 3:4, God spoke to Moses and called unto him out of the bush, and said, "Moses, Moses." And Moses delivered Israel out of Egypt. The same "love of God" is manifested in the Psalms, "Hear, O my people, and I will speak" (50:7); "And call upon me in the day of trouble; I will deliver thee" (50:15). And Isaiah 6:8, "I heard the voice of the Lord, saying, Whom shall I send? . . . Then I said, Here am I; send me."

The rest of the Old Testament elaborates on the "love of God." In the New Testament, God is calling and seeking Jews and Gentiles, "The Son of man came to seek and to save that which was lost" (Luke 19:10).

Paul now correlates Abraham and David. What opposites! What contrasts! Yet both stand on the same level with God. God calls Abraham "a friend," and David "a man after my own heart." Amazing, isn't it? "But for the grace of God," it would be a different story. You see, in the sight of God, all have sinned at all times or ages, under all circumstances, regardless of race, creed or color. Abraham with his maturity, with his steadfastness and faithfulness, although he wavered at times, is compared with David, with his courage, his trust in God, his immorality, his immaturity, and all his debauchery. Abraham lived under "Grace," David under "Law," yet both stand in the presence of God on the merits of imputed righteousness.

The Greek word for "blessing" in Romans 4:6, is the same word that is used in the Hebrew in Psalm 1:1, where it is translated blessed. Actually, the word means happy. Oh, the happiness that comes to people when they rely upon God for salvation and justification! Out of the degradation of sin and shame, David rejoices over the realization that God has forgiven him, God has pardoned him, God has brought him into His holy presence justified, just as-if-he-had-never sinned. It was done by God's divine process of imputed righteousness. This has always been so. The Cross is Eternal! The Plan of Redemption is Eternal! The Saviour is Eternal! God's Word is Eternal! Man may change, but God never does (Malachi 3:6; Hebrews 13:8). This is what brings bliss and blessing, comfort, consolation and peace to every believer of all ages.

Verse 7: . . . saying, Blessed are they whose iniquities are forgiven, and whose sins are covered.

The same word for "blessed" appears in verses 6, 7, 8 and 9. In verse 7, as in the other verses, it is the same Greek word that basically means happy. This word is the highest term which a Greek could use to express joy and happiness. Aristotle, the Greek philosopher, applied it to the state of the gods and those nearest to the gods among men. In verse 7, "blessed" means not only forgiven, but remission, and also pardon; and in the last part of the verse, ". . . and whose sins are covered," the Hebrew equivalent of the Greek word for "covered" is not the word that means atonement. The word actually means to cover so that it cannot be seen. Therefore, it is not that sin is being atoned for, but rather it is forgiven, forgiven and removed far away, "for thou hast cast all my sins behind thy back" (Psalm 38:17).

Again, ". . . whose sins are covered." The better translation is "were covered." It is in the past tense. The Saviour did it over nineteen hundred years ago. The word cover is used as a figure of speech, meaning to conceal or hide under something else. Our sins are forgiven and are removed "As far as the east is from the west" (Psalm 103:12); ". . . and thou wilt cast all their sins into the depths of the sea" (Micah 7:19) so they shall never be found again.

There is a Jewish teaching that on the Day of Atonement Satan comes to accuse Israel, and he particularizes their sins, and the Holy Blessed God particularizes their good works, takes a pair of balances and puts their sins against their good works and weighs one against the other; when the two scales of the balances are alike, Satan goes to bring in another sin to overweigh the good works. What does God do? He takes the sins out of the scale and hides them under his purple garment. When Satan comes and finds no iniquity there, then it is said "The iniquity of Israel shall be sought for, and there shall be none" (Jeremiah 50:20); and when Satan sees this he says before Him, the Lord of the world, "Thou hast taken away the iniquity of thy people, Thou hast covered all their sins, Selah."

The Jews explain the phrase, "under his purple garment," to mean his garments of mercy. This is true of the mercy of God as covering the sins of His people through the purple blood of His Son, which is the purple covering of Christ (Song of Solomon 3:10). (Gill, *Commentary on Romans* — Lexicon in Decem. Rhetores, page 266. Ed. Maussac.) However, the whole quotation concerning this circumstance is completely out of context with the Song of Solomon 3:10. As this writer's mother would have said in Jewish, "It doesn't stand, nor does it fly."

Verse 8: Blessed is the man to whom the Lord will not reckon sin.

This is another rung in the stepladder of joy. Paul again repeats the word "blessed," but this time it is happiness brought about by the realization that sin is not imputed. In fact, sin cannot be imputed since all believers of today, as well as Abraham and David of the past, are already reckoned or imputed righteous. This was done once for all believers. The Greek of this text should be rendered, "Whose sins the Lord will in no wise (by no means) reckon." In the Greek this is in the future tense, meaning, that at any future time God will by no means reckon sin to the believer when he shall stand before the judgment-seat of God (Romans 14:10).

Verse 9: Is this blessing then pronounced upon the circumcision, or upon the uncircumcision also? for we say, To Abraham his faith was reckoned for righteousness.

This "blessing" or blessedness, is it only for the circumcision, i.e., the Jews; or is it also for the uncircumcision, i.e., the Gentiles? To a Jew, this is a very important question. His entire faith is built around the fact that circumcision brings him into the covenant relationship with God. The Old Testament speaks of the "God of Israel." To the Jew circumcision is the main factor in this concept. Uncircumcision is *the* alienating factor, since a

Jewish child is not considered an Israelite unless and until he is circumcised. To the Jew, an uncircumcised individual can never be called a child of God or an Israelite. How could the "blessedness" of God rest upon an uncircumcised Gentile? To the Jew this is unthinkable! — impossible! The problem brings to the forefront the question of faith and works — works in the form of circumcision. Is circumcision really a prerequisite to justification? asks the Apostle. The answer to this question can be found only in the life of Abraham and his experience with God. Was it not Abraham's faith that was counted — or reckoned, or imputed — to him for righteousness? Is this not what the Old Testament states? Just what part did the principle of circumcision have in Abraham's standing before God?

Bishop Lightfoot, in his published commentary on *Galatians*, p. 157 ff., Ed. 2, shows that Genesis 15:6 was a standing thesis for discussion in the Jewish schools. The same thought, although differently expressed, is found in I Maccabees 2:52 of the Apocrypha, "Was not Abraham found faithful in temptation, and it was imputed unto him for righteousness?" And in the Talmudic treatise, *Mechilta,* the verse is expounded at length and even made the subject of an elaborate allegory, as follows: "Great is faith, whereby Israel believed on Him that spake, and the world was! For as a reward for Israel's having believed in the Lord, the Holy Spirit dwelt in them. In like manner thou findest that Abraham our Father inherited the world and the world to come solely by the merit of faith, whereby he believed in the Lord; for it is said, 'And he believed in the Lord and He counted it to him for righteousness'" (Ibid. p. 160; also Sanday on *Romans,* p. 104).

Verse 10: How then was it reckoned? when he was in circumcision, or in uncircumcision? Not in circumcision, but in uncircumcision . . . :

In other words, the Apostle is asking, was Abraham's righteousness imputed to him before or after his circumcision? He replies by saying that it was *before* his circumcision, "Not in circumcision, but in uncircumcision." Abraham was reckoned righteous years before his circumcision. Abraham was 99 years of age when he and his son Ishmael, who was 13, were circumcised (Genesis 17:24-26). Over 13 years elapsed between Genesis 15:6 and 17:24, 25. This indicates that Abraham was "reckoned righteous" at least 13 years before he was circumcised. These are facts, not fiction. This no Jew can ever deny. It once and for all time settles the question of how "the righteousness of God" is obtained. It is by faith and not by works. It is done completely by God, independently of anything a person does.

Verse 11: . . . and he received the sign of circumcision, a seal of the righteousness of the faith which he had while he was in uncircumcision: that he might be the father of all them that believe, though they be in uncircumcision, that righteousness might be reckoned unto them . . . ;

The Greek word translated "sign" means a mark, a token, a pledge. This circumcision was for a token or a pledge of the covenant that God made with Abraham, and was to be a reminder to Abraham that God would keep His covenant with him. Circumcision was given to Abraham and his posterity as a constant reminder that Jehovah was a covenant-keeping God. It was also a reminder to Abraham and his descendants that God was the One to whom they should look to bring the fulfillment of the covenant to pass. They were merely to rely on Him, to place their implicit trust in the God of Abraham, Isaac and Jacob, and He would fulfill the promise that He made to Abraham for which circumcision was the sign.

"So absolute is circumcision as a mark of God's favor that if an Israelite practiced idolatry his circumcision had to be removed before he could go down to Gehenna" (Weber, Astyn, Theol. p. 51 f.). When Abraham was circumcised God Himself took part in the act (Ibid., p. 253). It was his circumcision and anticipatory fulfillment of the Law which qualified Abraham to be the father of a multitude of nations (Ibid., p. 256). Indeed, it was only through Abraham's circumcision that Isaac was born a "holy seed." This was current doctrine among the Jews; and Paul in this portion of Romans is striking at the very root of this doctrine by showing that Faith was prior to circumcision, that circumcision was ". . . wholly subordinate to Faith, and that all the privileges and promises which the Jew connected with circumcision were really due to Faith" (Sanday, *Romans*, p. 109).

Baptism was never meant to be a substitute for circumcision. It could never be. First of all, circumcision, of necessity, was administered to males only. Secondly, circumcision never displaced baptism, and baptism never displaced circumcision. They, the Jews, practiced both circumcision and baptism before the New Testament was ever written. Thirdly, in New Testament times Jewish Christians practiced both, i.e., they circumcised their male children and then when they became believers they baptized them, never before. Baptizing male and female infants and children is merely a carry-over into Protestantism of the false practice of Roman Catholicism. If baptism ever could mean to the Christian what circumcision means to the Jew, then in the name of common sense, why baptize a female infant? The whole idea must be like an evil odor in God's nostrils. It is a denial of imputed righteousness which we previously discussed. The New Testament does not teach infant baptism. It teaches baptism of *believers.* It is to be administered to a person after he has been born again, not in order *to be* born again. It is to show that the believer, because he has accepted and confessed his faith in the Lord Jesus Christ as his Messiah and Saviour, testifies to the world by being publicly baptized that he has died to the world. Baptism is the picture of the burial of the old Adam, and the birth of a new creation in Jesus Christ.

Circumcision is not the covenant itself but the sign and seal of the covenant. Signing and sealing a covenant can never be a substitute for the thing signed and sealed. Neither is baptism regeneration, but merely the sign and the seal of the fact that regeneration has already taken place. Circumcision came after God had made the covenant with Abraham. So baptism, in like manner, must come after regeneration, as it is the sign of what has taken place between God and the believer. The believer is sealed by the blood of Jesus Christ.

V. 11 ". . . a seal of the righteousness of the faith which he had while he was in uncircumcision. . .". The Greek word for "seal" means not only a seal, but also a seal of impression, a token of guarantee. Circumcision was given to Abraham afterwards, like the seal on a document, to authenticate the state in which he already was; viz., imputed righteousness, which he had previously received of God by faith before he was circumcised. Jewish Christians and the Jews themselves, were fully aware of the meaning of the term seal. The Jews taught that the seal was circumcision upon their flesh, as Abraham was sealed in his flesh (Targum, Cant. 3:8). The Talmud (Hometh R, 19) states, "Ye shall not eat of the passover unless the seal of Abraham be in your flesh." But, as we have previously stated, Abraham received this seal of righteousness which he had, as Paul says, "while he was in uncircumcision."

V. 11 ". . . that he might be the father of all them that believe, though they be in uncircumcision. . . ." Thus Abraham becomes the "Father of many nations" (Genesis 17:4 KJV) or literally, "the father of a multitude of Gentiles" (Genesis 17:4). Besides

this title bestowed upon Abraham by God in Scripture, he was
also the father, or progenitor, of the Jews in the course of nature,
or by natural descent. This is an elaboration of Jewish teaching;
namely, that Abraham is the "Father of the whole world," or, to
quote Caphtor, fol. 121-1, "(those) who enter under the wings of
the Shekinah"; and a comment in Misn. Biccurim c. 1, sect. 4,
"(Seeing) he was taught the true faith." (*Gill Commentary*,
Vol. 6, p. 27.)

The Apostle is merely restating in Romans 4:11 what the
Rabbis of his age were teaching, and proves that the reality of
justification comes not only on the Jews, but on the Gentiles as
well. Or, to paraphrase the last statement of verse 11, "that
righteousness should be reckoned (imputed) unto all them that
believe, though they (Gentiles) be in uncircumcision also."

**Verse 12: . . . and the father of circumcision to them who not
only are of the circumcision, but who also walk in the steps of
that faith of our father Abraham which he had in uncircumcision.**

Moreover, in a very real sense, Abraham was also the father,
the progenitor and ancestor, of the people of Israel. Israel could
indeed claim him as their physical ancestor, as they did according
to John 8:33. The thought here is that Abraham may be the
father of those who are the circumcised in the flesh, which is one
characteristic, but also of those "who walk in the steps of that
faith," which is a second characteristic. The Greek word for
"walk" is a military term. It means to walk or march in file.

In passing, it is interesting to note that God does not beg or
plead with people to accept Christ as Lord. He "commandeth
men everywhere that they should all repent" (Acts 17:30). "Repent" is a military term meaning an about-face, a change of
direction. In Romans 4:12, the implication is that having made
"the about-face," we are to "march in file" and follow that faith
which Abraham followed. As Abraham marched in file of that
faith so we both, the circumcised and the uncircumcised in the
flesh, Jew and Gentile, are also to march in file of that faith.
Abraham becomes the father, the ancestor, the progenitor of that
great army of God. The word "walk" is better translated, "are
walking." This is our present pilgrimage. We form part of that
great company of believers who are walking or marching in file
with Abraham at the head. While we march, we ask others to
join in this triumphant march that leads to eternal life. With
whom are you marching? Who is at the head of *your* line? Unbelief has no place in this file of faith made up of those of the cir-

cumcision and the uncircumcision. "If ye were Abraham's children, ye would do the works of Abraham" (John 8:39). The last clause of verse 12 again emphasizes the fact that Abraham had this faith, "which he had in uncircumcision."

Verse 13: For not through the law was the promise to Abraham or to his seed that he should be heir of the world, but through the righteousness of faith.

Paul starts another chain of thought here, using Abraham as his proof. It is the discussion of the difference between "works" and "faith" as the principle of obtaining righteousness. Paul is quoting a Jewish teaching regarding Abraham as "the father of the whole world." (See comments on verse 11.) Other Jewish teachings are that Abraham "was the foundation of the world," "And that for his sake the world was created." It is interesting to note here that the Talmudic teaching states that, "The world was not created but only for the Messiah" (Sanh. 98b). God said to Abraham, "Unto thee and thy seed will I give this land." Also, "In thee shall all the families of the earth be blessed." The "in thee" would most certainly imply his seed. All this, of course, was promised to Abraham before there was the Law. It was given to Abraham by Jehovah and he (Abraham) accepted it by faith, "Abraham believed God." The motivating factor in Abraham being the recipient of God's gifts, promises and blessing was faith. Bear in mind that Romans chapter 4 in its entirety deals with the doctrine of justification. Justification is not obtained by means of circumcision or personal obedience, but only through faith. "If there had been a law given which could make alive, verily righteousness would have been of the law. But the scripture shut up all things under sin, that the promise by faith in Jesus Christ might be given to them that believe" (Galatians 3:21, 22).

Verse 14: For if they that are of the law are heirs, faith is made void, and the promise is made of none effect . . . :

In other words, if Israel, who are the recipients of the Law, could by obedience to that Law become the heirs of righteousness, then faith would be nullified. Or, stated another way, if the people whose life principle is the Law and who wish to be justified by the Law, and who are the adherents of the Law, that is, legalists — if such could be heirs to the promises, nothing but confusion and contradiction would result and the plain teaching of Scripture would be done away. To put it in plain language, faith would be nullified and Abraham placed in jeopardy, for it is by faith that Abraham was justified. These legalists (they that are of the Law) seek justification by means of obedience to the Law. If this could be the case, then the Abrahamic covenant would be broken and faith thereby "made void." The Greek word for "void" means to empty, to evacuate, to deprive a thing of its proper function, to be without foundation, to falsify to no purpose. The tense of the verb is such that it could be translated to read, "has been voided or emptied."

V. 14: ". . . and the promise is made of none effect . . ." Legalism would not only make the promise to Abraham null and void and render faith powerless and useless, but it would also destroy it completely. Moreover, if legalism were in fact true, the promise to Abraham is already destroyed, for such is the tense of the Greek verb.

Verse 14 is of great importance. If legalism were ever meant to be the principle of justification, the entire plan and program of salvation, which God has wrought for mankind, from the first verse of Genesis through the last verse in Revelation, is groundless and useless. It would mean that Abraham was not justified; in fact, no Old Testament saint was justified (Hebrews 11). We of the New Testament are still in our sin, "separate from Christ, alienated from the commonwealth of Israel, and strangers from the covenants of the promise, having no hope, and without God in the world" (Ephesians 2:12). If this were true, the cross would be the greatest calamity and catastrophe the world has ever seen. Just the thought of its being true is enough to make the child of God shudder; and with the Apostle Paul we could shout, "God forbid!" which means, Impossible! Unthinkable! Perish the thought! But, instead, the child of God, knowing Faith to be the principle of Justification, and not Legalism, may confidently ascend to earth's highest pinnacle and shout the words of the prophet, "The righteous shall live by his faith" (Habakkuk 2:4).

Verse 15: . . . for the law worketh wrath; but where there is no law, neither is there transgression.

The Law was given for no other reason than to reveal God's holiness. The breaking of that Law brings "the wrath of God." The Law was never given as a means for justification. When one realizes what the Law is and what it does, it should fill one with fear and dread of the wrath of God. The realization of this will do one of two things, either (1) it will bring one to Christ, as we are told by Paul in Galatians 3:24, "the law is become our tutor to bring us unto Christ"; or (2) it "worketh wrath," in the words of verse 15. The tense of the Greek verb is better translated, "it is working right now," or, "it is already in the process of working wrath."

Realizing all this, we can see the danger of procrastination. It is as though a person were to walk into the mouth of hell. The unbeliever is on the road to eternal destruction. Why will you perish? The door is open! Flee to God! The Law is either the schoolmaster or the judge. Choose!

V. 15: ". . . but where there is no law, neither is there transgression." The Law expresses what may be done, or what may not be done. There is now no hope of escaping the Law. It has been given and it is now working. "Sin is the transgression of the law" (I John 3:4 KJV). So now, everyone sins, the Jew (Ecclesiastes 7:20), and the Gentile (Romans 3:23). Sin is prevalent. Sin is obvious. The Law reveals it. The Law is the preparation for Faith. But, alas, Israel has made it the antithesis of Faith and in so doing has brought the wrath of God. Thus the Law brings to the forefront the sinner's wrath toward an avenging God.

Verse 16: For this cause it is of faith, that it may be according to grace; to the end that the promise may be sure to all the seed; not to that only which is of the law, but to that also which is of the faith of Abraham, who is the father of us all . . .

The inheritance which the descendants of Abraham were to receive must either be through Grace, by Faith, or through the works of the Law. It has been conclusively proven in the preceding verses of this chapter that it cannot be obtained by the works of the Law, for such "worketh wrath." Therefore, and for this cause, it must be of Faith according to Grace. No person can boast of obtaining an inheritance by working for it, because an inheritance cannot be earned. It can be obtained only by birth or because someone has bequeathed a gift. In Abraham's case, it was by birth, i.e., by being "born again." That is how we, too, become heirs of the promise made to our father Abraham. This is exactly what the Greek says in verse 16, "For this cause it is of faith, that it may be according to grace . . .";

V. 16: ". . . to the end that the promise may be sure to all the seed. . . ." Since this "promise" is given to the believers by God Himself, we do not have to be concerned about the "receiving" of the promise. That is why the Apostle says, "that the promise

may be sure to all the seed." The Greek word for "sure" means
firm, stable, certain and established. We need have no apprehensions about receiving it. In Him (God) there is "no shadow
of turning," and no wavering. We are "heirs" right now and
forever. Notice, it is a "sure promise to all the seed." Whose
seed? Abraham's seed, of course, comprised both of those who
are "of the Law," i.e., believing Jews, and of those "who are of
the faith of Abraham," i.e., believing Gentiles. Bear in mind
that Abraham was not a Jew. He *became* a Hebrew. Basically
the word Hebrew means one who crosses over. Originally, Abraham was a Chaldean, a Gentile (See: tract "Was Abraham a
Jew?" by Joseph Hoffman Cohn, published by the American
Board of Missions to the Jews, 236 W. 72nd Street, New York.)

V. 16: ". . . not to that only which is of the law, but to that
also which is of the faith of Abraham, who is the father of us
all. . . ." "The father of us all." A high privilege of New Testament saints is to be partakers of the inheritance promised to
Abraham.

**Verse 17: . . . (as it is written, A father of many nations have I
made thee) before him whom he believed, even God, who giveth
life to the dead, and calleth the things that are not, as though
they were.**

"A father of many nations have I made thee." The word
Abram means "exalted father." The word Abraham means
"father of multitudes." In this text, verse 17, if Abraham were to
be "the father of many nations," it would imply that these nations would have to include other nationalities than just Israelites.
The Hebrew word for nations in Genesis 17:5, and in almost
every place where it is found in the Old Testament, does not
include Israel. Since this is so, Gentiles of necessity become the
beneficiaries of Israel in the Abrahamic covenant. (This is discussed in our commentary on verses 11 and 12.) The statement
contained in verse 17 is parenthetical. God's promise to Abraham
is understood by Paul to have a spiritual application which is
typical of its temporal application, and is made by way of confirmation.

V. 17: ". . . before him whom he believed, even God, who
giveth life to the dead, and calleth the things that are not, as
though they were." The phrase, "before him," in this verse is
one Greek word, the Hebrew equivalent of which is "before
God," and would be better translated this way. The statement
found in verse 4:17 could be re-worded as follows: "before God

whom he believed, the (One) quickening the dead." Abraham was looking at the result of his faith, which was the quickening power of God, so that he (Abraham) would become the
"father of many nations," "Who giveth life," or "who quick-
eneth" (KJV). The Greek word means to make alive or to
quicken. The Apostle must have had in mind the birth of Isaac
and, as well, the resurrection of Christ of whom Abraham was
the progenitor. ". . . and calleth the things that are not, as
though they were." In God's sight, there is no yesterday or
tomorrow. God is Eternal. God told Abraham that his (Abraham's) seed would be as numerous as the stars, and multitudinous as the sands of the sea. Yet, at the time that God said
this to him, Abraham was 99 years old, and Sarah was barren.

God called "the things that are not, as though they were"
already in existence, and Abraham believed God's word, God's
promises and God's faithfulness. It is interesting to notice that
the structure of the Greek verb "calleth" is such that it reads
calling. God is still calling today. He has never stopped! He
called in the Garden of Eden; He called Abraham; He called
Moses; He called Israel; and He called the Prophets. All this is
in the Old Testament. God continues this calling in the New
Testament. The disciples were called, and He called blind
Bartimaeus (Mark 10:46). He calls us today. Will you answer?

God is omniscient, omnipotent and omnipresent. When He
formulates a plan, in His sight it is already an accomplished
reality. That is God's way of doing things, and it is God that
does it. He does not leave it to man. When God calls, we had
better answer! Abraham believed all this, and God is still, even
today, fulfilling His promise. God looked at Abraham, and in
God's sight he (Abraham) was already surrounded by multitudes. This should be a great comfort to the "born again" child
of God. In the midst of a troubled world we stand firm, we
stand sure, we stand trouble-free. "Be of good cheer; I have
overcome the world" (John 16:33), are the comforting words of
the Saviour. We rest serenely in His finished work (Philippians
1:6). What impetus this should give to our lives, our witnessing,
and our preaching!

**Verse 18: Who in hope believed against hope, to the end that
he might become a father of many nations, according to that which
had been spoken, So shall thy seed be.**

The expression in the opening clause of this verse, "Who in
hope believed against hope," is called an oxymoron (Webster's

Dictionary, "A figure of speech in which opposite ideas or terms are combined, e.g., thunderous silence"). Abraham believed God implicitly, even when it was against all human reason or hope, and this, humanly speaking, means when there is no basis for hope. Such, indeed, was Sarah's condition. She had been barren all her married life, and had already experienced menopause. It was not logical for Abraham or even Sarah to hope for a son; it was foolish to hope. But in spite of all this, Abraham hoped, Abraham trusted, and Abraham believed that God would keep His word that he (Abraham) would become the "father of many nations." Abraham was convinced beyond any shadow of doubt that the God he now worshipped was a supernatural God, and that his God would perform for him what no other so-called gods could ever perform for any man. This, Abraham's God did! Abraham became the "father of many nations," and God fulfilled His word as recorded in Genesis 15:5.

This fact should gladden the hearts of believers. Our God does the impossible. He has revealed Himself as a miracle-working God, e.g., as shown in the burning bush, the plagues in Egypt, the parting of the Red Sea, the manna in the wilderness, and in many other miracles. This same God has promised us eternal life and has promised to keep us through our earthly trials and tribulations. Amid trials, we hope; amid tribulations, we rejoice; amid sorrows, we sing; and in the face of the death of our body, we despair not; inasmuch as all these are but the prelude to a greater life, a better life, and a perfect life. Our God walks beside us, "I will never leave thee nor forsake thee" (Deuteronomy 31:6; Joshua 1:5; Matthew 28:20; Hebrews 13:5). Fellow Christians, let us unfurl the blood-sprinkled banner of our Saviour in spite of every obstacle to our faith, as the night is fast approaching on this sin-cursed world. Let us be faithful to Him as He is faithful to us. We have the evidence! We have the proof! Hallelujah, what a God and what a Saviour! He lives with us, through us and in us.

Verse 19: And without being weakened in faith he considered his own body now as good as dead (he being about a hundred years old), and the deadness of Sarah's womb . . . ;

Abraham's faith never weakened in God and in His promises. The Greek word for "weak" means deficient in strength, to doubt, to hesitate. Abraham did not doubt that God would fulfill His promises of a "seed" from his loins and the womb of Sarah, even though Abraham "considered his own body now as good as dead" . . . "and the deadness of Sarah's womb."

The Sinaitic, the Vatican, the Alexandrine, the Nestle, and the Nestle Revised texts, all eliminate the word *not* in verse 19 of the King James Version, "And being not weak in faith, he considered not his own body." Abraham's body, for reproduction, was now dead. He was "about an hundred years old." Sarah's body was barren and all possibility of conception was, therefore, removed. That Sarah could bear Abraham a son was unthinkable; in fact, it was impossible. However, in spite of all these human impossibilities, Abraham's faith was "not weak" (KJV); or, not weakened (ASV). Abraham believed God implicitly. Abraham trusted God to fulfill every "jot and tittle" of His promises. Abraham's God is our God. He is the same yesterday, today, and forever, "I, Jehovah, change not" (Malachi 3:6).

Verse 20: . . . yet, looking unto the promise of God, he wavered not through unbelief, but waxed strong through faith, giving glory to God . . . ,

Abraham was not in strife with himself in reference to the promise of God, "but waxed strong." The structure of the Greek text is such that it should be translated, "but was empowered by faith," or "was made strong by faith" (Hodge). If Abraham "was made strong," it would have had to be accomplished by the force or power of the Holy Spirit acting within Abraham. His strength had to be attributed to the Holy Spirit for the Holy Spirit is the energizing power of the God-Head who energizes each of us as He did Abraham. This resulted in Abraham "giving glory to God." In like manner, if we yield ourselves to God we, too, shall be empowered to overcome all our doubts and fears, thus glorifying God in every facet of our lives through our faith. Bear in mind that even our faith is a gift of the Holy Spirit.

There must have been apprehensions in the life of Abraham. Certainly there were times when he questioned *when* God would fulfill His promise of a seed. Abraham never doubted the credibility of God's promises. After all, Abraham was as human as we are. Have there not been times when we have become impatient — when we have wondered how long it would be before our prayers would be answered? As a man, Abraham "laughed" at the thought of Sarah and him having a seed. But, as a man of God, he was encouraged, strengthened and empowered by the Holy Spirit. Abraham's faith was victorious and he gave glory to

God. Unbelief is not always the product of intellectual doubts; but doubts are the result of loss of faith. This, to be sure, was not Abraham's experience. He did not doubt.

Verse 21: . . . and being fully assured that what he had promised, he was able also to perform.

The Greek from which the opening phrase — "and being fully assured" — can be translated, "to be fully established as a matter of certainty; to be fully convinced." Abraham was "being filled with conviction." Since Abraham was "being filled," it points to someone filling him which, of necessity, would point to the working of the Holy Spirit. Abraham did not doubt God's Word or His promise. This is a "missing ingredient" in the believer today. We are filled with doubts, fears, apprehensions and questions. We do not seek to be "fully assured" or "fully convinced," which assurance or conviction the Holy Spirit is able to accomplish for us today, even as He did for Abraham. Thereby, Abraham became victorious. We are not fully convinced, or "assured," in the way that Abraham was and, therefore, we live defeated lives. Abraham rested on the power of God to bring to pass that which God had promised him, even though it was humanly impossible. Abraham's God and ours is the God who performs the impossible. He is Omnipotent.

Verse 22: Wherefore also it was reckoned unto him for righteousness.

Here again, the Apostle brings to the forefront the doctrine of Imputed Righteousness. Faith is the principle of that imputation. Like Abraham we, too, must place implicit trust in God and the accomplishments of the cross. Bear in mind, that the "righteousness of Christ" is not infused into us, but, rather, "we are clothed, reckoned, counted," as righteous. It is Christ's righteousness which covers us. (See our note on Romans 4:3.)

Verse 23: Now it was not written for his sake alone, that it was reckoned unto him . . . ;

In other words, the Apostle is saying, this was not written in the Scriptures for an historical record, but, rather, for a spiritual assurance for all who will place their trust in Jesus Christ as Lord (God Incarnate in the flesh); as the true, sinless, spotless Lamb (or Sacrifice) of God, who died on the cross for the sins of those who believe, who rose from the dead and is now seated at the right hand of the Father as our Mediator.

Abraham is the one person who stands out in the revealed program of God as the reality of the fact that God uses the principle of Faith as the means, the vehicle, the instrument of justification. Abraham is the fulfilled evidence of the promise, "The just shall live by faith." That faith must be in Christ, not in the teachings and the concepts of men. The revealed will of God is in His record, as recorded in John 5:9-12. God's plan is so completely revealed, so simply stated, that, as the Scripture says, "yea fools, shall not err therein" (Isaiah 35:8b). Faith, then, must be pointed in the right direction.

Verse 24: . . . but for our sake also, unto whom it shall be reckoned, who believed on him that raised Jesus our Lord from the dead . . . ,

Thus Paul reminds us that the record of Abraham's faith was written for our admonition, that all mouths might be stopped forever. This is the believer's assurance, the believer's comfort, that God does save us on the principle of faith. Surely, the words of the Saviour are comforting to every child of God, "Let not your heart be troubled: ye believe in God, believe also in me . . . I am the way, and the truth, and the life" (John 14:1, 6). If Abraham was justified by faith, so are we. God does not, and never has changed His plan and program of salvation. At no time, under no circumstances, has God ever saved anyone except by faith. God is not a changing God (James 1:17b). He was, He is, and always will be the same. (See Malachi 3:6; Hebrews 13:8.)

V. 24: ". . . unto whom it shall be reckoned . . . ." The object of Abraham's faith was redemption. There can be no redemption without a Redeemer; hence, "Your father Abraham rejoiced to see my day" (John 8:56). This writer believes that the "day" is the day of the resurrection of our Lord. Redemption is based on the Resurrection, "If Christ be not raised, your faith is vain; ye are yet in your sins" (I Corinthians 15:17 KJV). Since this was "saving faith" for Abraham, it is also saving faith for us today, we who base our faith on the *physical resurrection* of Christ. This is what Abraham looked forward to, and we look back to the same reality. The resurrection of Christ is the focal point in the history of God and man. Here God and man could meet, did meet, and do meet. This is the "Eternal Day" that has become the Day-Star of history, the divine Emblem of Hope. This is the day on which all creation shouted "Hallelujah"!

The blessed reverberations of that shout will be heard through all eternity.

V. 24: ". . . who believe on him that raised Jesus our Lord from the dead." Throughout this Epistle Paul continues to use the word "Lord" to describe the Person of our Saviour. He seems to stress it consistently. This should not be overlooked. Our Saviour is not just a human being. He is God Incarnate in the flesh. Since this is so, it embraces many relevancies such as: What constitutes the incarnation? How did the incarnation materialize? Who and what were the agencies that made it possible?

These are very important questions. They require careful scrutiny. Since our Saviour is the Lord Jesus Christ (for comments on the word "Lord" see our notes on Romans 1:4), He could not have had a human father. That Jesus did not have a human father, demands a "super-human" conception. So it was. Jesus was conceived of the Holy Spirit (Matthew 1:20). This was in fulfillment of Genesis 3:15, where it is the "seed" of the woman that is referred to, not the "seed" of the man (not male, hence, no ovum and no sperm); and it was also a fulfillment of Isaiah 7:14, "A virgin shall conceive." To the unregenerate, this is a paradox: to us who are the saved, it is the *foundation* of our faith. Jesus Christ was very man and very God. This Man had to be of Jewish blood. The Jewish blood came from His mother, the Virgin Mary. Medical science states that the *type* of the blood is determined by the sperm of the male. In Mary's case there was no sperm. The blood is manufactured in the embryo by the process of elements in the body of the mother to which the infant is connected by the umbilical cord. This, too, is the fulfillment of a number of prophecies, one of which is summarized by the Saviour Himself in one verse, "Salvation is from the Jews" (John 4:22). This fulfills the requirement of Ezekiel 18:4, ". . . the soul that sinneth, it shall die." The Hebrew word for "soul" is translated in a number of different ways. When we look at the various passages in which this word appears, it seems to add up to the meaning of *man*.

Since the blood of bulls and goats was not able to cleanse from sin, a human creature had to die as a substitutionary sacrifice. It had to be a *perfect* sacrifice. Man is a partaker in the Adamic sin and could not meet the requirements of a *perfect* sacrifice. Our Saviour, being *perfect* Man, met this requirement in becoming God Incarnate in the flesh (Philippians 2:6). He fulfilled the requirements of the soul, and died on the cross for the sin of the world (John 1:29).

The other aspect of salvation is that "Salvation is of the Lord" (Jonah 2:9; Psalm 3:8). This makes it essential that the Saviour be a God-Man. Thus, inevitably He has to be God Incarnate in the flesh. He is so described in Philippians 2:5-11. The basis of all this is the fact of the resurrection which the Apostle speaks of in Romans 4:24.

Verse 25: . . . who was delivered up for our trespasses, and was raised for our justification.

In the first part of verse 25 — "who was delivered up for our trespasses" — Paul summarizes all of the Mosaic sacrifices. All the sacrifices that Jehovah requested are restated in these few words. Every sacrifice in the Old Testament, under all dispensations, looks forward to the day when Christ was delivered up for our trespasses or sins. That was the day when the sin question was settled for all time. That was the day of which Isaiah spoke when he said, "and the Lord hath made the iniquity of us all to meet on him" (53:6, Hebrew, literal). That was the day that Moses looked for, all during his latter life here and hereafter, Luke 9:30, 31, ". . . who were Moses and Elijah; who appeared in glory, and spake of his decease." The Greek word for "decease" is literally the word exodus. Is it a wonder that John the Baptist (John 1:29) pointed to the passover lamb when he knew all the time that it was Christ who was the real "exodus" for every believer of every age regardless and irrespective of dispensation? "Moses, when he was grown up . . . looked unto the recompense of reward" (Hebrews 11:24-26). That was the day that Zechariah 9:9 spoke of, ". . . behold, thy king . . . having salvation." That was the day that the Magi from the East came to Jerusalem asking, "Where is he that is born King of the Jews?" (Matthew 2:2). That was the day of which Simeon said, "For mine eyes have seen thy salvation" (Luke 2:30). That was the day that the Saviour had in mind when He said, "If thou hadst known in this day" (Luke 19:42).

The words of Romans 4:25 stand out like a mountain peak in a valley of promises. "In the beginning was the Word, and the Word was with God, and the Word was God" (John 1:1). But these were only promises. The penalty — the *full penalty* — had not yet been paid. That day was not yet come. Sin and death loomed larger and larger on mankind's horizon. The imminence of death hung like the sword of Damocles over humanity. Death was still on the throne — it was still reigning — Romans 5:17.

Just as sure as night follows day, God's Word would not fail. His sovereign plan had to come to fruition. It did! "The Word became flesh" (John 1:14). The mills of God began to grind slowly but surely. The millenniums became centuries, the centuries became decades, the decades became years, the years became days, the days became hours, and, finally, the hour arrived — "The hour is come" (John 12:23), and "For this cause came I unto this hour" (John 12:27).

When that hour came, it was one of the darkest hours in history. Where there is night, there must be day. The day came! "On the first day of the week . . . early, while it was yet dark" (John 20:1). This was the day that all eternity waited for. The realization, the manifestation of that day that became the hour, was fully come, when the Saviour arose and fulfilled the words He had spoken to His followers, "Because I live, ye shall live also" (John 14:19). What a change this made! What blessed promises became realities! Death was no longer on the throne! The Usurper was dethroned! Life triumphant now reigned! Life became the divine Potentate and "he giveth it to whomsoever he will" (Daniel 4:17). This is what Paul meant when he said in Romans 4:25, ". . . who was delivered up for our trespasses, and was raised for our justification."

The resurrection is unique to Christianity. No religion bears this unique stamp of God's approval. Every religion or religious movement has a dead founder; i.e., Judaism's, Moses; Confucionism's, Confucius; Zoroastrianism's, Zoroaster; Christian Science's, Mary Baker Eddy; Seventh Day Adventism's, Ellen G. White; Jehovah's Witnesses, Pastor Russell and Judge Rutherford; Bahaism's, Mirza Husayn Ali; and Islam's, Mohammed. But only Christianity has a *living* Christ. The resurrection of Christ proves the truth of the Christian message, and at the same time proves all other so-called religions false.

The resurrection proves the claims of Jesus Christ as the Lord and Redeemer of mankind. It proves the Virgin Birth; it proves Christ's vicarious sacrifice; it proves Him to be the God-given Mediator; it proves His promise of His return and Second Coming; it proves the resurrection of every born-again believer; and it authenticates the restoration of Israel and the introduction of the Millennium. In addition to the foregoing, the resurrection guarantees the destruction of sin and the casting of Satan into the lake of fire; it proves there is a hell, and that the sinner is going there unless he repents and is born again; it demonstrates the importance of the Gospel; it substantiates the depravity of man; and it clearly portrays the righteousness of God as the Gospel proclaims it.

The resurrection of Christ further proves that the sacrifice of Christ was, and even now is, the only satisfactory propitiation in God's sight for a lost mankind, and that the blood of God's own Son, Jesus Christ, is the only cleansing agent for sin. It authenticates the Old Testament, its sacrifices and its promises. It substantiates the truth that no Old Testament or New Tesament saint has died or will die in vain. It gives the power of the Holy Spirit to the believer to "go into all the world and preach the Gospel." It makes the preaching of the Gospel imperative in this present hour as this age hastens to its cataclysmic end.

The hour of Christ's return is upon us. Sin is prevalent all around us. The signs that our Saviour spoke of are visible in every avenue of life. There is murder, thievery, dishonesty, idolatry, fornication, divorce, truce-breaking and lawlessness — all signs that spell the time of our Saviour's return. The sad part of it is that these signs are not only visible in the world, but they are visible even in some of our so-called fundamental churches. "The night cometh, when no man can work" (John 9:4), and the sun is fast approaching the western horizon. Tomorrow may be too late to preach the Gospel. Doors are already being slammed shut. The urgency of the hour impels us to make haste. It is needless to pray that the Lord open the ears and circumcise the hearts of the unbelievers, unless we realize that we, every blood-bought born-again child of God, are God's hands, His feet, and His lips. We are His instruments that He must use to bring His redeeming message to a lost world. All these truths are embraced in the second half of Romans 4:25, ". . . and was raised for our justification."

Fellow Christians, let us rise to this momentous occasion and work, looking for the moment when we shall be swept into His Eternal Presence. May ours be the joy of hearing from His lips the words, "Well done"! This blessed joy will be ours if we obey His voice.

5

Verse 1: Being therefore justified by faith, we have peace with God through our Lord Jesus Christ ...;

The first part of this verse is better translated, "having been justified by faith." The Greek verb is in the past tense. The doctrine of Justification has been fully dealt with in Chapter 4 wherein the Apostle carefully elaborated upon this doctrine and fully explained it. In the verse before us, he summarizes what he has said in the preceding chapter. The Greek word for "justified" has two Hebrew words which clarify the meaning. The first word means judgment, the act of judging, sentence, decision, court of justice. The second word means justice, equality in the administration of justice, righteousness, justification, acquittal.

The meaning of the clause is, in the court of justice, where impartial administration of justice is to be practiced, God has declared the believer justified and acquitted him of guilt through the principle of faith. This is God's method of righteousness. The Law of Jehovah is an order of life which cannot be challenged or changed. This Law must be administered by God on His own terms. The terms are all included in the one word, faith. However, we must bear in mind that faith is the principle, the method, the means, the vehicle that God uses to justify each believer. The justifier is God.

V. 1: ". . . we have peace with God through our Lord Jesus Christ . . ." Before being justified, a sinner is an enemy of God, separated from God, tossed about on the turbulent sea of sin, filled with apprehensions, doubts, and fears, and not ready or willing to face a just God. The sinner is ever trying to flee and hide from God. As sinners, we are at enmity with God. We are rebellious; we are unwilling to believe in God. We are horrified at the thought of death, knowing that we shall have to face a righteous Judge who is impartial in His judgments, who

135

is just in His punishment. God is the last One a sinner wants to meet.

How different it is with the one whom God has justified. Because we have been made righteous, we have peace. Jehovah has become our Friend, our Father, our Protector in all our trials, and our Defender in every battle. He leads, He guides, He guards every footstep. He has even numbered the hairs of our heads, and He knows us by name. Death is no longer a fear, it is but the door into the very presence of God Himself. He has become our Father, i.e., in the analogy of our human father-and-son relationship. This is the new conception of Jehovah which our Lord Jesus brought to us when He taught us to pray, "Our Father," and in such teachings as the prodigal son (Luke 15:11). God in His love, in His mercy, in His compassion, is to be thought of as a tender, compassionate, forgiving human parent, but on a far grander, far more exalted scale than any human relationship could possibly be, as God's nature is infinitely greater than ours. Every believer is able to flee to God in the face of danger, trial, and tribulation. Like a child in fear may cling to its earthly parent, so every believer may turn not in fear but in trust to God. All this has been accomplished through our Lord Jesus Christ. What peace! What joy and assurance! "O Love that wilt not let me go," is the first line of a precious old hymn in which the hymn-writer caught the vision of this truth and then penned these tender words. These are the eternal words of comfort for every believer. They form the silver lining of every troublesome cloud of life's vicissitudes. Praise His Name!

Verse 2: ... through whom also we have had our access by faith into this grace wherein we stand; and we rejoice in hope of the glory of God.

There is much discussion over the Greek word that is translated, "we have had" in the American Standard Version, and "we have" in the King James Version. The consensus is for "we have had." Every person, the moment he becomes a believer, enters into all the blessings entailed in salvation. We enter in once for all time and eternity, never again to leave this position or the presence of the Lord Jesus Christ.

In view of this, is it not time for us to re-examine our methods and habits of prayer? When believers pray, the average prayer begins with the words, "Lord, we come into Thy Holy Presence," when, as a matter of fact, the believer, since the day he became a believer, has never left God's presence. The moment we believe, God's Holy Spirit enters into our being and never leaves us. We are the Holy Spirit's eternal abiding place. No matter where we are, no matter what we do, He is there. We "have had our access," and we are still there. We shall be there changed from glory to glory. This is the heritage of every blood-bought child of God. We speak to God out of the abundance of our hearts and not with the excellency of words.

Another rendition of Romans 5:2 is, "through whom we have obtained our access into this grace wherein we stand." We did not obtain this position through our own strength, but through Christ and His completed work on the cross and His sprinkled blood on the eternal mercy-seat. He did it all! "Wherein we stand," means to fix, to establish, to confirm, to stand fast, to be permanent. The tense of the Greek verb is the perfect indicative, giving it a double meaning. It implies a past action, and affirms an existing result. The statement means that when the believer is saved, he is brought into this position, and is permanently fixed there. We stood in the Grace of God yesterday, we stand in it today, and we shall stand there eternally.

V. 2: ". . . and we rejoice in hope of the glory of God." Because we have been permanently fixed, we rejoice, we glory, and we boast. We are doing this all along. This verb, being in the present indicative tense, means that we are constantly rejoicing or glorying in our position. We boast in the glory of God. The Greek word for "glory" has a Hebrew equivalent which means honor, splendor, or majesty. We boast that we are secure in God because His Honor, His Splendor, and His Majesty is our assurance. If we were not "once for all" kept in this position, God's very nature as a covenant-keeping God, could be in question. He has made this covenant through the death of our Saviour, by the sprinkling of His blood on the eternal mercy-seat, and by the Holy Spirit sealing us in this position. The complete fulfillment of this will be realized when every believer is translated into His presence, in his resurrected body (Romans 8:23).

Verse 3: And not only so, but we also rejoice in our tribulations: knowing that tribulation worketh stedfastness . . . ;

By "tribulations" the Apostle, no doubt, has in mind physical hardships. The word means pressures, afflictions, distressing circumstances, and trials. If these experiences are brought about because of the believer's standing for the truth, for righteousness, for the Gospel's sake, then the believer can boast, can glory, and can rejoice. These experiences will prove to be polishing stones for the child of God. Indeed, he can "rejoice in tribulations."

There is another type of tribulation that we should consider at this point. It is this: Many times we are, ourselves, the cause of our own annoyances or misfortunes. We sometimes carry not only a chip on our shoulder, but often it is also a board, when no one is able to approach us without knocking it off. This is not "suffering for Christ's sake" but, rather, the result of our own sensitiveness or foolishness.

There is still another type of tribulation to consider of which we ourselves are the cause, and it has nothing to do with suffering for righteousness' sake. A very striking example of this is that of an Old Testament saint who is described in the Scriptures as a "righteous man" whom God delivered from final condemnation (II Peter 2:7-10). The righteous man was Lot. All the "vexing" circumstances in which Lot found himself during his stay in Sodom were brought about by Lot's unwillingness to separate himself from his wicked neighbors and associates; in fact, Lot chose Sodom. It was his own doing. This is a classic example of thinking "the grass is greener on the other side of the fence." Lot knew where he was going (Genesis 13:9-11). All the heartaches that Lot experienced were caused by his unwillingness to separate himself. This was his ruin. Lot was the cause of his wife's death because of this choice. He even lost his sense of right and wrong. It is almost impossible to imagine a man of God being willing to expose his own daughters to mob violence and rape (Genesis 19:8). Yet Lot stooped to this depth of wickedness. How low can one sink?

Let us look further into this man's life. The adage that "the apple doesn't fall far from the tree" for good or evil in accounting for inherited traits of human beings, seems to apply in the case of Lot's progeny. His two daughters deliberately planned and committed the crime of incest with their father, first making him drunk (Genesis 19:31-38). The degradation and bestiality of this man and his daughters is revolting to every decent member of society. Look at the results! Because of this immorality, Lot fathered two heathen nations, Moab and Ammon. But for the Grace of God, Lot would have suffered all the torments of hell. But God delivered him!

Moreover, Lot persisted in his sin, even after God delivered him out of Sodom. Sodom should have been a stench in the nostrils of himself and his family. All of them ought to have been thrilled to leave this cesspool of abomination. Lot should have

left the area long before he did, but he refused to leave his family
who would not consent to go, and he, therefore, chose to remain
in the midst of sin. When they did leave, it must have been with
heavy hearts. Sodom was, in a sense, their native land, the
homeland of their choice. Lot's wife took just one lingering,
backward look, and what a costly look it proved to be! What
dire consequences! She became a pillar of salt! (Genesis 19:26).
That last look cost her her life. What effect did this act of God
have on Lot's mind and heart? None. He fled with his daughters
to a cave in the mountains, far from the haunts of mankind, and
became the victim of a plot on the part of his adulterous daughters
to perpetuate the family seed by incest, as already described. The
lesson in this bit of ancient history is for us all, i.e., the evil
consequences which may follow a simply act of carnality by a
righteous man (II Peter 2:8). Let us hearken to God and not to
the world.

There is still more to this story, a side-effect, so to speak, of
Lot's deviation from the path of righteousness which should be
taken into account because of the deep scar it left on the heart
of Abraham. Abraham, too, was disobedient. God called Abraham and Sarah, his wife, and specifically told him, "Get thee out
of thy country and from thy kindred, and from they father's
house" (Genesis 12:1) and come out alone. Did Abraham obey
God? No. He brought Lot with him. Abraham, too, refused to
separate himself from the world. Just one sinful act, just one
foolish move, is often sufficient to set off a chain of experiences
that brings with it endless heartaches. It did just this to Abraham. What heartaches! What pain! What anxiety! How many
sleepless nights, and how many tears the sins of Lot must have
cost Abraham. All could and would have been avoided if only
Abraham had obeyed God. But the grace of God delivered him
just as it delivered Lot.

And God's grace will deliver each of us if we will only let God
have His way and His say in our lives. The epitaph on Abraham's
tomb was written by the Saviour Himself, "Abraham rejoiced to
see my day" (John 8:56). One wonders what epitaph God
wrote on Lot's tomb. What will be yours, what will be mine?
We know God's epitaph for Paul. He rejoiced in tribulation.

In Romans 5:3, the Apostle writes with the thought of glorying
in tribulation for the sake of righteousness. To stand firm for the
faith, to contend for the faith, to suffer for the cause of Christ,
are experiences for which every believer will thank God. The
Apostle Peter also states that it is blessed to suffer for righteous-

ness' sake (I Peter 3:14). These two Jewish Christians, Paul and Peter, knew what it meant to suffer trials and tribulations for the sake of the Gospel. This is a high calling! It is a privilege that not many of us know today. Yet it was a daily experience for the first Christian martyrs, who were Jewish. For them it was the goal toward which to press (Philippians 3:14). For most of us, it is the goal to shun. Christ, the Gospel, the Church, the Word of God, all these are apt to be regarded as "cunningly devised fables" (II Peter 1:16) for most of us, rather than stones builded around a chief corner-stone upon which we, as living stones, may build a spiritual house offering up sacrifices, even our lives, that will be acceptable to God through Jesus Christ (I Peter 2:4, 5). Suffering for Christ should be a daily experience for every believer (II Timothy 3:12). According to this passage in Timothy, it is imperative that the Christian suffer daily tribulations for the cause of Christ.

V. 3: ". . . knowing that tribulation worketh stedfastness . . ."; The meaning of the Greek word for "worketh" is, will bring out, will produce, will result in. "Worketh" in modern English is work, or working, in the present tense. The word for patience (KJV) is better translated perseverance, endurance, or stedfastness (ASV). Tribulation should drive Christians away from the world, thus causing us to flee to God. Tribulation should cause us to lean on the Lord more consistently, resulting in a closer walk with God as we seek to do His will. This should cause us to search His Word, to witness, to live exemplary lives at all times, under all circumstances, never counting the cost. Living this way, we will be clothed with the whole armor of God, our loins girded with truth, our breastplate the righteousness of God, our feet shod with the preparation of the good tidings of peace, with the sword of the Holy Spirit as our weapon (Ephesians 6:10-17). To be thus prepared is the meaning of Romans 5:3.

Verse 4: . . . and stedfastness, approvedness; and approvedness, hope . . . . :

The Apostle continues with the thought introduced in verse 3. He says, "and stedfastness, approvedness." In other words, this patience (KJV) or stedfastness (ASV) which could also be translated perseverance or endurance, results in approvedness. The Greek word for "approvedness" is a very strong word. It means the state or disposition of that which has been tried or proved. It denotes that a person has been found reliable, tested in battle and found to be trustworthy and genuine. It is only this kind of person whom God has approved who is to be entrusted with the Gospel (I Thessalonians 2:4). This is the believer who has been tried, tested and approved, who will receive the crown of life which the Lord has promised to them who love Him (James 1:12). This approvedness results in hope. This hope is to be placed in one Person only, Jesus the Messiah, who died and was buried, who rose the third day and ascended unto the Father as our Mediator, and who will return for us "who wait for His appearing," to receive us unto Himself. This is forcefully stated in the first verse of this chapter, "through our Lord Jesus Christ."

Verse 5: . . . and hope putteth not to shame; because the love of God hath been shed abroad in our hearts through the Holy Spirit which was given unto us.

The hope that "putteth not to shame" is the hope that the believer has in the Lord which will prevent him from ever being put to shame. He need never blush, he need never be frustrated; he will never be disappointed or disgraced. This is the meaning of the Greek words which are translated, "putteth not to shame."

The Septuagint of Isaiah 28:16 reads, "Behold I lay for the foundations of Sion a costly stone, a choice, a cornerstone, a *precious stone*, for its foundations; and he that believes on *him* shall by no means be ashamed." This LXX text caught the attention of the Jewish Christians in the early church as a clear Messianic prophecy. Paul must have had this in mind in writing Romans 5:5 and also Romans 9:33. The Tried Stone, the Sure Stone, the Precious Stone, is none other than the Lord Jesus Christ. Whosoever places his trust in Him need never be ashamed. Let us make sure and certain that our faith is built upon this Precious Stone, the Lord Jesus Christ.

V. 5: ". . . because the love of God hath been shed abroad in our hearts . . ."

Basically, there are three words for "love" in biblical Greek: the first word is "Eran," which refers to the love between the sexes, sometimes called romantic love or sensual love or lust (Matthew 5:28) either within the marital state or without, such as illicit love. The Greeks had a god called Eras, or Eros, from which name the word erotic is derived; a statue for Eros was placed at the heart of the Greek fertility rites during which festivity the young of both sexes were permitted or invited to indulge in shameful and degrading acts in the name of love. However, some of the Greek philosophers, such as Plato and

Aristotle, tried to divest the word Eran of its original purely sexual connotation and invest it with a nobler meaning. This word is not in the New Testament.

The second Greek word is "philain." This is a New Testament word which means human love apart from the implication of sex relationship. It also means romantic love, but on a higher level than that of sex only, such as the love between husband and wife, love for children, family love, brotherly love, and the love of one's neighbor. Such love applies to all our human relationships, the equivalent meaning of which is friendship.

The third Greek word for love in the New Testament is "agapan," which is used to signify purely spiritual love, that is, the love of God (I Corinthians 13). This word takes on the meaning of complete selflessness, as, "Greater love hath no man" (John 15:13). This is the meaning of the word love in Romans 5:5. The Greek word means to prefer, to set one good or one aim above another, to esteem one person more highly than another. This word may be used for God's love for a man, as in Daniel 10:19, "O man greatly beloved."

It is not possible for the writer to develop fully the complete meaning of the various Greek words in this present commentary on the book of Romans. However, let us look at this one word "agapan" in the sense already given. It is God's love at the infinitely highest, coming down to man through Jesus Christ and lifting up to God the man who accepts it, that he may "be with me where I am" (John 17:24) and placing him in the heavenlies. This is done by God's choice, who thus bestows His love on the believer in Christ. Certainly, this shows that God is indeed love (I John 4:8, 16), which is also expressed again and again in the Old Testament, and proclaimed with such power and clarity by the Apostle Paul in this tremendously important book of the New Testament. God esteems the believer in Christ above everyone and everything.

When God's love has been shed abroad in the believer's heart, the Holy Spirit's work has just begun. The Greek word for "has been shed abroad" is in the perfect tense, indicative mood, passive voice. The whole statement points to the action that took place at Pentecost when the effusion of the Holy Spirit occurred. The believer must yield himself, dedicate himself to God in the fullest sense in order to reap the full benefit of God's glorious love. This is something which each and every believer can experience; it is not reserved for the few. The Greek word for "has been shed abroad" in the tense in which it appears in this text, means to gush out. It is a literal pouring out, as water is poured out. Paul could have had in mind Isaiah 44:3, which expresses the thought of this verse. God's love has been poured out to us, i.e., to all believers, without reservation. The believer can either accept all that God has for him or reject it.

Many times after a Sunday service we hear people say, "I didn't get anything out of the message this morning." When this is not the fault of the preacher, it is the fault of the hearer. If the hearer fails to give the preacher his attention, or comes to the service with a shallow mind, or a mind too full of temporal things, is it any wonder that he has little or no capacity for the preacher's message, even if the preacher were the Apostle Paul in person? Or, if the hearer comes with a thimble-size amount of attention, how can he expect to go away with a bucket-full of spiritual food? Frequently we come to a worship service with minds and hearts filled with self. There just isn't room for God in our lives. We are too full of the world with all its cares, its trials, its frustrations, its torments, and apprehensions, to permit us to hear God speaking to us through His ministers. Only a few of us are able to experience fully what Paul means in Philippians 1:6, "Being confident of this very thing, that he who began a good work in you will perfect it until the day of Jesus Christ."

Fellow Christians, let us yield to God so that His effulgent love may lift us from the "lower" plane of our mundane selves to the "higher" realm of His eternal dwelling place so that we may enter into the joy of His presence, reserved for every believer who will accept His gracious offer. It is a challenge; will you accept it? This can be done by the working of the Holy Spirit within your life. For the first time in this Epistle, we find the Holy Spirit mentioned in this particular verse.

Verse 6: For while we were yet weak, in due season Christ died for the ungodly.

The Greek word for "weak" means helpless, imperfect, and inefficient. It fully portrays man's sinful condition in relation to God's Holy Law. If the Law did anything at all, it vividly portrayed man's sinfulness and God's holiness. It showed man that no matter how perfect or righteous he thought himself to be, his best deeds, in God's sight, were as ugly as the bandages from leprous wounds, i.e., "filthy rags" (Isaiah 64:6 KJV). This was the intent of the Law, the purpose of the Law, the genius of the Law. Whenever man thinks himself to be good, the Law shows him his sin and brings him to the cross for cleansing (Psalm 19:7; Galatians 3:24).

God gave man plenty of time in which to try to work out his own righteousness, but the more time God gave him the deeper he sank into sin. Man had all the time necessary, but when time had run its course he was deeper in sin than ever before. This was precisely in accordance with God's own plan, formed before the world ever came into existence, that at the exact moment when time had run its course, "when in due season Christ died for the ungodly," and when, according to John 12:23, Jesus Himself said, "the hour is come," at the very moment set by God in the beginning, the Righteous One was lifted up and the crucifixion was accomplished. It was "in due season" and in accordance with God's plan. It was the time that Daniel foretold, 9:26 KJV, "And after threescore and two weeks shall Messiah be cut off." This was written hundreds of years prior to the Incarnation. God's plans and programs are always according to schedule (Galatians 4:4). His plans can never be thwarted, upset, or interfered with. Satan and his imps are given their liberty only within fixed limits set by God, just like a puppy at the end of a leash (Job 1:12). When all mankind had carefully planned its program, and its every act had been studied and finally executed, when it was all over, it was nothing more than fulfilling what God had planned ages before (Acts 4:28).

In a shifting world, in a constantly changing world, how comforting are the promises, the prophecies, the plans and programs of a changeless God! He has built on a solid Rock a kingdom that needs no change now or ever. Our God knows the end when He hasn't even come to the beginning (Revelation 3:8). He has given us a perfect revelation of Himself. He has given us a perfect Book, the Bible, which is inerrant, infallible, plenary in its every jot and tittle. He has revealed Himself in the perfect revelation, i.e., His Son. His perfect plan of eternal salvation will ultimately bring us into His presence in a perfected state (I Corinthians 15:53, 54; I Thessalonians 4:13-18; Hebrews 9:28; I John 3:2). In the midst of a turbulent world, in this maelstrom of sinful humanity with death all about us, the child of God, the blood-bought, born-again individual can shout with joy and with full assurance, "I know him whom I have believed, and I am persuaded that he is able to guard that which I have committed (deposited) unto him against that day" (II Timothy 1:12). And all this is "according to schedule."

"Christ died for the ungodly." What a profound statement!

What wonderful words! The Apostle is exalting the gratuitous nature of God's love. Christ died for us while we were yet in our sinful state. "How unsearchable are his judgments, and his ways past tracing out" (Romans 11:33). But God's ways are never like man's ways. This is the way the God of Abraham, Isaac, Jacob, Israel and our God always works. God's ways are beyond human ken, we are unable to plumb their depths. The mystery of God's love is that He loved us while we were yet in our sins. But that was His plan. That God should love the righteous, the pure, we can easily understand. But to love the sinner enough to send His Son to die for him on the cross, to suffer all humiliation, to endure all pain, to experience all trials, to feel all anguish — this transcends all human reason and understanding. It is baffling to the unregenerate human mind, but blessedly reassuring to the believer, and sublimely expressed by the Apostle John, "Herein is love, not that we loved God, but that he loved us, and sent his Son to be the propitiation for our sins" (I John 4:10).

Let us pursue this subject further: If God were to love us because we love Him, then He would love us only as long as we love Him. This would place the believer in jeopardy. The whole plan of salvation would have to be taken out of God's hands and thrust upon man. The whole plan of salvation would be lost to sinful man, and the sovereignty of God would be minimized, yea, nullified! We would be lost sinners, not saved ones. That "Christ died for the ungodly," makes salvation possible for everyone regardless of race, creed or color, or social standing. The Love of God is all-sufficient, all-embracing, and eternally enduring. Our salvation was accomplished by God and given to us while we were yet in our sinful, ungodly and impious state. God had to do it all. He did. Do you believe it? Will you accept it? Then heed the loving invitation of a living Saviour, "Come unto me . . . and I will give you rest" (Matthew 11:28).

Verse 7: For scarcely for a righteous man will one die: for peradventure for the good man some one would even dare to die.

The death of Christ is unique, unparalleled, and unequaled in the history of the world. We hear of heroic deeds and sacrificial acts among friends. A mother, father, brother or sister will endanger his or her life to save the life of a loved one. We hear of a parent running into a burning home to rescue a child, or a parent running into the path of a train or automobile to save the life of a child. This kind of selfless and courageous action is understandable. It is not an uncommon occurrence.. Once in a great while, very rarely, we hear of a person losing his life in an effort to save the life of a man or woman who, in the eyes of society, is regarded as a "righteous" person, one who in the sight of man is upright, of moral character, as "touching the righteousness which is in the law, blameless," one whose conduct is reputed to be right, whose actions and deeds are exemplary, one who contributes to all good causes, to the church, to missions, and all the rest. All these traits of character come within the meaning of the Greek word which is translated "righteous" and would apply to an upright individual who is greatly respected in his community. All these traits in a person may fulfill man's concept of righteousness, but the person might not necessarily be kind, loving, sympathetic and compassionate.

We do not often hear of a person dying or even being willing to die for even such a "good man" as is mentioned in the latter portion of verse 7, ". . . for peradventure for the good man some one would even dare to die." There is a possibility — a very remote possibility — that someone would be willing to die "for a good man," a generous man, a beneficent man, a virtuous man, an excellent and fine man. Such a person might possess spiritual and moral qualities of considerable magnitude. The Greek philosophers understood the word which is here translated "good" to be a "magnitude" which gives meaning to life and existence. The word "good" is applied to God or to Christ, as well as to man, in the New Testament. This word is used to describe an individual possessing moral qualities. Such a one must be charitable, compassionate, understanding, kind, lovable, and loving. The person who possesses this quality called "good" has in his possession that which constitutes the life of a Christian (Romans 15:14; II Thessalonians 1:11). For the person possessing all of these characteristics the Apostle says of such a person, "someone would even dare to die." This is possible. This is understandable. It is not beyond human comprehension. The thought contained in this verse is continued in verse 8, which follows:

Verse 8: But God commendeth his own love toward us in that, while we were yet sinners, Christ died for us.

Thus the Apostle, in a most striking manner, presents the love of God and the love of man in vivid contrast. God's love toward us, in our sinful state, is a love beyond human apprehension and comprehension. God did this for us "while we were yet sinners" — while we were yet in our godless, depraved, sinful state. This is the meaning of the Greek word for "sinners." We were then the enemies of God. We neither loved Him, nor possessed the capacity to love Him. The love of God had not yet "been shed abroad in our hearts."

We were filled with unrighteousness and with all the myriad seeds of sin that infect the sinner which are spawned by unrighteousness. While we were in this state of degradation, "Christ died for us." The depth of the Love of God will never be plumbed by the human mind. It is fathomless! Only God can love as God loves. He vividly portrayed this love at Calvary. Christ suffered all the physical and mental torments of hell. He suffered pain, humiliation, thirst, separation, ridicule, and desertion. Grasp it, sinner! Christ died for you! Will you accept Him? He waits to receive you. What love!

Verse 9: Much more then, being now justified by his blood, shall we be saved from the wrath of God through him.

The phrase, "being now justified," implies more than just being pardoned or forgiven. We forgive a person for a misdeed, or if we have been wronged by him, but from that moment on, in the majority of cases, we are on guard against him. His lawless or discourteous action against society or ourselves tends to create in us a feeling of doubt, if not fear. There is mistrust on our part in one form or another when we are in the presence of a person who has wronged us. The old adage describes the situation, "Fool me once, shame on you; fool me twice, shame on me!" When we are justified by His blood, we are so thoroughly cleansed from our sin that there is never a trace of sin left. We are so placed in the presence of God as though we had never committed one sin or wrong, i.e., just-as-if-I've-never sinned — justified! This has all been accomplished for us by the Lord Jesus Christ through the cross. We have been brought into filial relationship with God. This is a marked difference from being just forgiven. How wonderful and comforting it is to know that this is our own personal possession!

How has all this been accomplished? What has brought all this about? It is "by his blood." You see, the God who is revealed in the Old Testament is the very same God who is revealed in the New; therefore, remission and salvation are the same. The program of God still is "without the shedding of blood is no remission" (Hebrews 9:22 KJV; Leviticus 17:11). The author of the book of Hebrews (this writer believes it was Paul) was steeped in the teachings of the Old Testament and thoroughly versed in all its sacrifices. He was fully aware that Israel was "cleansed" only once a year from all her sin (Leviticus 16:30).

V. 9: ". . . shall we be saved from the wrath of God through him." But this sacrifice, that "while we were yet sinners, Christ died for us," is a different type of sacrifice than that found in the Old Testament. The sacrifice and ceremony of the Day of Atonement in Leviticus 16:30 could take place only once a year. The ceremony took a great deal of preparation, and had to be perfect. It was the most important service of the year because it was the *sin-cleansing* service of the year. It was really no atonement, as the Hebrew word for atonement is *kophar* and means, in its primary sense, a cover. This is the word from which we get our English word "cover." This is what the sacrifices during the entire year did for the people of Israel, they "covered" their sins. The sprinkled blood in the Holy of Holies cleansed the nation of its sin.

The word for "cleansed" in the Hebrew is *tohar* and means to purify, to pronounce or declare clean. What a service it was! What preparation! The high priest rehearsed it over and over again. There must be no room for error. When the high priest entered into the Holy of Holies, the people were tense, their hearts beat with excitement. Would the sacrifice be acceptable to God? Would the high priest come out alive, or would the alternate priest take his place? This was the one time of the year when the character of the high priest's life must stand the supreme test! First he had to sprinkle the blood of the sacrifice for his own sin. If this was acceptable to God, he then continued with the service which would cleanse Israel from her sin. When the services of the Day of Atonement were over, what rejoicing there was in Israel's camp! Years later, when the Temple was built, the young Israelites, after the service was over, escorted their high priest from the Temple to his home with music and dancing in the street. The day ended with a party in the garden of the high priest's home. What joy! What mirth! Another year had come and gone. The high priest was alive; Israel's sin was cleansed.

Contrast what has just been written, with the Reconciliation of the New Testament! Our Lord's Reconciliation was no yearly or recurring ceremony to be prepared for and rehearsed in advance. It reached its awful climax as the fulfillment of ancient prophecy, "that the scripture might be fulfilled." The eternal High Priest was on the cross. His life was not taken from Him but was yielded up for the sins of the whole world. The earth quaked and darkness engulfed the land. The holy Victim announced His own death, "It is finished!" The words echoed throughout the world, and will continue to echo throughout eternity. Then all was quiet from Friday before sundown until Sunday. Our great High Priest's body was in the tomb. His frightened and scattered followers could only wonder and wait. Would He rise from the dead, as He promised? Had God forgotten them? Of what use now was the earthly Holy of Holies with its veil rent, the tombs opened and nature convulsed? (Matthew 27:50). This was no Temple ceremony. This was a tragedy of incalculable portent not only for Israel, but for all mankind, the greatest catastrophe in the annals of time.

Three days later the darkness lifted. Creation was born anew. Again the earth quaked, the stone was rent, the tomb was opened, and all nature took on a new lease of life.

It was early in the morning, and while it was yet dark Mary found the stone taken away and the tomb empty. The Eternal High Priest had risen! "He is not here!" (Mark 16:6). The cross was triumphant! It had conquered death and the grave! The High Priest was alive! He showed Himself, "See my hands and my feet (with the nail prints), that it is I myself: handle me" (Luke 24:39). He entered into the Holy of Holies once for all. He obtained eternal redemption for us (Hebrews 9:12). Once for all time and eternity the blood was sprinkled and we need no longer wait for an annual Day of Atonement. We have been washed, we have been cleansed, we have been made alive for eternity "by His blood," "Because I live, ye shall live also" (John 14:19), and thereby our eternal salvation is certified. We may now enter into His presence with boldness because we are now justified. Our entrance and our justification both have been obtained for us "by his blood" (Romans 5:9; Hebrews 10:19).

The price that Christ paid for our justification is the most treasured possession the believer has on this earth, i.e., His life's blood. To lay down one's life for the love of another is the highest sacrifice a person can make (John 15:13). When one gives his life, he gives everything. The price that God paid for our redemption was in reality everything that He had. He gave His Son to die on the cross for us — in our behalf. The Old Testament required more than the sacrifice of bulls and goats, it required obedience and surrender to God's will and word. The animal blood of the sacrifices did not meet the requirement of that which God demanded in the Old Testament, as stated in Ezekiel 18:4, "The soul that sinneth it shall die." This requirement negates the concept of good works as a means for salvation. Nothing that an individual can do will mediate his sin. Death is the requirement for every sinner regardless and irrespective of how deep or how shallow the sin is. Since "it is impossible that the blood of bulls and goats should take away sins" (Hebrews 10:4), it was necessary to have a *sinless* individual die in the place of a sinner. Since every sinner in the Old Testament had to die for his own sin, the only solution was the Incarnation, resulting in the Crucifixion. Inasmuch as *all* men (Jews and Gentiles) are sinners, the Incarnate Son of God had to die for all. How would this be accomplished? God accomplished it! "Behold, the Lamb of God, that taketh away the sin of the world!" (John 1:29).

At the crucifixion both the Gentiles and the Jews were identified with the death of Christ. Both were equally guilty. One was the perpetrator; the other the accomplice (Acts 4:27). Both fulfilled the Old Testament requirements by laying their hands upon Him, "And he shall lay his hand upon the head of his oblation" (Leviticus 3:2), and both Gentile and Jew identified themselves as sinners in the crucifixion of our great High Priest, not for the sins of Israel, as did the high priest of old, but once at the end of the ages so that the sins of both Gentiles and Jews might be put away by the sacrifice of Himself (Hebrews 9:25, 26). Had the Jews alone been guilty of the crucifixion no Gentile could ever have been saved, for then Christ would not have died for all mankind. But Christ died for the sin of all. This was the price our Eternal Father paid to redeem men of all ages, races, creeds and colors. "God so loved the world, that he gave his only begotten Son" (John 3:16). All this is contained in the phrase, "being now justified by his blood," or better translated, "in his blood" (Romans 5:9a).

V. 5:9b: ". . . shall we be saved from the wrath of God through him (Christ)." Commentators on the Roman epistle explain this "wrath" as meaning hell. Is this the only wrath that we know of? This writer does not want to seem dogmatic, but it appears to him that the word "saved" entails more than just being saved from hell. Will not the wrath of God be made manifest during the Tribulation period? Is such period not the time when God's fury is to be poured out on sinful men? How terrible will be the judgments of God as depicted in the book of the Revelation! Surely, if it were possible for us to bring back to life one of the ancient Egyptians who lived through the plagues of Exodus 7-12, he would tell us that the experiences of that time were as though hell had broken loose. The book of Revelation tells us

that because of the fury of God's judgments during the Tribulation period, the inhabitants of the earth will wish themselves
dead. They will want to die and will not be able to die. The
darkness of that hour, the devastation, the destruction, the bloodshed, the turmoil and the anguish will be indescribable. Can
the human mind conceive of a river of blood two hundred miles
long and deep enough to reach up to the bridle of a horse?
(Revelation 14:20). No human eye has ever seen such a spectacle.

And that other spectacle described by the prophet Ezekiel
(39:11-16) — can the human mind conceive of a catastrophe more
horrifying than that of beholding a multitude engaged in the
business of burying the dead bodies of the slain for seven months
without intermission, or by "men of continual employment"?
What an awful funeral! This is a revelation of the wrath of God
literally poured out upon a sinful generation, lost in hopeless
misery and wilful defiance of God. Surely even all right-minded
worldly parents would avail themselves of every precaution within
their power to guard their children from the awful judgments of
the Tribulation. Is it not reasonable then to believe that our
heavenly Father will rescue His own, for whom He has paid such
a priceless ransom as the life of His Son, the Lord Jesus? This
is assurance beyond all human doubt that God will save His
children from the terrors of such a holocaust.

This writer believes in a loving God who will do what He has
promised. How is it possible to believe that our loving heavenly
Father would abandon His children at such a time? It is difficult
to believe that God will not spare every believer from the horrors
of the Tribulation. The word "saved" implies more than just
not going to hell.

If the saints of God, living at the time of the Tribulation are
to go through this trying period, then why believe in the imminent
return of Christ? We should first look for the anti-Christ, then
start counting the days. This negates the incentive for Christian
living. The hope of Christ's return would not be a purifying
hope in such a case, it would be bleak despair. It would be the
last thing upon which a Christian could build his hope of heavenly bliss. Why hope for our Lord's return if there lies in store
for us the sufferings of a thousand hells? This writer is more than
ever convinced of the pre-Tribulation Rapture concept of
Eschatology. Thank God for His bountiful love! The imminent
return of Christ was the belief of the first century saints. It gave
meaning and impetus to their lives. They could sing in the face

of death in the arenas of Rome. This purifying hope of our Lord's return still does the same for us. "Even so, come, Lord Jesus," is the hope of each and every believer who trusts that God will not permit him to experience His wrath and His fury poured out. This, the writer believes, is the meaning, the portrayal, and the truth contained in Romans 5:9b, we shall "be saved from the wrath of God through him."

Verse 10: For if, while we were enemies, we were reconciled to God through the death of his Son, much more, being reconciled, shall we be saved by his life . . . ;

The Apostle, in this verse, is showing how far the law of God reaches. He is elaborating on what he stated in verse 8. Like an artist, he is completing the picture of the condition of every sinner prior to salvation. What contrast there is between the Love of God and the attributes of sinful humanity! The Greek word translated "enemies" means hated, hostile, inimical, an adversary. There can never be any compatibility between virtue and vice. God in His nature, in His character, in His attributes, is more than virtuous; He is sinless. Man in his sin nature is the extreme antithesis of God. Man is filled with sin, vice and corruption; he is depraved, immoral, degraded and literally loathes God and His righteousness. Sinful man, if it were in his power, would even destroy God. Since man loathes righteousness, he is an enemy of God. The Greek word for "enemy" is used in the New Testament for that which is hostile to God and his Christ (Luke 19:27; Acts 13:10; Philippians 3:18). The word "enemy" or "enemies" is used with the same thought in mind as presented in Psalm 110:1, "Until I make thine enemies thy footstool." The Jewish scholars who translated the Old Testament from Hebrew into the Greek Septuagint, understood this word to mean an enemy of God. Psalm 110 is quoted in the following passages: Mark 12:36; Acts 2:34; I Corinthians 15:25; and in Hebrews 1:13; 10:13. Paul considered death with this same thought in mind; namely, as an enemy (I Corinthians 15:26).

All of us were enemies of God when He, in His mercy and compassion, reached down to save us. What a loving God we have! How grateful we ought to be! He demonstrates this by reconciling us "while we were enemies." Bear in mind that we, the sinners, enemies of God, need to be reconciled to Him. God was never our enemy; therefore, He does not need to be reconciled to us. "God and man are never on equal terms in relation to reconciliation. Reconciliation is not reciprocal in the sense that both equally become friends when they were enemies. The supremacy of God over man is maintained in every respect" (*Theological Dictionary of the New Testament*, by Gerhard Kittel, pub. Wm. B. Eerdmans Pub. Co.). The "reconciled" of verse 10 is parallel to the "justified" of verse 9. Our sinful and selfish state, which sought only evil, is now changed, and seeks, or should seek, to live only for Christ. Being justified and reconciled results in our becoming new creations in Christ and living for Him (II Corinthians 5:15).

There is still one more thought that should not be overlooked in this verse. The clause, "while we were enemies," means that while we were still God's enemies, He had already perfected His plan and program of salvation, and we were included among that number chosen "in him before the foundation of the world" (Ephesians 1:5). For the reader who understands the grammar of the Greek, this is an extremely interesting and rewarding study. It is all the more so for those of us who believe in the Sovereignty of God, the Depravity of Man, and reject the doctrine of Sinless Perfection.

V. 10: ". . . much more, being reconciled, shall we be saved by his life. . ."; The believer being reconciled through the death of the Saviour receives much more through His life, i.e., having been reconciled by His death we shall be saved by His life. The structure of the Greek verb, "we shall be saved" (KJV), is such that it applies not only to the resurrection of the believer who has "fallen asleep in Jesus" (I Thessalonians 4:14, 15), but also to the translation of the believer who is alive at the coming of the Lord. Coming back with the Lord when He "shall descend from heaven, with a shout," lies in the future of every believer, including those who have "fallen asleep." So far as God is concerned, that which lies in the future for us is from the first a completed reality with God (I John 3:2).

If the death of Christ reconciled us to God while we were enemies, and accomplished so great an achievement, how much more an achievement does being saved by His life accomplish for us? The contrast between these two is very great.

The death of our Lord wrought miracles. His life accomplishes greater miracles, i.e., the resurrection and the translation of every believer (Philippians 1:6). "Wherefore also he is able to save to the uttermost them that draw near unto God through him" (Hebrews 7:25). The word "uttermost" has been so changed with wrong implications in some evangelical circles, that it has lost all semblance of its true meaning. For one thing, it certainly does not carry the meaning of "guttermost" as if depicting the degradation of the sinner. On the contrary, it is more properly applied to the duration of our salvation, which is *forever*, that is, to the utmost of time and the uttermost of our salvation. The Lord Jesus Christ is our Living Saviour, who saves the sinner; and our Living High Priest, who is constantly interceding for those whom He has saved, i.e., for us. Moreover, He has promised to return to receive us unto Himself (John 14:3). There would have been no resurrection, no salvation, no intercession at the throne of grace, and no promise of His return to receive us unto Himself, if His life had ended with His crucifixion. All this has been accomplished only because He lives. The promise of His return is the hope of every believer, a sure promise and one in which he can glory. How unique and extraordinary is our Christian faith and heritage! The challenge and responsibility of this faith and heritage are equally as great. Go! Preach! Witness! Live! Occupy! Each one of these words is a battlecry in our Christian warfare. What have we done with these commands? We will have to give an account to our Lord and Master.

Verse 11: . . . and not only so, but we also rejoice in God through our Lord Jesus Christ, through whom we have now received the reconciliation.

Verses 9 and 10 look back to the time of our salvation, the day when we acknowledged Christ as Lord and Saviour; and forward to the day when we shall be saved from "the wrath of God"; namely, the Tribulation and hell itself. But verse 11 now looks at the present status of the believer, who lives in this sinful world. Although this world is permeated with trials and tribulations, with torments and tears, with uncertainties and apprehensions, the believer can say with Paul, "we also rejoice" right now. The tense of the Greek word for "rejoice" requires that the rejoicing, the glorying, the boasting, the exulting, and the lauding be *right now*. No matter what the condition, no matter where the believer is, no matter what the circumstances may be, he can and does boast in God, believing that he is a child of God, and that his Heavenly Father will always watch over him under all circumstances (Psalm 139:1-10). The reality and possibility of this rejoicing and glorying is not dependent upon anything the believer has wrought through his own efforts. If this were the case, then the Christian could not rejoice in all the perplexing problems that occur in a lifetime. The flesh is weak and is incapable of doing this. But this has all been wrought through

Christ, and was accomplished by the Saviour Himself. It is
through Him that the believer can do all things (Philippians
4:13).

V. 11: ". . . by whom we have now received the atonement"
(KJV) (or "reconciliation," as in ASV). This verse (Romans 5:
11) is the only place in which the translators of the King James
Version have used the word "atonement" in the New Testament.
The work of our Saviour on the cross and His resurrection did
not bring about atonement. The Greek word which in Romans 5:
11 is translated "atonement" in KJV is the same Greek word
which is translated "covered" in Romans 4:7, "Blessed are they
. . . whose sins are covered." (See comment on 4:7 on page
116 and on Leviticus 16:30 on page 148, Romans 5:9.) Hence,
the work of our Lord on the cross and through His Resurrection
has not *covered* our sins but has *cleansed* the believer from every
vestige of sin; it has washed him "whiter than snow"; it has
brought him into the presence of God just-as-if-he-had-never-
sinned. The believer has not received *atonement* — perish the
thought! Therefore, Romans 5:11 is better translated in the
American Standard Version, ". . . through whom we have now
received the *reconciliation*." We have been reconciled to God!
Our Saviour's work in behalf of the believer has removed and
cleansed every trace and particle of enmity and guilt from the
heart and mind of the believer, and has *reconciled* him to God
the Father. Having, therefore, received reconciliation, we now
love God and worship Him. In trials and tribulations, we flee to
Him, because our Lord is a living Saviour, and, regardless of
circumstances, our joy in Him is complete. He is the Author and
Perfector of our Faith. Hallelujah, what a Saviour!

The Greek word used here for "atonement" in the King James
Version of the New Testament is never used to refer to an offering,
which is the meaning of the word atonement. It is always used
to mean *reconciliation.*

Introduction to verses 12-21

By some commentators, Romans 5:12-21, taken as a whole, is
regarded as the most difficult portion in the New Testament.
This entire section is the comparison of the chain of consequences
from the Fall of Adam, with the chain of consequences from
the Work of Christ. It deals with the two great representatives
of mankind, Adam and Christ, and the contrast between the
sin of Adam and the salvation in Christ. The sin of Adam
brought the doom of death to humanity. The work of our

Saviour which was wrought for us through His death, burial and resurrection, brought redemption to humanity. It is a succinct history of the human race from God's standpoint. This portion of Scripture is a masterpiece of argument from premise to conclusion. It contains truths assembled together with such skill as to lead one to believe that the master mind of the Holy Spirit had guided the hand of the Apostle in putting the history of our fall and redemption into such a short but inspired record. Volumes have been written on these ten verses. From verse 12 to verse 21, doctrines are dealt with, such as original sin, imputation, salvation, and justification, thereby preparing the way for a life-union of the believer with Christ. Moreover, these verses set the stage for introducing the doctrine of sanctification and glorification in the chapters following. Paul shows in verses 12 to 21 that in Adam all die, and in Christ we are made alive (I Corinthians 15:22). From Adam proceeds the power of sin and of death; from Christ proceeds the power of righteousness and life. The superiority of the Second Adam, Christ, over the First Adam is made clear, and also that Adam's sin was not an isolated case. He was a corrupt tree that brought forth evil fruit; whereas, our Lord is the good tree that brings forth good fruit. So Christ's righteousness is made manifest in the believer.

Verse 12: Therefore, as through one man sin entered into the world, and death through sin; and so death passed unto all men, for that all sinned . . . : —

Although sin was introduced by Eve, the Apostle does not separate Adam from Eve. In God's sight, Adam and Eve became "one flesh" (Genesis 2:24); "And called *their name* Adam" (Genesis 5:2). Thus, the sin and the consequences of that sin are placed on the shoulders of both of them as one titular head of humanity. Both sinned; both are, therefore, responsible for that sin. I Timothy 2:14 does not exonerate Eve. She is just as culpable as Adam. The sin was so great in God's sight, the ramifications of their sin had such far-reaching consequences, their actions were so contrary to God's will, that God did not deem them worthy of honorable mention in His Hall of Fame, Hebrews 11.

When they were both created, it was in the image of God. They both shared in that image and in all its benefits. When they sinned and defaced God's image, they shared in the punishment of the sin. They broke the command that God gave to them (Genesis 2:15-17). The penalty for breaking that com-

mand was, "Thou shalt surely die." That this was a "covenant"
seems obvious from the literal translation of Hosea 6:7, "but
they like Adam have transgressed the covenant."

V. 12: "Sin entered." Sin made its appearance. Sin entered
and took possession. The possession was God's creation. If sin
made its entrance into the Garden of Eden, sin must have existed
before the Fall. This writer believes that the Scriptures teach
just that (Ezekiel 28:12-19; Isaiah 14:12-15). A careful look at
Ezekiel 28:13 will reveal the fact that it speaks of Satan making
his appearance in the Garden of Eden. The entrance of sin into
the world resulted in sin becoming the inheritance of humanity, as a father leaves his wealth as an inheritance to his children. The Bible uniformly connects sin and death as cause and
effect (Ezekiel 18:4; Jeremiah 31:30; Romans 6:16). By "death"
this writer believes that it is both physical and spiritual, temporal and eternal.

Because "sin entered," Adam and Eve with all their possessions now became the property of sin (Romans 8:10; Matthew 4:
9). They were now, because of their sin, the slaves of sin (Romans 6:16). The rewards or wages of sin is death (Genesis 2:17;
Romans 6:23) and the wages have never been reduced. Death
has been the potentate from the Garden of Eden onward, "dust
thou art, and unto dust shalt thou return" (Genesis 3:19).
Death, this writer believes, is death in the general sense, i.e.,
physical and spiritual. Even believers are subject to death, and
death will not be conquered for the believer until Christ returns
for His own (I Corinthians 15:54). What a price Adam and
Eve paid for just a few moments of pleasure! What a contrast
God shows between them and Moses! (Hebrews 11:24-27).

The Rabbis and scholars of old believed and taught the "Depravity of Man." They taught that death was introduced into
the world through the serpent and brought upon Adam and his
posterity. By way of illustration, just a few Talmudic passages
will suffice: Tal. Bab. Sabbat., fol. 55:2; Bava Bath., fol. 17:1.
One quotation will serve as an example: "Adam and Eve, through
the evil council of the serpent, were the cause of death to
themselves and to all the world." (See Gill's Commentary, Vol.
IV, for more references.)

The Rabbis today have changed this concept, and have written the following prayer: "I thank thee, Oh God, that thou didst
not create in me an evil spirit." Nothing but presumption could
inspire such a prayer to God. However, Rabbis have taught that
the passage in Genesis 4:7, "sin lieth at the door," means that

sin pursues a person as soon as he is born. The door being the womb.

V. 12: ". . . and so death passed unto all men . . ." Death is the consequence of sin. Death has made its way to every member of the human race, from Adam and Eve on. We must not overlook the fact that in the Greek there is the definite article (the) before "sin" and "death." This definite article denotes that each act is a power or principle which controls man, and reveals itself in every form of actual sin and hereditary corruption. In Romans 5:17, the definite article appears before the Greek words for "grace" and "righteousness," showing each of these virtues to be a controlling principle over man in Christ. Had there been no sin, there would be no death, either spiritual or physical. But sin and death are the inheritance that we have received from Adam, who is the generic head of mankind. Sin is the principle that brought death to Adam and his posterity.

In today's society we hear that slums, poor housing, lack of education and recreation are the contributing factors in the immoralities of our society. This writer does not believe this. Adam and Eve had perfect surroundings; and God gave them dominion over every living thing upon the earth and set Adam in the Garden of Eden to dress it and to keep it, with permission to eat of every tree in the garden except one. That one restriction was the tree of the knowledge of good and evil. There were no slums or delinquents, juvenile or adult, in the Garden, only a beautiful paradise created by God for His newly-created children. What more perfect surroundings could any human beings desire? Yet in the midst of such a paradise, Adam and Eve yielded to the sin of disobedience, the parent sin, Satan-inspired, from which all other sins are born.

How strange it is that our world leaders, our philosophers, our social do-gooders and over-zealous instructors in ethical culture, cannot see the folly of the outward reformation of the human creature and his environment, apart from his spiritual rebirth through faith in God, the Lord Jesus Christ. The specious programs for the moral and social improvement of the inhabitants of our slums and ghettos are, in God's sight, an offense and mockery.

Verse 13: . . . for until the law sin was in the world; but sin is not imputed when there is no law.

There is not a single page in human history that does not record sin. The longer history continues, and the older mankind becomes, the deeper in sin will society sink. It is becoming more and more obvious that man is incapable of extricating himself from the miry clay of sin. The Apostle says, "for until the law sin was in the world." Sin moved into the realm of humanity, and humanity has been unable to evict it. Ancient history, before the Law was given at Sinai, records that sin was prevalent. Some examples are the immorality of Sodom and Gomorrah, the evils of Egypt, the licentiousness of Mesopotamia, and the lasciviousness of the provinces surrounding it.

Verses 13 through 17 are a parenthesis and should be taken as one whole. We shall, however, look at each verse separately. To be sure, the Law that was given to Moses was not in operation from the Fall until Sinai. But there were laws! There were sacrifices! There were even tithes! How else would Joseph have known that it was wrong to have illicit relations with Potiphar's wife? Why was Cain's sacrifice rejected? Why did the patriarchs offer tithes? Surely there were laws in operation.

Paul did not say that the absence of the written Law did away with all responsibility. He clearly stated that the Gentiles who "have not the law . . . are the law unto themselves" (Romans 2:14). Israel must have occupied a similar position prior to the time when they received the Law and its institutions. Law, in Paul's mind, chiefly entails punishment. It increases the degree of guilt. The Fall was the result of the inclination, the tendency, the susceptibility to sin; it linked together sin and death. What the Apostle seems to bring out is that prior to the giving of the Law, the fate of humanity was linked to Adam's Fall.

V. 13: ". . . but sin is not imputed when there is no law." The Greek word for "imputed" means to enter in an account, i.e., to charge in a ledger against one's account. This word appears only twice in the New Testament, here and in Philemon 18. We inherit sin from our progenitor, Adam. Mankind, i.e., all men, do not become sinners when they sin; men sin because they are born sinners.

Verse 14: Nevertheless death reigned from Adam until Moses, even over them that had not sinned after the likeness of Adam's transgression, who is a figure of him that was to come.

The reason for this "reign of death" is obvious from the contents of verse 13. Since we are all descendants of Adam, having been born after the Fall, we have inherited the sin nature. We are the fellow-heirs of our progenitor, Adam. Sin inevitably brings death. Adam broke the law that God had given him. Knowingly he disobeyed God's Word, which was Law, ". . . thou shalt not eat of it" (Genesis 2:17). If he ate of that tree, death would ensue. Because he broke that law, death became the punishment as God said it would.

Paul's object is to show that through our natural birth we became partakers of sin and its consequences, viz., death. We are born sinners and are subject to death. It is not brought about by any deeds of our own. In that same way, we become righteous in God's sight by being born again. We become the partakers of the life of Christ. We inherit His (Christ's) righteousness. We become joint heirs with Christ through our second birth (Romans 8:17). The result is that we become a "new creature" in Christ (II Corinthians 5:17). The Greek word for "reign" means to reign as a king, kingly power, dominion. It is used to designate both the kingdom of God under the regal authority of the Messiah, the kingdom of Satan and the anti-Christ, as in Matthew 4:8; 9:34; Revelation 16:10; 17:17, and other places in the New Testament. Death most certainly reigned as a potentate from Adam to Moses. The Law intensified this reign in that the Law revealed the sinfulness of man and the absolute Holiness of God. When Christ came, He provided mankind with the way out. He constantly preached the kingdom of God, eternal life, eternal rest, and salvation from sin and death, in the midst of a restless humanity. He even promised the sustenance for it by stating that He was the Bread of Life; that He was the Water of Life; that He was the Way of Life; and that He was Life itself. He presented Himself as God (Matthew 26:63, 64; Hebrews 1:8), the Regal Authority over the kingdom of righteousness, in contrast to the kingdom of Satan with its sin and death. Our Lord invited men to accept His offer of everlasting life, as a gift. COME! was the keynote of His message.

The herald of that message today is the blood-bought, born-again saint of God, and the keynote of that message is still the same, *come!* And what is the message? Jesus Christ is life everlasting to all who will accept Him as Lord and Saviour. Will you accept Him? And if you will, what is the categorical imperative of that acceptance? *Go!*

V. 14: ". . . even over them that have not sinned after the likeness of Adam's transgression . . ." Death has touched every human being born after the Fall, regardless of age. Even infants who have not sinned as Adam sinned, are subject to death. Death reigns over everyone, including those who do not hear

God's command as Adam heard it, i.e., "Thou shalt not!" (Genesis 2:17). We must not lose sight of the fact that even though there was no specific law or code of laws given by God to man during the span of time between Adam and Moses, there was a law operating, as is plainly set forth in Romans 2:14, 15. Moreover, in every human being there is an inclination to sin, regardless of age. Even an infant will reveal its Adamic nature when denied its own way. Put a toy or bottle of milk within reach of two small children, give the article to one or the other, then take it away from the one and give it to the other, and watch the effect. The result is invariably an outburst of temper, tears, or even screams from the dispossessed infant. We never have to teach children how to lie, to cheat, or to steal. It is their innate nature. Each of us was born a sinner. This is our inheritance from Adam.

V. 14: ". . . who is a figure of him that was to come" (or the one coming). The Greek word for "figure" appears a number of times in the New Testament. In John 20:25, it is the same Greek word that is translated "print," the print of the nails made in the hands of the Saviour. In I Thessalonians 1:7 and II Thessalonians 3:9, this Greek word is translated "ensample," as an "example" to be followed.

The Apostle, this writer believes, had the following thought in mind: Adam as a human being merely, was not a type of Christ, but the *results* of Adam's sin are a type of the *results* of the work of Christ (I Corinthians 15:22). As in Adam all men are born in sin and die, so in Christ all sinners are born again and live! Adam's sin reached all mankind, and the results of his disobedience are prevalent throughout the human race in every age. Sin is rampant in the world today, and has permeated every inhabited area of the globe. There is not a community on this earth where at least some of the people of that community do not commit acts of disobedience, lawlessness, and vice. The world has become a breeding place of anarchy, riots, demonstrations, strikes, revolutions, and rebellions. What are these evils? Are they not the offspring of the parent sin of *disobedience?* All these acts of violence and lawlessness may be traced back to that one act of Adam when he refused to obey God's explicit command, "Thou shalt not eat of it" (Genesis 2:17).

So in Christ, we who are born-again believers must live an obedient life, clothed in His righteousness. The child of God must not be energized by the flesh, but, rather, by the Spirit of God. We must so live that we may be epistles read of all men

(II Corinthians 3:2), so that in reading us all men may see Christ, whom to know is life eternal. The sacrifice of Christ, the "once for all" act of God for us must saturate the life of the Christian, who is presented to the Father, clothed with His Son's righteousness; in fact, the work of Christ is far more effective than the sin of Adam. The one is the very antithesis of the other. As in the first Adam, all die, so (in like figure) in the Second Adam, all will be made alive (I Corinthians 15:22). This is the parallelism presented in the latter part of verse 14. Now notice how superior the work of Christ is in the following verses:

Verse 15: But not as the trespass, so also is the free gift. For if by the trespass of the one the many died, much more did the grace of God, and the gift by the grace of the one man, Jesus Christ, abound unto the many.

The Greek word translated "tresspass" means offense, to fall by the side of, a false step, a transgression. This word appears in many passages in the New Testament (Matthew 6:14, 15; Mark 11:25; Romans 4:25).

The Apostle here is comparing the sin of Adam and his posterity with the free gift of God. The Greek word Charisma is translated "free gift" in English, and it entails every phase of salvation. In many theological circles, the Gospel is referred to as "The Charisma." The difference between the trespass and the free gift, is as wide as life and death. The benefits that we derive from God's free gift and the evils brought upon mankind through the Fall are as far apart as heaven and hell. By the *one* sin of Adam, through that *one act of disobedience,* the many (the article "the" is omitted in the KJV) are dead. So through the *one* act of the Messiah, through the *one act of obedience,* the many are made righteous. The free gift given to man by the grace of God supersedes all that the Fall brought on. This is why the Apostle uses the phrase, "much more," in comparing the offenses of the one (Adam) with the gift by grace of the other (Christ). The action of one brought death, while the action of the other brought eternal life.

Verse 16: And not as through one that sinned, so is the gift: for the judgment came of one unto condemnation, but the free gift came of many trespasses unto justification.

In this verse the Apostle makes a vivid contrast of the difference, first, between judgment on the one hand, and a free gift on the other; and, second, between condemnation on the one hand, and justification on the other; and, third, the difference between the *one* and the *many*.

Through the single act of Adam came the Fall. From the one sinner came the judicial sentence which resulted in the condemnation of many. The contrast is that through the one sin of Adam came the sentence of condemnation on all men; the justification received from Christ's Work is from many sins or offenses.

There is much discussion on the text of verse 16 by many theologians. In very simple form the verse aims to show the superiority of Christ's finished work covering the many sins of man, whereas Adam's one sinful act caused the judicial sins to be passed on to the sinner. The evil from which Christ saves us is far greater than that which Adam brought upon us. We are all sentenced to death on account of the Fall. The death and resurrection of Christ seals the truth that the one act of Christ is sufficient to deliver us from all our sins and to justify us. The superiority of the accomplishments of the Saviour is merely the attestation of His Deity. The very fact that He is God Incarnate gives the assurance that His every work would supersede and overcome all the undoings from the Fall in the Garden of Eden. His last words on the cross, "It is finished," were the shout of a victor over the vanquished. The sentence would be more clearly translated and better understood if it read, "It is accomplished." He, alone, accomplished all that the Father had sent Him to do. He left nothing undone. He brought to the full completion everything that the Father had requested. The Saviour never stopped short of any phase of His Work. He discharged every duty, every word, every jot and tittle that the Father desired. Need we wonder that the Father said of Him, "This is my beloved son, in whom I am well pleased?" This could never be said by the Father if it were not true.

At the close of the Saviour's ministry on earth, we hear Him say, "Father, the hour is come; glorify thy Son, . . . I glorified thee on the earth, having accomplished (the same word in the original as finished) the work which thou hast given me to do" (John 17:1-4). The word for "is come" in the Greek carries the thought that the hour was the expected hour, the anticipated hour, the coming hour. How comforting to the believer is the reality that God's program is never late, not even for one moment. The world shifts, the world vacillates, the world changes, but God moves unwaveringly in His planned program and He sees its completion to the split second (Acts 4:28).

Take heart, fellow Christians! It is wonderful to surrender your life to a God who is Sovereign, never changing, always moving forward, sure-footed, toward that moment when the Saviour will shout, not from the cross, but from heaven, with the trumpet of God, "It is finished!" The last soul will have been saved — the Church, blood-bought, born again, saints only — completed; the Tribulation about to begin, the anti-Christ about to be revealed, bloodshed looming on the horizon of a sinful civilization, the Gentile world about to have its last fling, and the Jews decimated, but not devastated. Then, approximately seven years later, the return of the Lord to establish His Kingdom on earth. This should fill our hearts with joy, our lives with zest to win the lost of the world, including the lost sheep of the House of Israel. "Even so, come, Lord Jesus," should be the heart's cry of every believer.

Verse 17: For if, by the trespass of the one, death reigned through the one; much more shall they that receive the abundance of grace and of the gift of righteousness reign in life through the one, even Jesus Christ.

Thus the Apostle continues the comparison of the consequences of Adam's sin with the grace and righteousness brought into the believer's life through faith in Christ. The superiority of the work of the Saviour over Adam's sin and its degenerative processes is further amplified. The grace of God always is and always must be superior to the sin of man.

The phrase, "by the trespass of the one," can also be translated, by the one trespass. The Greek word for "trespass" is the genitive singular, masculine or neuter. It points either to Adam or to Adam's one trespass. In either case, Adam or his one act of disobedience in eating the forbidden fruit — this one act — is what brought sin and death upon the human race. Death has been reigning ever since as a potentate, as a king, over humanity. (See notes on Romans 5:14 on the word "reign".) The King James Version translates this "by one man's offence."

Even Jewish teachers of old taught, "Adam transgressed one commandment of the Law, and was the cause of death to himself, and to all the world" (Zohar in Num. fol. 52.). Modern Judaism does not accept this. The Jews, like all religionists, change "with every wind of doctrine." Like all the unregenerate theologians, the Jewish Rabbis teach that their own works will save them. They feel that they can pull themselves up by their own bootstraps. The Bible teaches the contrary. Man is incapable, in his sinful condition, of meeting, face to face, a Holy, Righteous and Immutable God.

The Bible teaches that unregenerated man is the victim of sin and death, and that he is subject to these powers until he repents and yields himself to God; in fact, man is the bond-slave of sin and death (Romans 6:16).

V. 17: ". . . much more shall they that receive the abundance of grace and of the gift of righteousness reign in life through the one, even Jesus Christ." Here the conclusion follows with an even greater logical inference that God's grace must be more powerful in its effect than man's sin. And it is! We, who have experienced the power of God's grace know it. We haven't merely felt it; we have experienced it. We know it!

The blessings received from God are so superior to earthly good fortune that we are unable to make any just estimate of their value. What we receive from God is so "much more" than any earthly treasure (Matthew 6:19), that nothing in this world can be compared with it. Outside of Christ, our life here on earth offers us only sin's degradation and death's putrefaction; whereas being born again in Christ brings us righteousness, holiness, sanctification, justification, security and eternal life. The good that we have received from God through our Lord Jesus Christ cannot be compared with the evil consequences of sin and death which are the very antithesis of the good which is ours through Christ.

Dear reader, have you accepted this? Have you really experienced this? Has Christ become the Potentate of your life, and a living Reality in your life? He must become your very life itself. Suppose you were to become ill and called a doctor; and suppose the doctor examined you and prescribed a medicine; and suppose you had that prescription filled. With the medicine in your hand, or at your bedside, you might feel confident that it would cure your illness. However, unless you took that medicine and it became a very part of you, it would do you no good. So it is with the Saviour. Unless He becomes your life, righteousness through the Grace of God cannot and will not "reign in life" in your life or in the life of anyone else. This is the meaning of being born again, of becoming a child of God, and a believer in the Lord Jesus Christ.

Verse 18: So then as through one trespass the judgment came unto all men to condemnation; even so through one act of righteousness the free gift came unto all men to justification of life.

The words, "the judgment came," and "the free gift came," are in italics in both ASV and the KJV, signifying that they are not in the original Greek and were added by the translators for clarification. Verses 18 and 19 are a brilliant and convincing comparison between the disobedience of Adam and the obedience of Jesus Christ; and verses 20 and 21 portray the contrast and supremacy of the abounding blessings of grace over the abounding spread of sin because of the Law. One is the extreme opposite of the other. One brought condemnation to all men; the other brought them justification of life. One act resulted in death; the other in life. One brought evil and all the consequences of evil; the other brought righteousness and all the blessings of righteousness which God freely gives to the believer.

It was imperative that the Saviour's action be in complete accord with the righteous characteristics of the God-head, so as to undo all the evil which Adam's sin brought upon mankind. The work of the Saviour had to excel in every avenue of life where evil had been introduced by Adam's fall. Satan, sin and death became the supreme governing power over man and man's dominion. This governing power was no ordinary dictatorship to be endured until overthrown or exhausted in a few years, but was a miasma of evil, ever-spreading and intensifying. The Epistle to the Ephesians (6:12), states that we do not wrestle against "flesh and blood, but against the principalities, against the powers, against the world-rulers of this darkness, against the spiritual hosts of wickedness in the heavenly places." To withstand this power of evil, we need the whole armor of God. It took God Himself to conquer this Satanic power. Christ, the Incarnate Son of God, conquered it! The resurrection of our Lord sealed the doom of sin and death, and the kingdom of Satan. The Second Coming of our Lord is the victorious possession of what rightfully belongs to God, which Christ purchased with His own life's blood (Romans 8:22, 23; Philippians 2:6-11).

There is one further observation that should be made in connection with the two phrases in Romans 5:18; namely, "all men to condemnation . . . all men to justification." The word "all" in the first phrase means all men who are in Adam are under condemnation. Adam's actions resulted in sin and death. Death is the wages of sin and the wages have never been reduced. Therefore, death reigns in the unregenerate, viz., the lost.

In the second phrase the word "all" means only the men who are in Christ have justification of life. This writer does not believe in a "converted community." Some who call themselves theologians, and the Universalists as well, have taught that this verse teaches that "all men" are saved, and that all the preaching of the Gospel does is to make all men believe that they are already saved. In fact, the head of the Department of Évangelism of one of the denominations believes this. Is it any wonder that God does not bless such wishful thinking? This "converted community" idea has not even reached first-base, as baseball fans say when a batter strikes out; and the idea is not entitled to any better name than "hogwash." And what have Jews to do with hogs? "Salvation is from the Jews" (John 4:22). This writer is Jewish, and he believes that every person is lost until and unless he repents of his sin, accepts Christ as Lord and Saviour, and confesses that belief publicly. The fruits of this justified life in the individual person will be visible and obvious through progressive sanctification, which is wrought by the Holy Spirit.

Verse 19: For as through the one man's disobedience the many were made sinners, even so through the obedience of the one shall the many be made righteous.

This verse continues to show the comparison between the actions of Adam and Christ. One disobeyed; the other obeyed. One refused to do God's will, and the results were disastrous to himself and his posterity. The other delighted to do His Father's will and the result was everlasting life to all who believed. Our Lord's chief aim and object throughout His ministry was to fulfill and accomplish the Father's glorious purpose to save the lost. The results of the Son's work in carrying out His Father's will did not only delight our heavenly Father, but it also brought peace, joy, happiness, righteousness and eternal life to every one who accepted Him, who became the saints of God.

Adam disobeyed. The Greek word for "disobeyed" means to hear amiss, to fail to listen, to neglect to obey, to disregard. Each meaning elaborates upon the fact that Adam willingly, knowingly and fully realized the consequences of his act, and completely disregarded what God had commanded him not to do. In spite of this, he proceeded to disobey God's will, with no thought of what his disobedience would bring upon him and his descendants. This one man's disobedience hurled mankind into the dismal swamp of sin from which the human race has never been able to extricate itself through its own efforts. Like Israel of old, "They have sown the wind, and they shall reap the whirlwind" (Hosea 8:7). All creation has been caught in this whirlwind of sin, energized by Satan. This sinful world, hardened and still disobedient, is moving farther from God and deeper into sin as the centuries roll on. It will continue to get worse "until the times of the Gentiles be fulfilled" and God finally calls a halt. The "times of the Gentiles" are drawing to an end. Sin with its hideous consequences is evident all about us. Every vestment of morality and decency is being discarded. Mankind is scraping the bottom of the barrel of sin under the delusion that sin in modern dress is progress; whereas, in God's sight man has lost all semblance of progression and has turned it into retrogression. All this has come about "through one man's disobedience."

The folly of Adam, in verse 19, is compared with Christ's judicious actions. The Apostle states that "through the obedience of the one," Christ obeyed! The Greek word for "obey" means to give ear, to hearken, to render submissive acceptance, to heed, to regard, to comply, and to conform. Each word speaks volumes of the obedience and submissiveness of Christ. This procession of synonyms is like climbing a ladder, the top rung of which brings one into the very presence of God. Christ's every move proclaims obedience, compliance and submission. The words, the prayers, the tears, the steps and actions of the Saviour, are all as the very presence and spirit of the Father Himself being flashed like lightning out of heaven and enveloping His Son and all His saints in every age, and are like a rampart of protection, from the time of His visitation on earth until now and unto the end. What demonstrations of omnipotence! What deliverances from human failures! Only God can perform such miracles!

Will you accept God's holy Son? Will you acknowledge Him? Will you live for Him? Only He can deliver you from the shackles of sin and bring you out of a world that is engrossed and enslaved in evil. Only He, Christ, can offer you the way, the truth and the life, clothe you with His righteousness and make you an inheritor of eternal life. Accept Him and live. Reject Him and die.

Verse 20: And the law came in besides, that the trespass might abound; but where sin abounded, grace did abound more exceedingly . . . .

Another translation of this verse is, "the law entered, that the offence might abound" (King James Version). The Greek word "entered" means to supervene, to come in as something additional. The classical Greek uses this word as meaning to introduce with a notion of secrecy.

The Law of Moses entered or was introduced, and sin became more obvious, more visible, more definite. The Law that came by Moses clearly and more vividly exposes the results of Adam's disobedience. The words, *thou shalt*, and *thou shalt not*, are the foundation of the Decalogue, but they are also found in the warning that God gave Adam, Genesis 2:17. To repeat what has previously been said, the distinct purpose of the Law was to reveal man's sinfulness and God's Holiness. Man, seeing how righteous God is through the eyes of the Law, would seek the Grace of God and be converted through the very same medium that revealed his sin, "the Law of the Lord is perfect, *converting* the soul" (Psalm 19:7 KJV).

Verses 20 and 21 compare the work of Christ with the sin of Adam. These verses show the superiority of Christ's accomplishments over the accomplishments of Adam. Sin abounds, but Grace is super-abounding in its work, and is triumphant over sin. Grace to be victorious over sin and death, had to excel, it had to surpass and outweigh, it had to have the upper hand to attain superiority and victory over sin. Grace accomplished this in that it replaced sin and death with righteousness and eternal life. The contrast is very great in the respect that Grace outran, outdistanced the evils of sin, and supplanted sin with the Holiness of God.

Verse 21: . . . that, as sin reigned in death, even so might grace reign through righteousness unto eternal life through Jesus Christ our Lord.

This is the summarization and conclusive analogy of the work of Adam with its evil consequences over against the work of Christ with all its glorious benefits.

For the believer, sin reigned. It is in the past tense. It does not and need not reign in our life any longer. We have been bought; we have been redeemed; we have been washed; we have been justified; we have been and are sanctified daily; and we are waiting to be glorified. All this God has done for each and every believer through and with the blood of Jesus Christ. This is an accomplished reality with God, who did it for us, i.e., for believers only, while we were still His enemies, Romans 5:10. What a wonderful reality! All our sins, the sins committed by the believer before and after his salvation, have already been cleansed by Christ's blood. Even now, the believer is already a child of God, complete in Christ, as though he were already in the very presence of God (I John 3:2). We have already passed from death unto life eternal (John 5:24; I John 3:14). When life on this earth ceases, we merely step from the glories we have experienced here as a child of God, into the very presence of His Glory. Hallelujah! What a Saviour! Do you know Him? You can!

6

PAUL HAS JUST COMPLETED, in chapters 1 to 5, a searching and comprehensive study of sin, condemnation, death, righteousness and justification; and a comparison of Adam's work and its consequences with our Lord's work and its consequences, both being elaborated and explained. The conclusion Paul reaches is that one cannot have a true conception of sin without a true understanding of God and His righteousness. Sin is incompatible with godliness, and is an affront to God. The sinner must be reconciled to God.

The Apostle also discusses the reactions of sin upon man and the super-abounding reactions of Grace. In chapter 5, Paul compares the first Adam with the second Adam, Christ, and shows us clearly that the tendency to sin is present in every person the moment he is born, and that in order to achieve the power, the means and the method to overcome the inherent sinful nature, every person must be born again. However, the impulse to sin is ever present, but the born-again believer has the weapon and the power to keep this impulse in subjection.

In chapter 5 Paul goes on to discuss fully the doctrine of justification. The results of justification, he points out, are righteousness and sanctification which the believer obtains through faith in the Lord Jesus Christ (I Corinthians 1:30).

We must not and dare not lose sight of the fact that righteousness and sanctification have practical aspects in the born-again believer, i.e., a visible reality that accompanies righteousness and sanctification. There are Christian principles and ethics which must demonstrate the fact that we are the children of God. He that is born of God does not habitually continue in sin (I John 3:9). Believers need to return to the principles of the Bible. God requires — God demands — holy living. We must be careful not to hang out our soiled linen for the world to see, where it will be visible to both saint and sinner. The standards of the pew

171

must equal the standards of the pulpit. But, alas, the standards
of some pulpits, even some fundamental ones, are not much higher
than the standards of many pews. Let us, who have taken the
shadow of the cross for our abiding-place, lift the blood-sprinkled
banner high enough for the world to see that both the banner
and the bearer proclaim the righteousness of God. This is what
the Apostle speaks of in chapter 6.

**Verse 1: What shall we say then? Shall we continue in sin,
that grace may abound?**

What a question this is! Volumes might be written to explain
these words. "Shall we continue in sin?" the Apostle asks. The
Greek word for "shall" in the Nestle's text, which this writer is
using, means may we stay longer, may we prolong our stay, may
we remain on, may we continue to embrace, may we persist. All
these expressions end with "in sin." Need there be an answer
to this question? The faintest and most fleeting apprehension of
the nature of God would return an answer of complete and utter
denial. Continuing in sin — just the thought of it — is incompatible with all that we know of God. Grace is not a license to sin,
but the demand to relinquish all manner of sin. The Grace of
God saves a sinner from sin, i.e., enables him to abandon sin.

**Verse 2: God forbid. We who died to sin, how shall we any
longer live therein?**

The two words, "God forbid," are one in Hebrew. The Hebrew
word carries the thought that the idea expressed in verse 1 is
unthinkable. (See comment on this expression in Romans
3:4, page 80). The root verb for "forbid" means to make common,
to profane, to defile, to pollute, and that the thought itself is blas-
phemous in God's sight. If we are under Grace, the thought of
continuing in sin is blasphemy.

V. 2: "We who died to sin." Dying to sin is the only position
of the believer, and it looks back to the time of our unsaved past.
If we died to something, something died, the death is final. It
cannot be brought to life again. The demands of the Saviour are
imperative to a holy life. He continually said, "Follow me"
(Matthew 8:22; 16:24; Mark 8:34; 10:21; Luke 9:59; John 10:27).
If we die to sin, then it is not possible for us to live in it. We
either die to it or live in it.

How the necessity of holy living needs to be repeated over and
over again! How neglectful we are! Dedication and consecration
are two of the great essentials in our lives. Repentance is not an

emotional experience, but a devotional *sine qua non* to Christian living. Consecration and holiness are the missing ingredients in too many Christian lives. We have died to sin, the Apostle says. To die to sin is not a call to sinless perfection, but is a call to sainthood in Christ Jesus, a striving to live as close to Christ as possible in the midst of a sinful world.

Holy living is a goal to strive for, "I press on toward the goal unto the prize of the high calling of God in Christ Jesus" (Philippians 3:14). Paul says that he has run the race, and fought the "good fight of faith." He never claimed to have been a winner, but everything short of this striving brings dishonor to God's grace and to the Gospel. The very name Christian calls for an exemplary holy life. We are urged to avoid the very appearance of evil.

Verse 3: Or are ye ignorant that all we who were baptized into Christ Jesus were baptized into his death?

The Apostle here is asking the question, "Don't you know what baptism portrays? Why you were baptized? Don't you know the purpose of baptism?" The Greek word for "ignorance" means, inability to discern, failure to understand. These are the various shades of meaning of the word ignorant in both classical and Koine Greek.

This writer is not only Jewish, but he is also biblical. Baptism to a Jewish Christian of Orthodox background is not what it is to all Protestants or to all Protestantism. He will never accept any other form of baptism than total immersion of the believer *after* he has publically confessed Christ as Lord and Saviour. The New Testament teaches *only a believer's baptism.*

It is interesting to note that no less a contemporary scholar than Dr. William Barclay, Lecturer in New Testament Language and Literature in the University of Glasgow, states in his book, *The Letter to the Romans*: "We must remember that baptism in the time of Paul was different from what baptism commonly is today. *a.* It was *adult* baptism. . . . In the Early Church a man came to Christ as an individual, often leaving his family behind. *b.* Baptism in the Early Church was intimately connected with confession of faith. . . . Baptism marked a dividing line in his life. *c.* Commonly, baptism was the total immersion, and the practice lent itself to a symbolism which sprinkling does not so readily lend itself to. When a man descended into the water, and the water closed over his head, it was like being *buried* in a grave. Baptism was symbolically like dying and rising again. The man died to one kind of life and rose to another kind of life" (pages 83 & 84). *Why sprinkle?* The clause, "we were baptized into," retains a literal as well as a figurative meaning of baptism. It means, strictly, *"to immerse into Christ"* (Ruckert, Romans 6:3).

Other forms of baptism in Protestantism have been brought over from the Roman Catholic Church. The doctrine of baptism to which Paul holds is different from many modern denominational teachings. Where in the New Testament is there any authority for sprinkling? There is no such authority! Where in the New Testament is there any authority for infant baptism? Nowhere. Where in the New Testament does it teach that baptism in the New Testament is the same as circumcision in the Old Testament? Nowhere. If baptism corresponds with circumcision then why baptize females?

The whole practice of infant baptism is contrary to the teaching of the New Testament, and it must be a stench in the nostrils of God because it nullifies the cross and makes baptism a means of salvation and, therefore, a matter of works! All this is completely refuted by Paul in chapters 3 and 4. To this writer, the Doctrine of Baptism cannot and must not be compromised. It is all true, or there is no truth in it. It means, symbolically:

The *immersion* of the believer . . the *death* of Christ

The *submersion* of the believer . . the *burial* of Christ

The *emersion* of the believer . the *resurrection* of Christ

Baptism is *not* a sacrament, *it is an ordinance*. The Saviour said, Go! Preach! Baptize! The preaching must be the proclamation of the Word of God; the message, the Gospel of God; the motive, the Love of God; the means, the Grace of God through the Blood of Christ. Baptism, as this writer has explained it, is not Baptist Doctrine, but Bible Doctrine! Thank God, there is still a host of Bible-believing people who believe and practice it. We shall not compromise on the Scriptures! To believers, the Scriptures will always be the final authority. In these trying days it has to be, "Thus saith the Lord." Paul was not a sacramentarian; neither are we who believe the Scriptures to be the final authority.

Verse 4: We were buried therefore with him through baptism unto death: that like as Christ was raised from the dead through the glory of the Father, so we also might walk in newness of life.

"The picture in baptism points two ways, backward to Christ's death and burial and to our death to sin (v. 1); forward to Christ's resurrection from the dead and to our new life pledged by the coming out of the watery grave to walk on the other side of the baptismal grave." *F. B. Meyer.*

The Apostle is again referring in verse 4 to what he said in verses 2 and 3, i.e., "We who died to sin . . . were baptized into his death." The fact that baptism is the portrayal of the believer's burial signifies that the believer is dead to the world and to the power (or reign of death, 5:17) of sin. The Christian can live a victorious life (or reign in life, 5:17) in and for Christ in the midst of a sinful world. He has the weapons of warfare, the Bible and the power of the Holy Spirit, plus the assurance of victory. There is every reason for a Christian to live a victorious life; and no reason, when in Christ, why he should fail (Romans 8:31).

We must bear in mind that we do not become Christians through an emotional experience, but by being born again and by being indwelt by no less a Person than the Incarnate, Omnipotent Son of God. The Lord Jesus Christ is not an emotion that passes away, but rather a Person whose Spirit abides with us and in us eternally (Hebrews 1:8). Need we give any more reasons why we can achieve a victorious life through our Lord?

When we were born again, we were buried to sin, to fears, to doubts. Our sinful nature died. When we are baptized our immersion typifies that death and burial, and is a symbol of Christ's death for us. This is the reason why we who are truly born again believe in baptism by immersion, not by sprinkling. How can death, burial, and resurrection be portrayed by sprinkling with a few drops of water?

V. 4: ". . . that like as Christ was raised from the dead through the glory of the Father, so we also might walk in newness of life." This is the second aspect of baptism. Just as the first aspect symbolizes Christ's death, so also the second aspect symbolizes our Lord's resurrection from the dead; and this again is a symbol of one's change from death to life when he is born again. As a sinner he died to worldly lusts and fleshly desires, and as a new creation he rose again to walk in newness of life in Christ Jesus our Lord. As the Saviour's resurrection was "the Crown of glory of the Father," so when one is born again, his new birth is symbolized by rising from the baptismal waters to a new life that will glorify the Father and the Son.

We cannot live *for* Christ until and unless we have died *with* Christ. This is the prerequisite for Christian living. The only person who can live as a Christian is one who has been born again. Before one can walk with God, he must be born of God. Godly living can be energized only by God Himself, through the Holy Spirit. Life for God requires Godly Power, and that is supplied by the indwelling of the Holy Spirit. This can be accomplished only by God through the new birth. Baptism is the outward testimony of an inward change and reality. We have been buried, we have been raised, now we must "walk in newness of life."

The Greek word for "walk" literally means to maintain a certain walk of life and conduct. It is the first person plural aorist subjunctive mood, and is used in exhorting others to join in the doing of an action, i.e., that we might "walk in newness of life" with Christ. This is beautifully typified in the ordinance of baptism when the believer is raised out of the waters. This act of coming up out of the waters constitutes the completed testimony of the believer's new birth which is so graphically portrayed in baptism by immersion.

Just one further point on baptism by immersion: It is interesting to note that the scholars of old spoke of total "immersion into the bath of baptism." *Lange — Rom.*, p. 202. "The main intention of the verse is to bring out the idea of resurrection following death in our case as in Christ's. The sense, therefore, is: As our burial (or total immersion) in the baptismal water was followed by entire emergence, so our death with Christ to sin which that immersion symbolized is to be followed by our resurrection with him to a new life." *Pulpit Commentary — Romans* — Pages 156 & 157.

We have been given, by the second birth, a new heart, a new mind, a new goal, and a new life. All the ingredients of this newness have been supplied by God through Christ and the Holy Spirit. Every believer receives this newness the moment he accepts Christ as his Lord and Saviour. The urgency of the times and the impelling power of the Gospel should move us and cause us to become living epistles for our Lord. The world will hear only what we tell it, and will see only what it sees in us. As death hath reigned in us (this is in the past tense), Christ's Life now reigns in us, that we "might walk in newness of life" (II Corinthians 5:14, 15).

Verse 5: For if we have become united (been planted KJV) with him in the likeness of his death, we shall be also in the likeness of his resurrection . . . ;

The Greek word for "united" or "planted" means planted together, grown together, closely entwined or united with; the word expresses a process by which a graft is made in a tree or a bush. It becomes united with and becomes one with what it is grafted into. Here it is used as a metaphor. As Christ died to the world, so must we, the believers, die with Him.

Baptism is a true symbol of *our* death and burial, symbolizing our likeness to Christ in *His* death and burial. It is also a true picture of our new birth from sin and death to life and holiness, symbolizing our likeness to Christ in His resurrection. Thus the ordinance of baptism is the outward and visible sign to the world of the death of our old nature, and our being united with or grafted into Christ.

V. 5: ". . . we shall be also in the likeness of his resurrection . . ."; As the lowering of the body into the baptismal water typifies our death and burial, in like manner the raising of the body out of that water typifies our new life in Christ. This life has to be a new and different life. Our old life was a life of selfishness and sinfulness, filled with sensuality. Now that we have been born again, our new life has to be a completely different one of righteousness and holiness, and an example of what a Christian should be. Our new life must substantiate what our baptism symbolized! There must be no hesitancy, no turning aside (Luke 9:62). There can be no excuses for not living for Christ. God has given us the weapons for that life and the power to sustain it in and through Christ. This new life is ours to use, and it must be used for Him.

The last half of verse 5, to be "in the likeness of his resurrection," also points to the completion of our salvation. It gives assurance and zest to our present life here on earth regardless of how difficult and trying it might be. As Christ died and was buried, in like manner (as a type) we, too, have died and were buried. This is in the past tense. Here is the goal that is set before us, sealed and signed by the Holy Spirit with the blood of Jesus Christ. Our text states that, "we shall be also . . of his resurrection." The words, "in the likeness," are in italics, and therefore are not in the Greek New Testament. The words, "we shall be," are one word in the Greek, and this one word is in the first person plural, indicative, future. The meaning of this future tense here is that there can be no "maybe," no "if," no "perhaps." It means that God through Christ is guaranteeing our resurrection to be just as real and concrete as Christ's was. "Because I live, ye shall live also" (John 14:19), is the promise of the Saviour. Need we more assurance?

Verse 6: . . . knowing this, that our old man was (or is in KJV) crucified with him, that the body of sin might be done away, that so we should no longer be in bondage (or serve KJV) to sin . . . ;

The Greek tense is one that states a past action or event. It is used to express a past event viewed in its entirety, i.e., the old man, or nature, *was* crucified. For the believer this past tense of the verb refers to an historical fact in life that cannot be repeated. To state it more emphatically, the old nature *was* crucified. It died! It cannot be resuscitated! It is done with! When a person confesses his sins and accepts Christ as his own personal Lord and Saviour, his old nature dies right then and there. He is now a new creation in Christ. The old nature is then not only dead, but also buried, just as it was portrayed in his baptism. From then on, the believer begins to live a new life and must continue to do so, energized by the Holy Spirit who is the motivating Power of the believer's new life. This is the reason that a believer does not habitually continue to practice sin (I John 3:9), neither can he raise from the dead his old nature which was buried. God is a God of the living and He expects His children to keep on living for Him. We might stray, we might misbehave, but God's chastening hand will always bring us back to walk in His path. To put it in human thought and language, God's reputation is at stake in the life of every believer. That life can no more be lost than God can deny His own nature. Our life now is Christ's life in us. What a plan! What a program! What a prospect!

The expression, "our old man," that Paul uses in this verse, meaning "our old nature," is a Rabbinical expression. According to Rabbi Aba, "The 'old nature' is based on Genesis 19:31, where it is called the evil imagination, or (a) corruption of nature based on Ecclesiastes 4:13, because it is born of man." (*Midrash Haneelam in Zohar* in Gen. fol. 68:1.) "This is joined to him from birth and remains with him to his old age." (*Midrash Kobeleth*-fol. 70:2.) "The evil imagination will not cease until the Messiah comes, Who will destroy it." (*Zohar in Exodus,* fol. 94.4.)

For the believer this has already become a reality. The Messiah *has* come. As a Victor over the vanquished, He has conquered sin. His resurrection certified that victory. The believer in the Messiah "should no longer be in bondage to sin," or as in KJV, "should not serve sin." The Greek word for "bondage" means to be enslaved or subservient to. We have been bought by Christ (I Corinthians 6:20; 7:23) and we are His. As bond-slaves we are subservient to Him. We do not and we need not serve sin.

Verse 7: . . . for he that hath died is justified from sin.

The Greek word for "hath died" is better translated "having died." In and with Christ the believer died to sin. Even according to human law a person who is dead can no longer be punished or held accountable for the deeds done while he was alive. He is then dead (Ecclesiastes 12:7).

Verse 7 expresses the same idea which is expressed in verse 6. The two ideas are analagous. The sinner was a bond-slave to sin prior to his new birth. At his new birth his old nature died to the power of sin, and a new creature was born. The new creature is no longer under the jurisdiction of sin, or subject to its ever-varying forms of temptation. He has been set free! "If therefore the Son shall make you free, ye shall be free indeed" (John 8:36). The thought expressed by Paul in verse 7 is based on a Rabbinical teaching that states "when a man dies he is free from the law and commandments."

V. 7: ". . . is justified from sin." The Greek word for "justified" in this verse means to be held acquitted. The tense of this verb indicates that an action which has taken place in the past cannot be brought up again. It is a "once-for-all" action.

We should bear in mind that this, too, has been accomplished by God for the believer, by a God Who is Sovereign. His actions are indisputable; His character immutable; His judgments irrefutable. He has decreed to free the sinner from the power of sin through the blood of His Son. The force of His power is immeasurable and eternal. Through His power He saves each and every sinner, and keeps him throughout life's trials and tribulations until that blessed time when He shall bring him into His Presence (I Peter 1:4, 5).

Verse 8: But if we died with Christ, we believe that we shall also live with him . . . ;

The Greek tense of the verb "died" expresses an historical action in the past. The sinner's old nature died with Christ.

This fact is thoroughly established in the preceding verses, and expressed in the tense of the verb in this verse.

The Apostle continues by saying, "we believe that we shall also live with him." The Greek word for "believe" denotes action in progress. We believe *now* and we *continue* believing. This faith is not in some dubious nonentity but rather it is in the Eternal entity of God, who has given us an Eternal Saviour and indwells us with His Holy Spirit to give us this assurance. This is the same God who so energized the early believers whose faith could not be shaken even by death in the arenas of Rome. This is the same God who today gives His believers that same assurance. We, too, who face the stark reality of death believe *now* and *continue* to believe that we shall most certainly live with Him. The Greek expression for "we shall also live with him" is in the future indicative, and is used to affirm that an action is to take place some time in the future.

We have the Saviour's promise, "If I go . . . I will come again, and receive you unto myself" (John 14:3). "The Lord himself shall descend from heaven . . . and the dead in Christ shall rise first; then we that are alive, that are left, shall together with them be caught up in the clouds to meet the Lord in the air" (I Thessalonians 4:16, 17; I Corinthians 15:51-58).

Verse 9: . . . knowing that Christ being raised from the dead dieth no more, death no more hath dominion over him.

Christ came not only to die, but also to be raised. Early in His ministry, He assured His followers that He would be raised the third day, "Destroy this temple, and in three days I will raise it up" (John 2:19b). He proved it unequivocally by coming out of the grave on the first day of the week. His own words substantiate the truth that He shall never die again. "I was dead, and behold, I am alive for evermore" (Revelation 1:18). There can be no reason or necessity for Him to die again (Hebrews 10:12). In the fulness of time — not one moment too late or one moment too early — God sent forth His Son (Galatians 4:4). When the hour arrived (John 12:23), He was crucified. When the hour arrived, He stepped from His tomb alive, and never again need this miracle be repeated. He did this once for all time, and has given His followers life that will last for all time and eternity. The gifts that God gives His followers are without repentance (Romans 11:29 KJV), or, as in ASV, "are not repented of." His one act was sufficient to perfect His saints forever (Hebrews 10:14).

"Death no more hath dominion over him." Because He died
and rose again death could not lord it over Him. The Greek
word for "dominion" means to be lord over, to exercise sway
over. In Classical Greek, it means to act like a master or lord with
full authority.

Death and sin reigned and does reign right now. Mankind
is under the lordship of Satan, death and sin, which have dominion at the present time. Death and sin never had that authority over the Lord Jesus Christ. Satan could do nothing to Him
unless the Father willed it. No one could take the Saviour's life
from Him (John 10:17, 18) until the moment arrived. Even then
it wasn't taken from Him, He laid down His own Life as a voluntary act, "I lay it down of myself" (John 10:18). His enemies
would have slain Him before, but they could not, as the hour
had not yet arrived (John 7:30; 8:20).

We must always remember that the Lord was not mere man.
It is true that He was *very* man, and at the same time, He was
very God. Satan, death and sin are not God's Frankensteins —
inventions to scare mankind, and to eventually destroy the human
race. Satan and death can touch man only as God allows (Job
1:12). When the time arrived for the Saviour to die, He laid
down His life. When the moment of the resurrection arrived, He
had the power within Himself to step out of the tomb. He said
so! "No one taketh it away from me . . . I have power to lay it
down, and I have power to take it again" (John 10:18). These
words were spoken by the man Christ Jesus, who was also God
Incarnate in the flesh. No one can have dominion over, or lord
it over, God!

What divine assurance! What comfort this affords the believer!
Since He is our Lord, since it is He who gives eternal life to every
believer, we have the assurance that the life He gives us will last
forever, and no one can take it away from us, nor can we lose it.
He gave us that life and He is the Keeper of it. Is it any wonder
that the Apostle Paul says, "I know whom I have believed, and
I am persuaded that He is able to guard that which I have committed unto him against that day" (II Timothy 1:12). Let us
shout it from the rooftops!

**Verse 10: For the death that he died, he died unto sin once:
but the life that he liveth, he liveth unto God.**

The death of Christ on the cross accomplished that which the
Mosaic institutions could not. The animal sacrifices had to be
repeated over and over again, daily, monthly, annually. The

high priest repeatedly had to obtain atonement for sin through the animal sacrifices. The work of the cross is not atonement but cleansing (see comments on Romans 5:11).

The Old Testament sacrifices were but shadows or types of the cross. They were the temporary expiation waiting for the real cleansing to bring reconciliation to fruition. Reconciliation was a once-for-all-time action. It never needs to be repeated again (Hebrews 7:27; 9:12, 26, 28; 10:10; I Peter 3:18). It is a completed action. The work of the Lord Jesus Christ met every requirement for reconciliation. His work satisfied God in every facet of righteousness. All the necessary sacrifices for sin He offered in His one sacrifice of Himself. When He died on the cross all Eternity shouted, Enough!

It was impossible for the Lord Jesus Christ to be a sinner even though He took the sinner's place. He knew the meaning of sin and all of its ramifications. Understanding sin fully, He became the sin offering (II Corinthians 5:21). The Saviour in His death on the cross fulfilled all the requirements for the sin offering.

"But the life that he liveth, he liveth unto God." The KJV is more accurate, "but in that he liveth, he liveth unto God." The tense of the Greek verb "liveth" is such that the literal translation is, "but in that he liveth right now, he liveth right now unto God." We have a living Saviour, not a dead founder. This is the great difference between all other religions in the world and Christianity. No other faith has a living Saviour. This is the uniqueness of Christianity. It is only for the Christian. Only a Christian is able to sing to a living Saviour, "I need Thee every hour." It is impossible for a follower of any other faith to sing to its founder. The founders of all other faiths are dead, and one doesn't sing to a dead person. The founder of Christianity is a living God, "God is not the God of the dead, but of the living" (Matthew 22:32).

The Saviour, seated at the right hand of the Father, is merely waiting for the time to be fulfilled when He shall come for His own, not as He came the first time, to suffer for sin and our salvation (Hebrews 10:28). He now lives to God. He is in the Eternal Holy of Holies as our Mediator, doing that which we are unable to do for ourselves (Hebrews 7:25). Are we eager for His coming? Are we anxiously expecting Him? Are *you* ready?

Verse 11: Even so reckon ye also yourselves to be dead unto sin, but alive unto God in Christ Jesus.

We are to consider ourselves dead to sin and the punishment

of sin and any of its damning potentialities. The death of Christ
paid for every sin of the believer. He met the sin question at
Calvary. He took all the guilt and punishment of sin — "the Lord
hath laid (met or hath caused to fall upon, so the Hebrew) on
him the iniquity of us all" (Isaiah 53:6 KJV). Since our Saviour
died for sin, we are now to reckon ourselves dead unto sin in Him.
Is this not what was portrayed in baptism?

If we are to reckon ourselves dead to sin, then we are to
separate ourselves from it. We are to have no part in it. The refusal to separate ourselves from sin brings horrible consequences;
and the consequences of disobedience should make the child
of God shudder. The history of Israel is a history of consistent
disobedience. All the trials and tribulations, all the torments and
tears, all the persecutions and privations, all the bloodshed and
barbarism that Israel suffered, are the evil fruits of disobedience.
God has repeatedly beseeched Israel to return and to harken unto
Him (Jeremiah 3:1, 12, 22; Hosea 14:1). The history of Israel
should be a lesson to every believer to avoid sin in every form as
one avoids a plague. Therefore, the Apostle is saying in this
verse (11), let us be dead unto sin; hence, sin can no more speak
to us, inasmuch as it is impossible for the dead to hear.

The deadness that this verse speaks of has another aspect.
We are urged to avoid the practice of sin, the evil fruit of which
is death, because we are challenged to live according to the glorious principle of life in Christ Jesus. The Apostle writes, "But
alive unto God in Christ Jesus." The Greek word for "alive" is
better translated but living unto God.

There is a negative and a positive approach to the Gospel.
Prior to our new birth, we were dead to God and alive to the
world, to sin. After our new birth we became alive to God and
dead to the world and to sin. We are, therefore, either one or
the other. We cannot be both at the same time. When we are
born anew, God supplies us with all the essentials for growth in
our new life. Let us avail ourselves of these essentials.

As born-again believers we are dead to sin, but alive unto
Christ, and the fruit of this transition is life everlasting, the
complete opposite of sin or death everlasting. In Christ the old
nature is dead because it was crucified with Him. Now, because
Christ rose from the tomb, our new nature is alive in Him. He
has imbued it with life, for "in him we live, and move, and have
our being" (Acts 17:28). Unless we are in Christ we cannot live
a life for God. Christ is Life itself.

Have you made your choice? We still hear the voice of God

today. "Choose you this day whom ye will serve" (Joshua 24:15). If the Lord be God, serve Him, but if Baal, then serve him. Shall it be life? Or death? Make your choice! God waits!

Verse 12: Let not sin therefore reign in your mortal body, that ye should obey the lusts thereof . . . :

This is an elaboration of verse 11. The word "therefore" points to what the Apostle said in the preceding verse. The Greek word translated "let . . . reign" is in the present imperative mood, and with the word "not" states a prohibition. The statement means, prohibit sin to reign over your mortal (death-bound, corrupt body) with regal authority. This body of flesh is prone to sin, the propensity to sin is prevalent in every fiber of our bodies, for, ". . . in my flesh, dwelleth no good thing" (Romans 7:18).

Paul is referring to what he has previously stated; namely, that the old nature which dwelt in the flesh prior to our new birth has been crucified and buried. The new nature is to have the dominant authority over our bodies. After all, when we are born again we become the bond-slaves of Christ. He will then have the authority over us. He has bought us and all that we are and possess are His, "For ye were bought with a price: glorify God (not sin) therefore in your body" (I Corinthians 6:20). The mature Christian knows that living this new life in Christ is a battle that must be fought continuously. We cannot and we must not let up for a moment. This was the admonition of Paul in his letter to the Corinthian church wherein he states that he has to buffet his body in order to bring it into bondage (the Greek word for "bondage" has the thought of bond-slave), so that his body may continue to be used for and by the Lord and not be rejected (I Corinthians 9:27; Romans 12:1). All this is implied in the imperative, "let not sin therefore reign in your mortal body." This we accomplish through the love of God which has been shed abroad in each believer's heart.

V. 12: ". . . that ye should obey the lusts thereof. . ."; Before we leave this verse let us scrutinize it a little further. Man is so made that he must worship something. Even an atheist worships himself or his ideas. Man either worships sin in one form or another, or else he worships God. There seems to be no middle ground. It is either Satan and sin, or God and His righteousness. This writer believes that even a godly man can be lost. Surely Nicodemus was the personification of a godly man, yet he was lost and doomed to hell unless he was born again (John 3).

God has decreed that the work of His only begotten Son on the cross, and His resurrection from the dead, and the belief in and acceptance of that work on the part of the sinner, is the only basis of salvation for the human race. Christ Himself said, "I am the way, and the truth, and the life: no one cometh unto the Father, but by me" (John 14:6). In the final analysis man serves either Christ or sin, either the way of life or the way of death. We repeat, *there is no middle ground.*

Verse 12 admonishes the believer not to obey the flesh or its lusts. The Greek word for "obey" means not only to obey or to harken, but it also means to render submissive acceptance. The Greek word for "lust" means earnest desire, irregular or violent desire. Lust is sensual in its every aspect.

What graphic words the Apostle uses! — "sin," "lust," "reigning" in our "bodies." And what do we see all about us — in society, in business, in politics, in the realm of sports and entertainment and, most alarming of all, in the religious sects and churches — living examples of sin and lust demonstrating their ascendency in every imaginable devilish aspect.

Nevertheless these conditions ought not to discourage the child of God. As the age draws to its close, sin and lust will be everywhere present. Sinful heathenism is in the throes of its last fling. Sinfulness is to saturate every avenue of life prior to our Lord's return. Sin is to prevail when the anti-Christ makes his appearance (II Thessalonians 2:1-12).

Take heart, my fellow Christians! We are living in the last days. Let us covenant to serve God and His Christ who loved us, who gave Himself for us, who bought us, who makes intercession for us, and who is soon coming to take us out of this maelstrom of sinfulness. Are you ready? Is this *your* hope? Make your election and your calling sure!

Verse 13: . . . neither present your members unto sin as instruments of unrighteousness; but present yourselves unto God, as alive from the dead, and your members as instruments of righteousness unto God.

The Greek word for "present" means also to place beside, to have in readiness, to place at the disposal of. The tense of the Greek word forbids the continuance of the action, and means, in the literal sense, *not* to present your members now, or continue to present your members as instruments of sin.

V. 13: ". . . but present yourselves unto God, as alive from the dead, and your members as instruments of righteousness unto

God." The Apostle is now enlarging, in emphatic. statements, what he has stated previously. This, again, is a call to holy living, to separation, to devotion, to dedication and consecration of ourselves to righteousness, holiness, and usefulness to the cause of Jesus Christ and the Gospel. In a previous passage (on Romans 6:4) we spoke of our death, burial and resurrection in Christ and His righteousness, as being so accurately portrayed in baptism. After this clear picture the Apostle now points the believer to the practical aspects of our Christian life. Christ and Christianity are not merely an emotional experience, but, on the contrary, the only way of life with God. As another writer has stated, "Christianity can never be only an experience of the secret place; it must be a life in the market place."

Such a Christian life must be lived by each and every believer. In verse 12, where the Apostle points out that the believer is not to serve the flesh or its lusts, the tense of the verb in the expression, "ye should obey," denotes that the believer must not now or at any future time permit himself to be used as a weapon for sin. God has promised to give us the strength and ability to overcome the evil propensities of the flesh by the indwelling, abiding presence of the Holy Spirit. Christianity is not a lackadaisical faith, but, rather, it is a perilous, unending, and offensive warfare against sin. It calls for superhuman weapons, which God has placed at our disposal (Ephesians 6:10-20), to fight this vicious battle with evil and evil-doers. It is a call to vigilance and twenty-four-hour duty. Therefore, we are to choose sides!

Christianity has both a negative and a positive side. God, in His Word, always tells His children what they can and what they cannot do; what they should and should not do. The first half of verse 13 is the negative side, what we must not do — "neither present your members unto sin" —; the last half is the positive, what we must do — "but present yourselves unto God."

To have electricity for heat and light we must have both negative and positive forces or currents. In order to live a life of godliness, God gives us the modus operandi, and the course that we are to follow.

If a Christian is occupied with the things of God, he will not have time for the things of this world and its sin. People who don't know how to witness for Christ, don't witness; people who quibble about tithing, don't tithe; people who complain about too many church meetings are not regular church-goers; and people who find fault with someone else's lack of Christian attributes, don't practice many of these attributes themselves. It is a case of the pot calling the kettle black. It is either Christ or chaos; it is either right or wrong; it is either sin or holiness. There can never be a middle ground.

A half-truth is either one or the other; it is either a truth or a lie, and is often as dangerous, if not more dangerous, than an outright lie. An inconsistent Christian life is a hazardous life both for the inconsistent Christian himself, and for the lost sinner who can never be sure when such a Christian is living the truth and when he is not. And when the sinner is sure it is the truth he is being told today, how can he be sure that the inconsistent Christian will tell him the truth tomorrow? This is the world's dilemma when it looks at Christians who should be the walking examples of the living truth of Christianity. "What you are thunders so that I cannot hear what you say," said Emerson, the American philosopher.

V. 13: ". . . but present yourselves unto God, as alive from the dead, and your members as instruments of righteousness unto God." Thus the Apostle describes the positive aspects of Christian devotion and service. The word for "present" in the Greek is the same Greek word that is used in the first half of the verse, but in a different tense. In the last half of the verse it means to present your members *now* and *completely*. The Greek word for "alive" is more accurately translated living. The whole statement reads like this: "But present yourselves now and completely unto God, as living from the dead, and your members as instruments or weapons of righteousness unto God."

God invites and challenges us to holy living. The Holy Spirit indwells every believer, and here the Father is urging His followers to engage at once in the warfare with sin and unrighteousness. These words are a call to arms! There is a battle which must be fought, a battle in which the enemy never tires. The conflict is constant and relentless, and recruits are needed to replace those who have borne the heat of battle in the good fight of faith. We cannot live on the laurels of other Christian warriors. Each soldier of the cross has his own burden to bear in this warfare, and he will be able to win if he uses the power and the weapons which God will supply to those who have the faith and courage to ask for them, for "every one that asketh receiveth" (Matthew 7:8). No soldier of the cross need ever be defeated. The victory is within reach of every child of God. Thus we see from verse 13 that there is an unending war between sin and righteousness. As the soldiers of sin are legion, so must the soldiers of God be legion. No one can stand idly by. "Why stand ye here all the day idle?" (Matthew 20:6).

We must choose! There is no room for neutrality! This is a fight to the finish. There are no "peace feelers," and there cannot be any "peace tables." There can be no coexistence with sin. Compromise is suicide! There is now no question as to which army will be the winner. God is Sovereign. Let us join the winning side!

Verse 14: For sin shall not have dominion over you: for ye are not under law, but under grace.

Sin does not now and cannot ever lord it over the born-again child of God. We have been redeemed by the blood of Christ. We are His bond-slaves. We should be constantly trying to satisfy Christ who is our Lord. He lords it over us now, and will lord it over us, or have dominion over us, forever. We should no longer try to satisfy anyone other than Christ.

V. 14: ". . . for ye are not under law, but under grace." The Grace of God dominates our lives. God is no longer our Judge, but our Father. Because He is our Father, He now bestows His love upon us. We have passed from the powers of death with all the punitive actions of the Law. The hymn writer of old expressed it properly, "Free from the Law, oh, happy condition!" We no longer hear God's thunderous voice from Sinai. We are hearing His love from Calvary.

Love is what motivated God at Calvary, and God's loving Grace motivates us today. Bear in mind that the Law demands obedience, but the Grace of God demands our all. Love is a greater power than Law could ever be. Law instills fear, dread, apprehensions, and inhibitions. Love knows no bounds; it transcends all laws to protect the loved one; it never counts the cost; it never stops loving; and it always seeks to please the loved one. Love loves constantly with no selfish motives. God revealed at Calvary what true love is, and all that love will do. Because God loved us so much He gave His Son and never stopped to count the cost. What have we given to Him? "I am satisfied with Jesus, but the question comes to me as I think of Calvary, Is my Master satisfied with me?" are the words of a hymn. Let us search our hearts! Let us surrender to Him! Let Him lord it over you!

Verse 15: What then? shall we sin, because we are not under law, but under grace? God forbid.

In the Nestle's Greek text the question, "shall we sin?" is better translated, "may we sin?" It is in the mood that expresses a prohibition. The implied answer is, No.

The Arminian School of Theology holds that a believer can be saved today and lost tomorrow. The adherents of this school believe that persons who are born again may lose their salvation by yielding to sin, and they criticize us because we believe in the Bible doctrine of the perseverance of the saints, or eternal security.

We do not believe that our salvation depends in any degree upon our own efforts, but that everything pertaining to our salvation depends upon God who not only saves but keeps, as it is clearly stated in John 10:27, 28, "My sheep hear my voice . . . and they shall never perish"; and in Ephesians 4:30, "And grieve not the Holy Spirit of God, in whom ye were sealed unto the day of redemption."

When we are once born again our salvation is preserved by God, and we can never lose it. The Arminian School of Theology, therefore, points to this and says that if a born-again believer may sin without losing his salvation, then we believe that a born-again believer may continue to live in sin. The writer takes exception to this ridiculous claim. If the doctrine of *eternal* salvation does anything at all for the believer, it impels him to live a far more holy life than the teaching that a saved person can lose his salvation.

The sovereignty of God is one of the most humbling doctrines in the Bible. It makes a saint realize that any misdeed or improper behavior is dishonoring to God. Such actions degrade everything that God is and stands for. The fact that God is Sovereign and we are His children, is the great impelling force that challenges every believer to live a holy life. It will cause us to scrutinize the way we live and everything we do. It brings to the forefront the imperative command of God to His followers, "Ye shall be holy; for I am holy" (Leviticus 11:44 KJV; I Peter 1:16). The believer *must* exemplify God's Holiness, God's Righteousness and Purity in his life and by his life. If the believer doesn't live this way, he shames God.

Arminianism teaches that a man can lose his salvation. If this is true, if a man *can* lose his salvation, then being born again is not being born into eternal life (John 3:16). If a saved person can be lost again, then even God cannot save him. If God is unable to keep those whom He has saved, then God cannot save at all, in which case the cross becomes a sham, the Bible a confusion, and man is more powerful than God! The Arminian school talks of holiness, but its concept of God and Holiness is full of another kind of "holiness," which is to say, it is full of holes. Arminianism is the teaching of a Roman Monk, Pelagius, A.D. 360-410, and a little Scripture. His teaching was perpetuated by Jacobus Arminius, 1560-1609, from whom the doctrine gets its name. Arminianism is fundamentally nothing but works, and a complete denial of the super-abounding accomplishments of God's Grace for the believer.

Verse 15 is a summarization of the preceding verses of this chapter. It closes with the words, God forbid. In other words, God forbid the thought that the blood-bought sinner should habitually practice sin in order to amplify the super-abounding powers of God's Grace. The verse demands that the saint should *refrain* from sin. Baptism portrays the line of demarcation between the death of the old nature and the birth of the new in the life of the believer. His old nature is buried with Christ, symbolized by his going under the water; and his resurrection or rising with Christ, is symbolized by his emersion from out of the water; both together symbolizing that the believer becomes the new creation in Christ. The Sovereignty of God now operating in our lives does not give us the freedom *to* sin, but the freedom *from* sin and its powers.

Verse 16: Know ye not, that to whom ye present yourselves as servants unto obedience, his servants ye are whom ye obey; whether of sin unto death, or of obedience unto righteousness?

The law of the bond-slave was common knowledge in the days when Paul's words in this Epistle were penned. When a person voluntarily sold himself as a bond-slave in that day, this one act could never be nullified. It was for life and the authority of the master was absolute. The bond-slave of Paul's time was at the beck and call of the master whom he served. Thus in like manner the bond-slave of sin has a life of misery; a life of distress; it is a life of despondency and hopelessness; and its goal is death. The life of God's bond-slave is the very antithesis of that kind of a life. His life is filled with confidence, hope, righteousness, and holiness, resulting in eternal life, because he has already passed from death unto life. This is the completed reality in the life of the believer. What contrast with the life of sin's bond-slave!

The child of God cannot help but obey the Lord because he is His bond-slave. We repeat, it is either obedience to sin with death as the objective; or it is obedience unto righteousness, to which belong all the benefits that God can bestow on His child, including life eternal.

Notice that here, too, there is no middle ground. We must choose our master. Sin is the master of destruction. God is the master of love and eternal life. It is impossible to have two masters. Whichever one we choose, we become his bond-slave, and we have no moment that belongs to us. All of time and all of self and all of our possessions belong to the master whom we choose. Either sin has exclusive possession of each of us, or God has exclusive possession. With God it is all or nothing. A Christian should completely yield himself to the Lord and withhold nothing. Nor should he count the cost in serving the Lord. "Choose ye this day whom ye will serve." But choose well, as Eternity is at stake.

Verse 17: But thanks be to God, that, whereas ye were servants of sin, ye became obedient from the heart to that form of teaching whereunto ye were delivered . . . ;

The "whereas" is omitted in the KJV, making it read, "But God be thanked, that ye were the servants of sin," which seems to give the meaning that the Apostle was grateful that his Roman converts were at one time servants to sin. Verse 17 in the ASV, however, includes the "whereas," which is a conjunction, meaning, "in view of the fact that," or, "while on the contrary," so that the Apostle's meaning becomes clear that he is thankful his Roman converts, although formerly servants of sin, are now servants of righteousness.

From time to time it is good for the believer to take a retrospective look at his life. Doing so will make him more grateful to God for all that God has done and is doing for him. This look will send the believer to his knees in gratitude to God for His mercy, His love, and His compassion, and will cause the believer to make an introspective appraisal of the depth and genuineness of his service as a bond-slave of Christ. This look will also cause the believer to live more closely to the Lord, and result in a life of deeper devotion, more complete dedication, and greater fruitfulness for the Lord who bought him at such colossal cost, viz., His life's blood.

The first half of verse 17 clearly depicts for us the condition that we were all in prior to our salvation. We were indeed "servants of sin" at *that* time; in fact, literally bond-slaves to sin. This is an enslavement from which we could not extricate ourselves. It was not only a condition of helplessness, but also

one of hopelessness. Within our own ability there was no way
out. We were impotent to free ourselves from all the entanglements of sin and its consequences, death. Realizing this now,
and fully comprehending our former lost condition, should send
a chill of fear throughout our being. What a frightening condition we were in! How blind we were! The quicksand of sin
would inevitably slowly but surely engulf us were it not for the
Grace of God! How comforting and consoling is this precious
Grace of God! Thanks be to God that we are eternally in His
power. Nothing — no human power, our own or others, or the
power of Satan and his imps — can ever wrench us from the
power of our God! We are guarded by God Himself in this
security, through the principle of faith, whereby we are kept in
the spirit of readiness to be revealed in His presence (I Peter
1:5).

What bliss! What joy! Let us sing with the hymn-writer:
"O happy day that fixed my choice on Thee, my Savior and
my God. Well may this glowing heart rejoice, and tell its raptures
all abroad!"

V. 17: ". . . ye became obedient from the heart to that form of
teaching whereunto ye were delivered . . ."; The structure of
the Greek word for "obedient" is used most frequently to express a
past event viewed in its entirety. It expresses this thought: We
became obedient when we believed, and will continue to be
obedient no matter how long we live. That is to say, our obedience becomes an historical fact which cannot be altered. It happened and remains that way! This obedience was the work of
God's Grace in our hearts. It was accomplished by the indwelling and abiding presence of the Holy Spirit within us, who shall
never leave us. This is what it means to become obedient from
the heart. Because we have rendered such heartfelt obedience
to God, He has delivered us from sin. We shall never need this
deliverance repeated in our lives. It is an accomplished reality —
"ye were delivered"! This is God's achievement. Our impotence
is swallowed up in His Sovereign omnipotence. With God this is
an historical actuality. Thus was His glorious endowment brought
to its consummation. Need we say more?

When we were born again, God delivered us from sin, and we
turned from our old sinful paths and practices. Our hearts, our
minds, our lives were changed. We had a new path to walk in, a
new direction. Our old life was a life of sin and death. Our
new life became a holy and dedicated life.

It is one thing to receive a new life, and quite another

to learn how to walk in it. God has supplied this guidance in His Word, the Holy Scriptures, which contain His full teaching down to the minutest detail as to our daily walk. This is the form and pattern we are to follow. The urgency of the present hour, with all its threatening perils confronting the believer at every turn, demands our constant vigilance. If we are tempted to forget, we must return to the Great Commission of our Lord. He said, "Go ye into all the world, and preach the gospel to the whole creation" (Mark 16:15); "make disciples . . . baptizing them . . . teaching them to observe all things whatsoever I commanded you" (Matthew 28:19, 20). (The Greek word which is translated "teaching" is the same as the word for doctrine.)

We are commanded to "Preach the gospel!" Preach in season, out of season, in any season — but Preach! This is the most essential ingredient in our preaching — preaching the Word! The reason we are losing our power and our people is that we are preaching *about* the Word, *about* the cross, and *about* the Saviour. Let us stop preaching *about* these great subjects and return to preaching *them*. We must preach them — the Word, the cross, the Saviour. When we do this we shall see the demonstration of God's saving power in our midst. Preaching these great truths was valid in the age of the apostles and the early church, and it is still valid today. The cross may be a stumbling block to the world, but it is the stepping stone into God's Eternal Presence. If Paul, in his time, had to urge Timothy to preach the Word, how much more pertinent is the preaching of the Word today!

Fundamentalism today is divided into two groups. One group emphasizes nothing but *teaching* the Word. This group holds to all the doctrines; they are pre-millenarians, and some are even pre-tribulation rapturists. They have a form of evangelism, and even hold evangelistic meetings. But the *spirit* of evangelism is not prevalent among them. They console themselves with the thought that we are living in the last days. However, in this era there is a falling away. The result is that they who rely on teaching don't have many conversions, and the spirit of evangelism is restrained.

The second group of fundamental Christians believe not only in *teaching*, but also in *preaching*. The Spirit of Evangelism among this second group is vibrant. Souls are being won to Christ. Their churches are growing by leaps and bounds. They are not, as a rule, devisive. They do not split churches but, rather, organize new ones. They hold to all the cardinal doctrines in the

Scriptures. However, a great number of the people in these churches are not taught the deeper truths of the Bible, truths essential to consecrated living and Christian maturity.

This writer believes that all through the centuries, from the Ascension of our Lord until His return, the Gospel has not lost and never will lose any of its power. It is still God's power to salvation. It will accomplish the work which God planned for this entire age. This writer further believes that an established and mature Christian will not be moved by winds of false doctrine.

During the first century A.D., the apostles were both soul-winners and teachers. Among them were a number of prophets. When the first century ended, the books of the New Testament had all been committed to writing, the apostles had run their earthly course, and there was no longer the need for the type of ministry which had been laid to their charge by our Lord, or for the miraculous acts they had been empowered to perform in His name (Mark 16:17, 18) which were necessary to establish the church during that latter half of the first century. God's methods are clearly revealed in concrete form in His immutable Word, where they have been recorded in written form.

The churches which had been established were carrying on their testimonies. To further His Work, God ordained these early Christians in the local churches to the work of ministering and to building up the body of Christ. He gave some who were evangelists; some who were pastors; some who were teachers (Ephesians 4:11). These three groups of the Lord's servants are still available to the local church. It takes all three to accomplish the work of perfecting the saints (Ephesians 4:12). Seldom are three offices given to one individual. The Apostle states that the saints were delivered unto this pattern of teaching. Let us return to that pattern and fulfill the program of God's redeeming Grace.

Verse 18: . . . and being made free from sin, ye became servants of righteousness.

The literal translation of this statement is, "And having been freed from sin." It is in the past tense. We had been freed from the guilt, the punishment, the entanglements of sin which would have resulted in death. This was accomplished for us at our conversion. When we were born again we were saved.

How foolish even to think of such impossibilities as being unborn and un-saved! Or, as Arminianism teaches, to believe that a man can lose his salvation. Common sense rebells against such nonsense. Verse 18 states that we *have been freed.* Who did this? God, of course. Is there any power in all creation that can supersede the Power of God? Of course not. We have been freed by the Lord Jesus Christ Himself. "If therefore the Son shall make you free, ye shall be free indeed" (John 8:36). His work will suffice and endure for all eternity.

V. 18: ". . . ye became servants of righteousness." This, too, is in the past tense, but a·different kind of past tense. It is the pluperfect tense which the dictionary defines as a past perfect, more than perfect. Because we have been freed from sin, we are no longer subject to any of its authority or biddings. We are now under the jurisdiction of our new Master, the Lord Jesus Christ, and all of His protective care and righteousness. This accomplishment can never be improved upon. Through the Holy Spirit we have become devoted to the service of righteousness.

This is the doctrine of repentance in action. To repent means to make a complete about-face in life. It is a change of heart, a change of mind, a change of direction, and a change of motive and purpose in life. These changes are the out-working of repentance in the life of every believer. They are being worked out for us and in us by the Holy Spirit, ". . . being confident of this very thing, that he who began a good work in you will perfect it until the day of Jesus Christ" (Philippians 1:6). Notice that it is not the individual believer who does this work but, rather, it is He, the Holy Spirit.

Our Arminian friends will immediately quote such passages as Philippians 2:12, ". . . work out your own salvation with fear and trembling." They say, "See, you have to work it out for yourself." It is true that every believer must be willing to work; but why stop short with only half of the thought expressed? The KJV divides the thought into two separate sentences, whereas the ASV translates the passage into one sentence with two clauses, the latter dependent upon the former, thus, ". . . work out your own salvation with fear and trembling"; and the second clause, ". . . for it is God who worketh in you both to will and to work, for his good pleasure." So you see, separating the first clause from the second, and building up a false doctrine on an incomplete pronouncement of the Apostle, is an attempt to make Scripture seem to say something it does not say. It is ignoring God's part in salvation, something to be done only "with fear and trembling." A literal translation of Philippians 2:13 would be ". . . for it is God who is the One operating in you right now, both to will and to continue operating in you on behalf of His good will."

Though the infirmity of the flesh is ever present, God will continue working in it to accomplish His Will (Romans 8:28-30). These inspired words of the Apostle Paul, clear and triumphant, should settle the question of whether a person can be unsaved after a Sovereign Almighty God has saved him and is keeping him.

Verse 19: I speak after the manner of men because of the infirmity of your flesh: for as ye presented your members as servants to uncleanness and to iniquity unto iniquity, even so now present your members as servants to righteousness unto sanctification.

Many commentators claim that this is an apologetic statement. As one commentator puts it, Paul is apologizing "for his use of the image of truth, on the ground of their (his hearers') imperfect spiritual comprehension." (From *Word Studies in the New Testament*, by Vincent and A. T. Robertson.)

Whatever the reason may be for Paul's statement, humanly speaking, he is comparing the former state of the believer as a slave to sin, with the present state of the believer as a slave to righteousness. This writer believes this to be sound analogy. The unbeliever is a slave to sin. Sin is his taskmaster. Notice the second clause of the text, ". . . for as ye presented your members as servants (slaves) to uncleanness and to iniquity unto iniquity . . .". Here the tense of the Greek verb, "presented," puts the state of the unclean believers in the past, or represents it as a past event viewed in its entirety. Was not sin the potentate which was their god and, as such, were not the members of every believer's body at the disposal of the sin-god? The Apostle is stating an inescapable and convicting truth which clearly portrays the unregenerate state of every believer before his conversion. All the members of the sinner's body become slaves to uncleanness from "iniquity unto iniquity." Sin constantly pollutes the depraved soul. One sin begets another until the soul is conquered and every semblance of righteousness vanishes, as it does in the case of the dope addict and the confirmed alcoholic. This is the total depravity of sin. It does not stop until it completely dominates the soul. There is only one way to stop it, "Ye must be born again" (John 3:7) through the power of God, for there is no other way under heaven

"wherein we must be saved" (Acts 4:12) from the degeneration
of body and soul.

The same Greek expression as to sinners becoming servants to
uncleanness and iniquity is found in I John 3:4, in which sin is
identified with lawlessness. Sin is the personification of lawlessness. How descriptive of our age is this word lawlessness. It has
crept into every avenue of our life — social, commercial, political, financial, and moral. No matter where one turns it is prevalent. Lawlessness will continue to permeate the fabric of this
world's affairs until it becomes almost triumphant. Why "almost" triumphant? Why not completely triumphant? Because
this writer believes in the pre-millennarian return of our Lord,
and that God will call a halt to the complete and utter takeover
of lawlessness. The Lord will return with His saints and set up
the Davidic Kingdom which was promised to Him by God's angel
prior to the birth of our Lord (Luke 1:32). As to our members,
when we were sinners, becoming servants to uncleanness and
iniquity (in v. 19a), compare this passage with I Peter 4:3, 4.

V. 19b: ". . . even so now present your members as servants to
righteousness unto sanctification." This is the change from uncleanness and iniquity. The Apostle is now stating what a Christian should do. He is saying in effect, now that you have been
born again; now that you have repented and God has justified
you through the work of the Cross by the blood of Jesus Christ;
present your members, or, rather, keep on presenting your members, as slaves or servants of righteousness unto sanctification.
This is the structure of the Greek text. Or to state it another
way, having been delivered from the enslavement of sin, in
your new relationship you should become obedient to Him, your
new Master. This is an imperative challenge.

Since Christ was willing to give up His Own Life and undergo
a horrible death on the cross to free us from the bondage of sin,
we should be willing to present our members to Him and place
our very lives at His disposal to be used for righteousness. This
is a transaction which, to the unregenerate eye, may look like
slavish subservience, but to us who are born again it is a precious
privilege, an exalted relationship, one which should make us all
eager to comply with Paul's advice to Timothy and become "a
vessel unto honor, sanctified, meet for the master's use" (II Timothy 2:21). This we must do, yea, we should be *eager* to do.
God gives us His power and His ability to do it by the indwelling,
abiding presence of the Holy Spirit.

By yielding or presenting our members to righteousness, God

will ultimately, by constant use, bring our members unto that perfect state of sanctification when we are translated into His presence. This is the ultimate goal of achievement provided by the Gospel in the life of every believer.

The Greek word for "sanctification" in Romans 6:19 ASV, and "holiness" in the KJV, means moral purity or sanctity. The grand objective, or terminal point, of the believer's transformation from the lawlessness of sin to the righteousness of God — or, to put it another way, when the believer presents his members to God for God's own purposes and use — is sanctification; or, as verse 19b reads, "even so now present your members as servants to righteousness unto sanctification." This is what the tense of the verb "present" is saying. This presenting of our members is a continual process that God is carrying on in the life of every believer. The culminating day when every believer will be crowned with *perfect* sanctification, is the day when we are brought into God's presence. The Rapture of the Saints will bring this to pass. Now we are *being kept,* not keeping ourselves, from the power of sin. In God's presence we shall be delivered from the presence of sin into the presence of perfect sanctification.

Verse 20: For when ye were servants of sin, ye were free in regard of righteousness.

This verse is concise, but it expresses volumes. There is no compromise with God. Sin is the very antithesis of righteousness. There is a constant battle between the two. It has been so since the Fall in the Garden of Eden (Genesis 3:15). There God planted the enmity between the two, and there will never be a reconciliation. Moreover, the ultimate defeat of one and the triumph of the other can never be doubted. God and righteousness will be victorious over Satan and sin.

God is not broadminded in the sense that He is tolerant of sin. The cross is the proof of His utter and complete abhorrence of sin. God and sin are opposites, diametrically opposed to each other, as light is opposed to darkness. The world through sinning is being swept into sin's awful vortex until God shall destroy sin and its power. This is the reason that the Scriptures always call upon God's people to separate themselves from sin and to abstain from all appearance of evil. This call is not merely an invitation to separate, but is a *command* of God Himself (Leviticus 11:44). It was God's command to Israel, and she refused to obey. Israel's disobedience to this and other of God's

commands has resulted in the dispersion of her children to the
four corners of the earth. The evil fruits of this disobedience
are recorded on the pages of history throughout the past 2,500
years. What awful fruits! And what an awful record of disobedience!

God's standards are not lowered in the New Testament. They
are identical to those of the Old Testament. The same command
that God gave to Israel is the command for His saints of the New
Testament (I Peter 1:16). As Israel refused, so, seemingly, have
the New Testament saints refused. We are as stubborn and as
stiff-necked as Israel. Is it a wonder that the spirit of restlessness
is as prevalent in the church among God's people as it was
and still is in Israel? The Apostle states that when we were
servants (slaves) of sin we were not subject to the dictates of
righteousness. He says that we were "free in regard to righteousness." Fellow Christians, this is a call to separation, to devotion,
to consecration, and to a holy and righteous life. God commands! God challenges! God invites! Will you accept or reject?
Choose you must!

**Verse 21: What fruit then had ye at that time in the things
whereof ye are now ashamed? for the end of those things is
death.**

The Apostle asks a probing question. If we would take a retrospective look at our lives, it would make us blush. The best of
our lives, while we were yet in our unregenerate state, was
nothing but indulgence in attractive sins. In God's sight, the best
in our sinful life was as putrid as bandages from leprous wounds
(Isaiah 64:6). Is this anything to be proud of?

This writer rebels against hearing life-stories of people who
delve into their past and describe habits and indulgences they
have given up for Christ. When one listens carefully it usually
turns out that when such life stories are not complete fabrica-
tions, they are gross exaggerations. This writer has heard testimonies that were shameful distortions of certain scriptural inci-
dents like the one referred to in Acts 8:9-12. Such testimonies
are generally calculated to exalt the persons who give them,
rather than to exalt the Christ who bought them. Let us leave
the things which are behind and press on toward the goal unto
the prize of the high calling of God in Jesus Christ (Philippians
3:13, 14). The prize can be ours if we have the courage to press
on toward the goal. Let us forget the past, which is something
that will only make us ashamed. The prize can be obtained only

by the mature, seasoned, and dedicated life of a Christian. This is a goal and a prize worthy of all effort. Let us press on!

V. 21: ". . . for the end of those things is death." How probing and thought-provoking are these words! The end of our unregenerate lives is death, when we were yet in our sin, separated from Christ, alienated from the commonwealth of Israel, strangers from the covenants of the promise, having no hope and without God in the world (Ephesians 2:12). The end of our unregenerate lives, the Apostle says, is death.

It is shocking to the child of God when he reflects upon the dangers, the pitfalls, the snares and delusions that beset his life during his lost condition. The recollection of these past assaults of the enemy and his deliverance from them should cause the child of God to fall to his knees in thanksgiving for the abundant mercies that God has showered upon him. How grateful every born-again believer ought to be to Christ who emptied Himself unstintingly for only one purpose, that we might have an eternal life and an eternal abode with God. How niggardly we are with our time, our talents, our possessions and our lives! All these are Christ's for us to use for His glory. The end of our former unregenerate life was death. Then we were born again and death was done away. Thank God! We have a new life to live in Christ. All is changed! What glories lie ahead!

Verse 22: But now being made free from sin and become servants to God, ye have your fruit unto sanctification, and the end eternal life.

The literal translation of the Greek is, "but now having been freed." Such is the emancipated position of the child of God. Prior to our salvation we were under the jurisdiction of a taskmaster. We were kept in bondage and in a constant state of serfdom. We were slaves bereft of all freedom. We were kept, as it were, under the thumb of sin. But thank God, we have been made free. Notice very carefully the wording of the verse, that we were "made free." By whom? By the Incarnate Son of God the Messiah. He, alone, can free a person from the enslavement of sinfulness. This emancipation required the payment of a ransom. We were bought and paid for in the slave-market of sin. Our new Master and Lord sought us in love, "As a father tenderly loves his children with compassion, in like manner the Lord loves them that revere Him" (amplification of Psalm 103:13). The motivating power of our new Master is love. To serve this Master is a joy and privilege. In essence it is like being made free. Such is the position of every believer. How do *you* serve Him Who did this for you?

V. 22b: ". . . ye have your fruit unto sanctification, and the end eternal life." The phrase "ye have" in the Greek denotes action in progress. The Apostle is urging the Christian to have fruit now and to keep on having fruit. The only excuse for not having fruit is laziness, indifference, and lethargy. Every Christian *can have* fruit. This fact can become a sad commentary on a great number of fruitless Christian lives. It is not that Christians are unable to lead souls to Christ, it is simply that they won't! They refuse to put forth the effort. The Gospel is still God's power unto salvation. It has never lost any of its power. The Gospel has all of the potency and efficacy that it had on the Day of Pentecost. Its outreach has increased today. Through the mediums of radio and television we are able to reach untold thousands. These are at our disposal; let us use them. God uses and will continue to use every means of reaching people with the Gospel. We must put forth the effort. The Gospel must be preached! When it is, it always produces fruit. The Gospel is God's principle for having fruit (I Corinthians 1:21). Will you put forth that effort?

V. 22b: ". . . unto sanctification . . ." There is much that can be written on these two words. In the light of the preceding words, "ye have your fruit," the Apostle is exhorting the Roman converts to bear fruit unto sanctification. Having fruit is the result of heeding this exhortation. There is nothing that a Christian can do that will prove of greater value in purifying his life than soul-winning — having fruit. To be an effective soul-winner one must not only speak the Gospel, but one must *live it* as well. Words are meaningless if they are not substantiated in the life of the person speaking them. Soul-winning not only purifies a Christian's life, but it also cleanses his life and makes it more efficient in the work of God (John 15:2). This admonition should goad every Christian to become a soul-winner.

V. 22b: ". . . and the end eternal life." What a contrast this is with the closing words of the preceding verse, "for the end of those things is death"! The evil fruit of sin is death. The good fruit of righteousness is eternal life. Between the two it will be eternal separation with no hope of reconciliation. A person is a fool not to choose life.

Verse 23: For the wages of sin is death; but the free gift of God is eternal life in Christ Jesus our Lord.

The wages of sin have never been reduced! Indeed they cannot be. The judgment of God has always been death. God's standards never change. He never tolerates sin. Inevitably and eventually God's retributive decrees are always executed. The penalty for sin has remained the same throughout all dispensations, beginning at the Garden of Eden (Genesis 2:17). It is still the same today, and will continue to be the same until Satan, the father of sin and death, and the consequences of sin, are cast into the lake of eternal fire (Revelation 20:10).

V. 23: ". . . but the free gift of God is eternal life in Christ Jesus our Lord." The Greek word for "free gift" is Charisma. In theology this is the Gospel, and it covers the full scope of salvation and every benefit the believer receives through faith in Jesus Christ. What a contrast is presented in verse 23! The first part of the verse speaks of death, "the wages of sin." The wages are paid by Satan the taskmaster, and the sinner is the slave; and the wages are the only pay the sinner receives for a lifetime of work, namely, death. Satan has nothing else to give his subjects but death in a lake of eternal fire in which he, too, must suffer forever and ever and endure all the torments that fire and brimstone can inflict,

Then consider the second part of the verse, "the free gift of God," eternal life in Christ Jesus our Lord! Compare the free gift of God with the wages of sin. Satan, the potentate of evil, pays his servants the horrible wages of death, whereas God Almighty, the King of Glory, bestows upon His servants the gift of life everlasting, joy unspeakable and full of glory. God in dealing with His own is motivated by love and love only. He is continuously giving gifts to His children, and never ceases to shower them upon His own. He is the God of the *living*. He gave His only Son, and the Son, when He rose from the dead, became the Heir of all of God's possessions. At His resurrection He revealed Himself to be the personification of life. Whoever accepts Him as Lord and Master becomes co-heir with Christ, and shares with Him the rewards that God gave His Son. Since life is our Lord's eternal possession, He gives it freely to anyone accepting Him. This free gift, which is totally free and unearned, is eternal life. Christ is the Master and Keeper of that life. We become God's children, and, if children, then joint-heirs with Christ (Romans 8:16, 17). Since God's Eternal Life is also in Christ, all that Christ has, we have. He is Life itself. Hallelujah, what a Saviour!

7

Verse 1: Or are ye ignorant, brethren (for I speak to men who know the law), that the law hath dominion over a man for so long time as he liveth?

Paul is still pursuing the discussion of Law and Grace. He is asking in effect, "Are you, my brothers, ignorant of how the Law operates? Don't you understand Law? Can Law affect a person who has died?" In verse 14 of chapter 6, Paul points out that the believer is not under the Law, written or otherwise, but under Grace. The Grace of God becomes the motivating power in the life of every believer.

The Apostle is addressing himself to believers, for he calls them brethren, meaning spiritual brethren. In this group there were undoubtedly a number of non-Jews, but there were also a number of Jews, Paul's brethren of the flesh, who were believers, and who possessed a full knowledge of the Law. Many of them were still zealous for the Law, and continued to observe Jewish customs (Acts 21:20). This writer, as a Hebrew Christian, is fully aware of this, and knows that even today there are many Hebrew Christians who continue to practice the ancient customs of Judaism. Many Hebrew Christians do not eat pork; they eat only unleavened bread at Passover, or abstain from eating leaven during the Passover festival. However, Hebrew Christians, when they observe these ancient customs, do not do so in order to be saved, but because such customs have been a part of their lives from childhood. Does an American Jew or Gentile, because he may be living in a foreign country, forget the 4th of July? Not if he is an American who loves his country. By the same token, neither does the mere observance of the 4th of July by one not born in this country and unnaturalized, make one an American citizen.

The Law cannot and does not have a prior claim over the Hebrew Christian, neither does it have jurisdiction over him. The believer, Jew or Gentile, has died with Christ, and no power other than Christ's can have any claim upon him, as there is no power higher than Christ's, He who yielded up His life voluntarily for us. The Law has no claim on any person, whether he be Jew or Gentile, after he has accepted the Messiah as his own Lord and Saviour. The authority of the Law ends when a person dies. Even the Talmud states: "When a man is dead, he becomes free from the Law, and the commandments" (Talmud Bab. Sabbat. folio, 30.1).

V. 1b: ". . . the law hath dominion over a man for so long time as he liveth?" The Law demands obedience of every unsaved individual so long as he lives. The Greek text has reference to *every* unsaved individual throughout his entire life. But the one who is saved, the believer, has died with Christ, and the Law is stripped of its power. This is the position of the believer in relation to the Law. And, conversely, this is the position of the Law in relation to the believer. The conclusion is that the believer and the Law are dead to each other.

Verse 2: For the woman that hath a husband is bound by law to the husband while he liveth; but if the husband die, she is discharged from the law of the husband.

This is the only place in the New Testament that the Greek word for "woman" appears. However, in the Septuagint Old Testament it appears in Numbers 5:19, 30; Proverbs 6:24, 32. The Greek word means a married woman. The Apostle states that the married woman *has been* bound and not *is* bound. The Greek verb is in the past tense. No doubt the Apostle is making a comparison between a married woman who becomes a widow, and a believer in relation to the Law. The married woman who becomes a widow is free from the Law of her deceased husband in the same manner as the believer who has died with Christ is free from the Law. This must be the reason for the use of the past tense of the Greek verb in the phrase, "has been bound." In like manner, the Law is powerless in the case of the believer, since he is dead to the Law after he is saved.

Let us digress for a moment to look at some greatly neglected truth. What verse 2 implies is that there is no room for divorce. The indissolubility of marriage is God's changeless edict. It is as binding today as it was in the Garden of Eden: "they shall be one flesh" (Genesis 2:24).

In these days of lawlessness we hear many sins denounced in a number of pulpits, but only infrequently do we hear the subject of divorce mentioned or discussed. Even in fundamental circles the subject is avoided. Why? Is it because so many church members are divorced or are considering divorce? Statisticians tell us that one out of every three marriages ends in divorce. Seemingly this fact is an accepted norm in our society. It is rapidly becoming the norm even in so-called Christian circles. Grace does not nullify the "law of the husband." When God's decree, "they shall be one flesh," was made in the Garden of Eden there was no Law. It was the imperative command of God under Grace.

There is no excuse for divorce in the married life of Christians. It negates the testimony that Christ is sufficient for every problem in life, because in the life and home of a Christian there is no sorrow or tragedy that cannot be resolved with prayer. Divorce is the repudiation of God's standard for every Christian home. Only a timid heart of wavering faith will not listen to the still small voice of God's eternal love.

This writer's Christian experience and conviction compel him to regard the very thought of divorce with revulsion. Married Christians should always frown upon it. Only those who are unbelievers or heathen should resort to it. We who are Christians must remember and must teach others that marriage is a sacred contract ordained by God, and it must not be dissolved by man. Even as our Lord said, "What therefore God hath joined together, let not man put asunder" (Matthew 19:6).

A minister of the Gospel is the last person on earth who should seek to end his marriage by divorce, or to recommend that another do so. Any minister who divorces his wife should immediately resign from the ministry. He no longer belongs in the pulpit, but rather in the pew, inasmuch as putting away his wife in defiance of God's edict against divorce is notice to the world that his faith in Christ was not strong enough to help him keep his marriage vows. For such a minister to retain his sacred office and continue preaching the Gospel of salvation would be nothing less than sham and a denial of his faith in the Shepherd and Bishop of his soul (I Peter 3:7).

V. 2b: ". . . but if the husband die, she (the wife) is discharged from the law of the husband." Death abrogates all laws. As soon as the husband dies, the wife has been discharged from the "law of the husband." The Greek word translated "is discharged" (ASV) or "is loosed" (KJV) means to render null, to abrogate, to cancel, and to free. This states clearly that death is the only thing which ends marriage in God's sight (I Corinthians 7:39).

Verse 3: So then if, while the husband liveth, she be joined to another man, she shall be called an adulteress: but if the husband die, she is free from the law, so that she is no adulteress, though she be joined to another man.

A more accurate translation from the Greek would be, "as long as the husband is living, she will be called or treated as an adulteress." These are strong words, and this admonition should be carefully considered and heeded by every believer now married or contemplating marriage.

The Apostle is building, in Romans 7:1-6, an analogy between marriage and the "law of the husband," on the one hand, and the works of Law and Grace on the other, to show more clearly how Grace is the governing factor in a Christian's life. As Christ died for our sins, so do we, when we are born again, die to the Law, and our life is motivated by the Grace of God now that we are living under Grace. Death of our old nature separates us from all legalism when we are born again, in the same manner that the death of the husband or wife voids a marriage contract.

Verse 4: Wherefore, my brethren, ye also were made dead to the law through the body of Christ; that ye should be joined to another, even to him who was raised from the dead, that we might bring forth fruit unto God.

With this verse the Apostle continues the simile which he previously introduced. The Greek word translated "wherefore" proceeds to explain more clearly the analogy between the Christian's death to the Law through the death of Christ and the death of the husband which frees the wife from the "law of the husband." "Ye also were made dead." The Greek for this statement expresses a past action viewed in its entirety. It is a once-for-all-time statement, and means exactly what it says, i.e., we *were* put to death to the Law. The Law is not what was put to death to the believer, but, rather, the believer was put to death to the Law through the body of Christ. The meaning of the phrase, "the body of Christ," is the crucified body of Christ. The believer participates in the death of the Saviour by dying with Him. The old sinful nature is crucified with Christ (Romans 6:6).

The Law is the means and method by which a person is led to Christ (Galatians 3:24; Psalm 19:7); and, by the same token, the Law condemns the one who rejects Christ. Christ and His **work** on the cross is the only propitiation for sin that God recognizes. Notice that we are made dead — we do not make ourselves dead. That we are put to death to the Law is the accomplishment of the Godhead. The Father gave the Son as His acceptable sacrifice, and the accomplishments of this sacrifice were imputed unto us by the Holy Spirit. With Christ the believer dies, with Christ he rises again, and with Christ he now lives.

V. 4b: ". . . that ye should be joined to another, even to him who was raised from the dead, that we might bring forth fruit unto God." Since we are put to death to the Law, this frees us that we may be joined to another, namely, Christ (Ephesians 5:23).

The expected result of marriage is children. In like manner the believer's joining with Christ should result in fruit, "that we might bring forth fruit." This is expected of every believer. The only reason that God leaves His children here upon this sinful earth after they are saved, is that they may bear fruit for Him. He has given us all the essentials for fruit-bearing. Our Christian life need never be sterile. If our life be sterile and remain barren, "He taketh it away" (John 15:2). Undoubtedly, this is the meaning of John 15:6, and the reason why many barren Christians die early is that they are "cast forth as a branch . . . and they gather them, and cast them into the fire." Beware! Take inventory! Don't be spiritually barren. To be so is dangerous. God expects us to be fruitful.

V. 4b ends with the words, ". . . unto God." What a difference there is between the evil fruits of sin and the good fruits of righteousness! The evil fruits of sin are humiliation, degradation, covetousness and lust, resulting in sorrow and death (Romans 6:21). The good fruits of righteousness which God enables us to bear are the fruits of His enabling so long as we abide in Christ, the true Vine. These good fruits are the exact opposite of the evil fruits of sin. The good fruits exalt our lives, fill them with dignity, love, joy, peace, kindness, goodness and faithfulness, and enable us to crucify the flesh and attain eternal life (Galatians 5:22). The repentant sinner seeing the life of the saint and its fruits of love and peace, will become jealous and desire to possess the same attributes, we hope and pray. This jealousy of a God-given life will result in fruit to the glory of God.

Verse 5: For when we were in the flesh, the sinful passions, which were through the law, wrought in our members to bring forth fruit unto death.

This verse reminds us vividly of what we were prior to our new birth before we were put to death to the Law; and at the same time it reminds us of what our new life in Christ must be, that we may "bring forth fruit" unto life.

Our sinful nature was always bearing evil fruit. In our sinful state we were occupied in a quest for things that would satisfy our sensual passions. Sin operates contrary to Law. God told Adam to refrain from eating "of the tree of the knowledge of good and evil" (Genesis 2:17). Although God provided an ample number of trees which were filled with fruit which he could eat (Genesis 2:16), God's prohibition against the tree of knowledge incited Adam to disregard God's admonition. Adam ate and death ensued. The old adage, that forbidden fruit is the sweetest, probably originated because of the memory of Adam's temptation and fall. (See Proverbs 9:17, 18.)

The prohibitions of the Law excite our Adamic nature to disregard the laws of God. The fruits of Adam's sin and our sin are identical — *death*. "Sin operated." Our members passively permitted sin to work in them, producing fruit unto death. The fruit of righteousness is eternal life as compared with the fruit of sin, which is death. What a contrast! What a choice! Which do you choose? (Deuteronomy 30:19).

Verse 6: But now we have been discharged from the law, having died to that wherein we were held; so that we serve in newness of the spirit, and not in oldness of the letter.

The Greek expression for "we have been discharged," means rendered useless or powerless, has been severed. The Greek tense implies a completed action, an accomplished reality, i.e., we have been rendered dead to the Law, and the Law has lost all of its persuasive powers over our members. This fact should make the legalists realize that we Christians are no longer subjects *of* the Law or subject *to* the Law. Service under the Law, and the temptation to disregard God's laws, are warnings to the believer not to return to the legalism of the Law. This should cause every believer to cherish the Grace of God all the more and to hold to it more tenaciously.

Death has severed our relationship to the Law and to all of its jurisdictional powers — "having died." The clause immediately preceding this completed action, this accomplished reality, is "we have been discharged." This clause tells us why, namely, "having died." Death in all cases renders that which has died useless to that which was subject to its power prior to death.

"Having died," there was nothing left in us which the Law could use. This is why verse 6 states that we have been discharged from all the powers of the Law, powers which were operative in our members before we were saved. We must not forget that it is not the Law that died. We, the flesh, the old sinful self, died. The Law still operates in the members of all who are still sinners.

V. 6: ". . . we were held . . ." The Greek for these words means to be in the grasp of, or to be bound by; it is like being chained in a prison. The flesh, our old state, was subject to and held in the grasp of the Law. But now, since the flesh died, the Law has lost its hold. Thank God that we Christians have been freed from the Law and are no longer subject to any of its punitive measures ordained by God (Galatians 3:23).

V. 6b: ". . . so that we serve in newness of the spirit, and not in oldness of the letter." Because the believer has been freed from the Law, does not mean that he can do whatever he pleases with his life. He has not been freed to serve the flesh or its lusts, his previous taskmasters. Freed from the Law, he was bought by his new Master, Christ. He must henceforth be obedient to this new Master. The believer was bought off the auction block of sin to a glorious service which, when compared with the service to his former master, is like being set free from slavery. Having been freed from the Law, we Christians are to serve right now. This is the meaning of the words "so that we serve." The Greek tense denotes a continuous service or continuous action. We have been completely discharged from serving the Law and are now free to serve our Master and Redeemer.

V. 6b: ". . . newness of spirit . . ." The Dispensation of Grace and the giving of the Holy Spirit ushered in the preaching of the Gospel (Acts 1:8; 2:2-4). This is the "newness of spirit," the new message with a new Power to proclaim it. It differs greatly from the Dispensation of Law which the Apostle refers to as the "oldness of the letter," by which is meant the Law with all its prohibitions. This old letter or covenant, the Dispensation of Law, was confined to a *rebellious nation,* Israel. The new message or covenant, the Dispensation of Grace, energized by the Holy Spirit, is God's gracious offer to a *rebellious world,* regardless of race, creed or color. Of this new covenant the Apostle says, it is "not of the letter, but of the spirit: for the letter (Law) killeth, but the spirit (Grace) giveth life" (II Corinthians 3:6).

The Holy Spirit is the "breath of life" and is the creator of life. He breathed life into Adam's nostrils, and Adam became a living being (Genesis 2:7). Prior to the Holy Spirit breathing into the nostrils of Adam he, Adam, was nothing more than a body of clay. When the Holy Spirit breathed into that body of clay, it "became a living being."

So it is today. When the believer lived in sin he was considered dead to God, but when the time of salvation arrived, the Holy Spirit moved (breathed) into the life of the sinner, he made his confession of faith in Christ Jesus, and the sinner was quickened or made alive unto God (Ephesians 2:5).

Before leaving verse 6, there is one more observation that should be made. The struggle of the believer, described in verses 7 to 25 of this chapter, can be overcome only by the indwelling, abiding presence of the Holy Spirit. The Holy Spirit is Christ's Representative during this Dispensation, dwelling in the believer, encouraging him, and energizing him in this great struggle. Since the believer is not struggling with flesh and blood, but with principalities, powers and the world-rulers of darkness, against spiritual wickedness in heavenly places, he needs the super-human power of the Holy Spirit to fight a victorious battle (Ephesians 6:12).

My fellow Christians, take heart! Victory is promised. We will win, we will overcome, if we faint not. Yield yourself completely to God our heavenly Father, and He will give you the victory (Galatians 6:8).

Verse 7: What shall we say then? Is the law sin? God forbid. Howbeit, I had not known sin, except through the law: for I had not known coveting, except the law had said, Thou shalt not covet . . . :

The Apostle puts himself in the place of one asking such a question. Paul knows better. "Is the Law sin?" To a Christian Jew, especially one of Paul's background and training, this is an unthinkable question. To a Pharisaic Jew, and before his conversion Paul was a Pharisee, the mere suggestion of the thought that the Law could be sin was abhorrent and an affront not to be endured. How could anyone make such an appalling error? Surely such a question could come only from the lips of one totally unfamiliar with the Law and its jurisdiction.

V. 7b: "Howbeit, I had not known sin, except through the law . . .": The Law reveals sin and vividly portrays what sin really is. It identifies sin. ". . . for I had not known coveting, except the law had said, Thou shalt not covet . . ." If "Thou shalt not covet," had not been part of the Decalogue, no one would have known that coveting was a sin. The Law removes

all the excuses for not knowing what sin is. The revelation of the
Law shuts every mouth that faces God (Romans 3:19). There is
no ground upon which to claim ignorance as an excuse. The
Greek word for "lust" carries the thought of a constant quest for
the unrestrained gratification of sensual desires. In the Greek the
command, "Thou shalt not covet," is in the future indicative,
meaning that when the Law says that "thou shalt not covet," it
means that from the day the commandment was given, to covet
was definitely a sin. No one was permitted to covet thereafter
forever and be innocent of sin. The Law drove sin out of concealment and brought it into the open for everyone to see.

The reason the Apostle used the tenth commandment is that
all sin stems from covetousness (Colossians 3:5). It was the
cause of the sin of Potiphar's wife (Genesis 39:7). Covetousness
is the cause of stealing, killing, war, envy and strife. This is the
second word that described the spiritual decline of our present
civilization and of every previous one. The first word is lawlessness. Covetousness is the underlying cause for the unrest, greed,
and crime now prevalent in the cities of our country, as well
as in the whole world. This spiritual decline is satanically inspired. It was nothing less than covetousness which led to Satan's
pride and greed, and resulted in his fall from heaven. He, who
was called, "son of the morning," in Isaiah 14:12, became Lucifer
(KJV) or "day-star" (ASV).

Satan was greedy, he coveted the powers of God. His envious
heart said five times, "I will!" What was Satan's goal and the
object of this five-times repeated, "I will"? To be like God and
to possess the powers of God (Isaiah 14:13, 14). Pride and greed
were Satan's downfall. God brought him low, cut him down to
the ground, and will ultimately consign him to hell forever (Isaiah
14:15; Revelation 20:10).

Covetousness and lust are the instruments of pride and conceit.
Throughout the world's history, nations and their rulers have
disappeared into oblivion because of covetousness. The pages of
of history present a graphic picture of the downfall of nation
after nation and the underlying cause of the downfall. Let us
beware of this sin of covetousness. Shun it! Flee from it! It is the
agent of destruction, and its victims will most surely be cast with
Satan into the bottomless pit (Revelation 20:2, 3 KJV).

**Verse 8: . . . but sin, finding occasion, wrought in me through
the commandment all manner of coveting: for apart from the
law sin is dead.**

The phrase in the Greek for, "finding occasion," means a starting point, an opportunity, a base of operation for an expedition. In classical Greek, "finding occasion" is used when describing a base or starting point for war, a place of origin, or the source. The Law did not make the occasion, it was sin that gave rise to coveting.

Satan and sin are always opposed to holiness and righteousness. The moment the Law came into existence, Satan and sin began to work through the instrument that was affected by Law, namely, man. Therefore, sin "finding occasion," began to operate in man through devious methods. Man, becoming a slave to sin, yielded his members as instruments or weapons to sin, and sin began more intensely to operate; and lust began to show its results in every avenue of life. The Law tends to put a man into subjection to holy living, and holy living is the antithesis of sin. When sin meets Law, sin springs to active opposition.

Satan and sin are the bitter enemies of holiness and righteousness. The conflict has been evident throughout the history of mankind since the Fall. Sin will not be defeated until Christ returns and Satan is chained for the Millennium, after which he will be cast into the lake of fire (Revelation 20:2, 3, 10). The forbidden fruit of righteousness and holiness, is sin and Satan.

The Law was not dead and, in a very real sense, neither was sin, for sin ruled from Adam to Moses. The Apostle uses the first person nominative pronoun "I" in verse 7, and the objective pronoun "me" in verse 8. Paul is saying that he did not at first realize the spiritual reality of the Law. When there was no Law sin was a dormant thing to him, and it laid as though it were dead. But when Paul came under the Law and realized the ramifications and meaning of the command, "Thou shalt not covet," then his sin nature sprang to life and began to operate. He knew then what the prohibition against coveting really meant.

When a person is told not to eat certain kinds of food, as when a diabetic is denied food containing sugar and carbohydrates, he craves these elements more intensely because he must refrain from eating food containing them. In like manner sin came into reality, as it were, when Paul comprehended the meaning of coveting as taught by the Law.

Verse 9: And I was alive apart from the law once: but when the commandment came, sin revived, and I died . . . ;

A more accurate translation of the Greek for, "And I was alive," is, and I was living. Paul states that he was living apart from the

Law. What Paul is really saying is that when he, as a Pharisaic Jew, looked at the Law, he looked at the *letter* of the Law. In the light of this concept of the Law, he *was* living. He was zealous for the Law. Jewish jurisprudence looks at the *letter* of the Law. Under this system of exegesis, Paul observed the Law. Under this system of interpretation, he was truthfully living apart from the Law. This is not God's meaning of the Law or its objective. The inherent purpose of the Law is not its letter merely, but that the Law is the schoolmaster, to bring us to Christ (Galatians 3:24 KJV).

V. 9: ". . . but when the commandment came . . .", or, "but at the coming of the commandment," whenever that time was, the Apostle states, "sin revived," or sprang into action. Sin began its sinful activities. When Paul realized what the Law meant with all of its ramifications and implications, he said, "I died." He realized that he was incapable of meeting the requirements and standards of the Law. He saw death looming on his life's horizon. It was like the proverbial "sword of Damocles," and death was his inevitable end. He undoubtedly knew the text, "the soul that sinneth, it shall die" (Ezekiel 18:4). To Paul this meant that so far as the Law was concerned, he was as good as dead; in fact, he said so, "I died." In the Greek this term expresses a past event in its entirety. In other words, when Paul realized this, he died, not physically, of course, but so far as his Adamic nature was concerned.

What a transition there is in this one verse! From life to death; from error to truth; from man's concept of light to sin's darkness and death; and from fiction to fact. What an awakening this must have been to Paul! It should be the same to every sinner. "What then is the law? It was added because of transgressions, till the seed should come to whom the promise hath been made" (Galatians 3:19).

In other words, the Law awakens the reality of sin in the person who turns to Christ for salvation. Since we realize that the Law is dead, Christ is the sure Way to eternal life. The Law reveals sin and slays; Christ reveals sin and saves. Choose! You cannot be neutral. If you do not accept Him, you reject Him. Sin and death will find you out and slay you. Christ and His righteousness will seek you out and offer you salvation and eternal life. The Saviour said, "Come!" Will you?

Verse 10: . . . and the commandment, which was unto life, this I found to be unto death . . . :

This commandment the Apostle, as a Pharisee, believed was the principle of life. The keeping of the Law, if it were ever possible, the Apostle, as a Pharisee, thought would earn one eternal life. This keeping of the Law is what he learned at the feet of Gamaliel. This same keeping of the Law is the false hope that is supposed to give life and impetus to Judaism. But how tragic! Israel missed the entire purpose of the Law. She failed to recognize that the Law was not God's principle of salvation. What God recognizes and responds to is found in the Psalm 34:18: "Jehovah is nigh unto them that are of a broken heart, and saveth such as are of a contrite spirit." Also, in Psalm 51:17: "The sacrifices of God are a broken spirit: A broken and a contrite heart, O God, thou wilt not despise." See also Psalm 86: 5, 15; Isaiah 57:15.

"Is the Law then against the promises of God? God forbid: for if there had been a law given which could make alive, verily righteousness would have been of the law" (Galatians 3:21). The entire purpose of the Law was to humble man and make him see that within himself there was no ability to work out his own salvation. Realizing his own inability, he would cast himself upon the mercy of God.

What consternation there must have been when Paul realized that the very principle which he thought would bring him life, brought him death! What a frightening experience this must have been to him! His fear must have been indescribable. It was a changed Paul that penned the words, "and the commandment, which was unto life, this I found to be unto death." In other words, he is here speaking of himself as a saved and commissioned apostle. He came to know the difference and is proclaiming it. He saw the inherent purpose of the Law operate in his own heart and life, since the Law was the result of his complete acquiescence to God's Will and brought him salvation. Have you realized this in your life?

Verse 11: . . . for sin, finding occasion, through the commandment beguiled me, and through it slew me.

The first part of this verse is a repetition of the first part of verse 8. The Apostle states that it was sin that beguiled him, not the Law. The Law is not the cause of sin which results in death. Sin, through its devious and deceptive methods, is what slew the Apostle.

The Greek word for "beguile" means to delude, deceive thoroughly; in the classical Greek it means to cheat or to swindle. In the Septuagint Old Testament, the same language is used which Eve used when she said, "The serpent beguiled me, and I did eat" (Genesis 3:13; II Corinthians 11:3; I Timothy 2:14). The devil has not changed one bit. He is constantly deceiving people and misinterpreting God's Word to them. Satan is always attempting to mislead us by his devilish ability to twist God's Word, and to make it say what God never said or meant. Sinners are foolish enough to believe the devil, and this belief always results in death. When God's Word is broken the consequences to the sinner are disastrous. It was so in the Garden of Eden, it was so in Paul's time, and it is the same today. Sin and Satan, deception and death, are the evil forces still lurking in the shadows along life's highway.

Mankind has always lived under a delusion. Great numbers of people have lived and are living according to the Decalogue or the Golden Rule, believing obedience to the commandments or the Golden Rule to be an assurance of salvation or eternal life. All who live thus are laboring under a great deception. Man's sinful nature can never meet the requirements of a holy law. The inhibitions and prohibitions of the Law are contrary to the flesh, and the flesh incessantly rebels because its freedom is hindered. The sinful nature of man is the instrument and the weapon of sin. The only power that can thwart the inherent evil tendency of the flesh is the Holy Spirit. This is why the child of God finds it so difficult to live a holy life. Resistance to evil becomes a continuous battle that cannot be halted for even one moment. The Holy Spirit must supply the power and the weapons for this warfare. The child of God must constantly rely upon the Holy Spirit for help in this fight to the finish. Sin and Satan are always relentlessly pursuing the believer. Satan never gives up. Therefore, the child of God must be ever vigilant.

How true this was in the life of the Apostle before his conversion! He was so beguiled, bewildered and bedeviled by sin, that when he thought he was doing God's will and fulfilling the Law, he was actually fighting God, His righteousness and holiness. Through the working of sin in Paul's life, sin so deceived him that he became guilty of murder (Acts 8:1; 9:1, 4). How tragic are the results when we yield our members as instruments of sin!

Dear reader, repent before death overtakes you! The only way of escape is the way of the cross. It leads home unto eternal life. The Saviour invites you. Will you come?

Verse 12: So that the law is holy, and the commandment holy, and righteous, and good.

Under no circumstances could the Law be anything else. The inclination to sin, due to our Adamic nature, is constantly opposing and rebelling against the holiness of the Law. The Law is the ever-present barricade to sin. It is also the holy monitor reminding the sinner of his evil deeds, and the consequences of his impious actions. The Law is also the still small voice of an Omnipotent God reminding the sinner that his sinning will result in death and hell. The flesh rebels against the holy Law.

"The commandment, Thou shalt not covet, is holy, righteous, and good." The flesh not only rebels against the whole Law, but it defies every prohibition of the Law. The flesh is the enemy of *every word of every commandment.* The evil nature of the flesh carries on a continuous warfare with everything that God stands for and all that He is (Romans 8:7, 8).

What goodness would result if mankind followed God's prohibition, Thou shalt not covet! If man obeyed the Law, this would be a transformed world. But this is wishful thinking. Certainly, there shall come a time when evil will be subdued and righteousness will prevail. Every word of God is permeated with goodness and righteousness, and clothed with His garment of love. This is God! This is His character! This is Calvary! "Why will ye die?" is the eternal question that God asks a sinful world and Israel (Ezekiel 33:11).

The Apostle voices the same truths regarding the Law and the precepts of God that the Psalmist recorded more than seven centuries before him: "The law of Jehovah is perfect, restoring the soul: The testimony . . . is sure, making wise the simple. The precepts . . . are right, rejoicing the heart: The commandment . . . is pure . . . The fear . . . is clean . . . The ordinances . . . are true, and righteous altogether. More to be desired are they than gold . . . sweeter also than honey" (Psalm 19:7-10). These are the words of a child of God whose soul has been converted, whose eyes have been opened, whose taste has been sweetened by His Word, and whose ears have been unstopped to the call of God. What transformation this is! The ultimate goal of achievement of the Law, the genius of the Law, is to bring the sinner into complete fellowship and relationship with God. God has sought this throughout all ages. His quest began in the Garden of Eden when Jehovah God called unto the man, "Adam, where art thou?"

God asks the same question today, "Where are you? On what path are you traveling?" Won't you answer Him who is the Way, the Truth and the Life? He — Christ — is the *only* way back to the Father's house.

Verse 13: Did then that which is good become death unto me? God forbid. But sin, that it might be shown to be sin, by working death to me through that which is good; — that through the commandment sin might become exceeding sinful.

The Apostle is answering a hypothetical objection to what he has stated in the preceding verses. Nothing but good can result from anything that God does. Only an evil heart and a perverted mind misconstrue God's righteous actions and words. This has always been so. Evil does as evil thinks. Paul is saying that God's actions are always righteous.

When Abraham tried to intercede in Sodom's behalf, he asked God to spare Sodom and Gormorrah because their sin is very "grievous" in God's sight. Abraham asked God, "Shall not the Judge of all the earth do right?" (Genesis 18:25). Abraham knew that every judgment of God *is* right. The Apostle Paul states the same truth more emphatically. He says, "God forbid." The Greek term for this expression, which is thus translated into English, is meant to represent an emphatic denial that a holy law could bring death to a believer such as Paul. Or, to put it in other words, do not contemplate such a possibility! Or, in plain language, do not even *think* such a thought! It is altogether evil.

V. 13b: "But sin, that it might be shown to be sin, by working death to me through that which is good . . ."; Sin, no matter under what colors it might hide, or how attractively it might be camouflaged, always has death as its objective. In this verse Paul says that the true nature of sin became obvious to him only when he realized that sin (coveting) so distorted the commandment against it as to make it appear that it was the commandment, not sin, that brought death to him. Sin was working all the time to bring about its evil results. The Greek tense of the phrase "by working death to me," is a present participle, thus portraying the fact that sin is constantly working. It works in the flesh of the believer. This is an unending battle in which the believer is engaged, and during which he must continue to call upon the Holy Spirit for assistance. The devices of Satan and his evil deceptions are the everpresent enemies that will keep the child of God always alert and ever vigilant.

V. 13c: ". . . that through the commandment sin might become exceeding sinful." Nothing so completely reveals sin as the commandment of God. Black is most obvious when it is on a white background. The moment the commandment of God is revealed, sin springs up in violent opposition. All its evil potentialities are instantly brought into action, and all its infuriated resentments begin their war against righteousness. Thus sin works out its own undoing, because this unremitting warfare reveals the fulness of sin's evil nature which, after all, is the very purpose of the Law, namely, to disclose sin's vileness. Only an Omnipotent God can use evil to reveal His righteousness, thus exposing the true nature of sin and its evil consequences. By revealing sin, God shows every man that he is a lost sinner and doomed, unless he repents. Truly, God uses the wrath of man to praise Him (Psalm 76:10).

Sin and misery are inseparable companions, and diametrically opposed to salvation and righteousness. The culmination of sin is death, and the culmination of salvation is eternal life. Choose you must.

Verse 14: For we know that the law is spiritual: but I am carnal, sold under sin.

Verses 14-25 of this chapter of Paul's epistle have provoked much discussion through the centuries among Christian writers and commentators. It was discussed by the early Christian Fathers: Augustine (354-430) struggled with it, and the followers of Pelagius (360-410) stated their views, making this portion apply to the unregenerate. Segments in Arminianism (Arminius 1560-1609) take the position of Pelagius, since they believe in sinless perfection. See comments on Romans 6:15, pp. 189, 190.

This writer has never met a Christian who does not sin, and does not expect to meet one until he gets to heaven. One thing we can be certain of is that the Christian's cast-off fleshly tabernacle which is buried in the cemetery never sins. Verses 14-25, this writer believes, illustrate the struggle of every blood-bought, born-again child of God, whether he is in his spiritual infancy or his spiritual maturity. The flesh is ever present with all of us, and is constantly warring against the new nature which we received by our new birth. The Christian life is a battle with victory in sight, and obtainable for every follower of Christ. We have the assurance of such victory in our risen Lord and Saviour. We must be on guard at all times in this endless conflict with the flesh. Sin must be kept in subjection, and must not be permitted to get the upper hand in the believer's life. If it ever does, the consequences are tragic. Thank God for our protected position. We are no longer in bondage to sin. To be in conflict with sin is one thing, but to be its bond-slave is an altogether different thing.

V. 14a: "For we know that the law is spiritual . . .": Every Christian will admit that the Law breathes the very holiness and righteousness of God. Every jot and tittle of it has been given by God, and the Holy Spirit moved the writers of God's Word to record it accurately, just as God wanted it recorded; therefore, the Law is good and pure and holy in every word.

V. 14b: ". . . but I am carnal . . .", When the Apostle wrote these words he was the self-confessed bond-slave of Christ, the called apostle, separated unto the Gospel of God, the victim of many persecutions and privations, "in deaths oft" (II Corinthians 11:23-27), and even though he had endured all these terrible experiences, he could say in this letter to the Romans, which was written *after* his second letter to the Corinthians, "I am carnal." It was the heart-cry of this soldier of the cross. Surely he had passed through the fires of the refiner's furnace (Malachi 3:3); surely his body bore the marks and scars of his testings; surely these experiences would have been sufficient to purify a believer. Yet Paul knew that his flesh — his carnal nature — was still with him. He knew that as long as he lived he would never reach the state of sinless perfection.

If this Christian warrior did not and could not claim that he had never sinned while he was in this life, how, in the name of common sense, and in the light of Scripture, can any person who is a follower of Christ, claim sinlessness? Either such a claim is unadulterated presumption or the result of willful ignorance of Scripture. Only this would lead anyone to make the empty boast of sinless perfection. To make this boast is to negate such passages as, I Corinthians 15:35-58; and I Thessalonians 4:13, 18. Sinless perfection contradicts I John 1:8-10.

V. 14c: ". . . sold under sin." The classical Greek word for "sold" shows this word to mean to pass right across and through space, to pass over boundaries or barriers secretly or by force, or to pass through one place to another. This Greek word has also a second meaning; namely, to export captives or political prisoners to foreign parts for sale as slaves. Hence, being "sold under sin" is the condition of the flesh, making it imperative that before we can become sinless and inherit the Kingdom, we, the flesh, must be changed. See I Corinthians 15:51-53. **The**

Greek word "sold" in this verse is in the past tense and expresses a more than perfect past, that is, in the state of completion. As long as the Apostle was in the flesh he was prone to sin, and the disposition to sin was ever in his flesh, i.e., his flesh was permanently sold to sin. In other words, his flesh was a slave to sin and, like every other believer, he must wait for the resurrection (I Corinthians 15:42). The living saint must wait for the translation or the Rapture (I Thessalonians 4:15-17).

Observe carefully, this is the condition of the flesh *only*. The inner (new) man, viz., the soul and spirit, is saved and eternally kept by the Holy Spirit through and in Christ. Only the believer in Christ has the two natures, and they war. The unregenerate has only the sin or Adamic nature.

Verse 15: For that which I do I know (allow KJV) not: for not what I would, that do I practise; but what I hate, that I do.

Paul is saying in this verse, for that which I work out, that which I produce, that which the flesh produces instinctively, I do or do not allow. The innate inclination of the sinful flesh always reacts intuitively and powerfully. Even before a person thinks, he acts, almost simultaneously. How many times have we said or done things for which we were sorry? If we had only taken time to think we would have avoided many pitfalls and embarrassing experiences. But, the sinful self, the "I," always springs so quickly into action, producing sad results. The one imperative rule for the Christian is to be alert at all times to quell his sin nature. The believer cannot let his guard down for even one moment lest his flesh do that which his inner man would never allow. Our better judgment knows better, but the flesh moves too readily.

V. 15: ". . . but what I hate, that I do." Doesn't this sound familiar? Everyone of us has said at one time or another, I hate myself for doing thus and so; or I wish I had never done this; or my better judgment told me not to do that; or I wish I had listened to my better judgment and not acted on impulse. Isn't this exactly what the Apostle is saying, and he an experienced soldier of the cross? He had been through this war with sin, and said what many of us have thought and said on similar occasions.

Verse 16: But if what I would not, that I do, I consent unto the law that it is good.

In other words, Paul is saying, if one does that which the born-again man should not do, then it is not the new man that acts, but the former unregenerate nature. The new nature consents to the truth that the Law is good. The flesh constantly springs into action. Because this is so, Paul says in another place, "I buffet my body, (literally — I beat my body black and blue) and bring it into bondage" (I Corinthians 9:27). Struggling against the impulse to sin and forcing — buffeting — ourselves to resist the sinful impulse, is the daily experience of every believer who desires to live a life that is pleasing to the Lord. Thus we can all say, "I consent that the law is good." Every child of God agrees that the Law is good. There is not one thing wrong with the Law. It is sin that rebels against the Law because the Law reveals sin and brings it out of concealment. The new nature endeavors to live a holy life and shuns the very appearance of sin. This is God's pattern for His followers. The believer is to live an exemplary life in the midst of this sinful world.

Verse 17: So now it is no more I that do it, but sin which dwelleth in me.

Because it is "no more I that do it," does not permit the believer to sin, and is no excuse to continue in sin habitually (I John 3:9).

The Greek word for "do" means to work out, produce or practice. The Apostle states here that his new nature ("I") is not the one that is producing or practicing sin. His new nature is striving to please his Master. This conflict between sin and the new nature is the never-ending battle in which each believer must take part from the moment he is born again. There can be no respite in this warfare which we must carry on relentlessly. The old nature of the flesh is ever present, and takes advantage of every opportunity to "practice evil." Our carnal members are the weapons of sin in this battle. However, God gives every Christian the assurance of victory over sin and death through His son who died, who rose, and who is now living in every Christian. The Apostle states that he "can do all things through Christ which strengtheneth me" (Philippians 4:13 KJV).

Our new nature can never be conquered by sin. The believer is even now as though he were in heaven and in the presence of God. This new creature is invincible because he is energized and guarded by the Holy Spirit. Victory is assured.

But the Adamic nature of the believer has not been eradicated.

This is why Paul says, "but sin which dwelleth in me." Sin is the evil-doer. The Greek word for "dwelleth" is better translated dwelling, since it is a present participle. Sin keeps on dwelling in the believer until his physical death, or until he is "caught up" in the Rapture. This warring sin nature of the believer must, by all means, and under all circumstances, be kept in subjection, and this can be accomplished only at the price of constant vigilance.

Verse 18: For I know that in me, that is, in my flesh, dwelleth no good thing: for to will is present with me, but to do that which is good is not.

Paul is again elaborating on the evil tendencies that are ever present in the flesh. That there is evil present in every man is something that Paul learned at the feet of his Rabbis. They taught him that in each Jewish man there are two natures, i.e., the good imagination and the evil imagination. So innate, so inborn in humanity is the evil nature that the Rabbis believed God created it. The "imagination of man's heart is evil from his youth" (Genesis 8:21); "And it repented Jehovah that he had made man on the earth, and it grieved him at his heart" (Genesis 6:6). Rabbi Abahu interpreted this "repentance" and "grief" of God to mean that God actually regretted having put "the bad leaven in the dough," i.e., the evil in man; and that this evil was waiting on man as he emerged from the womb, for "sin coucheth (lieth) at the door" (Genesis 4:7; Sanhedrin 91.b.) and all through man's life it remains "his implacable enemy" (Tanhumah-Beshalla 3). This warfare in the soul was part of the heritage of Jewish belief.

Modern Judaism has changed this idea that God created the evil in man. In the Jewish prayer book there is this statement: "I thank thee, O God, that thou didst not create in me the evil nature." What an idle boast this is! If there is no evil nature in Israel, then why do they continue to deny that the Messiah has already come; why are the Jews still in dispersion; why are they still falsely accused and persecuted; why do they not possess the entire land as God promised it to Abraham; why is there bloodshed; and why is there war? All this is an affront to God! It is denial of the Pentateuch, the Torah. The Torah is the foundation of Judaism. If there is no evil nature in the Jews, why is the book of Leviticus still accepted by them as the third book of the Law? This book deals with sin offerings, intercessory priesthood, a tabernacle, an altar and other accompaniments. These laws and services were instituted by God for the purpose of expiating sin. If the evil nature is not present in Jews and Gentiles alike, then God made a horrible mistake. What Rabbi would have the audacity to make such an absurd claim in the presence of a Holy God? In the very heart of Leviticus is this declaration, "for it is the blood that maketh atonement" (17:11). If sin does not exist, then why the blood on the altar for atonement? Sin will prevail in the world and even in Israel until the Messiah comes. "In those days, and in that time, saith Jehovah, the iniquity of Israel shall be sought for, and there shall be none; and the sins of Judah, and they shall not be found: for I will pardon them whom I leave as a remnant" (Jeremiah 50:20). This is not the place to enter into an exegesis of this text. Suffice it to say that the phrase, "in those days, and in that time," certainly points to the days of the coming of the Messiah. Even the Rabbis will admit this interpretation.

The Apostle states that in his flesh "dwelleth no good thing." In his flesh is the abiding evil nature that is the root of his dissatisfaction with himself, and the cause of his confession of failure. This evil nature which he calls "no good thing," defeats his will to do that which is good and continues to present problems and difficulties. He is continually fighting it, and trying to subdue it. The conflict is an endless one and will trouble him until his Lord calls him home. Verse 18 contains the words of this veteran soldier of the Gospel. Even though he is born again, regenerated, he still has to fight the sin nature that abides in his flesh.

V. 18b: ". . . for to will is present with me, but to do that which is good is not." The Apostle's will to do good is in him; it is his new nature. This Christ-nature is given to him by the Holy Spirit. It is always present. But, the will to work out the good that will be pleasing to the Lord, is not present. Why can't Paul do that which is good? Because the flesh is in the way, it is weak, "the spirit indeed is willing, but the flesh is weak" (Matthew 26:41). The flesh is "sold under sin" (verse 14), and it cannot do that which is good. The words "I find" in verse 18 of the King James Version are omitted in the Sinaitic MS., the Vatican, the Alexandrine texts, and, therefore, also omitted in the American Standard Version.

There is in verse 18a further truth which is foundational to Christianity. When Paul says, "that in me, that is, in my flesh, dwelleth no good thing," he is emphasizing the doctrine of the

Total Depravity of Man, the same doctrine spoken of in Romans 3:23; namely, "all have sinned."

Is there any person in this world with any respect for God who would dare claim that a human being never sins? Even the blood-bought child of God, one who may have but little knowledge of the Scriptures, is cognizant of his ever-present sinful nature and knows that he must do his utmost to subdue it. The Apostle is using his own experience as an example of man's total depravity. Every Christian strives to live a life pleasing to God, but he is at the same time keenly aware of the weakness of the flesh.

Verse 19: For the good which I would I do not: but the evil which I would not, that I practise.

This verse is a continuation of Paul's discussion of the subject of verses 15-18. The conflict between our wills to do good and the evil nature which defeats our purpose, is the warfare in which every believer is engaged as he endeavors to live a holy life. The old sinful nature is constantly maneuvering for a position in which to overcome the new nature. The believer must be constantly on guard to live a victorious life.

The warfare that is perpetually being fought in the life of the believer, if carried on victoriously, will prove to be for his greatest good. It keeps him spiritually alert, in the spirit of prayer, searching the Scriptures, relying upon the Holy Spirit, witnessing to others of the love of God, looking for the coming of Christ. Last, but not least, it will prove to be the purifying ingredient in living a holy life. This alertness of the Christian is the weapon or instrument that God uses for His Glory, an alertness which can be relied upon for the spreading of the Gospel.

Some years ago there was a story told about a Scotch fisherman who always managed to get a higher price for his catch than did his fellow fishermen. How he did this was a carefully-guarded secret which he divulged only to his granddaughter on the day of his death.

The secret was in keeping his fish alive until he brought them to market. Whereas other fishermen dumped their catch into the holds of their boats where the fish died almost at once, this canny Scotchman kept his fish alive until sold, and, as a consequence, the fish were firm and fresh and brought a higher price.

How did he do it? This was the carefully-guarded part of the secret. First, he always retained a vicious dog on his boat to keep his inquisitive fellow fishermen away; second, he had the bottom of his boat arranged to hold a shallow amount of running water, and a net into which the fish were dumped. In this water and inside the net he kept a very large live catfish. When the Scotchman dumped the contents of his net into the hold of his boat, the fish fell into the shallow water with the live catfish which at once began fighting with them. The catch was thus kept alive and moving briskly until the boat reached port, and was therefore in far better condition for market than the catch of other fishermen whose fish had died almost immediately after being caught.

This is only a story, but it serves to illustrate an important factor in the Christian's earthly warfare; that is to say, the temptations and harassments of Satan serve, like the catfish in the story, the purpose of keeping the Christian under pressure in his spiritual life, impelling him constantly to witness and work for the Lord, keeping his spiritual life in action, as the catfish kept the other fish alive, preventing his becoming dormant and his life almost useless in the hands of the Living Christ.

The Apostle is stating this truth by saying that now, having become a child of God, he wants to do good, is *determined* to do good, but the flesh is the ever-present stumbling block to the fulfillment of his will to do so. In this persistent frustration of his best efforts, his evil nature is doing the very things that defeat his efforts in holy living.

If the struggle for victory in the Christian life was so difficult for a stalwart Christian like Paul, as he here confesses it to be, what a challenge it presents to every believer! We must be vigilant, we must be wide-awake, and on our spiritual toes, so to speak, every moment of our lives. We must be cautious of every move we make, lest we prove to be stumbling-blocks instead of stepping-stones for Christ. Becoming a Christian is not an invitation to a life of ease, nor can we be lackadaisical in our Christian conduct in the midst of an evil civilization. We must be on guard and spiritually fit for this fight to the finish.

Verse 20: But if what I would not, that I do, it is no more I that do it, but sin which dwelleth in me.

If the new nature, which is the Christ-nature, is opposed to what the sin nature, the flesh, is doing, then it is not the new nature which is doing the evil. Evil works incessantly. It never stops. It is this sin nature which is dwelling and working in the believer.

The tense of the Greek verb "dwelleth" is a present participle and conveys the thought that sin abides in the Christian all the time, and will continue to abide in him as long as he lives in his body. It expresses an action in progress, and further states that sin continues to abide in his body. The Christian *is in* the flesh! This is his earthly habitation. His spiritual nature lives in an earthly tabernacle. So then, just as sin abides and works unceasingly, so must the spiritual nature, since it, too, abides in the believer and works unceasingly. The new nature does not sin and the old nature never stops sinning; hence, the continuous warfare in the believer's life. Because of this ever-present conflict in his life, it behooves the believer to be always watchful of the evil nature within him, and to use his new nature, with the help of the Holy Spirit, to subdue the indwelling sin.

Verse 21: I find then the law, that, to me who would do good, evil is present.

There is much discussion among Bible students over this verse; in fact, more than over any of the other verses in this chapter, because the article "the" before the word "law" leads many expositors to believe it refers to the Law of Moses. "There are just as many (expositors) who feel that it means the 'law of sin' or a law with the article *the* preceding it. The constant rule of experience imposing itself on the will. Thus, in the phrases — law of faith, works, the spirit. Here the law of moral contradiction." Vincent — *Word Studies in the New Testament.*

This writer believes that verse 21 speaks of the "law of evil" that is present in every believer. The Rabbis taught of the two natures, the good and the evil, always present in every Jew. This teaching was based on Genesis 6:5, ". . . and that every imagination (thought, counsel, design, project) of the thoughts of his heart was only evil continually." "The heart is deceitful above all things, and it is exceedingly corrupt" (Jeremiah 17:9).

The believer is the *only* person who has two natures. One always wills to do good, while the other always seeks to do evil. This is what the Apostle is confessing in this verse. The "law of evil" is ever present, and rises in opposition whenever his born-again nature, which he calls good, wants to do that which is pleasing to God. Verse 21 is the experience of every follower of Christ who seeks to do His will. It challenged the Apostle's purpose as he walked in the service of his Master, and until this very hour it is the experience of every child of God who serves Him. We can overcome it in the same manner as the Apostle did, if we use the spiritual weapons that God has placed at our disposal to fight the law of evil dwelling in our flesh. Have courage, my fellow Christians, the Lord is on our side!

Verse 22: For I delight in the law of God after the inward man . . . :

The Greek word for "delight" is a very strong word which expresses delight or approval. It differs greatly from the word "consent" in verse 16.

What a difference there is between the inward man, which is the regenerated or converted man, and the carnal man! The regenerated man has been born again to fellowship with God. Resurrected ("Ye were dead through your trespasses," Ephesians 2:1.) to live for God, he has been re-fashioned into a living example of God's super-abounding grace in the midst of a sinful world. He has been radically transformed to conform to God's standards and has become a new creation in Christ for a testimony to the miraculous powers of God in this present evil civilization. He is to live as a pilgrim on a pilgrimage to a "city that hath foundations," an ambassador of the Theocratic Kingdom of God, to exemplify a righteous and holy life such as God requires of His ambassadors, in contrast to the kind of life lived by members of the evil generation in which such persons abide.

This "inward man" delights in and approves of the Law of God, and God rejoices with him. The righteousness of God is not revealed only in the Gospel or Good News itself, it is also revealed in the accomplishments of the Gospel in the inward man. This man can now delight in the Law of God because he does it out of a heart of love instead of fear. It is no longer the thunderous voice of Jehovah at Mt. Sinai speaking to the believer, it is now the tender voice of God the Father speaking to His children, enabling them to call Him Abba, Father (Romans 8:15). (Abba, Father, a form of address suggesting a loving filial relationship, used by our Saviour during the agony of the garden, Mark 14:36, combining Abba, our Lord's Aramaic mother-tongue, with Father, the Greek. Abba, therefore, has a loving connotation as of a loving child to a loving parent, love engendering love. Abba, Father, thus becomes a term of endearment signalizing "the glory which I had with thee before the world was . . . for thou lovedst me before the foundation of the world," John 17:5, 24. The Son loves the Father, the Father cherishes the Son, each delighting the other.)

Verse 23: . . . but I see a different law in my members, warring against the law of my mind, and bringing me into captivity under the law of sin which is in my members.

This "law of sin" that the Apostle sees in his members is an entirely different law than the one in which he delights, i.e., the "law of my mind." The "law of sin" is dissimilar in every respect because it is contrary to the law of God, by which law the Apostle means the "law of my mind," different in its standards, its objective, and its purpose. The "law of sin" is corrupt, contemptible, vulgar, and dishonorable, bringing death to its members. No wonder the Apostle says it differs from the "law of my mind" in which he delights after the inward man. One is the exact opposite of the other.

The "different law" which Paul refers to, the "law of sin," was operating in him at the time he was writing this Epistle, even though he was a mature Christian. Is this not sufficient evidence that there is no validity to the unscriptural teaching of sinless perfection, and the eradication of the sin nature of the believer while he still is in the flesh? The "law of sin," inherent in this flesh is constantly warring against the law of God, i.e., the "law of my mind," and opposing it as though on the battlefield. This war is going on perpetually, an endless conflict in which the Christian must never abandon his vigilance or relax his efforts. He must pray always to the Holy Spirit to help him maintain his spiritual fervor. Never for one moment should he let down his guard. He must be ever on the alert against sin.

In verse 21 Paul states that, "the law of evil" was ever present; in verse 22 he states that he delights in "the law of God"; and in verse 23 he speaks of the "law of my mind." By the term, the "law of my mind," Paul is referring to his spiritual, born-again nature. He tells the believers in Philippi to "Have this mind in you, which was also in Christ" (Philippians 2:5), which is a command, not an invitation. The Greek verb which is translated "have" is in the imperative mood, meaning that we *must* think like Christ. This "law of my mind" is the bitter enemy of the law of the flesh, the sin principle, the laws the Apostle says are "warring against" each other. How could it be otherwise? Sin and righteousness cannot be at peace; they are incompatible. Neither can there ever be a compromise. It is not amazing that the Apostle was deeply conscious of this conflict

from which there is no respite, and which is still existent in
every sincere child of God. The "me" in verse 23, "bringing me
into captivity," is not this "me" that part of Paul's personality
which he refers to as the "inward man" in verse 22, and "my
mind" in verse 23, which is continually serving God without
ceasing? It is his flesh which he refers to in verse 14 as "carnal,
sold under sin."

As this writer pointed out in his commentary on verse 21,
the Rabbis taught of this conflict between the good and evil in
every Jew (Bereshit Rabba. Prash.9. fol.7.4.). The two expressions in verse 23, the "law in my members" and the "law of sin,"
must be synonymous since both are opposed to ("warring
against") "the law of my mind." "The law of sin which is in
my members" is bringing Paul into captivity. Being in captivity
is far different from being a slave.

The thought expressed in verse 23 is that one's members are
taken into captivity like a prisoner of war, that is, taken by force
and manacled, or made to walk through a prison camp with a
bayonet in one's back. In similar manner sin deceives our members and brings them into captivity. They are held in this
condition by the evil enemy while awaiting release or the opportunity to escape. Our members may be held captive, but
our mind is always thinking of home. From personal knowledge
we are fully acquainted with what it means to be a prisoner of
war, waiting for the defeat or destruction of the enemies' armies,
and subsequent release from prison.

Such is the burden of the Apostle's argument in verse 23.
We are aware that our salvation is in three phases: (1) We
were saved from the *penalty* of sin. (2) We are being saved
from the *power* of sin. (3) We shall be saved from the *presence*
of sin.

In this warfare of the power of evil against the power of
righteousness there is no question as to which power will have
the victory. We do not fight this battle alone. The Holy Spirit
is *in* us and *with* us. We are the instruments that He uses to
overcome the enemy. No matter how feeble the instrument may
be, it is the hand of the Omnipotent One that holds our hand
and wields the weapon. The thrust is not ours but God's, He
who wields the weapon.

The flesh is the captive of sin. The mind is the bond-slave of
God in Christ. We are His eternal possession, and no power,
human or satanic, can ever overcome the sovereignty of God
who is continually, unwaveringly, and unalterably moving to-

ward His goal of victory. We may be and we are being held
captive by sin, but we shall be delivered. We have the promise
of God's Word, ". . . greater is he that is in you than he that is
in the world" (I John 4:4); ". . . be of good cheer; I have overcome the world" (John 16:33); "Let not your heart be troubled;
. . . I go to prepare a place for you . . . I come again, and will
receive you unto myself; that where I am, there ye may be also"
(John 14:1-3; also Isaiah 41:10).

This teaching of the Apostle in verse 23, being brought into
captivity under the law of sin, is based on the teaching of the
Rabbis. They also teach of a "captivity of the soul" (Caphtor,
fol.14.2). (See our commentary on verse 18, and the teaching
of the Rabbis, that in every Jewish man there are two natures,
the good imagination and the evil imagination.) "That there is
warfare between the two natures, good and evil, in man, and
that one is *carried captive* by the other" (Zohar in Genesis
fol.56.3). The Rabbis also teach that the good imagination is
like being "bound in a prison." They, therefore, ask the question,
How shall I serve my Creator while "I am held captive to my
corruption and a bond-slave to my lust?" (Machzor Jud. Rispan
apud 1). Capell, in Romans 6:16.

There is a great deal of difference between the religionist
and the Christian. The religionist must hold on to the founder
of his religion and to his beliefs in that religion. His religious
life is an endurance contest. The founder of Christianity is the
living Christ who is ever at the Christian's side. The Christian's
life is a fellowship walk in which he is led and encouraged by
the Spirit of his Master. The founder of Christianity is the
Author and Perfector of our faith, and His life is hidden in our
lives (Colossians 3:3).

**Verse 24: Wretched man that I am! who shall deliver me out
of the body of this death?**

The last phrase, "the body of this death," may be translated,
"this body of death." The Greek word, which is here translated
"wretched," is used only twice in the New Testament, here and
in Revelation 3:17. It is the cry of a man in distress, as though
he were caught in a trap from which he is unable to extricate
himself. Some expositors have thought that the expression, "deliver me out of the body of this death," may have occurred to
Paul because he had probably heard of the practice of an ancient tribe of savages whose practice consisted of strapping the
body of a dead person to a criminal when executed. A similar

practice is mentioned in Roman mythology, and is recorded in
the eighth book of Virgil's "Aeneid," where it is written that
one Mezentius, a cruel Etruscan king, "bound living persons
face to face with dead ones, leaving them to starve." Hence
the adjective, "Mezentian," which according to the dictionary
means extreme cruelty.

V. 24: ". . . who shall deliver me?"

The Greek word for "deliver" means to drag out of danger,
to rescue, to save, or to deliver. This verse, and verse 25, sets
the stage for chapter 8. In verse 24 the Apostle shows that the
flesh is permeated with death. It is dying in every fiber and
there is no stopping the process. The flesh must ultimately and
surely die. It is corrupt. The new nature, the inner man, is
carrying this body of death like a dead body strapped to a
living human being. It is dead weight; it is hindering the inner
man and hampering him at every turn; it is frustrating him. He
is unable to get rid of this cumbersome and useless load. Like
the Apostle in verse 24, our inner man is ready to cry in despera-
tion, "I am miserable, I am wretched, I am trapped! Who will
help me, who will deliver me out of this body of corruption
and death? I am groaning and travailing in pain under this
heavy load of misery" (Romans 8:23).

The Jewish translators of the Septuagint version translate
Isaiah 6:5, "Woe is me." "O, wretched I," even as Paul, a saved
man, cried, "Wretched man that I am!" And surely no one will
deny that Isaiah who uttered almost identical words in 6:5, was
a saved man.

Verse 24 records the despairing cry of the Apostle as one who
is on the battle front in his Christian warfare and is in constant
conflict with the enemy, sin. Paul gives us in this portion of
chapter 7 a graphic picture of the struggle of the spiritual man
with the carnal flesh. This struggle is an arduous one filled
with pitfalls and difficulties, and is very trying, full of hardships
to the point of tears, and at times almost hopelessly frustrating,
seeming to be on the verge of overwhelming the inner man,
which it is never able to accomplish fully because God is above
us, His Son beside us, and the Holy Spirit within us. Our God
is Omnipotent, He is Sovereign, He is invincible!

The powers of the Godhead thus give us the unconquerable
energy with which to fight this conflict. The believer cannot be
defeated because the God whom he trusts will bring him to
victory (Philippians 1:6). The God whom we serve will, beyond
a shadow of a doubt, deliver His own from the power of sin.

Verse 25: **I thank God through Jesus Christ our Lord. So then I of myself with the mind, indeed, serve the law of God; but with the flesh the law of sin.**

This chapter closes on a triumphant note. Instead of a lament over defeat, Paul's "I thank God" is like a shout of exultation, as if he had cried, "Praise the Lord, the victory is won!" Even though bound by sinful flesh with all its evil desires, the Apostle is assured of victory. He has no fears, no doubts. Whereas life in his flesh is filled with difficulties, with apprehensions, his life in Christ, the regenerated inner man, the "I myself," is certain of victory, because the believer is able to testify that behind every cloud of anxiety there is always the silver lining of redemption in the Person of a living Saviour who is able to deliver His redeemed (John 10:28, 29). Sin will not dominate the believer.

The source and reservoir of the Apostle's gratitude is his Saviour, the Lord Jesus Christ. He sold himself to the Saviour on the road to Damascus, and accepted Him as his Lord. Having been thus bought, Paul committed his life and every talent he possessed to the service of his Master. He became Christ's bond-slave. He had no fears, no apprehensions, no anxieties as to what his Master would do for him. Though a self-confessed captive in the "body of this death," he thanked his heavenly Father for his victorious deliverance through Jesus Christ his Lord.

The price that the Master paid for this bond-slave made Paul too great a treasure to be lost. After all, did not the Saviour step down from His Father's Throne to convert this persecutor into an inspired Apostle? This bond-slave was to play the part of a chosen vessel in God's plan. He was, and still is, the most illustrious servant in the economy of God's New Testament.

The Master used His servant Paul as an example of what He will do for every believer who will place his implicit trust, his devotion, and his life into the sovereign hands of an Omnipotent Saviour, and thereby empower him to conquer every foe, no matter how formidable the foe may be. Even the gates of hell cannot prevail against those who are the Saviour's own.

In the midst of trials, testings, torments and apprehensions, caught on the dangerous edge of the maelstrom of a sinful civilization; hindered and hampered at every turn by the sinful flesh when attempting to do good, encumbered by privations, faced by apparently unsurmountable hurdles, and chafed by a tyrant's yoke, the child of God has ever a song in the night. This indomitable courage of the believer to outride pitfall and discouragement is the acid test of his faith. Trials and tribulations are the inspiration of the song-writers of God. Under the hardships and privations of this earthly pilgrimage the redeemed of the Lord sing the loudest. When the carnality of the flesh is being whipped into submission, the inner man, the spiritual ego, the "I myself" breaks forth with thanksgiving and praise to our Master who bought us with His own precious blood. This is the Apostle's "Hallelujah Chorus," but it does not voice itself until he realizes his own inability to extricate himself from what he calls "the body of this death." So it is with each of us. When we realize and acknowledge the incapability of our flesh, then the Lord will use us to His glory. Have you experienced this? It is wonderful!

In verse 25 the Apostle proclaims with a cry of thanksgiving that he, himself, on one hand, serves the Law of God with his mind, which is the inner man, while on the other hand, with his flesh, he is held captive by the law of sin which his flesh unceasingly serves. The mind is the enemy of the flesh. The struggle of righteousness versus sin was relentless and unending in the life of the Apostle, and continues to be so in the life of every believer.

Sin cannot conquer any child of God. Victory is assured no matter how discouraging the struggle may often seem to be. Christ removes all doubts and allays all fears. "Let not your heart be troubled" (John 14:1) are the comforting and reassuring words of the Saviour to every troubled believer. Verse 25 is the summary of verses 14 to 24 of this chapter.

Are you tired and weary of sin? Is your burden too heavy? Is your life filled with frustrations? Then come to the Saviour. He invites you, "Come unto me, all ye that labor and are heavy laden, and I will give you rest" (Matthew 11:28).

8

Verse 1 (KJV): **There is therefore now no condemnation to them which are in Christ Jesus, who walk not after the flesh, but after the Spirit.**

Much has been written discussing the last half of this verse. Some expositors believe that it should be omitted, while others believe that it should be retained. The Sinaitic and the Vatican texts eliminate the clause, "who walk not after the flesh, but after the Spirit." The Alexandrine text eliminates the phrase, "but after the Spirit." The Nestle's and Wescott and Hort texts eliminate the entire line, "who walk not after the flesh, but after the Spirit." Dean Henry Alford, in *The New Testament Commentary,* feels this clause is an interpolation and should be omitted. However, the present writer believes that the second clause is part of the verse and should be retained.

V. 1: "There is therefore now no condemnation to them which are in Christ Jesus . . ." That is to say, there is no condemnation of the believer whose life is motivated and energized by the Holy Spirit. The believer, who is "in Christ Jesus," is constantly endeavoring to please God and to serve Him in every way possible. He is living for Christ, and his life is to be an exemplification of what a Christian's life should be. His life must mirror the Christian virtues of faith, hope and love, and be winsome enough to awaken the admiration, if not the envy, of his non-Christian friends and neighbors, and perhaps cause some of them to exclaim as the old Roman theologian Tertullian once did, "See how these Christians love one another!" Every believer should be able to live serenely in the midst of the present-day sinful and turbulent society and thereby arouse curiosity, if nothing more, among his unbelieving acquaintances.

A Christian's life is governed by the Word of God. He lives according to God's standards. There is no condemnation for such a meritorious life. Indeed, there can be no condemnation.

Moreover, such a life is rewarding and holy. It glorifies God and the Saviour who paid for it with His blood. It is a challenging life, it is a noble life, which should be the ideal of every born-again child of God.

However, what has just been said cannot be true of a carnal Christian. A life given over to the sensual indulgences of the world is the extreme opposite of a godly life. A carnal Christian's life is filled with pitfalls and inconsistencies. It lacks spiritual virility and it does not make unbelievers desirous of becoming Christians. It does not ring true, since the observer cannot be sure what a carnal Christian actually believes, or whether his life is lived for God or for the flesh. When a life is permeated with carnality it lacks all semblance of spiritual fervor, and is a stumbling-block to the sinner. It does not exemplify the Gospel or Christ; it does not bear fruit for Christ; it is not energized by the Holy Spirit; it is not interested in the Word of God. On the other hand, it is carnally motivated by the insatiable desires of the flesh and its gratification.

In view of the foregoing evidences of failure in the life of a carnal Christian, should not all this carnality be condemned? Was not this the problem with which Paul was confronted by the church at Corinth? The licentious carnality of the members of the Corinthian church was their undoing. They were motivated by their fleshy desires, and were adulterous in their practices and worship. Paul wrote their leaders scathing denunciations of their degrading conduct, calling attention to their lack of spiritual discernment and their unwillingness to separate themselves from the evil practices of their friends, and to cease from their own sin.

Is this not the keynote of the Corinthian epistles? Does not Paul warn these carnal Christians of the dangers, the pitfalls, and the diabolical consequences that would ensue if they persisted in their evil acts? Is not this Paul's compassionate heart-cry to his erring brethren in the Corinthian church to come out from among their adulterous brethren and separate themselves from the unregenerate customs of their society? Does he not caution them to beware of the dangers and the judgment that will befall them? Is this not the condemnation that awaits the carnal Christian that Paul speaks of in I Corinthians 5:5?

The last clause of Romans 8:1, although it speaks of the Christian's walk as being "after the Spirit," does not speak of the gift of eternal life. This priceless gift cannot be lost even by carnality. God's gift of life everlasting is a transaction that endures for eternity regardless of the evil desires and acts of the flesh. Eternal life is a contract initiated by God and offered to the believer (John 3:16), and not one which the believer initiated and offered to God. The saving and keeping of this contract is dependent upon an Eternal God, and not upon the instability of the believer's sinful flesh. God cannot and will not repudiate His part in the contract. Life everlasting is an eternal gift given by an eternal God and lasts as long as God Himself. God does not change His mind toward His children, or change His gifts, "For the gifts and the calling of God are not repented of" (Romans 11:29); "Every good gift and every perfect gift is from above, coming down from the Father of lights, with whom can be no variation, neither shadow that is cast by turning" (James 1:17).

God is immutable in all of His gifts and calling. If the carnality of the believer could sever relationship with God, then Moses would be lost because of his bad temper and disobedience. If carnality could annul eternal life, then David would be doomed because of his adultery and murder. If carnality negates God's Word, then Samson would be in jeopardy of losing his salvation because of his willfulness, sensuality and self-destruction. If a believer's sin can forfeit his salvation, then God's Word is nullified, His promise is meaningless, and the cross the most tragic disappointment in history. God forbid that this could be true. It is a loving Father who bought us with His most treasured possession, His own Son, and sealed us with the immutable Person of the Holy Spirit, and who revealed and recorded it in His inspired Word. "By faith Moses . . . and what shall I more say? . . . if I tell of . . . Samson . . . of David" (Hebrews 11: 23, 32). With Israel of old we can shout, "Praise the Lord! Hallelujah!"

The truth of verse 1 gives meaning to our faith and to God's character. We must be motivated and energized by the Holy Spirit. Every step we take, every deed we do, every word we speak, must be an act of worship guided by the Holy Spirit in order that Christ may be glorified in us, His followers. Because "there is therefore now no condemnation to them that are in Christ Jesus . . ." let us make doubly sure that we "walk not after the flesh, but after the Spirit." We must be living examples because we have "passed out of death into life" (John 5:24). To live for God we must walk after the Spirit. The Apostle is saying that *now, right now, at this present moment,* there is no condemnation for the child of God.

What comfort this is! What consolation! But notice this, that only a Christian can have this assurance. Only the born-again believer can say this. Dear reader, do you have this assurance? You can have it. Accept the Saviour and He will give you this assurance. He is saying even now, "Come!" Will you?

Verse 2: For the law of the Spirit of life in Christ Jesus made me free from the law of sin and of death.

The reason for there being "no condemnation to them that are in Christ Jesus" (v. 1) is that the believer has died with Christ and is "free from the law of sin and of death." Here, as in chapter 7, Paul speaks of law. He has used the word "law" repeatedly, that is, the law of the mind; the law of sin; the law of God; the law of the husband; and to this list must be added the Law of Moses or the Decalogue. In verse 2, it is the law of the "Spirit of life."

The law of the "Spirit of life" operates in the life of the believer, and this law is life activated by the Spirit of God. The Spirit of God always brings life, because the Holy Spirit is the personification of life. The Greek word for "life" is in the genitive case, making life the possession of or belonging to the Holy Spirit. The Holy Spirit is the life-giver. Whenever He enters a person it is for the purpose of giving life (Genesis 2:7); or for the purpose of creating eternal life (John 3:5, 6); or for the purpose of calling one to receive the Word of God (Exodus 19:9); or for the ministry of the Gospel (Acts 13:2-4). In Romans 8:2 it is for the purpose of leading the believer to live a righteous life in Christ.

The contrast between the law of the "Spirit of life" and the law of "sin and of death" is strikingly obvious. The old Law brought with it the thunderous "Thou shalt nots" of Sinai. That Law brought sin to the forefront, and vividly exhibited the evil nature in man. Man is incapable of meeting the requirements of the Holy Law of righteousness through his sinful flesh alone. This law condemns him (Romans 7:9b) and makes his sinful flesh fearfully aware of its existence. Sinful flesh cannot be reformed or adapted to live with the Holy Law. The Law excites and aggravates it, causes it to react violently in opposition to the Law, and death is its end result. In contrast to this, God provides a law that gives life. This is the "law of the Spirit of life in Christ Jesus." The Spirit gives this life through Christ. Christ Himself said, "I am the way, and the truth, and the life" (John 14:6). The ministry of the Holy Spirit in this Dispensation of

Grace is to take the things of Christ and reveal them to a regenerated sinful humanity (John 16:7-15). These "many
things" contain the truth of the holiness of the Law, which is
pure and good, in contrast with man who is permeated with sin.
These "many things" contain the judgment that results in death;
the way of forgiveness and cleansing from sin; the restoration
of fellowship and relationship with God; and the way back home
to God. All these "many things" are in Christ Jesus, and we are
led into them by the Holy Spirit, who is Christ's Agent on the
earth in this Dispensation.

Because of the foregoing, the Apostle says, "There is therefore
now no condemnation to them that are in Christ Jesus." When
we accepted the Saviour we passed out of death into the glorious
life-giving power of the Holy Spirit, and, therefore, we do not
come into judgment. The Apostle John uses the word "judgment"
in John 5:24 that Paul uses for "condemnation" in Romans 8:1.
Since we do not come into judgment, there can be no condemnation to the believer whose life is motivated by the Holy
Spirit. The believer has been "made free," loosed or unfettered.
The Greek word which is here translated "made free" is the
aorist indicative, or the historical, which expresses a past event
viewed in its entirety. Being "made free" is an historic fact;
the believer has been set free from the law of sin and death. He
has been freed from its tyranny and despotic power.

**Verse 3: For what the law could not do, in that it was weak
through the flesh, God, sending his own Son in the likeness of
sinful flesh and for sin, condemned sin in the flesh . . . :**

What could not the Law do? It could not then, and it cannot
now, work out righteousness and salvation. Why? It was not
the purpose nor is it the program of the Law to save. The Law
was not given as the means of salvation. Sinful flesh is incapable
of meeting the standard of the Law in its innate nature; the
flesh is weak and is prone to sin. The whole of chapter 7 deals
with the corruption and sinfulness of the flesh. The flesh is
evil-minded. How can corrupt flesh be brought into harmony
with the holiness, righteousness and purity of the Law? The
Law radiates holiness in the same manner as the heart circulates
blood. The flesh is the direct opposite of the Law. The Law
cannot convert the flesh. The believer's flesh is changed only
through the grave or the Rapture. The Mosaic moral Law is
continuously engaged in warfare with the flesh and sin. The

Law is not to be blamed for failure to obey it; the failure to obey is due in full measure to the weakness of the flesh.

There is another fact that must be re-emphasized. Was the Law given for the express purpose of working out man's salvation? Could the observance of the Law mean salvation for the one who diligently obeys it? This writer does not believe that the keeping of the Law could save the person keeping it. It is not the purpose of the Law, nor is it within the power of the Law to save. Does not the writer of the book of Hebrews say, "and without faith it is impossible to be well-pleasing unto him" (11:6)? We also read "whatsoever is not of faith is sin" (Romans 14:23).

The purpose of the Law was to reveal to sinful man the holiness of God, and the corruption of sin. Seeing his own inability, and the impossibility of keeping the Law of God, which is good, holy and pure in every detail, man would cast himself upon the mercy of God. God's answer to this act of repentance and confession of faith is the accomplishment of Calvary. The mercy of God, the love of God, and the compassion of God are fully displayed on the cross. By the same token, so is the righteousness of God revealed on the cross. The sinner, seeing all this and realizing the holiness of the Law, will seek forgiveness through the accomplishments of the cross. The Scriptures state, ". . . by the works of the law shall no flesh be justified" (Galatians 2:16); ". . . for if righteousness is through the law, then Christ died for nought" (Galatians 2:21); "So that the law is become our tutor (schoolmaster) to bring us unto Christ, that we might be justified by faith" (Galatians 3:24).

V. 3b: ". . . God, sending his own Son in the likeness of sinful flesh and for sin, condemned sin in the flesh. . . ." The words, "his own Son," are very emphatic. They mean the Son of Himself, God's very own Son. The Greek for these words is a reflexive pronoun. There is far more meaning conveyed in this phrase than appears at first glance. The name, Christ, who is called the Son of God Himself, implies co-equality with God; it implies His pre-existence; it implies His Deity; it implies His sinlessness; and, of necessity, it implies His conception by the Holy Spirit and His Virgin Birth.

To the author, the whole structure of the Gospel, the unique position of Christ as being the only begotten of the Father, the complete program of salvation, and the whole glorious revelation of mankind's redemption, rests upon the Virgin Birth. Negate this one truth, and the Bible is meaningless, the cross is a disaster of misconception, the Resurrection a fable, the Ascension an illusion, the Second Coming a figment of the imagination, and the disciples the victims of a satanic hoax. Granting all this to be a cruel mirage, then it must follow that Israel is not a nation, Palestine is not the Promised Land, the discoveries of archaeology are not true, and, last but not least, and the most horrible thought of all, we are not saved, there is no revelation of God, and the whole race of mankind is utterly lacking in spirituality, and no better off than cavemen. The Virgin Birth is the *foundation* and the cornerstone of the Deity of Christ, and the pledge of life everlasting for all who accept Him as Saviour and Lord.

Christ is God's Own Son in both the Old and the New Testament. "Yet I have set my king upon my holy hill of Zion. I will tell of the decree; Jehovah said unto me, Thou art my son; this day have I begotten thee" (Psalm 2:6, 7). The Hebrew word for "set" is a most interesting one. The phrase, "yet I have set my king," can be translated thus: "Yet I have offered as an oblation" (Daniel 2:46); "poured out as a libation" (I Chronicles 11:18); "as a drink offering" (Ezra 7:17; Deuteronomy 32:38). These verses from the Old Testament contain the complete prophecy of the Sonship of Christ, and His satisfactory offering for sin. It is fulfilled in Matthew 17:5; II Peter 1:17; and in other verses.

The Saviour is God Incarnate in the flesh. Because He is that, He did not and could not have come in sinful flesh or in flesh of sin, but came in the *likeness* of sinful flesh (John 1:14; Philippians 2:7; Hebrews 2:14; I John 4:2). He did not become a sinner. He knew all the protean-like shapes and disguises of sin, and all the appalling, repulsive, disgusting, detestable consequences of sin. But He never committed sin. "Which of you convicteth me of sin?" (John 8:46). He was, He is and always will be the spotless Lamb of God "that taketh away the sin of the world" (John 1:29).

V. 3b: ". . . and for sin, condemned sin in the flesh. . . :"

And concerning sin, or because of sin, He condemned and judged sin and all of its fatal allurements in the one perfect and acceptable sacrifice that paid the complete price for all sinners. Christ was God's sin-offering for all eternity. He, by offering Himself, became our Eternal High Priest. ". . . who needeth not daily . . . to offer up sacrifices . . . for this he did once for all . . . which was after the law . . . perfected for evermore" (Hebrews 7:27, 28); ". . . there is no more offering for sin" (Hebrews 10:18).

Verse 4: . . . that the ordinance of the law might be fulfilled in us, who walk not after the flesh, but after the Spirit.

The Greek word translated "ordinance" means justice, equity, the state of righteousness; so that the meaning of the English phrase, "the ordinance of the law," is to be understood as meaning, "the justice (or righteousness) of the law might be fulfilled in us who are motivated by the Spirit." Notice that it is not *by us* but *in us*. Christ, through the working of the Holy Spirit, does this for each and every believer who yields to Him. This is another way of saying "imputed righteousness." The believer can fulfill these righteous ordinances of the Law if he permits the Holy Spirit to lead, and yields to the righteous promptings of the Holy Spirit. This is the reason for the need of crucifying the flesh, which is a daily responsibility, and a constant and continuous task in which every believer must engage. In fact, if a person claims to be a Christian and does not yield to the leading of the Holy Spirit, there is every reason to doubt that he is actually a Christian.

We face a serious problem in all Christian circles, among carnal Christians as well as among those who regard themselves as fundamentalists. We have so lowered the standards of the Gospel, we have so cheapened the cross, that we not only condone carnality in the local church, but have also brought about a serious lethargy among true believers. Instead of encouraging believers to be "perfect, as your heavenly Father is perfect" (Matthew 5:48), by seeking to fulfill the lofty spiritual standards set forth in the New Testament, "according to my gospel" (Romans 2:16), we put our own faulty human interpretation upon these standards and delude ourselves into believing we are following Paul's example when he said, "I determined not to know anything among you, save Jesus Christ, and him crucified" (I Corinthians 2:2), and by so doing invite and encourage carnality in our membership. We may be filling the pews in our churches on Sunday mornings, as well as the chairs in our Sunday schools, but where are our people on Sunday evenings, and during the week-night meetings? The pastors of our congregations and we, as ministers of God, are much to blame for this lamentable "falling away" among the once faithful followers of our Lord, and, like Adam, we blame everyone and everything except ourselves; whereas, we have, ourselves, been unfaithful to our high calling by helping to create this deplorable condition in the Body of Christ. Who shall say we are not most to blame?

The New Testament does not say that all a person needs to do to become a Christian is to confess Christ as Saviour, to be baptized, to join a church, and to tithe. No! The New Testament tells us that we must walk after the Spirit; we must crucify the flesh; we must witness for Christ; we must live holy lives; we must study the Word of God; we must not forsake the assembling of ourselves together; we must look for Christ's imminent return; we must separate ourselves from worldly lusts; we must be pilgrims on this earth, not settlers; and we must be ambassadors for Christ. All this can be done only if we walk after the Spirit. Thus and thus only can the ordinance of the law be fulfilled in us.

Unless the believer is willing to walk "after the Spirit" and to do that which the New Testament sets forth in the clearest language, he is not appropriating the cross and salvation through faith in Christ which is offered him on God's terms. This is what it means to be a Christian according to God's standards as proclaimed in the New Testament. And this is precisely what Paul means in Ephesians 2:10, "For we are his workmanship, created in Christ Jesus for good works, which God afore prepared that we should walk in them." If we are to be God's workmanship in Christ Jesus, how else can we attain to this high honor except by walking "after the Spirit?"

Verse 5: For they that are after the flesh mind the things of the flesh; but they that are after the Spirit the things of the Spirit.

Carnality serves the flesh, awakens and stimulates its appetite for ever-greater indulgence in sensual enjoyments. The more the flesh is ministered to, the greater becomes its craving for more and more pleasurable indulgences. The flesh is full of lusts, it is full of sin, it is filled with envy and strife, it is activated by Satan, and is contrary to God. The flesh, being God-less, has an evil bent to its every motive, and its end is death (Philippians 3:19; Colossians 3:2).

V. 5: ". . . but they that are after the Spirit" are born again in newness of life in Christ Jesus and are alive and far removed from the ones who are "after the flesh." The lines of demarcation are drawn. Henceforth for the believer it is "either or" — either the flesh or the Spirit. The ones led by the Spirit will seek to please God in every act of life. They will live exemplary

Christian lives. They always will be about their Father's business no matter how grievously they are tempted to forget it. They will live serenely in the midst of an evil generation which is destined to be engulfed in the maelstrom of sin, but the guiding light of the Holy Spirit will save them from confusion and bring them safely into the harbor of God's eternal love in heaven.

Conversion must be followed by a holy life. God's righteousness is not revealed only at Calvary, but it is also to be illustrated in the Christian's life. "Ye are our epistle . . . known and read of all men" (II Corinthians 3:2). Just as truly as Christ was crucified on the cross, that thereby we might be saved by His Sacrifice, so must the believer be crucified with Christ and portray that crucifixion in his own Christian life.

Sanctification follows justification. So must holy living follow conversion. Justification includes the pardon of our sins and the imputation of Christ's righteousness in us, and should be followed by sanctification which comprehends separation and dedication to God in Christ Jesus. So should holy living follow conversion.

Believers who have yielded themselves to God are guarded and protected by the sovereign hand of an omnipotent God. There can be no fear in this blessed relationship since the end is eternal life with God.

Do you, who are reading these words, know this experience? Are you occupied with the things of the Spirit? Will you accept the challenge of God's Word? What is your decision? The evil consequences are great if your answer is in the negative.

Verse 6: For the mind of the flesh is death; but the mind of the Spirit is life and peace . . . :

This verse settles any doubt that might remain after reading verse 5, as to exactly what the "mind of the flesh" and the "mind of the Spirit" mean, that is, in one case death; in the other, life and peace. The mind that is occupied with earthly and carnal things is the mind that leads to death. To be carnally minded is to be without Christ. To be without Christ is to be without eternal life, which can only mean that death and hell are the inevitable end. To be carnally minded is to be dead in trespasses and sins, the condition of the lost. The works of the carnally minded are dead in God's sight. They are an abomination to God because they are the works of the flesh, "The sacrifice of the wicked is an abomination to Jehovah" (Proverbs 15:8).

The works of the flesh are all about us. There is not a place on this earth where sin and carnality do not flourish without let or hindrance, and where men and women are not living in the unrestrained lusts of the flesh, lost in licentiousness and debauchery. The end is death.

V. 6: ". . . but the mind of the Spirit is life and peace. . . ." Compared with the "mind of the flesh," what a contrast, and what dissimilarity! The "mind of the flesh" bears no resemblance to the "mind of the Spirit," and, therefore, there is no basis of comparison between them because they have nothing in common. It is like trying to find a resemblance between life and death. How can they be compared? The only thing that they may be said to have in common is that each is at the end of a path. One path is filled with turbulence, shame, dishonor, remorse, degradation, and all the evil concomitants of a carnal life, resulting at the end in death. But notice where the other path leads, and see what God does for His own! They that mind the things of the Spirit are empowered by the Holy Spirit. Their path is a path of life and peace. It is devoid of all the distressing anxieties and temptations of the first path, but is filled with the tokens of God's bountiful goodness. When a saint suffers, God comforts him and gives the grace to endure all trials (II Corinthians 12:7-9). As a father provides all the good things he can afford for his family, so our Heavenly Father gives unstintingly of heaven's blessings to those who are the followers of His Own Son.

The Psalmist when he recorded God's proclamation against the kings of the earth revealed this truth in the words, "Worship, kiss the kiss of mouth to mouth, join yourself with the Son . . . Happy are they who take refuge, who take shelter, who put their trust and confidence in Him" (elaborated translation, Psalm 2:12). Those who worship and put their trust in the Son are the ones who are motivated by "the mind of the Spirit." The end result of these redeemed ones is eternal life that begins now and never ends, plus the inward joy of their salvation all along the path of love and peace and into eternity. The showers of God's blessings upon His children begin the moment we are saved, and continue to pursue us all the days of our life until we are brought into the mansion of God's love prepared for us from before the foundation of the world (John 14:2; Psalm 23:6).

Verse 7: . . . because the mind of the flesh is enmity against God; for it is not subject to the law of God, neither indeed can it be . . . ;

This verse was dealt with in the seventh chapter, verses 21-25. Carnality is always opposed to spirituality, because each is the eternal enemy of the other, and their standards are opposite and hostile. The mind of the flesh and its enmity against God are the evil attributes which are constantly fighting against the mind of the Spirit. God detests carnality because it is the implacable foe of righteousness, and impervious to the power of the Holy Spirit, therefore beyond the reach of the Holy Spirit to do the will of God. In Christ the mind of the flesh has been slain, and God gives His believing children the weapons whereby they also may slay the mind of the flesh in themselves; namely, His Word and the Holy Spirit with which to overcome this treacherous enemy of God (Ephesians 2:15, 16).

Carnality is the adulterous child of sin, and it must be slain in the believer's life in order for him to be used as an instrument for righteousness in God's hands. Even God Himself will not slay the carnality in the believer's life, or subject the mind of the flesh to His purpose. Carnality and all of its evil spawn is sold to sin (Romans 7:14). This is why the Apostle adds the phrase, "neither indeed can it be."

The child of God who refuses to yield to the wooings of the Holy Spirit jeopardizes his usefulness to God. He misses the fellowship and comfort that God affords every follower of Christ in a world overflowing with turbulance, trials, uncertainties, and sin.

Verse 8: . . . and they that are in the flesh cannot please God.

This is the natural, logical and expected result of what the Apostle states in the preceding verses 5-7. Since the flesh is at enmity with God, they who mind the things of the flesh, who occupy themselves with worldly practices, who are actuated by carnality, who concern themselves with temporal things rather than eternal, cannot under any circumstances please God. Thus the impotency of the flesh renders it a hopeless ally in the Spirit's campaign for righteousness. The flesh must be put to death.

This contagion of carnality and all its evil accompaniments were prevalent in the church at Corinth. Like a cancer, sin was consuming the moral and spiritual fiber of the church and sin became the accepted practice of its members. The corruption that prevailed in the Corinthian church made its testimony a noxious mockery and an abomination to the Apostle. All semblance of holiness and spirituality among the members was being slowly and surely destroyed, wherefore the Apostle's denunciations were specific and scathing as recorded in the fifth chapter of I Corinthians. He dealt with their sinful practices fearlessly and mercilessly, and demanded an immediate halt to their evil conduct. Like Belshazzar's misuse of the vessels of the Temple in a licentious feast (Daniel 5:1-4), the Corinthian believers were perverting the ordinances of God in the church. The carnal mind never yields to God, nor does it know the things of God (I Corinthians 2:14).

Verse 9: But ye are not in the flesh but in the Spirit, if so be that the Spirit of God dwelleth in you. But if any man hath not the Spirit of Christ, he is none of his.

The word "ye" points directly to the believer whose life must be governed by the Holy Spirit. Carnality is not an attribute of a Spirit-led Christian. He must manifest the Spirit of Christ in every contact with his fellow Christians, and also toward his worldly friends and associates. He must be constantly striving to live a holy life which will glorify the Father and magnify the Saviour. This can be accomplished only by the Holy Spirit who dwells in every believer (I Corinthians 6:19; Galatians 4:6; Ephesians 2:22).

The child of God whose life is not motivated by the Spirit is faced with difficulties and pitfalls. He is frustrated by the temptations of the flesh, and kept in a state of indecision. He is like the man described by the Apostle James who, he said, "is like a wave of the sea driven with the wind and tossed" (1:6 KJV). How different is such a life, torn this way and that by the mind of the flesh, from a life guided and dominated by the Holy Spirit! The fruit of a Spirit-led life is love, joy, peace, resulting in a life of serenity, and making the happy believer a useful instrument for righteousness. Temptations, trials and testings are but stepping stones to a life of joyful service for the Saviour (James 1:2) and become the God-inspired incentives to holy living. As a consequence, the comfort, consolation and companionship thereby showered upon the life of the believer through the Holy Spirit gives life its zest and meaning, and causes the darkness of carnality to fade away before God's holiness in the sunlight of His presence. This is the true meaning of the words, "the Spirit of God dwelleth in you."

The Spirit of God and the Spirit of Christ are synonymous titles used to designate the Person of the Holy Spirit. God the Father, God the Son, and God the Holy Spirit is, not are, the

Triune Godhead. This holy Three-in-One is the monotheistic Trinity of the Scriptures, and is the unequivocal Scriptural affirmation of the Deity of Christ. Moreover, the abiding presence of the Holy Spirit in the life of the believer evidences the fact that He is the child of God, the possessor and inheritor of eternal life in Christ. This possession of the Holy Spirit is the "great gulf" of difference between the regenerate life and the unregenerate life (Luke 16:26). The regenerate life is motivated by the Holy Spirit, and portrays holiness, righteousness and peace in the midst of an unholy society. It is characterized by serenity, while the life of the unregenerate is turbulent, and filled with discontentment, unrest, and sin, ending in death and hell, forever separated from God.

What contrast! Which will you choose? The Saviour says, "Come!"

There is another truth in verse 9 that must not be overlooked. Paul is the apostle whom God is using to elaborate the doctrine of Justification by Faith. Yet the Holy Spirit never ceases to impress upon the believer the truth of the necessity of good works as the result and consummation of salvation. Antinomianism (the Greek word for which means "against law") is foreign to the Christian faith and the Bible. It is false teaching espoused by Johann Agricola, German Protestant teacher (1492-1566) who broke with Martin Luther, maintaining that Christians justified by faith have no need to regard the moral Law of the Old Testament. The adherents of Antinomianism pervert the Scriptures and negate the doctrine of Grace. The great argument against Antinomianism is the sixth chapter of Romans. Works are always the *result* of salvation. To this end salvation always presses (Ephesians 2:10). As sin has its evil fruits in unrighteousness, so salvation has its good fruits in righteousness. God enables His children to bear fruit through the abiding presence of the Holy Spirit in the believer (John 15:5). The believer being called a "saint" (Romans 1:7), demands that he live a life which depicts righteousness and holiness. The Holy Spirit not only *dwells* in the believer, but He also *lives* and *works* in him. This is the office of the Holy Spirit. He not only unites the believer with Christ, but He also impels the believer to work for Christ (James 2:18).

Verse 10: And if Christ is in you, the body is dead because of sin; but the spirit is life because of righteousness.

In the Greek the translation reads, "the body indeed is dead."

The word "indeed" is omitted both in the King James and the American Standard Versions. The meaning of the Greek is this: "Indeed, it is to be admitted," or, "Indeed it is true" that the unrenewed nature of man is spiritually dead before conversion under the influence of the flesh. Barnes — *Notes on Romans.*

We should bear in mind that the body of the believer is not delivered from mortal death. Every believer's body dies a natural, physical death. Only those believers who are alive in living bodies escape death at the Rapture. Death of the human body of flesh is inevitable. The marked difference between the bodies of believers and unbelievers is that the bodies of believers will be resurrected to dwell in glory forever with Christ and His saints.

In verses 9 and 10 the Apostle uses the phrases, "the Spirit of God," "the Spirit of Christ," and "Christ" interchangeably. What he is saying in verses 9 and 10 is the sum and substance of chapter 6, in which Paul presents in graphic detail the fact that the difference between life and death, sin and righteousness, eternal bliss and eternal hell, is Christ. But notice, it is Christ in *us.* Christ must live, Christ must act, Christ must speak *through* the believer. But before He can do this *through* the believer, He must be *in* the believer. For Christ to live, to move, to act in the believer, the believer must reckon all of himself, that is to say, his body, his sinful flesh, as dead. He must not yield his body as an instrument for sin. He must keep his body in subjection (I Corinthians 9:27). Carnality never represents the spirituality of Christianity. Christ is personified in the holy, dedicated and consecrated life. The believer must submit himself as an instrument for righteousness so that he can exemplify Christ in his daily life. This can be done only by the transforming power of the Gospel through the working of the Holy Spirit. The body of flesh has the seed of death within it because of sin which was transmitted to us by the sin of Adam. On the other hand, the spirit of the believer, when born from above, has Christ within it, and Christ is Life — "I am the . . . life" (John 14:6). The flesh and Christ cannot be reconciled. Although the power of Christ can overcome the flesh and ultimately destroy it, the flesh is able only to resist or ignore Christ, it can never destroy Him.

V. 10b: ". . . but the spirit is life because of righteousness." The word "spirit" in this part of verse 10 does not refer to the Holy Spirit, but to man's spirit. The phrase, "the spirit of life," is parallel to the phrase, "the body is dead," in the first half of verse 10. The word "spirit" should not be spelled with a capital "S" as shown in the King James Version. Man is an eternal soul the moment he is born whether he is saved or not. An unsaved soul will be reunited with his body at the end of the Millennium and will spend eternity in torment. The saved soul will be reunited with his body, or translated in his body from this earth at the beginning of the Tribulation, which occurs seven years prior to the Millennium, to spend eternity in bliss with Christ. Therefore, the spirit of man is life, and Christ makes the difference between heaven and hell.

The "righteousness" mentioned in verse 10b is the righteousness which the believer receives through Christ. It is the righteousness which is worked out in the believer by the Holy Spirit. Because this righteousness is worked out in us and for us, because this righteousness is not dependent upon our sinful flesh, and because it is secure in the hands of an omnipotent sovereign God, the Apostle rises to a height of sublime ecstasy in the grand ascription of praise recorded in verses 38 and 39 of this chapter.

"Where do I stand?" is an eternal question all must answer.

Verse 11: But if the Spirit of him that raised up Jesus from the dead dwelleth in you, he that raised up Christ Jesus from the dead shall give life also to your mortal bodies through his Spirit that dwelleth in you.

These words constitute a comforting promise to every believer. The Apostle is elaborating on the preceding verses of this chapter. The abiding, indwelling presence of the Holy Spirit in the believer is his assurance of eternal life and the resurrection of the body. The one thing that an individual must ascertain in his own heart is that he is saved. He must be sure that he is saved, and he can be sure because this is clearly confirmed by Scripture: "These things have I written unto you, that ye may know that ye have eternal life, even unto you that believe on the name of the Son of God" (I John 5:13); "Wherefore, brethren, give the more diligence to make your calling and election sure: for if ye do these things, ye shall never stumble" (II Peter 1:10). In view of these two pronouncements of Scripture, no one could ever doubt the reality of his salvation.

The Holy Spirit is the life-giver and He is the One who raised Christ from the dead. This same Spirit dwells in the believer at the very moment of his re-birth. He lives, He moves, He acts in every believer. The dwelling place of the Holy Spirit is

the believer's body (I Corinthians 6:19). Since this is so, it is
imperative that the believer keep his body from every defilement.
The word "if" in verse 11 does not raise a question, but, rather,
states a fact which confirms the conclusion that the Holy Spirit
indwells every believer. Verse 11 may be said to iterate this
truth, and is like a double affirmation of assurance and comfort
for every child of God.

V. 11: ". . . he that raised up Christ Jesus from the dead shall
give life also to your mortal bodies. . . ." The resurrection of
the believer is assured in this statement. God is not a God of
the dead but a God of the living, and the Holy Spirit in the
believer is a living witness to the reality of this truth. The
Holy Spirit is life and gives life. Since He raised Christ from
the dead He will do the same for us. He is the One who gives
life to every believer in all dispensations (Matthew 22:31, 32;
Mark 12:26, 27; Luke 20:37, 38). We must not lose sight of the
fact that God has reconciled us through Christ who is the
"effulgence of his glory, and the very image of his substance"
(Hebrews 1:3), who with the Father shall endure throughout
eternity (John 10:28; 14:19). As the soul, spirit and body is a
composite man here on earth, so the soul and spirit will be reunited with the new, the resurrected, body (Romans 8:23; I
Corinthians 15:49-57; I Thessalonians 4:14-18).

The Greek word which is translated "shall give life," is so
constructed that it states a positive action in the future. The
believer, Scripture assures us, need have no apprehension about
his own resurrection — ". . . being confident of this very thing,
that he who began a good work in you will perfect it until
the day of Jesus Christ" (Philippians 1:6).

V. 11: ". . . through his Spirit that dwelleth in you." The
Holy Spirit dwells in every believer, comforting him in his earthly
walk and assuring him of his eternal life. No wonder then that
the Apostle Paul with this certainty in his heart and mind wrote
to Timothy, "I know him whom I have believed, and I am
persuaded that he is able to guard that which I have committed
unto him against that day" (II Timothy 1:12). Consider what
this veteran "warrior of the cross" endured throughout his ministry! Amidst trials, torments, testings and tears, cut off from
converts and earthly friends, often shut up in prison with every
avenue of escape guarded and death looming always before
him, he could still write words of precious comfort and consolation to the believers of his own day, and to others in all succeeding ages. Thus every child of God today, as well as in Paul's

day, in spite of privations, in spite of sin, and in spite of doubts and fears may be sure of victory over sin and death. This physical body of ours is mortal and the essential essence of sin and death. Every deed performed in the flesh, every move made, every breath taken, is one step closer to the body's inevitable end. Death is the last enemy to be encountered, as well as the last enemy to be abolished (I Corinthians 15:22, 26).

Satan can do what he will, but the Holy Spirit will bring the believer through to the triumphant day of resurrection in Christ. The Spirit who raised Jesus the Man, that same Jesus, who, because of His resurrection, is the Messiah, is the self-same Spirit who lives in the believer, and will resurrect him in the same manner as the Messiah was resurrected. For the believer to be absent from the body is nothing less than to be present with the Lord (II Corinthians 5:8).

We must not lose sight of the truth that there are no differences in the actions of the Godhead. They act as One. What the Father does, the Son does, and so also does the Holy Spirit. The Father gives life (John 6:37, 44). The Son gives life and raises from the dead (John 6:40). There are many other passages in the Scriptures showing that the Father, Son and Holy Spirit act as One. Paul harmonizes the work of the Trinity in II Corinthians 13:14.

Verse 12: So then, brethren, we are debtors, not to the flesh, to live after the flesh . . . :

The flesh and its carnality are the bitter foes of the Spirit-led life. When the believer has died with Christ, he receives a new nature which becomes the life-giving principle. He is then no longer dominated by the flesh. The new birth ended that domination. He owes the flesh nothing, and is under no compulsion to cater to its appetites. The demands of the flesh need no longer be consulted inasmuch as the believer is then free to ignore its desires and lusts. What the Apostle is actually saying is, "do not let the flesh lord it over you."

We must bear in mind that the believer is the bond-slave of the Lord Jesus Christ. He is obligated to serve his new Master. The believer is a debtor to Christ, and now owes Christ everything he possesses. Every moment of his time must be devoted to his Lord. This relation of Lord and bond-slave is binding and cannot be nullified; it is kept alive by the Spirit who abides in the new nature.

Verse 13: . . . for if ye live after the flesh, ye must die; but if by the Spirit ye put to death the deeds of the body, ye shall live.

This text contains a solemn warning and a glorious promise. The warning, "ye must die," is a danger-signal of disaster — eternal death. The promise, "ye shall live," is a blessed hope — everlasting life. If this warning and promise go unheeded, grave consequences are in store for the professing Christian. There is more to being a Christian than mere confession, baptism, church membership, and tithing. Being a Christian means living "by the Spirit," and this means dedication, devotion, consecration, holy living, witnessing, fellowship with God through prayer and Bible study, and assembling together for worship with others of like precious faith. These are the essential qualifications that must distinguish every individual who dares to call himself a Christian.

V. 13a: Beyond question, these words mean that God does not tolerate carnality — "if ye live after the flesh, ye must die." The believer must segregate himself from all carnality. The Saviour's work on the cross vividly portrays the repulsiveness of sin in God's sight and thereby reveals God's holiness as the lofty goal toward which every Christian must strive. Philippians 3:8, 9: "Yea verily, and I count all things to be loss for the excellency of the knowledge of Christ Jesus my Lord: for whom I suffered the loss of all things, and do count them but refuse, that I may gain Christ, and be found in him. . . ." This exultant outburst of personal testimony on the part of the Apostle is not to be regarded as describing a state of spiritual achievement reserved only for missionaries and ministers of the Gospel, but rather as a consummation within the reach of every born-again believer. Anything less than this is failure, failure that might be dangerous and end in catastrophe.

If we are to establish New Testament churches, then let us establish them according to God's New Testament standards. Programs, drives, campaigns and schemes might bring crowds and puff up our ego, but these material manifestations of activity do not build Christian character and devotion, nor do they help to nourish the new man within the child of God. The magnificent Roman Catholic cathedrals and many costly Protestant churches are eloquent testimonies of carnality which degenerates into idolatry. Over these doors the eternal finger of God has written, "Ichabod." These blatant displays of wordliness throughout Christendom are danger-signals of God's disapproval.

The Apostle says, in verse 13a, "for if ye live after the flesh," by which he means, "according to the standards of the flesh," or "if you seek to satisfy the flesh," or to put it still another way, "if the motivating and productive powers of your life are being used to gratify the flesh," then you are living a carnal life, and, verse 13a concludes, "ye must die."

The Greek word for "ye must" is in the present indicative which denotes action and progress in the present time. This means that everyone living according to the standards of the flesh is already in the process of dying. It is as much as to say, "death to you is inevitable and you *must* die."

"The death here spoken of, as it appears from the context and from the nature of life with which it is contrasted, cannot be the death of the body either solely or mainly. It is spiritual death, in the comprehensive Scriptural sense of the term, which includes all the penal consequences of sin here and hereafter" (Chapter 6:21; 8:6; Galatians 6:8. *Epistle to the Romans* — Hodge). "If you live to indulge your propensities you will sink to eternal death" (Chapter 7:23 *Barnes' Notes* — Romans). "Ye are on the point of dying. Eternal death" (*Word Pictures in the New Testament* — A. T. Robertson). (See also Haldane — *The Epistle to the Romans*.)

The alternatives of true Christianity are sin, carnality, sensuality, and death. The seventh chapter of Romans deals with carnality. It is the evil offspring of sin, its very essence. Sin is the enemy of God and every believer must fight it in his own life. The carnality of the flesh must be kept in subjection and must never be permitted to get the upper hand. The flesh can never be harnessed for good or for God. The end thereof is death. Such is God's decree, so vividly portrayed at Calvary.

V. 13b: ". . . but if by the Spirit ye put to death the deeds of the body, ye shall live." How charged with glorious promise are these words! What comfort they contain! What a striking contrast they present to clause "a" of verse 13! What a loving Father is our God. His love transcends all human perception and imagination. God never does anything for His children that He does not see to its completion. The moment a person is saved the Holy Spirit is at work in his life. The moment we cry, "Father," we have in us the power of the Spirit to keep in subjection all carnality and sin in our lives. The Holy Spirit is that Power. He is God and He is Omnipotent. With Him at our side we cannot be defeated, because He is invincible. We can be victorious in every encounter with sin. The child of God is under no compulsion to live a defeated life. Sin and death have no dominion over the believer (Romans 6:9, 14). Indeed, they cannot have dominion since we have been bought by the Saviour. We are His and He gives us the Holy Spirit as His Representative to indwell us, and to guide us in our struggle to win victory over sin and carnality.

The believer is admonished to "put to death the deeds of the body." The body is the slave to sin and its end is death (v. 10); therefore, the fleshly activities must be put to death. How can carnality and spirituality co-exist when they are eternal enemies engaged in constant warfare? The believer need not be dejected nor give up in despair. He has the Holy Spirit to help him conquer the deeds of the body. Unless the believer puts to death the deeds of the body he shall die, is the obvious explanation of this verse.

The last three words of the second clause of verse 13 contain the glorious promise previously pointed out, the greatest of all rewards, "ye shall live," or, "ye shall have eternal life." God, the Holy Spirit, certifies this truth to the heart of every believer. He leads us now, and will continue to lead us until He brings every believer into the presence of the Saviour. The Holy Spirit is the enabling power in every born-again child of God.

Let us consider again the striking contrast presented by the alternative promises contained in verse 13: The end of carnality is death. The end of spirituality is life. The first, death, is wrought by the flesh; the second, life, is wrought by the Holy Spirit. Looked upon in the light of eternity, the pleasures of the flesh can be enjoyed only for a fleeting moment, but the punishment for this so-called enjoyment is eternal hell. On the other hand, the privations we endure in overcoming the pleasures of the flesh are likewise of but a fleeting moment's duration, but the reward for enduring these privations is the joy of righteous living here on earth, guided and guarded by the Holy Spirit, and, in the life to come, eternal joy, heaven. Which do you choose? Christ or chaos? Eternal life or eternal hell?

Verse 14: For as many as are led by the Spirit of God, these are sons of God.

The Greek word for "are led" is in the present passive. This puts the responsibility of the leading on the Holy Spirit who is the motivating power in the life of the believer. The passive form of the Greek verb gives the supremacy to the Holy Spirit in determining and directing the actions of the believer, and this is done voluntarily by the believer. The Holy Spirit is the One acting on and in the believer, and the believer must permit Him to exercise His authority, for "He who began a good work in you will perfect it until the day of Jesus Christ" (Philippians 1:6); ". . . for it is God who worketh in you both to will and to work, for his good pleasure" (Philippians 2:13).

Since the believer has been purchased by the Saviour, the believer's life is not his own. It belongs to Christ and must be empowered by the Spirit of God. He will lead the believer in the truth of God; He will bring the believer's life up to God's standards; He will lead the believer away from sin; He will conduct and accompany him along the way, and also comfort him. Lastly, He will make the believer's life productive for God in soul-winning. It will be a life pleasing to God, and will fulfill His purpose in the believer.

V. 14: ". . . these are sons of God." This is a sobering thought and negates the concept of liberalism that *all* humans are the sons or children of God. It also refutes the neo-orthodox theory of a "regenerated community." The Scriptures teach that, in the main, there are two kinds of people in the world, the saved and the lost. The ones who deny that Jesus is the Christ are the children of the devil, and they are destined to dwell with the devil in eternal hell. The ones who believe that Jesus is the Christ, who accept the accomplishments of the cross, who accept the physical resurrection of the Saviour, whose lives are dominated by the Spirit of God, and who believe in the Deity of Christ and His Virgin Birth, these, and only these, are the sons or the children of God. That the devil also has his children, see Matthew 13:38; John 8:44; Acts 13:10; I John 3:10. They are motivated by carnality, sensuality, lasciviousness, lewdness, lust, and greed. They are unthankful, unholy, lovers of pleasure, and their lives are devoted to the pursuit of sin. The devil's children are to be found in every walk of life, in every stratum of society, and in every part of the globe. They are found not only in the slums of the poor, but also in the high places of society, as well as in the courts of authority. They are the devil's possession; in fact, ". . . the whole world lieth in the evil one" (I John 5:19b).

Reader, which side are you on? Why do you halt between two opinions? Choose this day whom you will serve. If you choose the pleasures of this world with the devil, then death and hell are your inevitable end. If you choose Christ, then eternal life is your destiny. Choose you must!

Verse 15: For ye received not the spirit of bondage again unto fear; but ye received the spirit of adoption, whereby we cry, Abba, Father.

The word "ye" has direct reference to the born-again follower of Christ. When a person is saved, he does not receive the spirit of slavery or bondage that places him in a servile position. He does not become the slave of a tyrannical master who fills him with fear and dread, thereby placing him under unbearable burdens and laws. Such would be the position of the unregenerate, from which position the believer has been delivered. He has been purchased from the slave-market of sin, never again to be returned to the bondage of evil.

V. 15: ". . . but ye received the spirit of adoption, whereby we cry, Abba, Father." The believer becomes a child of God. He is liberated from fear, sin and death. He has received the spirit of adoption placing him in God's family, and he becomes an heir of God's possessions. God has not purchased him from the slave-market of sin merely to make him the slave of another taskmaster. Rather, God has redeemed the sinner and placed him in the position of His child. By sealing him in this position, God has made sure that his position will never be altered (Ephesians 1:4). God does not become the slavemaster, the judge, or the executioner from whose presence the redeemed sinner would flee. God becomes the believer's Father — Abba. The word Abba appears only three times in the New Testament, in Mark 14:36; Romans 8:15; Galatians 4:6. In the sight of God the believer becomes a child of God and is placed in a father-child relationship. Paul writes out of a Jewish heart, as the Jews always address God as Father which, in the Hebrew, is *"Av,"* and this when translated into our Lord's Aramaic mother-tongue, becomes Abba; and Abba, combined with the Greek word for Father, becomes, in English, "Abba, Father." (See comment on Romans 7:22.) The believer, therefore, is elected to a filial relationship of love. The very fact that God is now the believer's Father brings him within the protective power of God, similar to the family relationship between a human father and his child.

As our Father, God watches over us, He cares for us, He guides us, He provides for us, and showers upon us His bountiful blessings. It is a wonderful feeling to know that in the midst of our turbulent human existence, permeated as it often is with fear, dread, hate, and blood-shed, we have an Omnipotent

loving Father who watches over His own. He who notices the
fall of a sparrow, watches over His children so carefully that He
knows the number of the hairs of their head (Matthew 10:29-
31).

What a Father we have! What a wonderful Redeemer is our
Lord! What a wonderful Guide is the Holy Spirit! Let us make
sure that evidences of this "wonderful" relationship may be seen
in us, the children of our heavenly Father.

**Verse 16: The Spirit himself beareth witness with our spirit,
that we are children of God . . . :**

The Holy Spirit abides in every truly born-again believer and
He never leaves us. He is there to comfort, to guide, to instruct,
to correct, and to chastise us under all circumstances. He is
there in our joys, and also there in our adversities, no matter
how catastrophic they may seem to be. He never leaves us.

The Greek expression which is translated "beareth witness
with," is made up of two Greek words and means to testify, to
bear witness together with another, to add testimony, to be in
support of another. It is in the present indicative, denoting action in progress at the present time.

The Holy Spirit is not an emotion nor is He an idea. He is
the Third Person in the Godhead. He is real. He lives and
moves within us. He illumines the mind and comforts the heart
of the believer. The Holy Spirit does this by guiding the believer in the truth of the Word, constantly assuring the believer
that his life is secure in God. There is no need to waver or to
be in doubt as to the reality and certainty of salvation. The
Word of God states, "He that believeth on the Son of God hath
the witness in him: . . . And the witness is this, that God gave
unto us eternal life, and this life is in His Son" (I John 5:
10, 11).

The realization of this eternal life in the Son of God stabilizes
the Christian during his pilgrimage through this sin-cursed
and dying world. Since our human fears and doubts are thus
allayed, we Christians need concern ourselves only with our testimony and witness by taking advantage of the opportunities
that the Holy Spirit gives us to let our light shine to the glory of
God (Matthew 5:16). To be lackadaisical in our service is to
be unworthy of the precious gift God has bestowed upon us.
The Holy Spirit within the believer is the co-witness with "our
spirit, that we are the children of God." If we are children of
God and born from above, *and we are,* then we are positively

certain of our relationship with God, in which case we must live godly lives even in the midst of an un-Christian society that is permeated with sin, immorality and profanity, even though we are surrounded by a shameless, defiled and degenerated people. We must, in short, live our lives by the power of the Holy Spirit as though we were constantly in the presence of God.

Whether or not we acknowledge the fact of God's presence or realize its truth, we are, nevertheless, continuously in His presence. He knows our every move. He knows our every thought. He is aware of our indifference to holy living and of our lethargic attitudes. God is not unmindful of our failures, but is ever cognizant of them, and sorely grieved because of our spiritual somnolence, for all of which we are accountable to our heavenly Father. Our super-highways have signs admonishing the motorist to stay awake in order to stay alive; to drive as though a patrolman were right behind him. How much more pertinent and apropos are the warning signs of Scripture in our Christian living! They may be likened to the eternal Voice of God reminding us that His eternal Eye is always upon us no matter where we are or how occupied.

The doctrine of the Perseverance of the Saints, or Eternal Security, in which we believe, is not a license to sin. The Arminian School of Theology (see our commentary on Romans 6:15) deprecates this very important doctrine. Because Arminianism discredits this doctrine, its adherents are unaware of the fact that the Christian who believes in eternal security and cannot ever be lost, will never continue in sin habitually. Faith in a sovereign God — the God of the Bible — comprehends humility as a basic principle, the fruits of which are love for others, witnessing to them, and otherwise living exemplary lives in the midst of an evil generation and maelstrom of sin.

Does the Holy Spirit convict you of sin? Or, does He comfort you when you are confronted with it? Examine your heart, your mind, your character and your life. God's directive to us is, "Ye shall be holy; for I am holy" (I Peter 1:16). This is not an invitation, it is a command.

Verse 17: . . . and if children, then heirs; heirs of God, and joint-heirs with Christ; if so be that we suffer with him, that we may be also glorfied with him.

In Jewish law the eldest son receives the greater portion of the father's estate and becomes the head of the family after the father's death. In Roman law all children share alike. Paul was familiar with both laws, and fully understood the ramifications of and the differences between Jewish and Roman law. In Romans 8:16, 17, Paul refers to the saints as children being "joint-heirs" with Christ, which would seem to negate the Jewish Law, the law that God uses. Actually it does not. God, in the Old Testament, is the Father of Abraham, Isaac and Jacob, and of Israel. In the New Testament the Saviour likewise refers to God as Father, and Paul states in Romans 8:15, "whereby we (believers) cry, Abba-Father." God's laws have not changed. They are the same under Law and under Grace.

The Apostle refers to all born-again believers as children. Under Jewish Law, Christ is the Father's first-born and inherits all things (John 13:3; 16:15; Hebrews 1:2, "hath at the end of these days spoken unto us in his Son, whom he appointed heir of all things . . ."). Therefore, our Lord has received all of the Father's possessions. Since this is so and we are in Christ, we have become the co-heirs and co-participants with Christ, or, as Paul says, "joint-heirs." We have all that Christ has. We share in all His eternal possessions, including eternal life. What a heritage we possess! (Ephesians 1:11).

However, there are two sides to this heritage, just as there are two sides to every coin. Looking again at verse 17 ". . . if so be that we suffer with him . . ." let us examine it more closely: The Greek word for "if so be" is a conditional participle in the indicative mood which assumes a fact, so that the expression "if so be," means, as is really the case.

To suffer with Christ is a privilege; in fact, every believer who has really lived for Christ has suffered. This suffering for Christ is not the exception but the rule, and is inevitable. The world is so permeated with sin and debauchery that it literally loathes those who strive to live the Christian life. Sin is the mortal enemy of holiness and righteousness. Anyone who takes his stand beneath the banner of true holiness will be the target for all the venomous darts of Satan. Beyond all doubt there is no limit to the suffering to be endured for Christ. History records innumerable cases of the suffering of true Christians for Christ. Suffering and persecution are the believer's earthly companions. This is the accepted norm (II Timothy 3:12), and is the refining and polishing process that God uses to condition His children for the glory that lies ahead.

We do not fully appreciate physical health until we lose it. Nor do we appreciate joy to the fullest extent until we know the meaning of sorrow. Neither can we fully comprehend the meaning of eternal life until we are born again, and are able to grasp the full realization of our escape from the doom and anguish of eternal hell. When all this is fully understood and in some degree experienced, then, "the things of this world grow strangely dim." They are revealed to be immaterial and irrelevant to the true life of the spirit. The things of this world are like chaff that the wind of tribulation and suffering blows away, because these things are of transitory importance and meaningless in the light of the Gospel and in the sufferings of Christ. To live *for* Christ is to suffer *with* Christ. In the final analysis, to lose one's life for Christ is but to find it in Him and to reign with Him (Matthew 10:39; 16:24; II Timothy 2:11, 12; Revelation 3:21, and 21:7) and to participate in His glorification. We, who are the saints, will be exalted to the same glory to which Christ has been raised.

Verse 18: For I reckon that the sufferings of this present time are not worthy to be compared with the glory which shall be revealed to us-ward.

Privations, persecutions, discomforts, distresses, hunger, and suffering, have produced some of the greatest saints in the history of our planet, "of whom the world was not worthy." A person who has never been hungry, persecuted or ill, cannot completely sympathize with those who have experienced these vicissitudes; nor does such a person know what life really is. How can one fully appreciate a mountain-peak experience unless one has previously dwelt in the valley of life? This is what the Apostle is saying when he makes the comparison between the suffering for Christ's sake and the glory that awaits the sufferer. The glory to "be revealed to us-ward" transcends all present sufferings. Our sufferings and sorrows are only temporary. At best they cannot last much longer than three score and ten years of our earthly duration. The glory that awaits us is eternal. Our trials should be nothing more than stepping-stones to glory.

If the child of God were to put in a balance all the sufferings that he must endure for Christ, the glories of eternity would far outweigh the sufferings. God uses the trials of our earthly life as the whetstone upon which to sharpen our hope for the glories of eternity. Without these sufferings and the blessed hope of joy to come, life would be dull, drab, meaningless and flavorless. And, in the final analysis, adversities are inextricably a part of earthly existence, and the struggle to overcome them is the exercise that builds the muscle of life. Without this spiritual muscle life's adversities would be insurmountable.

These are the hazards that attend a life of true Christianity in our generation. The average Christian does not know the meaning of privation and suffering, and has never had to endure any of these "inconveniences." He is generally preoccupied with a desire for the luxuries of life, which, in the light of the cross, are trivial and meaningless. This preoccupation with the "creature comforts" of life is one reason why the great majority of Christians live lethargic lives. They are spiritually listless and indifferent. Some of them have reached a state like that of the Lotus-Eaters where "slumber is more sweet than toil," and they refuse to be aroused. Others, like Jonah, have become totally indifferent to the spiritual storms of this world, and are as fast asleep as Jonah was: "But Jonah was gone down into the innermost parts of the ship; and he lay, and was fast asleep" (Jonah 1:5). Like Jonah, so we may be cast into a sea of storm. Will the Lord prepare a great fish to swallow us up even as Jonah was swallowed up, and bring us to usefulness as a witness for Christ? Prepare! Take heed! Awake! Why sleepest thou?

If a Christian has not suffered for Christ he is not interested in Christ's return. He is comfortable in this sinful world. One way for a Christian to be comfortable in this sinful world is to live as an unbeliever and not as a Christian. A godly life is invariably a persecuted life. The Apostle was fully aware of this. He was despised, maligned, jailed, beaten, chained, and starved for the cause of Christ. He said, ". . . I bear branded on my body the marks of Jesus" (Galatians 6:17; I Corinthians 4:9; II Corinthians 11:23). He was finally martyred.

However, Paul never despaired. He fought the fight of faith, he ran the race, he pressed on toward the prize of the high calling of God. He could boast of his genealogy, he could boast of his religious background and training; and he could also have boasted of his membership in the Sanhedrin, of his life as a religious Jew, and of his dedication and devotion to his religious convictions. But all these human honors and glories he considered as refuse in the light of the Gospel and Christ (Philippians 3:8). He was willing to suffer all humiliations and privations and didn't even deem them worthy enough to be compared to the glory which he was to receive with Christ.

When the Apostle speaks of "the sufferings of this present time" (verse 18), he is speaking of the sufferings of the saints in the first century. The early saints knew what suffering meant.

They were tortured and torn to death by wild beasts in the arenas of Rome. They were persecuted in prisons; beaten with stripes; burned at the stake; executed on crosses; and starved in dungeons. Yet Paul says that these experiences are not even worthy of mention when compared with the glory that lies ahead for the saint. What do we know of such trials and experiences? If we suffer with Christ, we shall reign with Him. If we do not, then what? Ponder these truths: If the saints in the first century considered it a privilege to suffer for Christ, we should have the same mind in our generation. No mathematician could possibly produce an equation that would show the sufferings of the saints in this present life as worthy of comparison with the glories to be enjoyed in the life hereafter.

At Christ's return the glories that are His shall be fully revealed. Christ in all His splendor, in all His deity, in all the glory that He had with the Father from eternity shall be disclosed, uncovered and made manifest. The Greek word for "revealed" has an eschatological implication. When will this revelation take place? At His Second Coming, of course; "When the Son of man shall come in his glory . . . then shall he sit on the throne of his glory" (Matthew 25:31). Is this to be at the Rapture (I Thessalonians 4:17) or at His visible return to this earth? It will be when He comes to the earth in His full glory and honor, to assume His Regal Power and the throne promised Him prior to His birth (Luke 1:31-33).

We must take a second look at the conditions attending these events. Paul states (verse 18), "the glory which shall be revealed to us-ward." This being the case, all believers will have to be brought into Christ's presence before He can come with them. He will have given the saints their rewards after they have given their accounts of the deeds done on earth, as recorded by Paul in I Corinthians 3:10-15, and II Timothy 4:8. These are the chosen ones who will return to earth with Him. This phase of eschatology being completed, the saints are then ready to participate in His glory on earth, since His Heavenly Glory has already been revealed to us.

When our Lord returns to earth He will be accompanied not only by His saints, but also by an angelic host (Matthew 25:31). Here He will judge the Gentile nations and set up His Messianic Kingdom, restoring the glories of the Davidic Throne; and the people of Israel will become the earthly ambassadors of His Kingdom (Isaiah 2:2-4; 60:13; 61:6; and Zechariah 8:23). Christ will then be in His full glory as King of kings and Lord of lords, and His glory will be seen by all the peoples of the earth.

Fellow Christians, let us awake from our spiritual lethargy, let us take the Gospel of Christ to a world engulfed in sin. Be willing to suffer all privations and persecutions for Him. Be willing to go even to regions beyond the camps of our friends and relatives. Let us be willing to forsake the pleasures of this life for the cause of Christ, and to yearn with purer hearts for the glories of eternity. Count it all joy, count it a precious privilege to suffer for Christ, for if we ". . . are partakers of Christ's sufferings, rejoice; that at the revelation of his glory also ye may rejoice with exceeding joy" (I Peter 4:13).

Verse 19: For the earnest expectation of the creation waiteth for the revealing of the sons of God.

The Greek word translated "earnest expectation" appears only twice in the New Testament, here and in Philippians 1:20. The term means to watch with neck outstretched, concentrating on one single object so intently as to disregard everything else, as if one were standing on tiptoe and straining forward to get a closer and better look.

Moreover, Paul expresses in verse 19 the truth that in the Fall in the Garden of Eden all mankind, as well as all creation, animate and inanimate, was affected by Adam's sin. The ramifications and ravages of sin are prevalent in everyone and everything.

When the Messiah returns in all His Glory, He will not come alone, but He will come with His own to rule and to reign over a redeemed creation. This is in fulfillment of all the prayers, hopes, and prophecies of the prophets of the Old Testament: Isaiah foresaw it, 2:2-4; 11:6-10; 45:14-17, 22-25; and 60:4-9. Jeremiah foreshadowed it, 30:18-24; 31:31-34. Micah foretold it, 4:1-5. Zechariah prophesied it, 8:20-23. Israel hopes for it, Isaiah 43:9-21, and the saints of the Lord must be ready for it, "looking for the blessed hope and appearing of the glory of the great God and our Saviour, Jesus Christ" (Titus 2:13). A large number of saints in this generation have lost sight of this glorious hope. Have you?

The Greek word that is translated "waiteth" (verse 19) is a comprehensive word not easily explained. The thought implied is that creation is looking away from itself, eagerly expecting and welcoming "the revealing of the sons of God." It is a hope that keeps constantly hoping, i.e., it is now existing and will continue until the event is consummated. In other words, creation is now eagerly waiting for the fulfillment of this great event. If creation is living in this state of expectancy, what should be the attitude of the sons of God?

Verse 19 brings to the forefront all the hopes, ambitions, desires, and longings of the Apostle. He looks away from his imprisonments, persecutions and privations, from his sufferings and heartaches, from all the tormenting trials he has endured since his salvation and dedication to the preaching of the Gospel, and is now obsessed with an insatiable desire to be with his Lord and to accompany that Lord upon His return to this earth when He comes back to destroy all the cancerous corruption of sin. To Paul, the best of this life on earth is hell, compared with the joys to be his in heaven.

There is also a prophetic truth stated in verse 19 that is in chronological order according to premillennial interpretation. The Revelation of the sons of God, which must be preceded by the Rapture, occurs prior to the Restoration of the creatures, or humanity, the order being; first, the Rapture; second, the Revelation; third, the Restoration. As to the word creation, meaning creatures, the Jewish teachers referred to the Gentiles as "creatures": "all the prayer of the creatures" (Bereshit Rabba Tarash, 13, fol. 11. 3.; also, Mark 16:15; Colossians 1:23).

Most of the right-minded Gentile nations have sought for peace. Every right-minded person in this world longs for peace. Only the morbid and perverted individuals among us, the demon-possessed, and the satanic-inspired nations have not sought for and do not now seek for peace. In the main, peace has been the heart cry of all peoples. Except for predatory savages and nations, peace is the hope and desire of all creatures. However, many law-abiding peoples and nations fail to realize that peace can be had only according to God's terms and standards. Christ is the world's only hope for peace. He is the creator, possessor and maker of peace. "The earnest expectation of the creation," (verse 19) will be realized, as when God spoke to the residue of His people and said, ". . . I will shake all nations, and the desire of all nations shall come" (Haggai 2:7, KJV).

This writer believes that the word "creation" embraces all creation, and includes the earth and all created beings and animals as well as man. This entire creation is subject to sin and will be redeemed only when the Messiah returns and sets up the Davidic Kingdom on earth with Jerusalem as its capital and Israel as its earthly emissary.

When the Gentile nations see "the revealing of the sons of God," the Saviour will have been accepted by Israel, and not only will there be peace between Israel and her Messiah, but among the nations also. (See my commentary on Romans 2:9, 10 — another place in this Epistle where the pre-tribulation-rapturist position is substantiated.) It is evident that this truth was believed by the Apostle Paul. Do we need a better authority for this truth?

Verse 20: For the creation was subjected to vanity, not of its own will, but by reason of him who subjected it, in hope . . .

This verse is an elaboration of the Fall. Because of the willfulness of Adam, because of his disobedience, because of his one sinful act of eating the prohibited fruit, God cursed the ground, and the whole creation was made subject to a blight, a blemish, a flaw, and an imperfection from which it has not recovered. The consequences of that one deliberate sinful act of Adam was more far-reaching than he could possibly have foreseen. His sin unleashed the power of Satan so that it reached every part and aspect of creation.

Creation was placed under the dominion of Adam, ". . . Be fruitful, and multiply, and replenish the earth, and subdue it; and have dominion over the fish of the sea, and over the birds of the heavens, and over every living thing that moveth upon the earth" (Genesis 1:28). When Adam sinned all creation was made subject to sin, Adam included. The sentence of God's subjection is recorded in Genesis 3:14-19. The defects and the degradation of creation, because of sin, are prevalent and obvious. Creation moans and groans because of its subjection to the folly and vanity of the Fall (Isaiah 24:4-7; Jeremiah 12:4; and Joel 1:15-20). How far-reaching is that one sinful act of Adam! ". . . cursed is the ground for thy sake . . ." (Genesis 3:17). This was God's reaction to Adam's action.

But notice the last words of verse 20: ". . . in hope . . ." Far above all sin and degradation, as high as heaven is from earth, reigns a Holy God Who is ready to offer and provide the way out of this sin-cursed creation; a Holy God, shining like the Morning Star above the devastating consequences of sin, and holding out salvation and hope to all who will accept it: ". . . he shall bruise thy head, and thou shalt bruise his heel" (Genesis 3:15). The wounding of the Messiah's heel is not a permanent wound, but the wounding of Satan's head is fatal.

The Rabbinic commentary by Onkelos on this verse is, "He

shall pound to pieces thy head and thou shalt pound to pieces his heel." The Palestinian Targum testifies that in Genesis 3:15 there is promised a healing of the bite in the heel from the serpent, which is to take place "at the end of the days, in the Days of King-Messiah." In the Palestinian Midrash of Genesis, Bereshita Rabba 12, we find these words: "The things which God created perfect, since man sinned, have become corrupt, and do not return to their proper condition until the son of Perez, the Messiah comes." This is what the Apostle John states in I John 3:8.

When God said, "Look unto me, and be ye saved, all the ends of the earth; for I am God, and there is none else" (Isaiah 45:22), God put the cross and Saviour in the very center of salvation. Thus did our God provide a way out of the corruption brought about by the Fall.

The New Testament says the same things that the Old Testament says. The same God speaks in both Testaments. In the Old Testament God says, "Look unto me, and be ye saved," and this is repeated in the New Testament by God the Son, "As Moses lifted up the serpent in the wilderness, even so must the Son of man be lifted up; that whosoever believeth may in him have eternal life" (John 3:14, 15). The writer of the book of Hebrews says, "looking unto Jesus the author and perfecter of our faith" (12:2). The plan of salvation has always been the same, whether in the Garden of Eden or in Gethsemane, whether from the cross on Golgatha's Hill, or on Mt. Olivet at the Ascension, or at the revelation of our Lord's final glory when He returns to the Mount of Olives.

It is to the Mount of Olives that all creation looks. This is where the "hope" of verse 20 will be fully realized. As creation now groans, it will yet sing. The groaning is neither final nor fatal. Creation will sing her song of redemption, but it must have its minister of music. Who is its minister of music? It is none other than Israel: "Sing, O heavens; and be joyful, O earth; and break forth into singing, O mountains: for Jehovah hath comforted his people, and will have compassion upon his afflicted" (Isaiah 49:13, 61:6; Psalm 98:3-9). The eyes of creation have been fastened on this sight for millenniums. Reader, where are *your* eyes fastened?

Verse 21: . . . that the creation itself also shall be delivered from the bondage of corruption into the liberty of the glory of the children of God.

As the Fall brought creation into subjection and made it the slave of corruption, so creation will be liberated from this slavery when the saints, referred to in this verse as "the children of God," are delivered and brought into the liberty of the rightful glory which the Saviour has accomplished. (This writer believes that the word here should be translated "creation" as it is in the ASV, rather than "creature" as in the KJV, in the light of what follows in verse 22.)

The Greek word which is translated "shall be delivered" is in the future indicative passive, making the phrase to mean that deliverance "from the bondage of corruption" is already an accomplished fact. Our deliverance is certain, and nothing can alter this future condition, since it has been sealed with the blood of God's Own Son. But it must wait for the appointed time when this will be fully realized and fulfilled. ". . . Sit thou at my right hand, until I make thine enemies thy footstool" (Psalm 110:1). (Also look at commentary on 8:19, 20, page 263 ff.)

Verse 22: For we know that the whole creation groaneth and travaileth in pain together until now.

The Apostle in this verse is explaining verse 21, as verse 20 explains verse 19. Or, to put it another way, the truth contained in verse 19 is substantiated in verse 20, just as the truth presented in verse 21 is substantiated in verse 22. The Greek phrase translated "groaneth and travaileth in pain together," which appears here is the only place it appears in the New Testament. The word "travaileth" has the meaning of travailing with birth pains. Every segment of creation groans and moans in pain, waiting to be delivered from its subjection to vanity, as a woman in travail hath sorrow, ". . . but when she is delivered of the child, she remembereth no more the anguish, for the joy that a man is born into the world" (John 16:21). Everything in creation is looking for deliverance "from the bondage of corruption" (v. 21) which will be the day of redemption.

Judaism believes that the days preceding the coming of the Messiah are to be turbulent, marked by destruction, devastation, persecution and bloodshed. The killing will be so great that blood will flow like rivers. The Apostle John foresaw the very same thing in Revelation 14:18-20, which Jeremiah foresaw six centuries before and recorded in his prophecy 30:6, 7. What a day of groaning that will be! But the pain of tribulation shall give birth to the day of Glory. And Israel "shall be saved out of it"!

When the persecutions of the Israelites in Egypt became too difficult to bear, God heard the cry of His people and sent Moses to deliver them. These persecutions under Pharaoh gave birth to the nation Israel.

When the turmoil of the howling mob at the crucifixion ceased and Christ's followers laid His body in the tomb, all their glorious hopes of His triumphant reign on earth died within them. At the blackest hour of disillusion and despair, overwhelmed with discouragement, grief-stricken and heart-broken, their very lives shattered, our Lord's followers fled in fear and trembling and disappeared into hiding. Furtively, on the third day, in the dark of early morning, one of the women crept back to the tomb, and, seeing the stone rolled away, ran and called two of the disciples. A few others had come with spices for anointing (embalming) the crucified One (Mark 16:1-3; Luke 24:1). These few faithful ones, filled with grief and pain, came to the tomb expecting to find their Lord's body, but when they saw the place was empty they supposed, at first, the body had been stolen, and, not knowing the Scripture, that "he must rise again from the dead" (John 20:1-10) returned to their homes.

But Mary remained, weeping. ". . . so, as she wept, she stooped and looked into the tomb; and she beholdeth two angels in white sitting, one at the head, and one at the feet, where the body of Jesus had lain. And they say unto her, Woman, why weepest thou?" (John 20:11-13). She turned and beheld the living Christ! He was risen! He spoke to her! "Mary! . . . Touch me not; for I am not yet ascended unto the Father: but go unto my brethren, and say to them, I ascend unto my Father and your Father, and my God and your God" (John 20:16, 17).

In an instant, despair was turned to joy for Mary. As the news of the resurrection reached the disciples, hopelessness was turned into rejoicing. And where did this miracle start? At the tomb where "death is swallowed up in victory." Grief and loss turned out to be the birthpangs of redemption.

So shall it be in the days preceding the coming of the Lord. The world will be torn in strife. Ruin and devastation will be on every side. Death will be rampant among the inhabitants of the earth. Dead bodies will be seen everywhere, stacks of them in astronomical numbers. Sixty million, six hundred and sixty-six thousand, six hundred and sixty-six people killed in just *one* battle (Revelation 9:16-18). It will take seven months to bury these corpses (Ezekiel 39:12); and seven years to burn the debris (Ezekiel 39:9). Gentile sin will then have filled its cup to the brim, and a world-wide revolution against Jehovah and His Messiah will be in full force (Psalm 2). The battle lines will be drawn, the slaughter will begin, the earth will quake, the heavens tremble, and the sun and the moon will be darkened. But Jehovah is on the scene. See Joel 2:4-11; Isaiah 13:9-16; 34:1-8; and others. These are but the birth-pangs of redemption for "all creation," in the full meaning of verse 22. The creation has already begun its groaning and travailing for that day.

Verse 23: And not only so, but ourselves also, who have the first-fruits of the Spirit, even we ourselves groan within ourselves, waiting for our adoption, to wit, the redemption of our body.

Although the clarity and compactness of Paul's language cannot be improved upon, it is always a joy to the believer to "amplify" Paul's phraseology in order to apply it more specifically to our own condition, thus: "Not only does creation groan, but we the saints, the blood-bought believers, who have tasted the eternal joy and bliss of the 'things God prepared for them that love him' (I Corinthians 2:9), also cry and groan in this sin-surrounded life."

The saint of God who lives close to the Saviour longs for the day when he shall be taken out of this world. The ungodliness and the sensual lusts of this life make godly living an unending battle. It is far from an easy task to live soberly and righteously in the midst of degradation and sin, but doing so has its glorious reward because of the "earnest expectation" (v. 19) which we have of "looking for the blessed hope and appearing of the glory of the great God and our Saviour Jesus Christ." (Titus 2:13).

The expression in v. 23, "who have the first-fruits of the Spirit," is better translated, "having the first-fruits," since it is a present participle. The believer is in constant and continuous possession of the first-fruits of the Spirit, which are listed in detail in Galatians 5:22, along with the promise of increased fruit-bearing in John 15:5. The realization of the possession of these first-fruits *by* the believer is testified to by the indwelling and abiding presence of the Holy Spirit *in* the believer.

Every saint who is constantly striving to live a truly Christian life in this sin-laden world is often troubled and deeply saddened because of the sinfulness around him; or, as Paul so graphically puts it, the unrighteousness of this present world and the bondage of corruption which holds the entire creation in thrall, causes us to "groan within ourselves" (v. 23).

The thought in the Greek phrase, "waiting for our adoption," portrays the idea of "earnest expectation" expressed in verse 19 (as the verb "waiteth" in v. 19, is the same verb as "waiting" in verse 23). The thought contained in this phrase, "waiting for our adoption," expresses the idea that the saint of God is eagerly waiting to receive his inheritance, just as a son might wait to receive his inheritance from his earthly father. In biblical times the family estate, in the main, was divided among the sons. So here, in this passage, the thought is that the saint of God will receive his inheritance for which he has been waiting with "earnest expectation." The Greek word for "adoption" means being accepted as a son.

The phrase in this verse (23), "the redemption of our body," also has reference to our "adoption" when we believers receive our *completed* adoption at the time of the Rapture or the Resurrection. This Greek word for redemption means to loosen or to unbind, to set free, to liberate as from a prison. The flesh hinders, limits, and is a burden to the new man. The Rapture will be the liberation for which the mature Christian waits and longs. What a day that will be when we believers are freed from our body of death and enter into our complete inheritance as the sons of God! (Ephesians 1:14; II Corinthians 1:22). When we are released from our earthly bodies we enter into our completed redemption which was begun by the Holy Spirit through the accomplishment of the cross (Philippians 1:6).

Verse 24: For in hope were we saved: but hope that is seen is not hope: for who hopeth for that which he seeth?

Webster's dictionary defines the word "hope" thus, "to desire with expectation or with belief in the possibility of obtaining; desire, trust, reliance."

Our faith in the Lord Jesus Christ is the foundation for our hope. But the word "hope" in the Scriptures is not an empty abstraction, but a concrete reality in that it is based upon the Word of God both living and written (Hebrews 6:18, 19). Our hope *is in* a Sovereign God and an Omnipotent Saviour, "For thou art my hope, O Lord Jehovah:" (Psalm 71:5; 39:7; Jeremiah 14:8; 17:13; 50:7; Ephesians 4:4; I Thessalonians 5:8; Colossians 1:27; ". . . which is Christ in you, the hope of glory").

The Greek word translated, "we are saved" (KJV), is more accurately translated, "were we saved" (ASV), since it is in the past tense. Our faith in the Messiah gave us eternal life the moment we placed our trust in Him. We received salvation immediately and we have it now. The *completion* of our salvation, when we are brought into our full inheritance as the mature sons of God upon the redemption of our body, can be stated with such full assurance that Paul puts it in the past tense. We have this full assurance now, but the actual accomplishment of our *completed* salvation must wait for the Rapture or the Resurrection. (The Alexandrine and the Sinaitic manuscripts use the word "expect" instead of "hope.")

At the present time this hope of our completed salvation, the redemption of our body, is not visible to human eyes. If it were we would not have this "earnest expectation" or hope for it. One does not hope for something that he already possesses. The Christian has this hope certified to him by the Holy Spirit written with the blood of Jesus Christ our Lord. The believer has already experienced the first-fruits of it and waits for its completion. In God's sight, it is already a completed reality. Praise His Holy Name!

Verse 25: But if we hope for that which we see not, then do we with patience wait for it.

The Gospel gives meaning and content to a believer's life. It is only a Christian who is certain of eternal life. Only a Christian can look forward to eternity without apprehension, fear, doubt, or qualm. The abiding presence of the Holy Spirit allays all fears of an after life. He is our Comforter whom the Saviour promised to send (John 16:7). He is our Paraclete, our Intercessor, the One appointed to be our Advocate. He is the One called to aid and support the believer. Every Christian hereby knows his own destiny. He is certain that even though every step he takes brings his body closer to the grave, that same step brings his spirit closer to eternity and into God's eternal Presence. Even in this life, permeated as it is with tears and trials in the midst of an adulterous generation and surrounded on every hand by the lusts of the flesh and the pride of life, the child of God is at peace because his eternal destiny is covenanted by God Himself.

This hope, this exultant confidence, is a living reality in the life of the saint. He waits for the fulfillment of his salvation with joy, stedfastness, longsuffering, meekness, temperance and fortitude, purified by that blessed hope (I John 3:3) of a day to come when he shall see Him and be like Him. This is the amplified meaning of the Greek word translated "patience."

What assurance! What bliss! If you, who read these words, will put your trust in Him, this blessed hope can be yours.

Verse 26: And in like manner the Spirit also helpeth our infirmity: for we know not how to pray as we ought; but the Spirit himself maketh intercession for us with groanings which cannot be uttered . . . ;

As hope is the sustaining factor in the believer's life, so, in like manner, is the Holy Spirit the sustaining power in the believer's life. Within himself, in his own strength, through his own ability, the believer is unable to maintain the spiritual power he needs to achieve a righteous life. The abiding presence of the Holy Spirit gives him the divine energy he must have to overcome the evil inherent in his flesh. The text before us (v. 26) states the source of all the spiritual power needed in the believer's life. The saint of God has the Holy Spirit on his side. With God as his constant companion he can overcome all evil. This is the meaning of the Greek word translated "helpeth"; it also means to take hold with another. The Holy Spirit shares the believer's burdens.

We know not how to pray. We do not know what is necessary for our good. We may ask for the wrong thing at the wrong time. We may ask for something that might lead us into problems and difficulties. The Holy Spirit intercedes for us, and, as our censor and prayer partner, brings only that which is best for us into the presence of the Father.

The intercession of the Holy Spirit on our behalf, as stated here, is made "with groanings which cannot be uttered." Even the Holy Spirit struggles with the carnal nature of the believer, the flesh, and He does it with unutterable groanings.

It is interesting to note that the classical Greek gives a second meaning to this word "unutterable," or "cannot be uttered." It is used by various writers with the meaning of a shout of victory, a war-cry, or battle-shout. This could make the phrase mean that the "groanings" of the Holy Spirit are really shouts of victory in this war against the flesh. God is invincible; therefore, the victory of the Holy Spirit is assured. The believer must permit the Holy Spirit to work through him.

Verse 27: . . . and he that searcheth the hearts knoweth what is the mind of the Spirit, because he maketh intercession for the saints according to the will of God.

The Greek word for "searcheth" is better translated searching since it is a present participle. The searching of the heart of man can be done only by God, for He not only searcheth, but He also *knows* what is in a man's heart, I Samuel 16:7; I Kings 8:39; Jeremiah 17:9, 10).

God the Father is man's heart-searcher. The saint of God is indwelt by the Holy Spirit. Therefore, God the Father and God the Holy Spirit know what is best for the saint. The Father fully knows and understands the unutterable groanings of the Holy Spirit. The Apostle urges the saints at Philippi to, "Have this mind in you, which was also in Christ Jesus . . ." (Philippians 2:5). In other words, think as Christ thinks. Set your mind on things that are above. We are to have godly thoughts because we are God's children. This thinking will be done under the guidance of the Holy Spirit, and He is constantly making intercession for us according to God's will.

To be in God's will is the most important thing in the Christian life. God's will and God's work are not the same. A saint can be in God's work and be completely out of God's will. (By God's work this writer means full-time ministry.) The two must be kept separate.

The Holy Spirit is the only One who knows God's will in every believer's life. The Spirit of God, alone, must guide the believer. He will do so if the believer permits Him. The Christian who is desirous of doing God's will must think, act, and move by the guiding power of the Holy Spirit. Only then will the saint be in God's will. Is not all this the true definition of the word saint? Does not the Psalmist voice the heart-cry of the saint, "Search me, O God, and know my heart: Try me, and know my thoughts: And see if there be any wicked way in me, And lead me in the way everlasting" (Psalm 139:23, 24)?

Verse 28: And we know that to them that love God all things work together for good, even to them that are called according to his purpose.

To the young saint who is experiencing dire need under trying circumstances, this is a perplexing verse. The mature saint, on the other hand, who knows sorrow and suffering, disaster and distress, takes great consolation in this verse. Saints who love God and are the called ones do not ask Why? Asking why denotes hesitation and wavering (James 1:6 KJV), and is characteristic of Christian immaturity. God does not entrust a weak and vacillating Christian with difficult and important tasks. For such

God chooses only the perfect and upright, ... who is able to hold fast his integrity in the face of merciless temptation. A classic example of such a man in the ancient world was the patriarch Job (2:3-6). God permitted Satan to take everything away from him except his life and a foolish wife who urged him to "curse God, and die" (2:9 KJV). But Job showed his spiritual maturity and integrity by replying, ". . . the Lord gave, and the Lord hath taken away; blessed be the name of the Lord" (Job 1:21 KJV). A cursory reading of the first few verses of Job chapter 1, gives us God's estimate of Job. Job thanked God for considering him trustworthy and willing to endure the difficult and trying experiences he suffered at the hands of Satan. Polycarp, the apostle of John, at his martyrdom said, "I thank thee, my Father, that Thou hast chosen me worthy for this hour."

V. 28: "To them that love God" is better translated "to them loving God." It is a present participle in the Greek. To this writer this phrase "to them loving God," means to them whose love is a God-given love, and to whom loving God is their pursuit in life, their objective. The Greek word for love, *agapao*, is the love of God to man and man to God. It is a holy love and born of the Holy Spirit, ". . . because the love of God hath been shed abroad in our hearts through the Holy Spirit . . ." (Romans 5:5).

Since loving God is the Christian's grand purpose in life, God will work everything for his good. We might not understand at the time why difficulties are being heaped upon us. None of us possesses perfect vision when it relates to the future, but we all have 20-20 hindsight. We walk through the valley of trials with our sight beclouded by tears, but when we reach this mountainpeak and are able to look back from this new vantage point, we can clearly see God's loving hand and heart. God uses our tears in this life to mix the mortar for the stairs leading to eternity. "They that sow in tears shall reap in joy" (Psalm 126:5). "Yea, and all that would live godly in Christ Jesus shall suffer persecution" (II Timothy 3:12). The devil hates the child of God whose life is spent in love and labor for God.

Jewish teachers believed in a life of love and labor for God, and taught it on the authority of Deuteronomy 32:6: "Is he not your Father, who created you?" God's love for His children is often revealed more clearly during times of hardship and trouble. "Whatsoever heaven does is for the best" (Berahhot 60b). "This is also for good." The Hebrew expression, *Gam zeh Ltovah* (even this is for good), is a Jewish idiom which this writer has heard from childhood from his parents and grandparents. The

Old Testament is the history of Israel and their dealings with God. Through slavery and bitter suffering, through fire and desolation, through dispersion and captivity by their enemies, the victim of God's overflowing wrath because of sin and disobedience, God has been dealing with His people to one glorious end, that He might bring them into complete fellowship with Himself in everlasting lovingkindness, and shower upon them the overflowing measure of His mercy and blessing (Isaiah 54:1-8, 17; 63:9).

V. 28b: ". . . to them that are called according to his purpose." Not any are called but those whom God purposes to call. In the New Testament the word "call" is used of the divine call or invitation to enter into the Kingdom (Hebrews 3:1). It is a call that comes from God. Therefore, the called ones are the saints of God. No one is ever born again apart from the Holy Spirit who calls every child of God to repentance and eternal life. This is a call to true Christianity (Romans 1:7; I Corinthians 1:2; ". . . called saints").

The Apostle is beginning to develop the doctrine of the Sovereignty of God in this verse (28). This doctrine is one of the truths that Paul said he wanted to impart to the saints in Rome ". . . that I may impart unto you some spiritual gift, to the end ye may be esablished . . ." (Romans 1:11). The Sovereignty of God is Old Testament teaching: God called Abraham, Genesis 12:1-3. He called Moses, Exodus 3:1-6. He called Israel, Deuteronomy 7:6; Isaiah 42:6; 48:12; 51:2. It is the same God by whom we are called in the New Testament (I Corinthians 1:9; Ephesians 1:11; II Thessalonians 2:14; II Timothy 1:9; Hebrews 9:15; I Peter 2:9). God called Jeremiah and separated him from his mother's womb, "Before I formed thee in the belly I knew thee, and before thou camest forth out of the womb I sanctified thee; I have appointed thee a prophet unto the nations" (Jeremiah 1:5). Paul makes the same claim in Galatians 1:15, 16. It is God who does the calling, who does the saving, and who does the keeping. We stand like faithful and obedient servants and passively watch God's hand move us and mold us, and finally bring us into His eternal presence. Verse 28 (of Romans 8) must not be separated from verse 29, which rounds out and completes its meaning.

The verses immediately following substantiate the truth that the called ones are the saints of God. This is not Calvinism, but rather it is Biblical doctrine. We shall consider the Sovereignty of God at further length in chapter 9. However, we shall not go into a full discussion of it, since it is not the purpose of this commentary to investigate the doctrine exhaustively. It should be borne in mind, as it is stated here, that extremism in any direction is dangerous. It is always well to avoid it wherever possible. Extremism in one direction leads to Arminianism, while extremism in another direction could destroy evangelism. It is just as dangerous to swing too far to the right as to the left. Let us always keep in mind the three crosses of Calvary with the Saviour of the world in the center, a malefactor on either side of Him, and each malefactor representing a contradiction of the other. Both sides are wrong.

Verse 29: For whom he foreknew, he also foreordained to be conformed to the image of his Son, that he might be the first-born among many brethren . . . :

The Greek word which is translated "foreknew," means an act of divine intelligence and creative knowledge, a knowledge which includes affection and choice, and is thus a *voluntary* action on the part of God; hence, when the Apostle says that God "foreknew" and also "foreordained," he means that God is acting according to His own wisdom, and included in His wisdom is His affection and choice.

This is not the place, and it is not the writer's intention, to develop the Doctrine of Predestination as a subject within the scope of this commentary. Volumes have been written on Predestination and are available to any reader. Each of us has to decide for himself what he wishes to believe about Predestination. This writer believes in a Sovereign God who acts and moves according to His Own will and purpose, and not according to the whims or wishes of men.

We had nothing to do with the plan and program of salvation. God did it all, "Salvation is of the Lord" (Jonah 2:9 KJV; Psalm 3:8 KJV). The Saviour was born into this world of a virgin; He lived a holy, sinless life; He proved His Deity by His miracles; He died on the cross for sin; He was buried and rose the third day; and He ascended unto the Father where He makes intercession for every saint. He is returning to this world to set up the Davidic Kingdom promised Him at His birth (Luke 1:30-33); and seven years prior to His coming again He will come for His saints and receive them unto Himself (John 14:1-3; I Corinthians 15:50-58; I Thessalonians 4:13-18). God does all this without man's help, and He does not need man's assistance in order to bring it to pass. We heard the story of the Gospel; the Holy

Spirit convicted us of our sin and gave us the faith to believe and accept it. We did not originate it. God planned it. God brought it to pass, and is perfecting it in every saint. He will continue perfecting it until every saint will "be conformed to the image of His Son," who is God's Own Son in character, in attributes, and in His Person.

Verses 28-30 are addressed to believers and apply only to those who have been genuinely born again. Some years ago this writer heard the late Dr. H. A. Ironside make the following statement, "Over the door of heaven is written the phrase, 'Whosoever will.' After entering heaven one sees, over the inside of the door, the words, 'Chosen in Him from before the foundation of the world.'" These words should satisfy every Christian.

The Syriac translates verse 29 thus, "And from the beginning He knew them, and sealed them with the image of His Son that he might be," etc. See Ephesians 1:4, 5, 11. Every saint can sing to God's glory, "Isn't He wonderful!"

Verse 30: . . . and whom he foreordained, them he also called: and whom he called, them he also justified: and whom he justified, them he also glorified.

This verse continues to show the results and the accomplishments of predestination or foreordination. All who are thus in the mind of God are called to participate in all the privileges and blessings of the Gospel. The calling results in justification, which is the first accomplishment of the Gospel. To be justified in the sight of God means to be cleansed of every sin. It means being placed in the presence of God, and never again to be out of God's sight. It means that the person must so live that God may be glorified in the life of this justified one. It is the requirement of this position that this one must live and move and be conscious of the reality that God is watching every move, and that He is aware of every thought of this justified one (Psalm 139: 1-3). It demands a righteous life guided by the Holy Spirit. It further demands a separated life that must not be tainted with worldliness and sensuality. The rewards are great, to be sure, but, at the same time, the burden of obligation is just as great.

V. 30c: ". . . them he also glorified." This is the final result of our salvation. All the foregoing acts are viewed as already completed in God's sight. They are accomplished realities with God. However, the reader of these words is not yet glorified. He is still living and moving in sinful society. If he is living a holy life he is longing to be delivered from the sinfulness around him. Thank

God, we need not be worried about God completing what was started by the Holy Spirit, "being confident of this very thing, that he who began a good work in you will perfect it until the day of Jesus Christ" (Philippians 1:6; Hebrews 9:28).

Isn't it comforting to know that we have a God who knows the end from the beginning, a God who has formulated a plan that cannot be changed by vacillating man? We have an eternal Saviour who has graciously and lovingly purchased eternal life for us, and grants it unstintingly to "whosoever will," never considering our condition or station in life, who guides our faltering footsteps "in the paths of righteousness for His Name's sake" to bring to completion His own foreordained plan for our eternal destiny. He conceived it, He directs it, He will complete it. We must, with loving obedience, permit Him to work in us, if we are to enjoy to the fullest our Saviour's purpose for each of us.

Verse 31: What then shall we say to these things? If God is for us, who is against us?

What conclusion are we to draw from the statements in verses 29 and 30 wherein Paul refers to "these things"? These verses reveal the actions of God in the life of the believer. The only conclusion that we can draw from "these things" is that God has placed a protective hedge about us. If God is for us, then, in order to harm the believer, the enemy must be stronger than God. God is invincible. He has planned the believer's salvation. He has saved him, indwells him, energizes him, and is working in him in order to conform him to the image of His Own Son, with glorification as the end result. The conclusion that the Apostle arrives at is expressed by the Apostle John, ". . . greater is he that is in you than he that is in the world" (I John 4:4).

Verse 32: He that spared not his own Son, but delivered him up for us all, how shall he not also with him freely give us all things.

If God, filled with compassion and love for His creatures, was so moved that He was willing to sacrifice His greatest possession, His Own Son, on our behalf and in our place, then, we are to understand, He will withhold nothing from His chosen ones. God did not stop to count the cost of this great sacrifice, and this cost was His most cherished possession. God did not stint. God did not withhold anything in order to redeem us. He opened the windows of heaven and poured out His greatest treasure of

love and bliss by permitting His Son to be nailed to the cross for
our salvation. All this God did for us.

Divine love transcends human comprehension. The Greek word
for "own," in verse 32, expresses the thought of co-equality.
When the Saviour faced the multitude and claimed co-equality
and pre-existence with the Father, the Jews understood this to
mean Deity and took up stones to kill Him (John 8:31-59). By
the term, "his own Son," the Apostle means that the Saviour was
God's own peculiar treasure, His own essential nature, One with
God Himself (Hebrews 1:8), but He gave the Saviour to us out
of a heart of love. What a price this was! In the light of this
price God has a right to demand of us our all. Anything short
of this is not giving the Father and the Son that which is no
longer ours but, rightfully, theirs.

V. 32b: ". . . shall he not also with him freely give us all
things?" He who, indeed, is our divine Benefactor, who, in the
past, made the astonishing surrender of His own Son will, in the
future, supply us freely with all the glorious blessings of eternal
life through His Son. We shall not lack one thing promised us
by our heavenly Father "who made us meet to be partakers of the
inheritance of the saints in light" (Colossians 1:12). What would
God possibly refuse to give us after giving us His Son? The
answer is, nothing!

Since He did so much for us what are we willing to do for
Him? He gave so unstintingly, ought we to withhold anything
from Him? The hymn-writer asks the searching question, "I
gave my life for thee, what hast thou given for me?" Surely,
we can do no less than those Macedonian Christians who "gave
their own selves to the Lord" (II Corinthians 8:5).

**Verse 33: Who shall lay anything to the charge of God's elect?
It is God that justifieth . . . ;**

The Greek word translated "charge" is in the future tense, and
means to bring a charge against, to accuse, to institute judicial
proceedings, to come forward as an accuser against. Inasmuch
as the believer has been saved and justified, who can bring any
charge of sin, and institute judicial proceedings, against him?
The believer is "God's elect." Since we are God's chosen-out-ones,
His selected ones, it means that God has chosen us to be the
recipients of special privileges, that we are, in fact, His especially
beloved. We are His chosen as Christ was God's chosen, and,
therefore, elect and precious as in I Peter 2:4, 6. Incidentally,

the Greek word translated "chose" appears in the Septuagint version of Deuteronomy 4:37 where it implies that it is God's choice, and is not affected by human whim. The same word is used of the saint in the New Testament (Ephesians 1:4). God has signally chosen us to set His affection on us, has justified us by the gift of His Own Son, and has hedged us about with His protective love. Who, then, can bring any charge against God's choice ones? Not even Satan, because God is the Judge of all creation, including Satan.

V. 33b: "It is God that justifieth . . ." The word "justifieth" in the Greek is a present active participle and should be properly translated "justifying." The expression has this thought: God has chosen the believer and is "justifying" him all the time; in other words, God continues to keep the saint in this most choice position of being just.

Verse 34: . . . who is he that condemneth? It is Christ Jesus that died, yea rather, that was raised from the dead, who is at the right hand of God, who also maketh intercession for us.

Who, then, or what is condemning? Excepting God, who has a right to condemn? Is not unbelief the condemning factor in God's sight? It condemns even now. The Greek word for "condemneth" is a present active participle, and is more properly translated "condemning." Unbelief is always condemning and will continue to do so. The only means of stopping this action is the acceptance of the Gospel.

The death of Christ on the cross was the sacrifice for sin, but this is only one aspect of the Saviour's sacrifice on the cross. His death for our sins was not all that He did to accomplish the program of salvation. It is not a dead Christ whom we worship, but, rather, a living Christ, because He was raised from the dead. After His resurrection He remained on the earth for only a short time, and then ascended into heaven and is right now at the right hand of the Father (Hebrews 1:3; 10:12) where he is interceding for us as Sovereign Mediator. Paul was fully versed in the Old Testament, and based his thinking on Isaiah 50:8, 9; and Psalm 110:1.

The believer is so situated and protected in the plan and program of God that nothing can alter this position. God is the Planner, He is the Keeper, and He alone will consummate this plan and program for every believer. All this is unalterable because it is in the Sovereign Hands of God.

Verse 35: Who shall separate us from the love of Christ? shall tribulation, or anguish, or persecution, or famine, or nakedness, or peril, or sword?

The Apostle continues to pursue the theme of a Sovereign God Who has granted eternal life to every believer. He asks, "Who shall separate us from the love of Christ?" or, Who can sever our relationship with Christ? or, Who can disunite the believer from Christ? or, Under what circumstances in all creation can the believer's relationship with Christ be severed? What power can sever a born-again child of God from his Saviour?

Surely the believer's faith is not entrusted to a mere human being who died on a cross and was buried. If that were the case, ". . . your faith is vain; ye are yet in your sins" (I Corinthians 15:17). The believer would be no better off than any unsaved person. The saint has put his trust in a risen and an ascended Christ who is Omnipotent. He holds us in His grasp. What can alter that position? He is seated at the right hand of the Majesty on high (Hebrews 1:3; Colossians 3:1), not as the saint's prosecuting attorney, but as his Advocate, his Intercessor, and his Mediator. What comfort and consolation this is for the child of God who must live in a world of sin and turbulence!

This writer believes that the love spoken of here is not the love that the saint has for Christ, but, rather, it is the love that Christ has for the saint. The saint is still living in the flesh, and "the flesh profiteth nothing" (John 6:63), because it cannot be harnessed for God or for good. At times the saint's faith may falter. Trying circumstances or dire need may cause a saint to doubt, to question, or to waver in his faith, but it is the love of Christ for the saint that is the saint's guarantee that his life is hid with Christ in God (Colossians 3:3).

This being the case, the Apostle asks, under what circumstances can the saint be separated from Christ? Can he be separated by tribulation? Tribulation can be brought about by external circumstances, such as famine, war, the destructive unheavais of nature, starvation and nakedness. By anguish? Anguish can be suffering brought about by disease or accident. By persecution? Persecution can be anything from defamation of character to bodily harm by an enemy. The Apostle enumerates a list of almost every perilous and hostile condition inimical to human life — conditions to be shunned by every normal human being.

Verse 35 asks a question. Suppose a saint is put to this test of enduring one or more of these calamities? Suppose he wavers under the test? Suppose he endures all of Satan's machinations? Will these experiences sever the relationship of the saint and the Saviour? Paul's shout of triumph in verse 39 is the answer.

Do not the pages of Scripture glow with glorious examples of the faithfulness of the saints under severest testings? Was not Job tried almost beyond endurance? Yet he remained steadfast! Was not Peter tried at the trial of Christ, and actually tried beyond endurance (Matthew 26:34)? Was not Peter tried again and found faithful (Acts 4:19-21)? And did not Paul speak out of his own experiences when he wrote the words of verse 35? He knew what hunger was, what it meant to be in peril, and to lack clothing. No matter what the testings may be, no matter how severe the persecutions, Christ is always there and will provide the grace to see us through all tribulation if we will but ask for it. In fact, enduring such conditions as Paul describes is what helps to make a soldier of the cross. It is during the darkest hours of life when the saint is able to understand what Elihu meant when he said to Job, of God, ". . . who giveth songs in the night" (Job 35:10). The true saint of God uses the trials of life as stepping stones to greater service for his Lord. Nothing in life will do more for the saint in bringing him to greater heights of loving service to the Saviour than persecutions. "Count it all joy, my brethren, when ye fall into manifold temptations" (trials, calamities, afflictions — in the Greek) (James 1:2). The glorious promise for the child of God is, "If we suffer, we shall also reign with him: . . . yet he abideth faithful: he cannot deny himself" (II Timothy 2:12, 13 KJV). (Look at my commentary on Romans 5:3).

Verse 36: Even as it is written, For thy sake we are killed all the day long; we are counted as sheep for the slaughter (Psalm 44:22, Septuagint Version).

The Apostle has been laying the foundation for the succeeding chapters in the book of Romans. He began the groundwork in verse 29 of the present chapter, and is still pursuing this doctrine of a Sovereign God who uses the failings and falterings of faithless men to praise Him. The text, verse 36, before us, is taken out of the 44th Psalm which depicts the Divine intervention in Israel's history. Though Israel has gone so far as to stretch out her hands in the worship of pagan gods, though Israel has forgotten her covenant relationship with Jehovah, yet God has not forgotten her. Israel's sin has brought upon her all her calamities. Seemingly, to Israel, God *has* forgotten her. By the same token, does

not every child of God who is living in disobedience feel that
God has forgotten him? Nevertheless, sin cannot go unpunished.
Sin will find us out and do one of two things, punish and restore
us, or render us useless. And God has been punishing Israel only
for her own good, "In overflowing (or little — KJV) wrath I hid
my face from thee for a moment; but with everlasting lovingkindness will I have mercy on thee, saith Jehovah thy Redeemer"
(Isaiah 54:8).

When God restores Israel she will soar to greater spiritual
heights than she has ever experienced. Is this not true for all of
God's chosen ones? And is this not the truth proclaimed in
Romans 8:28 and applicable to Israel in full force and effect —
Israel, who are the called according to God's eternal purpose?
Stop! Think!

There is a vast difference between suffering because of sin,
and suffering for righteousness. Sin will lead one into paths that
righteousness will never tread. The sufferings endured for sin are
grievous and maiming, and must be borne alone. But the sufferings endured for righteousness' sake are rewarding (Matthew
5:10; II Timothy 2:12), and the righteous sufferer is not alone,
but has the comforting presence of the Holy Spirit in and with
him. The hymn-writer expresses this thought accurately, "There
is a balm in Gilead that makes the wounded whole." What comfort! What consolation for the saint of God!

**Verse 37: Nay, in all these things we are more than conquerors
through him that loved us.**

The Greek word translated "more than conquerors" means to
overpower in victory, to be abundantly victorious. For the saint,
persecutions and privations are steps that lead to glory. We are
more than conquerors. When a battle or a war is won the commanding general and the political dignitaries have the pre-
eminence. The "buck privates" stand at attention and form the
background for the celebration ceremony and applause. In Christian warfare the saint of God is not only a "buck private," he is
also a conqueror in the army of the Lord, for in Christ we have
become ". . . kings and priests unto God and his Father . . ."
(Revelation 1:6 KJV). This is a quotation from Exodus 19:6.

The Jewish teachers paraphrase Exodus 19:6 and render it as
it is in the King James Version, Jerusalem Targum, "And ye shall
be unto me kings and priests"; or, as it is rendered in the
Targum of Jonathan ben Uzziel, "Ye shall be before me kings and

priests." Surely, this must have been in the mind of Paul when he wrote Romans 8:37.

Verses 38, 39: (38) For I am persuaded, that neither death, nor life, nor angels, nor principalities, nor things present, nor things to come, nor powers, (39) nor height, nor depth, nor any other creature, shall be able to separate us from the love of God, which is in Christ Jesus our Lord.

The Greek which is here translated, "I am persuaded," is in the perfect indicative passive tense, so that what the Apostle is actually saying is, "I have been persuaded," inasmuch as Paul has been persuaded for a long time, long before he began to write these words. Paul stands firm on the promises of God. He had been born again. He had been saved on the road to Damascus. From that day on, his position remained unaltered. His salvation was a completed transaction, a once-for-all-time contract. To lose one's eternal salvation after one has been born again is as impossible — to use a homely comparison — as it would be to unscramble an egg. Once an egg has been scrambled it cannot be restored to what it was before it was scrambled. So with salvation and being born again. God's word is inviolable. To believe on Christ is to be born from above and to live forever (John 3:16).

This writer has been confronted, as no doubt the readers of these pages have been, with the question of the eternal character of our salvation. Will our salvation ever end? Christ died *once* as a satisfactory sacrifice for sin, and thereby completed that transaction. Christ ascended to the Father once for our justification, and, thereby, completed that transaction. Christ sat down at the right hand of the Father and is thereby continuing that transaction for every believer for all eternity. "Wherefore he is able saving for ever them that draw near unto God through him being ever alive to continually make intercession for them" (Hebrews 7:24 Greek). Christ will come again for His saints to complete the physical union of the true Church. The Rapture and the Resurrection complete our glorification. He will restore Israel one more time never to be scattered again. He will restore peace to the world, and sit down on the throne of His father David never again to entrust it to another human. All these are once-for-all-time acts that God will perform, and they are not dependent upon the actions of men for their fulfillment. This is the same God who planned an eternity of glorious life for all believers, and no power, human or satanic, can alter it.

It is not necessary for us to elaborate on any one or more of the opposing forces which Paul names, of "things present, nor things to come" — death, life, angels, principalities, heights, depths, "nor any other creature" — powerful enough to sever our relationship with God and separate us from His love in Christ Jesus our Lord. Why? Because God saved us through Christ, and every believer is in Christ from the moment he believes, and throughout all eternity. For it is as the Apostle says in verse 38, "For I have been persuaded" and, therefore, his position is unaltered through endless ages, as is the position of every born-again believer. We are placed in the heavenlies the moment we believe, and God has been looking upon us as already completed in Christ. As we bear the image of the earthy Adam, we shall, without a doubt, bear the image of the heavenly which is Christ (I Corinthians 15:49). As the first is a certain reality, so also is the second. It rests upon the completed accomplishments of the Saviour.

9

ALL THAT THE APOSTLE HAS SAID in the preceding eight chapters of Romans he is substantiating in chapters 9, 10 and 11 which follow. Paul must now prove beyond the shadow of a doubt that what he has previously written in this Epistle is wholly and completely based upon the Word of God; namely, the Old Testament. All the doctrines and truths that Paul has established are not the creations or imaginings of his own mind, but they are, rather, the established truths of God, in the recording of which Paul has been guided by the Holy Spirit.

Romans 9, 10 and 11 have been referred to as a "parenthesis" by some highly-regarded commentators of the past and present, but this writer does not believe that one jot or tittle is out of its divinely-chosen place in God's Holy Word. Does not Paul claim, "All scripture is given by inspiration of God . . ." (II Timothy 3:16 KJV)? This being the case, every word in the Scriptures is in its proper place. These three chapters are *not* a parenthesis. They are *pivotal*. The whole Epistle to the Romans revolves around these three chapters. They are to this Epistle what the center-post is to a tent or the keystone is to an arch. Remove these three chapters and the Epistle collapses at its center and falls to pieces. Remove these three chapters and all that is left are words and doctrines without any substantiating evidences of their truth.

The doctrines of justification, sanctification, baptism, the two-fold nature of the believer, the believer's victory over his Adamic nature, the call to separation and to a holy life empowered by the Holy Spirit, and the perseverance of the saints — all these truths must be substantiated, and the evidences of such substantiation are to be found in these three chapters, which we shall now study.

CHAPTER 9: In the ninth chapter we are brought face to face with the Sovereignty of God. The reality of the truth of this great doctrine means that the saints of God do not compel a Holy God to react to the whims and wishes of vacillating humanity, but, rather, that man moves according to the will of an Omnipotent God. This God moves, plans, throws down, builds up, chooses, and motivates according to His own divine plan, program and pleasure.

CHAPTER 10: In the tenth chapter we are confronted with man's (in this case Israel's) responsibility to a Sovereign God. Israel has become faithless, and is now faltering and failing in her own foolishness and stubbornness, and has degenerated to a righteousness which has no semblance to God's righteousness (verse 3). It is a righteousness that Israel has manufactured. Instead of accepting and yielding to the plan and program of God, instead of obeying God's Word, she has gone so far astray that someone must come and show her the way back to God. Instead of being the emissary to a heathen world, instead of being the herald of God's Word, Israel must now have someone to teach her God's word (verses 14 and 15). Israel has lost both her message and her position. Because Israel has failed, does that mean that God is foiled? Because Israel has turned her back upon God and strayed into the world of sin, does it mean that God must now devise a new plan, a new program, with a different motive and objective? Is God's plan for Israel now thwarted; is God helpless and Israel hopeless? – verse 21. Has God's covenant been nullified and abrogated through Israel's failings? Does God now have to beg and plead with Israel not to destroy His plans? Is God brought to His knees by mere sinful humanity? Certainly not!

CHAPTER 11: In chapter 11 we are shown that God's plan for Israel stands, inasmuch as He did not cast off His people – verse 1. The God who has planned is a Sovereign God, and the nation which has failed, is a frail, faltering nation that will be compelled to come back. God's will in Israel must and will be done even if severe measures have to be executed. The failings of Israel will be used to accomplish God's plan for a great number of Jews and Gentiles – verse 11, which was God's plan even before the foundation of the world (Ephesians 1:4). Israel has merely acted according to God's plan. Centuries before, these actions were predicted by the Holy Spirit through the prophets (Isaiah 6:9, 10; 29:10; Deuteronomy 29:4; Psalm 69:22; and Romans 11:8-11, 25 ff.). (God used His people in ancient times to fulfill a plan for a Gentile people – Genesis 15:13-16.) When God's plan for the Gentiles, in times soon to come, has been completed, Israel will be brought back to her rightful place – verses 25-27. Are not God's wisdom and plans rich and beyond human comprehension? (11:33). God formulates His plans, and man acts in accordance with them — verse 32. God knows what He is doing. He does not make mistakes. Everything is moving along on schedule even to the minutest detail. No one can thwart or upset God's design for His creation throughout the ages. The blueprint is ever before Him, and man moves in accordance with God's will at the right time and in the right place — verses 33-35.

With this proof before us no saint need fret, worry, or doubt God's omniscience. With the saint in God's omnipotent hands he may wander, but he will never be lost, and sooner or later he will come back. No saint of God can continue in sin (I John 3:9). His carnal nature may put up a fight, but the flesh will not prevail, and the spirit will be victorious (Romans 7:25). The power and the weapons of warfare with sin are motivated by God the Holy Spirit, and through His mighty power every saint will be victorious (Philippians 1:6; Ephesians 6:10-20) because his God is invincible. "Fret not thyself because of evil-doers . . . Delight thyself also in Jehovah; and he will give thee the desires of thy heart" (Psalm 37:1, 4). Read the whole Psalm for it is a vindication of the first eight chapters of Romans.

We repeat, chapters 9, 10 and 11 of Romans are not *parenthetical*, but *pivotal*. They authenticate the Apostle's theology, and substantiate all that he has said thus far in this Epistle.

Verses 1, 2: (1) I say the truth in Christ, I lie not, my conscience bearing witness with me in the Holy Spirit, (2) that I have great sorrow and unceasing pain in my heart.

What the Apostle is saying here is that the truthfulness of the statement he is about to make, and the genuineness of his belief in it, are so real to him that he is ready to declare these words to the whole world, and before heaven in the presence of Christ Himself. In other words, Paul's "great sorrow and unceasing pain" in his heart for his brethren after the flesh are so great that he dares to call the Saviour to witness to their reality. He also calls upon his conscience, his God-given nature, his Holy-Spirit-filled nature, as another witness to the truth of his sorrow and unceasing pain, in addition to putting God on the witness-stand, so to speak, to testify to the truthfulness of his words concerning the deep sorrow of his heart. With such an august host of witnesses the Apostle proceeds to bare his heart concerning the burdens that lie upon his mind.

The spiritual struggle is a consuming burden, it preys upon his mind, it weighs upon his heart, his grief is incessant, it is with him day and night, he cannot escape it, it disturbs his peace and undermines his hope. His state of mind concerning his brethren after the flesh may be compared to that of a person who watches a loved one wither away and is helpless to save or to provide a remedy.

This writer speaks out of a heart of experience as one who stood at the bedside of his loved one as cancer was eating away her strength. One cries to God for help in such an hour as this. We struggle in prayer, and feel like tearing everything to pieces, even life itself, in order to stop the awful agony. As we grapple with the problem the heart is stricken, the mind is bewildered, and we cry out, as so many have cried out, "God Almighty, help us in this tragic hour! O Lord, take my life but spare my loved one!"

Only some such extremity as the foregoing can explain what the Apostle is saying. It is like a cry to heaven for help to rescue his people. The Apostle knows they are lost, they are doomed, and that hell is ahead. Israel is perishing! The Satan-inspired rout must be halted, and only faith in Christ, which is God-given, has power to check Israel's headlong course toward destruction. Human willfulness inevitably leads to madness unless restored to newness of life by faith in Christ. Otherwise, Israel would stand consigned to everlasting death before the bar of divine judgment.

The certain knowledge of this was the cause of Paul's heart-rending cry as he stood helplessly by watching Israel stumbling blindly along the path of sin toward the insatiable jaws of hell. Paul's conviction of the truth of Israel's danger is the reason why he spent his life and health preaching the Gospel, "in labor and travail . . . in hunger and thirst . . . in cold and nakedness" (II Corinthians 11:27).

The certain knowledge of Israel's lost condition is also the consuming passion of many present-day Hebrew Christians working among their own people. Israel today still continues to stumble along the awful road to hell. We believers who are aware of the plight of modern Jewry are sending forth a cry for help, which may be likened to the Macedonian call of old. But it is falling on many deaf ears, even among the ranks of our Fundamental brethren. Pray earnestly to our heavenly Father that you who read these lines may be found worthy to answer this call.

A similar cry comes also from a sinful world. The apathy, the lethargy, the Laodicean lukewarmness of many nominal Christians today is distressing. They have lulled themselves into a sleep of indifference from which they refuse to be awakened. How tragic this is in the light of the needs of sinful humanity, Jews and Gentiles alike!

However, this writer is a Hebrew Christian who has spent decades of time as a field evangelist in the active work of Jewish missions. He has been, literally, to hundreds of Christian meetings where missions of all kinds, domestic and foreign, have been presented. Rarely in his experience has he ever heard any mention made of the plight of the Jews, and their need of the Gospel. The Jew is the forgotten ingredient in the great majority of Christian missionary programs. He is joked about, and, in many cases, slandered when he isn't maligned, and often pointed to as an example of disobedience, but scarcely ever prayed for, and almost never represented as a people needing the Gospel. With Jeremiah of old, and the Apostle Paul, this writer cries to believers everywhere, "Is it nothing to you, all ye that pass by? Behold, and see if there be any sorrow like unto my sorrow, which is brought upon me" (Lamentations 1:12). If you have never thought before of the Jew's need of the Gospel think of it now, and lay the subject on your heart with earnest prayer for God's direction in giving your personal support to the work of reaching God's ancient people with the Gospel of salvation through their Messiah the Lord Jesus Christ. Will you help? You can if you will.

Verse 3: For I could wish that I myself were anathema from Christ for my brethren's sake, my kinsmen according to the flesh . . . :

The Apostle is continuing to explain the grievous burden that he has for his people Israel. He places himself next to Christ only in his willingness to become a sacrifice for his people, if such a sacrifice on his part would close the flood-gates of Divine judgment and result in Israel's salvation. The Greek word "anathema" denotes the object of a curse (I Corinthians 16:22; Galatians 1:8).

Paul is saying that he *could be willing* to wish himself separated from Christ and given up to judgment, if by the means of such self-sacrifice Israel would be saved. Paul does not say that he actually wishes himself to be anathema. He says that he *could wish* himself to be so. In God's sight Paul knows that he could never actually be accursed from Christ; therefore, he says that he would be willing *to wish himself* accursed for his kinsmen

according to the flesh if such self-sacrifice would be in accord
with God's will and plan. But even if it had been in accord with
God's will and plan it would have been to no avail; hence, it was
never fulfilled. In Greek the verb for "I could wish" is in the
imperfect tense, and expresses an incomplete action. Paul was
never anathema or accursed from Christ, so his wish was never a
completed action. The action remained imperfect, and is expressed beautifully in the English by "I could wish."

In the latter portion of Romans 8 Paul began to lay the foundation for the elaboration of the doctrine of the Sovereignty of God.
He knew that frail humanity could never thwart the plan of God.
He knew that he was God's chosen vessel, and he constantly
moved with that fact in mind. In the succeeding verses of the
chapter before us he goes on to explain the doctrine and to
elaborate upon it.

**Verse 4: . . . who are Israelites; whose is the adoption, and
the glory, and the covenants, and the giving of the law, and the
service of God, and the promises . . . ;**

The Apostle wants to make absolutely certain that no one will
mistake his words, "my brethren" (in v. 3), to mean Christians
rather than Israelites. He uses three terms by which he refers to
his brethren: (1) "my brethren"; (2) "my kinsmen according to
the flesh"; (3) "Israelites." The term "Israelites" applies only to
the nation of Israel which is the descendant of Jacob. It does not
and cannot mean the Church of the New Testament, in any
sense of the word. To apply the term Israelites to the Church
does violence to the Word of God.

After naming the three terms by which Paul refers to his
brethren he proceeds to specify seven God-bestowed gifts which
distinguish his brethren from the rest of mankind: (1) the
adoption, (2) the glory, (3) the covenants, (4) the giving of
the law, (5) the service of God, (6) the promises, (7) the
fathers.

Post-millennarians and A-millennarians have so spiritualized
the Scriptures that the Word of God at times is made by them to
mean the very opposite of what it teaches. Origen, in the third
century A.D., introduced the Alexandrine method of Biblical interpretation, or exegesis. The Post-millennarians and A-millennarians of the present day consider themselves masters of
exegesis, and because they lack *spiritual* eyes they have produced
spiritual lies. In spiritualizing the Scriptures they have carried
their exegesis beyond the literal and historical meaning to the

point where the interpretation is no longer "spiritual" in its true sense, but almost entirely allegorical, and the truth is thereby distorted. A careful scrutiny of Galatians 6:16 will show their failure. Paul is speaking of two groups of people in this Galatian verse, "And as many as shall walk by this rule, peace be upon them (the Gentile Christians), and mercy, and upon the Israel of God (the Jewish Christians)." The Apostle is writing to a *local* church in which there are both Jewish and Gentile Christians.

The name Israel is unique, and is the name of Jacob and his descendants (Genesis 32:28). Exodus 4:22 applies to Jacob's descendants, ". . . Israel is my son, my first-born." (See also the following: Deuteronomy 14:1; Isaiah 43:1, 4, 5; 44:1-8.) The name Israel is the eternal possession of the children of Jacob who are God's eternal earthly people, ". . . since I established the *eternal* people? ". . . (Isaiah 44:7). This is the true translation of the Hebrew. (See also I Chronicles 17:22; Ezekiel 43:7.) Israel is an eternal nation which has never ceased, and her destiny lies in her future when she will fulfill God's purposes as His emissary.

V. 4: ". . . whose is the adoption . . ." This is the first of the seven God-bestowed gifts which distinguish Israel from the rest of mankind, and denotes Israel's eternal relationship to Jehovah. The sons of Jacob — Israel — are the earthly sons of Jehovah, and such is their status in His service; therefore, of Israel it must be said, "whose is the adoption," or theirs the right to claim the exalted position accorded a son. In their present state, in these "times of the Gentiles," they have failed to claim their adoption as sons, but a time is coming when they will claim their adoption and be restored as sons. Jeremiah, speaking of Israel's restoration, says, ". . . for I am a father to Israel, and Ephraim is my first-born" (31:9). Deuteronomy 14:1, "Ye are the children (sons) of Jehovah" . . .; 32:6 . . . "Is not he thy father that hath bought thee?" See also Hosea 11:1.

V. 4: ". . . and the glory . . .". This is the second of the seven God-bestowed gifts previously mentioned. The "glory" is that peculiar Shekinah Glory that hovered over Israel as a cloud by day, and led the Israelites as a pillar of fire by night, in their flight from Egypt (Exodus 13:21, 22). That Shekinah Glory was still prevalent in the tabernacle. Exodus 40:34: "Then the cloud covered the tent of meeting, and the glory of Jehovah filled the tabernacle." (See also Leviticus 16:2; I Kings 8:11; II Chronicles 5:14.) The Shekinah Glory will be returned to Israel when she is restored to her proper place and position. Haggai 2:7: ". . . and I will fill this house with glory, **saith**

Jehovah of hosts." Verse 9: "The latter glory of this house shall
be greater than the former, saith Jehovah of hosts . . ." Ezekiel
describes the Millennial temple in greater detail, and shows
that Jehovah's glory will return to Israel (Ezekiel 43:5) ". . .
and, behold, the glory of Jehovah filled the house." There are
many other passages which clearly state the truth that the Shekinah Glory will return to Israel.

V. 4: ". . . and the covenants. . ." This is the third of Israel's
seven God-bestowed gifts. It should be noted that Paul names
all the covenants as Israel's possession, not one of them only.
Every covenant that God made with the sons of Jacob, from the
one with Abraham on, is the possession of Israel, whether it be
the Abrahamic, Mosaic, Davidic, Palestinian, Messianic, and even
the New Covenant. These are all the *eternal* possessions of the
nation Israel. God, Who is a covenant-keeping God, is the One
who deals with Israel. The land is their eternal possession (Genesis 17:7, 8); the Davidic throne shall be their eternal posession
(II Samuel 7:16; Psalm 89:34-37); Isaiah 9:6, 7; ". . . for unto
us (Israel) . . . unto us (Israel) . . . Of the increase of his
government and of peace there shall be no end, upon the throne
of David . . . from henceforth even for ever." Also see Jeremiah
23:5; Hosea 3:5; Luke 1:30-33, ". . . the Lord God shall give
unto him the throne of his father David; and he shall reign over
the house of Jacob forever. . . ." As pointed out in our comment
on verse 3, on Paul's use of the terms, "my brethren" and the
"Israelites," these terms are not to be confused with the Church
of the New Testament. Surely, it must be evident to even the
most careless reader of Scripture that the "House of Jacob"
cannot possibly mean the Church!

Even the New Covenant is Israel's possession, and we, as
born-again believers, share in it (Jeremiah 31:31; compare with
Hebrews 8:6-12). This passage from Hebrews is taken from
the Septuagint Version of the Old Testament, which is not a
good translation of that portion of Scripture, and is not even
complete. The Septuagint Version has never been accepted as a
whole by students who believe the Bible to be the inspired
Word of God.

V. 4: ". . . and the giving of the law . . ." The fourth of the
seven gifts. The law is Israel's peculiar possession, Exodus 19
and 20; Romans 2:17; 3:2. This "giving of the law," we must
realize, is a high and holy privilege. The New Testament never
speaks disparagingly of the Law, but, on the other hand, the
Law is always referred to in the New Testament as being **good,**

and as being holy. ". . . the law was our schoolmaster to bring us unto Christ . . ." (Galatians 3:24 KJV). It was the Law that showed us our sinfulness, and vividly displayed the holiness of God in the midst of a sin-cursed and dying world. It was the Law that convicted us of our sin and caused us to seek refuge in the Grace of God "that we might be justified by faith." Israel's misuse of it, their misunderstanding and misinterpretation of that Law ought not and does not in any sense of the word bring the Law into disrepute, or discredit its efficacy in the heart and mind of the child of God. The Law is still one of the greatest guidelines to holy living. The only difference in the place and function accorded the Law in the New Testament as opposed to its place and function in the Old Testament is that the driving force throughout the Old Testament was the fear of judgment. The driving force in the New Testament is love. Assuredly, love is not only the greatest force in the universe, but also the grandest. Love inspires instant and full-hearted obedience, eager and utter sacrifice, and adoring gratitude for every one of God's gifts. This is the force that inspires the Christian and makes him even grateful for the Law, as the traveler is grateful for guideposts along the way. We are to live holy lives, not out of fear but out of love of Christ.

V. 4: ". . . and the service of God . . ." The fifth of the seven gifts. The service of God is the position that God chose for Israel (Exodus 19:5, 6). Isaiah 61:6: "But ye shall be named the priests of Jehovah; men shall call you the ministers of our God: ye shall eat the wealth of the nations (Gentiles), and in their (Gentiles) glory shall ye boast yourself." The Exodus passage is prophecy; the Isaiah passage is the fulfillment. See also Zechariah 8:23; Habakkuk 2:14.

This "service of God" which was Israel's peculiar privilege is vividly portrayed in the tabernacle services and in the Mosaic institutions. The beauty, the majesty, and the glory that were portrayed in this "service of God" laid the foundation for the preaching of the Gospel of the Grace of God. Only God knows how many countless thousands of souls have been saved through the preaching of the tabernacle and its sacrifices as a picture of the work of the Saviour and the accomplishments of the cross. My fellow Christians, do not minimize "the service of God," for this service made it not only possible but also easier for you and me to preach the Gospel of salvation through faith in Jesus Christ, and to see the atoning sacrifice on the cross as the grand foundation stone upon which the Gospel rests. Truly the Lord Jesus Christ was the tabernacle alive as He hung on the cross, as He died, as He rose from the dead, and as He ascended into the Holy of Holies, and into the presence of the Father where He sits now as the Eternal High Priest, our mediator. All this is seen in "the service of God," which millenniums ago God gave to the nation of Israel. Some day both the *living tabernacle* of Christ and the temple made of stone shall be side by side in that great city of Jerusalem where He, who loved us and gave Himself for us, shall be the Eternal High Priest and the eternal King of kings and Lord of lords.

V. 4: ". . . and the promises . . ." The sixth of the seven gifts. All the promises that God has made to Israel, God Himself will fulfill. His warnings are prevalent and His promises are sure. He will restore Israel to her own land, and none shall make her afraid (Ezekiel 20:33-38; Isaiah 43:5; 49:22-26; 54: 8, 17; 60:7-9; Jeremiah 30:16-22; 31:10-40; etc., etc.). God promised her a land; He promised to protect her; He promised her the Messiah; He promised her a kingdom with Jerusalem as its capital. God Himself will bring this to pass (see Isaiah 9:1-7). Bear in mind that these promises are as sure and as real as God Himself.

Verse 5: . . . whose are the fathers, and of whom is Christ as concerning the flesh, who is over all, God blessed for ever. Amen.

This is the seventh of Israel's seven gifts, "the fathers." Israel has always boasted in her fathers, Abraham, Isaac nd Jacob. This was her boast as recorded in John 8:31-39. The Rabbinical teachings are numerous supporting the claim that Israel rests on the merits of the fathers. "Israel lives and endures because it supports itself on the Fathers. As the vine supports itself on the trunk which is dry, while it, itself, is fresh and green, so Israel supports itself on the merit of the fathers, although they are already asleep. So the merit of the fathers is a general possession of the whole people of Israel, and the protection of the whole people in the day of Redemption" (Shemoth rabba, c. 44; Beresch rabba c. 70). "The Holy One spoke to Israel: My sons, if ye will be justified by Me in the judgment, make mention to Me of the merits of your fathers, so shall ye be justified before Me in judgment" (Pesikta 153b). See also Acts 3:13 and 7:32.

V. 5b: ". . . and of whom is Christ as concerning the flesh . . ." This is better translated, "and of whom as concerning the flesh is the Messiah." Messiah is not a personal name. The Messiah had to be of the stock of Israel. If He were not a Jew according to the flesh He could not have wrought salvation, ". . . for salvation is from the Jews" (John 4:22). See also Matthew 2:2; Luke 1:30-33; 2:11; etc.

V. 5c: ". . . who is over all, God blessed for ever. Amen." This verse has been discussed perhaps more than any other passage in the New Testament. The problem is the punctuation. Where to put the comma, that is the question! The MSS. of the New Testament were written without punctuation. Moving the comma would make the text read, "who is over all God, blessed for ever." The latter reading is the one this writer accepts. Paul has traced the salient points in Israel's history, and climaxes it by proving that the Messiah, according to His human nature, is Jewish, but at the same time is deity. He is God! Even in the Incarnation, Jehovah has so joined Himself with His people Israel that He has, as God the Son, clothed Himself in Jewish flesh. The Messiah is the crowning glory in Israel's history. He is the capstone in their historic succession.

In writing to Titus, Paul states, ". . . looking for the blessed hope and the appearing of the glory of the great God and our Saviour Jesus Christ . . ." (2:13). Here, as in Romans 9:5, Paul uses the title "Theos" for the Saviour. He is very God and very Man. The same idea was previously presented by the Apostle in this Epistle in 1:3, 4. In verse 3 the humanity of Christ is presented and in verse 4 it is His deity. This is the same truth that Isaiah records in 9:6. The "child born" and the "son given" are the Saviour's humanity. The Wonderful Counsellor, the Mighty God, the Everlasting Father, the Prince of Peace, are His deity.

In the opening verses of Romans 9 Paul has lifted the curtain of history and given us a glimpse of Israel's past as well as a glimpse of her prophetic future. The greater glories of Israel are still in the future. Paul shows this clearly in chapter 11.

Verse 6: But it is not as though the word of God hath come to nought. For they are not all Israel, that are of Israel . . . . :

Because a number, no matter how great or small that number may be, of the people of Israel and their leaders have not accepted Jesus as the promised Messiah, does not nullify or abrogate the Word of God. The faithlessness of those who reject Jesus the Messiah does not mean that the Word of God has failed. In the history of Israel there has never been a time when the *whole* nation has believed God, His Word, His prophets or His promises; in fact, God's faithful ones have always been a remnant.

On the other hand, we must not lose sight of the fact that

the many thousands of converts recorded in the first nine chapters of the book of Acts were all Jews. It is not true to say
that the Jews, *as a people,* rejected Jesus as their Messiah. The
Jewish leaders and their politicians rejected Him, but the multitudes, the common people, as recorded in the Gospels and the
book of Acts, followed Him. In the light of this, it is no wonder
that we read in Acts 21:20 of the "myriads" (Greek) of Jews
that believed. The Greek word which means "myriads," is translated *thousands* in both the King James Version and the American Standard Version, and means thousands of thousands. Josephus, the Jewish historian (37-95 A.D. *circa*), estimates that at
least one-third of the Jewish population in the world were followers of Christ at the end of the first century. The passage in
Acts confirms this.

The Apostle proves that all Jews did not believe in Jesus the
Messiah, by saying, "For they are not all Israel, that are of Israel." That is, all Israel are not believers, and, by the same token,
all Gentiles are not Christians; and, also, by the same token,
Gentiles who become Christians do not become *spiritual* Israelites.

This writer is of Orthodox Jewish parents and training. When
living in Poland, and even after we came to the United States in
1921, we did not consider the Reform Jews as truly Jews. We
called them "German Jews" because the Reform movement came
to life in Germany. In fact, the German Jew boasted, "Ich bin
Deutsch" (I am German). So, today, the Jews in the United
States say, "I am an American of Jewish extraction or persuasion."
These people are called Jews, or Israel, but they are not, as Paul
so graphically expresses it, *of Israel.* "If I forget thee, O Jerusalem, Let my right hand forget her skill. Let my tongue cleave
to the roof of my mouth, If I remember thee not; If I prefer not
Jerusalem above my chief joy" (Psalm 137:5, 6).

There always has been a faithful remnant in Israel. To paraphrase verse 6 of Romans 9 it would read thus, "For not all
who are of Israel *are Israel,* there is a true Israel *within* the nation Israel, namely, the remnant." To be a Jew, Jewish sentiment
alone is insufficient; there must be a Jewish practice and observance. There has always been a divinely-called handful of
Jews who have been true to God. This has been true in history;
it is true today (Romans 11:5); and it will be true in God's
prophetic tomorrow (Romans 11:25; Jeremiah 50:20; Zechariah
12:10; etc.)

The Church of the New Testament does not and will **not**

replace Israel in God's economy. This concept is a distortion of Scripture. If the Church is Israel, then the Church is blind; it is ignorant of God's righteousness; and it is in a fallen and sinful condition.

The falseness of both the A-millennial and Post-millennial positions is revealed in just three chapters of Romans, namely, 9, 10 and 11. If the Church is Israel, what about all the curses and judgments that have befallen and are still to befall Israel during the awful days of the great tribulation, the time of Jacob's trouble (Jeremiah 30:7)? Is the Church of Jesus Christ under this condemnation? One cannot take the name of Israel upon one's self without inheriting the consequences; namely, the curses and judgments which are to precede the blessings. The judgments and the blessings are to the people of Israel. The nation is now and has been for centuries experiencing God's punitive dealings because of her unbelief, but during all these centuries there has always been a faithful remnant.

However, after the judgments, Israel's future is bright. God has promised to restore and redeem Israel (Isaiah 43:1-5; 49: 25, ". . . I will save thy children"). Since time is meaningless in God's sight, He says, "In a little wrath I hid my face from thee for a moment; but with everlasting kindness will I have mercy on thee, saith the Lord thy Redeemer" (Isaiah 54:8, KJV). Because the first half of this verse is being literally fulfilled, the last half will likewise be fulfilled: "I, Jehovah, change not; therefore ye, O sons of Jacob, are not consumed" (Malachi 3:6). In view of these plain statements of Scripture in which the name of Israel is unmistakably spelled out, how is it possible to make these prophecies apply to the Church of the New Testament?

Verse 7: . . . neither, because they are Abraham's seed, are they all children: but, In Isaac shall thy seed be called.

Because the sons of Jacob are the progeny of Abraham this does not make them the *children of the promise*. Paul is here quoting the Septuagint Version of Genesis 21:12. What the Apostle is saying in verse 7 is that the rightful heir, the child whom God will recognize as the one who will inherit the blessings that He promised Abraham, is Isaac and not Ishmael. Ishmael was the result of the unbelief of Sarah and Abraham. God will not recognize Ishmael as Abraham's seed promised in Genesis 12:3. It was not up to Abraham to choose the son who would be the recipient of God's blessings.

Man cannot and does not dictate to God. Our God is a Sovereign God who chooses upon whom He will bestow His blessings. Isaac was God's choice, not Abraham's. In fact, Abraham tried to change God's mind: ". . . Oh that Ishmael might live before thee!" (Genesis 17:18). But God rejected Abraham's plea and said, ". . . Nay, but Sarah thy wife shall bear thee a son; and thou shalt call his name Isaac; and I will establish my covenant with him for an everlasting covenant for his seed after him" (Genesis 17:19). In God's sight Isaac is the true seed of Abraham.

Verse 8: That is, it is not the children of the flesh that are children of God; but the children of the promise are reckoned for a seed.

This verse is an elaboration of the preceding verse. Ishmael was born as a result of impatience and unbelief, both of which traits are alien to the very nature of God. Abraham and Sarah refused to wait until God would fulfill His promise to them. Their loss of patience and lack of faith caused them untold grief and remorse. Sarah became angry, as well as jealous, which brought strife in the home, and finally division. The consequences were recrimination and unhappiness for all concerned (Genesis 21:8-11).

Imagine the poignancy of such a situation occurring in any family, to say nothing of having it occur in a family such as Abraham's, a father who was the most venerable of the patriarchs — an old man, the revered head of his family, having to throw his own flesh and blood out of his own home! Sin will have its pound of flesh. Sow the wind and reap the whirlwind. Sow doubt and disobedience and reap tears and trouble. The sin of Sarah and Abraham spawned other sins because they acted contrary to God's purpose for them. They responded to the instincts of the flesh, and God would have none of it. Like Sarah and Abraham we sometimes get ourselves into difficulties because of sin, and then God turns a deaf ear to our pleas for help and lets us see the fruits of our wrongdoing. This was the case with Abraham and Sarah. God's choice was Isaac as the child of promise, and nothing could alter His decision. God decreed that Isaac was to be Abraham's true posterity.

God's judgment was final even though it grieved Abraham's heart (Genesis 21:11). It must have been a grief-stricken Abraham to whom God spoke (Genesis 21:12-14). What tears, what remorse, what pathos are expressed in these few verses of

Genesis 21! But what a lesson it was! Abraham had to yield to God's wishes. The lesson for the believer in this story is that it is better to cry in our youth than to weep in our old age, as was the case with Abraham who was a very old man. God's ways are best if we will only wait for His guidance.

The first half of verse 8, and its reference to the "children of the flesh," was Abraham's plan, but the last half of the verse, and its reference to the "children of the promise," was God's plan and His decree. The Apostle continues this thought in the next verse.

Verse 9: For this is a word of promise, According to this season will I come, and Sarah shall have a son.

Paul is quoting Genesis 18:10 of the Septuagint Version: "And he said, I will return and come to thee according to this period seasonably, and Sarah thy wife will have a son; . . ." (The Septuagint Version — Samuel Bagster and Sons, Ltd.).

This is in fulfillment of God's promise in Genesis 17:21, "But my covenant will I establish with Isaac, whom Sarah shall bear unto thee at this set time in the next year." A translation of the Hebrew of Genesis 18:10 would read, "And he said, I will most certainly or positively return, when the season liveth, and behold a son to Sarah thy wife . . ." etc. (Literal Hebrew.)

Why is God so specific about the time and the season and the seed? This writer believes it is because God wants Sarah and Abraham to know that it will be according to His plan and His choosing; that is to say, according to God's sovereign pleasure. It is God's prerogative to choose the time, the place, and the person: ". . . but when the fulness of time came (this set time in the next year) God sent forth His Son, born of a woman . . ." (Galatians 4:4).

Abraham pleaded with God, offering God a plan of his own, "Oh that Ishmael might live before thee!" (Genesis 17:18). To Abraham this made no difference whether the mother of his son would be Sarah or Hagar. Ishmael, born of Hagar, was Abraham's own flesh and blood. Abraham could say, "This is my son. What difference should it make to thee, O God?" But to God it did make a difference. God never promised to bless the seed of Abraham that was planted in the womb of any woman other than Sarah. The promise of Genesis 12:2 was to Abraham and his wife Sarah. In time Abraham, after years of childlessness, began to lose patience and to doubt God's promise, ". . . O Lord Jehovah, what wilt thou give me, seeing I go childless . . ." (Genesis 15:2)? Sarah lost patience also, as we see in Genesis 16:1, 2.

Abraham and Sarah had given up hope. They laughed at the thought of having their own son when they were both so old. "Then Abraham fell upon his face, and laughed . . ." (Genesis 17:17). "And Sarah laughed within herself . . ." (Genesis 18: 12). But God's promises are not to be laughed at. What a price this "friend of God" and his wife paid because they laughed, and what a burden of self-reproach they had to bear as their doubt and rebelliousness bore its bitter fruit through the centuries that followed! God's rebuke to Sarah's levity was very stern, a denial of her denial: ". . . wherefore did Sarah laugh, saying, Shall I of a surety bear a child, who am old?" (Genesis 18:13). "Then Sarah denied, saying, I laughed not; for she was afraid. And he (God) said, Nay; but thou didst laugh" (Genesis 18:15). God made a covenant and He will keep it, "Is anything too hard for Jehovah?" (Genesis 18:14).

V. 9c: ". . . and Sarah shall have a son." The Apostle quotes the concluding part of Genesis 18:14, ". . . and Sarah shall have a son" — in God's time, according to God's plan, and not one moment sooner. A Sovereign God ignores the desires of a vacillating humanity when its desires are not in accordance with His will. Romans 9:9 proves that God's Word must always be trusted even when we, because of the weakness of our faith, think He has forgotten.

Verse 10: And not only so; but Rebecca also having conceived by one, even by our father Isaac — . . .

The Greek of this verse presents a great truth not apparent in the English translation. In Sarah's case her conception was miraculous. Sarah had been sterile all her life and undoubtedly had passed the period in life called the menopause, or change of life. In order for Sarah to conceive and bear a child, God had to perform a miracle. In Rebecca's case this was not necessary. Verse 10 states in the Greek that Rebecca *had the power to conceive,* because of her physical youth and good health. The two Greek words translated "having conceived" really could be translated "having the facilities of being ready to conceive." In other words, she was physically able to become pregnant, which is generally normal for every woman before it has ceased to be with her "after the manner of women" (Genesis 16:11). God did not have to open Rebecca's womb. She was young and in good health, which was not true in Sarah's case.

The reasons for God's choice of Isaac instead of Ishmael are self-evident and inevitable in order that God might override Sarah's premature and almost-successful coup to introduce a "pretender" to the office of Isaac in God's plan, even as He explained to Abraham, "in Isaac shall thy seed be called" (Genesis 21:12). It was only through the miraculous intervention of God that Isaac was born, and, therefore, foreordained to be the one upon whom God would shower His blessings. To this end God used Abraham and Sarah, not Abraham and Hagar, to bring Isaac into this world. This condition was not operative in Rebecca's case, for she "conceived by one, even our father Isaac."

When God chose Jacob, the younger son of Isaac, again it was God's sovereign will as well as His good pleasure to make the choice. This was a different choice than the one God exercised in making His choice of Abraham's seed. With Abraham's seed there was one father and two mothers. But with the choice of Isaac's seed there was but one mother, and she gave birth to twins, Jacob and Esau. God's sovereign will was again demonstrated in this choice. It was God's elective choice which decreed that Jacob, the younger, was to be served by Esau, the older.

Verse 11: . . . for the children being not yet born, neither having done anything good or bad, that the purpose of God according to election might stand, not of works, but of him that calleth . . . ,

This verse is not a parenthesis, as the King James Version has it. It is a continued explanation of God's election, and an elaboration of the truth that God's purpose in election is unalterable because established in the beginning by His sovereign will.

Jacob and Esau "being not yet born," were still in their embryonic stage, in process of development in their mother's womb, and unable, as yet, to display any indication of their true character. Whether the soul of one was more noble than that of the other, no one but God could know, for at this time their characters as human beings, whether upright or evil, had yet to be developed and displayed before the eyes of the world. Nevertheless, while they were still in this stage, God already had chosen the one upon whom He would shower His blessings. God, and God only, does the calling and selecting.

This election to which the Apostle refers in verse 11, is not something new, that is, it was not made just at the conception of the twins in Rebecca's womb, or even at their birth, but it was made millenniums ago. God's election of one of the twins instead of the other was merely a further development of His promise of the "seed" that was to crush the evil brought into the world by the Fall in the Garden of Eden (Genesis 3:15). The Fall rendered man incapable of extricating himself from the spider's web of evil in which he had enmeshed himself. Shackled by sin, man became the slave of Satan. Utterly impotent and beyond human help, man could do nothing for and by himself. But God, being omnipotent, chose His own means whereby His fallen creature might be saved. God's method and the instrument by which He would accomplish this redemption are shown in verse 11. God alone must apply the implements of salvation. He does this by means of His own sovereign will, independent of human help.

Since "all have sinned" (Romans 3:23) and "there is none that seeketh after God" (3:11), it is understandable that "the purpose of God" must be "according to election." Man is incapable of working out a righteousness that is pleasing to God. It must be "not of works, but of him that calleth."

How else could it be? Does not Paul state this truth over and over again? ". . . having been foreordained according to the purpose of him who worketh all things after the counsel of his will" (Ephesians 1:11); ". . . but according to his own purpose and grace, which was given us (we did not get it ourselves) in Christ Jesus before times eternal" (II Timothy 1:9).

Most commentators admit that Paul teaches in Romans 9:11 the truth that election rests in the sovereignty of God. Why did God choose Noah even though He knew that Noah would get drunk? Why did God choose Abraham, Isaac and Jacob when He knew they would lie? Why did God choose Moses even though he was a murderer? Why did God choose Israel when He knew that they would be a stubborn and stiff-necked people? Why did God choose David when he knew that David would commit adultery and murder? Why did God choose Peter when He knew that Peter would deny the Saviour? Why did He choose the disciples when He knew that they would forsake the Saviour at His most crucial hour? Why did God choose us when He knew that we were vile sinners and our righteousness was a foul odor in His nostrils? Why? In order "that the purpose of God according to election might stand, not of works, but of him that calleth."

Verse 12: . . . it was said unto her, The elder shall serve the younger.

Verses 10-12 are one complete sentence. This declaration in verse 12 is contrary to Law and Jewish custom. The older son was always the accepted heir who received the greater portion of his father's estate. The family recognized the older son as the head of the family at the father's death. But God never acts according to human laws and concepts. God is not subject to the rules and regulations of man. He is God! He is supreme! He does what He wishes, when He wishes, and with whom He chooses. God acts according to His sovereign will. He does not need the advice of sinful men.

God chooses the very opposite of that which man chooses, and has always done so. God did not choose Abraham's Ishmael, but Abraham's Isaac. He did not choose Isaac's Esau, but Isaac's Jacob. He did not choose Jacob's eldest son Reuben, but Jacob's fourth son Judah. He did not choose Jesse's first-born son Eliab, but Jesse's youngest son David. And He did not choose the throne of Solomon, but the throne of David to be the inheritance of the Messiah upon which David's greater Son would reign over the house of Jacob forever (Luke 1:32, 33). In all these instances God's choice was contrary to human law and Jewish custom. God's action and election are always according to His own will. God is not obligated to anyone, and He acts independently of everyone. God also acts according to His own counsel. Through God's will and by God's own choice Jacob became the head of Isaac's house, and received the blessing as the head of the house from God's own hands. He became the recipient of all the promises that God made to Abraham and Isaac (Genesis 28: 13-15). God placed His approval on Jacob, and confirmed His preference for him. This was in accordance with His will.

Verse 13: Even as it is written, Jacob I loved, but Esau I hated.

One must read the first chapter of Malachi to understand the full meaning of this verse. The blessings that God promised to shower on Jacob included his descendants, that is to say, the nation of Israel (Genesis 25:23). The reader must not lose sight of the truth that in the blessing that God promised to shower on Jacob and his posterity is included the glorious blessing of the Messiah and the Messianic Kingdom.

In the Malachi passage Israel questions God's love, "Wherein hast thou loved us?" (Malachi 1:2). God proceeds to answer Israel's complaint by describing the desolations that He will bring to pass upon the Edomites, who are the descendants of Ishmael and Esau (Genesis 28:9). Devastating judgments will befall those whom God rejects, even among the children of the sons of the patriarchs, like Ishmael who was the son of unbelief on the part of Abraham and Sarah; and Esau, Isaac's son, and Jacob's brother. God chose Jacob and rejected Esau. Both of these men, Ishmael and Esau, were born in the line of messianic descent, and were sons of the patriarchs Abraham and Isaac, chosen by man, but rejected by God. God will have no part or parcel with Ishmael and Esau and His destroying judgments lie ahead for both of them. They will not be among the saints who are to live and reign with Christ in the Millennium (Ezekiel 35).

In Malachi 1:3, God says, "but Esau I hated." This passage and many other passages in the Old Testament tell of God's punitive measures to be carried out against Edom and the unfaithful ones of Israel. In Malachi, God promises to make desolate the heritage of the Edomites, and states that He has indignation against them forever (Malachi 1:4). In other words, when God says, "Esau I hated," it means God's indignation is an eternal indignation and is active forever. (It is like playing anagrams with God's Word to give this word "hate" any other meaning than the clear meaning it has in Malachi 1:3.) It is used in the New Testament to mean not merely to hate, or to dislike, but to hate with wrath (John 3:20; Romans 7:15).

If chapters 38 and 39 of Ezekiel are a description of God's attitude toward Russia, and His dealings with that nation, and this writer believes that they are, then verse 3 of chapter 38 would certainly seem to be a confirmation of this fact: "Thus saith the Lord Jehovah: Behold, I am against thee, O Gog, prince of Rosh, Meshech, and Tubal"; and verse 9 of chapter 39 would be a result of the horrible destruction of Gog and the tragic consequences (39:12). The great majority of Bible scholars agree with this interpretation. In Ezekiel 35 God uses the very same language to describe His intentions toward the descendants of Esau and Ishmael. Mount Seir is a mountain range in Edom (Genesis 36:1-30). In Ezekiel 35 God's judgments are completely and utterly obliterative: v. 3 — ". . . I will make thee a desolation and an astonishment." In v. 4 — ". . . thou shalt be desolate . . ."; v. 6 — "I will prepare thee unto blood, and blood shall pursue thee . . ."; v. 9 — "I will make thee a perpetual (eternal — Hebrew) desolation . . ."; v. 14 — "When the whole earth rejoiceth,

I will make thee desolate." In v. 15 — "As thou didst rejoice over the inheritance of the house of Israel, because it was desolate, so will I do unto thee. . . ." See also Jeremiah 49:17-19; Obadiah 17-19.

Now look at the promise that God has made to the descendants of Jacob: Isaiah 43:1, ". . . O Israel: Fear not, for I have redeemed thee; I have called thee by thy name, thou art mine." Verse 2: "When thou passeth through the waters, I will be with thee; . . . when thou walkest through the fire, thou shall not be burned . . ." Verse 4: "Since thou hast been precious in my sight . . . I have loved thee." See also Isaiah 54:8, 17; 63:9; Jeremiah 30:16, 17; 31:1, 3 ("Yea, I have loved thee with an everlasting love"); 32:37-44.

What conclusions are we to deduce from the foregoing texts which express God's denunciation of the descendants of Ishmael and Esau, and those which express God's everlasting love for Jacob? Surely there can be but one answer: God has chosen Israel and placed His love on this people forever. God has rejected and hated the Edomites with destructive abhorrence, and this, too, is forever. We should never try to change the meaning of the word "forever," for wherever it is used in Scripture it means eternity — everlastingness. How can we dare to alter the meaning of this word when the inspired Word of God links it with endless life in heaven, and with endless life in hell?

This unmistakable and unchanging expression of God's hate toward the descendants of Ishmael and Esau must be understood to be toward them as a nation, not as individuals. We must never lose sight of the truth that the grace of God is still able to grant eternal life to the individual descendant of Esau and Ishmael. By the same token, we must also never lose sight of the truth that every Jew who rejects Jesus Christ is lost and is doomed to a sinner's hell forever. But, on the other hand, because God has set aside the Jewish nation does not mean that the individual Jew who accepts the Lord Jesus Christ as his Saviour and Messiah cannot be saved. Natural descent from parents to offspring does not transmit faith in God, as Romans 9:13 declares in language so plain it can hardly be misunderstood, "Jacob I loved, but Esau I hated," both of them sons of a father beloved of God, Isaac. The fundamental principle of the new birth is the same in the Old Testament as it is in the New Testament. Israel as a nation *must* and *will* be born again, and God will perform this miracle in one day! (Isaiah 66:8; Zechariah

3:9; 12:10; Romans 11:26, 27). So the individual sinner must be born again (John 1:13; 3:1-6; I Peter 1:23).

God invites each and every one of us to accept the Saviour and receive eternal life. God's hands are open and extended with love and compassion to every sinner. Decide not lightly or too hastily, for the holy Judge who will say, "Come, ye blessed of my Father," is the same Judge who will say, "Depart from me, ye cursed." Refuse, and you spend eternity in hell. Choose you must!

Verse 14: What shall we say then? Is there unrighteousness with God? God forbid.

The Apostle is asking a hypothetical question such as an unbeliever might ask, to which the Apostle instantly supplies his own answer, "God forbid!" Because God acts according to His own sovereign will in choosing one person and rejecting another, an unbeliever might be disposed to wonder whether such action is fair or right when directed to an unbeliever like himself. He might even think it uncommendable, or unjust, or iniquitous, or even downright bad. An unbeliever is one who doesn't believe in God, or believes God to be a fictitious or imaginary being with unstable human judgment who could be wrong as often as right especially in making an act of election, sometimes choosing one person and rejecting another, depending upon the mood or whim of the moment. Not believing in God, and, therefore, being ignorant of God's true nature, such an unbeliever could hardly be made to understand that God does not reason like a man. God's ways are not man's ways; therefore, the yardstick that a man uses is incapable of measuring God's ways.

"God forbid!" This characteristic expression of Paul's is understood by this writer to mean, "Don't even let this kind of foolish reasoning be generated in your mind!" There is no unrighteousness in God's administration of election because His nature radiates grace and mercy. These attributes are God's possessions, and what He does with them is His innate prerogative. God is not answerable to man. What God does is His own business. When God acts in mercy and grace He does it out of sheer love, since He is under no compulsion from man to be merciful or gracious. Man has no merit in himself upon which to lay claim to God's grace.

Anyway, does not man have the privilege of free choice? Do we not have a right to choose our friends? Would anyone be foolish enough to accuse a man of injustice in his choice of friends, a co-worker, or a mate? Does not a king choose his ministers and heads of state; a president his cabinet; or a pastor his staff? Who is to say that a man is unjust in choosing one person as a friend, as a co-worker, as a mate, in preference to another? Does not God have the same right as man? God's rejection of any man is merely His act of preterition or the passing by of the non-elect, such as God's rejection of Ishmael and Esau. Thus God called David and rejected Saul; thus He called Paul and rejected someone else (Galatians 1:15, 16; Acts 9:15). God did the same with Jeremiah (1:5). Man acts on the level of humanity, and God acts on the level of Deity, a realm into which the slightest thought of unrighteousness could never enter — ". . . shall not the Judge of all the earth do right?" (Genesis 18: 25).

There is another aspect to the question asked in verse 14 that ought not to be overlooked. The question, "Is there unrighteousness with God?" could be asked by Jewish Christians with this thought in mind; namely, God set the nation of Israel aside because of sin, on the one hand, whereas, on the other hand, He permits the Apostle to exalt Israel as the possessor of the God-bestowed gifts described in verses 4 and 5 of this chapter. God at one time used the descendants of Jacob to bring judgment upon a Gentile nation (Genesis 15:13-16). God's choice of Israel in one case, and His setting her aside in another, are both acts of God's sovereign will. The answer, therefore, to the hypothetical question of Jewish Christians, "Is there unrighteousness with God?" may still be answered with even greater emphasis, "God forbid!"

Verse 15: For he saith to Moses, I will have mercy on whom I have mercy, and I will have compassion on whom I have compassion.

This is the Septuagint Version. In making this statement to Moses God was merely exercising His divine prerogative. We must realize that God has a right to act as He wills just as a king may choose to do that which seems right to him, thus exercising his regal powers. Do not governors of our individual (U.S.) states sometimes grant clemency to a convicted felon and refuse to grant it to another? Is this not exercising the power that is vested in the office to which they have been elected? Cannot God do the same? We cannot imagine depriving God of His freedom to act in any way that is pleasing to Him, anymore than we can imagine depriving a mature human being of his right to his freedom of choice.

It is needless to argue that verse 15 means something different than what it says. The Apostle could scarcely have meant anything else but that it is God, and God only, who chooses those to whom salvation is offered. God alone chooses the recipients of His bountiful grace, and a sinful humanity cannot alter that choice. A sinful humanity cannot dictate to a Holy God. The Apostle is proving that God's choice is in accord with His own freedom and independence as the Omnipotent Creator of the world. What man is there who can claim that he has a right to God's mercy? No human being merits God's grace or favor. "There is none righteous, no, not one; . . . there is none that seeketh after God" (Romans 3:10, 11, quotes Psalm 14:1-3). This being the case, how can a sinful humanity choose to do right or to make wise spiritual decisions? God gives us the faith and the ability through the Holy Spirit to say, "Our Father."

Realizing this truth should cause every born-again child of God to fall to his knees to thank God for salvation. God has done this in spite of the sinner, "for by grace have ye been saved through faith; and that *not of yourselves* . . ." (Ephesians 2:8).

Verse 16: So then it is not of him that willeth, nor of him that runneth, but of God that hath mercy.

In verse 15 God said to Moses, "I will have mercy . . . I will have compassion . . .", words which refer to the nature of God's act in bestowing forgiveness. Paul expresses the same idea in I Timothy 1:13; in Romans 11:30-32; and again in Hebrews 4:16.

Whatever interpretation one puts on these verses it must be admitted that they present a truth which cannot be disputed. This truth is that God through His own choice, exercising His own prerogative, which is His exclusive sovereign privilege, bestows mercy and grace upon whomsoever He wills. God is all in all — Father, Son and Holy Spirit. Our Father gives us the faith to believe; the Holy Spirit bestows upon us the power of conviction; and the Messiah saves us, "Salvation is of the Lord" (Jonah 2:9 KJV). God asks no created being to counsel with Him in administrating this authority, nor can any created being find fault with God over His choice. This right of individual choice is not only a right possessed exclusively by God as an attribute of the God-head, but individual choice is also a right exercised by man in human affairs, and no one can deny to man the right of exercising this privilege. So that in view of verse 16, we must conclude that God dispenses His benefits to whomsoever He pleases. This is God's inalienable prerogative.

The phrase in verse 16 in the Greek, "so then," is a "Paulism" not found in the writings of any other author of the New Testament. It introduces a conclusion. The verse in the Greek is better translated, "So then it is not of the one wishing, nor of the one running, but of God the one having mercy." Wishing, running and having mercy are all present participles. Each expresses the characteristics of a verb and an adjective. The first two describe man's actions of running and wishing, whereas the final action is God's right of choice, which is having mercy.

There is an element of timelessness in God's words as He speaks to man. He spoke, and He still speaks, to Israel in and through the Scriptures. The Bible has never stopped speaking, and still speaks to mankind today.

The truth set forth in verse 16, that it is not the one that wills, or the one that runs, but that it is God, has always been so. It is not a New Testament concept; it is merely an affirmation of an Old Testament truth. "There is a way which seemeth right unto a man; but the end thereof are the ways of death" (Proverbs 14:12; 16:25). But God has provided a sure way and the end of that way is life. ". . . I am the way, and the truth, and the life; no one cometh unto the Father, but by me" (John 14:6). The reader may be asked at this point, which way seems right to you, the way "which seemeth right to a man," or the way which leads unto Him who said, "I am the way"? Which way will you choose, for choose you must!

Verse 17: For the scripture saith unto Pharoah, For this very purpose did I raise thee up, that I might show in thee my power, and that my name might be published abroad in all the earth.

The word "saith" (said) is better translated "says." To the Apostle the Scripture was still speaking. God spoke to Adam in the garden; He spoke to Cain and Abel; He spoke to Noah; He spoke to Abraham, Isaac and Jacob; He spoke to Moses and the prophets who, in turn, spoke to Israel; He spoke to the apostles and the saints; He speaks to us today through His Word.

Verse 17 is a quote of Exodus 9:16. In order to understand this more clearly, we must go back to an earlier chapter in Exodus. Before Moses ever set foot in the land of Egypt, before he ever set out upon his journey to Egypt, God said to him, ". . . but I will harden his (Pharaoh's) heart, and he will not let

the people go" (Exodus 4:21). God's motive in His actions with
Pharaoh is clearly set forth. God's purpose in His dealings with
Pharaoh reveals His intention to carry out His program with
Israel.

God again said to Moses that He would harden Pharaoh's
heart so that God would be glorified, "And I will harden Pharaoh's
heart, and he shall follow after them (Israel); and I will get me
honor upon Pharaoh, and upon all his host; and the Egyptians
shall know that I am Jehovah" (Exodus 14:4). Didn't this
hardening of Pharaoh's heart bring glory to God? There can be
no doubt of it. How much poorer Israel's history would be, and
the history of the whole world for that matter, if there had been
no Passover! But how could there have been a Passover if there
had been no hardening of Pharaoh's heart? Israel is the walking
proof of the authenticity of the Bible and the sovereignty of
God. The world knows of the God of Israel only because of
what God did for Israel. Israel is the shining example of what
God can do and does. She is *living* evidence of the truth that
God uses His chosen vessels to glorify Him, and in the way most
pleasing unto Him. God sent Israel into Egypt for two purposes:
(1) Until the sin of the Amorites be full (Genesis 16:16; II
Chronicles 20:10). (2) To get honor and glory through Israel's
deliverance out of Egyptian bondage and through the hardening
of Pharaoh's heart.

The story of Redemption is contained in the contest between
God, Moses and Israel, on the one hand, and Pharaoh, on the
other. When the Jewish nation lifts its Passover cup she tells the
story of her deliverance out of Egypt. In the same manner,
when the born-again believer lifts the communion cup he, too,
tells the story of deliverance out of the clutches of sin, Satan
and hell. Overnight Israel was transformed from a life of torments and tears, of suppression and slavery, to a life of freedom
and fellowship with God. So the sinner, upon conversion, is
transformed from slavery to sin to freedom in Christ; from a
child destined for hell to one destined for heaven. God did it all
for Israel, and He does it all for the sinner.

The Apostle states in verse 17 that God's action in Pharaoh's
life was, "that I might show in thee my power, and that my
(God's) name might be published abroad in all the earth." So
it was! Wherever the story of Redemption is told it tells the
story of Israel's experiences and her deliverance out of Egypt. Is
this not what John the Baptist says, "Behold, the Lamb of God,
that taketh away the sin of the world!" (John 1:29)? Is this not

what the Saviour said when He spoke to Nicodemus, "And as Moses lifted up the serpent in the wilderness, even so must the Son of man be lifted up" (John 3:14)? Is this not the fulfillment of the story of Redemption as recorded in Matthew 26:26-29? Is not the Communion as explained and presented by Paul in I Corinthians 11:26, ". . . eat this bread, and drink the cup . . ." the story of the Passover? How could all this have come to pass if God had not raised up this particular Pharaoh, and had he not hardened his heart? This was God's plan, this was God's method, this was God's instrument. Who would have the temerity to question the power and wisdom of our omnipotent God?

Every child of God will agree with the Prophet Daniel when he wrote, "And he changeth the times and the seasons; he removeth kings, and setteth up kings; . . ." (Daniel 2:21), that he was setting forth the Sovereignty of God. Paul says the same in verse 17. God raised up Pharaoh, God hardened his heart, God was glorified in Egypt, and magnified in the parting of the waters of the Red Sea which Israel passed through dry-shod. For this purpose, and for this purpose alone, God raised up Pharaoh. As another writer stated, "In this sense was Pharaoh 'raised up.' He made his appearance in the world. God said 'Let him be,' and he was. *He became a man and a monarch.*" Chapter 15 of Exodus tells the story of God's glorification.

Verse 18: So then he hath mercy on whom he will, and whom he will he hardeneth.

The Apostle is drawing a conclusion from what he has previously written. He makes a similar statement on other occasions (Ephesians 1:5; Philippians 1:6; 2:13). That God does what He wills is, therefore, not something new that Paul is saying to the church at Rome in Romans 9:17.

Jehovah has always acted according to His own wisdom and purpose. The Old Testament bears this out. He promises to do to Israel as a nation what He is doing for every New Testament saint. In Jeremiah 31:31-34; 33:6-8, 26, are recorded a series of God's "I wills!" "*I will* make a new covenant with Israel . . . this is the covenant that *I will* make . . . *I will* put my law in their inward parts . . . and *I will* be their God . . . *I will* forgive their iniquity . . . (33:6-8, 26) . . . *I will* bring it health . . . *I will* cure them . . . *I will* reveal unto them abundance of peace and truth. *I will* cause the captivity to return, and will build them. And *I will* cleanse them . . . *I will* pardon . . ." (also Jeremiah 50:20; Ezekiel 34:11-17). It is sheer ignorance to say that God acts one way in the Old Testament, and another way in the New Testament, when it is with salvation in view. The plan of salvation is never altered from Genesis through Revleation. It is the same God working with His own in both Testaments. God does not vacillate, nor is He irresolute (Malachi 3:6; Hebrews 13:8).

What the Apostle is saying in verse 18 he has said in verses 11 and 15. This doctrine is fully established. Man does not have any claim on God because God is man's Creator. If God could harden Pharaoh's heart, then He can harden the heart of any other person.

V. 18b: ". . . and whom he will he hardeneth." The Greek word, which is translated "hardeneth," means to make stubborn, to render obstinate, headstrong.

The prophet Isaiah was told to make the heart of Israel fat, their ears heavy and to shut their eyes (6:10). (See also Deuteronomy 29:4; Isaiah 29:10; Psalm 69:23.) The most striking passage in the New Testament containing this thought is Romans 11:8 KJV, ". . . God hath given them the spirit of slumber. . . ." That this blindness or hardness will prevail is God's will, "until the fulness of the Gentiles be come in" (11:25), and God's will cannot be questioned. Does God act differently with a Jewish soul than with a Gentile soul? Certainly not! Have not most of us said that some people, meaning both Jews and Gentiles, are "Gospel-hardened?" The doctrine of the Sovereignty of God is the greatest incentive to preaching the Gospel. Since no one knows who will accept, it is imperative that the Gospel be proclaimed everywhere and at all times, to all classes of people. It is still God's good pleasure to save them that believe through "the foolishness of the preaching" (I Corinthians 1:21). "So belief cometh of hearing, and hearing by the word of Christ" (Romans 10:17). In the light of this truth the preaching of the cross is mandatory. The accomplishments of this kind of preaching must be left to the Holy Spirit. This writer preaches like a Calvinist, and gives an invitation like an Arminian. Thank God for the good results. The preaching of the Gospel is done only for the purpose of salvation. Man is already condemned whether he hears the Gospel or not (Romans 1:18-32). Therefore, a person is not lost after he hears the Gospel. He is hearing the Gospel in his lost condition; he must be given faith to believe it. Is not faith a gift of God? Then why doesn't God give faith to everyone, since no one has it of himself? (Read the *Epistle to the Romans,* by Sanday, page 257; and Henry Alford's *New Testament for English Readers,* page 294.)

Verse 19: Thou wilt say then unto me, Why doth he still find fault? For who withstandeth his will?

Paul is putting these questions into the mouth of an objector because of what has previously been said in our comment on verse 18 about God hardening Pharaoh's heart. This objector could be any man, and not necessarily a Jew. Even today there are many who ask the same questions.

Every man, from the fall in the Garden of Eden to this very moment, is born in sin (Romans 3:10-12). He is lost and doomed to hell, and is even now on the road to hell, that is, every man who does not believe in God and his Messiah, or who is not even concerned about God. For all he cares, God is dead, even as some so-called theologians are saying. Unsaved man is constantly seeking to satiate his flesh which is anti-God. This is the mode of life of every unregenerate man. Every human being is born in a lost condition. This is his natural state. From the moment of birth until the last breath of life on earth, every unsaved person moves closer to death and hell.

In the light of the foregoing, the questions in verse 19 are absurd and futile. Sin is disobedience to God's law, "and every transgression and disobedience" receives its just recompense of reward in hell, sin's final destination (Hebrews 2:2), "where their worm dieth not, and the fire is not quenched" (Mark 9:48). The hardening of the heart is the concomitant of a life of sin. God abhors evil and His nature cannot endure its presence. God is just and He must mete out His punishments justly. Sin cannot go unpunished.

It is only an evil and perverted generation such as ours that justifies sin or regards it as an illness. We call an alcoholic or a dope addict, sick; we say that a sexual pervert is a psychopath, which implies that he is, perhaps, the victim of bad advice; a juvenile delinquent we say is the result of an unhappy home or poor education; one who is lazy, who won't work and who lies and steals to get out of working, we call a schizophrenic or a paranoid, or we say that he has "delusions of grandeur" or a misdirected imagination.

But all these deviations from decency and virtue are designated by one or more simple terms in the Bible — sin, demon possession, the work of Satan — each and all punishable, by God's edict, with death.

The questions which Paul put into the mouth of an objector in verse 19 are answered by the Apostle in the verses which now follow. What was said in verse 15 must be repeated; namely, God will have mercy on whom He will have mercy, and compassion on whom He will have compassion, which is to say that it is God's innate and irrevocable right to select whom He will for blessing or punishment. Would anyone be foolish enough to question a potentate's selection of a staff, or the people's selection of a president, a senator or a congressman? Then why question the King of the universe? (See Daniel 2:21; 4:35.) God chooses out of this mess and mass of humanity a people upon whom He wishes to shower His blessings.

It is only a stubborn, sin-hardened, Christ-denying individual who would have the audacity to accuse God of a human weakness such as ill-treatment. Such a person would do this only because he refuses to abandon his sin and humble himself by confessing he is a sinner. He wants to have his cake and eat it too. One cannot live in sin and practice all the sinful acts of the flesh and have God, Christ, and salvation. Sin prepares for its victims a bed in hell, and unrepentant sinners are destined to lie in it.

The born-again believer, the child of God who has been washed by the blood of the Saviour ought always to sing, "Isn't He Wonderful?"

> Wonderful Name He bears
> Wonderful crown He wears,
> Wonderful blessings His triumphs afford;
> Wonderful Calvary,
> Wonderful grace for me,
> Wonderful love of my wonderful Lord!

Is this your testimony? It can be!

Verse 20: Nay but, O man, who art thou that repliest against God? Shall the thing formed say to him that formed it, Why didst thou make me thus?

The Greek word which is here translated "Nay but," is a difficult one to put into English, and is considered a Greek untranslatable idiomatic expression. This Greek word is used in the following places, Luke 11:28, where it is translated "Yea rather"; in Romans 10:18, where it is translated "But I say," and in Philippians 3:8, where we find it rendered, "Yea verily"; whereas in verse 20 of Romans 9, the English equivalent is "Nay but."

The Greek expression might be characterized as expostulatory, a mixture of surprise, impatience and exasperation, that any person should *think* of asking such a question of God, let alone actually asking it.

What mortal creature, what intelligent human being, would dare to question God whose very being is the perfection of holiness, righteousness and justice, whose word and power sustain all life, all light, all beauty from eternity to eternity? What is man but an infinitesimal point of consciousness whose lifespan is as nothing in the unending vastness of eternity? How can such a creature question God? And if he could, on what compulsion must God answer? Is God under any obligation to answer every fatuous question hurled at Him by depraved or feeble-minded sinners?

Or looked at from another point of view, is God man's enemy? Did God create man only to destroy him? A ridiculous question in view of John 3:17, "For God sent not his Son into the world to condemn the world; but that the world through him might be saved" (KJV). Is then sinful man God's enemy? Yes! God does not flee from man. Did not God say to Adam, "Where art thou?" But sinful man flees from God. Only a feeble-minded or sin-perverted creature would strive with his maker. Only a foolish son would say to his father, "Why did you bring me into the world?" or ask his mother, "Why did you give birth to me?" When Paul asked the question in verse 20, "Shall the thing formed say to him that formed it, Why didst thou make me thus?" he was no doubt inspired by the words of Isaiah in 45:8-12, to which the reader is referred.

We must realize that all mankind is at God's mercy. It is sheer folly and extreme irreverence to question the Creator's actions. He alone knows what is just and proper. His actions, His deeds, and His motives are beyond human ken.

The Old Testament is full of God's dealings with His chosen vessels who carry out His purpose in accordance with His divine will. Noah built an ark at God's command; Abraham left Ur of the Chaldees, and cast out Hagar and Ishmael, both at God's express command; God told Moses to bring Israel out of Egypt; God ordered Jonah to go to Nineveh; and so on throughout the Old Testament, God commanded His chosen ones and they obeyed. God, the Master Potter, makes what He pleases of His human clay. Rarely, in Scripture, does the clay revolt and question the heavenly Potter's wisdom, as did Jonah when God had to command him twice to go to Nineveh (Jonah 3:1-3). Jonah re-

volted against God's authority. Thus Paul's imaginary objector
to God's authority is told in verse 20, "O man, who art thou?"
which might be paraphrased, "What are you, O man, to hurl
charges at God?" to which there can be but one answer; namely,
"Clay in the hands of the Master Potter!" God's dominion over
men is absolute, and His power over their wills irresistible. This
is the doctrine of the Sovereignty of God.

To a Jewish person versed in his beliefs the doctrine of the
Sovereignty of God is not a strange one. It forms the backbone
of God's dealings with Israel. It is the same God who deals with
a nation in the Old Testament (II Chronicles 20:6-8; Daniel
4:35) that deals with individuals in the New Testament. Moreover, He also deals with individuals in the Old Testament as well
(Genesis 50:19, 20; Isaiah 29:10; and Daniel 2:20-22; 3:16-18).

**Verse 21: Or hath not the potter a right over the clay, from
the same lump to make one part a vessel unto honor, and another unto dishonor?**

God esteems the believer as precious in His sight as He does
the blood of the Saviour (I Peter 1:18, 19, 21). The Greek word
which is translated "dishonor" is written "a-honor," with an "a"
preceding the word "honor," thus negating the word honor. The
Greek word which is translated "honor," means to place a price
upon, to value, to dignify. See I Peter 2:7 where the word
honor is translated "preciousness." Again the word "a-honor" is
translated dishonor in II Timothy 2:20.

The Apocrypha (the books between the Old and New Testaments) contains one book entitled, "Wisdom of Solomon," 15:7,
in which are these words: "For the potter, tempering soft earth,
fashioneth every vessel with much labour for our service: yea, of
the same clay he maketh both the vessels that serve for clean uses,
and likewise also all such as serve to the contrary; but what is the
use of either sort, the potter himself is the judge" (KJV).

The illustration of the potter and the clay is an Old Testament
illustration that God has used of Israel (Isaiah 64:8; Jeremiah
18:1-6). God, the heavenly Potter, took a piece of Gentile clay
and fashioned out of it one human vessel whom He named Abraham. Out of this vessel of Gentile clay named Abraham, God
fashioned a nation called Israel, a people made for His honor,
His glory, and His own eternal purpose. No Christian theologian
or historian will dispute these truths. No one can question God's
right and privilege to deal with Israel after His own will. God
has been shaping and molding Israel for over 3,000 years. He

has taken her through the fires of persecution and the waters of tribulation, by trial and torment, in order to mold the nation to His program and purpose according to His divine will. These are undeniable historic facts. Israel's destiny is to become the universal evangelist in God's program (Zechariah 8:23), and to have an international ministry (Isaiah 61:6), as the priests of the Gentile nations, and the Levites of the millennial temple (Isaiah 66:18-21). All of which is in accordance with God's sovereign will.

The same God who worked with His people in the Old Testament, and still works with them, is the same God who is now working with the born-again believers of the New Testament. He is the same omnipotent, omniscient, and omnipresent sovereign Creator of the universe. He exercises today the same right, the same authority, the same power and freedom to do that which is pleasing to Him, even as He has done through the millenniums of eternity. This is exactly the meaning of what the Apostle is saying in verse 21 in his use of the potter-and-clay figure. Out of the mass of sinful human clay God takes one piece here, and another piece there, and fashions these pieces for His glory, to conform to the image of His Son. He molds them and covers them with His Son's righteousness so that His chosen ones may be adopted as His workmanship in Christ Jesus according to His own will and pleasure (Ephesians 1:5, 9; 2:10; Philippians 1:6; 2:13). The record is clear that God does not do this for every human being.

If God acts according to His Own eternal counsel, have we the right to question Him? The Apostle is comparing a human potter and his lump of earthy clay to God the heavenly Potter and His human clay. Does the earthy clay in the hands of the human potter possess the intelligence and speech to enable it to question the potter's right to make of it a particular kind of vessel? Certainly not! Then how can the human clay have the intelligence to question God the heavenly Potter as to His right to make of the human clay a particular kind of vessel, whether unto honor or unto dishonor? How unreasonable we humans often become! No human being has the spiritual right to question God.

The child of God should thank his eternal Father that He has chosen him, a depraved sinner, for such an exalted destiny as to be made a "joint heir with Christ," rather than to question God's sovereign prerogative. God has not counseled with man to find out what He (God) should do. God commands, God orders, God instructs, God moves the universe, and man moves according to His will. God "commandeth men that they should all everywhere repent" (Acts 17:30). For, "except ye repent, ye shall all in like manner perish" (Luke 13:3). But bear in mind, no one has any claim on God's mercy and grace. They are His to give to whomsoever He chooses.

There is one more thought that must be considered in verse 21. The Apostle was fully aware of the meaning of being a "vessel unto honor," and "another unto dishonor." Paul was the vessel chosen unto honor. The Lord Jesus left the Father's throne to talk to Paul and to bring him to his right senses. From his birth he was the clay which was fashioned "unto honor" (Galatians 1:15, 16) to be one thing, ". . . this man is a vessel of choice to me to bear my name both before nations and kings and the sons of Israel" (Acts 9:15, Literal Greek). Paul was a choice vessel indeed. But what trials and torments he suffered as the heavenly Potter fashioned him into a choice vessel! It took tears and tribulation, persecution and privation, discouragement and disappointment to scrape and polish this lump of human clay named Paul into a vessel of honor in the hands of the eternal Potter.

Verse 21 is of such grave importance in this study of the Epistle to the Romans, that it has been necessary to emphasize its implications over and over again. God acts independently of man, and man has no claim upon God's actions of mercy and grace. Nevertheless, God has no pleasure in the death of the wicked (Ezekiel 33:11); whereas, the death of His saints is precious in His sight (Psalm 116:15), because "to be absent from the body" is "to be at home with the Lord" (II Corinthians 5:8).

Verse 22: What if God, willing to show his wrath, and to make his power known, endured with much long-suffering vessels of wrath fitted unto destruction . . . :

The Apostle continues the discussion of God's attributes and His sovereignty. The meaning of verse 22 might be somewhat clearer if the phraseology could be slightly extended, as follows: What if God, choosing to manifest or display His wrath and indignation, and to reveal His power and His might, endured with much long-suffering and unwillingness to avenge too hastily the wrongs committed by the vessels of wrath having been fitted for destruction? Love that is blind to immorality, debauchery and sin is not love, but, rather, it is sheer stupidity. Evils, if they are not stopped, harnessed or eradicated, will wreak destruction.

Sin in the world is like a "bull in a china shop" — it destroys. Unless sin is torn out by the roots, it poisons whatever it comes in contact with. It is like a cancer that infects the tissues until it destroys the whole body.

Paul says that God is long-suffering and patient. God does not reconcile and balance His accounts every week. But when He does, He overlooks no errors. Mercy and long-suffering are as much attributes of God (Exodus 34:6 KJV; Numbers 14:18 KJV; Psalms 86:15 KJV) as justice, namely, ". . . Jehovah is a God of justice . . ." (Isaiah 30:18). He is also a God of wrath, but to wrath He must be provoked. (See Deuteronomy 9:7; II Chronicles 28:11; Zechariah 7:12; John 3:36; Ephesians 5:6.) These vessels and nations upon whom the wrath of God is to be poured are deserving "of the fierceness of the wrath of God, the Almighty" (Revelation 19:15). It is the punishment that fits the crime. Sin has fitted them unto destruction. However, this does not mean annihilation, but rather eternal damnation ". . . reserved unto fire against the day of judgment and perdition of ungodly men" (II Peter 3:7 KJV; Matthew 10:15; Jude 1:7; Mark 9:44 KJV).

The judgment that falls upon these sinful vessels demonstrates and illustrates the power of God. "The wrath of man shall praise thee (God)" (Psalm 76:10). The hardening of Pharaoh's heart revealed the power of God, and His omnipotence was demonstrated in such fashion that the whole world was cognizant of it. ". . . but in very deed for this cause have I made thee to stand, to show thee my power, and that my name may be declared throughout the earth" (Exodus 9:16).

Verse 23: . . . and that he might make known the riches of his glory upon vessels of mercy, which he afore prepared unto glory . . . ,

What the Apostle is saying here is that the actions of God spoken of in verse 22 had an ulterior motive; namely, God's love. The comparison made in verse 21, of God's actions in dealing with mankind, are like those of a potter molding a vessel. God's wrath was revealed in order that His power and His long-suffering might be demonstrated even in the vessels that were ripe for eternal punishment. God did all this, the Apostle says, "that he might make known the riches (or those abundant blessings) of his glory upon vessels of mercy." Or, to put it another way, God's motives and actions are always inspired by the very nature of His being, or, as Paul expresses it, "the riches of his glory," that

He may demonstrate upon His own children, whom He calls "vessels of mercy," His grace, by pouring it out abundantly upon those He loves. God plans and acts with this purpose in view so that all creation may know the good that He gives to His own here and in the hereafter. Is this not what Paul said in Romans 8:28, ". . . all things work together for good, even to them that are called according to his purpose"?

Did not God's wrath and His devastating judgments upon Pharaoh and the Egyptian hordes merely reveal in a striking and awe-inspiring manner His love for His people Israel? Was not God's deliverance of Israel from Egyptian bondage a mighty revelation of His purpose in calling Israel to be His chosen people? Was not this deliverance of Israel the culmination of God's purpose in sending the descendants of Abraham into Egypt? Certainly! Then, looking back at verse 22, God's actions upon the "vessels of wrath" are based upon the same reasons set forth in verse 23, in order that He might show to the whole world what He does for the vessels which are the recipients of His mercy. God's righteous means always justify His holy ends.

Now the facts we have been considering in our study of verses 22 and 23 concerning God's method of dealing with "vessels of wrath" and "vessels of mercy," have nothing to do with a condition that might arise unexpectedly and require an emergency solution. God does not plan things "at the last moment," so to speak, or act on uncontrollable impulses. From what we are permitted to know of God's methods, as revealed in Scripture, it is evident that His plans for mankind were made millenniums ago. Paul says of God, in verse 23, "which he *afore* prepared unto glory," the word "afore" meaning "previously"; "for whom he did foreknow he also did *predestinate*" (Romans 8:29 KJV). This same truth is expressed in Ephesians 1:4, ". . . he chose us in him before the foundation of the world . . ."; and, again, in Ephesians 2:7, ". . . that in the ages to come he might show the exceeding riches of his grace in kindness toward us in Christ Jesus." (See also Ephesians 2:10.)

The Apostle had few earthly possessions. In the main he worked for his support, and preached to the glory of God. Having little of this world's goods, he never lost sight of "the riches of his glory" that God had laid up in store for him. He speaks frequently of God's "riches" in his various epistles: Romans 2:4; 11:12, 33; II Corinthians 8:2; Ephesians 1:7, 18; 3:8, 16; Colossians 1:27. Included in these *riches* that God so generously gives to his saints is the *richness* of His forgiving mercy and grace which He "freely" gives to us (Romans 3:24; 8:32; I Corinthians 2:12). We must never lose sight of the truth that we did not obtain all these "riches of his glory" by our own efforts. God "freely" gave this wealth to us. God alone is the "Giver," He alone plans, prepares, and distributes according to His sovereign will. Mankind cannot demand it.

Verse 24: . . . even us, whom he also called, not from the Jews only, but also from the Gentiles?

Here is the true picture of the New Testament Church. It is comprised of Jews and Gentiles whom God has called unto salvation through the blood of Jesus Christ, and made of both one body and one local assembly. This is a call from God to which man is to respond. When God calls He does not invite, He does not plead. God *commands* as a general commands the military forces under him. God "now commandeth all men everywhere to repent" (Acts 17:30 KJV). Commanding certain persons to perform particular tasks is not something new in God's dealings with humanity. Such has always been God's method. He called Adam; He called Noah; He called Abraham; He called Moses; He called Israel; and He calls every believer. Because God commands as a military officer commands those under him, so the command "to repent" must be regarded as a military command.

Since God is no respecter of persons, since all have sinned and fallen short of God's requirements for righteousness, inasmuch as there is not even one righteous person on earth who consistently practices righteousness, it stands to reason that man, to become acceptable to God, must change his nature and his mode of living. Therefore, God summons men to repent, to make an about-face, and completely change their direction of mind, of heart, and of life. This summons is the Gospel which is not only God's power unto salvation, but also the cohesive element uniting Jew and Gentile into such close relationship that they become one in Christ. Thus they become blood-brothers in the truest sense through the blood of the Saviour.

This union of Jew and Gentile into one being in Christ is the true local church, and will ultimately become the "body of Christ" when the Rapture takes place. Such a union is what the Apostle refers to when he says, "even us . . . not from the Jews only, but also from the Gentiles."

V. 24: ". . . whom he also called . . ." is another manner of saying, "whom he has elected." God's order in calling His

elected ones is recorded in Romans 8:30, and He calls Jews and
Gentiles without discrimination. It is apparent that some of these
classes of mankind, whether Jews or Gentiles, are not called, and
are given up to live in debauchery and sin. God's order of calling
His elected ones is millenniums old, and is, therefore, not a new
truth introduced by Paul in this epistle. God chose Isaac, and
not Ishmael; He chose Jacob, and not Esau; and a long list of
Old Testament saints, for which see my commentary on Romans
9:10-12. God gave up Esau and Ishmael to sin, death and
judgment, just as He gave up the men described in Romans
1:24, 26, 28. God is still doing this today. Some of Israel have
been blinded, and some have not (Romans 11:7, 25). Some
Gentiles are saved and some are not. This selection has been
operating throughout all ages regardless and irrespective of dispensations. To you, therefore, who read these words, be advised,
and make your "election and calling sure" (II Peter 1:10).

**Verse 25: As he (God) saith also in Hosea, I will call that my
people, which was not my people; and her beloved, that was
not beloved.**

This verse is a reference to Hosea 2:23, which is a prophecy
relating to the restoration of the people of Israel to their rightful
position at the Second Coming of our Lord Jesus Christ. Hosea
2:23 in Hebrew and in the Septuagint differs from Romans 9:25,
the text before us. The phrase, "not my people" and "not (my)
beloved" are the names respectively of the prophet Hosea's son
(Hosea 1:3) and daughter (Hosea 1:6). Paul changes the word
"mercy" (in Hosea 2:23) to "love" (or "beloved") in Romans
9:25. In the Hebrew, the phrase in Hosea 2:23 is, "hath not
obtained mercy." The prophecy in Hosea does not make any
reference to the Gentiles, but rather to the ten tribes of Israel
who became idolatrous. God is promising their restoration in the
Hosea passage (See Hosea 1:11). In Romans 9:25, however, the
Apostle is applying this passage to Gentiles who have accepted
Christ as Lord and Saviour, and who are now recipients of God's
love. In the past, "God gave them up" (see Romans 1:24, 26, 28).
Even though they were dead in their trespasses and sins (Ephesians 2:1) and were separated from Christ, alienated from the
commonwealth of Israel, strangers from the covenants of the
promise, and without God in the world (Ephesians 2:12), yet
these Gentiles, who were in this despicable and hopeless condition, "that once were far off are made nigh in the blood of
Christ" (Ephesians 2:13). From the Biblical standpoint of the

total depravity of man, these Gentiles were doomed. In spite of this fact, through divine intervention, this seemingly hopeless people became the beneficiaries of God's love, mercy and grace. Twenty-three years before this, Paul had borne testimony before the council at Jerusalem in these words, "Symeon hath rehearsed how first God visited the Gentiles to take out of them a people for his name" (Acts 15:14). As for the Jews who were saved, Paul refers to them as a "remnant" in Romans 11:5, "Even so then at this present time also there is a remnant according to the election of grace."

The New Testament Church is comprised of a remnant out of Israel and a remnant out of the Gentiles. Of these two groups God has made one new creation; namely, the Church. As every living Jew who hears the Gospel will not inherit the Messianic Kingdom, neither will every living Gentile who hears the Gospel enter into the benefits of eternal life. In both cases there will be only a remnant.

Returning now to Romans 9:25 and Paul's words, "As he (God) saith also in Hosea," the verse in Hosea 2:23 which has *implication* to the restoration of the lost ten tribes, but which Paul in Romans 9:25 by *application* now applies to the Gentiles who have accepted Christ as Saviour.

Humanly speaking, Israel's lot among the nations is not an enviable one. Jews are hated, persecuted, discriminated against, and, from all appearances, they are bereft of God's protection, mercy and love. Yet the prophet Hosea states that through divine intervention Israel will be restored by God to His love, care and protection. (Peter makes the same *application* of Hosea 2:23 in I Peter 2:10 as Paul makes in Romans 9:25.)

Every Bible student should be aware of the difference between the *application* of a text and the *implication* of the same text. There are numerous ways in which a text can be applied. But there is only one true interpretation and *implication*. The apostles Paul and Peter are applying the passage in Hosea to the New Testament saint. They do not negate its true meaning. Hosea 2:23 as it appears in the Old Testament destroys the A-millennial position. It promises Israel's restoration to their "peoplehood" and to their land *before* the millennium. Romans 9:25 places the saint on the same basis as God places Israel. Israel is God's eternal earthly people, and the born-again believers are God's eternal heavenly people. The same God grants eternal gifts to both. God does this without human intervention.

Verse 26: And it shall be, that in the place where it was said unto them, Ye are not my people, there shall they be called sons of the living God.

As verse 25 is an *application* of the original text, so is verse 26. As verse 25 will be literally fulfilled, so will verse 26 have its completion in Israel. The word "place" in verse 26, this writer believes to be Israel's literal place, the Promised Land. Although a great number of Gentiles and the Arab nations do not believe that the land of Palestine belongs to Israel, God emphatically states that it does (Ezekiel 37:21). The nation Israel will be restored to her land just as sure as every born-again believer will be brought into the presence of Christ.

As to God's restoration of Israel to her land, see: Jeremiah 31:11; 32:36, 37; Ezekiel 20:34; 34:12; 37:21; Hosea 1-10; 2: 14-16; and others.

As to God's love for every born-again believer, see: John 13: 1-3; I Corinthians 15:50-58; I Thessalonians 4:3-18.

God's Word is irrevocable; God's promises indisputable; God's character and personality immutable (Malachi 3:6; Hebrews 13:8; James 1:17).

Verse 27: And Isaiah crieth concerning Israel, If the number of the children of Israel be as the sand of the sea, it is the remnant that shall be saved . . . :

This passage in Isaiah (10:22) is part of a section (10:20-23) that constitutes the promise of the restoration of Israel. However, Isaiah 10:20-23, from the Septuagint version, is considerably shorter than the Hebrew, and is, therefore, incomplete. The phrase "in that day" in Isaiah 10:20 is prophetic. The Rabbis of old claimed that this phrase in Isaiah, and the phrase, "in that time," in Jeremiah 50:20, speak of the time when the Messiah will come. Since "in that day" is a phrase in Isaiah 10:20, it is clear that Romans 9:27 presents the truth that only a remnant in Israel will return to God and accept God's promised Messiah. This return of the remnant will occur at the end of the Tribulation when the nations of the world will muster their forces in the vain attempt to destroy Israel from the face of the earth (Joel 3; Zechariah 12:2-11).

This stupendous event is the great moment in prophecy when Israel reaches her extremity and turns to God and accepts the Messiah whom they have pierced and rejected in ignorance (Zechariah 12:9, 10; Acts 3:17). But it is only a remnant that

God pardons (Jeremiah 50:20). This saving of the remnant is what Paul states in verse 27. Although Israel has become a multitudinous nation, it is only a remnant that will be saved — only those upon whom the "spirit of grace and of supplication" is poured. Zechariah 12:10 and Isaiah 10:22 are other ways of stating the truth of Romans 9:6, "For they are not all Israel, that are of Israel." Only after Israel has experienced the hell of tribulation and has been through the fires of trials and testings, and is refined and purified by these fires, as gold and silver are refined, will the remnant of that nation turn to God and His Messiah (Malachi 3:1-6).

God watches over the remnant and purifies and preserves those who comprise that remnant. They are the God-chosen converts who return, and it is God's own doing ". . . for I will pardon them whom I leave as a remnant" (Jeremiah 50:20). God restores them to the land and sustains them, "And I will bring Israel again to his pasture . . ." (Jeremiah 50:19).

In verses 27, 28 and 29 the Apostle continues to bring further evidence to substantiate the doctrine of the Sovereignty of God. He is showing that the God of the Old Testament, who is watching over and preserving the nation Israel, is doing the very same thing with His saints of the New Testament. The God who saves Israel *as a nation* is the God who saves the *individual saint*.

Verse 28: . . . for the Lord will execute his word upon the earth, finishing it and cutting it short.

This verse (28) is the second half of verse 27 which Paul is quoting from the Septuagint version of Isaiah 10:20-23. Here is the quotation from the Septuagint, "He will finish the work, and cut it short in righteousness; because the Lord will make a short work in the world." This verse in Isaiah 10:23 ASV, is as follows: "For a full end, and that determined, will the Lord, Jehovah of hosts, make in the midst of all the earth," which is the completion of the particular prophecy begun in verse 20 of Isaiah chapter 10. Romans 9:27, 28, and its source in Isaiah 10:20-23, is the proof that God Himself will have to bring peace into the world. He has decreed it and He will see to its fulfillment. The Lord Himself, and only the Lord, will determine when this will take place. He said to His Messiah, ". . . Sit thou at my right hand, until I make thine enemies thy footstool" (Psalm 110:1). "I will overturn, overturn, overturn it . . . until he comes whose right it is; and I will give it him" (Ezekiel 21:27. In the Hebrew it is 21:32).

God says that He, God, will overturn and overturn and overturn it "until." God's Word is plain that sin and perverseness can go only so far, and then God calls a halt. When the Gentiles *"re-fused"* to have God in their knowledge, "God gave them up unto a reprobate mind" (Romans 1:28). By the same token, when Israel refused to harken to God's Word, and to His prophets, God scattered them to the four corners of the earth, and left them there among the Gentiles where they are being persecuted to the present hour (Deuteronomy 28:15-68).

The day must come when all this evil will be stopped. The Gentiles will plan their last world-wide revolution against Jehovah and His Messiah, and God will destroy this revolution, breaking it into pieces like a potter's vessel (Psalm 2:9). This Gentile revolution is sin's last fling. The nations will try to destroy every semblance of Godliness and righteousness, and even try to exterminate the Jews so completely that even the name of Israel may not be remembered (Psalm 83:1-4). In the midst of the attempted decimation of Israel, Israel will awaken to her sin, will acknowledge her offense, and seek God's face (Hosea 5:15). Then she will say, "Come, let us return unto Jehovah; for he hath torn, and he will heal us; he hath smitten, and will bind us up" (Hosea 6:1).

Unless God does intervene and cuts short the devastation of sin, man will destroy himself. "And except those days had been shortened, no flesh would have been saved" (Matthew 24:22). If no flesh were saved then the kingdom of the Messiah which was promised at His birth (Luke 1:30-33) could never be established in Jerusalem. But notice again the verse in Matthew 24:22. God intervenes and shortens those days "for the elect's sake," the "elect" being the remnant of Israel which God Himself has preserved (Jeremiah 50:20).

Hence shortening those days "for the elect's sake," is what the Apostle is saying in verse 28, ". . . For the Lord will execute his word upon the earth, finishing it and cutting it short." It must be "thus saith the Lord," "one jot or one tittle shall in no wise pass till all be fulfilled" (Matthew 5:18 KJV).

Verse 29: And, as Isaiah hath said before, Except the Lord of Sabaoth had left us a seed, we had become as Sodom, and had been made like unto Gomorrah.

This verse quotes Isaiah 1:9 which reads "Except Jehovah of hosts had left unto us a very small remnant, we shall have been as Sodom, we should have been like unto Gomorrah."

Because of her sins, her iniquity and idolatry, her stubbornness and disobedience, Israel deserved the same fate as Sodom and Gomorrah. Because of sin the wrath of God descended upon Sodom and Gomorrah. God is just, He is long-suffering, He is righteous. Because these are His attributes, sin is hateful and abhorrent in His sight, and punishable. Were it not so, if God were tolerant of sin and did not punish the sinner, He would not be our just and loving Father. Obedience is God's first prerequisite, ". . . Of every tree of the garden thou mayest freely eat: but of the tree of the knowledge of good and evil, thou shalt not eat of it: . . ." (Genesis 2:16, 17). Adam and Eve disobeyed God and God punished them. What God did to Adam and Eve He is still doing to every descendant of theirs. This punishment for disobedience is what God did and is still doing to Israel. Verse 29 quotes from the first chapter of Isaiah which contains a vivid portrayal of Israel's disobedience and of God's displeasure.

Even though God promised the patriarchs that their seed would be as numerous as the sands of the sea and as multitudinous as the stars in the heavens, He did not promise that He would tolerate their sins and let them go unpunished. Because He is God and is omnipotent, He will guide the course of history by His will so that even though Israel would be severely punished, there would always be a faithful remnant left, thus fulfilling God's promises to the patriarchs that Israel would have a seed and a land. Thereby God maintains His standards and fulfills His promises to His people. Because God kept His promises so faithfully in the Old Testament, He can be trusted implicitly to keep them in the New Testament. In the Old Testament God promised Israel a seed, a land, and a blessing. He is keeping that promise. In the New Testament God promises His saints resurrection from the dead, eternal life, and a home in glory. All these gifts are the heritage of every saint who will put his trust in Jesus Christ as Saviour (Philippians 2:13).

The Apostle is not only portraying the Sovereignty of God in verses 27, 28 and 29, but he is also substantiating God's trustworthiness to Israel and His saints. God has promised eternal life to every saint who will accept His Son, "He that believeth on the Son hath eternal life . . ." (John 3:36). Will you accept Him? The choice is yours.

Verse 30: What shall we say then? That the Gentiles, who followed not after righteousness, attained to righteousness, even the righteousness which is of faith . . . :

What conclusion is to be drawn from what the Apostle has been saying in the preceding verses? The conclusion must be that the Gentiles who are not even now pursuing righteousness according to the method and means of Jewish standards, have obtained righteousness. The word translated "followed" in verse 30, is a present active participle which should be translated following. The word translated "attained" expresses a continued action which states the truth that the Gentiles are even now in the process of obtaining ("attaining") the righteousness which Israel has been seeking through all these centuries. The righteousness spoken of in verse 30 is a God-given righteousness, which the Apostle states as being "not of him that willeth, nor of him that runneth, but of God" (9:16). It is *an imputed righteousness* which no individual can obtain through his own efforts or by his own ability.

Why? Because it is "even the righteousness which is of faith." The faith itself is a gift of God. Human frailty in itself does not have the ability to muster a faith pleasing to God because of the weakness of the flesh. Then, too, the Scriptures state, "There is none righteous, no, not one; . . . There is none that seeketh after God" (Romans 3:10, 11; Psalm 14:1-3; 53:1-3; Ecclesiastes 7:20). Is a burglar eager to see a policeman while in the process of burglarizing? Is a murderer convicted of first-degree murder and sentenced to die, eager to see the electric chair? By the same token, is the sinner eager to come into the presence of a holy and righteous God?

Only God can alter this attitude of spirit in the sinner. And He does! He supplies the faith through the Holy Spirit; He supplies the method through the new birth; He supplies the means through the blood of His Son. All a person needs to do, whether he be Jew or Gentile, is to cast himself upon the mercy of God. God receives all who come to Him through the Son. Will you?

Verses 31, 32a: (31) . . . but Israel, following after a law of righteousness, did not arrive at that law. (32a) Wherefore? Because they sought it not by faith, but as it were by works.

The saved Gentile obtains by faith that which the Jews fails to obtain by works. The problem with Israel is, and has always been, a lack of faith. The Jewish people do not lack morals, or standards, or laws. They boast having all of these. The divorce rate among Jews is low; dope addiction among Jewish teen-agers is surprisingly low; the number of Jews in penal institutions is insignificant; and alcoholism is rare among Jews. They are a moral people. Works of righteousness supersede faith in the Jewish mind. To a Jew, no matter what a man believes, so long as he is morally upright he is a righteous individual. "Prayer, charity and fasting overcometh all evil deeds." This brief prayer summarizes the Jewish concept of righteousness — *works!*

But seeking righteousness by works is foreign to God. God's problem with Israel is now and always has been the same. The Jews refuse to hearken to God's Word and His messengers. They have always lacked faith from the time of Moses to the present hour, whether in Egypt, the wilderness, or the modern State of Israel, slave or free, yesterday or today. They have always had their own ideas, and "every man did that which was right in his own eyes" (Deuteronomy 12:8; Judges 17:6). Lack of faith in God has been Israel's undoing. This is the reason that Paul states so emphatically in verse 31 that Israel, "did not arrive at that law," which Israel thought would make her righteous.

In verse 32a Paul asks a question and immediately preceeds to answer it, "Wherefore?" he asks. Why didn't Israel "arrive at that law?" (v. 31). Then he answers his question: "Because they sought it not by faith, but as it were by works." And ". . . by the works of the law shall no flesh (Jew or Gentile) be justified in his (God's) sight; . . ." (Romans 3:20). Faith is the primary factor which leads to salvation, but it must be faith in Christ as the promised Messiah and Redeemer (Isaiah 53:6, 11). This faith Israel lacks even today. She has faith and confidence in her own ability, but refuses to trust God and His ability for deliverance. We must say to Israel today, ". . . Fear ye not, stand still, and see the salvation of Jehovah . . ." (Exodus 14:13). All that God ever wanted of Israel was faith and obedience. ". . . Hearken unto my voice, and I will be your God, and ye shall be my people; and walk ye in all the way that I command you, that it may be well with you. But they hearkened not . . ." (Jeremiah 7:23, 24; 42:5, 6). Would to God that Israel might believe the song of her redemption that she sang millenniums ago in the wilderness (Exodus 15:1-8). God says she will! (Revelation 15:3, 4). God speed the day! "Oh that thou wouldest rend the heavens, that thou wouldest come down . . ." (Isaiah 64:1). "Even so, come, Lord Jesus" (Revelation 22:20 KJV).

Christ is the answer to every individual's problem, Israel's included. Let us preach it from the housetops of the world (Matthew 10:27). Preach the Word, both living and written.

Verses 32b and 33: (32b) **They stumbled at the stone of stumbling; (33) even as it is written, Behold, I lay in Zion a stone of stumbling and a rock of offence: and he that believeth on him shall not be put to shame.**

In this verse the Apostle is stating the truth that Israel has taken offense and rejected the stone which she wrongly concluded to be an embarrassment. Yet all this is prophetic, inasmuch as it lay in the omniscience of God before the foundation of the world, who revealed it to Isaiah the prophet six hundred years before it occurred. Paul was fully aware of this. After all, Paul did not figure out the cause of Israel's stumbling all by himself. It was the Holy Spirit who enlightened and illuminated the Apostle's mind and enabled him to write these words. This Epistle is verbally inspired by the Master Author Himself, the Holy Spirit.

Here is the prophecy as recorded in Isaiah 8:14: "And he shall be for a sanctuary; but for a stone of stumbling and for a rock of offence to both the houses of Israel . . ."; and Isaiah 28:16: ". . . Behold, I lay in Zion for a foundation a stone, a precious cornerstone of sure foundation: he that believeth shall not be in haste." The Septuagint ends with "shall not be ashamed."

The Apostle takes two different texts and puts them together. The Stone that Jehovah laid in Zion has not only become an offense to Israel because of their rejection of Him who is the Rock of their salvation, but it has become grievous, it has troubled them, it has caused them untold suffering. In His, the Lord Jesus Christ's Name, Israel has been persecuted, tortured and tormented. In this twentieth century, six and a half million Jews have been slaughtered as sheep. This mass murder came about because of Israel's rejection of the Stone that should have proved to be their shelter in time of storm, one of the worst storms in Israel's history. They have been called "Christ killers" across the centuries. Surely our Saviour's prophecy has been fulfilled with almost terrifying exactitude, ". . . and ye shall be hated of all nations (Gentiles) for my name's sake" (Mark 13:13).

Though Israel has stumbled over this "Stone" it has become a "rock of offence." The Greek word in verse 33 which is translated "offence" could be translated scandal. To Israel, Christ and all His accomplishments on the cross, His Resurrection, His Ascension, and His Return, are nothing less than a scandal. Christ, say the Jews today, has become the Gentile's God. His coming on the world's horizon, and that which people have made of Him are, to Israel, disgraceful, shocking, outrageous, and iniquitous. All these implications are contained in the Greek word *skandalon,* which is translated in verse 33 "offence."

In spite of what Israel thinks of Jesus Christ, God says of Him, "This is my beloved Son, in whom I am well pleased" (Matthew 3:17; 17:5). What a contrast is here between Israel's opinion and God's declaration! Blinded Israel says of Him, *skandalon* (offense), but God commands, ". . . hear ye him"!

Notice the wonderful benediction in the closing words of chapter 9, "And he that believeth on him shall not be put to shame." The Greek word here translated "believeth" is a present participle which could be more accurately translated believing. Faith in Christ has always been the principle of God's plan of salvation. There are no dispensations in God's plan. Abel, Enoch, Noah, Abraham, Isaac, Jacob, Moses, Rahab, Gideon, Samson, David, and every New Testament saint, was saved the same way. "Believe on the Lord Jesus, and thou shalt be saved" (Acts 16:31; Romans 10:9). This is the only way of salvation in the whole Bible. And as the wonderful benediction which concludes verse 33 of chapter 9 says, all who trust Jesus Christ as Lord, "shall not be put to shame." The Greek which is translated, "will not be put to shame," is so constructed as to mean that faith in Christ has never in the past, or will never in the future cause a saint to blush or fear disgrace. He may face ridicule in the world, but his faith will be honored in the presence of God.

What truths! What joy! What revelations of God's wisdom and omnipotence are recorded in this chapter! The Apostle has plumbed the depths of God's omniscience and sovereignty. He has done a masterful work. And in doing it, Paul has brought the saint of God to the mountain-peak of God's majesty and glory.

What a God! What a Saviour! Do you trust Him?

10

THE TENTH CHAPTER of the Roman Epistle deals with the results of chapter 9, and portrays vividly Israel's adamant disobedience. This disobedience is apparent in Israel today, and has brought upon her people untold privation, agony, and persecution. Throughout her history Israel has trod the paths of hardship and suffering, slavery and savagery, torment and torture, stubbornly enduring endless privations and dispossessions which have invariably climaxed in tragedy and disaster. Yet, despite these experiences, horrible and revolting as they were and still are, Israel's obstinate disobedience continues unchanged right up to the present time. She is still the stubborn, stiff-necked people of Jehovah that she was in the wilderness journey out of Egypt. Israel, like the Gentile nations of the world, has refused to humble herself, and to acknowledge her transgressions. She is still endeavoring to develop her own righteousness, which is a righteousness diverse from the righteousness of God. Israel wants to be the captain of her own soul, the master of her own ship.

But Israel has lost both her rudder and her compass, and now, with her vessel of state careening about in a maelstrom of sin, what is to save her from being drawn into the vortex of hell? Yet this is the condition of Israel today, even as it was in Paul's day. What a price she has had to pay for self-righteousness! What a sad state of confusion and depravity for a people once chosen by the Lord for His own peculiar treasure (Psalm 135: 4)!

Verse 1: Brethren, my heart's desire and my supplication to God is for them (Israel), that they may be saved.

The Sinaitic, the Vatican, the Alexandrine and the Nestle texts all substitute the word "them" for Israel. This writer is using the Nestle's text. However, there can be no doubt that the word "them" in verse 1 unmistakably stands for Israel, and that this is certainly one of the reasons why the translators of the King James Version rendered the middle portion of the verse, ". . . my heart's desire and prayer for *Israel* is . . .". Hence, the word "them" in the American Standard Version, as quoted in the preceding paragraph, stands for *Israel* and this is the obvious intention of the translators of the ASV in verse 1 of the chapter now before us.

The Greek word which is translated "desire" in verse 1 expresses more than want or hope. It has in it the thought of choice, and is so used in the Septuagint and in the Rabbinical writings. There is even an element of emotion in the Greek word. Thus, the word expresses more than desire. This is why the Apostle states that it is his "heart's desire" as well as "on his mind" and in his prayer of supplication. Because Paul is praying for his people Israel is evidence that Israel's plight was not without remedy and that the *whole* nation was not lost. Only part of that nation was blinded, as witness further on in this Epistle and in Ephesians: "But if some of the branches were broken off, and thou . . . wast grafted in among them, and didst become partaker with them . . ." (Romans 11:17; Ephesians 2:14-16; 3:6).

Although Paul was the "Apostle to the Gentiles," he never lost sight of the plight of his own people, Israel, whose plight was always before him. Did not the Lord Himself tell Ananias, the Damascus disciple, that Paul was "a chosen vessel unto me, to bear my name (as Jesus the Messiah) before the Gentiles and kings, and *the children of Israel*" (Acts 9:15)? The Apostle's dearest hope for his people — his heart's desire — was "that they may be saved," or "on behalf of them for their salvation." Why, it may be asked, was Paul so deeply moved on Israel's behalf? Simply because Israel's salvation is the forerunner of the future salvation of the Gentiles and all creation, at which time, according to prophecy, the nations of the world will beat their swords into plowshares and their spears into pruning-hooks, hostilities among the nations will cease, there will be an end to wars and bloodshed, and the Davidic kingdom will be established — all coming to pass as the result of Israel's salvation. The world will never see Israel's Messiah in human form again until Israel invites Him. ". . . Ye shall not see me henceforth, till ye shall say, Blessed is he that cometh in the name of the Lord" (Matthew 23:39).

How much poorer the saints of God are because they have either willfully neglected or ignorantly rejected the importance of Israel's salvation through the ministry of the Gospel and the promised Second Coming of Christ! It is needless to talk to Israel about the awful day of trouble soon to come upon her, "such as never was since there was a nation" (Daniel 12:1), without first pointing out her place in the Body of Christ. First trying to terrorize a person and then showing him how to escape that terror is "putting the cart before the horse." The Rapture of the saints is interwoven with the salvation of Israel. This is why the Apostle states in verse 1 that he yearns, he prays, he works for Israel's ultimate salvation. All that Paul told the church at Corinth (I Corinthians 15:50-58) and the church at Thessalonica (I Thessalonians 4:13-18) concerning the Rapture of the saints, is descriptive of that which will precede the salvation of the nation of Israel. Dear reader, what are you doing for Israel?

Verse 2: For I bear them (Israel) witness that they have a zeal for God, but not according to knowledge.

What other apostle is better qualified to bear more convincing testimony to Israel's zeal than Paul? It was his zeal, both before and after his conversion, that consumed his time, his mind, his heart and his soul. It was Paul's passionate zeal as a Pharisee (Philippians 3:5, 6) when he caused Jewish Christians to be killed. He counted himself blameless as touching the righteousness which is in the Law, and he thought he was doing God's will in fulfilling the very letter of the Law. How blind Paul was before his conversion! How misguided was his zeal! But after his conversion, his zeal purified and restored, and after deep remorse and self-incrimination, he bore witness that Israel's zeal for God, which he once shared, was misdirected and not according to knowledge. Paul, before his conversion, was a perfect example of the perverse zeal that is now destroying Israel. It was a misconceived zeal for God; that is, as clearly stated by Paul, "not according to knowledge."

The Jewish people through the centuries have not been devoid of knowledge and education. Even today they have more college graduates in proportion to the size of their racial group than do other racial groups in all population centers. They have always boasted of their achievements in the field of knowledge, achievements to which they point with pride and joy. Jewish parents urge their children on to higher education, encouraging them to keep in mind that persecution and privation may rob them of their material wealth, but can never rob them of their education.

However, this talent for distinction in the realm of knowledge is not what the Apostle has in mind. He is not writing about secular knowledge. The knowledge Paul has in mind is the knowledge of God, His Word, His righteousness, His salvation, and His hatred of sin. Lust and dishonorable passions were the cause of the downfall of the people spoken of in Romans 1:28, people whom God "gave up unto reprobate minds." Israel refused in time past and refuses now to accept God's principle for righteousness, endeavoring instead to develop a system of their own. Therefore, even as Paul declared in his day, so also it can be repeated and insisted upon today, "they have a zeal for God, but not according to knowledge," exactly as it is revealed in God's Word. Israel's wrong-headed zeal is ever seeking, yet never arriving, a quest for a system of righteousness that has been Israel's downfall. They have refused and still refuse to follow God's revealed purpose and plan. Throughout Israel's history they have been obsessed with the determination to work out a system whereby they could make themselves righteous. This zeal for their own plan caused them to miss God's plan whereby He *imputes* His righteousness to the believer. Israel's plan, therefore, is not and never can be "according to (God's revealed) knowledge."

Verse 3: For being ignorant of God's righteousness, and seeking to establish their own, they did not subject themselves to the righteousness of God.

The Greek word which is here translated "ignorant," means not to understand. In the classical Greek it means not to perceive or recognize, fail to understand, to be unaware of what is right, to act amiss.

Israel as a nation has always failed to recognize and to understand God's mode of righteousness. Their determination to work out a system of their own has resulted in their utter failure to understand God's righteousness. Israel failed to recognize God's righteousness during their wilderness journey (Exodus 19). They did the same during Jeremiah's time (Jeremiah 7:21-26), walking "in their own counsels and in the stubbornness of their evil heart." They "made their neck stiff" and refused to hearken unto God's counsel and His voice. Their eyes were focused on their own abilities rather than on God's plan, or mode and method of righteousness. They erred and acted amiss and failed completely to perceive and to understand God's righteousness.

All this was the cause of their "seeking to establish their own" righteousness. What wasted effort and energy! What wasted zeal! What a multiplicity of evil consequences! The cost to Israel has been a vast amount of wasted time and energy, resulting also in wasted lives, in needless bloodshed, in dire want, as well as in horrible privations and persecutions. The greatest cost of all to Israel has been that millions of Jews have gone to a hopeless and Christless eternity. What an awful price to pay for the sin of disobedience!

V. 3b: ". . . they did not subject themselves to the righteousness of God." Israel's difficulty has always been their refusal to subject themselves to the rule of God. Submission and subjection are concepts which are contrary to Israel's thinking. They "murmured" when they were subject to Moses' jurisdiction. They sinned under Joshua's rule. They did what they pleased under the Judges. Finally, they rejected Jehovah's rule, and eventually Jehovah Himself (I Samuel 8:7-9; 10:17-19). And eleven centuries later as a nation they said in Pilot's presence, "We have no king but Caesar" (John 19:15). This denial of God's sovereignty is exactly what is stated in verse 3b before us. They "did not subject themselves" to the righteous rule of Jehovah millenniums ago, and they do not now. But the time is coming when they will (Matthew 23:39). Christ was the answer then, and He is the answer now as verse 4 states.

Israel's attempt to work out a system of righteousness can only result in a righteousness which they hope to attain *by works*. This is the very antithesis of God's righteousness which is to be achieved only *by faith* (Romans 9:30). The two can never be reconciled. Israel will have to submit to God's righteousness, and in Christ they will obtain that which they have sought for all these centuries. ". . . but that which is through faith in Christ, the righteousness which is from God by faith . . ." (Philippians 3:9).

Verse 4: For Christ is the end of the law unto righteousness to every one that believeth.

Christ is the culmination of our fondest hope, the consummation of the highest law, the realization of life's grandest goal, the acme of human destiny, the *ne plus ultra* of righteousness; or, as verse 4 describes it, "the end of the law unto righteousness." The accomplishments of the cross not only "rent the veil" of the Law, but they swept aside the barrier separating God and man, and cleared the way for direct communication between God's children and their heavenly Father. Christ fulfilled the purpose of every jot and tittle of the Law. In His person and in His work

He is the personification of virtue, "the way, and the truth, and the life."

V. 4b: ". . . to every one that believeth." The Greek is more accurately translated "to every one believing." Notice the "every one." The phrase is sufficient to disprove the neo-orthodox false teaching of a "converted community." How far-fetched are the ideas of these so-called Christian scholars! They always twist the Word of God from its plain and obvious meaning so as to make it say the opposite. They are not exegetes at all! They do not explain the Bible, they twist it. They are eisegetes!*

"Christ is the end of the law unto righteousness" to the *believer only*, or, according to the more accurate translation of the Greek phrase, to the *one believing right now!* This is the Gospel; this is the message of the Bible; this must be the message of the pulpit. Paul was no compromiser. He did not vacillate or temporize. He stood for the truth of the Gospel and wrote to the Galatian church, ". . . so say I now again, If any man preacheth unto you any gospel other than that which ye received, let him be anathema" (Galatians 1:9). If a minister does not preach the Gospel, he fails to do so for one of two reasons, or both. Either he is trying to please the pew, or he doesn't believe the Gospel himself. In either case, he ought not to call himself a minister of the Gospel. We who preach the Gospel must not and cannot deviate from the revealed inspired Word of God. Our every message must be, "Thus saith the Lord."

The person who has not placed his trust in Christ is under the Law with all of its multitudinous restrictions. He is subject to its rules and regulations, and to the strict compliance of the Law, otherwise he must suffer the consequences. Christ has not abrogated the Law; He fulfilled it. The believer in Christ is free from the punishment of the Law, since he is in Christ. Henceforth, he lives eternally in Christ and ultimately will live with Him.

Verse 5: For Moses writeth that the man that doeth the righteousness which is of the law shall live thereby.

The Law says, "do this and you shall live." Christ has redeemed the believer from this injunction, and has placed him under grace which says, "Believe and you are saved."

---

*An *eisegete* is a Bible commentator or interpreter who, instead of bringing out the true meaning of a text, introduces his own thoughts and ideas into the interpretation as if they were those of the original author. Eisegesis is the opposite of exegesis.

The earlier chapters of this Epistle to the Romans are devoted to Law. They clearly explain the conditions and requirements of the Law. The Law is strict. It demands scrupulous compliance. Every letter must be kept. Man is incapable of fulfilling the requirements of the Law. The "flesh is weak." While the Law demands strict compliance, man cannot and does not possess the ability to comply.

This writer does not believe that the Law was given as a means by which an individual might work out righteousness and justification that will obtain eternal life. The Law points to Christ. It is the tutor or schoolmaster that brings one to Christ. Verse 5 quotes Jehovah as saying to Moses in Leviticus 18:5, "Ye shall therefore keep my statutes, and mine ordinances: which if a man do, he shall live in them: I am Jehovah," or, as Paul states it in verse 5, "that the man that doeth the righteousness which is of the law shall live thereby." "Doeth" is better translated doing. However, keeping the Law that a man may live is not possible in the light of the Scriptures (Ecclesiastes 7:20; Isaiah 64:6; Psalm 14:1-3; 53:1-4; 143:2). Since Scripture is quite clear on this point it is understandable why the Psalmist should ask, "If thou, Jehovah, shouldst mark iniquities, O Lord, who could stand?" (Psalm 130:3). We are not left without comfort. The Psalmist continues, "But there is forgiveness with thee. . ." (Psalm 130: 4; see also Psalm 51:1, 9; Isaiah 43:25; 44:22). God does forgive the repentant sinner, "Blessed is he whose transgression is forgiven, whose sin is covered. Blessed is the man unto whom Jehovah imputeth not iniquity" (Psalm 32:1, 2).

V. 5b: "Shall live thereby." Even the Jewish scholars wrote that this verse means eternal life. But eternal life worked out by man himself is impossible. Man is unable to develop a system of righteousness whereby he can obtain eternal life. Salvation is beyond human abilities, and, therefore, it must be of the Lord. Confirming the truth of this fact is why Isaiah wrote, "Look unto me, and be ye saved, all the ends of the earth; for I am God, and there is none else" (Isaiah 45:22). The Lord says unto us, Come! Will you? If you do, you "shall live."

Verses 6, 7: (6) But the righteousness which is of faith saith thus, Say not in thy heart, Who shall ascend into heaven? (that is, to bring Christ down:) (7) or, Who shall descend into the abyss? (that is, to bring Christ up from the dead.)

The Apostle is quoting Deuteronomy 30:12 here. He is using this Old Testament text as a Midrash, which is the Jewish method of teaching and does not always explain the text quoted. The Midrash is used at times to explain and illustrate the thought that the teacher wishes to convey to his pupils. The Rabbis often used the language of the Old Testament to express their meaning in familiar language. In Deuteronomy Moses is reaching the end of his ministry and life, and in chapter 29 he is rehearsing his last counsels to Israel as he reaches the end of his forty years of leadership, and Israel's experiences with God. He describes the miracles, the wonders that God had performed to bring Israel to their present hour. He reminds them of God's marvelous and varied provisions; he rehearses the victories that God gave them; he tells of their inheritance; and he recalls the covenants that God has made with the patriarchs and the nation itself. He warns them of the dangers and pitfalls that will befall them should they not obey God's voice and words. Though their inheritance is before them there is the possibility of losing it because of disobedience. Their children must remain faithful. Should the children of Israel become disobedient they will be scattered among the nations, and will find themselves in the same trying condition that Israel was in when the nation was in Egypt. But Moses assures them that their children will be delivered in the very same manner and by the same means as their fathers were.

No one will need to ascend into heaven to obtain God's law and commandments. Moses brought them to the people in the early days of their deliverance out of Egypt. Similarly, the Apostle says that Christ has been brought down to earth, and has revealed the righteousness of God which is obtainable through faith. This is the *true* righteousness, the only righteousness that God accepts. Human frailty, through its own efforts, is incapable of achieving a righteousness that is pleasing to God. Then, too, we must always keep before us the biblical truth that "without faith it is impossible to be well-pleasing" to God. This faith must be centered in Christ, and in His accomplishments on the cross. This is exactly what the Saviour asked of the people of Israel (John 10:22-39 ff.). This Christ did once for all time even as Moses brought down the Law to Israel. God has always had only one program for righteousness resulting in salvation. That has been the righteousness which is obtained through faith in the Messiah. This is God's unalterable and eternal program, ". . . but the righteous shall live by his faith" (Habakkuk 2:4). It must be *imputed* righteousness (Psalm 32:1, 2).

V. 7: ". . . or, Who shall descend into the abyss? (that is, to bring Christ up from the dead.)" Paul makes, in verses 6 and 7, a deeper and more far-reaching application of the words of Moses in Deuteronomy 30:13, that God's righteousness is not "beyond the sea." Christ has not revealed God's righteousness only through the Incarnation, but He obtained it by the Crucifixion and rose from the dead for our justification, eternally certifying God's righteousness by His Ascension.

What striking and beautiful comparisons the Apostle makes in our text! Christ is not only "the end of the law for righteousness"; He ends our fears and allays our doubts and obliterates our apprehensions. He did this once for all time and eternity. It need never be repeated. Indeed, it cannot be!

Dear reader, do you believe it? Have you appropriated the accomplishments of the cross for your own sin? Christ can be the end of your fears and doubts just as He is the end of the Law for righteousness. He is the personification of life, of peace, and of truth, and He will give you eternal life freely if you will only accept Him. He invites you, "Come . . . and I will give you rest" (Matthew 11:28) from your burden of sin.

Verse 8: But what saith it? The word is nigh thee, in thy mouth, and in thy heart: that is, the word of faith, which we preach . . . :

God's Word, says Moses in Deuteronomy 30:14, is "in thy mouth, and in thy heart," and God's voice Israel knew and possessed. The Apostle makes the same application. We have God's Word, and in it is revealed His will. We can read it with our eyes, and it is preached so that we can hear it.

We need not climb heights or cross oceans to hear God's Word. It has been brought to us, we see it, we hear it; but, we must believe it, and we must confess with our lips that which we believe in our hearts. It is faith. It requires implicit trust and surrender of self. Faith is God's principle for attaining righteousness. It has always been so, even in the Old Testament. God's plan of salvation in the New Testament is not the innovation of a new method of obtaining the righteousness of God. The New Testament merely elaborates and reiterates the principle established in the Old Testament (Genesis 5:6). (Also see commentary on Romans 4:3.) God has accomplished it, and He asks us to believe Him and His Word which His messenger must preach. This is why the servant of God must preach God's Word. He cannot and must not depart from it. God has promised that His Word "will not return unto him void." He has promised to bless it and to use it as His means of salvation. It is God's will that it be preached. ". . . it was God's good pleasure through the foolishness of the preaching to save them that believe" (I Corinthians 1:21). If one does not preach it, he is a fool.

Verse 9: . . . because if thou shalt confess with thy mouth Jesus as Lord, and shalt believe in thy heart that God raised him from the dead, thou shalt be saved . . . :

The Greek structure of the word "thou shalt confess" is better translated "thou confesseth" (right now). The Greek verb denotes an action taking place *right now*. The action is in the process of taking place.

The tenses and moods of the Greek verbs, "confess," "believe" and "saved," are interesting and instructive. They express this thought: if you confess *now* with your mouth that Jesus is Lord (denoting the fact of His Deity), and believe *now* that God has raised Him from the dead (the resurrection actually presents His humanity) (Philippians 2:5-8), you shall be saved eternally just as certainly as you were saved when you put your trust in Jesus as Lord and were born again.

The Resurrection of the Saviour is the unique message of Christianity. No other religion has a resurrected founder. Only the Christian can be sure of his own resurrection and can vindicate it upon the authority of the Saviour Himself, ". . . because I live, ye shall live also" (John 14:19). The Resurrection is the heart of the Christian message (I Corinthians 15:14, 16-20).

Verses 8 and 9 answer the questions presented in verses 6 and 7. Christ has come down from heaven, has died and been buried, and has risen from the grave. The two greatest foundational truths of the Gospel are the Incarnation and the Resurrection of Christ. All other doctrines and dogmas of Christianity are based on these two truths.

What is meant by the word "confess"? It means more than just walking down the church aisle and confessing Christ as Lord. It also means witnessing to others of the saving grace of Christ; it means leading people to Christ; it means spending time in prayer and Bible study; it means fellowship with God's people in God's house; and it means living a life of devotion and dedication to God, to Christ, and to the Gospel. Confessing Christ in these ways must be done at all times, under all circumstances, regardless and irrespective of the cost. All this is entailed in our profession and confession of faith in Christ.

It must be a living and vibrant faith. It must be a fruit-bearing life that is empowered and guided by the Holy Spirit, a life portraying righteousness and holiness. We must not forget that when we were saved we became, ". . . his workmanship, created in Christ Jesus for good works, which God afore prepared that we should walk in them" (Ephesians 2:10). If we have not the *fruits* of righteousness, which must be the result of our profession of faith, can this profession of faith save us? James asks this question in his epistle, ". . . if a man say he hath faith, but have not works? can that faith save him? . . . Even so faith, if it have not works, is dead in itself" (James 2:14, 17). This is biblical Christianity. This is what the Apostle Paul meant by the words, "confess" and "believe," in verse 9.

Paul continues throughout the Roman Epistle to affirm and reaffirm the truth that God saves a person once and that it lasts throughout eternity. He is a Sovereign God who saves us and thereby places us in an unalterable position. Just as Christ died on the cross once for all time, and rose from the dead, so every person who puts his trust in Christ receives *eternal life*. It lasts forever! We are saved by Christ; we are being kept in the state of being saved by Christ; and just as surely as we have been saved we shall most certainly be brought into the completion of our salvation at the resurrection or translation by Christ Himself (I Thessalonians 4:13-17).

What a wonderful plan and program God has prepared for His saints! What a wonderful God and Saviour the saints have! Do you believe in the Saviour? Is this hope the motivating power in your life? It can be, ". . . Christ in you, the hope of glory" (Colossians 1:27).

Verse 10: . . . for with the heart man believeth unto righteousness; and with the mouth confession is made unto salvation.

This verse is one of the salient points in this Epistle. It spotlights attention upon two of the most important members of the human body, the heart and the mouth. These two members reveal what a person really is. A person's speech tells exactly what is in his heart, ". . . for out of the abundance of the heart the mouth speaketh" (Matthew 12:34).

To this writer it has always been a mystery how a person can call himself a Christian and not try to lead others to a saving knowledge of Christ. Such a Christian, in my opinion, is traitorous and treacherous to the Gospel and to Christ. Such a person commits a greater crime in the sight of the Gospel than a murderer does in the sight of society. There *cannot* be such a thing as a *silent* Christian. If he is silent, he is not a Christian. If he is a Christian, he is not silent.

There are two phases to a Christian's life: First, he must, with all his heart, trust Christ implicitly as Lord and Saviour. It must be a heart belief. Scripture states that a man speaks, believes, thinks, understands, and reasons with his heart. The Bible does not separate the mind from the heart, as some theologians do. The Hebrew usage of the words, "heart and mind," at times equates the heart with the mind. Trust in Christ is the primary phase of a Christian's life. The second phase is what a Christian does after he accepts Christ as Lord and Saviour. He must *publicly confess* his faith, and be baptized. His baptism portrays the truth that he has died to the world and is now living for Christ. He must be a living example of the transforming power of the Gospel, and this is done in two ways — by his life, and by his witness to others.

Faith is the fountainhead of Christianity, and witnessing is the stream into which its waters flow. A fountain cannot function without a stream or outlet. Stagnant water becomes foul and is a menace to health. The life of a Christian must be guided by the "new heart" that God gives him at his new birth, and his witnessing must be guided by the Holy Spirit. This is *true* Christian living. Anything short of this places the believer in jeopardy since he is unfaithful to God.

The Greek verbs, "confess" and "believe," are constructed so as to convey the meaning that a Christian is a person who *keeps on confessing*. Though the verbs express an action taking place in the past, they also express that same action as taking place *in the present*. A Christian keeps on believing, and keeps on confessing. This believing and confessing is the divine imperative in his life and makes him keep on preaching and living the Gospel. It constitutes the impetus in Christian living that forms the very foundation of a life of devotion to God and His method of proclaiming the Gospel to a lost world. This is what Paul meant when he wrote, ". . . it was God's good pleasure through the foolishness of the preaching to save them that believe" (I Corinthians 1:21).

The world laughs at the preaching of the cross. It scorns the Gospel. But God commands us who are the believers to preach it regardless and irrespective of the attitude of worldlings. The Saviour ordered His followers to Go! Preach! Baptize! Teach! It is still the order for today.

Verse 11: For the scripture saith, Whosoever believeth on him shall not be put to shame.

Paul is quoting again Isaiah 28:16 of the Septuagint version. (See commentary on this text in Romans 9:33.) The Apostle makes a change in the text. The Isaiah passage reads, "He that believeth." Paul makes the change to "whosoever" believeth, in order to state the biblical truth that the Gospel is a universal call.

Since "all have sinned" and all are lost in their sin, the call of God to believe is extended to all. The truth of Scripture is that "God is no respecter of persons." The word translated "believeth" in v. 11 is a present participle which is more accurately translated believing.

The Gospel today has in it all the potency that it ever had. The Gospel saved yesterday, and just as surely it saves today. The Greek word translated "shall not be put to shame" carries the meaning that belief in Christ never disgraced anyone in the past, nor will it do so in the future. If we take the banner of the Gospel to a sin-laden world, we shall be honored in God's sight now and throughout all eternity.

Whosoever will may come, and whosoever comes will in no wise be refused or rejected. A person does not go to hell because God failed to provide the way to heaven. John 14:6 is God's way, and its acceptance results in eternal life. Proverbs 14:12 and 16:25 is man's way and it results in death. Choose! Whoever you may be, Jew or Gentile, black or white, yellow or red, you must make a choice.

Verse 12: For there is no distinction between Jew and Greek: for the same Lord is Lord of all, and is rich unto all that call upon him ... :

This text surely proves that the Jew is just as lost as the Gentile. If he is as lost as the Gentile why have we so neglected taking the Gospel to the lost Jew? The Apostle is restating what he has said in Romans 3:23, 30. The Lord is Lord of all Jews and all Gentiles alike. The word Lord refers to Christ. He is called "Lord of all" in Acts 10:36. Also in Philippians 2:11 and Romans 1:4 He is called Lord, thus establishing His Deity. Paul never loses sight of the important truth that Christ is not only the Son of God, but that He is also God the Son, the Incarnate Jehovah. Only this kind of a Saviour is rich enough to bestow salvation "unto all that call upon him."

Sinners must call upon Jehovah in the Person of Christ to

receive salvation. "And in none other is there salvation: for neither is there any other name under heaven, that is given among men, wherein we must be saved" (Acts 4:12). The word translated "call upon" in Romans 10:12 is better translated "calling upon." This states the truth that all who call upon Him even today are just as saved as Paul himself was, and just as sure of inheriting the riches in Christ. (Ephesians 1:18; 2:7; 3:16; Philippians 4:19; Colossians 2:2, 3.) The riches of this world can never be compared with the riches that God has in store for His saints.

Verse 13: . . . for, Whosoever shall call upon the name of the Lord shall be saved.

The Apostle is quoting Numbers 12:7; Joel 2:32, which is a prophecy of the Second Coming, which will be the time of the setting up of the Messianic Kingdom. This is the *implication* of verse 13, and is the primary exegesis of Joel 2:32.

However, we must not overlook a proper *application* of the same text. Just as the prophet Joel states that when the Messianic Kingdom is about to be set up, ". . . whosoever (be he Jew or Gentile) shall call on the name of Jehovah shall be delivered," so now the message of salvation is extended to all peoples regardless and irrespective of race, creed or color. Paul is merely re-stating in Romans 10:13 the established truth in the Gospels (Matthew 11:28-30; Mark 16:15, 16; John 3:16, 36.) The invitation to eternal life is open to all. No one is excluded.

For the reader who has a working knowledge of the Hebrew and the Greek this passage is quoted from the Septuagint version. The Hebrew word for "saved" is *molat*. Basically it means physical deliverance or escape. The Septuagint version uses the word *sotso*, which means not only physical deliverance but also salvation in the spiritual sense, which means eternal life. The Greek word is in the future indicative passive, meaning the person who calls upon "the name of the Lord," is saved immediately and will be kept in the state of salvation throughout eternity. The word Lord in the Hebrew is Jehovah. This is another place in this Epistle where the Apostle reaffirms the truth that the Saviour is God incarnate in the flesh.

God's gift of life is secured eternally by Him. Hallelujah, what a God and Saviour we have! Do you know Him? Have you accepted Him? If not, why not now? Whoever you may be, His arms of love are open and His invitation is extended to you.

Verse 14: How then shall they call on him in whom they have not believed? and how shall they believe in him whom they have not heard? and how shall they hear without a preacher?

Let us not lose sight of the burden of this chapter. It describes graphically the *present* condition of Israel. How is Israel going to call upon the Lord Jesus Christ as their Messiah when all they have known of Christ and the hordes of His false followers through the ages and until now, has been persecution and proscription, torture and torment, bloodshed and butchery? Throughout the centuries Israel has been hearing of Christ in mockery, primarily from the lips of their persecutors. They have called Jews Christ-killers. They have repeatedly taunted the Jews with the gibe, Why don't you go back to your own country? meaning Palestine. Jews have not even heard that Christ could be the Messiah of Israel. Christendom, that is, Christian countries collectively, and even vast numbers of true Christians have denied that the Gospel is for the Jews.

The Jew has repeatedly asked the question, How can Jesus Christ be the Messiah of Israel when His followers hate us and persecute us? Jews believe that everyone who is not a Jew is a Christian. As a nation they have not heard the true message of the Gospel. Even fundamental groups of Christians are not too much interested in supporting Jewish Missions. Missionaries in other fields traverse mountains, oceans, and continents to go to the far reaches of the earth to preach the Gospel to the heathen. But very few of us, who are the believers, try to reach the Jew next door. Why? Until this is answered and corrected the Jew will not hear the message of Christ.

No one can believe the Gospel who has not heard it. This is what is stated in the second question of verse 14, "How shall they believe in him whom they have not heard?" If Israel has not heard, then is it not understandable why she has not believed?

The third question of verse 14 relates to a preacher. The Gospel must be preached in order for people to believe. Acts 8:26-40 is a good example. Philip was instructed by an angel to go to Gaza in the desert, and the Holy Spirit told him to "join thyself" to the chariot of the Eunuch. When Philip did so he noticed that the Eunuch was reading Isaiah, chapter 53. Why couldn't the Eunuch understand that this chapter speaks of Christ? After all, he had just left Jerusalem, and without a doubt he had heard many people talking of what had happened at Golgotha. He was aware of the crucifixion. Yet he could not correlate Isaiah's prophecy in the Scriptures with the crucifixion. Why? Because ". . . the natural man receiveth not the things of the Spirit of God" (I Corinthians 2:14); and ". . . it was God's good pleasure through the foolishness of the preaching to save them that believe" (I Corinthians 1:21).

If a man is to call on Christ he must have faith in Him. In order to have faith he must hear the Holy Spirit calling. And, lastly, someone whom the Holy Spirit has sent must preach the Word of God to him. This is the method God uses. When the Word of God is preached to the Jews it will be as effective with them as it has been with the Gentiles. What a harvest has been reaped by those who have taken the Gospel to the Jews!

This method of preaching is the method that God Himself has ordained to use as the means of reaching people for Christ. The divine imperative is to go and preach to the whole world. This must be so, since "all have sinned, and fall short of the glory of God" (Romans 3:23).

The Greek work for "preacher" in verse 14 is a present participle, which is better translated (one) preaching. It must be the preaching of the cross even today, as this is God's plan and program for the present age. We must keep on preaching until we are called home.

Verse 15: . . . and how shall they preach, except they be sent? even as it is written, How beautiful are the feet of them that bring glad tidings of good things!

Paul has been asking a series of questions that constitute the prerequisites for obtaining salvation. He brings them all down to the starting point of an established Old Testament truth: "Look unto me, and be ye saved . . . for I am God, and there is none else" (Isaiah 45:22). "Salvation is of Jehovah" (Jonah 2:9). (See also Joel 2:32.)

A person must call upon and look unto Jehovah for salvation, but the message of salvation must also be *preached*. The messenger of God must be commissioned and instructed. The messenger must obey his commission and bring the true message of God. This is precisely what the Apostle has been developing in the four questions asked in verses 14 and 15.

The Apostle quotes Isaiah 52:7 and Nahum 1:15a. Isaiah 52:1-10 looks forward to the establishment of the Davidic Kingdom, which is the everlasting kingdom of the Messiah. Even Jewish Rabbis have taught that this passage is Messianic, a prophecy to be fulfilled at the time when the King Messiah will come (Vajirka Rabba, Parsha, c. 9, fol. 153.2; Perek Shalom, fol. 20.1). Not only will Israel rejoice, but the Gentile nations will also rejoice at the completed revelation of the Salvation of the Lord in the Person of Jesus the Messiah. What joy! What gladness this will bring! The whole earth will be able to sing that beautiful hymn, "When peace like a river attendeth my way." What music this will be! Israel will be the conductor of this universal chorus. The baton will be in the hands of the Jews as they lead the nations of the world in this song of redemption (Isaiah 52:8-10).

In verse 15 the Apostle makes *application* of the world-wide nature of the Isaiah passage to its personal and immediate relevancy. Just as the world will rejoice in the millennial Kingdom over Jehovah's salvation, so does the individual Jew and Gentile in this present hour rejoice in his personal salvation. Just as it will be the Jewish message of redemption which will initiate the universal rejoicing over the establishment of the Millennium, so it must be the Jewish message of salvation which will at this present hour bring rejoicing to Jew and Gentile that the Saviour of the world is the seed of Abraham, of the tribe of Judah, of the house of Jesse, of the loins of David, according to the flesh. ". . . for salvation is of the Jews" (John 4:22 KJV).

Verse 16: But they did not all hearken to the glad tidings. For Isaiah saith, Lord, who hath believed our report?

We must not forget that in this chapter (10) of the Roman Epistle the Apostle is speaking of Israel's present condition. Notice that he does not say that *all* Israel did not hearken. He merely states that "they did *not all* hearken," meaning that some did. A cursory look at the book of Acts will reveal that multitudes in Israel accepted the message of the Gospel and placed their trust in Christ. The three thousand converts on Pentecost were all Jews (Acts 2:37-42); the five thousand *men alone* were all Jews (Acts 4:1-4); "the multitudes of them that believed" were all Jews (Acts 4:32); "and the believers were the more added to the Lord, multitudes both of men and women" (Acts 5:14; 6:1); "And the word of God increased; and the number of the disciples multiplied in Jerusalem exceedingly; and a great company of the priests were obedient to the faith" (Acts 6:7). These were all Jews. Then the "thousands" (myriads) spoken of in Acts 21:20 were all Jews. The Greek word for "myriads" means thousands, or innumerable, an immense number, thousands upon thousands, upon tens of thousands. Josephus, the Jewish historian, states that more than one-third of the Jewish population of the world at the end of the first century were followers of Christ.

"Who hath believed our report?" (Isaiah 53:1 KJV). The answer must be, multitudes! If the Gospel is presented properly and intelligently to the Jew, there wll be conversions. The Jew is not illiterate, immoral or unintelligent. But he is neglected.

To this writer it has been obvious for many years that the Gentiles have not been more receptive to the Gospel than the Jews. The first Gentile convert recorded in the New Testament is Cornelius (Acts 10). His conversion occurred approximately sixteen years after the Ascension. The lack in the Church today is an interest in reaching the Jew. Many Christians have been lulled to sleep by the unscriptural philosophy of the "Gentile Church," claiming that we are now in the "Gentile Church age." Paul's Epistle to the Ephesians is a powerful contradiction of the "Gentile Church" fallacy. Isn't it more logical to trust the Holy Spirit and the Bible rather than to listen to the false doctrines of self-styled Bible teachers? "Let God be found true, but every man a liar" (Romans 3:4). Is it not easier to lead a blind person than a dead one? Does not the Bible say that the Gentiles are "dead" spiritually? But the Bible says that the Jew is only "blinded." The Gospel is to *all* for *all*. Let us neglect no one.

(*Note*: For the student of Hebrew there are many Hebraisms in this chapter that make interesting subjects for study.)

Verse 17: So belief cometh of hearing, and hearing by the word of Christ.

This text is the greatest challenge to the Christian in urging him to proclaim the Gospel. Spreading the Gospel by means of the printed word, popularly called reaching a person's understanding by means of the "eye gate," as invaluable a method as it is, is of secondary importance to preaching, which has been called spreading the Gospel by the "ear gate." It was the Saviour's method, "And Jesus went about all the cities and the villages, teaching in their synagogues, and preaching the gospel of the kingdom" (Matthew 9:35). Thus, *hearing* the Gospel was God's means from the beginning of Jesus' ministry of spreading the Gospel and making it known. We, His followers, must not overlook the example set before us. The Gospel *must be preached*. Preaching and teaching is an elaboration of the Great Commission (Mark 16:15). Preaching is God's unalterable method. Bear in mind, however, that the preaching must be "the word of Christ," about Christ, and it must point men and women to Christ. When the Gospel is preached there *will* be conversions. God has promised, and verse 17 substantiates it.

Verse 18: But I say, Did they not hear? Yea, verily. Their sound went out into all the earth, And their words unto the ends of the world.

The foundation for chapter 11, next following, is being laid in verse 18; in fact, these words can be called the introduction to chapter 11. The Apostle is showing here that Israel's failure to give any credence to God's Word did not and does not foil God's plans for Israel. Did not Israel hear? Certainly! Of course they heard! Their utterances have been released throughout all creation and all over the world.

But has Israel *really* heard? Has Israel as a *nation* really heard the Gospel? A person may hear and yet actually not hear. Is this not what God told Isaiah to do in his commission as a prophet? "And he said, Go, and tell this people, Hear ye indeed, but understand not; and see ye indeed, but perceive not. Make the heart of this people fat, and make their ears heavy, and shut their eyes; lest they see with their eyes, and hear with their ears, and understand with their heart, and turn again, and be healed" (Isaiah 6:9, 10; Romans 11:7-11).

The message of redemption has indeed gone into the far reaches of the world, but Israel's ears have not been tuned to this message. God had a purpose both in the message and its reception, and He still has His plan. It will come to fruition in spite of Israel's indifference to God's program. His will must be done on earth, even as it is in heaven.

Verse 19: But I say, Did Israel not know? First Moses saith, I will provoke you to jealousy with that which is no nation, with a nation void of understanding will I anger you.

Did Israel not know what God wanted or expected of her? Yes, she knew. But spiritually and experimentally Israel, as a nation, never put it to practice. Through Moses God repeatedly warned her of all the tribulations that would befall her if she continued to disobey God's voice. This is what the Apostle is quoting in verse 19.

The Rabbinical interpretation of Deuteronomy 32:20, 21, is as follows:

And he said, I will hide my face from them (leave them to themselves), I will see what their end shall be: for they are a very froward generation (literally, a generation given to perverseness, evasions of truth and right; a falsehood-loving race), children in whom is no faithfulness (with no loyalty to a tender parent). They have provoked me with their vanities (literally, breaths, something insubstantial, vaporous, unreal, hence false gods). And I will rouse them to jealousy with a no-people (measure for measure; just as they had angered God by adopting a no-god, so would God anger them by bringing against them a no-people, a horde of barbarians); I will provoke them with a vile nation (or, foolish nation (KJV and ASV), ignorant and hence barbarous and inhuman in its habits and methods. (Ibn Ezra). And this people will win successes over Israel. (*The Soncino Edition of the Pentateuch and Haftorahs, page 899.* See also Romans 11:11.)

Because Israel became such a disobedient nation, the occasion was thereby presented for preaching the Gospel to the Gentiles, a people who "refused" to have God in their knowledge, and had surrendered themselves to vile passions and abominable habits — a people whom God had long before given up to evil minds, evil hearts, and evil practices (Romans 1:24-32). God, in fact, considered these Gentiles a no-people. How vividly these truths explain the fact that God uses even "the wrath of man" to praise Him (Psalm 76:10a).

Verse 20: And Isaiah is very bold, and saith, I was found of them that sought me not; I became manifest unto them that asked not of me.

Since God had given the Gentiles up to vile passions and unrighteousness, they did not seek after God. Because of the perverseness of their hearts and minds they became absorbed in wicked machinations, engrossed with carnality, and obsessed with the gratification of evil lusts. God was farthest from their reprobate hearts and minds.

While the Gentiles were in this depraved condition, God manifested Himself to them. He called the Apostle Paul to go and preach the Gospel to the Gentiles (Acts 9:15), and then commanded Peter to visit a Gentile's house and preach to him and his family. Peter was shocked and amazed to think that God would bestow His mercy upon a depraved Gentile, one who was of a people who were "no-people," and yet this Gentile (Cornelius) was empowered and indwelt by the Holy Spirit. To Peter and the other Jewish Christians this was a surprise, and almost unthinkable (Acts 10:44, 45). Cornelius fulfilled before the very eyes of these Jewish Christians the text before us in Romans 10:20. God prepared both Peter and Cornelius for His own purpose and honor.

Verse 21: But as to Isreal he saith, All the day long did I spread out my hands unto a disobedient and gainsaying people.

Thus Paul ends chapter 10 of his Epistle to the Romans with this quotation from Isaiah 65:2. It is as though Paul were saying:

"I'll grant you that God has extended His hands of mercy, His hands of compassion, His hands of invitation to His ancient people. I'll grant you that God has constantly been inviting Israel as a nation to return to His service and love. I'll grant you that nationally Israel has turned her back upon God; has spurned His love; has disregarded His invitation; and has refused to hearken to His word. I'll also grant that Israel, in spite of God's patience and promises of forgiveness, has pursued her stubborn and willful course even to this present hour. Does this mean that God made a mistake when He led His chosen people out of Egyptian slavery and into the Promised Land of Canaan? Have God's plans, program and purposes for Israel gone amiss? Have God's covenants and promises to the patriarchs and Israel been negated through Israel's sinful actions? Has God been caught unaware? Is God's program now nullified because of Israel's refusal to hearken to His Word?"

All this is contained in the quotation of Isaiah 65:2, and in Romans 10:21. And all of the questions which may have been in Paul's mind are answered in chapter 11.

God is never thwarted. His plans are never altered. His purposes are never foiled. His promises are sure and can never be negated. His love never fails. His character can never be disgraced. His possessions can never be taken from Him. His gifts are eternal. His Word is settled forever.

This God, who is the Creator of the universe, presents to the world an unalterable plan of salvation. He has given His Son. He has permitted a sinful world of Gentiles and Jews to crucify that Son, only so that this "offering for sin" would work out for their good. Because of the Crucifixion there is the Resurrection. Because there is the Resurrection there is life everlasting. It is in God's Son. God says to a sinful humanity, "Accept Him and live; reject Him and die." Which do you choose? Life or death? Choose you must!

11

In this chapter the Apostle is not only continuing the discussion that he began in the closing portion of chapter 10, but he is also substantiating all that he has written in the Epistle to the Romans thus far. He is now re-stating in chapter 11 the following truths which he established in preceding chapters; namely, (a) God's unalterable plan for Israel, vss. 1-4, 25-32; (b) the doctrine of election, vss. 5-7; (c) the sovereignty of God, vss. 8-10; (d) the plan for the Gentiles and the Jews in this dispensation or age, vss. 11-20; (e) the challenge and warning to the New Testament saints, vss. 21-24; (f) God's retribution and His eternality, vss. 32-35.

Verse 1: I say then, Did God cast off his people? God forbid. For I also am an Israelite, of the seed of Abraham, of the tribe of Benjamin.

Because Israel spurned God's love, she disregarded His invitation and hearkened not to His Word. Is God through with the Jews? Because Israel went the way of the Gentiles, did her actions negate God's covenants and nullify His promises? Because Israel indulged her evil desires and became backslidden have her actions in the past compelled God to devise a new plan and program which is called the "new covenant" in Jeremiah 31:31, but which today is called the New Testament? Does this mean that the promises of God made to the Patriarchs and to Israel must now be altered, that is to say, spiritualized, to suit this age? Must the names Zion, Jerusalem, Caanan, now be made to mean Heaven? The Apostle's answer rings from the rooftops of eternity, No! God forbid! Impossible! The Old Testament is not nullified, and God is not through with the Jews (Jeremiah 31:37).

If God were through with the Jews His Word would be meaningless. If God's promises in the Old Testament have not and are not being fulfilled in the nation of Israel literally, which they are, are not His promises in the New Testament going to be fulfilled in the same manner? Is it not the same God who said to Abram in Genesis 13:15, ". . . for all the land which thou seest, to thee will I give it, and to thy seed for ever"; and who said in I John 2:25, "And this is the promise which he promised us, even the life eternal" (see also John 10:28; 17:2; I John 5:11).

If we alter the words "for ever" in the Old Testament, should not the word "eternal" in the New Testament be altered? It is the same God who speaks in both Testaments, it is the same Word. If because of the disobedience of some of Israel ("they did *not all hearken,*" Romans 10:16), God cast off the entire nation, will not God do the same with the New Testament Church because of the disobedience of some of the saints? If some of the Jews refused to obey God and the whole nation was cast off, does not the same God and the same principle work for the Church? Since when has the plan and program of salvation been changed? Were not Abel and Abraham saved the same way as we are today, according to Romans 4 and Hebrews 11?

The exclamation, "God forbid," runs recurrently throughout the Pauline Epistles. The Greek term means, don't permit it to come into existence; don't permit it to be created; don't let it occur. In the Hebrew it is one word which means profane or profanity. In other words, the Apostle is saying that it is profane even to think that it would ever be possible for God to be through with the Jews. The thought of God casting off His people Israel is profanation. Is it possible for language to express more strongly the thought of impossibility or improbability? (See I Samuel 12:23 for the Hebrew word "God forbid.") God did not abrogate His promises to Israel, nor is God ever going to be through with Israel nationally. If one says that God is through with Israel he is literally profaning the name of God. The same applies to the New Testament saint. A saint can never lose his relationship with God. It is absolute profanity to state that a child of God, a born-again believer, will be cast away or lose his salvation. Salvation was wrought by God through the blood of Christ. God did this, and it is God who completes it, and Christ brought it to pass in a once-for-all-time-and-eternity action (Philippians 1:6).

V. 1: "For I also am an Israelite, of the seed of Abraham, of the tribe of Benjamin." The truth that God is not through with national Israel, which implicates every individual Jew, is substantiated in this declaration in verse 1. If the Jews rejected Christ (and they did not all reject Him; see commentary on

Romans 10:16), when did this rejection take place? Did it occur
in Pilate's hall when the Jews shouted, "Let him be crucified"
(Matthew 27:11-26)? Are the Jews reaping today the harvest of
hate and persecution that spawned from their answer to Pilate's
denial of guilt for the execution of Jesus, "His blood be on us,
and on our children"? If God heard this self-invoked imprecation,
and the Jews have been and still are the victims of its consequences, although the people who uttered it were encouraged
by their leaders, how can a Jew be saved? If God's condemnation has fallen on the Jew because of this angry invocation, then
the blood of Christ cannot save the Jew. It condemns him!

But, Paul asks in verse 1, "Did God cast off his people?" and,
he replies immediately, "God forbid! For I also am a Jew." If
God is through with the Jews in this so-called "Gentile Church
Age," the Apostle asks, "What will you do with me? Am I not a
Jew of the seed of Abraham and of the tribe of Benjamin?" He
might well have added, what about the thousands of Jews saved
at Pentecost; and what about the five thousand Jews in Acts 4
who were saved? And what about the multitudes through the
centuries who believed and were saved? If all of these Jews were
not saved, then neither was Paul. If the blood of Christ is not
able to save a Jew, how can it save a Gentile? Is not the Gentile
just as guilty of the crucifixion of Christ as the Jew?

Does not Luke state in Acts 4:27 and 28 that both Jews and
Gentiles are responsible for the death of Christ? Does not Luke
also state that the crucifixion of Christ was to have been perpetrated by the Jews and the Gentiles according to God's plan,
"to do whatsoever thy hand and thy counsel foreordained to
come to pass" (Acts 4:28)? If God answered the plea of that
angry mob — "His blood be on us, and on our children" — then
the reader must conclude that this writer, who is a Jewish
Christian, is not saved. If this writer, who is of the seed of
Abraham, a son and a grandson of a Pharisee, is not saved, then
how can a Gentile, who is separated from Christ, alienated from
the commonwealth of Israel, a stranger from the covenants of
God, without hope and without God in the world, and who is
considered spiritually dead in the sight of God, be saved? If this
writer is not saved, then how can any reader who is of Gentile
extraction become a child of God through faith in Christ? Is not
every Gentile who is reading these words just as guilty of the
crucifixion as is the writer?

The reason for the strong words, "God forbid," in verse 1 is
that the question, "Did God cast off his people?" brings into

question the validity of the Old Testament convenants. If Israel made the agreement and became a willing party to God's covenant to become His people, to possess His land, and to become His emissaries, then the *keeping* of this would be incumbent upon Israel. But the Old Testament states that it is Jehovah who made the promises and the covenants, and He has not released Israel nor does He intend to do so. God stated that He would go and return to His own place until Israel would acknowledge her sin and seek Jehovah's face (Hosea 5:15). God said that His wrath would persist for a short time, and then He will restore Israel to her possessions and position (Isaiah 54:7, 8; 61:1-6; Zechariah 12:10; 13:1).

We must also consider another matter: The angry mob of Jews demanded the crucifixion of the Saviour. They taunted Him on the cross with the words, ". . . if thou art the Son of God, come down from the cross . . . He saved others; himself he cannot save. He is the King of Israel; let him now come down from the cross, and we will believe on him" (Matthew 27:40, 42). Christ could have come down from the cross if that would have been necessary to complete God's plan and program of salvation, but it wasn't. Our Saviour answered the angry mob with an intercessory prayer, "Father, forgive them; for they know not what they do" (Luke 23:34). In other words, the crucifixion was caused by blindness and ignorance. Peter accuses the Jews, "And now, brethren, I know that in ignorance ye did it, as did also your rulers" (Acts 3:17). God used Israel's stubbornness, blindness, and ignorance to bring to fruition His plan of redemption. The Gentiles joined in, and they, too, were ignorant (I Corinthians 2:8) and fulfilled God's plan.

Verse 2: God did not cast off his people which he foreknew. Or know ye not what the scripture saith of Elijah? how he pleadeth with God against Israel . . . :

Israel's disobedience did not come as a surprise to God. He was not taken unaware. God knew that Israel, as a nation, would refuse to follow His Messiah. God knew every act of violence that would be perpetrated against His Son. He knew the time, the place, and the people that would bring it to pass. The Messiah's miracles were accomplished according to plan (John 9:3). The Last Supper was established according to plan (Matthew 26:17, 18), as was also the hour of Messiah's death, "To this end have I been born, and to this end am I come into the world . . ." (John 18:37). Isaiah 53 paints a profoundly moving picture of Israel's actions and Messiah's sufferings. God foreknew the events that transpired at Golgotha. Psalm 22 was not an after-thought, but, rather, a minutely-detailed prophecy written hun-dreds of years prior to the crucifixion, a prophecy fulfilled to its very jot and tittle. God also knew the victory that would issue from the tomb. The Saviour's birth, ministry, death, burial, resurrection, and ascension was God's foreordained plan.

The Apostle introduces in verse 2 the experience of Elijah during his flight from the wrath of Jezebel. Elijah thought he was the only righteous person left in Israel who remained true to Jehovah. But Elijah was wrong. Paul quotes the texts of I Kings 19:14 and 18 in the next two verses of Romans 11:3, 4. Had Elijah not fled from the wrath of Jezebel, had he stood his ground as a prophet of God and trusted Jehovah to deliver him from this vile and evil-minded woman, he would have seen that he was not the only righteous person left in Israel who remained faithful, and he would not have had to accuse the whole nation of Israel of infidelity. He was blinded and cowed by the crafty and murderous Jezebel, and this blindness and fear drove him to a wrong conclusion. Had he stood his ground he would have seen the host of "seven thousand men" that God still had in Israel. Fear often drives people to wrong conclusions, and Elijah was no exception.

Paul draws an analogy in verse 2. God foreknew Israel. They are His "chosen people." God could not cast them off. Just as Elijah had arrived at a wrong conclusion, Paul warns the Roman saints not to follow Elijah's example. The condition was the same in Israel at Paul's time as it was in Elijah's time, and he cautions the saints at Rome not to make the same mistake Elijah made. Paul stated in Romans 10:16 that "they (Israel) did not *all* hearken," which implies some in Israel *did* hearken to the Gospel.

The whole divine program of salvation and its culmination in the Messianic Kingdom lay in the foreknowledge of God. Know-ing in His eternal wisdom that Israel would fail in her faithfulness to Him, God's plan of salvation held provision for such failure, and thus precluded the necessity for any subsequent modifica-tion of His plan. God's plans are eternal and unalterable, and all of them, so far as this world is concerned, are centered ir-revocably around His people Israel. God foreknew their history, and their every breach of loyalty and service to Him through the ages before the crucifixion. The enduring peace of this world, as well as the salvation of creation itself, God has entrusted to Israel. He cannot and He will not cast off His people.

Verse 3: Lord, they have killed thy prophets, they have digged down thine altars; and I am left alone, and they seek my life.

Jezebel killed many prophets. Did not Obadiah hide "a hundred prophets" in a cave to save their lives? (I Kings 18:4). Israel, as a nation, may have been guilty of killing prophets, digging down altars, but *not all* of Israel was guilty, only some of them. However, Jezebel was not a Jewess, she was the daughter of the Gentile King Ethbaal of Zidon. She never embraced the faith of Israel — the faith of her husband, Ahab, an Israelite. Ahab was a more evil king in Israel than any of his predecessors (I Kings 21:25, 26). However, he repented in his later years (I Kings 21:27-29).

Elijah was not the only good prophet left in Israel. His fear for his own physical safety got the better of him, however, and as he pleaded with God against Israel he spoke as a self-righteous individual, rather than as a prophet of Jehovah inspired by the Holy Spirit. Paul shows in verse 3 the falsity of Elijah's accusation.

There is a lesson in this for every child of God. No saint can walk self-righteously with a chip on his shoulder believing that if someone knocks it off, he, as a saint, is suffering for Christ. Not so! He is suffering for his own presumption; so let us beware!

Verse 4: But what saith the answer of God unto him? I have left for myself seven thousand men, who have not bowed the knee to Baal.

What a shocking surprise this must have been to Elijah! This was God's rebuke to His prophet, delivered by God Himself to Elijah for his unworthy estimate of God's people Israel. Did not God promise Abraham a seed as numberless as the stars in heaven? How could Elijah shrink this "seed" down to himself alone? Would God have to start all over again and use Elijah as a second Abraham? How absurd! The Greek word for "the answer of God" in verse 4 appears only here in the New Testament, and means a response from God, a divine communication, an oracle. Elijah's plea to God that he was "left alone" could not have been more wrong. He was not left alone. There were seven thousand men in Israel who were faithful to Jehovah. Verse 4 does not mention the number of women and children who were also faithful to Jehovah. There must have been a sizeable number in Israel who had not bowed the knee to the image of Baal.

This writer may be permitted to draw a personal analogy from Elijah's complaint. He has been approached a number of times by people who have said, "You are the first Jewish Christian I have ever met." Well, the truth is that God has a considerable number of Jewish Christians. The writer has also had the joy of speaking to many groups of Jewish Christians, numbering in the aggregate hundreds of men, women and children. The reason there are not more Jewish Christians is that true believers, and many fundamental Christian churches, do so little in bringing the Gospel to the Jew. One cannot reap more than one has sown. The fact that there are not more Jewish Christians is a sad commentary on our indifference to and negligence of God's people Israel. This condition should be a challenge to every born-again believer.

Verse 5: Even so then at this present time also there is a remnant according to the election of grace.

This completes the analogy that the Apostle introduced in verse 3. Just as God had a faithful remnant in Elijah's time, God also had a faithful remnant in Paul's time, and we have a faithful remnant out of Israel today. God has always had a faithful remnant of true followers in Israel. There never was a time during this present dispensation, or in any other dispensation, that God has not had a faithful remnant in Israel.

This faithful remnant in Israel has always been the fruit that was "meet for the master's use" (II Timothy 2:21). This fruit, this remnant, this handful of faithful souls out of the great host of the twelve tribes, are the saved ones "according to the election of grace." Herein is further proof of the truth that God has not "cast off his people." These faithful ones are the elect of God who comprise the three thousand, the five thousand, and the multitudes of Jews who became Christians that are recorded in the book of Acts. This is a further proof that the parable of the fig tree in Matthew 24:32, when placed beside Luke 21:29 and this verse before us, cannot be Israel. The nation Israel has had not only buds, but fruits, as well.

This saved remnant out of Israel was, therefore, saved according to God's election and by God's grace from everlasting. God kept, and is still keeping, a watchful eye over them, and calls them by His grace. (Look at the commentary on Romans 9:6-13). These Jewish saints form an integral part of the true New

Testament Church. They are the half of the ones of whom God "made both one, and brake down the middle wall of partition . . . that he might create in himself of the two one new man . . ." (Ephesians 2:14, 15). Without them there can be no true completed Church in Christ! They are included in the word "us" of Ephesians 1:4, 5. We Christians have, for the most part, excluded them from the missionary program of the Church. But God has included them, and by His grace and His own good pleasure He is daily adding to His Church from that remnant out of Israel. Are you?

Verse 6: But if it is by grace, it is no more of works: otherwise grace is no more grace.

The Sinaitic, the Alexandrine, the Syriac, and the Nestle's texts do not contain the last half of the verse. Such omission, however, by no means alters the meaning of the text. If salvation is by grace then it stands to reason that it is not of works, and vice versa. Grace excludes all works. The doctrine of election spoken of in verse 5 is by the grace of God. The Apostle is emphasizing in verse 6 the all-sufficiency of grace. We must never lose sight of the supreme truth that election resulting in salvation is wrought for every person by the grace of God alone. None of our "filthy rags" of human righteousness ever assisted God in this achievement. "Salvation is of Jehovah" (Jonah 2:9). ". . . for by grace have ye been saved through faith; and that *not of yourselves* (human righteousness), it is the *gift of God*" (Ephesians 2:8). If it is a *gift,* then it is unmerited and gratuitous. No human being can boast of its attainment through any merit or righteousness of his own.

It was by the grace of God that the remnant of Israel was reserved. What the Apostle is implying in verse 6 is that in spite of Israel's national disobedience, stubbornness, and sinfulness, resulting in the rejection of the Messiah, God had and still has a remnant out of this nation that He elects *for* Himself and *by* Himself. Only an Omnipotent and Sovereign God could achieve this divine miracle. Salvation is not a reward; it is a gift. It must be so. Either it is *all grace,* or else it is *all works.* If salvation can be attained by works, then "grace becomes no more grace." This was true in the past, and is true today.

The Greek word translated "is" in verse 6 is the present indicative, and is more accurately translated becomes. Grace and works cannot be mixed. It must be one or the other.

The first six verses of chapter 11 add up to the conclusion that

God is not through with the Jews; that He has not cast them off as a nation; that there is a faithful remnant in Israel and that there always has been and will continue to be; that this remnant has been reserved by God in this age; that there will be a remnant reserved by God through the Great Tribulation for the Millennial Kingdom (Jeremiah 50:20); that this remnant has been reserved by the pure grace of God; and, lastly, that this salvation is a gift of God by His grace, and He bestows this gift through His own choosing on whomsoever He wills.

What a wonderful God we have! Do you know Him? You can. The way is open to whosoever will. "There is a fountain filled with blood, drawn from Immanuel's veins; and sinners, plunged beneath that flood, lose all their guilty stains."

Verse 7: What then? That which Israel seeketh for, that he obtained not; but the election obtained it, and the rest were hardened . . . :

What conclusions are we to draw from the statements in this verse? Israel has been seeking to establish a code of ethics of her own by means of which she could become righteous in the sight of God. Israel has never veered from this objective, and still pursues what must of necessity always be a hopeless quest. The Greek word translated "seeketh" in verse 7 is in the present indicative action, thus acknowledging the truth that Israel is *still* seeking righteousness through her own efforts. That she has not obtained it is obvious, for if she had she would not be scattered among the nations as she is, and still rejecting her promised Messiah, the Lord Jesus Christ. However, this condition is true only of *national* Israel, and is not true of a goodly number of individuals in Israel.

V. 7: ". . . but the election obtained it," that is, righteousness; and the "election" is that remnant upon whom the eternal eye of God has ever been fixed with unwavering vigilance. This choice remnant was and is a goodly number. The thousands upon thousands, the multitudes, the myriads that are spoken of in the book of Acts were all Jews who comprised this remnant. It wasn't until sixteen years after the Ascension that we read of the first Gentile, Cornelius, being converted.

The church in Jerusalem was not rich in this world's goods; in fact, Paul took up offerings in other churches for the saints at Jerusalem. But how rich they were in praise, in faith, in hope, and in devotion to their Messiah! Do not forget that these Christians, the Church, the Body of Christ, many of them martyrs, spoken of in the first nine chapters of the book of Acts, were all *Jewish* Christians. Paul, the Pharisee, was persecuting *Jewish Christians* not *Gentile Christians*. The "threatenings" spoken of in Acts 4:29 and 9:1 were against the Jewish Christians in and about Jerusalem. This Jewish remnant of the faithful followers of Christ "loved not their life even unto death" (Revelation 12:11). They were poor in the eyes of the world, but they possessed riches in their risen Messiah. This is the "remnant" that obtained righteousness (Mark 6:52; 8:17; John 12:40).

V. 7: ". . . and the rest were (blinded KJV) hardened (ASV) . . .": The Greek word translated "hardened" means to petrify, to become callous. Only in a figurative sense can the word be made to mean blind, as in the expression, "blind with rage." The word "hardened" in v. 7 is in the aorist indicative passive, expressing the biblical truth that Israel was acted upon rather than acting. In other words, the hardening process was brought upon them by an outside agency, in this case, God (see verse 8). What sobering words! What awful separation between those who obtained the election and those who obtained it not! The human mind cannot fathom it. It is beyond our ken. The word "harden" rolls like thunder through the eternal ages. Pharaoh's heart was hardened before Moses ever started on his journey. That same "hardening" is prevalent in Israel.

The Psalmist's words should still ring in Israel, "Today, oh that ye would hear his voice! Harden not your heart . . ." (Psalm 95:7b, 8a). What tribulations Israel has experienced because she refused to heed this warning! The evil consequences of her blindness are recited with terrifying exactitude and completeness in Proverbs 1:24-32 in language far better than this or any other writer could possibly describe them. The words, called, refused, set at naught, laugh, calamity, mock, fear, storm, distress, anguish, and, shall not find me, are words of solemn condemnation, filled with warning that can be heard across the centuries.

"O Love that wilt not let me go," are the words of a hymn that constitute a beautiful commentary on Proverbs 1:33, "But whoso hearkeneth unto me shall dwell securely . . .". God's hands are still stretched forth to Israel and His voice still pleads with His ancient people. The remnant hears now, and the nation will also hear at the end of the Tribulation. ". . . in their affliction they will seek me early" (Hosea 5:15 KJV). The word "early" means diligently, or earnestly (ASV) or the dusk before dawn. As the Eternal Son of God, who is the Day Star of Israel, returns to earth, the darkness that has hung over Israel all these millenniums will be dispelled.

Have you accepted the Saviour? He is the Light of Life, the Bread of Life, the Water of Life. He invites you, "Come unto me" — His eternal invitation to you!

Verse 8: . . . according as it is written, God gave them a spirit of stupor, eyes that they should not see, and ears that they should not hear, unto this very day.

The Apostle is alluding to Deuteronomy 29:4 and Isaiah 29:10. There should be no parenthesis around Romans 11:8, as shown in the King James Version. The words in verse 8 should be joined to verse 7. Verse 8 explains who the hardening agent is. It is God Himself.

Let us not try to inject our own ideas into verse 8. This text is to be taken literally, the same as the other texts. It states that, "God gave them a spirit of stupor." It does not say that this condition was brought to pass by the Pharisees, the Sadducees, or the Scribes, or by any agent other than God. It was God's doing then, and God is choosing to do it now. This "spirit of stupor" is prevalent in Israel even today. The Gospel, to the average Jew, is only for the Gentiles. To the average Jew it is also meaningless. He is indifferent to its appeal, and he feels that, as a Jew, it does not apply to him. He is blinded to its truth (II Corinthians 3:14, 15). This is what the Apostle is saying in Romans 11:8, that the "spirit of stupor" is prevalent in Israel at this present hour.

A careless reader of Scripture could, at this point, stumble into a false assumption that the "hardening" process in Israel was the result of her own human frailty or the work of her self-willed leaders, whereas a careful study of the succeeding verses will show that the "hardening" process was brought about wholly in accordance with God's plan and purpose, as operative today as it was in the past. We shall see God's motive for this "hardening" in verse 11, as well as God's purpose in continuing to harden the hearts of His people. Israel could, if God so willed it, recover her sight today and avail herself of God's revealed truth.

Verses 9 and 10: (9) And David saith, Let their table be made a snare, and a trap, and a stumbling-block, and a recompense unto them: (10) Let their eyes be darkened, that they may not see, and bow thou down their back always.

These two verses are a quotation from the Septuagint version of Psalm 69:22, 23.* The Greek words translated, "be made a snare," "let . . . be darkened," and "bow thou down," are in the imperative mood. This mood expresses the idea that; (a) the will to influence the behavior of another, as in a command, entreaty, or exhortation; (b) expressive of being a command (*Webster's Third New International Dictionary*).

This is what the Apostle began to state in verse 8. God had a purpose, as we have just seen, in blinding or hardening Israel. If God had not, how would the Gentiles have heard the Gospel? Consider Peter: He spent more than three years at the feet of the Saviour; he witnessed the trial and crucifixion; he saw the empty tomb and the resurrected Saviour; and he saw the Ascension. In spite of all this, the Holy Spirit had to give Peter the vision of a "great sheet" (Acts 10:9-23) to get him to preach the Gospel to a Gentile, Cornelius. If God had to have so much patience in awakening Peter's obedience, how much more patience and loving kindness did the Saviour have to have to get a Pharisee like Paul to go to the Gentiles?

God's eternal purpose is the motivating factor in the blinding and hardening of Israel. Because of God's great love for Israel, upon which His purposes for her salvation are based, the Gentiles are made to be the recipients of God's love, mercy, and grace, as we shall see. This truth is developed further along in this chapter. What we need to remember is that we are not to despair or neglect our witness because of this "hardening process" which is still Israel's lot under God. Let us rather rejoice that there is still "a remnant according to the election of grace," and preach the Gospel to Jews and Gentiles alike.

Israel's back has been "bowed" down with the burden of sin. Their persecutions and privations have broken their back and decimated their numbers by millions. Christians cannot console them with the words, "But the way of the transgressor is hard" (Proverbs 13:15). Nor can we quote the words of Solomon to them, "The way of him that is laden with guilt is exceeding crooked; . . ." (Proverbs 21:8). Until God takes away the hardening of their hearts, they will admit neither to guilt nor to transgression. One thing they do know: The Gentiles, from the beginning of Jewish history until the present time, have far exceeded the sum total of Israel's transgressions and guilt. The

---

*For the Greek student the tenses in these two verses shed a lot of light on a great truth in Scripture.

guilt of one Gentile nation, Germany, in just ten years has been a million times greater than the guilt of all the Jews throughout their entire existence. The history of the Roman Empire, the Roman Catholic Church, Spain, Italy, France, England, and Russia, teems with Jewish persecution, murder, and exile.

We should realize that when God permitted His Son to be crucified He was at the same time crucifying His own people Israel. God's relationship to Israel is that of the "potter and the clay." The clay cannot question, nor does it have the intelligence to question, God, "Why didst thou make me thus?" (Romans 9:20). But we must not forget that Israel's insensibility to God's Word and warning is the direct cause of His punitive measures against His people. Sin must be punished. God's righteousness is not dulled by His love. Its true character is displayed in His justice. God's punishment is the corollary of sin.

Israel as a nation may be wallowing in sin. She may be scattered among the nations and seemingly lost in the maelstrom of iniquity. Nevertheless, God has His remnant and His plan for the redemption of the nation. He has never abrogated His plan, nor nullified His promises, nor repudiated His covenants. God's will must be done on earth as it is in Heaven.

Verse 11: I say then, Did they stumble that they might fall? God forbid: but by their fall salvation is come unto the Gentiles, to provoke them to jealousy.

This is the answer to the question in verse 1, "Did God cast off His people?" and God's purpose for His people, in verses 7 through 10. The Apostle is asking these questions: Have the Jews fallen to their eternal destruction? Is national Israel dead? Because Israel has incessantly sinned, have God's punitive measures brought this nation to extinction? Are God's plans and purposes for national Israel now annulled? All these questions are pertinent to the question in verse 11, "Did they stumble that they might fall?"

The Apostle's answer is, "God forbid." (See the commentary on 11:1.) Notice that the word "fall" occurs twice in verse 11, and that each is translated from a different Greek word. The Greek word for "fall" in the first part of the sentence, "Did they stumble that they might fall?" means to fall prostrate, to fall dead, to become null and void. The Greek word for "fall" in the second part of the sentence, "but by their fall," means a false step, a trespass, an offense, a transgression. The Apostle is saying that Israel's sin did not make her "fall" final or fatal, but rather a fall that created an opportunity for God to bring salvation to the Gentiles.

The promises of God to Israel are sure. God has not altered His mind nor His program. Israel's sin opened the way for the Gospel to be preached to the Gentiles. God's purpose in permitting the Jewish nation to stumble and fall was not the destruction of Israel, but, rather, the salvation of the Gentiles. We must also remember that only part of the nation fell. There was and still is this "remnant according to the election of grace" (verse 5). In this "fall" of Israel God fulfills His promise, ". . . who would have all men to be saved, and come to the knowledge of the truth" (I Timothy 2:4). But the promises to national Israel are still to be fulfilled.

V. 11: ". . . to provoke them to jealousy." The word in verse 11 translated "jealousy," also means, in the classical Greek, to admire and strive after. Divine wisdom has used the stumbling of the Jewish nation to facilitate the preaching of the Gospel to the Gentiles. By the preaching of the Gospel, the Gentile's conversion would produce so marked a change in the life of the Gentile that the Jew would become jealous of that Gentile's change and desire that that same experience take place in the life of the Jew. Nothing is so effective in preaching the Gospel as a life that has been transformed by Christ through the Holy Spirit.

God does not take pleasure in seeing anyone go to an eternal hell (Matthew 18:11, 14). He has done everything possible to provide salvation for everyone. The Gospel is *to all, for all.* "Whosoever will may come" (Revelation 22:17 KJV) is written on the parchment of eternity by the sovereign hand of God, with the quill that He dipped in the blood of His Son. There is no need for anyone to go to a Christless eternity. God has placed all obstacles possible on the road that leads to hell.

By blinding Jewish eyes and hardening Jewish hearts God has opened the door of heaven to the Gentiles, and has not shut the door to the Jews. The life of the saved Gentile should be so changed, so different, so revolutionized, so diverse from the unregenerate Gentile that even a spiritually-blinded Jew should be able to see the difference. This is what the Gospel will do and must do for every born-again child of God. In this way the blindness and hardness can be removed from the eyes and heart of the unsaved Jew and he, too, will be converted. God is grieved because Israel is dying in her sin. He has extended His invitation, "Say unto them, As I live, saith the Lord Jehovah, I have no pleasure of the death of the wicked; but that the wicked turn from his way and live; turn ye, turn ye from your evil ways; for why will ye die, O house of Israel?" (Ezekiel 33:11; see also 18:23, 32).

Christians are slow to take the Gospel to the Jews. Seemingly they are not interested in seeing the Jews saved. God uses only one method in reaching people with the Gospel, "So then faith cometh by hearing, and hearing by the Word of God" (Romans 10:17 KJV). The admonition contained in Romans 11:11 is that by our changed life we "will provoke them to jealousy." Opening the door of salvation to the Gentile by the grace of God was to make the backslidden Jew jealous. The jealousy of the Jew toward the Gentile for this reason would have no relation to the conduct of the Jew which the Apostle has described as Jewish stumbling and falling. God moved them to jealousy once before, in the ages past (Deuteronomy 32:21; see Romans 10:19.) How have we lived? is the question every one of us shall have to answer in the personal presence of the Saviour.

Verse 12: Now if their fall is the riches of the world, and their loss the riches of the Gentiles; how much more their fulness?

If by the fall of Israel the Gentiles have become the possessors of so great spiritual blessings, how much greater will these blessings prove to be to all creation when the whole nation of Israel becomes converted and is restored to complete fellowship with God? Or to put it another way, if the remnant of Israel — that smaller number which comprises the remnant described in Romans 11:5 — proved to be such an incalculable blessing to the world as a whole, and their "hardened ones," being placed in an inferior or less favored position, proved to be the "riches of the Gentiles" in the form of such rich benefits and abundant blessings, then how much greater will these benefits and blessings be for the entire world when the whole Jewish nation is restored?

"The whole creation groaneth and travaileth in pain until" (Romans 8:22) the day of Israel's restoration. What joy, what blessing, what exultation the restoration of Israel will bring to pass! If being the "tail" of the nations has blessed so many individual Gentiles, how much greater will the blessings be when Israel becomes the "head"? (Deuteronomy 28:13). Scripture gives us the answer and we need not speculate. Peace will be universal; there will be no more hostilities; there will be no need for politics; and there will be no crimes committed. There will be one law, and one Law-giver seated at Jerusalem. There will be holy demonstrations; Israel will be the spiritual ministers in this kingdom; ". . . and the lion shall eat straw like the ox" (Isaiah 11:7). See Psalm 2; Isaiah 2:2-4; 9:6, 7; 11:1-12; 61:4-11; Jeremiah 23:5-8; 30:18-22; 31:1-14, 27-40; 33:14-18; Ezekiel 11:14-20; 34:25-31; Amos 9:11-15; Zechariah 14:9-11; Luke 1:30-33; and others. This is God's prophetic program. This is God's social order in prospect. This is the answer to the question in verse 12.

Verse 13: But I speak to you that are Gentiles. Inasmuch then as I am an apostle of Gentiles, I glorify my ministry . . . ;

The Apostle is addressing the Gentile Christians in the church at Rome. Perhaps some of the Gentile Christian members of that local church could boast of their position in Christ. They might even affect a superior attitude toward the Jewish Christians. The Apostle spoke to these Gentile Christians with authority. His position as the Apostle of the Gentiles was unique for he spoke as a Jew, a Christian, and an apostle. His position gave him complete authority to admonish every member in this local church when and if admonishing might be needed.

We must not overlook the truth of the fact that this text (verse 13) has application as well as implication for every believer in the local church today, even as it had in the time of Paul. This authority with which he speaks to these Gentile Christians is invested in every pastor of a local church. However, we have changed the order. In our day a church is governed by deacons and trustees and not by the pastor who is also under the authority of the deacons and trustees. This is contrary to every order and rule of the New Testament. When God's people fail to recognize the God-given authority of God's anointed shepherds they are sure to find themselves, sooner or later, out of God's will and on the road to disunity and questioning. Just a casual look at texts such as Exodus 14:11; 15:24; 17:2, 3; and Numbers 11:1-4; 21:5, gives us a picture of what happens when God's people murmur against the leader whom God has appointed. The pastor is the leader, not the deacons and trustees. He should lead, not follow. If he is true to his calling he will accept the pastor's office with all humility. Paul does not state that he magnifies himself. He says, "I magnify my *office*" (KJV), "I speak to you! For as much as I am an apostle of the Gentiles, I honor, I glorify, I laud, I give praise, I value my office, my ministry." The Christian ministry is the highest and holiest position that a man can attain to in God's plan and program. Let us not minimize its dignity and authority.

The high esteem Paul placed on the office to which God called him was the result of his devotion to the grand purpose of his life, the salvation of his people Israel. This man never lost sight of Israel's plight in his day or in their future restoration in God's plan. Unsaved Israel's position in God's program is not inimical to the hope of the believer. They are intertwined. The hope of the believer is the coming of the Lord and Israel's hope is the coming of the Messiah, although at present Israel does not recognize the Lord Jesus Christ as her Messiah. In this sense, therefore, the Lord is Israel's only hope for salvation and restoration, even though in her present backslidden state she would deny it.

Verse 14: . . . if by any means I may provoke to jealousy them that are my flesh, and may save some of them.

The Apostle could never divest himself of the great sorrow and unceasing pain that he carried in his heart for his people. In Romans 9:3 he states, "I could wish that I myself were anathema from Christ for my . . . kinsmen according to the flesh." In Chapter 10:1 he states, ". . . my heart's desire and my supplication to God is for them that they (Israel) may be saved." In chapter 11, verses 13 and 14, he glorifies and magnifies his ministry that he "may provoke to jealousy them that are my flesh." The goal of this jealousy is their salvation. What holy passion! He was willing to use any means and suffer every difficulty so long as some of Israel were saved. This servant of God would try every resource at his disposal even if it meant martyrdom for himself, as it did, in order that Israel might admit her sin and recognize the Lord Jesus Christ as her Messiah, the answer to her prayers and hopes. Paul was "the bondslave of Jesus Christ," and, as such, he determined to spend his life, his energy, and every moment of his time in the service of His Master. He reaped abundant fruit from among the Gentiles, and undoubtedly reaped much fruit from among his own nation, Israel, as well. He knew his goal and was certain of his reward. "I press on toward the goal unto the prize of the high calling of God in Christ Jesus" (Philippians 3:14; II Timothy 4:7, 8).

Verse 15: For if the casting away of them is the reconciling of the world, what shall the receiving of them be, but life from the dead?

If the casting away of a great majority of the Jewish nation, or their loss of life (as the Greek word means), results in the reconciliation of the world, what shall "the receiving of them be"? The word in classical Greek which is here translated "the receiving of them be," has also an added meaning; namely, to take to one's self a helper or partner. When God restores Israel to her proper position (Exodus 19:5, 6), she will then become the helper of God. "But ye shall be named the priests of Jehovah; men shall call you the ministers of our God . . ." (Isaiah 61:6). When Israel is restored by God Himself it will be as "life from the dead" for the world of nations and creation.

By "the casting away of them" (Israel) they have become the fugitives of the world, they are the undigested Jonahs among the Gentiles, they are the strangers and foreigners among the nations, they are in exile. Throughout the centuries they have not been assimilated. They have survived to the present hour, and are, therefore, a miracle of the ages. When the Greeks began to write history, Nehemiah was the last of the Old Testament historians.

The Jews have been the teachers of the world, ". . . they were intrusted with the oracles of God" (Romans 3:2); they were the instruments by which salvation and the Saviour were brought to the Gentile world (John 4:22; Romans 1:3); they have been the instruments of the blessing of God to the world (Genesis 12:3). In spite of all this they are still the haunted and the hunted, the despised people of the world. But they are the "chosen people" of Jehovah, and He has promised to restore them.

If the world is ever to experience "life from the dead," it will be dependent upon Israel's conversion and restoration. The hope of the world is wrapped up in Israel's restoration. Israel may claim and proclaim that ". . . Jehovah hath forsaken me . . ." (Isaiah 49:14), to which God retorts, "Can a woman forget her sucking child . . . yea, these may forget, yet will not I forget thee" (Isaiah 49:15). How can God forget with the Saviour at His side? The Saviour's hands bear the engravings of Israel (Isaiah 49:16). There is hope for Israel, "As a shepherd seeketh out his flock in the day that he is among his sheep that are scattered abroad, so will I seek out my sheep; . . . I myself will be the shepherd of my sheep . . . saith the Lord Jehovah" (Ezekiel 34:12, 15). Because there is hope for the nation Israel, the promise of life from the dead is certain for the world (see Isaiah 49:26b).

There will never be a world-wide revival until Israel is reconciled to God and the Messiah. When that event takes place, the world-wide revival will take place, and "life from the dead" will become a reality.

Verse 16: And if the firstfruit is holy, so is the lump: and if the root is holy, so are the branches.

The interpretation of the "firstfruit" and of the "root" is varied. It is not necessary to attempt a detailed explanation of these two words. The A-millennialists and the discredited Post-millennialists have difficulty with verse 16. The best they can do is to explain it away. They can not correlate their eisegesis* with the Scriptures, and this presents a real problem to one who tries to teach the Bible! Exegesis of· Scripture must always be, "thus saith the Lord."

This writer believes that the "firstfruit" and the "lump" represent either Abraham alone, or the patriarchs. There should be no difficulty with the thought that Ishmael and Esau are of the first two, Abraham and Isaac. Ishamel was not the promised seed of God, but was the fruit of the unbelief of Abraham and Sarah. Esau was rejected before he was born.

Out of the loins of Abraham, who was the "firstfruit" and the "root," the nation Israel came into existence. God set Abraham and his seed, Israel, apart. They are God's peculiar possession. Abraham was that peculiar "firstfruit" that God chose for Himself. In the same manner God chose Israel for Himself. (This writer remembers seeing his mother bake bread many times. She would always pinch off a piece of the dough, roll it into a ball, and then throw it into the oven. She would make a prayer over this piece or the "lump" of dough. This custom is all based on Numbers 15:19-21. Undoubtedly the Apostle had this in mind.)

Israel is likewise the "lump" and the "branches" (Deuteronomy 4:7; 7:6; 10:15; 14:2; 26:19; 32:8, 9). The word "holy" (Romans 11:16) does not always mean holy in the Greek and in the Hebrew. The word means set apart, as well. In this sense the word holy is used of the temple and the vessels in it. Israel is "set apart" from all nations, or Gentiles, ". . . Lo, it is a people that dwelleth alone, and shall not be reckoned among the nations (Gentiles)" (Numbers 23:9). That the nation Israel will become holy in the completed sense is promised in Jeremiah 50:20; Isaiah 43:25; and Micah 7:19. God has promised to cleanse, to redeem, to sanctify, and to restore the nation Israel according to His original purpose and plan. This restoration is not dependent

---

*A mode of interpretation in which the commentator introduces his own ideas as though they were the author's.

upon Israel, but upon a Sovereign God who promised it and who will perform it.

Verse 16 is a further substantiation of Romans 11:1, 2a. God's promises are sure; His covenants are indestructible; His Word is irrefutable, giving credence to the Gospel, and implicit confidence to every child of God. There can be no doubt as to the veracity of God's Word. This is why the Apostle states that, ". . . I am persuaded that he (Christ) is able to guard that which I have committed unto him against that day" (II Timothy 1:12).

Do you have this confidence and hope? Are you sure of your destiny? Christ says, "I am the way, and the truth, and the life" (John 14:6). Are you walking in the way? Do you know the truth of eternal life? You can. Christ is the answer.

Verse 17: But if some of the branches were broken off, and thou, being a wild olive, wast grafted in among them, and didst become partaker with them of the root of the fatness of the olive tree . . . ;

Let us not overlook the word "some" in this verse. Notice that verse 17 does not say *all the branches*. When one hears some so-called Bible teachers attempt to interpret this portion of Romans 11, one receives the impression that the Holy Spirit made a mistake, for they teach that verse 17 somehow contains a reference to the "Gentile Church" or the "Gentile Church Age," which is false reasoning and is a carry-over of A-millennialism and Post-millennialism into the clear teaching of Pre-millennial truth as it is in Scripture. How can there be such a monstrosity as a "Gentile Church"? If it is a Gentile Church it cannot be the Church that Christ started and which Paul describes in the Epistle to the Ephesians.

The "olive tree" spoken of in verse 17 is, perhaps, the olive tree in Jeremiah 11:16 and Hosea 14:6. Notice that the branches of the wild olive tree were grafted in *among* them, not *instead* of them. This is a further elaboration of Romans 11:5, 7. The faithful remnant was bearing fruit. If there had not been a remnant the Gentiles would never have heard the Gospel. It was the Jewish Christians who preached the Gospel to the Gentiles. They (the Gentiles) were "grafted in among them," and they (Gentiles) became a "partaker with them." In other words, the Gentile at his conversion was spiritually grafted into the good olive tree and became a *part*-taker, not an *all*-taker, with the Jewish believers. Jewish and Gentile believer became one. They partook of the root, Abraham, (Romans 4), and of the fatness (of the righteousness which is by faith, Romans 4:3) of the good olive tree.

The grafting as shown in Romans 11:17 is contrary to the science of horticulture. The ordinary process of grafting is to take a wild root and graft a good branch onto it. The good branch, drawing its strength from the wild root, will grow the type of fruit or flower from which it was cut off. It will not grow the type of fruit of the wild root, since it is a good branch. In this way, rose plants are grown in green-houses and nurseries.

God is a *super*-natural God. He takes the wild branch and cuts it off the wild tree (the Gentile) and grafts it into the good tree (Israel) among the good branches. Even though it is a wild branch, God performs a miracle and the wild branch bears the same fruit as the good branch; in fact, both produce fruit unto God (Romans 7:4). Thus the Gentile receives the blessings of God through the Jew.

Verse 18: . . . glory not over the branches: but if thou gloriest, it is not thou that bearest the root, but the root thee.

Here is a warning for the Gentile Christian. In this verse Paul is saying, Don't boast or vaunt yourself against, or glory over, or assume superiority over, the natural (Jewish) branches.

The Jewish Christian is not grafted into a Gentile Church. To a Jewish Christian the Church has become a Gentile Christian Church in its thinking and concept. It is a Church with the Jew left out. The Gentile who becomes a believer in the Jewish Messiah and accepts Christ as his Saviour, is grafted into the Church, the Body of Christ. If there could be boasting it would have to be on the part of the Jewish Christian since, "Salvation is from the Jews" (John 4:22). We must not forget that the Jewish nation, collectively and individually, is what Paul calls the natural good branches of the tree! Only some of the natural branches have been broken off. The stock is not sterile. It is still drawing the living sap and distributing it among the branches.

Verse 19: Thou wilt say then, Branches were broken off, that I might be grafted in.

The Gentile believer might feel that God loves him more than the Jew because the Jewish "branches" were broken off to make room for the Gentile, but this is not so. It is a false assumption. The succeeding verse explains why some of the Jews were broken off:

Verse 20: Well; by their unbelief they were broken off, and thou standest by thy faith. Be not high-minded, but fear . . . :

True. They were broken off, but why? Surely, not to make room for the Gentiles. The majority of the Jewish nation was broken off because of continued faithlessness. Never in the history of Israel has the whole nation been obedient to God's Word. They always rebelled and continued to pursue their own ideas and ends. They have not accepted, and do not accept, God's Word or His messengers. This is why so great a number of Israel was broken off.

In verse 20 there is a warning to the Gentile believer, "thou standest by thy faith." That which Israel lacks God has given to Gentile believers. Even faith is a gift of God, imparted to the believer by the Holy Spirit. It is not because God loves the Gentiles more than He does the Jews that He caused the Jews to be "broken off." It was their faithlessness that brought God's judgment upon them. This resulted in the grafting in of the Gentiles, but the grafting in is by faith alone.

"Be not high-minded, but fear . . ." is the warning, in verse 20, to every Gentile believer. In other words, Paul is saying, Don't be proud, don't boast, since you (Gentile believers) were not placed in this position of favor with God because you are better than the ones who "were broken off"; see yourselves as you are, and realize that salvation is a gift of God bestowed upon you as an unmerited favor. If Gentile believers will see it in this light, they will stand in fear, that is to say, in reverential awe. It is the simple truth that God in His mercy and love reached down and took us up out of the miry clay of sin and placed us on the Rock of our salvation, the Lord Jesus Christ. We did nothing; God did it all (I Corinthians 10:12).

Verse 21: . . . for if God spared not the natural branches, neither will he spare thee.

The Greek word translated "spared" means to be tender of, to forbear.

God's patience, love, mercy, and long-suffering can be tried, but only for a limited time. "My Spirit shall not stirve with man for ever . . ." (Genesis 6:3), God's mercy and long-suffering are enduring; He is patient and loving. However, God's righteousness, justice and holiness cannot be tampered with (Deuteronomy 7:4; 11:17; 28:20; Proverbs 6:15; Isaiah 47:11; and others.) God does not lower His standards, nor can sin flourish in His sight.

Israel tried God's love and mercy for generations, and He endured her infidelity. Yet we see throughout the Old Testament, for example, where God's justice and righteousness brought the judgment of God almost immediately upon Israel, in the slaying of all but two (Joshua and Caleb) of the male adults that were brought out of Egypt (Numbers 14:38) and the sin of Korah (Numbers 26:10). The righteousness of God brought down the gavel of God's wrath upon Israel.

The names which are sometimes used to convey the nature of God's relationship to Israel are thought-provoking! God, on different occasions, is called Father, Husband, Lover, and the Good Shepherd. These titles help us to understand, in part, some of the attributes of our God, His love, His patience, His beneficence, His mercy, and His compassion. With what infinite patience God permitted Israel to commit their last great sin, the rejection of His Messiah! Nevertheless, the love of God cannot be trodden under foot and go unpunished, not even in Israel. Israel had to be punished for their sins even though they were God's very own people. It was the last sin that God permitted Israel to commit; and the wrath of God came upon them inasmuch as the "natural branches" were not spared, as, indeed, they could not be. Israel's rejection of the Messiah in the presence of the Gentiles brought deprecation of God's character, and discredit to His Word. This could not be tolerated any longer. The Gentiles were laughing at God's Word, blaspheming God, and this was the fault of the Jews (Romans 2:24).

God must be glorified, His Name magnified, His character exemplified, and His judgments justified in the presence of all peoples. Sin ran its course in Israel, and God's anger blazed forth upon His disobedient and defiant people. No longer could Jehovah tolerate "the natural branches." He broke some of them off.

The Apostle warns the Gentile believer, in verse 21, "Neither will he spare thee." Boasting, haughtiness, pride, conceit, cupidity, apathy, indifference, and disobedience are the fruits of unbelief. They are the marks of faithlessness, the very opposite of true faith, and have no place in the lives of those who have been born again. If such vices have any place in the lives of those who call themselves Christians, such so-called Christians are either fooling themselves, or are guilty of hypocrisy, and, therefore, come under our Lord's condemnation, "But woe unto you ... hypocrites!" (Matthew 23:13). If they are merely careless they are lulling themselves to sleep in a fool's paradise. This is not even Christianity! It is shameless unbelief. How can a careless or hypocritical life reflect even feebly the agony and anguish of the cross? Such a one is a sham-Christian and will surely be cut off. When the Apostle says in verse 21, ". . . if God spared not the natural branches, neither will he spare thee," these careless and hypocritical ones are they whom the Apostle had in mind.

Show-Sunday church attendance is not Christianity. Pretense-Christianity cannot and will not be tolerated in the light of the cross any more than were the sins of Israel — in fact, even less! The Gentiles do not have a covenant relationship with Jehovah. The Gentiles cannot say, "Our father is Abraham" (John 8:39); nor can the Gentiles refer to God in the same way the Jews do when they say, ". . . the God of Abraham, the God of Isaac, and the God of Jacob" (Exodus 3:6). God is referred to in the Old and New Testaments as, "The God of Israel" (Exodus 24:10; Numbers 16:9; Joshua 13:33; I Chronicles 4:10; Psalm 41:13; Isaiah 45:3; Ezekiel 8:4; Matthew 15:31; Luke 1:68). No nation can call God "our Father" except Israel (I Chronicles 29:10; Isaiah 63:16).

The born-again believer, the genuine follower of Christ can, and, thank God, he does, call God, "the God of Abraham, Isaac and Jacob" and "the God of Israel" who is Jehovah, his Father.

Such a born-again believer is held in the grasp of the omnipotent, sovereign hand of God and need never fear. The perfect love of a perfect God casts out all fear. Do you know Him who is the personification of this love? He is the Lord Jesus Christ. Will you accept Him? Will you live for Him? He will enable you. He says, Come!

Verse 22: Behold then the goodness and severity of God: toward them that fell, severity; but toward thee, God's goodness, if thou continue in his goodness: otherwise thou also shalt be cut off.

The Greek word translated "goodness" means also kindness, gentleness, and generosity; the Greek word for "severity" means also to cut off or shear, or to fall from a height, as falling off a cliff. It is the only time the word severity, which occurs in this verse, is used in the New Testament.

To understand the true character of God one must look at all the attributes of God. The Apostle shows (in verse 22) the two extreme opposites of God's attributes, i.e., His goodness, as contrasted with His severity. The two are inseparably related in the vastness of God's nature, yet one is the antithesis of the other. A just and loving God must have both attributes. One without the other is inconceivable. To be a loving Father, God must also correct, punish, and give proper direction and warning.

The Apostle is saying in effect, Look at God's goodness, His patience, His love, and His beneficence! It is beyond human comprehension. We cannot understand how a loving and patient God can refrain from punishing a sinner, whereas a loving but impatient human father corrects his erring children many times, and at once! A human parent calls a stop to the wrong-doing as soon as he hears of it. God does not. God is patient and long-suffering. When God does punish, when God does call a halt to the evil practices of a person or a people, the punishment is some-times attended with catastrophic consequences. A graphic example of God's punishment of the wicked is described in Romans 1:24-32, where we have an illustration of God's dealing with the Gentiles, and in Deuteronomy 28:58-67, where we may read a record of God's dealings with Israel.

Paul is saying in verse 22, Look, see the goodness of God toward the good branches, and the severity of God toward the ones having fallen (so the literal Greek). This severity, of course, is directed toward the Jewish branches which were cut off. Though the Jews are God's own people, their covenant rela-tionship with God did not give them the right to continue in their sin. God warned them repeatedly. His warnings were not heeded, hence, their sin brought God's severity. These unbe-lieving branches in Israel had to be broken off. God had no alternative. His patience was tried, His character was being maligned and blasphemed (Romans 2:23, 24) by their unbelief and sin. God had to call a halt to the evil practices of these unbelieving Jews; therefore, He cut them off.

There is a warning in this judgment. The Apostle is calling this warning to the attention of the membership of the church at Rome. He is saying in effect, See the severity of God toward these branches which fell to their eternal destruction! The church at Rome knew what was happening in Jerusalem. Approximately twelve years after Paul wrote these words the Roman Emperor Titus destroyed Jerusalem. The city was sacked, the temple was burned, and the people were killed or carried into captivity by the Roman hordes. Every holy purpose for which this city was founded was outraged and its character obliterated. Behold what severity! What judgment!

Thus Paul writes in verse 22, ".... but toward thee, God's

goodness. . . ." God's goodness toward them that continue in His goodness is named as the complete opposite of God's judgment — His severity — toward them that fell. There is a note of caution in these words. "God's goodness" cannot be abused, it cannot be taken lightly. It is not a license for spiritual promiscuity. A Christian cannot trifle with sin and carnality. The grace of God *will not permit sinful indulgences.* One cannot buy off God with liberal offerings or absolutions, a practice in the Roman Catholic Church. The grace of God is a call to separation, to spiritual sobriety and consecrated living. It demands holiness of life, and requires a consistent daily walk. "Ye shall be holy; for I am holy" (I Peter 1:16; Leviticus 11:44). Holiness of living is imperative for every blood-bought believing child of God. A separated life in Christ is a far cry from the cheap "believism" we hear talked about today in many evangelical circles. The cross demands devotion, dedication, consecration, as the daily practice for every follower of Christ.

The keynote of our preaching must be *repent!* The keynote of our preaching *must not* be to *decide!* We must return to the New Testament concepts of Christian conduct lest the finger of God write "Ichabod" across the Christianity of the present day, just as it has written "Ichabod" across Roman Catholicism as well as many forms of Protestantism of the past and present. The message of redemption is, ". . . except ye repent, ye shall all in like manner perish" (Luke 13:3). To repent means that we must make an about-face on the world, turn our backs on worldly lusts, separate ourselves from unbelievers, and come out from among them lest we perish.

There is an old Jewish belief that if a person dies with his face to the wall and his back to the room, it is a good omen. It means that he has died to the world in order to live for God. If he dies with his face to the room it is a bad omen, and means he has lived for the world and died to God. Is this not a beautiful illustration of true Christianity as depicted in baptism when the old nature s buried *with* Christ in the waters of baptism, and the new nature is brought out of the waters alive *to* Christ? Thus we who have died to the world *must live* for Christ (Colossians 3:3; Galatians 6:14; I Timothy 2:11; and others).

Verse 23: And they also, if they continue not in their unbelief, shall be grafted in: for God is able to graft them in again.

There is a prophetic note in this verse which rests upon the promises of God made unto the Patriarchs, that their seed shall be as numberless as the stars or the sands of the sea, as compared with the number of the "remnant." There are also various promises that God made to Israel through the prophets, beginning with Moses. God will fulfill every promise that He has made to the Patriarchs and their posterity, Israel, ". . . there hath not failed one word of all his good promises . . ." (I Kings 8:56; Jeremiah 32:42, 33:14-18).

The prophetic note is struck in the last two clauses of Romans 11:23. The Greek verb which is translated "shall be grafted in" is in the future indicative passive, and thus substantiates the promises of God to the Patriarchs. Just as certainly as God broke off the unbelieving branches, God will graft them in again. That is, the nation will be restored to her prominence. Just as surely as God scattered Israel, He has the power to restore her. The Greek word for "is able" in verse 23 is the same word that is used in Romans 1:16, for "the power of God unto salvation." It is used to describe God Himself, "For he that is mighty hath done to me great things; and holy is his name" (Luke 1:49). These words are taken from the song of Mary in response to the praise of Elizabeth. The Roman Catholic Church calls this song, "The Magnificat," a title derived from the opening words, "My soul doth magnify the Lord."

Romans 11:23 is another instance where the Apostle strikes the death knell to A-millennialism. The promises of God are sure because they do not depend upon human frailty. A Sovereign God has promised to restore Israel. He has made that promise to be just as certain as the constellations in the heavens (Jeremiah 31:35, 36). Regardless of what many of our so-called theologians say, the prophet Jeremiah declared millenniums ago, "Hear the word of Jehovah, O ye nations, and declare it in the isles afar off; and say, He that scattered Israel will gather him, and keep him, as a shepherd does his flock" (Jeremiah 31:10). Zechariah tells us when, "And it shall come to pass in that day, that I will seek to destroy all the nations that come against Jerusalem. And I will pour upon the house of David, and upon the inhabitants of Jerusalem, the spirit of grace and of supplication; and they shall look unto me whom they have pierced; . . ." (12:9, 10).

These words from Zechariah 12:9, 10, are just as sure and certain as that the sun will shine. God has promised it. The Saviour reiterated that promise, "For I say unto you, Ye shall not see me henceforth, till ye shall say, Blessed is he that cometh in the name of the Lord" (Matthew 23:39). God will bring this to pass, as the Apostle states in Romans 11:23, ". . . for God is able to graft them in again." When this comes to pass, and God grafts them in again, the believers will have been brought into the presence of the Saviour. The Rapture will be history, the true Church will be completed, the seven-year Tribulation will have run its course. Millions will perish, rivers of blood will flow, cries of torture and torment will fill the air, destruction and devastation will be universal.

Dear reader, will you have to say, "The harvest is past, the summer is ended, and we are not (or I am not) saved" (Jeremiah 8:20)? You need not be without salvation. Today, if you hear the Saviour's voice, can be your day of salvation. Harden not your heart. He stands at your heart's door and knocks. Will you not let Him in? (II Corinthians 6:2; Revelation 3:20).

Verse 24: For if thou wast cut out of that which is by nature a wild olive tree, and wast grafted contrary to nature into a good olive tree; how much more shall these, which are the natural branches, be grafted into their own olive tree?

The Apostle is pursuing the discussion which he began in verse 23. He is speaking to Gentile believers and is saying, If you, Gentile believers, who were wild by nature, were grafted into the good tree, is not God able to graft the natural branches which were broken off into the good olive tree?

The question which the Apostle is asking is a trenchant one. What is implied by the words, "by nature a wild olive tree"? The wild olive tree is an accurate picture of Gentile heathenism. The cultivated olive tree was an evergreen reaching to the height of about thirty to forty feet, with stiff dark green narrow leaves and yellow flowers in small axillary branches. The wild olive tree was a scrubby bush with broad leaves, thorny branches, and its fruit produced an inferior grade of oil, which was used only for ointment. The wild olive tree, as its name implies, was worthless from a seedling. Its fruit could not be used for human consumption although its foliage may have been attractive. It grew wild in Palestine and in other countries. How true a picture that is of the Gentile world! Have not the Gentiles grown wild in their religious beliefs? The multiplicity of Gentile faiths over the world is startling, such as idol worship, statues of pagan deities, animal worship (India), self-immolation (Buddhism), and self-infliction, as practiced by some of the tribes in the Philippine Islands. The diversity of faiths in heathen Gentile countries is limitless, even some of the practices which have grown up in connection with so-called Christianity are revolting, such as kissing the toes of statues, kissing rings, and baptizing still-born infants. Roman Catholic nurses are even required to baptize the aborted and undeveloped human fetus. What wild and shocking perversions of true Christianity have been spawned by Gentile paganism!

This comparison of Gentile wickedness with the sinfulness of the broken branches of Israel might well have been in the Apostle's mind when he propounded the question presented in verse 24. If God can take a heathen, a savage head-hunting Gentile in whom the image of God has been all but obliterated, whom God has given up to vile passions and a reprobate mind, symbolized by the wild olive tree, and graft him into the good olive tree which can produce good fruit, is not God able to ingraft the natural branches which were broken off into the good olive tree?

It is interesting to note that the Apostle uses the same verb in the same mood and tense in verse 24 for "be grafted into" (literal, "shall be grafted in") as in verse 23, "shall be grafted in." Thus Paul is emphasizing again the certainty of Israel's restoration. If God has cast away Israel and will not restore her to her national position and possession; if God will not keep His promises which He made to the patriarchs and their posterity (Israel); if God is not bound by His word in the Old Testament, then by the same token God is not bound by His own word in the New Testament. It is the same God that speaks and acts in both Testaments. If God can cast away Israel to eternal dissolution, never again to become the chosen nation under God's protective care; if God can do this with Israel, then God will not keep His promises to His New Testament saints. What other assurance has a saint? If God's promises to Israel are not fulfilled, the nation is nothing more than a wild olive tree with its inferior fruit, with as little worth in God's sight as the Gentiles.

The Rapture of the Church of Jesus Christ is intertwined with the restoration of Israel by the same omnipotent God. He who has said in His own Word, "He (God) that keepeth Israel will neither slumber nor sleep. Jehovah is thy keeper" (Psalm 121:4, 5); hath also said to His New Testament followers, "For the Lord himself shall descend from heaven, with a shout . . . then we that are alive, that are left, shall together with them (the dead in Christ) be caught up in the clouds, to meet the Lord in the air; and so shall we ever be with the Lord" (I

Thessalonians 4:16, 17). This is the hope of every blood-bought believer and it rests upon God's own Word. Thank God that He can be relied upon to keep it.

The Apostle closes this section of chapter 11 with the positive assurance in verse 24 that God will keep His word, for he says, ". . . how much more shall these, which are the natural branches, be grafted into their own olive tree?" This olive tree had to be cultivated, had to be nurtured and protected. The oil it produced is one of the important ingredients of human consumption, for medicine, for anointing and for offerings to God. This olive tree is the true picture of Israel. God has nurtured and protected her. He has hedged her about with His love and compassion. "In all their afflictions he was afflicted, and the angel of his presence saved them: in his love and in his pity he redeemed them; and he bare them and carried them all the days of old" (Isaiah 63:9). He *will* restore Israel.

The Apostle has no misgivings concerning God's purposes for Israel's ultimate salvation, no qualms, no qualifications, no "ands, ifs or buts." God will do it because He has promised it. Isn't it comforting to worship this kind of a God? Is He your God? Do you know Him? He said, "He that believeth on the Son hath eternal life . . ." (John 3:36). Will you believe Him?

Verse 25: For I would not, brethren, have you ignorant of this mystery, lest ye be wise in your own conceits, that a hardening in part hath befallen Israel, until the fulness of the Gentiles be come in . . . ;

To most people a mystery is something that is unexplained, unknown, kept secret or concealed. To Paul a mystery is something revealed. To the average Christian the Jew is the greatest mystery of all, or so it seems to this writer. To the world the Jew is an unsolvable enigma. In short, the Jew is not understood, therefore he is misunderstood and continues to be the riddle of the ages.

Paul has been explaining in chapter 11 the position of Israel in the world and the Church. He addresses himself to the believers in Rome and is saying in effect, "My fellow Christians, my brethren in the faith, I want to explain to you the final result of God's dealing with my kinsmen according to the flesh, the Jews. The blindness that God has placed on the Jews is partial, but not final or fatal, and will continue until the fulness of Gentile sin has run its course in prophetic history."

We must always bear in mind that there is a great difference between *national* rejection and *individual* election. This truth was dealt with in verses 5, 7, 17, of this chapter. Only the remnant, the elect of Israel, is being saved now. Only *some* branches, not *all*, were broken off the good olive tree. This condition prevails in Israel today. The hardening process is affecting only part of the nation. The Apostle states that "a hardening in part hath befallen Israel." This God did ". . . and gave them a spirit of stupor . . ." (11:8). Was this not the message of Isaiah when he was called — Isaiah 6:9, 10?

When the Messiah came, Israel saw no beauty in Him; they despised and rejected Him because of the spiritual hardness that was operating in Israel. It is still operating in Israel even today. But it shall be removed. The "until" in verse 25 certifies to this truth. Jehovah Himself will remove it. But for now, some are hardened and some are not. There have been thousands in Israel who have accepted Jesus Christ as their promised Messiah, and some are accepting Him today.

Almost all expositors interpret the phrase in verse 25, "until the fulness of the Gentiles be come in," as meaning that the blindness will prevail in Israel until the last Gentile is converted and completes the body of Christ, the Church. The present writer does not believe this explanation for a number of reasons:

(1) The Church of Jesus Christ is not composed of converted Gentiles only, but rather it is composed of two converted peoples, Jews and Gentiles. Were this not so, both Paul and the Holy Spirit made a grave error in Ephesians 2:14-18; 3:4-6. This misinterpretation of Romans 11:25 is precisely what is wrong with the Church today. We have so filled the Church with Gentiles that it is an arduous task to find Christians in it.

(2) There is no difference between the terms, the "*fulness* of the Gentiles," and "the *times* of the Gentiles." Just because the New Scofield Reference Bible states at the bottom of page 1226 of that work that there *is* a difference, does not necessarily make it so. There is some Post-millennial thinking in the Scofield references, and there are a number of places where many Bible teachers disagree with Dr. Scofield. In the book of Daniel on page 910, 911 of the New Scofield Reference Bible, Dr. Scofield finds himself on the horn of a dilemma because he is trying to explain his own Pre-millennial position with a Post-millennial interpretation. Even as great a scholar as Dr. Scofield was, he was not always right. There is now a revised edition of the Scofield Reference Bible in which some of Dr. Scofield's questionable in-

terpretations were corrected. There must always be harmony of the Scriptures whenever a Bible truth is presented.

(3) If the phrase, *"fulness* of the Gentiles," means the completion of the body of Christ, the Church, then Israel is to be nationally converted at the *beginning* of the Tribulation. But the Bible teaches, and even Dr. Scofield believes, that all Israel will be saved at the *end* of the Tribulation. We must always study the context when we interpret Scripture. The Greek manuscripts are written without punctuation and do not show chapter and verse separations. Romans 11:25 in the American Standard Version does not end with a period, and therefore it is not a completed text. Verse 26 begins with a small "a" and states, "and so all Israel shall be saved . . ." This statement definitely means *national* conversion, and it occurs at the *end* of the Tribulation period. Even Dr. Scofield believed this and developed it in the notes of his Scofield Reference Bible. If it is true that the nation of Israel will not be saved until the end of the Tribulation — and Scripture clearly says it is true, and this writer believes that it is true — then Israel will not be saved until they go through "the time of Jacob's trouble" (Jeremiah 30:7); so there *cannot* be any difference between "the *fulness* of the Gentiles" in Romans 11:25 and "the *times* of the Gentiles" in Luke 21:24. What is the difference between a bottle full of milk and a full bottle of milk? And what is the difference between six, and a half dozen? No difference!

It is interesting to note the Rabbis taught the truth that Israel would experience "the time of Jacob's trouble" before the Messiah comes — "When thou shalt see the time in which many troubles shall come like a river upon Israel, then expect the Messiah himself" (Tract, Sanhedrin, f98:1).

Paul's statement in Romans 11:25 that a ". . . hardening in part hath befallen Israel" is a hardening which will prevail until ". . . they shall look unto me whom they have pierced . . ." (Zechariah 12:10), and say, "Blessed is he that cometh in the name of the Lord" (Matthew 23:39; Psalm 118:26). These passages from Zechariah and Matthew refer to Israel's conversion on a national scale. As the nation was represented by the leaders of the Jews in Pilate's hall in their rejection of Jesus as the Messiah, so likewise at Israel's national conversion, Israel will be represented by those "that turn from transgression in Jacob" (Isaiah 59:20), meaning the remnant. The confession is recorded in Isaiah 53: 5, 8.

The signs of the times are such that the conversion of Israel as a nation cannot be far off. Surely the sands of time are running out in which the saints of God will have the opportunity to take the Gospel to the Jew. Let us embrace every opportunity to witness among Israel.

Verse 26: . . . and so all Israel shall be saved: even as it is written, There shall come out of Zion the Deliverer; He shall turn away ungodliness from Jacob . . . :

Paul is quoting Isaiah 59:20 with some variation, but there is no doubt that this passage is a Messianic prophecy predicting the Second Coming of Christ, because it is obvious from the context.

The Greek word for "all" in the text before the proper name Israel means the whole. It does not mean every individual of the nation, but the mass, the great body. It is so used in Matthew 2:3; 3:5. This clearly points to national conversion.

If we look at Isaiah 59:20 in its context, the time when this national conversion takes place is pinpointed in 59:19. The sin of Israel was rampant. Many pledged their allegiance to the anti-Christ. Their number was so great that it seemed "that there was no intercessor" (59:16): "therefore his own arm brought salvation." Undoubtedly, this has reference to the Messiah (Isaiah 63:1-6). The prophet borrows the language used to describe the armor of warriors and applies it as the armor of righteousness with which the Messiah is clothed. (Compare the language of Isaiah 59:17 with Ephesians 6:10-17.) Isaiah 59:18, "According to their deeds . . ." And "to the islands . . ." refers to the Gentiles. (Perhaps Revelation 16:19, 20, sheds additional light on this.) Isaiah 59:19 describes the universal fear of all peoples at the revelation of the Messiah. When the anti-Christ will collect all his forces in his attempt to crush the people of God, Jehovah will intervene and "come as a rushing stream" or a flood. (Psalm 2:1-5 describes the last Gentile revolution prior to the establishment of the Davidic Kingdom.) The driving force in back of this "rushing stream" of destruction is none other than "the spirit of Jehovah" (Hebrew of verse 19). Then ". . . a Redeemer will come to Zion, and unto them that turn from transgression in Jacob, saith Jehovah" (Isaiah 59:20).

Why has not the Redeemer come? The following are several rabbinical answers: "Why has the son of Jesse not come, either today or yesterday? (I Samuel 20:27). The answer lies in the question itself: Why has he not come? Because we are today,

just as we were yesterday" (Esser Tzachlzochath, page 65).
"The Messiah could come today without being preceded by
Elijah, if we ourselves prepare our hearts without troubling the
prophet to do it for us. Let us make ourselves ready then to
receive the Messiah any day by obeying the Voice of the Lord"
(Esser Orth, page 60 by I. Berger).

Many more rabbinical passages could be quoted, but suffice
it to say they all speak of repentance. Is this not what the
prophet Zechariah wrote? "Be ye not as your fathers . . . Thus
saith Jehovah of hosts, Return ye now from your evil . . . doings:
but they did not hear, nor hearken unto me, saith Jehovah"
(Zechariah 1:4; Isaiah 1:16-19; Jeremiah 4:1, 2). Did not the
Saviour say the same? ". . . except ye repent, ye shall all in like
manner perish" (Luke 13:3). God's Word says they will repent.
(See Zechariah 12:10; Isaiah 59:21; Jeremiah 50:17-20.)

It is impossible for anyone to read Romans 11:26, 27, and not
realize that the Apostle is quoting Isaiah 59:20, 21. He does it
for the express purpose of proving that national Israel will accept
the Lord Jesus Christ as their Messiah. The Isaiah passage
(59:21) repeats a "covenant" in the same manner as Jeremiah
speaks of a "new covenant" in 31:31-34.

The chronology of Paul and Isaiah is identical. Isaiah shows
that Israel is lost in her darkness and gropes as blind people
because of her sin (59:9, 10). Israel is bereft of true righteousness and the multiplicity of her sins has brought evil upon her
(Isaiah 59:9-15; Psalm 14:7). Is not this what the Apostle has
been saying in chapter 11:20, 21? — ". . . by their unbelief they
were broken off . . . toward them that fell, severity." Verse 25
speaks of "a hardening in part hath befallen Israel. . . ." It shall
all be righted by the coming of the Messiah, when the cup of
Gentile sin has become full. Israel will then be unequivocally
restored to her proper position as the emissary of Jehovah. (See
II Corinthians 3:14-16, same as Romans 11:25.)

Would to God this were to happen today! With Isaiah of old
this writer looks to that day — "Oh that thou wouldst rend the
heavens, that thou wouldst come down . . ." (Isaiah 64:1). The
same plea, only worded differently, came from the lips of John;
the old Apostle in the loneliness of a stony and parched Patmos
Island, when he said, "Even so, come, Lord Jesus" (Revelation
22:20 KJV).

**Verse 27: . . . And this is my covenant unto them, When I
shall take away their sins.**

Some expositors claim that Paul is quoting the Septuagint version of Isaiah 27:9, while others think it is Jeremiah 31:34 (or verse 33, as it is in the Hebrew). However, the central truth of Romans 11:27 — that the sins of Jacob will be forgiven according to Jehovah's covenant — is in both the Isaiah and Jeremiah passages.

The Greek word for "take away" also means struck off, smote off, cut off, and is so used in Matthew 26:51 and Mark 14:47. The Hebrew equivalent is *quoras,* as used with the making of a covenant. When so used it has the meaning to "cut a covenant" (Genesis 15:18; Jeremiah 31:31,32; and others). Thus the Abrahamic covenant was sealed by cutting, that is, by circumcision.

The Apostle brings the covenant relationship that God has with Israel into view here in verse 27. He states that it is God's "covenant unto them," meaning Israel. As the blindness was placed upon Israel by God, in verse 8, so Paul states that the removal of that blindness is also the direct action of God Himself. God must act upon Israel and bring to pass her national conversion. Verse 27 assures us that it will come to pass.

God will so cleanse His people Israel that not even the slightest semblance of sin shall be found in her midst. "In those days, and in that time, says Jehovah, the iniquity of Israel shall be sought for, and there shall be none; and the sins of Judah, and they shall not be found; for I will pardon them whom I leave as a remnant" (Jeremiah 50:20; Zechariah 3:9; Psalm 130:8). The day upon which this event will occur cannot be far off. God speed the day! With the Psalmist we pray, "Redeem Israel, O God, out of all his troubles" (Psalm 25:22).

Will you not join us in Moses' prayer? ". . . come thou with us, and we will do thee good; for Jehovah hath spoken good concerning Israel" (Numbers 10:29).

Verse 28: As touching the gospel, they are enemies for your sake: but as touching the election, they are beloved for the fathers' sake.

According to the Gospel, they, Israel, are reckoned as enemies. In their blindness, in their stubbornness, in their unyieldingness, and because of the "hardening" process now active in Israel, they are hostile, inimical and considered enemies of the Gospel. But the deeper and more significant reason for Israel's hostility to the Gospel is that this hostility is in accordance with the plan and program of God. Thus the "hardening" process is fulfilling God's purpose in having the Gospel preached to the Gentiles.

The Apostle states in verse 28 that they, Israel, have become enemies "for your sake." If blindness and hardness of heart had not been placed upon the Jews, the Gentiles would not have the opportunity that they now have to hear the Gospel. The problem today, and it has been for centuries, is that some Gentile Christians have gone to extremes in claiming that the Jews have been, and still are, excluded from the Gospel. These Gentile Christians claim that the Jews have had their chance. How foolish and wild this idea is in the light of the clear teaching of Scripture!

By what stretch of the imagination can anyone claim that the Jews have had their chance and lost it, and that now they have been set aside in order that the Gentiles may have *their* chance during the present age? How can it be claimed by anyone familiar with the history of Christianity that the Jews have had their chance and lost it, when the Jews, at best, have only heard the Gospel in its entirety for about forty years, from 30 to 70 A.D.? The Jews, as a nation, rejected the Saviour and refused to hear the Gospel. The Gentiles, on the other hand, have had 1900 years of the Gospel. Have all the Gentiles accepted the Gospel? Let history speak for itself. How can anyone equate a 40-year period of time with a 1900-year period? Figures do not lie, although liars have been known to figure.

Let us go one step farther. At the end of the first century of the Christian era, there were in the neighborhood of one million Jewish followers of Jesus Christ. This number was about one-third of the Jewish population of the world at that time. When has there ever been a period in Gentile history during the past 1900 years when one-third of all the Gentiles in the world were followers of Jesus Christ? By "followers" this writer means true converts, as were the believing Jews of the first century. Where on God's green earth is there today, or has ever been at any time in history, one entire city, not to say state or nation, where every person living therein was a true believer in the Saviour?

These Gentile "wild olive branches" seem to have remained wild for the most part and have not heeded the warnings of the Apostle in verse 22. How distorted the Gospel has become among many of these "wild branches"! Is it any wonder that the poor neglected Jews, with the Law of Moses in their hands, are unable to recognize the Gospel, with its transforming power, and its godly requirements of holy living, in these so-called Gentile Christians who have reverted to their wild state? Perhaps some of them have not even been grafted in. How is the blinded Jew to

see the difference? What is there in the lives of many Christians
that should make the Jew jealous?

Truly, the word of the Apostle, ". . . for if God spared not the
natural branches, neither will he spare thee" (verse 21) ought
to be a warning to every blood-bought believer. Such a warning
should cause us to stop and think. It should cause us to look at
our lives *introspectively* so that our Christian walk and conduct
may be *prospectively* more worthy of Him who died that we
might live eternally. Repentance, conversion, holiness, righteousness, are the Christian virtues which should characterize every
born-again follower of the Lord Jesus Christ. Sinful desires and
habits must be replaced with the love of God and the brethren.
A Christian cannot continue in sin. The cross does not tolerate
a vacillating life in the believer. One who lives a worldly life all
week and puts on a pious cloak on Sunday for church and public
worship, is hardly a true believer. Godly living has its rewards
here and hereafter. Sin has its retribution in hell. Which will
you choose, heaven or hell? Choose well, eternity is at stake.

V. 28: ". . . but as touching the election, they are beloved for
the fathers' sake." The greater number of Jews have rejected the
Gospel and spurned God's call. However, this in no way negates
the truth that there has always been a believing remnant. (See
commentary on Romans 11:5, 7). There always *must be* a
remnant in Israel that is faithful to God, if He is to fulfill His
promises to the three patriarchs, Abraham, Isaac and Jacob. The
promises that God made were eternal promises. (See Genesis
17:7, 8; Leviticus 26:42; and others.)

The Millennial Kingdom will be centered about the fulfillment
of all the promises that God made to Abraham, Isaac, Jacob
and Israel. The Lord Jesus Christ Himself confirmed the truth
that Israel will be restored to her covenant relationship with
God (Matthew 23:39). Israel's restoration is imperative. There
is to be a Millennial Kingdom, with Jerusalem as its capital and a
restored Davidic throne. God promised the patriarchs "a seed
and a land." The patriarchs never possessed it as an eternal gift
and neither did Israel. Israel must possess it "forever" (Genesis
13:15). They are not in possession of it now. They only have
part of it. God must and God will bring about the eternal possession of the *whole* land for the fathers' sake.

**Verse 29: For the gifts and the calling of God are not re-
pented of.**

God called Abraham out of Ur of the Chaldees and made certain promises to him. God called Israel out of Egypt and made promises to her. God does not alter His mind nor does He retract His promises. The Greek word translated "not repented of" means irrevocable, without change of mind. This Greek word for "not repented of" appears in the New Testament only in Romans 11:29 and in II Corinthians 7:10. "Not repented of" means that under no circumstances are God's gifts and callings, to both Israel and the New Testament saints, revocable or abrogated, withdrawn or annulled. God's gifts and callings will never be repudiated!

This calling of Abraham and the promise of the seed and a land was in the form of a covenant which was sealed by circumcision (Genesis 17:9-14). When God spoke to Moses, He spoke as "the God of Abraham, the God of Isaac, and the God of Jacob" (Exodus 3:6). God informed Moses exactly what He wanted him to do and what He (God) would do for the "seed" of Abraham, Isaac and Jacob (Exodus 3:7-12). God was fulfilling the promises that He made to the fathers. God not only made promises to them, but He also made promises to Israel and to David. To the fathers it was a seed and a land; to Israel He promised the land and to be in their midst; that He would be their God and they would be His people (Leviticus 26:12; Jeremiah 11:4; 30:22; Ezekiel 43:7, 9). To David, He promised an everlasting throne (Psalm 89:36), and God sealed this promise with an oath (Psalm 89:35). God even calls the constellations to witness His sincerity (Psalm 89:5, 6, 36, 37), which means, of course, that these promises are irrevocable and as eternal as the "eternal life" that God gives to every born-again follower of Jesus Christ. As salvation is "a free gift" so are "the gifts" to Israel. The same Greek word for "the gifts" appears in Romans 11:29 as in 5:15, 16; 6:23, and elsewhere.

Paul certifies the sovereignty and the immutability of Jehovah in relation to His gifts and callings. What comfort this affords the believer! What anxiety this truth dissipates! In Christ those "whom he called, them he also justified: and whom he justified, them he also glorified" (Romans 8:30). Do you believe Him? He has promised to perform and to perfect it. Will you accept that promise?

Verse 30: For as ye in time past were disobedient to God, but now have obtained mercy by their (Israel's) disobedience. . . ,

In this verse the Apostle calls to the attention of the Gentile believer the Gentile's past position in the sight of God. Just a cursory look at Romans 1:24-32 reveals the former deplorable condition of the Gentiles and their evil practices. The Gentile world has not changed from ancient times to modern; it is still the same; and that world is still filled with "all unrighteousness, wickedness; full of envy, murder, strife, deceit, malignity," given up to vile passions, sexual perversity and promiscuity. Drunkenness and dope-addiction have permeated almost all strata of our society. Yet out of this pandemonium of sin, God has called the Gentile believer to salvation and showered him with abundant blessings.

Gentile believers are being reminded of what they were and where they were prior to their conversion. The Greek word for "disobedient" in verse 30 is in the historical tense, thus viewing disobedience in its entirety as a past event. Verse 30 is really an admonition to every believer that he cannot flirt with sin and serve God at the same time. One cannot ride two horses in opposite directions simultaneously. The narrow gate and the straitened way lead to God and righteousness, the wide gate and the broad way lead to Satan, sin and destruction (Matthew 7:13, 14).

The challenge to the Christian today is the challenge which Elijah made to Israel, ". . . How long go ye limping between the two sides? if Jehovah be God, follow him; but if Baal, then follow him. And the people answered him not a word" (I Kings 18:21). What thundering words these were in the midst of confusion and sin! What a challenge! It is a challenge that needs to be repeated from every Christian pulpit again and again even today. Christians must be reminded of God's call to holy living and awakened out of their spiritual somnolence and lethargy. Every true Christian must take up his cross and follow Christ. It is an "either or" proposition; that is to say, it is either Christ or chaos, righteousness or sinfulness. If Elijah's challenge were proclaimed today, what would be the average Christian's response? Would it be Israel's answer to Elijah — "And the people answered him not a word"?

The contrast between the first clause in verse 30 and the second is very pointed, ". . . but now have obtained mercy by their (Israel's) disobedience. . . ." God used Israel's disobedience as the occasion for showering the Gentile with mercy. However, we must never lose sight of the truth that Israel's disobedience was *national.* It was only that "some of the branches were broken off," and the Gentile believers were "grafted in *among* them," not *instead* of them The Gentile believer became a "partaker *with them*" not *instead* of them. The verb "to break" is in the passive mood and means "to be an object of gracious favor and saving mercy" (*Greek Lexicon,* Samuel Bagster and Son). The classical Greek gives the added meaning of compassion and pity and conveys the thought of giving charity. Is this not what God's grace means to us? Because of God's mercy and love for every sinner, He gave His Son to die on the cross and has given Him to each of us as an eternal gift through Whom we receive eternal life. What a God we have! What a wonderful Saviour He has given us! Do you love Him?

Verse 31: . . . even so have these also now been disobedient, that by the mercy shown to you they also may now obtain mercy.

This verse and verse 32 are re-stating a truth that was established earlier in this Epistle. The Apostle uses different words in verses 31 and 32 to state the truth which was established earlier in Romans 3:23, namely, ". . . for all have sinned, and fall short of the glory of God." Hence, both Jews and Gentiles are in need of God's mercy. The same Gospel saves both. Both are lost unless they repent and turn from their evil ways. Here is a definite challenge for tolerance, patience, love and understanding to the Jew in the light of the Gospel. Gentile believers may say in their hearts, "The Jews have had their chance; now it is our turn. The Jews rejected their Messiah and therefore they have lost their opportunity for salvation." But what says the Apostle? Four times in verses 30 to 32 he speaks of God's mercy toward the disobedient Gentiles. The Jew may be stubborn. Is the Gentile never stubborn? Let us show the same mercy toward the stubborn Jew that we show toward the stubborn Gentile. If it were not for the mercy of God, where would we believers be? Let us search our hearts. In God's heart there is only mercy.

Three times in verses 30 and 31 there appears the word "now." It has a prophetic connotation. *Now* Israel is disobedient. *Now* Israel is in unbelief. *Now* Israel is stubborn and stiff-necked and adamant in her refusal to accept Jesus as her promised Messiah. But it will not always be so. Israel's rejection of Jesus as Messiah is temporary. Her rejection may be of long duration and still continues, but time is running out. Rampant sin and sensuality are prevalent in every nation of the world. The mills of God are about to grind in judgment. Even the true Church is beginning to lose her evangelistic fervor and her call to separation. Some of the mighty warriors of the Gospel, who came out boldly for the verbal inspiration of the Word of God and the 24 hour day of Genesis 1 — "and there was evening and there was morning, one day" — grand old warriors of the faith, who never wavered in their courage "for the faith which was once for all delivered unto the saints," are now wavering. Not long ago one Bible teacher said, "We must re-think our doctrine of verbal inspiration!" God forbid that any of us who call ourselves Christians shall compromise our holy faith. Are we to be put to shame by those Christians of the first century?

God's Word is settled forever in heaven. There is no doubt among all the shining hosts of heaven as to the verbal inspiration of the Word of God, the scriptural doctrines of the Depravity of Man, the Virgin Birth, the Incarnation, the efficacy of the cross and the blood, the Resurrection, the Ascension, the mediatorial work of the Saviour, the Rapture of the saints, and the Second Coming of Christ. These are settled dogmas in heaven. Ought the faith and hope of every born-again child of God on earth be less than the faith and hope of the saints in glory?

The pendulum of time swings, the wheel of fortune spins. Soon the "times of the Gentiles" will be fulfilled. The "now" of Israel's unbelief will cease. Israel will accept Him whom in ignorance once they pierced. They will proclaim Him whom they once rejected centuries ago. It cannot be long. Are you ready? Are you living for the Saviour daily? Are you trying to win others to Christ? What is your answer? Search your heart!

Verse 32: For God hath shut up all unto disobedience, that he might have mercy upon all.

As a fisherman gathers his catch together in a net, so God has gathered both disobedient Jew and Gentile together that He might have mercy on both. Sin has entrapped mankind. Only God's mercy can release the sinner from the net of sin. There is no merit in any man, individually or as a race. Merit is of God only. God gave the disobedient, both Jews and Gentiles, up to unbelief. Because of unbelief God dispersed the Jews to the four corners of the earth. All is of God, both the giving up to unbelief and the dispersing. Thus God asserted His powers in these two judgments. Both Jews and Gentiles were the objects of God's judgment and His mercy. It was their sin and God's holiness that brought salvation unto the lost.

The Apostle places both Jew and Gentile on the same sinful ground in the presence of a holy God. Both are sinners, and are equally deserving of God's wrath and punishment. Both being guilty in God's sight, God is able to bestow His super-abounding mercy upon them both and thereby provide a way of deliverance from the quicksands of eternal death. Sin and its consequences gave occasion for the coming of the Messiah and His accomplishments on the cross. Thus our heavenly Father provided the only possible way in which both disobedient Jew and Gentile could be delivered from the consequences of sin. This provision is the Gospel.

The good news of salvation through faith in Christ needs to be proclaimed from every Christian pulpit today throughout the world. The Gospel is not to be thought of as merely "good advice" to sinful people which will help them earn their salvation, but rather it is the *good news* of the gravest importance to all people that Christ has already paid the price of redemption and offers it as a free gift to "whosoever will." This free gift is the Charisma of God, ". . . but the free gift of God is eternal life in Christ Jesus our Lord" (Romans 6:23).

Verse 33: O the depth of the riches both of the wisdom and the knowledge of God! how unsearchable are his judgments, and his ways past tracing out!

The Apostle is about to reach one of the topmost rungs of the spiritual ladder which he has been ascending step-by-step in the composition of this Epistle or letter to his beloved saints at Rome, when he yields to an outburst of joy as the riches of God's wisdom and knowledge are borne in upon him and cause him to utter this wonderful doxology of praise to God for His unsearchable judgments. The truths of God, as the Apostle here bears witness, are overwhelming, beyond human knowledge and apprehension. What depths of God's riches of wisdom and knowledge are in store for His blood-bought believers!

Christianity is life's greatest spiritual symphony, composed by the Master Musician Himself! It is the greatest drama of the ages, the most thrilling love story of time and eternity, filled with all the divine pathos that the Holy Spirit could reveal and record in human speech. What passion and compassion God has stored up for those He loves is fully revealed in the Saviour's suffering on the cross. Only the love of God which transcends human knowledge could have endured such extreme anguish and agony that He might redeem His own. Thus the holiness of God's love reveals His justice and righteousness. Since man is devoid of these divine attributes, God did it all. Truly, "Salvation is of Jehovah" (Jonah 2:9). God's mysteries are fathomless, as Cow-

per wrote, "God moves in a mysterious way His wonders to perform; He plants His footsteps in the sea, and rides upon the
storm." And so the Apostle, as he contemplates God's glory and
power, exclaims, "O the depth of the riches . . . and the knowledge
of God!" (v. 33). The vastness of God's intelligence and His
illimitable knowledge are beyond the comprehension of the wisest
philosophers and theologians. Where is there one of them, child
of God though he be, who can plumb the depths of God's sovereign omniscience? The love of God is infinite, beyond human
reason or logic and is therefore incomprehensible to the mind of
man. Does the love of God ever reason as we reason? God *is*
love (I John 4:8) and loves because of His very nature. God's
love is the keynote of creation and the motif or inspired theme
of His plan of redemption for the human race.

V. 33: ". . . how unsearchable are his judgments. . . ." The
Greek word for "unsearchable" means also inscrutable and appears only here in the entire New Testament. God's judgments,
and God's administration of justice, are beyond scrutiny. Are
not God's ways always superior to man's, so that the human mind
is unable to penetrate the depth and height of God's concepts?
(Isaiah 55:8, 9).

V. 33: ". . . and his ways past tracing out!" No human mind
can explore the mysteries of God's methods — His "ways." It
is only because of our God-given faith and the indwelling and
abiding presence of the Holy Spirit, that we can grasp as much
of the truth of God as we do (Isaiah 66:4 KJV; I Corinthians
2:9 KJV). This limitation of the human intellect is the reason
for so many controversies among Christians.

We always want to inject our opinions into God's doctrines,
His acts towards us, and His truths. What are God's doctrines
and acts, so far as He has permitted us to observe them? The
human mind exhausts itself in trying to list them, as, for example,
the doctrines of election, predestination, the sovereignty of God,
the Trinity, the perseverance of the saints, imputed righteousness,
the Deity of Christ, the indwelling of the Holy Spirit and His
office in imparting to the believer his two-fold nature; the blinding of the Jews and their restoration, the opportunity for the
Gentile believer to be grafted into the good olive tree. In short,
God's doctrines, His acts, and His truths, taken as a whole, are
God's justice and His righteousness. His specific gifts, the inheritance of the saints — all inherent in the Gospel — are so far
beyond the finite comprehension of man, that the listing of them
tends to deflate the human ego. We always try to help God out

because the flesh is impelled to rise and say, "This is what *I* want, think or believe," and not "What does God's Word say?" which must always be our final authority. (See Gill's Commentary, vol. 6, pp. 105, 106, on Romans 11:33-36.)

Even the Apostle was overwhelmed by God's wisdom and knowledge, and His dealings with man. If such a brilliant mind as Paul's could be overwhelmed by God's knowledge, wisdom and judgment, is it any wonder that our minds are also overwhelmed? Thank God that to be saved we do not need to understand everything about God and His ways. The plan of salvation is so simple that even the unwise can grasp it. Salvation is not based on knowledge, but rather upon faith in a risen and coming Lord.

Do you believe this? You must if you wish to inherit eternal life. The decision is yours to make.

Verse 34: For who hath known the mind of the Lord? or who hath been his counsellor?

This is the Septuagint Version of Isaiah 40:13. Thus Paul continues his "doxology of praise" which began in verse 33. The verb, "hath known," in the Greek is so constructed as to make it timeless so that Paul's full meaning is, Whoever knew, or who knows now, and who will ever know the mind of God? The inescapable answer is, No one! Can the human mind ever fathom the mind of God?

The second part of the question in verse 34 is, ". . . or who hath been his counsellor?" The Greek word for "counsellor" appears only here in all the New Testament. This rhetorical question which Paul asks about a "counsellor" for God may have led some of our ambitious leaders in the church to feel that because of their importance in the kingdom of God, God would be bankrupt without them. They act as though they are waiting for a vacancy in the Trinity, which may be said with no irreverence.

We must never forget that our God is a sovereign God, Who acts, thinks, plans and carries out His own program independent of fallible humanity. Where was man when God planned His program of salvation? Where was man when God carefully laid out His plan as recorded in Ephesians 1:4? Where was man "before the world was" (John 17:5) when the holy Word went forth that the Son of God would die on the cross for sin? The miracle of eternity is expressed by the Psalmist, "What is man that thou (God) art mindful of him . . ." (Psalm 8:4; 144:3)?

Verse 35: . . . or who hath first given to him, and it shall be recompensed unto him again?

This is the Septuagint Version of Job 41:11, but slightly changed. It is Paul's rendition of God's words to Job in which the Apostle enlarges upon the grandeur of God's character and attributes. Everything that man possesses has been given to him by God. However, mankind refuses to acknowledge this. The believer will never be able to thank God enough for His bountiful love and the gifts which God has showered upon him who loves Him (I Corinthians 2:9 KJV).

Do you know Him? Do you love Him? Do you serve Him?

Verse 36: For of him, and through him, and unto him, are all things. To him be the glory for ever. Amen.

Paul ascribes everything to God, creation and all creatures, redemption and its benefits. God saves us, God keeps us, and God will glorify us. God is the source, the sustainer, and the perfector of everything, including the saint and salvation. The Apostle was fully cognizant of the attributes of the Godhead. He ascribes all the honor, the glory, the praise to Him who alone is worthy of all praise. The Trinity is not overlooked in the closing words of this chapter. God the Father is the source of all creation; through the Son of God, God was made manifest to creation; unto the Holy Spirit is given the sustaining power of life in creation and redemption.

All the reverence, the awe, the worship, the glorification, the exaltation, the love, that this Hebrew Christian Apostle could express in a heathen language which he learned in his early days in the Hebrew language, giving God all the honor and glory, he endeavors to express in this verse in the Koine Greek. He closes with the "Amen," which is to say, Let us believe this!

Do you? You must if you want eternal life.

12

INTRODUCTION. The Apostle having presented the major doctrines of the Christian faith in the preceding chapters of this Epistle, now addresses himself in chapters 12 through 16 to the individual believer.

To review briefly the chapters already covered: In chapters 1, 2 and 3, Paul presents the doctrine of the depravity of all men. In the closing verses of chapter 3, and in all of chapter 4, he presents the justification of believers on the ground of faith, and summarizes his argument in the opening verses of chapter 5. In the closing verses of chapter 5 we find the doctrine of sanctification. Chapter 6 is concerned with the doctrine of baptism. Chapter 7 is devoted to the two-fold nature of the believer. Chapter 8 deals with the abiding indwelling presence of the Holy Spirit and the victory over sin.

Chapters 4 through 8, therefore, present God's work — His actions — His love for, His mercy toward, and His glorification for all believers.

Chapters 9 through 11 are the pivotal chapters of the Epistle to the Romans. Leaving them out, we have left the grand and glorious truths of the Christian faith but with no substantiating evidence. Without these three chapters the believer stands on unstable ground. With them, starting in chapter 9, all the proof the believer needs is proffered to give him full assurance that his faith rests in the hands of an omnipotent Sovereign God who will perfect him. Under no circumstances will any believer be put to shame, ". . . and he that believeth on him (Christ) shall not be put to shame" (Romans 9:33).

Chapter 10 deals with man's responsibility to a Sovereign God. Israel is used as a type of fallen man. She is ignorant of God's righteousness. Moreover, she is rebellious, and is in danger of losing her usefulness to God by straying out of His will, thus forfeiting her position as God's emissary. This straying has gone so far that Israel no longer realizes how dangerously far it is. Therefore she needs a rude awakening by an alien agency, namely, the Gentiles and God's program for their salvation through Israel. This program of salvation Israel was to have brought to the Gentile world. Israel was to have been the instrument in God's program to bring the Gentiles out of their depraved position and condition as described in chapter 1, verses 24-32. Israel failed miserably! Instead of being the instrument in God's hands to convert the Gentiles, Israel degenerated to the depraved condition of the Gentiles themselves.

Because Israel failed God so miserably — to her everlasting shame — is she lost eternally? Was it because God's plan for Israel went awry that she was lost? Did God indeed cast off His people, as Paul asks at the beginning of chapter 11? Is Israel now doomed and damned for all eternity? If this were the case, fear might assail the heart of every true believer, Jew and Gentile, and engulf him in a maelstrom of confusion and uncertainty. But the child of God need not fear. God will not permit Israel to be doomed. He is using Israel's disobedience and sin as the means of spreading the Gospel to all mankind. Israel must come to her spiritual senses, she must return to her former moorings of love and faith in God. God will not permit her to stumble eternally in her blindness and perversity. Gentile hostility and depravity will cause her to return to God and plead for forgiveness. She will pray for the return of the Messiah whom she ignorantly rejected. God's will shall be accomplished by the restoration of Israel to her rightful position as His chosen people.

This is the lesson that every child of God must learn. God's ways are not our ways most of the time, but God's ways are the best all the time. We have a loving Father, a compassionate Saviour and a patient Holy Spirit working in our behalf, with the goal of glorification always in sight. The child of God may slip and stumble along the way, but it is God's hand that grips him tightly, always leading him to his mansion in glory. The saint sees it in the distance. The road may be rough, but God will bring him into the heavenly abode which the Saviour has promised to prepare for him.

What blessed moments of glory we delight in and what lessons we learn in these experiences! What a wonderful God we have! What a wonderful plan He has laid out for us! What opportunities these lessons present to every believer! What challenges! Will you accept them? Before you accept the challenge for service, you must accept the Saviour who gives us life and the stimulus for service. Before we can live and work for God, we must be born of God. Before we can walk *for* God, we must walk *with* God. What is your decision?

The five chapters of Romans before us, namely, 12 to 16 present the obligation that rests upon every believer who would serve God properly. Because God has done so much for us, we must give concrete evidence of our love for Him in willing and joyful obedience. Chapter 12 contains instructions concerning a Christian's conduct in relation to God; chapter 13, a Christian's conduct in relation to the world; chapter 14, a Christian's conduct in relation to fellow believers; chapter 15, a Christian's conduct in retrospect and summarization; chapter 16, the Apostle's salutation and benediction.

This writer's commentary on Romans 12:1 now follows:

Verse 1: I beseech you therefore, brethren, by the mercies of God, to present your bodies a living sacrifice, holy, acceptable to God, which is your spiritual service.

The Apostle is not only challenging, he is also inviting and summoning, he is exhorting and encouraging his fellow believers in the faith, to present, or to place at God's disposal, their bodies as a sacrifice to God. And he is beseeching them to do it "by the mercies" of a living God.

To this writer, the Apostle's thought in the foregoing verse is that the believer should come to the place in his Christian life where he is willing to do anything, no matter what the cost might be, even if it be life itself, to serve his God and Saviour. We are to be ready to sacrifice our dearest possession, and to be mocked and ridiculed, if need be, and to become an outcast in order to serve the Saviour. We must stand ready, and to be, as it were, actually in the very presence of God and at His disposal for any purpose or service He may require of us.

The word "present" in verse 1 is also used in Luke 2:22; Romans 6:13; Ephesians 5:27; Colossians 1:28. A scrutiny of these texts will convey to the believer a clear understanding of true Christian dedication and consecration. The Apostle's use of the term, "living sacrifice," in Romans 12:1, makes a striking contrast with the Levitical sacrifices, and the verse as a whole is a challenge to the Christian who has been made alive (Ephesians 2:5) and quickened into a realization of God's grace and made willing to present his body a "living sacrifice . . . unto God." In the Old Testament, it was a living, perfect, spotless animal that was slain which became the acceptable sacrifice for sin. In the New Testament it is the depraved person, who when made *alive* by the Holy Spirit, is invited to present himself at God's disposal as a "living sacrifice" or for any purpose in the service of God.

In the giving of self — one's body — to God, the Apostle is inviting the Christian to give *all* of himself, body, soul and spirit, to God. The believer at the time of his conversion, became the bond-slave of Christ. Because the believer was purchased by the blood of Christ, he is *possessed* of Christ. He is Christ's completely. The Apostle is asking the Christian in verse 1 to surrender *all* to Christ. It is as absurd as it is impossible for a Christian to think that he can offer a hand, a foot, or any other part of his body, to God in sacrifice, any more than an Israelite in the Mosaic sacrifices could offer a part of an animal on the altar in the tabernacle. The animal's life was first taken, which means its consciousness or soul and all of its physical members. Similarly in verse 1, the complete man means his body, soul and spirit.

We have still another difference between the "living sacrifice" of verse 1 and the Levitical sacrifices of the Old Testament. In the New Testament it is a voluntary offering of self. The contrast between the believer's sacrifice of himself and the ceremonial sacrifice of animals is very great. The latter was death, a living animal slain; the former is life, a person dead in sin is quickened, made alive, becomes the "living sacrifice." For the animal, death, for the person, life; the animal destroyed in the service of God, the believer made alive *to serve* God.

God gave His best, His Son, as an offering for sin for each of us. He now asks that we do the same for Him. God is typified as a Shepherd, and not a slave-driver. He led the way and showed us what He expects of us. The Apostle invites and entreats each of us, in verse 1, to serve God, who loves us and gave His Son for us, by placing ourselves at God's disposal. After all, we are not our own, we have been bought with an incalculable price and we are to glorify God (I Corinthians 6: 19, 20).

V. 1: ". . . holy, acceptable to God. . . ." The Greek word for "holy" means not only just that, but also means to hallow or consecrate, to separate to God (John 17:9). At our conversion we are separated *unto* God through the accomplishments of the cross. This separation is what God did for us through the instrumentality of the Saviour's death, burial, resurrection and ascension. God was in this way working *for* us, a working which was begun by the Holy Spirit, who will complete this work of God in the life of every believer until He brings us into His presence. The work of the cross was a "once-for-all-time-and-eternity" work. It is all-sufficient, inasmuch as it meets every requirement of God's holiness, righteousness and justice. The work of the Holy Spirit in the believer's life is continuous and never-ending until the believer is brought ultimately into God's presence.

In chapter 12 the Apostle recounts almost every duty in the category of the believer's spiritual service toward his fellow believers in relation to God and one another. The believer is to exhibit to God and the world what God has done *for* him, *in* him, and what He can do *through* him. The believer must yield and be eager in his Christian conduct, and must always be in the position of willing readiness to be used by God at any time and in every manner in which God sees fit to use him. The work of the cross is God's wondrous spiritual gift to us. The exhortations of this entire chapter are addressed to every believer and describe what every believer should do in his earthly walk for God. Thus in our loving service we express our gratitude to God for His super-abounding grace toward His own in the presence of unbelievers and the world. By such loving obedience we are able to thank God in a concrete manner. Such a consecrated and devoted earthly walk is the very essence of holiness.

The word holiness as used in the preceding paragraph is not to be taken in the Arminian sense and practice. As here used, holiness is the biblical prerequisite for true service on the part of every believer. Holy living is an achievement of the Holy Spirit. He gives us the power and the weapons by which we can keep the flesh under subjection to the new nature which has been implanted in us. In this manner every believer can "work out" his "own salvation." Yet in the true sense ". . . it is God who worketh in you both to will and to work, for his good pleasure" (Philippians 2:12, 13), which is the only means whereby the "living sacrifice" becomes "holy, acceptable to God" (Romans 12:1).

We must bear in mind that the "living sacrifice" of verse 1 is not a propitiatory sacrifice to God. In no way does this "living sacrifice" earn salvation. Under no circumstances will *any* human sacrifice other than that of Christ's, expiate sin. The purpose of our "living sacrifice" is gratuitous, that is to say, it is our manner of expressing our gratitude to God for the salvation and grace that God showered upon us. In this manner, too, we become what Paul commends us for being, when he writes, "Ye are our epistle, written in our hearts, known and read of all men . . ." (II Corinthians 3:2; 5:9).

The Tabernacle in the Wilderness was permeated with God's holiness, because the Tabernacle was God's dwelling place when He led Israel. Every believer on earth at this moment is God's tabernacle. Only this kind of a holy life is "acceptable to God." It is "well-pleasing" to God (Hebrews 11:5, 6).

V. 1: ". . . which is your spiritual service." The Greek word for "spiritual" is the word from which the English word "logical" is derived. Paul's use of the Greek word for spiritual in this context is as if he had asked, Is not God's request of us a logical, reasonable and legitimate one? Did not God give His best for us? Since He did, His request of us to give Him *our* best is logical and reasonable. By presenting our bodies as a "living sacrifice," we not only express our gratitude, but also our logical and reasonable service, because the Greek word for "service," in its fuller sense implies our manner and method of worship.

The Greek word, "to serve," in the New Testament means to render religious service and homage, to offer and present sacrifices (John 16:2; Romans 9:4; Hebrews 8:5; 9:9), in the worship of God according to the requirements of the Levitical Law (Matthew 4:10, "thou shalt serve"; Acts 7:7, "serve me" or "worship me"; Hebrews 9:14, "to serve the living God"; Philippians 3:3 KJV, "which worship God in the spirit"). The strict sense of this Greek word, "to serve," is to perform sacred service, to worship God in observance of rights instituted for His worship, especially for priests. As believers, we are God's priests, and royal ones according to the New Testament (Revelation 1: 6; I Peter 2:5, 9).

There is another differentiation to be noted in connection with the word "sacrifice" in verse 1 which must not be overlooked. The religions of the cults in some sections of the world call for sacrifice in the form of self-infliction through starvation, or beating one's body, or suicide. God's requests of us have nothing to do with such sacrifices but are confined strictly to the presentation of our bodies in a spiritual sense as "living sacrifices." God wants us in every moment of our lives to be "living sacrifices," and thus it becomes our rational service for Him. Our old self died with Christ as depicted in our baptism (Romans 6), and is raised out of the baptismal waters to a newness of life with Him. We have been crucified with Christ. We have died *with* Him. We have been raised *with* Him, and now we must live *for* Him. "I have been crucified with Christ; and it is no longer I that live, but Christ liveth in me . . ." (Galatians 2:20).

How do you serve God? Have you accepted this challenge? If you have not accepted it as yet, will you? You must, if you wish to be "well-pleasing in his sight" (Hebrews 13:21).

Verse 2: And be not fashioned according to this world: but be ye transformed by the renewing of your mind, that ye may prove what is the good and acceptable and perfect will of God.

The Greek word for "fashioned" means to fashion in accord with, to conform or assimilate oneself. The word for "world" (age) has reference to the spiritual state of the world or age and not its material state.

The word "conform" is like a watchword which we hear on every level of society. Everybody is doing "it," we are told. Why, people ask Christians, must you be so puritanical? The world requires its citizens to conform, and when the world requests conformity of the believer, it strikes at the very heart of his faith. Christians must *not* conform to the world's standards because they do not represent the world's order. We have *repented* and have made an about-face on this world of sin and sensuality. We *have been made* a new creation in Christ. Being born again demands a change. The new birth requires an undaunted and unashamed stand for holiness in the midst of a sinful world. This is not easy, but neither was the cross easy for the Saviour. He stood alone before Pilate and His accusers in the midst of a jeering crowd and fulfilled the words of the prophecy, "I gave my back to the smiters, and my cheeks to them that plucked off the hair; I hid not my face from shame and spitting" (Isaiah 50:6). The Saviour walked into the jaws of torment and torture, never wavering, and set His face "like a flint."

Our Lord speaks to us today and says, "My sheep hear my voice, and I know them, and they follow me" (John 10:27). As He took up His cross and was willing to die for every believer, so every believer is requested to take up his own cross and follow Christ, even at the cost of life itself (Matthew 10:38, 39). We must stand firm and remain resolute in our convictions for the Gospel. As Christians we have no room for compromise. We cannot halt between the two opinions of evil and righteousness. We cannot straddle the fence between sin and holiness, between the worldly practices of society and the holy requirements of God. The tense of the Greek word in verse 2, "be not fashioned," demands a change in our nature. In other words, we are told to stop being "fashioned according to this world." We must walk with our feet on the ground and our eyes centered on the heavens.

V. 2: ". . . but be ye transformed by the renewing of your mind. . . ." The Greek word "but" is more clearly expressed by "but rather"; it negates the preceding statement to emphasize the succeeding one. The Greek word for "be ye transformed" means to change the external form, to undergo a spiritual transformation. This is the Greek word from which the English word "metamorphosis" is derived, and it means "a striking alteration as in appearance, character or circumstances, an abrupt change." This is the very same Greek word that appears in Matthew 17:2 and Mark 9:2 in telling of the Saviour's transfiguration.

In its true sense, is this not the meaning of being born again and of repentance? Is this not what God expects of us who are the followers of Christ? Is this not the meaning of II Corinthians 5:17, "Wherefore if any man is in Christ, he is a new creation . . ." (Literal Greek)? There must be a *complete* change in every one who accepts Christ as Lord and Saviour. This is the true exegesis of II Corinthians 3:18, "But we all, the face having been unveiled, beholding in the mirror the glory of the Lord, are changed into the same image from glory to glory, even as from the Lord the Spirit" (Literal Greek). The believer with the new nature and abiding presence of the Holy Spirit in him, must experience a radical change in his life, his outlook and his behavior. God does not merely expect this, but rather He *demands* it: "Ye *shall* be holy; for I am holy" (I Peter 1:16).

V. 2 cont.: ". . . by the renewing of your mind. . . ." There is contained in the Greek word which is translated "renewing," the thought that there must be a change for the better into a new kind of a life as opposed to the former corrupt state, ". . . and have put on the new man, that is being renewed unto knowledge after the image of him that created him . . ." (Colossians 3:10).

That there must be a complete change both mentally and physically is evident from the text itself. Just a glance at verse 2 shows this. The Greek word translated "mind" also means the faculties of perceiving and understanding, as well as those of feeling, judging, determining, the power of considering soberly, of recognizing goodness and hating evil. (See Romans 1:28; 7:23; Ephesians 4:17.) "Have this mind in you, which was also in Christ Jesus" (Philippians 2:5).

The Saviour's whole being was dominated by the one overriding purpose for which He came into the world, namely, the fulfillment of His Father's will. Our Lord's whole life was devoted to glorifying His Father and accomplishing "the work which thou hast given me to do" (John 17:1-4). The crowning day in the Saviour's life was the day upon which He said, "It is finished" (John 19:30). To the world, that day was a day of ignominy and defeat, but to the Saviour it was a day of triumph. Upon this day He completed His work and could now, as the victor over sin, ascend into the presence of His Father.

Something of the glorious accomplishment of our Lord upon the cross is felt in verse 2 as an example for the believer to be "transformed by the renewing of your mind," and to make such an example the driving force in the believer's life, a goal of achievement attainable through the indwelling presence of the Holy Spirit, even as the Apostle himself declared in Philippians 3:14: "I press on toward the goal unto the prize of the high calling of God in Christ Jesus." Will you accept this challenge?

V. 2 cont.: ". . . that ye may prove what is the good and acceptable and perfect will of God." The Greek word translated "prove" means also to test, to examine, to scrutinize, to see whether a thing is genuine or not, to approve and deem worthy; or as it is in the original Greek of I Thessalonians 2:4: ". . . but as we have been approved by God to be intrusted with the gospel, so we speak, not as pleasing to men, but God is the One who is proving our hearts." Will what *we* are doing for God stand this acid test?

The Greek word for "good" in verse 2 also means upright and honorable. This is the same word that appears in Romans 8:28, in which place it means beneficent. This word in the Septuagint Old Testament and New Testament expresses absolute moral goodness. The Saviour used this word in describing God (Mark 10:18). This quality of goodness must be the goal for which every believer should strive. Paul strove for it, yet he did not claim to have reached it, but said, "I press on toward the goal."

The Greek word for "perfect" in the Septuagint and classical Greek means to be brought to its end, finished, wanting nothing for completeness. This is the word that the Saviour used to state the fact that He had finished or completed His Father's work.

The same word is used to describe the perfect state of all things to be ushered in by the Saviour's return (I Corinthians 13:10). It is used to describe the mature believer in Hebrews 5:14, where it is translated "fullgrown." Every believer should strive for maturity lest he become a misfit in God's sight. Paul urges the believers at Ephesus to mature and to "be no longer children" (Ephesians 4:14). By heeding this admonition to the believer to become perfect, mature, fullgrown, we fulfill God's will in our lives. We are not to remain babes in Christ (Hebrews 5:14). It is a wonderful experience to have a baby in a home. It is a thrill for the parents to care for it and watch it grow. What a heartache it is for the parents when the infant does not mature. How much greater is the heartache of God when His children remain spiritual infants. It is only a mature believer who possesses enough spiritual discretion to know and to "prove what is that good and acceptable and perfect will of God" in his own life.

What have you done with your life? "Only one life to live; 'twill soon be past; only what's done for Christ will last."

Verse 3: For I say, through the grace that was given me, to every man that is among you, not to think of himself more highly than he ought to think; but so to think as to think soberly, according as God hath dealt to each man a measure of faith.

The Christian who has obeyed the challenge and has presented himself as a dedicated and devoted instrument in God's hands, and has permitted the transforming power of the Holy Spirit to operate in his life, must not become high-minded or conceited. Nor should he feel so important in God's work as to think that he is better than his fellow Christians or that he is indispensable in God's plan and program. It is the accomplishment of the Holy Spirit through the grace of God when a Christian reaches the place of usefulness in the work of the Gospel. We must never lose sight of the truth that we are but the clay in the hands of a Sovereign Potter. The molding process may still be carried on, if the clay is pliable, and become "a vessel unto honor" (Romans 9:21).

The warning contained in verse 3 is to avoid lofty thoughts of ourselves, not to over-estimate ourselves, not to think that we are better in God's sight than others. The classical Greek gives the added meaning to the words, "not to think of himself more highly," by translating it, to look down upon, despise, to be over-proud. This admonition should have a sobering effect on pride. Humility is the great virtue many of us lack. Usually those who boast of their humility practice it least.

The Apostle continues in verse 3 to admonish believers "to think soberly." The Greek for this phrase adds the meaning, to be in one's right mind, to be sane. How many times do we accuse someone of not being in his right mind? Spiritually speaking, the Christian who is proud, conceited, who looks down upon other Christians as not being his equal, who has a high opinion of himself, actually is *not* in his right mind. We all are where we are by the grace of God, "according as God hath dealt to each man a measure of faith."

Even faith itself is a gift of God. The measure, the alloted amount, the specific portion of that faith is likewise determined by God Himself. "But unto each one of us was the grace given according to the measure of the gift of Christ" (Ephesians 4:7). Is not Christ the Author and Finisher of our faith? (Hebrews 12:2 KJV). Is He not the one who brought us our faith? Is He not the One who is completing that faith in the life of every believer?

How much faith has been measured out to you? Christ has promised that we shall receive all that is necessary to fulfill our joy (John 16:24). We must ask! We must knock! Will you open the door and let Him in? The decision is yours to make.

Verses 4, 5: (4) For even as we have many members in one body, and all the members have not the same office: (5) so we, who are many, are one body in Christ, and severally members one of another.

The Apostle is comparing the body of believers in Christ to the human body. It is a simile. The various parts of the human body perform different functions, yet they are all one body. A leg, an arm, an eye, an ear, each has its particular office to perform and all together are the treasured members of the body. So are the believers in Christ His treasures and precious to Him. Every member is important to the local church. A custodian in the church is as important as any member of the official body. Each has his proper place in which he should function accordingly. In a similar manner, every believer has his place in the Body of Christ and his duty to perform as a member of that Body. This same thought is expressed in I Corinthians 12:12; Ephesians 4:15, 16, 25; 5:30; Colossians 1:18).

However, there is one point in this comparison of the physical with the spiritual that must not be overlooked. Although the body has many members, the values of the members are not equal. Who of us would not rather lose a finger than an eye, a hand than a foot, a toe rather than a finger? Since all Christians do not have the same talents, nor do they have the same abilities, the same truth must apply to the Body of Christ as applies to the human body. The union of believers is very real, in that all believers are motivated and held together by the same Holy Spirit. There is a diversity of gifts (I Corinthians 12:4-10), but they are all energized by the Holy Spirit. All members form one organic unit, namely, the Body of Christ.

Verse 6: And having gifts differing according to the grace that was given to us, whether prophecy, let us prophesy according to the proportion of our faith . . . ;

The words, "let us prophesy," are in italics, therefore not in the original Greek. No Christian has a right to prophesy today. God's revelation is complete. In the ages past when the Bible was in the process of being written, God spake to the fathers through His prophets. Now the Bible is complete, God "hath . . . spoken unto us in his Son . . ." (Hebrews 1:1, 2). This is a completed action. God now speaks to every Christian through His Word. There are no telephone connections to God!

V. 6: "And having gifts differing according to the grace that was given to us. . . ." This word, "having," or "to have" is a present participle thus expressing the thought that God is still in the process of giving gifts. Simply because God is still in the process of building the Church of Jesus Christ, God is still adding "to the church daily such as should be saved" (Acts 2:47 KJV).

No one can dispute the truth that Christians vary in abilities. Not all are called to be pastors, missionaries, or seminary professors. Not all are capable of fulfilling all these positions. There are differences between believers, as was shown in the preceding verses. We are not all equally endowed with the same ability. It is a special type of individual who can teach, or be a pastor, or a missionary.

However, *all* Christians are called upon to witness. This does not take a special gift or ability to perform. A witness merely tells what he has seen or experienced. To be a true witness a person needs only to be born again. There is a great deal of difference between preaching and witnessing. We must differentiate between the two.

Verse 6 states that it is God who is distributing these gifts.

He does this without the counsel of anyone. The person who is called to a position of eminence in the work of God has no right to boast of his gifts or ability. He is called through and by the grace of God. The honor is graciously bestowed upon him by God, thus removing all grounds for vaunting his personal superiority over his fellow believers. It is only because of the grace of a sovereign God that any of us receives gifts and appointments (Luke 18:14).

The Greek word translated "prophecy" in verse 6, does not always mean *fore*telling. It also means *forth*telling. A prophet is one who proclaims the truth of God, and the word prophet is so used in Matthew 11:9, 13:57, 23:37; Luke 13:33. A prophet also means one who imparts or interprets God's Word or who acts as His spokesman (Exodus 7:1), ". . . and Aaron thy brother shall be thy prophet." Surely we are well aware that Moses was "that prophet." In Exodus 7:1 Aaron is not referred to as "that prophet" but as "thy (Moses) prophet." God says to Jeremiah, ". . . Thou shalt be as my mouth" (15:19). The Messiah was referred to as a Prophet, and He not only predicted future events, but also, more times than He prophesied, He preached the truth of God (Matthew 21:46; Luke 24:19; John 7:52). Prophets were men who did not of necessity prophesy, they also instructed and encouraged their hearers (I Corinthians 14:3; I Timothy 4:14; John 11:51; Acts 2:17). A prophet is a person who takes the things of God and brings them to the people. In its true sense, this is what the Christian pulpit should be. We must "preach the Word." This writer believes that Romans 12:6 implies *forth*telling rather than *fore*telling.

V. 6: ". . . according to the proportion of our faith . . ."; or, in other words, according to the limits, dogmas, doctrines and teachings of our faith. Our preaching must be within the proper limits of God's Word. It should not be "what *I* believe," but rather, "thus saith the Lord." It should be according to the Word of God and according to context, and in harmony with the revealed truth of God. (Compare I Corinthians 14:37 with I John 4:1.) Too many times many of us make statements that cannot be substantiated by the one and only test of divine truth, "thus saith the Lord."

This writer has been surprised to hear people say that a person is lost "only after he hears the Gospel and ignores it," a shallow and completely false statement. Scripture presents the Gospel as a message of salvation, not of condemnation. The lost, regardless and irrespective of who, what or where they are, upon hearing the Gospel, are either convicted and converted or are not. Those who are not convicted and converted *continue in their lost condition*. The preaching of the Gospel is God's instrument by which He offers salvation to the lost. If *"all have sinned,"* then it stands to reason that *all* are lost, whether they *hear* the Gospel or not. This is the reason that every Christian should be witnessing. One reason why God permits us to remain on earth is that each of us may be witnessing to the saving power of the Gospel. "Then faith is from hearing and the hearing through the word of Christ" (Literal Greek for Romans 10:17).

The fundamental reason for the preaching of the Gospel is that sinners may be saved, not condemned. Winning the lost is the God-appointed duty of every missionary. Missionaries traverse oceans, mountains, continents, and penetrate jungles, encountering disease, wild beasts and savages. Why? To reach human beings who are lost in bestiality and sin. These human beings are generally ignorant and depraved natives — savages — bound for an eternal hell, to whom, in their lost condition, the missionaries seek to bring the Gospel. The only remedy that can save these lost souls from eternal death *is* the Gospel. In order that bringing the Gospel to the lost may be effective is the reason the Apostle states that our preaching must be in agreement with, or in proportion to, our faith as it is contained in the Word of God.

Verse 7: . . . or ministry, let us give ourselves to our ministry; or he that teacheth, to his teaching . . . ;

In verses 6 and 7 the Apostle mentions various offices in the service of Christ and in the work of the local church. In verse 6 he writes of the office of a prophet as the one who proclaims God's Word. In verse 7 he writes of the ministry which entails various phases of service, such as that of the minister, a deacon, and any devoted follower of Christ in the various services of the local church. Whatever the ministry may be, the one fulfilling it should give himself to perform it diligently.

V. 7: ". . . or he that teacheth, to his teaching . . ."; A more literal translation is, "the one teaching, to his teaching." A teacher is a person who has been given the ability to instruct, such as a public speaker when addressing an assembly. This teaching, too, must be in accord with the doctrines and precepts of the Word of God.

Verse 8: . . . or he that exhorteth, to his exhorting: he that giveth, let him do it with liberality; he that ruleth, with diligence; he that showeth mercy, with cheerfulness.

Again, the literal translation of the Greek for "he that exhorteth" is the one exhorting, in the teaching, and refers of course to one having the ability to inspire, to admonish, to entreat, and to comfort and console (Acts 4:36; 11:23; 15:32).

V. 8: ". . . he that giveth, let him do it with liberality . . ."; which might be better translated, the one giving, let him do it with sincerity or liberality, or with an open hand and an open heart, that is, unselfishly and unstintingly (II Corinthians 8:2; 9:7, 13).

V. 8: ". . . he that ruleth, with diligence . . ."; has reference, of course, to the one taking the lead, or the one who has been appointed to exercise authority or supervision over the local assembly; let him do it with diligence and earnestness, on his own initiative without help or urging, as a consecrated deacon ought to perform his duties.

V. 8: ". . . he that showeth mercy, with cheerfulness." Or the one showing mercy, or having compassion and pity, should do it cheerfully. In other words, showing mercy is not to be done out of a sense of duty merely, but out of a heart of compassion, with love and cheerfulness. The believers in the Roman church to whom Paul is writing, who possessed the gifts described in verses 6-8, were responsible to the disciples. The same rule holds true today. The various officers and workers in the local church do not have authority over the pastor. They are his advisors and assistants.

Verse 9: Let love be without hypocrisy. Abhor that which is evil; cleave to that which is good.

The infinite love of God for man is real, sincere, without sham; and the finite love of man for God must be just as real, sincere, and without sham. Man's love for God cannot be false, in which case it would not be love but hypocrisy and God is fully aware of the difference. God is able to differentiate instantly between true and false profession. Doubleness of heart and speech God does not tolerate or condone. True love of God and man is always ready for service. True love is permeated with compassion and sympathy, and must be always ready and unfeigned. Notice the word — unfeigned — in the following, I Timothy 1:5; II Corinthians 6:6; I Peter 1:22. Such love must be ever willing to

". . . restore such a one (who has fallen) in a spirit of gentleness" and humility (Galatians 6:1).

V. 9: "Abhor that which is evil. . . ." This is a strong admonition. The believer must, under every condition, look upon and believe that all manner of evil is an abomination to him. The Greek word translated "abhor" means to detest evil for the abomination which it is. Because holiness is the antithesis of evil, holiness is utterly devoid of any semblance of evil. The child of God cannot flirt with sin and serve God at the same time. Any evil practice, or tolerance of evil, negates the Christian's testimony. The Greek word for "abhor" is a present active participle that is properly translated abhor and keep on abhorring. (Romans 12:9 is the only place in the New Testament where this word appears.) To abhor evil habitually means a constant warfare from which there can never be any respite. Evil is always seeking either to destroy or besmirch righteousness and holiness. Paul exhorts the Christian to "put on the whole armor of God" for this battle (Ephesians 6:14-17).

The word for "evil" in the New Testament is used to describe the work and character of Satan, as in Matthew 13:19, 38; Ephesians 6:16; and elsewhere. Is not Satan the antagonist and the adversary of all that God stands for, and is he not against all God's standards of moral conduct for all believers? Is it any wonder that God admonishes the believer to "abstain from every form of evil"? (I Thessalonians 5:22).

The clause, "Abhor that which is evil," is so constructed in the Greek that the words comprising the clause demand that the abhorrence of evil must be expressed and demonstrated. The Christian must actively engage in his warfare and relentlessly destroy all the evil practices of his carnal nature. Chapters 7 and 8 of this Epistle to the Romans fully illustrate the nature of this warfare which elicited Paul's warning to "abhor that which is evil." Paul's exhortation definitely demands that the Christian *must* separate himself from sin. Sin must be repugnant to every born-again child of God. However, God's commandments for Christian living are not all negative. They are also positive, as the Apostle proceeds to state. The Christian is not only exhorted to abstain from evil practices, but he is also exhorted to pursue the virtues which make up the sum total of Christian living. He is not only told to *separate from* evil, but he is also informed as to what he is to be *separated unto*, while he is living in the midst of evil.

V. 9: ". . . cleave to that which is good." Again the Greek

would be more accurately translated, cleaving to that which is good, or attaching oneself to, or uniting and associating with. This is the positive aspect of Christian living. Active pursuit of the Christian life is what the Christian must devote himself to, and God supplies the means, the mode and method, by which the Christian is enabled to cleave to that which is virtuous and good. God expects and demands a commendable and scrupulous life of every one of His children, a divine postulate which applies to every believer in every age. God has never lowered His standards regardless of the person with whom He deals. It was just as wrong to sin under the Law as it is under grace. In fact, the sin under grace is doubly odious in God's sight as compared with the sin under Law, because grace is a manifestation or attribute of God, and is, in fact, the love of God, while under Law the lawbreaker must stand alone before the thundering voice of Jehovah at Sinai. God's love is a power or force greater than all other forces, for it is the *agape,* the Greek word for God's love, the love that God has "shed abroad in our hearts" (Romans 5:5).

Do you know this love? Have you experienced this love? Is it operating in your life now? It should. It must!

Verse 10: In love of the brethren be tenderly affectioned one to another; in honor preferring one another . . . ;

In verse 9, the Apostle speaks of the way the Christian life should be lived before God in the midst of a sinful world. The Christian's life is motivated by the love of God. In verse 10, the reference is to the Christian's life and walk with his fellow Christians. The Greek word for love in verse 10 is *phileo,* a different word for love from that which is used in verse 9 (*agape*). The love in verse 10 is the love which a person has for a friend, the love that exists between husband and wife, the love that parents have for their children. It is the affection which all humans feel or should feel, for one another. It is, at its best, a love that is warm, genuine, unselfish and unstinting. Genuine love of this kind is *understanding* love, and is devoid of selfishness. It is open-handed and open-hearted.

What a rare possession is human affection! How rewarding it is when one possesses such love! This writer has heard it said that the person who has six true friends is richer than a millionaire. How true, and how much truer it is among Christians! (John 13:35). This writer is blessed with a number of true Christian friends. If six true friends equate one millionaire, then this writer is a multi-millionaire! In the darkest hour of my life, my true friends rallied around me. Thank God for friends who know all our faults and shortcomings and still love us. This is one of the prerogatives of Christian friendship, imparting comfort and consolation in times of bereavement. Let us praise the Saviour for these friends who help us wipe away the tears of human sorrow. Thank God this friendship is made possible only through the love of God. There is a tie that binds our hearts in Christian love because it is bound by the hands of the Holy Spirit.

V. 10: "In love of the brethren be tenderly affectioned one to another. . . ." The believer is told to love with "tender affection." There are degrees of love, such as the love of the father for the prodigal son (Luke 15:30-32). Loving one's children all together as a group and loving one particular child with "tender affection" is a kind of double love, so to speak, made up of two words, "love" and "affection."

V. 10: ". . . in honor preferring one another . . ."; or, to prefer each of our brethren above one's self, in value, in preference, in estimation; that is, to give our brother precedence. In other words, to consider one's brother more valuable than oneself, by putting him first, or giving him the best and taking second best for oneself. This is real Christian friendship. Such love is genuine. It is the kind of love that should prevail and be demonstrated among brethren. According to the Scriptures, a believer can ascertain the strength of his faith by the manner in which he loves his fellow Christians. "We know that we have passed out of death into life, because we love the brethren" (I John 3:14; John 13:35). The whole phrase, "in honor preferring one another," means that each of us should set the example. We should not wait for our fellow Christians to do it first. Let us love our brother even if he hasn't begun to love. This is the true meaning of the phrase, "in honor preferring one another."

Verse 11: . . . in diligence not slothful; fervent in spirit; serving the Lord . . . ;

The King James Version translates the Greek of verse 11, "Not slothful in business," instead of, "in diligence not slothful," as in the American Standard Version. Because of the King James Version translation, "Be not slothful in business," this expression in the Apostle's advice has been misunderstood and wrongfully applied. The Greek word translated "diligence" does not mean business of a commercial nature. The identical Greek word is

also found in Romans 12:8, where it is translated "diligence."
In Mark 6:25 and Luke 1:39 the same Greek word is translated
"haste." (The classical Greek adds the meaning, to urge on, to
seek eagerly, to promote, to exert oneself.) This classical Greek
word appears in the following texts: II Corinthians 7:11; 12; 8:7,
16; Hebrews 6:11; II Peter 1:5; Jude 3. The Greek word translated "slothful" means, to hesitate, to be cowardly, to shrink or
hang back.

"Slothful" is a Rabbinism. In the Tractate, chapter 2, Mishnah
15, *The Saying of the Fathers,* Rabbi Tarfon states, "The day is
short, the work is much, and the workmen are indolent (slothful),
and reward much; and the Master of the House is insistent."

What the Apostle means by the phrase, "in diligence not
slothful," in verse 11, is that the believer should never hesitate
or relent in his strivings after his reward — the "Well done, thou
good and faithful servant," of his Lord. He must always stand
fast in his striving to maintain and to promote the standards of
God's Word and urge others who are Christians to do the same.
There is no room for cowardice in Christian conduct. A Christian
must under all circumstances be courageous, never shrinking
from his duty as a soldier of the cross. The Christian life is a
warfare in which every Christian must enlist for the duration,
armed with the power and the weapons of God, never hanging
back or shrinking from the fiery darts of the wicked one but swift
to charge with the sword of the Spirit which is the Word of
God. "Watch ye, stand fast in the faith, quit you like men, be
strong" (I Corinthians 16:13). "Finally, be strong in the Lord,
and in the strength of his might" (Ephesians 6:10-17; also Galatians 6:9; II Thessalonians 3:13). A Christian may burn out but
he must never rust out.

V. 11: ". . . fervent in spirit. . . ." Martin Luther states, "The
spirit is the highest and noblest part of man which qualifies him
to lay hold of incomprehensible eternal things; in short, it is the
house where faith and God's word are at home."

V. 11: ". . . fervent. . . ." The Greek word from which "fervent"
is translated means, to be hot, zealous, ardent, burning. A Christian should be a man with fire in his veins, his whole being
aflame for the cause of Christ. The phrase, "fervent in spirit,"
urges the Christian to strive to keep his spirit at white heat. God
despises lukewarmness; it is detestable in His sight and not to
be tolerated (Revelation 3:16). "Being neither cold nor hot,"
was the accusation against the Laodicean Church. Our churches
are filled with Sunday-morning Christians who are worthless to

God and the local church. Lukewarm Christians are useless and loathsome to God. If we do not keep our zeal burning at white heat with a passion for the lost, if we do not keep on witnessing for Christ, what use are we to God? The fuel that motivates a Christian life is witnessing, prayer, Bible study and fellowship. It takes all four to keep our spirits aglow for Christ.

A carnal life is cold, indifferent to the things of God. A Spirit-led life is warm, glowing, always distinguished by a deep and lively interest in the things of God, and quickly responsive to the power and guidance of the Holy Spirit, ". . . he shall baptize you in the Holy Spirit and in fire" (Matthew 3:11). A godly life is characterized by love and zeal. We must never lose our "first love" which is always evidenced by a warm spirit. To serve God properly we must be filled with the Holy Spirit.

V. 11: ". . . serving the Lord." A warm spirit, a compassionate heart and a constant perusal of the Word is what the Lord expects of everyone who serves Him. What can compare with the joy of bringing a soul to Christ? If heaven rejoices when *one* soul is saved, what does a revival mean in heaven? If God esteems the value of one soul so highly, does it not seem logical that witnessing and soul-winning should be the driving force of every local church and a powerful impetus in Christian living? In these days, we must always be "redeeming the time, because the days are evil" (Ephesians 5:16; Colossians 4:5).

What are we doing with our lives? Do our lives portray a burning passion for Christ? Are we winning the lost for whom Christ died?

Verse 12: . . . rejoicing in hope; patient in tribulation; continuing stedfastly in prayer . . . ;

The Christian life is radiant with hope. A true Christian life can never be hopeless. Its every heartbeat, its every step, its every breath, is activated by hope: A life so lived is energized by the Holy Spirit. A carnal life is not a hopeful life, since a goodly part of such a life is engrossed in worldly practices and ambitions. The things of this world are transitory, and the end of carnality is death (Romans 8:13).

In verse 12, the Apostle is urging the believers to be in a constant state of rejoicing. The Greek word which is translated "rejoicing" is a present participle. If our lives are motivated by the Holy Spirit, we shall be in a continuous state of rejoicing. The things of this world will become meaningless and unattractive. The note of jubilation is struck in the hope of the resurrection and the Saviour's Second Coming. The Christian is urged to live in a constant state of expectancy of the return of the Saviour. The believer's feet may be on the ground, but his eye is fixed on heaven, "looking for the blessed hope and appearing of the glory of the great God and our Saviour Jesus Christ" (Titus 2:13).

If it is this "blessed hope" which motivates a Christian's life, it will be filled with joy, since this hope is established upon an unwavering trust and confidence in the certainty (with the guarantee from the Saviour's own lips) that He will come again (John 14:3).

Christian character, faith, a life of devotion and consecration, are molded, fashioned and refined by tribulations and trials. When the things of this world begin to lose their attractiveness, when trying and adverse circumstances befall a believer, when he goes through afflictions and oppression, and the flesh becomes a prison instead of a dwelling place for the new man, then the saint of God begins to learn that these experiences are designed to teach him to bear calmly and bravely the hardships of life. He then learns to trust the guidance of the Holy Spirit instead of the flesh. Endurance and perseverance are the virtues he learns in the valleys of life's experiences. The believer never appreciates a mountain-peak experience until he has walked in the valleys of life's vicissitudes. Paul tells his fellow-Christians that in affliction they are to show endurance. The soldier of the cross must be at his best in affliction. Only in this manner can he prove his endurance. Adversity will always reveal what sort of a Christian a person is. Affliction will always develop a true child of God. "Before I was afflicted I went astray: but now I observe thy word" (Psalm 119:67, 71, 75). "Adversity is the diamond dust Heaven polishes its jewels with" (Robert Leighton).

V. 12: ". . . continuing stedfastly in prayer . . ." In this section of the Epistle, the Apostle is goading the saints at Rome to live in an attitude of expectancy of the Lord's return, as they continue, like good soldiers at the battlefront, to carry on their warfare in the face of hatred and persecution, which they could only accomplish by unwavering endurance and "continuing stedfastly in prayer." One does not need to stop working or to cease whatever he is doing to pray. A believer need not shut his eyes when he prays. The Lord hears the prayers of His saints no matter where they are or how their prayers are offered. Praying is not only communing with God, it is also praising and thanking Him for His wonderful provisions. "With all prayer and petition, praying all the time in the Spirit, and with this in view, watching with all perseverance and petition concerning all the saints" (Literal Greek of Ephesians 6:18). (Compare Philippians 4:6; Colossians 1:3; 4:2; I Thessalonians 5:17; Acts 1:14; 2:42; 6:4.)

A saint need not conform his life to the life-pattern of other saints. Just because David prayed seven times (Psalm 119:164), or Daniel three times (6:10), does not mean that we must do the same. Why not accept Paul's suggestion in I Thessalonians 5:17, "Pray without ceasing"?

Verse 13: . . . communicating to the necessities of the saints, given to hospitality.

Verses 9 through 12 show the spiritual composition of the Christian. The graces enumerated — love, goodness, hope, patience, prayer — make up a composite of the spiritual power-plant that motivates a Christian life, graces which in turn produce zeal, righteousness, abhorrence of evil, and the knowledge that a Christian has only duties and privileges, no rights. He must take advantage of every opportunity to serve the Lord. A lost opportunity can never be recaptured. In tribulation a Christian must prove that he is a stalwart soldier of Christ, one who must meet the dangers of life undaunted and unafraid because Christ is with him.

The courage to endure tribulation is the gift of the Holy Spirit, and can be acquired only by prayer through Christ. This is the *sine qua non* for Christian living.

Verse 13 is the practical exegesis of verses 9 through 12. Someone has said, "Christianity is a faith of an open hand, an open heart, and an open door," and this quotation is an excellent paraphrase of verse 13. The Apostle John states it in this manner, "But whoso hath the world's goods, and beholdeth his brother in need, and shutteth up his compassion from him, how doth the love of God abide in him?" (I John 3:17).

We are able to share with others our joys, our sorrows, our needs, our wants, and our provisions. "Bear ye one another's burdens, and so fulfil the law of Christ" (Galatians 6:2). This must be our pursuit, which is what the Greek word translated "given to," in verse 13, really means. An inner change through the new birth must manifest itself in a transformed attitude and relationship toward our human environment, the miraculous result of the new life created in us through Christ.

How are *you* living?

Verse 14: Bless them that persecute you; bless, and curse not.

The Greek word translated "Bless them," as used in this construction, is a Hebraism. It is used over four hundred times in the Septuagint Version of the Old Testament. In the Classical Greek it means, to speak well of someone.

To this writer the expression, "bless them," means, do not return evil for evil; or, do not try to get even with, or, to be revenged upon the one doing harm. In verse 14 Paul is urging his Roman believers to rise above the give-and-take practices of unsaved humanity. Unbelievers are prone to return evil for evil (v. 17), and worldlings whose lives are given to evil, fulfill the proverb, "evil does as evil thinks." The Christian is admonished to refrain from the evil habits of lost humanity. He is to live a life that will magnify and glorify God. The chasm between good and evil, between righteousness and wickedness, is wide and deep. We must stand on the side of righteousness.

The Christian is directed to go one step further. He must bless his persecutor. Not only is he admonished not to curse or return evil even upon his persecutor but he is also to bless him while the persecutor is in the act of persecuting him. The Greek word translated "persecute" is a present active participle that is better translated "persecuting." To bless those who persecute us requires added grace, and God has promised to supply the grace needed for every trial and temptation (I Corinthians 10:13).

V. 14: ". . . bless, and curse not." Do not "wish evil" on the one persecuting you as an enemy. Return good! Even bless him and in this way, "Thou shalt heap coals of fire upon his head, and Jehovah will reward thee" (Proverbs 25:22; Matthew 5:44 KJV; Luke 6:28; I Peter 3:9; Romans 12:20). We must not lose sight of the truth that a true and devoted Christian will suffer persecution at the hands of the world. This is a privilege, not a burden (II Timothy 3:12).

Verse 15: Rejoice with them that rejoice; weep with them that weep.

The literal Greek is, "Rejoice with the rejoicing (ones), weep with the weeping (ones)." Both words, "rejoice" and "weep," are present participles.

Isn't it easier to weep with someone than it is to rejoice? Isn't it easier to sympathize with someone in his grief, than it is to rejoice with someone who has received a blessing? If we are truthful with ourselves, then we all, at one time or another, have had such an experience. When we are with a person who is rejoicing over his good fortune or a blessing, there is the ever-present danger of jealousy. All of us, believers as well as unbelievers, are at times prone to become envious or jealous. Paul is cautioning believers not to become envious, jealous or covetous. Is not every believer a part of the body of Christ? Is the head of a human being jealous of the foot, or the eye of the ear? Certainly not! In the same sense, members of the body of Christ are urged and challenged to rejoice with fellow members who are rejoicing, and to weep with those who are weeping. Love, patience, sympathy and understanding are the vital elements of a Christian life. These virtues are not prompted by expediency or the hope of mitigating the pain or discomfort of misfortune, or inviting compromise. On the other hand, courageous endurance of temporal reverses and tribulation are evidences of *practical* Christianity.

Verse 16: Be of the same mind one toward another. Set not your mind on high things, but condescend to things that are lowly. Be not wise in your own conceits.

The Apostle continues to warn and to challenge the believer. Paul's words, "Be of the same mind," do not mean we are to do our thinking in the same way others do their thinking. Rather the idea carries over from verse 15, "Rejoice with them that rejoice," and so on. What Paul is saying in verse 16 is like Jesus' answer, "Go, and do thou likewise," when the lawyer asked Him, "Who is my neighbor?" (Luke 10:29-37). What Paul means is, "Have this mind in you, which was also in Christ Jesus" (Philippians 2:5; 2:2; 4:2). Think of a fellow-Christian as you think of yourself, is a judicious admonition. We are all redeemed the same way. Before we are saved, we are lost and doomed. Christ did it all for us. All believers are God's children by His accomplishments.

V. 16: "Set not your mind on high things. . . ." Do not think so highly of yourself as imagining that the only place in the church you can occupy is a high office. Do not strive to gain authority and prominence. It is far better to be in a humble position as a follower of Christ and *in* the will of God, than to be in an exalted position and *out* of the will of God.

V. 16: ". . . but condescend to things that are lowly." Christ Himself is the best exegesis of this exhortation. See Philippians 2:6-8: ". . . (6) who, existing in the form of God, counted not the being on an equality with God a thing to be grasped, (7) but emptied himself, taking the form of a servant, being made in the likeness of man; (8) and being found in fashion as a man, he humbled himself, becoming obedient even unto death, yea the death of the cross." (See also Matthew 20:26-28.)

V. 16: "Be not wise in your own conceits." This warning in verse 16 is a re-statement of what the Apostle has said in 11:25, ". . . lest ye be wise in your own conceits," which is as much as to say to those Christians at Rome, Don't be so high-minded as to think that your position is more secure than that of the Jews. Their God is the same God as your God. The same sin of unbelief that caused the Jews to fall from their lofty position can also cause your downfall. Israel refused to hearken to the voice of her prophets and her sages, "Woe unto them that are wise in their own eyes, and prudent in their own sight!" (Isaiah 5:21). "Be not wise in thine own eyes . . ." (Proverbs 3:7). Paul states the very same truth in verse 16, "Be not wise in your own conceits," or, in your own mind.

A timely warning! How meaningful are these words today! Will you heed?

Verse 17: Render to no man evil for evil. Take thought for things honorable in the sight of all men.

The literal Greek for verse 17 is as follows: "Recompense to no one evil in return for evil." The Old Testament states the same truth in Proverbs 20:22, "Say not thou, I will recompense evil: Wait for Jehovah, and he will save thee." See also Proverbs 24:29.

The carnal nature in each one of us is prone to by-pass this injunction not to recompense evil. We want revenge and recompense immediately for every wrong put upon us. This sentiment is an angry impulse and contrary to Christian ethics. When evil is inflicted upon us, we must ask the Holy Spirit for grace to bear it and leave the matter for Him to deal with the one inflicting the evil. Such self-restraint may be a difficult thing to put into practice, but the rewards are great.

V. 17: "Take thought for things honorable in the sight of all men." This may be a quotation from the Septuagint version of Proverbs 3:4 but with some alteration from the original which may be translated, ". . . provide things honest in the sight of the Lord and of men." It is quoted again in II Corinthians 8:21.

The expression, "take thought," is a present participle, better translated, recompensing to no one evil in return for evil, striving to exhibit good (upright, virtuous) things before men. This is the sense of verse 17. The Lord said, ". . . that they may see your good works, and glorify your Father who is in heaven" (Matthew 5:16). The Apostle puts it this way: ". . . wherein they speak against you as evildoers, they may by your good works, which they behold, glorify God in the day of visitation" (I Peter 2:12).

Verse 18: If it be possible, as much as in you lieth, be at peace with all men.

Sometimes it is not possible for a born-again believer to "be at peace with all men." Christianity, if it is in accordance with the New Testament, cannot and does not tolerate sin. The child of God cannot compromise with wickedness. Righteousness is to Christianity what the jugular vein is to the body: sever either completely and death ensues. When sin confronts a child of God, he must resist it with the determination to overcome it. This determination must be as sharp as an unsheathed Damascus blade. The Christian cannot be at peace with sin (Matthew 10:34), but the Christian must differentiate between sin and the sinner. Righteousness is the implacable foe of sinfulness and this warfare is without respite.

The Apostle states in verse 18 that the Christian is to strive to live peaceably with all men, as far as possible. The Christian is not to start a quarrel, or engender enmities, strife, jealousies, wraths, factions, divisions, or instigate hatreds (See Galatians 5: 19-23).

However, we must remember we cannot demand that worldlings have to conform to the precepts of Christian holiness and righteousness. "We know that we are of God, and the *whole world* lieth in the evil one" (I John 5:19). Satan is the "god of this age." It is not the program of the Gospel to convert the world in this age. This age does not end in peace, righteousness and tranquility. It will end with disillusion, devastation, destruction; it will end with the Battle of Armageddon, and the pouring out of rivers of blood (Isaiah 63:1-3; Matthew 24:1-29; Revelation 16:1-11; 18:1-9; 19:11-21); with a baptism of fire and global war; with the Gentile nations aligned against Jehovah and His Messiah (Psalm 2); with the final curtain of God's judgment falling on the last act of the drama of sin and its author, producer and chief actor, Satan.

The Gospel is calling out of this cesspool of corruption and immorality, a people for His name from among the Gentiles and Jews. God the Holy Spirit is building the true assembly with these blood-bought believers which is called the Body of Christ (Ephesians 2:16), and "a holy temple in the Lord" (Ephesians 2:21). It is this group of people called saints who are requested to live ". . . at peace with all men." A believer's life is to be exemplified by love, understanding, patience and peace, and not to compromise Christian standards of holiness and righteousness with the world's sin and iniquity (Titus 2:11-15).

Will you accept this challenge? You must if you are a born-again believer.

Verse 19: Avenge not yourself, beloved, but give place unto the wrath of God: for it is written, Vengeance belongeth unto me; I will recompense, saith the Lord.

This verse, of course, is addressed to Christians. The word translated "beloved," is the Greek word *agape*, which is the love that God has for man and man for God. It is the kind of love that God the Father designed to be the holy bond of unity among Christians. It is a God-given and God-motivated love. The injunction, "Avenge not yourself," is better translated, "Avenging not yourself."

In verses 9-17, 19, 21, the Apostle's style is that of the imperative mode, or, "direct command," form of address, such as, "Bless them that persecute you," "Avenge not yourself," and so on. In verses 18 and 20, however, Paul changes to the subjunctive mode of the verb, a command based on a condition introduced by "if," thereby indicating a softening of the command by a hint of compassion — "*if* it be possible," (v. 18); and, "*if* thine enemy hunger," (v. 20).

V. 19: "Avenge not yourself. . . ." The Psalmist states it this way, "Fret not thyself because of evildoers . . ." (Psalm 37:1). Solomon wrote, "Say not thou, I will recompense evil" (Proverbs 20:22). "Say not, I will do so to him as he hath done to me; I will render to the man according to his work" (Proverbs 24: 29. See also Proverbs 24:19.)

V. 19: ". . . but give place unto the wrath. . .". The American Standard Version wrongfully adds, "of God." The King James Version reads, ". . . but rather give place unto wrath. . . ." The American Standard Version distorts the truth, because the meaning of verse 19 is, Make room in your heart and life and disdain to notice the calumnies of men as they heap them upon you. "Learn to roll with the punches," is a current expression in the athletic world, and it conveys the truth of the clause, "but give place unto wrath." In other words, let slander roll off your back as water rolls off a duck. Don't let unjust criticism bother you. Again the Christian needs to be reminded that self-restraint may be difficult, but the reward is great.

V. 19: "Vengeance belongeth unto me; I will recompense, saith the Lord." Paul is quoting the Septuagint version of Deuteronomy 32:35 (See also Hebrews 10:13). The Old Testament passage is a mandate of Jehovah to His people Israel. The Apostle makes the application of this mandate to God's actions toward His children in the present age, and rightfully so. It is far better to let God judge the evil-doers than for the believer to attempt it. God's judgments are more effective. It is interesting to note that the Greek word translated, "will repay," in the King James Version of verse 19, is in the future indicative active, thus certifying the truth that God will repay. This "recompense" (ASV) or re-payment may not always be immediate, but it is certain. God's judgments for sin are inescapable, when the sinner fails to appropriate the accomplishments of the Saviour on the cross for his own sins. ". . . be sure your sin will find you out" (Numbers 32:23).

What consolations for us are to be found in the following verses: "Blessed is he whose transgression is forgiven, whose sin is covered. Blessed is the man unto whom Jehovah imputeth not iniquity" (Psalm 32:1, 2). ". . . the blood of Jesus his Son cleanseth us from all sin" (I John 1:7). See also Hebrews 9:14 and Revelation 7:17.

Have you accepted Him and His cleansing blood? You must if your hearts' desire is to find forgiveness for your sins.

Verse 20: But if thine enemy hunger, feed him; if he thirst, give him to drink: for in so doing thou shalt heap coals of fire upon his head.

This verse is the Septuagint version of Proverbs 25:21, 22, and is permeated with Rabbinical teachings. Compare II Kings 6:22 with verse 20; and what the Lord said in Matthew 5:44 and also Luke 6:27, 28. In the light of these, we should re-think the "Sermon on the Mount." This writer does not believe that the Beatitudes (Matthew 5:3-11) as well as the rest of the Sermon on the Mount are the laws that govern the "Kingdom Age." Chapters 5, 6 and 7 of Matthew apply to Christian living today because the entire Sermon on the Mount was delivered by the Saviour Himself.

Matthew 5:38-42 is another way of saying what is said in Romans 12:17, "Render to no man evil for evil." The idea contained in these verses is the exegesis of Proverbs 25:21, 22, by the Jewish teachers: "Rabbi Hama ben Haninah said, 'Even though your enemy has risen up early to kill you, and comes hungry and thirsty to your house, give him food and drink.' " The extract is based on Proverbs 25:21 (Midrash, Proverbs 21; f.49b).

V. 20: ". . . thou shalt heap coals of fire upon his head." This does not necessarily mean that it will bring God's judgment upon "thine enemy," but it could bring about his repentance and salvation. Shame will burn his conscience as fire burns coal. (Compare Psalm 1:4; 9:10; 11:6.)

There is also the truth in verse 20 that God's judgments are more punitive than man's. God in His own time will settle the score with the wicked. The next verse (21) is the elaboration of verse 20. The Christian is exhorted never to take the law into his own hands. He is to let God act in his behalf. In so doing, it is possible that the evildoer may plead for mercy and forgiveness, which could result in his salvation, in which case punishment might be avoided. Verse 20 reminds the Christian of what he can do through the power of the Holy Spirit.

Verse 21: Be not overcome of evil, but overcome evil with good.

Let not evil subdue you. Let it not conquer you so that your Christian testimony fails. Resisting evil is an arduous task for every believer. The flesh will always try to get the upper hand. The believer must follow the advice of Paul in Ephesians 6:11, "Put on the whole armor of God, that ye may be able to stand against the wiles of the devil." God not only supplies the weapons, he also supplies the power, namely, the Holy Spirit.

V. 21: ". . . overcome evil with good." Righteousness will always prevail over evil. Goodness and virtue will overcome sin just as the sun will melt ice. The believer who practices how to "overcome evil with good," will be rewarded in measure by the Saviour (Luke 6:38).

13

Verse 1: Let every soul be in subjection to the higher powers: for there is no power but of God; and the powers that be are ordained of God.

CHAPTER 13 HAS to do with the Apostle's instructions to his fellow believers as to how they are to behave under, and react to, their local governments. The Christian is to "be in subjection" to the government under which he resides. That is, he is to render obedience to, and be under, the jurisdiction of his government. He is to obey the laws of the state because the state is the "higher power" to which he is to "be in subjection."

Perhaps verse 1 was especially addressed to the Jewish Christians at Rome. In those days it was a disdainful thought to a Jew to have a Gentile in authority over him. The Jew longed for a Jewish government with a Jew in authority. Moreover, it is contrary to the teaching of the Torah to have a Gentile rule over the Jews (Deuteronomy 17:15; see also Matthew 22:17). Also present in the minds of Jews was the hope of a Messianic Kingdom with their Messiah as King. Undoubtedly this concept is what prompted the disciples to ask the Saviour, ". . . Lord, dost thou at this time restore the kingdom to Israel?" (Acts 1:6).

The Christian is the subject or the citizen of the state. He must abide by the rules and regulations of that state. In fact, a Christian should be a better citizen than the unbeliever. Righteousness, virtue, morality and integrity are the attributes that society admires and respects. The unbeliever, although he may not always covet these virtues for himself, nevertheless has a right to expect the Christian in his midst to possess them.

V. 1: "The powers that be are ordained of God" and the power or authority they exercise is only for human government. This does not give a ruler or dictator the right to demand worship for himself as an idol of his subjects. There is only one true and living God. He is Jehovah. When the early Christians were com-

428

manded to worship a human being as a god they chose martyrdom. In this same spirit the Jews throughout their history have
refused to accede to the demands of pagan Christendom in
submitting to baptism and pretending to accept faith in Jesus
Christ as God. This writer differentiates between the man Jesus
of pagan Christendom and Jesus the Christ, the incarnate God
of the Bible and true Christianity. The Jews of history and the
Jews of today do not know the difference between the two,
neither has the true Christian church ever made a determined
and unified effort to inform them of the difference.

V. 1: ". . . for there is no power but of God. . . ." That is to
say, for there is no authority but of God — by the direct hand of
God, His agency, or His permission. Or as it is in the literal
Greek, "and the existing (ones), having been appointed, ordained
and arranged by God." The Greek clause, "for there is no power
but of God," is so constructed as to mean that it is God who
places persons in positions of authority. Thank God that He
ever remains the Sovereign Omnipotent Ruler of this turbulent
world. Only an Omniscient God could bring any semblance of
order out of this maelstrom of confusion, because order is inherent in His being. Is this not what the prophet said to his
Gentile potentate, Nebuchadnezzar, ". . . Blessed be the name of
God for ever and ever; for wisdom and might are his. And he
changeth the times and the seasons; he removeth kings and
setteth up kings; he giveth wisdom unto the wise, and knowledge
to them that have understanding" (Daniel 2:20, 21)?

One day, and it will be much sooner than many think, the
last of this world's vacillating and self-aggrandizing rulers will
be removed. Then God will set His own Son, Jesus Christ, on
His eternal throne, a throne bought with His own blood, which
was promised to the Saviour prior to His birth (Luke 1:32, 33).
He now is waiting for the appointed moment to ascend that
throne. See Psalm 2:8, 9; 22:27, 28; 110:1, 2; and others. The
capital of that government will be Jerusalem.

**Verse 2: Therefore he that resisteth the power, withstandeth
the ordinance of God: and they that withstand shall receive to
themselves judgment.**

The literal Greek from which this verse is translated would
read, "So that the one that resisteth (or the one resisting) the
authority has opposed the ordinance of God." The mood and
tense of the verb "withstandeth" implies the action with finished
results in the present time. The warning here is strong and the

believer is urged to heed it. Obedience to the laws of the state is incumbent on the believer in his material realm, in the same way that obedience to God's laws is incumbent on him in the spiritual realm. The laws in both realms must be obeyed. This is exactly what the Saviour Himself clearly stated, "Then saith he unto them, Render therefore unto Caesar the things that are Caesar's; and unto God the things that are God's" (Matthew 22:21). This teaching undoubtedly was a bitter pill for the Jews to swallow. Anything pagan, and the Roman government and its officials were pagan, was detestable to the Jewish mind, and contradictory to the dogmas of the Old Testament. Paganism in any form was not to be tolerated. God's judgment was the bitter fruit of disobedience that Israel was reaping then, and reaps even now, as the result of the request made centuries earlier by their forefathers, ". . . now make us a king to judge us like all the nations (Gentiles)" (I Samuel 8:5). They asked for a king like the Gentiles had and God granted their request. The maxim, "For they sow the wind, and they shall reap the whirlwind" (Hosea 8:7), is the inevitable judgment of God.

V. 2: ". . . and they that withstand shall receive to themselves judgment." The literal Greek of this clause reads, "The ones having opposed shall or will receive to themselves judgment." The present writer does not believe that this clause speaks of *eternal* judgment but that it refers to *temporal* judgment, which would be executed by the civil governments whose laws have been broken.

The Greek word, *Krima,** which is translated "judgment," means the temporal or judicial sentence which is executed upon the one disobeying the laws of the state. The Christian must obey the laws of the state so long as they do not interfere with his faith as contained in the Bible (Titus 3:1; I Peter 2:13; Colossians 3:22).

Verse 3: For rulers are not a terror to the good work, but to the evil. And wouldst thou have no fear of the power? do that which is good, and thou shalt have praise from the same. . . :

The one invested with power, the ruler, prince or magistrate, is not a terror or one to be feared by the doer of a good work or

---

Krima, or *judgment* in English. For the student of Greek, there is an exhaustive study of the word *Krima* in the *Theological Dictionary of the New Testament,* by Gerhard Kittel, published by Eerdmans. Vol. III, pages 915 to 941.

by the one who obeys the law. The person who obeys the laws
of his state does not fear the state's officials or law-enforcement
agencies. A person driving on the highway has no fear of the
highway patrolman so long as the driver is obeying the traffic
laws. To the driver who obeys, the presence of an officer of the
law is a comfort. But to the one who disobeys, an officer of the
law is one to be avoided or feared, for he is "not a terror to the
good work."

V. 3: "And wouldst thou have no fear of the power?. . ." If
you want to dispel all fear of authority, then ". . . do that which
is good, and thou shalt have praise from the same. . .": Even
according to this world's standards, where is the community that
does not respect the honest law-abiding citizen? For the Jews
and the Jewish Christians, and especially for all born-again believers during the Middle Ages (476 A.D. to the seventeenth
century), dispelling all fear of authority was not an easy attitude
to maintain. The governments of Great Britain and Europe, religious hierarchies, heads of states and magistrates, before, during and following the Protestant Reformation in the sixteenth
century, minions of all the churches, Roman Catholic, Greek
Orthodox, Russian Orthodox, and the several Protestant move-
ments, all contributed their modicum of infection in spreading the
scourge of Jew-hate throughout the world. All are alike guilty
of the slaughter of millions of Jews. It doesn't matter what segment of history one studies, the Satan-inspired plague of Jew-
hate poisons all classes. Whether it be a Pharaoh, a Nebuchadnezzar, a Haman, a Titus, a Pope of Rome, a Czar of Russia, a
Martin Luther, a Rasputin, a Hitler of Germany, a Premier of
Poland, a Martin Niemoeller, a Bishop Diebellus of Germany, an
Ernest Bevin of England, every one of them, the dead and the
living, was or is a Jew-hater, and most of them have been guilty of
shedding Jewish blood.

If Paul were writing the Epistle to the Romans today, what
could he say to present-day Jews? What could he say to the
Jewish Christians and the millions of believers who love the
Saviour and love not their own lives unto death? Can anyone
doubt what Paul's attitude would be toward modern-day anti-
Semitism?

This writer is a Jewish Christian and he cannot be blind to the
Jew-hate of today and the experiences of his people Israel through
past and present ages. He knows from his own childhood what
it means to be called "a dirty Jew." The memory of this and
other painful experiences can never be forgotten. Opprobrious

epithets, such as "Christ-killer!" and the haunting words of the Polish people, "Why don't you go to your own country?" still ring in his ears. Who can blame the Jews in Israel if they do not want the Gospel preached to them? The terrors of past persecutions, ostracisms and banishments by those who called themselves Christians but never knew the meaning of the word, make it extremely difficult for Jews in Israel, and elsewhere, to tolerate the Gospel.

Would the Apostle state, "for rulers are not a terror to the good work," if he were writing this Epistle today? Could he say this to his "kinsmen according to the flesh" and to his "brethren in the Lord," who have been the victims of "Christian" hatred and persecution throughout the centuries of "Christian" history, right up to the present day, in Germany, in Russia, in China, in Korea, in the Congo, or wherever they may be? My fellow believers, ponder these thoughts and weigh these words. They are sobering in the light of past and present world conditions.

Thank God, the believer can sing, "This world is not my home." If a believer is persecuted by his governors who are evil, God will reward His followers for their submission to revilement and ostracism for His sake. He has even promised the gift of added grace to help them to bear these trials.

Verse 4: . . . for he is a minister of God to thee for good. But if thou do that which is evil, be afraid; for he beareth not the sword in vain: for he is a minister of God, an avenger for wrath to him that doeth evil.

Rulers are supposed to be men of character, of justice, who are motivated by the highest morals and God-approved standards of conduct. A ruler is called, "a minister of God to thee for good." The word in the Greek for "minister of God" is translated "deacon" in I Timothy 3:10, 13.

V. 4: "But if thou do that which is evil," then, inevitably, there must be fear, or "be afraid." The fruit of evil is fear. "Fear is the tax that the conscience pays for guilt" (George Sewell). We get our English word "phobia" from this Greek word "fear." Hence, fear is a phobia, but the believer is to have no such phobia, for ". . . perfect love casteth out fear . . ." (I John 4:18). "The fear of Jehovah is the beginning of wisdom . . ." (Psalm 111:10). If you are possessed by fear, accept the Saviour and He will dispel your fear.

V. 4: ". . . for he beareth not the sword in vain . . .". A ruler bears the sword like an executioner. In other words, justice must be meted out and the sword of justice is the weapon provided for arresting evil and punishing it.

God uses the person in authority as the avenger of evil. There must be retributive justice for all evil. Evil must be punished. To the believer who lives a Spirit-filled life and obeys the law of the land, this text presents no problem.

Verse 5: Wherefore ye must needs be in subjection, not only because of the wrath, but also for conscience' sake.

It is obligatory for everyone in the community to "be in subjection," that is, to render obedience to the local authorities. This subjection must not only be "because of the wrath," but also for "conscience sake," as well as for the sake of propriety. In every self-respecting and law-abiding individual there is an awareness of right and wrong, or moral sense, which directs and controls his own good conduct. Every believer also possesses this moral sense and self-respect through having been born again and sanctified by the Holy Spirit, thereby separating him from among men as an upright and self-respecting person. We are saved by the grace of God as revealed in Jesus Christ. His work on the cross saved each of us from the punishment and guilt of sin. Therefore, all of us who are saved, "are his workmanship, created in Christ Jesus for good works, which God afore prepared that we should walk in them" (Ephesians 2:10). This is the compelling force in every Christian (James 2:14; I Peter 2:19; 3:14, 17).

Verse 6: For for this cause ye pay tribute also; for they are ministers of God's service, attending continually upon this very thing.

The Greek word translated "ye pay" is literally, ye accomplish, or, ye fulfill, in the sense of discharging an obligation. It is obligatory for a Christian to pay taxes. In the Old Testament taxes were included in the tithes, and when all the tithes were added up they amounted to more than thirty-three per cent of the individual's income or possessions. Tithes in the Old Testament included every obligation, such as a tithe for the Lord, a tithe for the Temple services, a tithe for widows and orphans, a tithe for the Levites, and tithes for other objects.

In our New Testament dispensation, taxes and tithes are not to be evaded, they must be paid. God's plan includes the provision for our earthly governments, therefore the Apostle adds the statement, "for they (rulers) are ministers of God's service."

Even the Lord Jesus Himself told the people to pay taxes, "Render therefore unto Caesar the things that are Caesar's . . ." (Matthew 22:21). Government officials are by God's appointment and design, and, as such, they are "attending continually upon this very thing." Bear in mind that these officials are God's ministers in a purely secular sense.

Verse 7: Render to all their dues: tribute to whom tribute is due; custom to whom custom; fear to whom fear; honor to whom honor.

This verse concludes the first section of chapter 13 which deals with the believer's obligation to his government and its magistrates.

V. 7: "Render to all their dues . . ." or, discharge all the obligations to everyone to whom you are indebted, and do not be delinquent. This paraphrase conveys the full meaning of the two Greek words translated "render" and "dues."

V. 7: ". . . tribute to whom tribute . . ."; or, fully discharge your obligations to the ones to whom you are obligated, which obligations must be discharged to their full completion. Nothing is to be omitted. This is the full meaning of the Greek word translated "tribute."

V. 7: ". . . custom to whom custom . . ." ". . . fear to whom fear . . .". The Greek word translated "fear" means reverential fear, respect, awe, terror. Its Hebrew equivalent is *yoreh*. It appears in many places in the Old Testament; the two following texts give its true meaning, Genesis 28:17 and Psalm 111:10.

To this writer verse 7, in its entirety, covers every facet of a Christian's life: He is to pay taxes to his government, he is to discharge every obligation with honesty and integrity, including honor to his parents and to his government's officers. In the phrases, "fear to whom fear" and "honor to whom honor," the Apostle is pointing out two additional aspects in a Christian's life which must not be overlooked or neglected:

(1) "Fear to whom fear." The believer is admonished to revere God with reverential awe. Why should he fear his heavenly Father, whom he is permitted to address as "Abba, Father"? (See Romans 8:15 and Galatians 4:6.) His heavenly Father has showered him with untold blessings. He is not to be afraid of God — he loves God, and is over-whelmed by God's bountiful provisions. He stands in "reverential awe" as the Lord guides him, protects him, and leads him through the vicissitudes of life here on earth. God is ever present in our

joys, in our sorrows, providing all the grace and comfort necessary for every occasion. God perfects the believer's life until He brings the believer into His heavenly presence (Philippians 1:6). For the Greek word translated "fear," see the following texts: Matthew 14:26; 28:8; Mark 4:41; Luke 1:12; and others.

(2) "Honor to whom honor." The second aspect of the believer's life that must not be overlooked — and both are part of the ten commandments — is set forth in the phrase, "honor to whom honor"; see Deuteronomy 5:16; 6:5; Matthew 19:19; 22:37; Ephesians 6:2, 3. Here is the honor due to parents. The Greek word translated "honor" means also, to value, to hold precious, as used in I Peter 1:7, 19. God most emphatically commands every child of His to "honor thy father and mother." We are to prize our parents and hold them as a precious possession. God even promises all those who obey this commandment, longevity of life (Exodus 20:12; Deuteronomy 5:16; Ephesians 6:1-3).

If a person reveres God, honors his parents and his earthly rulers, he will fulfill every obligation to God, his parents, his government and its officials. If he does not, he is not true to God, or obedient to his parents and his earthly rulers. We see a denial of God's authority and disobedience of His commandments in the history and practical application of Communism, as a result of which children betray their parents, causing many of them to be put to death. Russia stands like a sinister monument to this awful denial of faith in God. America beware!

Verse 8: Owe no man anything, save to love one another: for he that loveth his neighbor hath fulfilled the law.

The literal Greek for this verse is, "To no one owe ye anything." Paul is telling his believers in Rome, "Now that you have become Christians, pay off all your debts and satisfy all your financial obligations, and hereafter owe nothing to anyone, but to love one another."

This writer believes that to love our neighbor is a God-given love which we believers are to have for our brothers and neighbors. The Greek word translated "love" here is *agapan,* not *phileou.* It is the kind of love that God has for man and vice versa, and is therefore the kind of love that Christians are to have for their fellow believers. Could "the law" spoken of in verse 8 be that "commandment" in John 15:12? Do not actions motivated by love preach the Gospel better than words? Did not this "neighborly" love astonish those people who beheld it during the early Christian centuries and cause Tertullian, the Roman theologian, to say, "See how these Christians love one another"! The Saviour's words in John 13:34, "A new commandment I give unto you, that ye love one another," in no way invalidates the Ten Commandments. The two commandments which the Saviour gave us in Matthew 22:37-40 concerning our love for God and our neighbor are the two pivotal commandments upon which the whole Law, including the Ten Commandments, hangs. The word "law" in Romans 13:8 does not have the article "the" before it in the Greek. Even though it does not, the phrase, "hath fulfilled the law," still points to the Mosaic Law, as the following verse (9) clearly indicates by quoting some of the Ten Commandments, or Old Testament Law. The perfect tense of the Greek word for "hath fulfilled" implies that the fulfillment is already an accomplished fact by the simple act of love.

Verse 9: For this, Thou shalt not commit adultery, Thou shalt not kill, Thou shalt not steal, Thou shalt not covet, and if there be any other commandment, it is summed up in this word, namely, Thou shalt love thy neighbor as thyself.

The ninth commandment (Exodus 20:16) which appears in the King James Version of Romans 13:9, "thou shalt not bear false witness," is omitted in the American Standard Version of Romans 13:9, as it is in most of the ancient manuscripts. It is interesting to note that the only other one of the Ten Commandments not mentioned in the Epistles is the one relating to the Sabbath. This is in accord with the decision reached by the disciples at the time the Law was brought up in relation to the Gentiles who became Christians (Acts 15:19-21, 28, 29). It is also in accord with what is stated and elaborated upon in Colossians 2:16.

The Law is an excellent guidepost for a Christian's conduct in the midst of apostasy. The Law describes God's moral standards for all dispensations. God has never lowered them. Believers must obey His Word which includes the Ten Commandments. The keeping of the Law is not the prerequisite for salvation. However, it is the criterion of Christian conduct for every born-again believer, and a goal not beyond our attainment with God's help (I Peter 1:9; James 2:14, 17, 18, 20; Leviticus 11:44). We should take a closer look at a favorite passage relative to salvation, namely, Ephesians 2:8, 9. We dare not stop short of verse 10, which is the corollary of verses 8 and 9.

V. 9: "Thou shalt love thy neighbor as thyself." The Apostle states that the commandments in this verse, and by implication, all of the Ten Commandments, are "summed up" in "love thy neighbor." In other words, all the commandments of the Law are brought together in the one commandment even as God "summed up" all things in Christ (Ephesians 1:10).

As a Christian you have no rights, only duties. You have died to the world, and as a bond-slave of Christ you have only one duty, which is bearing witness in word and in deed. If you love your neighbor as yourself you will try to lead him to a saving knowledge of Christ. Who is your neighbor? Everyone! (Luke 10:29-37). The whole Law is fulfilled in the keeping of this one commandment (Galatians 5:14). The Jewish teachers and Rabbis taught that the whole Torah was a commentary on this one Law. If one wishes to separate the two tables of the Law, it might be said that the first table, bearing the commandments 1 to 5, have to do with the love and worship of God; and the second table, bearing the commandments 6 to 10, have to do with man's duty toward his fellow man.

Verse 10: Love worketh no ill to his neighbor: love therefore is the fulfillment of the law.

The mood and tense of the verb "worketh" expresses a continuous action. Love worked in the past, love works now and will continue working "no ill (evil) to his neighbor." If one loves his neighbor, he has kept the Commandments and will not covet, steal, kill or commit adultery as regards his neighbor, as enumerated in verse 9. James called the love of our neighbor, "the royal law" (2:8). See Matthew 7:12. The most wonderful and completely satisfying exegesis of love is I Corinthians 13.

Verse 11: And this, knowing the season, that already it is time for you to awake out of sleep: for now is salvation nearer to us than when we first believed.

"Knowing the season." The Greek word translated "season" does not mean time in a general sense. It means a fixed period of time, a marked season characterized by particular circumstances, a time marked by an urgent call to waken out of apathy, out of indifference, out of lethargy, out of moral and spiritual slumber. This is a clarion call to spiritual alertness.

V. 11: ". . . already it is time . . ." means *at once — now* is the hour for you to be roused out of spiritual somnolence. Why is Paul suddenly addressing his Roman believers as though they were actually asleep? Why? Because, he says, "now is salvation nearer to us than when we first believed."

How timely and much more meaningful these words are today! We who are the born-again believers in Christ have lulled ourselves into a spiritual sleep of indifference, and we refuse to be awakened. Nothing seems to move us or stir us. The world is lost. People are dying in sin. Debauchery and corruption are all about us. Time is running out, doors are being closed to missionaries, the creeping paralysis of sin is spreading itself throughout all strata of society and like the tentacles of an octopus, sin is crushing mankind to death, yet the believer refuses to be aroused to the danger. Surely this must be the Laodicean age of the Church. Christ's return is upon us. "Awake thou that sleepest!" (Ephesians 5:14; I Thessalonians 5:6). How can we sleep when the Saviour's return is so close at hand?

How can anyone say that Paul did not teach and believe in the imminent return of Christ? This is precisely what the Apostle is saying in verse 11, and verse 12 confirms it. The present period *is* the time preceding Christ's Second Coming. Who will be foolish enough to say that Paul was not a premillennarian? Every premillennarian is in good company when he believes in the imminent return of the Saviour. He has Paul on his side. Are the teachers of today better expositors of God's Word than Paul? Paul's statement in verse 11 is irrefutable. The writer of the Epistle to the Hebrews believed this statement (Hebrews 10:25) and so did Peter (I Peter 4:7). Does one need greater assurance than the testimony of these witnesses as to the certainty of the pre-tribulation Rapture and the premillennarian teaching of eschatology? This writer, a Hebrew Christian, thinks not. He believes that such a distinguished group of Hebrew "eyewitnesses and ministers of the Word" as Paul, Peter and the writer of the Epistle to the Hebrews, whom many leading Bible teachers and scholars of today believe to have been Paul — that the testimony of such a group of devout Christian believers is good enough for this writer to accept as truth concening their conviction and teaching relating to the Second Coming of Christ.

What significant meaning these prophetic words of the apostles have today for the Christian! The signs of our Lord's Second Coming are evident in every area of today's life — spiritual, physical, political, economical, social and moral. How true it is that the whole world lieth in the lap of the wicked one (I John 5:19).

Verse 12: The night is far spent, and the day is at hand: let
us therefore cast off the works of darkness, and let us put on
the armor of light.

"The night is far spent" is a figure of speech. In fact, this
verse contains three figurative expressions. Here the Apostle is
speaking of spiritual darkness. Evil always prefers to work in
the dark since the light reveals its wicked deeds. Sin is a
thief. Sin robs its victims under cover of darkness because it
dreads the light (John 3:20) and to be seen of men. Both de-
ceiver and deceived prefer the shadows.

What a warning these words of Paul in verse 12 should be to
the believer! We must not relax and give up in spiritual drowsi-
ness, but be alert and vigilant, and fully armed to protect ourselves against "the wiles of the devil," our relentless enemy
(Ephesians 6:10-17). The reason for this warning is that the
contagion of sin has made devastating inroads along every
level of society. Evil has become so bold that it is actually endeavoring to dominate our social organism and is attempting to
legalize sin. The Greek which is translated, "The night is far
spent," means that the hour is far advanced.

V. 12: ". . . and the day is at hand . . . ," meaning that the
day when the believer is to be "called out" is at hand, and that
our redemption, our translation, the resurrection of the dead in
Christ and the rapture of the saints, and that the day when all
these wonders will come to pass is drawing ever nearer and
nearer. The call is urgent, the ominous hour of the Great Tribulation is looming on the horizon, about to engulf this evil generation. The day is so close at hand that haste is imperative. It
is almost daybreak and the daystar is about to irradiate the
souls of all believers.

V. 12: ". . . let us therefore cast off the works of darkness. . . ."
Because the hour is so late, the Apostle is here urging Christians
to alter their ways of living, to "cast off" and abandon their habits of spiritual slothfulness. These are the same warnings that
the Old Testament prophets made to Israel. Paul is saying in
verse 12, "Make up your minds to live lives of dedication and
devotion to God and the Saviour. Choose now, because the
hour is late." In a similar manner spoke the prophets of
old ". . . choose you this day whom ye will serve . . ." (Joshua
24:15). Elijah challenged Israel with these words, ". . . How
long go ye limping between the two sides? if Jehovah be God,
follow him; but if Baal, then follow him" (I Kings 18:21).

The results of Israel's indifference and disobedience are written on the pages of the Old Testament as well as upon the pages of the world's history up to the present hour. The results have been frightening, the punishments terrible, and the sufferings indescribable — trials-by-fire of an innumerable host of martyrs along with the slaughter of women and children.

The God of Israel, past and present, is the very same God of believers today. His warnings are to be heeded. Israel still stands as a living reminder to every blood-bought believer of the consequences of disobedience to God even as Paul wrote to the church in Corinth, "Now these things happened unto them by way of example; and they were written for our admonition . . ." (I Corinthians 10:11). God's standards have not been lowered for this Church Age.

V. 12: ". . . let us put on the armor of light." To the Christian who has *now* "cast off the works of darkness," Paul *now* urges him to "put on the armor of light." The armor of light and the sword of the Spirit are the spiritual weapons used in combat with evil darkness. It takes the power and the weapons of an omnipotent God to be victorious over sin and Satan. God provides His children with all the essential spiritual discernment to attain holiness and righteousness (II Corinthians 6:7; I Thessalonians 5:8). He even rewards them for using the weapons He has provided with which to fight the good fight of faith (II Timothy 4:7, 8).

Will you accept this challenge? You must if you have the desire to win the rewards. Or will you face Him empty-handed?

Verse 13: Let us walk becomingly, as in the day; not in revelling and drunkenness, not in chambering and wantonness, not in strife and jealousy.

Let us as Christian believers conduct ourselves before the world, and our brethren in the faith, in such manner that our behavior will be a credit to our Christian beliefs. Thus our lives will comply with all the social standards of decency and honor. As believers our acts and decorum must reflect God's righteousness and holiness, as becomes us as His children. Therefore our acts will speak louder than our words. When we live according to God's Word, He will lead us by His Spirit into His paths of righteousness. This is a *must* in every Christian's life. God's Word will find us out.

V. 13: ". . . as in the day. . . ." Our walk must be ". . . as in the day." Everyone will see it. Sin lurks in darkness.

Evil hides in the black of the night so that it may be concealed. The person living in sin prefers the night so that his evil deeds will not be visible. Righteousness and holiness never need to be concealed. Those who possess these virtues rejoice in the sunlight and invite the scrutiny of the world. A life so illuminated is the kind of a life that glorifies God (Matthew 5:16).

There are six sins which the Apostle names specifically in verse 13:

(1) *"revelling."* The word means licentious merry-making, especially in Paul's day, when revelling took place usually in honor of some Greek or Roman deity; or it could mean any kind of inebriated brawling. (2) *"drunkenness,"* that is, occasional or habitual drunkenness on the part of one person or a group. (3) *"chambering,"* that is, promiscuous and adulterous practices between the sexes. The Greek word means defilement of the conjugal bed (Hebrews 13:4). (4) *"wantonness."* The Greek word for this means intemperance, lasciviousness, lust and lewdness (Mark 7:22). (5) *"strife."* The believer is not to quarrel or cause contention, or sow discord, or participate in wranglings. (6) *"jealousy."* Arousing envy and creating rivalries.

The sins enumerated in verse 13 are the fruits of carnality. They are the result of yielding to the flesh and seeking to satisfy its desires. The flesh is the incessant foe of the spirit and must constantly be fought against and defeated in the life of every Christian (Romans 7:23). There is no respite in this warfare. What a list of solemn warnings this verse holds for every Christian!

Verse 14: But put ye on the Lord Jesus Christ, and make not provision for the flesh, to fulfill the lusts thereof.

"But put ye on" the Lord Jesus Christ as you would put on a coat to protect yourself against inclement weather. Putting on the Lord Jesus Christ in this spiritual sense will keep the believer from nurturing and yielding to the flesh. It will keep his spiritual fervor in tune with the Lord and will keep him from succumbing to the practices of sin as enumerated in verse 13.

V. 14: ". . . make not provision for the flesh.* . . ." Do not nurture the flesh or satisfy any of its desires. If we are able to succeed in doing this, then the lusts of the flesh will be sapped

---

*For the student of Greek there is a rewarding study on the words *sarz* and *sarkikos* in both the Koine and the Classical.

of their power to tempt us. The human, or violent desires — the cupidity of the flesh — can only be subdued through the power of the Lord. The believer is urged to so engross himself with the things of God and to let his life be motivated by the Holy Spirit that he will be able to say with Paul, "For I delight in the law of God . . . so then I of myself with the mind, indeed, serve the law of God" (Romans 7:22, 25).

The Rabbis speak of "putting on the cloak of the Shekinah." The language of the Rabbis and Paul is metaphorical and expresses a great truth.

Have you dedicated and devoted your life to Christ? If not, you have missed a great blessing. Crucify the flesh and you will enjoy the true meaning of "putting on the Lord Jesus Christ."

14

Verse 1: But him that is weak in faith receive ye, yet not for decision of scruples.

In this chapter the Apostle is instructing the believers how to conduct themselves and how they should act toward their fellow believers. The one being "weak in faith" is the person who has not been "established" in the faith. He is immature, he is still a babe in Christ. His mind has not been settled as to what he believes. He may be clinging, at least in part, to his old practices. If of Jewish faith he is probably adhering to some of his old beliefs. If he came out of heathenism he may not be altogether convinced that he ought to give up all his pagan customs (I Corinthians 8:7-12). Such a "weak-in-faith" believer was to be received into the fellowship of the church but not to be given any place of authority where spiritual matters had to be decided. He was not ready for such a position.

V. 1: ". . . yet not for decision of scruples." He was not mature enough as yet to distinguish, to scrutinize, to discriminate. As yet he did not have the spiritual faculty for rendering a proper estimate of an important matter. Because he was not yet established in his faith, he was still in his spiritual adolescence and could not be expected to have the spiritual discernment to make the proper distinction between right and wrong. The Greek word for "scruples" means disputations, doubts as well as scruples. What Paul is saying is this, "Receive the immature believer kindly and hospitably, take him into your midst and befriend him, and let him become a participant in the life of the church, but don't give him an office or a place of authority until he has matured spiritually. A little knowledge and a lot of zeal are the ingredients for trouble." Wranglings ought to be avoided, as stated in Romans 13:13. The weak and immature Christian is to be given the hand of fellowship and helped to grow to spiritual maturity.

Verse 2: One man hath faith to eat all things: but he that is weak eateth herbs.

A literal rendering of this verse is, "One is of the opinion and is persuaded in his own mind to eat all things." The person who understands the Word of God and the difference between Law and Grace and believes what the Bible states, can eat everything except that which Scripture prohibits, i.e., ". . . but that we write unto them (the Gentiles) that they abstain . . . from what is strangled, and from blood" (Acts 15:20). Paul elaborates on this same thought in Colossians 2:16.

V. 2: ". . . but he that is weak eateth herbs (or vegetables)." There is a diversity of opinion and much discussion as to who is meant by the "weak." Some commentators think it was a group of vegetarians in Rome. Others think it was the Essenes who were a group of ascetic Jews who practiced celibacy and lived chiefly on vegetables which they grew themselves.

We have vegetarians in the world today. The Seventh Day Adventists are vegetarians because they do not understand the difference between Law and Grace. They refuse to accept the accomplishments of the Saviour on the cross, namely, His death, burial, resurrection and ascension, as completely satisfying all requirements for righteousness and salvation. They do not believe the Word of God, thus they are "weak" and "eat herbs." They even doubt the Saviour's own words, "Hear, and understand: Not that which entereth into the mouth defileth the man; but that which proceedeth out of the mouth, this defileth the man" (Matthew 15:10, 11). Peter was given special instructions while on the housetop at Joppa as to what he could eat. Although this vision of Peter's had a higher application, nevertheless, Peter heard a voice which said to him, "Rise, Peter; kill and eat" (Acts 10:13).

Verse 3: Let not him that eateth set at nought him that eateth not; and let not him that eateth not judge him that eateth: for God hath received him.

Or, as it could be written in literal Greek, "Let not the (one) eating despise, scorn, treat with contempt, or consider him who doesn't eat, as nothing: and let not the (one) not eating judge, censor, or pass judgment on the (one) eating: for God received him (or became associated with him) and admitted him to His (God's) society and treated him with kindness and friendship." In other words, the mature and seasoned Christian who "hath faith to eat all things," is not to treat with contempt the believer who "eateth herbs" and is weak, or ignorant, or bigoted, or someone to be looked down upon, or to be ignored as though he didn't exist. On the other hand, let them who abstain from certain foods and feel that they are still bound by particular laws and superstitions, not judge or ridicule the ones who eat everything. These two types of believers are to love one another and have fellowship because God has received both of them. We are adjured "to love the brethren." God does not look on the outer man, He looks on the heart, and, ". . . him that cometh to me I will in no wise cast out" (John 6:37). If the Saviour receives everyone who comes to Him, ought we not do the same? We all have been adopted into the family of God. Who has a right to reject one whom God has adopted?

Verse 4: Who art thou that judgest the servant of another? to his own lord he standeth or falleth. Yea, he shall be made to stand; for the Lord hath power to make him stand.

The literal Greek of this verse reads: "Who art thou (one) judging right now, the servant who is an inmate of a house or the household servant that belongs to another lord?" No one person has a right to judge or call to account, or pass judgment upon, the household servant of another. A domestic servant is responsible to his or her own master or mistress, and what he does or how he does it while in service is the concern of the master he serves.

V. 4: ". . . to his own lord he standeth or falleth." To his own master, or in his own master's judgment, he stands, or is approved, or is deemed worthy to continue in his master's service. Or, on the other hand, in his own master's sight he fails or falls short, and is censured or dismissed. It is the servant's own lord who is the one to decide the value of his servant's services, and no one else can, or has the right to, evaluate the servant of another.

V. 4: "Yea, he shall be made to stand. . . ." The Greek structure of the verb *shall be made* is such that the action does not originate in the servant but that the power to stand comes from someone else. The Greek verb is in the future tense, indicative mood and passive voice. The second clause of the verse next following explains definitely Who the Person is that supplies the power.

V. 4: ". . . for the Lord hath power to make him stand." This servant, and the Greek word for servant means a household servant, is the kind of servant who is taken into the home; and which, by the way, beautifully expresses the position of the believer in the household of God — a servant who lives with the family. It is the Lord, as Master of this servant, Who has the power right now to make this servant of His to stand. God's purpose in the exercise of this power is twofold: (1) To demonstrate His omnipotence and sovereignty; and (2) to make His household servant strong enough to stand. Thank God, the believer never need rely upon his "weak flesh" to enable him *to stand* in the presence of his Master as one who is approved (Philippians 1:6).

Do you know the Master? He is the Lord Jesus Christ. Have you accepted Him? Now is the time. Tomorrow may be too late.

Verse 5: One man esteemeth one day above another: another esteemeth every day alike. Let each man be fully assured in his own mind.

There is no necessity to go into detail to explain this verse. Colossians 2:16 is a good commentary and an elaboration of its meaning. What difference do days make in the life of a Christian? None. Ash Wednesday, Maundy Thursday, Lent, are Roman Catholic innovations. In Israel church services are conducted on Saturday and everyone works on Sunday, thereby compelling Christians to work on Sunday. How foolish it would be for Christians elsewhere in the world to censure or condemn the Israeli Christians because they are in church on Saturday. This does not make them Seventh Day Adventists!

The Apostle in this chapter of Romans (14) is instructing weak Christians not to criticize mature Christians, and vice versa. Each one must be "fully assured in his own mind," and must not force others to conform to his convictions. We must practice what we believe without trying to make our convictions the standard for others. Let each of us "be fully assured," or "fully convinced," of our own beliefs and tolerate the beliefs of others. After all, the observance of a particular day, or days, does not determine one's salvation. It is possible that Paul might have been endeavoring to persuade his fellow Jewish Christians not to try to force the observance of the Jewish holy days and fasts upon the Gentile Christians. However, pagan religions also have holy days, or special days. The Roman pagans had a feast called Saturnalia which was celebrated during the month of December, and it was this feast which gave birth to the idea that developed into Christmas. Observing this or that holy day

is not a doctrinal question and is irrelevant to the question of
salvation. The cross, the Saviour, His blood, is resurrection, His
ascension — these are matters pertaining to salvation which cannot and must not be compromised. Days, feasts, fasts, holy
days, are meaningless in the light of the cross.

Some expositors go to great lengths in discussing holy days
and speak of the "Christian Sabbath." The Lord's Day is *not*
the Sabbath. We observe the Lord's Day to commemorate His
resurrection. There is no such day as a "Christian Sabbath" in
the Bible. For Christians there is no Sabbath Day on this earth.
The Christian Sabbath will be in glory, as referred to in Psalm
23:6, "And I will dwell in the house of Jehovah for ever," in
which the word "dwell" has reference to the Sabbath of rest,
and may be translated as follows: ". . . and I will sabbath in the
house of Jehovah all the days of my life," or "to the length of
days."

In this life on earth the Christian does not sabbath. He is constantly moving onward and upward in his pilgrimage towards
his heavenly mansion and must be continuously witnessing to
the saving grace of God through Jesus Christ. The Christian is
commanded to "Go, Preach, Baptize, Teach!"

Have you obeyed our Saviour's orders? Examine your heart
and life!

**Verse 6: He that regardeth the day, regardeth it unto the
Lord: and he that eateth, eateth unto the Lord, for he giveth
God thanks; and he that eateth not, unto the Lord he eateth
not, and giveth God thanks.**

The King James Version reads, "He that regardeth the day, regardeth it unto the Lord; *and he that regardeth not the day, to
the Lord he doth not regard it.*" The last two clauses of this
verse, printed here in italic type, are omitted in the American
Standard Version, as they are omitted in the Sinaitic, the Vatican, and the Alexandrine MSS. The first two clauses if translated literally would read, "The one minding the day minds it to
the Lord."

We must always keep in mind the special relationship between "the day" and "the Lord." There is a vast difference
between the two. It is only because of what the Lord Jesus
Christ accomplished on the cross and by His resurrection from
the grave on Sunday that make Sunday a special day for the
believer. However, it is wrong for the Christian to demand that
the non-Christian observe Sunday. What does Christ and His

resurrection mean to a follower of Confucius, to a Moslem, to a Jew? Nothing! Why should a non-Christian be made to conform to the convictions of a Christian?

V. 6: ". . . and he that eateth, eateth unto the Lord, for he giveth God thanks. . . ." Translating the Greek literally, this reads, "and the (one) eating he eats and continues to eat to the Lord, for he giveth thanks to God." That is to say, the one who is eating should so continue eating and giving thanks to God for what he is eating. One must always glorify God in what he is doing. Actions many times speak louder than words.

Abstaining from certain foods or eating certain foods does not make us better Christians in the sight of God. "But food will not commend us to God: neither, if we eat not, are we the worse; nor, if we eat, are we the better" (I Corinthians 8:8). Whatever we do or do not do, we must not be a stumblingblock to others (I Corinthians 8:9-13). "All things are lawful for me; but not all things are expedient" (I Corinthians 6:12). No matter what one does, he should "be fully assured in his own mind" (Romans 14:5) that he is in God's will according to God's Word.

Verse 7: For none of us liveth to himself, and none dieth to himself.

The Apostle is enlarging upon what he has written in the preceding verse (v. 6). A person can never completely disentangle himself from God or man. Our background, our environment, our own families, all have had a part in molding each of us. We are what we are today because of what we were yesterday. The future is determined by what we did in the past. We are today a mixture of our ancestors. A person cannot dissociate himself from his family tree any more than a branch can dissociate itself from a tree. All of us are the offspring of our forefathers. We cannot separate ourselves from our present society. Life is not an island. We do not live for ourselves and within ourselves, but we are in the midst of people and are part-and-parcel with them. And we influence others just as others influence us. We cannot escape from others any more than we can escape from ourselves. But we can *insulate* ourselves against the sinful practices of the world. Still we must not *isolate* ourselves from worldlings.

We cannot escape the future. The adage, "Tomorrow never comes," is the biggest lie the Devil ever concocted. Tomorrow always comes! Just as sure as the sun shines, just as sure will

tomorrow come. "Cast thy bread upon the face of the waters;
for thou shalt find it after many days" (Ecclesiastes 11:1).
". . . know ye your sin will find you out" (Numbers 32:23,
Literal). This is true for saint and sinner alike. Because the
future is inescapable, we must make provision for the future. A
person does not live or die to himself. The Bible states, "And
as it is appointed unto men once to die, and after this the judgment" (Hebrews 9:27 KJV). Physical death and judgment are
inevitable. Every sinner dies separated eternally from God,
unless that sinner's life has been one pleasing to God. Without
the proper faith in the plan, program, and the Person whom
God has sent, it is impossible to please Him (Hebrews 11:6).
A person may think that he can develop a system whereby he
can obtain righteousness, but this is catastrophic and ends in
death (Proverbs 14:12; 16:25).

There is only one way to escape eternal separation from God,
and that is by accepting the method and the means that God
has provided, namely, ". . . He that honoreth not the Son honoreth not the Father that sent him. Verily, verily, I say unto
you, He that heareth my word, and believeth him that sent me,
hath eternal life, and cometh not into judgment, but hath passed
out of death into life" (John 5:23, 24).

Dear reader, you need not die to yourself. The Saviour invites you. He is "the way, the truth, and the life" (John 14:6).
Will you accept Him? The choice is yours.

**Verse 8: For whether we live, we live unto the Lord; or
whether we die, we die unto the Lord: whether we live therefore, or die, we are the Lord's.**

This is an elaboration of the preceding verse (7). The negative
is stated in verse 7, the positive in verse 8. What comfort these
words bring to every believing child of God! Once we are born
into the family of God through our Lord Jesus Christ, we are
never separated from God in life or in death. We are His everlasting possession. For the Christian, death is not the yawning
chasm that separates him from God; it is the door that leads
into everlasting life and into the presence of God and the Saviour.
In every sense of the word the born-again believing child of
God is always in His presence. God never leaves him to live in
loneliness or to die unattended. Christ has promised never to
leave or forsake His followers. The Psalmist states it beautifully
in Psalm 139:1-18. The deepest chasm, the highest mountain,
the immeasureable depths of the sea, are not out of God's sight.

Neither can the darkness of death hide the believer from His presence. His God follows him all the days of his life and ultimately brings him into the mansions of glory (Psalm 23; Romans 8:38, 39).

Since this is so, the believer must live a life that will magnify and glorify God and the Saviour. The Holy Spirit is the energizer and motivator of that life which is holy and completely dependent upon Him. The believer is not the master of his own ship of life, nor is he the captain of his own soul. God the Father has bought the believer with the blood of the Lord Jesus Christ, and the believer has become the possession of God (I Corinthians 6:19, 20).

Do you know Him? Have you accepted Him? He stands at your heart's door. Will you invite Him in?

Verse 9: For to this end Christ died and lived again, that he might be Lord of both the dead and the living.

Or, "For this end Christ died and became alive." The death of Christ was the accepted sin-offering in God's sight. His resurrection brought to pass the justification of the believer (Romans 4:25). Because He "died and lived again," He is now Lord of "both the dead and the living."

In other words, the death of Christ and His resurrection was the fulfillment of God's purpose that the Saviour might become the Lord over the dead and the living, ". . . he humbled himself, becoming obedient unto death . . . Wherefore also God highly exalted him (by his resurrection and ascension), and gave unto him the name (Lord) which is above every name, that in the name of Jesus every knee should bow . . . and that every tongue should confess that Jesus Christ is Lord, to the glory of God the Father" (Philippians 2:8-11).

Verse 10: But thou, why dost thou judge thy brother? or thou again, why dost thou set at nought thy brother? for we shall all stand before the judgment-seat of God.

The Apostle asks, "Why judgest thou thy brother?" This same question can be addressed to each of us. Do we not judge? Do we not assume censorial power toward our brothers? At times, do we not make distinctions among Christians and question the nature or extent of their salvation? The Apostle pursues the questioning by asking, "And why do you treat with contempt and scorn, why do you despise, neglect and disregard your brother?" (Literal.)

The thoughts expressed in these words reflect the shameful weaknesses in the conduct of many of today's Christians. No artist could paint a truer picture of the all-too-prevalent nature of present-day Christianity than the picture reflected in verse 10. What open condemnations and scathing accusations are all too often heard in many Christian circles today against other Christians! How mean, how uncharitable, how condemnatory are the criticisms, implied and openly expressed, about the known or imagined misconduct of other Christians! Paul was no doubt confronted with this situation among the Christians of his day, but then he did not have what we have today, namely, the complete revelation of God. We should know better. The true blood-bought believing Church of Jesus Christ is today in her maturity and she need not falter in her faith and walk. There can be no excuse for the kind of weak-kneed Christianity that Paul refers to in verse 10, not only weak-kneed but hypocritical. The pleading words of the Saviour are drowned out in the bedlam of personal animosities and incriminations. The world is dying because of hate, and Christianity is in danger of losing her testimony in her neglect of Christ's commandments (Matthew 22:37-40), and, "This is my commandment, that ye love one another, even as I have loved you" (John 15:12, 13).

The importance of the two phrases in Romans 14:10, "But thou," and "or thou again," must not be overlooked. Each of these phrases is like a finger of accusation pointing to the individual believer by sharply emphasizing his disobedience of the Saviour's commandments to love one another. The faltering Christian derides, accuses, condemns. The Saviour loves, forgives, cleanses. What a contrast! Let each of us examine ourselves. It is better to do this behind the shut door of our inner chamber (Matthew 6:6) rather than in the presence of men or the hosts of heaven (I Corinthians 3:12-15).

V. 10: ". . . for we shall all stand before the judgment-seat of God." The Sinaitic, the Vatican, the Alexandrine and the Nestle's MSS. have the word "God" instead of the word "Christ," as it is in the King James Version. We shall all have to give an account of the deeds done in the flesh. We are all going to have to stand and be present before the judgment-seat of God. The word in the Greek for "judgment-seat" is *bema*. The fact that the word "God" is used in the American Standard Version and the ancient MSS. instead of "Christ," as it is in the King James Version, presents no difficulty. Is Christ not God incarnate? Is Christ not as much God as the Father or the Holy Spirit? Each Person in the Trinity is equal. Who can fully explain the Trinity in human speech? It is the mystery of the Godhead and in Christ is the fulness of that Godhead (Colossians 2:9).

We are not to judge our brothers. All judgment has been entrusted to Christ before whom the whole world will stand (John 5:22; Matthew 25:31-46; Acts 17:31; I Corinthians 3:13-15; Zechariah 12:1-10). Each of us shall be judged and we are not to usurp the prerogative to judge which belongs to Christ alone.

Verse 11: For it is written, As I live, saith the Lord, to me every knee shall bow, And every tongue shall confess to God.

This verse is a quotation from Isaiah 45:23 with but little variation, and is a prediction of the universal reign of the Messiah. Though the Apostle looks forward to that day, he applies the truth of it to the present-day life of the Christian. He also adds the very strong words, "As I live," which give special emphasis to the Isaiah text. The full meaning of this text is in Philippians 2:6-11.

The Jewish teachers taught this passage of Isaiah as a prediction of the reign of the Messiah in the "latter days," when the Davidic throne shall be set up in Jerusalem and Israel shall be regathered and restored.

Verse 12: So then each one of us shall give account of himself to God.

Every believer shall give a report, an account, a reckoning, of what he has done. This report will be "concerning himself." This is the reason that the Apostle warns and admonishes the Christian not to judge a brother. We shall have to stand before the tribunal of God. There is no escape from this divine Court of Justice. God is the Eternal Bookkeeper and there can be no juggling of His books. The fact that each of us must give an account of himself to God contains a measure of comfort for the Christian because the divine judgment upon our works will not alter God's position toward His child who has been given eternal life. He shall stand before the heavenly Tribunal with Christ as his Advocate.

Do you know Him? Have you accepted this Advocate?

Verse 13: Let us not therefore judge one another any more: but judge ye this rather, that no man put a stumbling block in his brother's way, or an occasion of falling.

Obedience to this commandment against judging one another is imperative even now. Therefore, let us refrain at once from judging or passing judgment on one another. Let not the strong brother who is established in the faith condemn the weak brother, and vice versa. Censorious actions are to be avoided by both classes of Christians, since all Christians are responsible to God alone.

It is interesting to note in passing how carefully God instructs His followers. He never tells His children what they *should not do* that He does not tell them what *they should do* (Psalm 1). If a Christian follows the admonition of God and proceeds to do what God expects of him, he will never have time to do wrong. The person who is busy serving God does not even have the time to consider what God reckons to be wrong. He is too preoccupied with God's work.

V. 13: The believer must be careful not to "put a stumbling block in his brother's way." The Greek word translated "stumbling block" is used figuratively. Paul is saying that the believer must not do anything that would give his brother "an occasion for falling." No doubt, Paul had in mind the words of the Lord in Matthew 18:6. The Apostle discusses this more fully in I Corinthians 8:9. The Greek word translated "occasion for falling" also means to set a trap or to give offense. We get our English word "scandal" from this Greek word. A Christian must avoid even the very appearance of evil lest it become a stumbling block (I Thessalonians 5:22 KJV).

Verse 14: I know, and am persuaded in the Lord Jesus, that nothing is unclean of itself: save that to him who accounteth anything to be unclean, to him it is unclean.

The word, "am persuaded," in the Greek is better translated, "have been persuaded." The Apostle did not arrive at this decision while he was in the process of writing this Epistle. He was confident of this truth sometime before. However, because there is *liberty* in Christ, there is no such thing as *license*. In Christ "All things are lawful; but not all things edify" (I Corinthians 10:23; 6:12). The Apostle did not arrive at this conclusion as the result of his own reasoning. It is an eternal principle, enunciated by Paul and inspired by the Lord Jesus Christ.

V. 14: ". . . to him who accounteth anything to be unclean, to him it is unclean." It is possible that Paul was addressing this advice to the "weak brethren," both Jews and Gentiles. These weak Christians who came out of paganism and legalism were not fully established in the faith. The treatment of these weak brethren was discussed at the meeting in Jerusalem (Acts 15:1-21). The Apostle had this problem of eating meat offered to idols with the weak brethren at Corinth (I Corinthians 8:1-13). The conclusion arrived at in both cases was through the leadership of the Holy Spirit and in Christ. In Christ nothing is unclean. However, to a "weak" brother, this may prove to be an "occasion for falling." So then, "to him it is unclean." This does not mean that either one of the brethren can go to extremes of either eating or abstaining. It is better to be a stepping stone to Christ than a stumbling stone, ". . . for ye were bought with a price: glorify God therefore in your body" (I Corinthians 6:20).

Verse 15: For if because of meat thy brother is grieved, thou walkest no longer in love. Destroy not with thy meat him for whom Christ died.

The Greek word translated "meat" does not mean meat only but rather any food. Just because someone may object to a Christian eating meat, does not necessarily mean that one must become a vegetarian. This is not what verse 15 states, nor does taking this text literally mean that one must refrain from eating any kind of meat and use liquids only (Galatians 5:1). If a Christian, Jewish or Gentile, is working and eating with unsaved Jews and eats pork, that would be a stumbling block to the Jews, in which case one must stop eating pork. If meat offered to idols was a stumbling block to the "weak" Christians at Corinth who had just come out of paganism, then Paul refrained from eating this sort of meat. If a certain practice offends a brother, the Apostle states that the one causing this offense, or distress, or feeling of pain, is no longer walking in the love that God is showering upon him. A Christian must not vex a brother. No personal satisfaction is worth the inflicting of sorrow upon a Christian brother in the matter of eating, or declining to eat, one kind of food or another.

V. 15: "Destroy not with thy meat him for whom Christ died." "Destroy not with your food him on whose behalf Christ died" (Romans 16:18). The liberty that the believer has in Christ must not be abused to the extent that it might endanger a soul or destroy the work of the Gospel. Abusing our liberty in Christ is hardly worth such a price. We should not live to eat but rather eat to live and not to make a god of our belly (Philippians 3:19).

If Christ gave His life for us, ought we not be more than willing to give up a certain practice, habit, or kind of food, for the sake of peace among the brethren? Since this chapter (14) is addressed to Christians and concerns our testimony among Christians, the words, ". . . if . . . thy brother is grieved, thou walkest no longer in love," does not make verse 15 mean that a Christian's salvation can be destroyed. Salvation cannot be lost any more than an egg can be unscrambled. What the Apostle is saying is, "Do not destroy the peace of heart and mind of your brother by vexing him with the liberty you possess in Christ." If you love the Lord, you should love the brethren and refrain from doing anything that would grieve them (John 15:12, 17; Hebrews 13:1; I Peter 1:22; I John 3:23; 4:7, 11, 12, 20, 21).

Verse 16: Let not then your good be evil spoken of . . . :

Let not the liberty and goodness you have in Christ be blasphemed. The English word "blaspheme" is a transliteration of the Greek word for "evil spoken of." Do not let your Christian liberty become so repulsive to your brother that it will be as blasphemy to him. Christian freedom does not override or walk on the freedom of others. What griefs, what heartaches, how many schisms could be avoided if every Christian observed and obeyed the admonition contained in verse 16! Let us so dedicate our lives that we may all become living epistles of the love of God. Let us so love one another that worldlings will become envious (I Corinthians 10:28-33). We are free to serve Christ and free to refrain from sin. This is true freedom in Christ.

Verse 17: . . . for the kingdom of God is not eating and drinking, but righteousness and peace and joy in the Holy Spirit.

The kingdom of God is entered into by faith, not formalism, or the observance of outward forms such as baptism, or eating certain foods and abstaining from eating others. Let us make sure that faith never gives place to formalism or that contrition and gratitude ever give place to cold ceremony. When the spiritual aspect (repentance) of the kingdom lost its entire meaning in the earthly and physical deliverance of the nation, then Israel lost sight of her mission to the world as recorded in Isaiah 61:6. Israel failed to recognize the true marks and meaning of the Messiah, His office, His message, His nature (Luke 19:44c) when her leaders brought Him before Pilate the Roman governor and shouted, "Crucify him! . . . we have no king but Caesar!" (John 19:15). Israel at that time had no comprehension of the universality of the Messiah's kingdom and in her blindness still fails to grasp the concept of a universal theocratic kingdom which cannot be confined to the physical limits of a sliver of soil called the Holy Land. If Jehovah is to be "the Lord of lords," then His Messiah must be "King of kings." (I Timothy 6:15; Revelation 17:14).

This is not the place nor is it the purpose of this writer to write a treatise on the "Kingdom of God." The reader can study for himself Matthew 19 where the terms "Kingdom of God," "Kingdom of heaven," "eternal life," "saved," and "everlasting life," appear in this chapter.

The kingdom of God does not stand or fall, nor is it occupied with eating and drinking. God does not look upon a person's digestive system to determine a man's destiny. The Lord Himself said, "Perceive ye not, that whatsoever goeth into the mouth passeth into the belly, and is cast out into the draught? But the things which proceed out of the mouth come forth out of the heart; and they defile the man" (Matthew 15:17, 18; also verse 11). God always looks on the heart (I Corinthians 4:20; 8:8; Hebrews 9:10; 13:9). Eating and drinking or the abstention from eating and drinking certain foods is not serving God (Colossians 2:16).

V. 17: ". . . but righteousness and peace and joy in the Holy Spirit." The Holy Spirit always instills righteousness and brings joy and peace. These three attributes are evidences of a Christian life and are "the fruit of the Spirit" described in Galatians 5:22, 23; Ephesians 5:9.

Righteousness, peace and joy manifest themselves in our lives not necessarily through our earthly possessions, our worldly accomplishments and the number of our influential friends in the world (Luke 6:26). Earthly possessions always bring problems and difficulties. Wealth and happiness are not synonymous. Righteousness, peace and joy are ours because of the love of God which has been shed abroad in the hearts of believers, and because of our gratitude to God for His Son and His love. This gratitude is expressed in the believer's life through the Holy Spirit.

The believer has peace with God and joy in fellowship with God. The believer also has peace and joy in fellowship with other believers. Nothing gladdens the hearts of believers more than the fellowship of believers when gathered around the Word and guided by the Holy Spirit.

Do you have this peace of God and joy in Him? The Saviour said, "Peace I leave with you; my peace I give unto you." Again, He said, ". . . that my joy may be in you, and that your joy may be made full" (John 14:27; 15:11). Will you receive Him who alone can give you joy and peace?

Verse 18: For he that herein serveth Christ is well-pleasing to God, and approved of men.

Or, as it might be equally well translated, "For (one) thus in serving Christ is well-pleasing to God." There is only one way to please God the Father and that is in serving Christ, "This is my beloved Son, in whom I am well pleased" (Matthew 3:17). When one is serving Christ, such service is always in righteousness. In fact, serving Christ *is* righteousness. There can be no greater joy and peace than when we are in the service of Christ and led by the Holy Spirit. This is well-pleasing to God.

Note in passing that the Apostle changes from Christ to God and from God to Christ. To the Apostle Christ is God and God is incarnate in Christ. Paul never loses sight of this cardinal doctrine of the deity of Christ. Neither should we.

V. 18: ". . . and approved of men." The Greek word translated "approved" means approved after examination and trial. What contrast there is between verse 16 and this phrase in verse 18! To stand approved of men after careful scrutiny is to be approved of God (II Corinthians 10:18; II Timothy 2:15). Even worldlings will respect men who serve God and righteousness in word and deed. "So shalt thou find favor and good understanding in the sight of God and men" (Proverbs 3:4; Luke 2:52).

Verse 19: So then let us follow after things which make for peace, and things whereby we may edify one another.

Or, "Let us make every effort and pursue by all means to obtain peace and harmony." "Behold, how good and pleasant it is for brethren to dwell in unity!" (Psalm 133:1; also Psalm 34:14).

We live in a turbulent world, torn by strife and hatred, war and bloodshed, vice and hypocrisy; in the midst of a people with broken hearts, lives and minds, in the midst of perversity, persecution and privation, with devastations looming on our horizon. The Christian is the only one who has the message of peace. The Gospel alone can mend broken hearts, quiet troubled minds, dry bitter tears and heal torn bodies. How needful is the Gospel today!

There is an Old Testament parallel to the present state of our world and the Christian now living in the midst of it. Over 2,500 years ago the prophet Jeremiah was living in Jerusalem under conditions just as bad as, if not worse than, those of today. Judah had her false prophets and perverted priests, and the distorted teachings of her scribes. Her rulers were misled and seeking self-aggrandizement. Jeremiah asked, "Is there no balm in Gilead? is there no physician there? . . ." (8:22).

Today, thank God, we have the "balm" of the Gospel and the living presence of the Great Physician in this troubled world. Are we taking Him to sinful men? We shall have to give an account. There is no escape!

V. 19: ". . . and things whereby we may edify one another." If we live peaceably with our brethren we will pursue every effort for spiritual advancement and the things whereby we may edify one another (Jude 20; I Corinthians 14:26; I Thessalonians 5:11). In Romans 14:19 the Christian is urged to make every effort to promote peace, and to use every means at his disposal to help his fellow Christian to reach spiritual maturity, which is the fruit of edification.

Verse 20: Overthrow not for meat's sake the work of God. All things indeed are clean; howbeit it is evil for that man who eateth with offence.

Or, literally, "do not tear down, like tearing down a building, the work and the course of God's workings for the sake of food."

V. 20: ". . . howbeit it is evil for that man who eateth with offence." This could have been addressed to the "strong" brother, the one established in the faith, who felt that it was proper for him to eat anything because he had obtained freedom in Christ, and therefore it did not matter what anyone thought, and who did not think it wrong for him to eat what he pleased. However, a brother established in the faith must not flaunt the freedom which he has in Christ in the face of a weak brother.

The Apostle is saying in verse 20 that he who "eateth with offence" has a wrong attitude and is following a wrong course of action. Paul is elaborating here on what he has stated in verses 13 and 15. The strong brother who eats, or insists that he can eat anything, is putting a stumbling block in the path of his weak brother. We must edify one another and never hinder anyone in his Christian life. The Greek word translated "offence" in verse 20 is the same word which is translated "stumbling block" in verse 13.

This whole warning against "eating with offence" has great ramifications in hindering a brother. Indeed, "eating with offence" can hinder the work of the whole church. It can cause divisions in the church and thereby hinder the church's program of evangelism and sidetrack the minds of its members by causing them to quarrel over food which can or cannot be eaten. How foolish this all seems when God has paid such a colossal price for our redemption in the gift of His Son, compared with the discussions over what to eat and what not to eat seem picayunish, and are apt to become stumbling blocks. Can the work of God in the Church of Christ be compared with food for the human body? It is fatal to do anything that hinders God's work. God calls us to peace but carnality engenders strife. The peace of God is the only "balm of Gilead" that will heal the restlessness of the flesh.

Verse 21: It is good not to eat flesh, nor to drink wine, nor to do anything whereby thy brother stumbleth.

The words, "or is offended, or is made weak," in the King James Version, are omitted in some older MSS., and do not appear in the Nestle's text which this writer is using.

It is wrong to assume from this verse (21) that Paul is urging the believers in Rome to become vegetarians. On the contrary, he is using his strongest arguments to show to what extent we must go in order not to hinder God's work among our brethren. We are not our own (I Corinthians 6:19, 20), therefore, every act of the believer must glorify God. How can one thank God for his food when this very food is a stumbling block to a fellow believer? (I Corinthians 10:30–11:1; II Corinthians 6:3). The Apostle is urging the saints at Rome not to hinder our brother's growth nor to hinder the Gospel.

If Christ was willing to become man, to suffer and endure shame and pain on the Cross in order to save us, ought we not to be more than willing to give up anything for Him? He gave up even His life for us. Ponder these words. They will bring you to your knees!

Verse 22: The faith which thou hast, have thou to thyself before God. Happy is he that judgeth not himself in that which he approveth.

The Apostle is saying to the one strong in the faith, "Do not boast of your faith and freedom in the presence of those who are not as strong as you are. Do your boasting and thanksgiving to God for what He has given you in your own privacy." We should rejoice in the very deep things of God, if we rightfully understand them. We must never boast about our knowledge in the presence of "babes" in Christ. The Apostle is not talking about faith in the Lord Jesus Christ as Lord and Saviour, which is a truth which must be proclaimed everywhere and at all times, under all conditions. We must so live our daily lives as if we were living in the very presence of God. We must use whatever God has given us as though He were watching our every move. The one possessing this kind of faith with firm convictions and firm assurance that what he believes is biblical, must not use it in any way that would hinder a brother.

V. 22: "Happy is he that judgeth not himself in that which he approveth." It is a wonderful assurance to know that what one does is right in God's sight (I Peter 1:7). One must be sure he does not himself practice what he condemns in others. Happy and blessed is the man who does not act contrary to his convictions about his food, whether to eat or not to eat. The best commentary on this matter is Colossians 1:9-16. This should settle the question and the meaning of Romans 14:22.

Verse 23: But he that doubteth is condemned if he eat, because he eateth not of faith; and whatsoever is not of faith is sin.

"But the (one) doubting, distinguishing, discriminating and hesitating whether to eat the food before him or not, if he eats has been condemned" (Literal). This person, if he eats, falls under the punitive measures of God. If his faith were strong, he would not be dubious about eating. To doubt is not a Christian attribute.

V. 23: ". . . and whatsoever is not of faith is sin." Everything which is not done with a clear conscience is sin. Doubt is on the borderline of agnosticism. If one studies the Word of God, he can know what is right and wrong. He need not doubt, and if he does, it is sin because he does not believe the Word of God.

Again, it should be stated here that verse 23 does not speak of salvation. It is dealing with the lives of Christians as they live day by day. Salvation is a permanently settled matter when a person accepts Christ as Lord and Saviour. Salvation is a completed act wrought by God Himself through the Lord Jesus

Christ upon the believer who is then thereafter permanently indwelt by the Holy Spirit. This relationship with God can never be altered any more than yesterday can be brought back into existence tomorrow.

We must exemplify Christianity and the meaning of the Gospel in our daily lives. We must constantly progress in our Christian maturity and behavior. It is needless for us to fret about our dead yesterdays. Let us press on to capture our living tomorrows, ". . . forgetting the things which are behind, and stretching forward to the things which are before, I press on toward the goal unto the prize of the high calling of God in Christ Jesus" (Philippians 3:13, 14).

What sort of a life are you living? Is it filled with fears and doubts? Surrender to the Saviour and He will grant you full assurance and give you peace.

15

Verse 1: Now we that are strong ought to bear the infirmities of the weak, and not to please ourselves.

Or, to translate the Greek literally, "We who are the established ones, confirmed and fully grounded in the faith (II Corinthians 12:10; 13:9), are obligated to continue to bear the infirmities of the ones (Christians, or 'babes in Christ') who are not fully established in their faith and must be helped."

The Greek word for "strong" in verse 1 does not mean politically or physically strong, but rather morally strong. The strong Christian must always help the weak Christian. The strong Christian must bear the weak Christian as one bears a burden. This duty to help must be inspired by the love of God which has been shed abroad in the hearts of all believers. Even in the world the widows, orphans, the poor, the sick and the disabled, are generally cared for, at least in part, by the communities in which they live. Therefore, if sympathy for the unfortunate and improvident members of a community leads the more fortunate folk of the same community to help them with gifts, so all the more ought the strong Christians help the weak brethren in their Christian living. This should be a privilege rather than a burden. "Bear ye one another's burdens, and so fulfill the law of Christ" (Galatians 6:2).

We are to bear the burdens of the weak in a figurative sense even as Christ bore the cross in a literal sense (John 19:17). This same Greek word for "bear" also appears in Luke 14:27, where it is used figuratively. Matthew uses this same word in 8:17 in quoting Isaiah 53:4. As Christ bore our sins, so we, who are the strong, must bear the weaknesses of our weaker brethren. This is a duty incumbent upon the mature Christian.

V. 1: ". . . and not to please ourselves." We should be willing to deny ourselves the many freedoms that Christ affords His followers in order not to offend the weak brethren, which is consistent Christian conduct. Christian principles are based upon the most important of all principles, namely, love (I Corinthians 10:23). Paul offers himself as an example of a mature Christian in this belief and behavior by seeking to "please all men in all things, not seeking mine own profit, but the profit of the many." A Christian cannot live for himself alone.

Verse 2: Let each one of us please his neighbor for that which is good, unto edifying.

Which is to say, let each one of us continue to make an effort to please our neighbor unto edifying. The Greek word for "good" carries a specific meaning, whereas the English word can mean anything from a "good" man to a "good" time. The Greek word for good as used in the context of verse 2 means not only good but also beneficent, upright, virtuous.

We should not lose sight of the truth that this "pleasing" of a neighbor must be for his spiritual advancement to the end that our neighbor may be more firmly entrenched and established in the Christian faith. A Christian cannot please his neighbor if he compromises his own Christian principles. We are all to live peaceably with all men "if it be possible." (See comments on Romans 12:18; 14:19. Also compare I Corinthians 10:33 with I Corinthians 9:22; 10:23; II Corinthians 13:9).

To this writer verse 2 is another clarion call for true Christian separation. A Christian must stand firm in his faith and constantly seek to please God rather than men. A believer cannot vacillate in his behavior. He must live a life of holiness and righteousness, always seeking to please God and striving to exemplify the Gospel in his every act and deed. This can only be done through the energizing power of the Holy Spirit. Pusillanimous and irresolute Christian living is a stench not only in the nostrils of God but of men as well. The classic example of the world's demand for the Christian to compromise his stand and message is the example of Peter and John, ". . . whether it is right in the sight of God to hearken unto you rather than unto God, judge ye: for we cannot but speak of the things which we saw and heard" (Acts 4:19, 20). A Christian cannot and must not please all men in the sense of Galatians 1:10. "Woe unto you, when all men shall speak well of you" (Luke 6:26). These words were spoken by the Saviour. My fellow Christians, take heed how you live!

Liberalism and modernism are the implacable foes of Christ and His Gospel. Their tenets are specious and incompatible with the truth of God's Word. False teaching and truth cannot coexist. If Paul meant anything at all by his words, "Come ye out from among them, and be ye separate, saith the Lord" (II Corinthians 6:17; Isaiah 52:11), he meant that a Christian cannot worship in a liberal, Christ-rejecting, Scripture-denying and worldly-practicing church. The Apostle John states the same truth in different words in I John 2:18, 19.

God requested separation of Israel when they came out of Egypt, and Israel refused (Exodus 12:38). God continued to make that same request and Israel has continued in her adamant refusal and is plunging into catastrophe after catastrophe (Isaiah 48:20; 52:11; Jeremiah 50:8; 51:6, 45; Zechariah 2:6, 7). God will use the relentless force of persecution to drive Israel out from among the Gentile nations (Ezekiel 20:33-38; Joel 3; Zechariah 12; Revelation 18:4).

There is a great lesson which the Christian should learn from Israel's long history of willfulness and disobedience. If a Christian refuses to heed this warning, the consequences can prove to be just as catastrophic (I Corinthians 10:5, 6).

Whom are you trying to please, God or man? Search your heart.

Verse 3: For Christ also pleased not himself; but, as it is written, The reproaches of them that reproached thee fell upon me.

The Apostle is quoting a Messianic prophecy of the first advent of Christ, "The reproaches of them, or the ones reproaching thee, fell on me" (Psalm 69:9 Septuagint).

As Christ bore the sin and the reproach of sin for the sinner, so each one of us must bear the reproach of our fellow-Christians. Christ was willing to suffer this reproach because of the end-result, namely, ". . . looking unto Jesus the author and perfector of our faith, who for the joy that was set before him endured the cross, despising shame, and hath sat down at the right hand of the throne of God" (Hebrews 12:2); "I gave my back to the smiters, and my cheeks to them that plucked off the hair; I hid not my face from shame and spitting" (Isaiah 50:6; 53:5). See also Philippians 2:6-8; Hebrews 10:7.

Christ never tried to please Himself. His every word and deed was for the sole purpose of glorifying the Father (John 17: 1, 4, 8, 12, 14, 19, 22, 24). Christ left heaven's glory, bliss, righteousness and perfection, and took upon Himself human flesh and moved in the midst of a sinful, depraved humanity, to save men and do His Father's will. All the pain, all the abuse, shame, torture and torment, was for the purpose of accomplishing His Father's will and to redeem man and creation. In the same manner, and if needs be to the same end, each and every one of us must be willing to do the Father's will (Matthew 10:38, 39).

Verse 4: For whatsoever things were written aforetime were written for our learning, that through patience and through comfort of the scriptures we might have hope.*

For whatsoever things were previously written were written for our learning (or, for our instruction and information), in order that through patience (or, a patient frame of mind, or, endurance and stedfastness), and through the comfort of the scriptures (that is, the Bible), we might have and keep on having hope (or, trust and confidence). Thus might verse 4 be literally translated.

A believer need never be despondent. On the other hand, an unbeliever, or one who does not accept the authenticity of Scripture and its verbal and inerrant inspiration, can derive no comfort from verse 4, because he could never be sure which part of the Bible is inspired by God the Holy Spirit, and which part is man's interpolation.

To this writer, and to every believer of like mind, there is a tremendous amount of comfort in verse 4 of this chapter, because the Scriptures are literally God-breathed. It is God who is speaking to us in every word and verse. Thank God that He has given to us His own Word from which to draw our comfort and assurance, and for the abiding, indwelling presence of the Holy Spirit to guide us in His Word (II Timothy 3:15-17).

We have a perfect God who has given us a perfect plan, wrought through a perfect sinless Saviour, who gave Himself to be the perfect sacrifice for the sins of the world, who has thereby cleansed us perfectly through His own blood, and who now lives and is now working in the life of every believer by the Holy Spirit to bring the believer unto perfection and to stand sinless in God's presence. Hallelujah!

---

*For the student of Greek who is interested in textual criticism, the following may be of interest: The Vatican text for verse 4 reads, (For whatsoever things) "were written, were all written for; and through comfort, might have hope of comfort." The Sinaitic and the Alexandrine MSS. also contain the phrase, "and through comfort."

All of this is the personal possession of every believer on the assurance of the Holy Scriptures which were written by holy men as they were moved by the Spirit of God. It is because of these promises and upon this assurance of the Scriptures that we draw through patience our comfort and our blessed hope.

Verse 5: Now the God of patience and of comfort grant you to be of the same mind one with another according to Christ Jesus . . . :

The two words, "patience" and "comfort," used in this verse, to describe God's nature are the same two words used to tell the believer how and where he can obtain "patience" and "comfort." God has revealed Himself in the Holy Scriptures, and only there can one find the perfect revelation of a Holy God and Saviour. God is inseparable from the Holy Scriptures, and vice versa. So likewise is the Saviour who is the Living Word revealed in the written Word. God speaks to us in and through the Scriptures.

V. 5: ". . . to be of the same mind . . ." can be translated, "the same thing to mind." The Greek word for "mind" is a present infinitive.

It seems as though all of chapter 14 is contained in this verse (5 of chapter 15), that is, the conduct and feeling of the Christian in relation to his fellow-believers because of his patience, his comfort and his hope, all to be done "according to Christ Jesus." "This is my commandment, that ye love one another, even as I have loved you" (John 15:12). If we would follow this admonition, we would be united and thereby avoid division and strife.

Verse 6: . . . that with one accord ye may with one mouth glorify the God and Father of our Lord Jesus Christ.

The Greek structure of the foregoing passage is such that it can be translated in the following manner: ". . . that ye may glorify and keep on glorifying the God and Father of our Lord Jesus Christ." For the last clause of this verse see II Corinthians 1:3; 11:31; Ephesians 1:3; I Peter 1:3).

Verse 6 is the cumulative result of verses 4 and 5, namely, to glorify God in unity of mind with praise and worship. This objective is what the Saviour prayed for in John 17:22. Obviously, such union will not be realized until all believers have been brought into glory as recorded in I Thessalonians 4:13-17.

Unanimity of body, soul and spirit of all true believers is
the great objective of the Gospel (John 17:21). This is the plan
of God and it is voiced in the New Testament. Paul states it in
Romans 15:5 and in the following verses: "For we are God's
fellow-workers: ye are God's husbandry, God's building" (I Corinthians 3:9; see Ephesians 2:21). Only when the flesh of every
believer is changed, either by death or by the Rapture, will
this objective be realized. Harmony is the crying need in the
true Church of Jesus Christ, and it should be the objective of
all believers.

**Verse 7: Wherefore receive ye one another, even as Christ
also received you, to the glory of God.**

The Greek word which is translated "receive ye" is the same
Greek word that is used in Romans 14:1. The thought expressed
in the two clauses of this verse (7) is contained in this Greek
word for "receive ye." That is to say, we are to receive one
another and to keep on receiving one another even as we are
being received by the Saviour who said, ". . . and him that
cometh to me I will in no wise cast out" (John 6:37).

The "weak" brethren of chapter 14 are to receive and to keep
on receiving the "strong" ones, and vice versa. The Gospel makes
no distinction between the "weak" and the "strong" just as there
is no distinction between Jew and Gentile in Christ. All are
received when they become Christians and are adopted into
God's family; and in the same manner, all Christians are to be
received into our fellowship. The Greek word for "receive ye"
means to receive all with kindness and hospitality.

When friendship, love and hospitality are prevalent among
believers, it always is "to the glory of God" (Ephesians 1:6).
When an unsaved Jew or Gentile is able to see that love is the
force that holds saved Jews and Gentiles together, he will become envious and the truth of the Gospel will become to him a
living reality. Such a sight will preach the Gospel to the unsaved
better than a sermon ever could.

That verse 7 is addressed to both Jews and Gentiles is obvious
because of what the Apostle states in the verses immediately following. It is only "in Christ" that "the middle wall of partition"
is broken down and the enmity abolished between the Jew and
the Gentile (Ephesians 2:14-17).

Let us search our hearts and confess our prejudices. God has
promised to cleanse us.

Verse 8: For I say that Christ hath been made a minister of the circumcision for the truth of God, that he might confirm the promises given unto the fathers . . . ,

In the program of God ". . . when the fulness of the time came, God sent forth His Son, born of a woman, born (this word 'born' is from the same Greek word as 'hath been made' in verse 8) under the law, that he might redeem them that were under the law . . ." (Galatians 4:4, 5). The Saviour Himself said, ". . . I was not sent but unto the lost sheep of the house of Israel" (Matthew 15:24). See also Matthew 10:6; Acts 3:26.

Every promise contained in the New Testament relative to the Saviour's birth is addressed to "the circumcision," that is, Israel (See Matthew 1:21; Luke 2:11; and so elsewhere). The Saviour confirmed the truth that God's promises made to the fathers are to be fulfilled to the minutest detail. Not one jot or tittle will be left unfulfilled. The Incarnation ratified, verified, established and confirmed every promise made to the fathers. God is faithful. "For the gifts and the calling of God are not repented of" (Romans 11:29).

Christ came into the world as a minister of God (Matthew 20:28) to fulfill all the promises that God made to the fathers (Genesis 12:1-3; 17:2, 4; Romans 9:4, 5). Christ ratified with all the guarantees of God Himself the covenants of God in the Old Testament.

V. 8: ". . . the promises given unto the fathers. . .". The word "given" is not in the Greek text (KJV "made"). The sentence should read, ". . . that he might confirm the promises to the fathers."

Verse 9: . . . and that the Gentiles might glorify God for his mercy; as it is written, Therefore will I give praise unto thee among the Gentiles, And sing unto thy name.

In this verse the Apostle begins to quote a series of Old Testament (Septuagint) passages to show the universality of the Gospel. The love of God was never meant to be confined to one nation, nor was it the plan of God to circumscribe it within the borders of the Holy Land.

V. 9: ". . . and that the Gentiles might glorify God for his mercy . . .". The blessings of God came to Israel "on behalf of the truth of God." It came to the Gentiles "on behalf of the mercy and lovingkindness of God." The revelation of the love of

God (I John 4:10) is that both Jews and Gentiles "might glorify God."

The Gentiles cannot lay claim to God on the basis of a "covenant" relationship, as the Jews can. The Gentile claim is merely mercy — "for his mercy." Though they do not merit it, the mercy of God crosses national and geographical bounderies. God's mercy includes "all." The Gentiles became the recipients of God's mercy and lovingkindness because God is merciful. They (the Gentiles) could not be overlooked if God's plans in the Old Testament were to be fulfilled. The Gospel, according to God's plan and purpose, now includes the Gentiles who became "the fellow members" and the "fellow-partakers of the promise in Christ Jesus" (Ephesians 3:6).

In verse 9 Paul quotes II Samuel 22:50 and Psalm 18:49, thus showing God's plan for the Gentiles in the Old Testament. The phrase, "as it is written," is better translated, "as it has been written." The tense expresses a completed action with finished results. The mood (indicative) expresses the certainty of reality. Thus Paul shows in verse 9 that the Gentiles, by adoption, become the children of God with the Jews, and both have Abraham as their father (Romans 4:11, 12, 16, 17). The Apostle is making certain that the Gentile Christians remember that Christ was "a minister of the circumcision," and, as such a minister, He devoted His ministry to the Jews. By the same token the Jewish Christians must remember that if the Gentiles are to "glorify God for his mercy," they must become the children of God through the same Messiah. To this end the Apostle brings in the Old Testament prophecies to prove that the Gentiles will praise God and glorify Him. "Salvation is from the Jews" (John 4:22), yet, ". . . God hath shut up all (Jews and Gentiles) unto disobedience, that he might have mercy upon all" (Romans 11:32).

The Theocratic Kingdom of God with its capital in Jerusalem and with the Throne of David as its seat of authority, and governed by the Messiah who is King of kings, is a Jewish kingdom with a universal outreach. *All* peoples are its subjects.

Verse 10: And again he saith, Rejoice, ye Gentiles, with his people.

This is the Septuagint Version of Deuteronomy 32:43. The Soncino Edition of the Pentateuch writes this verse thus, "Sing aloud, O ye nations, of his people." This is Israel's invitation to the Gentiles to join her in her song of deliverance. Some commenatators believe verse 10 to be Psalm 117:1. The Jewish

Targums translate this message to read, "Praise, ye nations his people." This writer would agree with the latter. However, the translation may not convey the meaning. The meaning is that the Gentile nations are to praise the God of Israel, not Israel.

It is possible to detect a prophetic note in verse 10 by reason of the context and the hope in the hearts of these early Christians for that Theocratic Kingdom when the Millennium shall be an accomplished reality and the Gentiles are invited to inherit the Kingdom with Israel. Then indeed will the Gentiles become "his people," and they shall all, Jews and Gentiles, praise God and His Messiah (Matthew 25:31-46; Psalm 67:3-5; compare I Peter 1:10).

The Apostle applies this text (Deuteronomy 32:43) to both Jewish and Gentile Christians. He urges them both to praise God.

Verse 11: And again, Praise the Lord, all ye Gentiles; And let all the peoples praise him.

This is the Septuagint Version of Psalm 117:1, and it conveys the Hebrew meaning. Rabbi David Kimchi states that this verse will be fulfilled and belongs "to the days of the Messiah." This is the time when all the people on earth will praise the Messiah (Philippians 2:6-8).

Verse 12: And again, Isaiah saith, There shall be the root of Jesse, And he that ariseth to rule over the Gentiles; On him shall the Gentiles hope.

Paul's reference to Isaiah's prophecy in the foregoing verse is to Isaiah 11:10, which in the Soncino Press Edition of the Pentateuch and in the American Standard Version is translated thus: "And it shall come to pass in that day, that the root of Jesse, that standeth for an ensign of the peoples, unto him shall the nations seek; and his resting-place shall be glorious." In the Septuagint Version, however, Isaiah 11:10 is translated: "And in that day there shall be a root of Jesse, and he that shall arise to rule over the Gentiles; in him shall the Gentiles trust, and his rest shall be glorious."

The Jewish commentators give Isaiah 11:10 a Messianic meaning, and state that he must be "the son's son of Jesse," or, "which goeth out from the root of Jesse." The Apostle retains the meaning that Christ "who was born of the seed of David . . ." (Romans 1:3) is "to rule over the Gentiles" (Romans 15:12). The tree of David's kingship has been cut down by sin. The root sprout of

Jesse (literal Hebrew) sprouts and restores through righteousness that which has been cut down by sin (Jeremiah 23:5).

If the Messiah has not already come, Israel is on the horn of a dilemma, because all the geneological records in Israel were destroyed in 70 A.D. under Titus; so what Jew can claim that he is a descendant of David? He may claim it but how can he prove it? Since all geneological records have been destroyed, the Messiah must have already come. He did indeed come! He is the Lord Jesus Christ.

The Jewish writers, such as Rabbi David Kimchi, Rabbi Aben Ezra, the Targums of Jonathan, the Prayer Book, all claim that the Messiah is to be a descendant of Jesse, a Son of David, and that He will rule over Israel and the Gentile nations.

It is interesting to note in passing that the Apostle calls the Old Testament to witness to the truth of Messiah's dominion over Israel and the nations in the last days, in the Torah (Moses) Deuteronomy 32:43; in the Prophets, Isaiah 11:10; and in the Writings, Psalm 117:1. The Lord did the very same thing in Luke 24:44. See also Luke 16:29 and Dr. Gill's *Commentary*, pp. 132 and 133.

Though all this is prophetic, Paul applies this truth to the Christians of his day. As the Jewish nation and the Gentiles shall praise the Messiah in the Millennium, the Jewish and Gentile Christians, the "weak" and the "strong" brethren, are to praise the Lord Jesus Christ now.

V. 12: "On him shall the Gentiles hope." Hope can never come through the efforts of a human being or any group of people. It must come from a source greater than humanity. It does! "On him (the Lord Jesus Christ) shall the Gentiles hope," ". . . which is Christ in you, the hope of glory" (Colossians 1:27; I Timothy 1:1; Romans 9:33; 10:11).

Verse 13: Now the God of hope fill you with all joy and peace in believing, that ye may abound in hope, in the power of the Holy Spirit.

Notice that Romans 15:5 begins this section of the chapter with a benediction and ends the section here (verse 13) with a benediction. Notice also that the Apostle states in verse 12, "*On him shall the Gentiles hope*," and that verse 13 begins, ". . . *the God of hope*." Paul never loses sight of the Deity of Christ. All the blessings of God are permeated with hope. We have our hope certified in Christ here and hereafter. "If we have only hoped in Christ in this life, we are of all men most pitiable" (I Corinthians

15:19), "Jesus said unto her, I am the resurrection, and the life: he that believeth on me, though he die, yet shall he live" (John 11:25). There are no disappointments in Christ. He is the author of hope and blessing. A Christian need not despair or drift hopelessly. A Christian need never resign to hopelessness. He needs to ask God to *re-sign*, or sign again, to hope and to be *re-assigned* to greater hopes. We are builders with God.

There are three kinds of bricklayers: One says, "I lay bricks." Another says, "I lay bricks to make a living." A third says, "I lay bricks in the household of God" (Ephesians 2:19-22). The first is without hope, the second has an earthly hope, the third has an eternal hope. So it is in this world. The first bricklayer lays bricks all his life. The second lays bricks only until he can get a better job. The third lays *living* bricks to build up a spiritual house (I Peter 2:4, 5). To carry the figure further, the first bricklayer is hopeless and *wrings* his hands in despair. The second becomes disheartened and like the agnostic or indifferent bricklayer *folds* his hands in discouragement. The third, filled with an eternal hope, *raises* his hands to God in praise and thanksgiving.

Where do you stand as a bricklayer? Christ is the hope of the world and He can be yours and the "chief cornerstone" in the house you are building. Will you receive Him?

There can be no "joy and peace" outside of faith in Christ (Isaiah 48:22; 57:21 compare with Isaiah 26:3). Only "in believing" is there perfect peace and joy. Christ is the answer to every problem and the Conqueror of doubts and fears. Only He can give peace and joy (John 14:27; 15:11). He does all this through His Representative whom He sent at Pentecost, that is, the Holy Spirit (John 16:7-14; Acts 1:8; Romans 15:19; Galatians 5:22; I Peter 1:8).

Verse 14: And I myself also am persuaded of you, my brethren, that ye yourselves are full of goodness, filled with all knowledge, able also to admonish one another.

Or, as it might be more literally translated, "But I have been persuaded, my brethren, that you yourselves are full of, or filled with, goodness and virtue, having been filled with all knowledge, being able also to admonish one another."

In this verse the Apostle begins his concluding remarks. He has made some strong comments about the schisms in the church. He has instructed the saints at Rome on how to behave toward one another — to be loving, considerate, tolerant of one another, even as Christ has shown His love toward them. Paul tells them that he was fully aware of the virtue and goodness they displayed. We are to realize that this is not the "goodness" of the flesh, but rather that goodness which is implanted in every believer by the love of God through the Holy Spirit (Galatians 5:22; Ephesians 5:9; II Thessalonians 1:11). They were filled with knowledge. Again, this is not the flesh, but ". . . the new man, that is being renewed unto knowledge after the image of him that created him . . ." (Colossians 3:10; see II Peter 1:5-8).

The church at Rome was a very effective church, its testimony was widespread (Romans 1:8). Paul is cautioning the believers at Rome to make sure that their lives are complementary to their faith. Nothing must be permitted to hinder their testimony in the midst of a lost community. They were filled with God's "goodness" and "knowledge" which was sufficient to maintain their testimony.

V. 14: ". . . able also to admonish one another." This goodness and knowledge of God enabled them "to admonish one another." The word "able" would be more correctly — and more literally — translated, "being able." God gave them "a mouth and wisdom" to counsel, to warn, to rebuke, and exhort one another. They were eminently gifted and supplied with the knowledge of Christian truth and had the power and wisdom to give good advice to one another.

Paul portrays one of the gifts that God gave him, namely, tact. He may have had words of criticism and correction, but he wanted to spur the believers on to greater heights, so that his words of correction to the saints at Rome were not "knockout" blows but "stepping stones" to help them achieve a greater and more effective testimony.

Verse 15: But I write the more boldly unto you in some measure, as putting you again in remembrance, because of the grace that was given to me of God . . . ,

Twice in this verse Paul uses words that do not appear elsewhere in the New Testament. They are "the more boldly" and "putting you again in remembrance," or, "reminding you." The literal translation of verse 15 is, "And more boldly I wrote to you in part, as reminding you by the grace given to me from God." Paul is also "more boldly" in his writing to them because they are filled with goodness and have the knowledge. The reminding is not remonstrative. It is done with kindly goadings and suggestions. It is done with love and compassion and not with anger. It is done by the grace, or because of the bountiful grace of God, of which Paul was himself a recipient (Romans 1:5; 12:3). He also received his apostleship at that same time. He writes here with the authority of a "called apostle" by the grace of God who must be faithful to his calling and to God.

Verse 16: . . . that I should be a minister of Christ Jesus unto the Gentiles, ministering the gospel of God, that the offering up of the Gentiles might be made acceptable, being sanctified by the Holy Spirit.

There is much discussion among Bible commentators over the Greek word translated "minister." The same word appears in Romans 13:6, "ministers of God's service." Here it is "a minister of Christ Jesus." Just as a civil minister has authority in civil matters, so Paul uses the same word to mean authority in spiritual matters. "A minister of Christ Jesus" is entrusted with the authority needed to discharge every duty relating to the work of the church. The "minister" is the authority. This is the proper office of the pastor today. We must bear in mind that a minister is not a priest. All *believers* are priests (I Peter 2:5, 9; Revelation 1:6; 20:6). The Christian pulpit is the voice of God's prophet proclaiming His Word and certifying it by "Thus saith the Lord!" Paul's peculiar position is that he was "a minister of Jesus Christ unto the Gentiles."

V. 16: ". . . ministering the gospel of God. . . ." The more literal translation is "sacrificing the gospel." This is the only place in the New Testament where the word "ministering" appears, a word used in the Old Testament in connection with the duties of the priesthood. Paul attaches the same significance to "ministering" the Gospel. As the priests in the Old Testament offered sacrifices continually, seeking atonement for sin, the "minister of Jesus Christ" is presenting the Gospel as the "once for all" satisfactory sacrifice for sin in God's sight. Christ is the fulfilled "sin-offering" to God, a sin-offering who was delivered up for our tresspasses" (Romans 4:25), ". . . and gave himself up for us, an offering and a sacrifice to God for an odor of a sweet smell" (Ephesians 5:2; see Hebrews 10:10).

V. 16: ". . . that the offering up of the Gentiles might be made acceptable . . ." (See Romans 12:1; Philippians 2:17; II Timothy 4:6), or, that the Gentiles, as a sacrifice, might be acceptable (see Isaiah 66:20).

V. 16: ". . . being sanctified by the Holy Spirit." Nothing is "sanctified" as far as God is concerned unless it is "sanctified by the Holy Spirit." The Greek word for "being sanctified" is more

accurately translated "having been sanctified." Whatever it is
that God can use, that is, a person as a priest or vessel (in the
Old Testament), and a person (in the New Testament), it must
already have been sanctified. It is not sanctified in the process
of being used. It must be sanctified prior to its being used in
order that it can be used.

Ministers are not mediators. There is only one Mediator and
He is Christ Jesus (I Timothy 2:5). Romans 15:16 is a touching
and beautiful simile in which the Apostle compares himself to a
priest and the Gentiles to an offering. Paul's language is purely
figurative and is not to be taken literally. Romans 15:16 is
the only place in the New Testament where "ministering" (or
sacrificing the Gospel) appears.

**Verse 17: I have therefore my glorying in Christ Jesus in
things pertaining to God.**

Anything that the Apostle achieved, whether material or spiritual, was not for his own personal glory. All of his possessions
and gifts were from God and he possessed them only because he
was in Christ. The wonderful story of the full meaning of Romans
15:17 is given in Philippians 3:3-14. Paul's personal testimony
should be the personal testimony of every believer. No one can
boast of having received a gift from God through his own human
efforts. Even salvation is a free gift (Ephesians 2:2-10; Romans
6:23).

Romans 15:17 is the summation of verse 16. Paul's calling,
his ministry, and the fruits of his ministry among the Gentiles,
everything he accomplished was his only because he received it
from God through Christ Jesus. And because he received all this
from God, he had the authority to "write the more boldly" and
to put the saints at Rome "in remembrance" (v. 15). Since Paul
belonged to Christ, and by his own confession was "the bond-
slave of Jesus Christ," Christ owns all that the Apostle has and is,
and Paul can therefore "boast, or glory" in Christ, and place
special emphasis on his "glorying in Christ Jesus" and "in things
pertaining to God."

**Verse 18: For I will not dare to speak of any things save
those which Christ wrought through me, for the obedience of
the Gentiles, by word and deed . . . ,**

Every accomplishment of the Apostle was through Christ. He
testified to this truth many times (Acts 15:12; 21:19; Romans
1:5; II Corinthians 3:5; I Corinthians 15:10). Romans 15:18 is

an elaboration of verse 16. The Apostle refuses to appropriate any accomplishment as his own. It is always Christ who is the Transformer and Converter. Paul is the instrument. Only a living Christ could transform a person like Paul and use him to bring about, or work out, effect, produce "the obedience of the Gentiles," whom God had considered dead in trespasses and sins (Ephesians 2:1), whom in ages past "God gave them up" (Romans 1:24, 26, 28). Only an eternal omnipotent Christ could accomplish this. What an achievement! What a God! What a Saviour! Do you know Him?

Verse 19: . . . **in the power of signs and wonders, in the power of the Holy Spirit; so that from Jerusalem, and round about even unto Illyricum, I have fully preached the gospel of Christ . . . ;**

A much clearer translation of the two opening phrases of this verse is *"by* the power of signs and wonders, *by* the power of the Holy Spirit" (Acts 19:11, 12).

The agency performing these "signs and wonders" (v. 19) was not Paul but the Holy Spirit. The Apostle is not taking any credit to himself. He gives all the honor and glory to Christ and the Holy Spirit. The flesh could never achieve the "signs and wonders" of which Paul speaks (Zechariah 4:6). The Apostle in verse 19 is stating again his conviction that it is the divine power of Christ and the Holy Spirit working in and through him in the performance of these "signs and wonders." Though he was the instrument through whom the miracles were accomplished and through whom the Gospel was preached to the multitudes, this was all done "by the power of the Holy Spirit." "And my speech and my preaching were not in persuasive words of wisdom, but in demonstration of the Spirit and of power" (I Corinthians 2:4; see also II Corinthians 12:12; I Thessalonians 1:5; Hebrews 2:2, 4).

The two words translated "signs and wonders," are two different Greek words that denote or describe the same events or miracles but of differing character, such as healing the body and converting the soul. No matter where Paul went he always and under all circumstances preached the Gospel. It was uppermost in his heart and mind (I Corinthians 1:23; 2:2; 9:16).

One of the phrases in verse 19 which has caused much discussion among the commentators is, "from Jerusalem, and round about even unto Illyricum." It is not this writer's intention to enter into a further discussion as to just what is meant by the phrase in question. It is enough to say that no matter where Paul went, whether to Illyricum or only to Thessalonica and Berea, on his second missionary journey, he always preached the Gospel. A good Bible dictionary will locate Illyricum, which was a Roman province across the Adriatic Sea from Italy.

Verse 20: . . . yea, making it my aim so to preach the gospel, not where Christ was already named, that I might not build upon another man's foundation . . . ;

It was a point of honor with Paul not to preach the Gospel where someone else had preached it before. He was not going to infringe on another missionary's territory. He made it his aim and eagerly strove to avoid evangelizing in places where Christ was already named, in order that he should not build on a foundation belonging to another missionary (II Corinthians 10: 15). The Apostle did not preach where other evangelists had organized churches. He went to preach in virgin territory. Paul devoted his time to the task of *founding* churches. He wrote to churches which others organized, such as the ones at Colosse and Rome. Paul at heart was a pioneer.

Verse 21: . . . but, as it is written, They shall see, to whom no tidings of him came, And they who have not heard shall understand.

The Apostle is quoting the Septuagint Version of Isaiah 52:15. The phraseology of the Septuagint differs from the Hebrew, but the meaning is basically the same. Paul is *applying* this verse to his own day and makes it the *primary* fulfillment. The verse in Isaiah 52:15 will be completely fulfilled when the Messiah comes the second time and Israel accepts Him of whom Moses and the prophets did write.

There are a number of Old Testament prophecies in the New Testament which are only partially fulfilled now. For example, Peter quotes Joel 2:28-30 and states, ". . . but this is that which hath been spoken through the prophet Joel" (Acts 2:16). A careful reading of the prophecy in Joel will clearly show that this prophecy will be completely fulfilled at the end of the Tribulation. There are a number of such passages in the New Testament. (See Hebrews 8:8-12 and compare with Jeremiah 31:34.) The passage in Isaiah (52:15) is fraught with Messianic prophecy. The ancient and semi-modern Jewish teachers taught that Isaiah's prophecy will be fulfilled when the Messiah comes and Israel is regathered. When this prophecy is fulfilled, the Messianic Kingdom will have been established. The Messiah, the Lord Jesus Christ, will then occupy the throne promised to Him prior to His birth, "He shall be great, and shall be called the Son of the Most High: and the Lord God shall give unto him the throne of his father David: and he shall reign over the house of Jacob for ever; and of his kingdom there shall be no end" (Luke 1:31, 32).

What a day that will be! Before that day comes, God's judgment will have been executed. The destruction will be appalling. The world will have been drenched in human blood. Now is the time to be saved. You can be! The Saviour invites you!

Verse 22: Wherefore also I was hindered these many times from coming to you . . . :

See Acts 19:21; 23:11; 28:16-24. Among the hindrances Paul refers to in verse 22 are those recorded in the texts noted. He was preoccupied with organizing new churches, which was the Apostle's calling and the Lord's will in his life.

Do you know the Lord's will for you? You can know, but you must make a distinction between the Lord's *work* and the Lord's *will*. They are not synonymous.

Verse 23: . . . but now, having no more any place in these regions, and having these many years a longing to come to you . . . ,

Paul evangelized the areas where the Holy Spirit led him. He visited these areas time and time again. His life as an apostle was fully yielded and possessed by the Holy Spirit along every step of his pilgrimage. He fulfilled his calling, the consummation of his highest hopes. This was his goal and the objective of his ministry, ". . . for he is a chosen vessel unto me, to bear my name before the Gentiles and kings, and the children of Israel" (Acts 9:15).

No trial, no persecution, no privation, veered him from his course. He directed his ministry toward one goal and never deviated from his purpose by one iota even when death stared him in the face, ". . . I press on toward the goal unto the prize of the high calling of God in Christ Jesus" (Philippians 3:14). The memory of the sufferings of Christ on the cross was an ever-present reminder. Undoubtedly, the face of Stephen as he was being stoned to death was a torturing memory. Paul counted it a precious privilege to suffer for Christ, and valued his own life as refuse, "For I reckon that the sufferings of this present time are not worthy to be compared with the glory which shall be revealed to usward" (Romans 8:18).

What is the nature of your life? Are you living for Christ or for the world? What is your answer?

Verse 24: . . . whensoever I go unto Spain (for I hope to see you in my journey, and to be brought on my way thitherward by you, if first in some measure I shall have been satisfied with your company) — . . .

Whether Paul ever went to Spain is debatable. It makes no difference to the twentieth-century Christian, and it is needless to discuss it. Paul is telling the saints at Rome that he is planning to see them on his way to Spain. He is looking forward to seeing them, that they may even be able to accompany him for a certain distance, and perhaps furnish him with things necessary for the trip. His hopes and ambitions did not materialize. He came to Rome not as a preacher, but as a prisoner (Acts 28:16-24).

Verse 25: . . . but now, I say, I go unto Jerusalem, ministering unto the saints.

The Greek word translated "ministering" does not necessarily mean preaching only, but other things as well, such as distributing that which the Apostle had received from the churches (Acts 19:21).

Paul postponed his trip to Rome and Spain in order that he might have the opportunity to preach to the Jewish Christians in Jerusalem, and to help them financially (Acts 11:29; I Corinthians 16:1-4). "Now after some years I came to bring alms to my nation, and offerings" (Acts 24:17). Helping his fellow Jewish Christians and collecting the offerings from the churches had been on Paul's mind for a good while (II Corinthians 8:4). This is repeated in a number of places such as II Corinthians 9:1, 2; and elsewhere.

Verse 26: For it hath been the good pleasure of Macedonia and Achaia to make a certain contribution for the poor among the saints that are at Jerusalem.

The churches at Macedonia, Philippi, Thessalonica and Achaia (Corinth was in this area), all were to have a part in this offering. Paul was passing through these places on his journey to Jerusalem (Acts 19:21).

Many of the Jewish Christians who were "the saints at Jerusalem" were very poor and were living in destitution. Many of them, when they took their stand for Christ, lost all they had. These Grecian churches were being admonished to help take care of "their own in Christ." It should be so today (compare Galatians 2:10). The Greek word for "contribution" in verse 26 means aid, relief, communion. Paul is reminding the churches of Greece that they are spiritually indebted to the saints at Jerusalem.

Verse 27: Yea, it hath been their good pleasure; and their debtors they are. For if the Gentiles have been made partakers of their spiritual things, they owe it to them also to minister unto them in carnal things.

Paul here makes a logical and a reasonable request. If the churches in Greece were so bountifully blessed by sharing in the spiritual gifts that were brought to them by the Jewish Christians at Jerusalem, is it not only fair but also proper for these Gentile Christians to share their material wealth with their poor "brethren in Christ"? This is why Paul states, in verse 27, translating his words literally, "For they thought it good, and debtors they are of them."

What a meager price to pay for such a wonderful and gracious return! Though this was to have been a "love offering" in the true sense, the churches at Greece were "debtors" and under obligation to help the saints at Jerusalem. If the Jewish Christians had not preached the Gospel to the Gentiles, at great personal cost in many cases, the Gentiles would have continued in their lost condition to be dead through their trespasses and sins, "separate from Christ, alienated from the commonwealth of Israel, and strangers from the covenants of the promise, having no hope and without God in the world" (Ephesians 2:2, 12). What a terrible destiny this would have been for these Gentiles! But because the Jewish Christians came and preached to them, these Gentiles partook of the Jewish Christian blessings and became ". . . fellow-heirs, and fellow-members . . . and fellow-partakers of the promise in Christ Jesus through the gospel" (Ephesians 3:6). Rightfully the Apostle now states that the Gentile Christians are indebted to the Jewish Christians.

Have you paid *your* debt to the Jew by giving him the Gospel? Are you sending missionaries and funds to win them? How negligent many Christians are! Are you among them? "Think you to face Him and to hear His 'Well done!' with Israel, His chosen, left dying alone?"

Verse 28: When therefore I have accomplished this, and have sealed to them this fruit, I will go on by you unto Spain.

When he had completed his work with the saints at Jerusalem, Paul planned to go to Spain via Rome. But before he did so, he was going to make doubly sure that the Jewish Christians received the "love offerings" from the churches. Paul states that he wanted to seal "to them this fruit." The Greek word here translated "have sealed," expresses antecedent action which is better translated "having sealed." The Greek word means to seal like a seal on a legal document, and in this case means insuring proper disposition of those gifts. (See John 3:33 for this word.)

Paul never visited Rome as he had planned. He visited Rome indeed but as a prisoner and not as a preacher. "Man proposes, but God disposes," which is a worldly form of the Proverb 16:9.

Verse 29: And I know that, when I come unto you, I shall come in the fulness of the blessing of Christ.

The Lord Himself assured Paul that he would go to Rome (see Acts 19:21; 23:11). Therefore, Paul was confident that he would go to Rome, but he never realized under what conditions he would go. One thing he was confident of and that was that his coming to Rome would be "in the fulness of the blessing of Christ." (The words, "of the gospel," which appear in the King James Version, are omitted in the majority of the ancient manuscripts as well as in the American Standard Version and the Nestle's Greek text.) Christ was his divine Master and Guide. This warrior of the cross was dominated and exalted and transformed by the love of Christ from the day of his conversion on the Damascus Road to the "time of his departure." His life and all he possessed he put in the hands of his Saviour. For him to live was Christ (see Galatians 2:20; 6:14; Philippians 1:6, 21; I Timothy 4:6-8). Paul spent his life serving his Master.

No matter what happened to Paul he was always confident that his Lord would work things out according to His will and for his (Paul's) good (Romans 8:28). No matter what happened to Paul, it was always for the furtherance of the Gospel (Philippians 1:12). He was completely dedicated to Christ and spent his life in Christ's service.

Are we spending our lives for Christ and the Gospel?

Verse 30: Now I beseech you, brethren, by our Lord Jesus

Christ, and by the love of the Spirit, that ye strive together with me in your prayers to God for me . . . ;

The opening phrase of this verse is the same as the one in Romans 12:1. Paul is requesting the saints at Rome to join together with him in intercessory prayer. The Greek word translated "strive together with me" means, you come to my aid by assisting me in this battle. The classical Greek gives this word the following meaning, contend along with, share in a contest, aid, succor or fight on the same side, a fellow-combatant. This "striving together" was to be done through the Lord Jesus Christ and through the love of the Spirit, that God will bless him in his proposed journey to Spain via Rome; and also bless his efforts as he goes to Jerusalem "ministering to the saints" there (v. 25).

Undoubtedly Paul was going to Jerusalem filled with questions as to how he would be received by his former associates with whom he had spent so much time at "the feet of Gamaliel." He wondered, too, what the Sanhedrin would say and do when they found out that he was in Jerusalem. Only one who has been in similar circumstances can understand what was going through Paul's mind when he made this request for prayer in his own behalf. This situation was Paul's "lion's den" experience. He was no superhuman individual but he was dedicated and devoted to his Lord and to his calling (Acts 9:15, 16). The Lord fully understood the apprehensions and doubts of this soldier of the cross. (See Matthew 26:36, 45; Luke 22:39-45 for our Lord's agonizing prayers.)

How comforting it is to know that when a saint is in the valley of trials and tribulations, or about to go through a trying experience, that the prayers of the brethren are bearing him up. One can "run the gauntlet" of misunderstanding and abuse when he knows his loved ones and friends are constantly praying for him (James 5:16, 18). In verse 30 Paul is asking his fellow-Christians to pray with him "by the love of the Spirit." This reciprocal love of the brethren was in compliance with the commandment of Christ Himself (John 13:34; 15:12, 17; Galatians 6:21; I Thessalonians 4:9; I Peter 1:22; I John 4:7).

Verse 31: . . . that I may be delivered from them that are disobedient in Judaea, and that my ministration which I have for Jerusalem may be acceptable to the saints . . . ;

The Greek word translated "I may be delivered" means to be dragged out of danger; and the Greek word translated "disobeying" means also to refuse to believe. Paul is asking that the saints at Rome join him in prayer for three things: (1) his safety; (2) that his mission may be acceptable or pleasing "to the saints at Jerusalem"; and (3) that he may go to Spain with a stopover in Rome.

This Apostle had borne tribulation and suffering beyond the experience of any of the apostles, and almost beyond endurance, so that now it is no wonder he is beset with fears and apprehensions. He knew what havoc he had wrought among believers prior to his conversion. He was fully cognizant of the many Jewish Christians he had caused to be killed and imprisoned. Now he was reaping painful memories of the sins he had sown in unbelief. The Saviour had had to teach him through suffering when the Lord told Ananias, the Damascus disciple, that Paul was a chosen vessel to bear God's name "before the Gentiles and kings, and the children of Israel" for His name's sake (Acts 9: 15, 16).

Paul had been beaten, shipwrecked, accused, ridiculed, throughout his ministry. Still ahead of him lay the experience of being chained and imprisoned. He went with apprehension yet with trust that the Lord would give him the grace to bear his ordeal. He did not flinch, for he knew that no matter what befell him, Christ would be glorified through it all (Philippians 3:10-16; II Corinthians 1:5, 7; II Timothy 2:12).

Verse 32: . . . that I may come unto you in joy through the will of God, and together with you find rest.

Or, according to another literal translation of this verse, "In order that in joy coming to you through the will of God, I may rest with you." The thought conveyed by the Greek word which is translated "that I may rest with you," means to experience refreshment in company with another.

The Apostle was looking forward to his journey to Rome which would permit him to spend time with the saints there. He would in such a case be refreshed in spirit by the meeting and able to provide himself with whatever material necessities he might require for his journey, and, most helpful of all, be sent on his way up-borne by the combined prayers of his faithful friends and loving co-workers.

How differently things turned out for him! The journey, as he planned it, never materialized. He came to Rome in chains and a prisoner (Acts 28:20). Notice how Paul always wanted to move "through the will of God" (v. 32). So it must be in every Christian's life.

What are your plans? What does the future hold for you? Is it eternal life, or is it death? Christ makes the difference. None of us knows what the future holds, but those of us who know Christ know that He holds our future.

Verse 33: Now the God of peace be with you all. Amen.

How wonderful and comforting it is to have peace with God! What solace there is in knowing that one can approach the God of the universe and address Him as Abba, Father (Romans 8:15). *You can!* God has made peace with man if man will accept God's plan, ". . . and through him to reconcile all things unto himself, having made peace through the blood of his cross . . ." (Colossians 1:20).

The Saviour invites you, "Peace I leave with you; my peace I give unto you . . ." (John 14:27). Are you apprehensive about your future? Are there doubts and fears in your life? Christ can allay them all.

16

VERSES 1 TO 16 OF CHAPTER 16 mention the names and location of many of Paul's fellow-workers, his beloved saints. These persons, their churches and households, including also his fellow-prisoners at Rome, make interesting historical reading and research. For the student who might wish to pursue this study there are many books at his disposal. This writer will not follow such a course. He will only deal with the verses that have a practical application for today's living and preaching.

Verse 1: I commend unto you Phoebe our sister, who is a servant of the church that is at Cenchreae . . . :

The Greek word for "servant" also means deaconess. Deaconesses could have been the female "servants" who ministered to the women of the church.

Verse 2: . . . that ye receive her in the Lord, worthily of the saints, and that ye assist her in whatsoever matter she may have need of you: for she herself also hath been a helper of many, and of mine own self.

The saints at Rome were to receive Phoebe with all Christian courtesy and stand by her, to assist and support her in whatsoever things she might need. She herself had succored many saints including Paul. He is now asking the saints at Rome to do the same for her. She could have been one of the wealthier women of the church at Cenchreae, which was the port of Corinth.

Verses 3-6: (3) Salute Prisca and Aquila my fellow-workers in Christ Jesus, (4) who for my life laid down their own necks; unto whom not only I give thanks, but also all the churches of the Gentiles: (5) and salute the church that is in their house . . .

(6) Salute Mary, who bestowed much labor on you.

Aquila was a Jewish Christian of Pontus and Prisca was his

485

wife. They had endangered their lives — "who for my life laid down their own necks" — in Paul's behalf (see Acts 18:1-3).

Verse 7: Salute Andronicus and Junias, my kinsmen, and my fellow prisoners, who are of note among the apostles, who also have been in Christ before me.

Paul refers to Andronicus and Junias as "his kinsmen" pointing to the fact that they were Jewish Christians (see Romans 9:3). They were fellow-prisoners with Paul. This should be taken literally. They were well known ("of note") among the apostles, and were followers of Christ before Paul had had his experience with the Master on the Damascus road.

Verses 8-16. (These nine verses are a continuation of the names of Paul's beloved fellow-workers and their households, concluding with the word) "Salute one another with a holy kiss. All the churches of Christ salute you." (No further comment on them is needed.)

Verse 17: Now I beseech you, brethren, mark them that are causing the divisions and occasions of stumbling, contrary to the doctrine which ye learned: and turn away from them.

The opening clause of this verse, "Now I beseech you, brethren," is the same as that used in Romans 12:1 and 15:30, and is followed by the words, "mark them," and the rest of the verse, an amplified literal translation of which would be, "watch them, keep an eye on them, and beware of those who are the ones causing the divisions and dissensions, the offenses and scandals that are inconsistent with the teaching and doctrine which ye learned; and turn away, shun, and avoid them."

How these words need to be heeded today! We hear the expression, "inclusive brethren," in the New Evangelicalism, which expression is something altogether opposed to the teaching of verse 17, in which Paul states that the true child of God should be *exclusive*, not inclusive. We are told to shun those who teach false doctrine, who cause divisions and dissensions. We must adhere only to the true doctrine as taught in the Scriptures. No Scripture should ever be taken out of its context and privately interpreted. We are to practice Scriptural separation, which means *exclusion*, not inclusion. Such is the admonition of the Apostle.

Verse 18: For they that are such serve not our Lord Christ,

but their own belly; and by their smooth and fair speech they beguile the hearts of the innocent.

The people who cause dissensions and divisions among God's people are not interested in serving the Lord because they use their energies for self-aggrandizement. There are many people in Christian circles who are guilty of this lust for gain and fame. They live in luxury and their incomes are far greater than the majority of the people from whom they gain their support. They live in mansions and own huge farms stocked with herds of cattle; they own properties and office buildings. They live like the pampered ones of wealthy society and know nothing about sacrifices. Yet they want others to sacrifice for them, for "their own belly" (compare Philippians 3:18, 19; II Timothy 3:5, 6).

They that flourish on the labors of others may not be evil in their own lives but they are motivated by a selfish zeal and an insatiable desire to promote their own prominence and good. They are actually parasites and are to be avoided and shunned because they do not serve the Lord Jesus Christ. Their "belly" is their god.

V. 18: ". . . and by their smooth and fair speech they beguile the hearts of the innocent." The two words, "smooth and fair," as applied to speech are essentially synonymous. They are generally used in a bad sense and this is the usage here and means they are used for deceitful purposes. Persons who use them are insincere and two-faced, double-tongued, treacherous and knowingly use these means "to beguile the innocent." From such turn away! (II Corinthians 11:13).

The reason for such strong admonition is that these men do not serve Christ but themselves. They do not honor Christ nor do they further the cause and the Gospel of Christ. They seek wealth, worldly applause and honor for themselves. (Compare the description of our Saviour in Philippians 2:5-11 with that of these men.) These causers of "divisions and occasions of stumbling" appeal to the emotions of the flesh rather than the devotions of the heart. Tears which are sometimes shed in pretended sympathy, do not always denote sincerity. Take heed! Let us as true believers serve the Lord with our hearts and lives. It is with the "heart that man believeth unto righteousness."

Verse 19: For your obedience is come abroad unto all men. I rejoice therefore over you: but I would have you wise unto that which is good, and simple unto that which is evil.

Or, as this verse might be expressed in an amplified and literal translation from the Greek: "For your submissiveness and obedience (to the faith Romans 1:8), has reached and has come abroad to all men. I rejoice therefore over you; but I would have you practically wise and spiritually enlightened in the pursuit of the good, upright and virtuous, and simple or unmixed, undefiled, to the evil or morally bad and corrupt."

Why, it may be asked, does the Apostle desire so earnestly to have his Roman believers possess this wisdom toward the good, and simplicity toward the evil? For the same reason apparently that he wrote to the saints at Philippi, "That ye may become blameless and harmless, children of God without blemish in the midst of a crooked and perverse generation, among whom ye are seen as lights in the world, holding forth the word of life . . ." (Philippians 2:15, 16; compare with Matthew 10:16). These words should be a warning to every saint who should heed them diligently. We must shun the people whom we are told to "mark" and to "turn away from" (v. 17) those who have made "their own belly" (v. 18) their god.

Verse 20: And the God of peace shall bruise Satan under your feet shortly. The grace of our Lord Jesus Christ be with you.

Dissensions and divisions among Christians are Satan-inspired. The Apostle has been warning the church at Rome to shun these evil brethren and avoid them. He now encourages them by saying that the God with whom peace has been made will bruise Satan, will crush and break him in pieces "under your feet shortly." Undoubtedly, the Apostle is alluding to Genesis 3:15, where God prophesies that the seed of the woman will crush and break in pieces the head of Satan. This is precisely what the Lord Jesus Christ came to do, "To this end was the Son of God manifested, that he might destroy the works of the devil" (I John 3:8). The saints are to rule and reign with the Messiah, and the devil is already a defeated enemy because he will be overthrown and trodden under foot.

Notice that this "peace" in verse 20 ("the God of peace"), is not a peace through negotiation. There is no note of "offer and acceptance" or compromise. God is *the* God of peace. Therefore, He is also holy, and righteous, and just. To call Him "the God of peace" is to give Him a title of victory, victory over sin. The words of the Saviour on the cross, "It is finished," are not words of defeat, but of accomplishment and triumph. "The God

of peace shall bruise Satan under your feet." In other words, the
devil and his angels, with all the evil they have brought into the
world, will be crushed forever. Then will God bring in His
peace (Isaiah 9:6, 7). The return of Christ to this earth, soon
to come, seals this promise. The Greek word translated "bruise"
in verse 20, is so constructed that it gives absolute assurance of
fulfillment. Beyond the shadow of a doubt, Satan will be
bruised under our feet.

Verse 20 is another place in this Epistle where Paul reiterates
his belief in the imminent return of Christ. He has done this in a
number of other places. It is interesting, to say the least, that
Paul should repeat it again as he closes this Epistle. He is saying,
"Good-by" with the word, "Maranatha," the Lord has come!
(See I Corinthians 16:22.)

"The grace of our Lord Jesus Christ," will keep every saint
through every trial and tribulation of life. The saint may have
to cross rivers of tears and climb mountains of doubts and experience many dangers in the vicissitudes of life, but he is given
the assurance that "the grace of our Lord Jesus Christ" will keep
him unto Christ and bring him into the mansions of glory (John
14:3; Matthew 28:20b; I Corinthians 10:13; Philippians 1:6;
Isaiah 26:3). Even the Psalmist David knew this peace, "Yea,
though I walk through the valley of the shadow of death, I will
fear no evil; for thou art with me . . ." (Psalm 23:4). That there
is no dying in the valley is proved because the Psalmist says he
walked through the valley.

Dear reader, do you have this peace and comfort? Christ can
and will supply it if you will accept Him.

**Verses 21-23. These three verses, like verses 1-16, mention the
names of some more of Paul's fellow-workers, including his kinsmen, and adds, "the whole church saluteth you."**

**Verse 24: The grace of our Lord Jesus Christ be with you all.
Amen (KJV).**

**Verse 25: Now to him that is able to establish you according
to my gospel and the preaching of Jesus Christ, according to
the revelation of the mystery which hath been kept in silence
through times eternal . . . ,**

To this writer it seems that the words, "to him that is able,"
apply to God the Holy Spirit. It is the Holy Spirit who takes the
Word of God and the things of Christ and reveals them to the
believer (John 16:7-14). It is through the vitalizing and il-

luminating power of the Holy Spirit that Paul has written this
Epistle. Only the Holy Spirit "is able" to establish and confirm
the saints at Rome according to the teachings and doctrines that
Paul has set forth in this letter to the Roman saints. He has
done so through "the preaching of Jesus Christ," whom the Holy
Spirit has revealed.

Moreover, it is only God the Holy Spirit who is able to establish and confirm the saint in the faith. It was also for this very
purpose — to establish and confirm the saints at Rome in the
faith — that Paul wrote this Epistle (1:11). This "preaching of
Jesus Christ" is a summary of what appears in Romans 10:8-12.
Paul spent his entire Christian life preaching Jesus Christ to the
Gentiles and showing, in his preaching to the Jews, that Jesus is
the promised Messiah of Israel.

The structure of the Greek word which is translated "is able"
in verse 25 is such that it states the truth that it is the Holy
Spirit who is able to establish the believer in the Gospel. The
Holy Spirit is able right now to establish a believer in Jesus Christ.
He is as powerful today as He ever was. He has never lost any
of His powers. (Compare Ephesians 3:20; Jude 24, 25, with
Romans 16:25.) The revelation of Christ, as the Apostle has
shown in this Epistle, was not so revealed in the ages past (Ephesians 3:3-9; Colossians 1:26; II Timothy 1:9, Titus 1:2; I Peter
1:20; Revelation 13:8).

In this last chapter (16) of Paul's Epistle and its concluding
verses (25-27), Paul is summarizing the entire Letter. The Epistle to the Romans is pregnant with spiritual truth, and brings it
to life with great power and with imperishable beauty.

V. 25: The ". . . mystery which hath been kept in silence
through times eternal . . ." is that the Gentiles should be brought
into full relationship with God on the same basis as the Jews.
When the Gentiles became Christians, they became ". . . fellow-
heirs, and fellow-members of the body, and fellow-partakers of
the promise in Christ Jesus through the gospel . . ." (Ephesians
3:6). Thus united in Christ Jew and Gentile became "one new
man." This was God's plan and program in "times eternal" and
"before the foundation of the world" (Ephesians 1:4).

In the ages past the Gospel was more or less in "mystery"
form. It is true that "Abraham rejoiced to see my day" (John
8:56) and that he looked for the city "whose builder and maker
is God" (Hebrews 11:10); and that Moses "forsook Egypt" (11:
27) and "kept the passover" (11:28); and that it is also true "of
Gideon, Barak, Samson, Jephthah; of David and Samuel and the

prophets (11:32) who "wrought righteousness, obtained promises" (11:33) . . . "And these all, having had witness borne to them through their faith, received not the promise, God having provided some better thing concerning us, that apart from us they should not be made perfect" (11:39, 40). This is the "mystery" which has been kept silenced through times eternal.

Verse 26 . . . but now is manifested, and by the scriptures of the prophets, according to the commandment of the eternal God, is made known unto all the nations unto obedience of faith . . . :

What was a mystery in the ages past has now been manifested through the prophetic writings. It still is manifested until the present time. The Old Testament prophetic writings are its proof and authentication (Luke 24:27, 44). It is all in accord with God's eternal plan and program that this message must not be kept within the confines of Israel but is to be made known unto "all the Gentiles" and many shall render submissive faith (Romans 1:5) in this Person and plan which is now revealed (Romans 1:2; 3:21; Hebrews 1:1, 2).

What then is this mystery? It is salvation and it is centered in one Person, "And in none other is there salvation: for neither is there any other name under heaven, that is given among men, wherein we must be saved" (Acts 4:12). "And the witness is this, that God gave unto us eternal life, and this life is in his Son" (I John 5:11). When God sent His Son into the world, "the mystery" was revealed and "in him dwelleth all the fulness of the Godhead bodily" (Colossians 2:9).

V. 26: ". . . according to the commandment of the eternal God. . . ." To this writer these words reveal the true source of divine inspiration. "All scripture is given by inspiration of God . . ." (II Timothy 3:16 KJV) ". . . but men spake from God, being moved by the Holy Spirit" (II Peter 1:21). The plan and program of salvation is not something new that God brought to pass because an emergency had to be met. It is an eternal plan (see Ephesians 1:4; I Peter 1:19, 20; Revelation 13:8). It is all centered in God's eternal Son.

Have you accepted God's eternal Son? To know Him is to love Him and be loved by Him forever.

Verse 27: . . . to the only wise God, through Jesus Christ, to whom be the glory for ever. Amen.

Paul is a Mono-Theistic Trinitarian and so is this writer. To believe in three gods is simple heathenism. There is only one God (Ephesians 4:4, 5) and no more. This being the case, and the Bible teaches this, ". . . yet to us there is one God, the Father, of whom are all things, and we unto him; and one Lord, Jesus Christ, through whom are all things, and we through him" (I Corinthians 8:6).

In the Godhead there are three Persons, God the Father, God the Son, God the Holy Spirit. The Holy Spirit indwells every person who accepts Christ, and the Lord Jesus Christ is the only way to the Father (John 14:6) and eternal life. This is what Paul is saying in verse 27. The way ". . . to the only wise God, (is) through Jesus Christ, to whom be the glory for ever." To whom else can a sinner give the glory for his salvation?

God gave His Son on the cross for the sinner. God works out our salvation for us with the righteousness belonging to Jesus Christ. He indwells us on this life's journey through the Holy Spirit and will ultimately bring us into God's presence, ". . . being confident of this very thing, that he who began a good work in you will perfect it until the day of Jesus Christ . . ." (Philippians 1:6).

Glory to God! We do not have to depend upon ourselves. Is this not the theme of this entire Epistle? Is this not the way the Apostle Paul began this Epistle? He never veered off his course from beginning to end. Christ was his incentive in life and his goal of achievement, "I press on toward the goal unto the prize of the high calling of God in Christ Jesus" (Philippians 3:14). "For me to live is Christ . . ." (Philippians 1:21).

What a wonderful way for this Hebrew Christian warrior of the cross to close his Epistle to the Roman saints! No wonder it has lived through the ages and has been the means of great encouragement for every saint through the centuries.

Dear reader, may this commentary bring you closer to Christ than when you first began to read it. This writer's testimony corroborates exactly such an experience for himself. Thanks be to God for His wonderful plan of salvation as revealed in Jesus Christ. And thanks be to God for choosing this writer, one from among the lost sheep of the house of Israel, for His own.

Amen.

BIBLIOGRAPHY

Alford, Henry, *The Greek Testament* (Moody Press: Chicago, n.d.)
    Anyalytical Greek Lexicon (Harper Bros.: New York, n.d.)

Barnes, Albert, *Romans* (Kregel Publishing: Grand Rapids, 1962)

Barnhouse, Donald G., *Epistle to the Romans* (Eerdmans: Grand Rapids, 1963)

Barclay, Wm., *Letters to the Romans, The* (St. Andrews Press, Edinburgh).

Brown, David, *Epistle to the Romans, The* (Zondervan: Grand Rapids, 1950)

Burton, Ernest DeWitt, *Syntax of the Moods and Tenses in the New Testament* (University of Chicago Press: Chicago, 1912)

Chamberlain, William Douglas, *An Exegetical Grammar of the Greek New Testament* (Macmillan Co.: New York, n.d.)

Coynbeare, W. J. and J. S. Hawson, *Life and Epistles of St. Paul, The* (Eerdmans: Grand Rapids, 1964)

Gill, Dr., *Commentary* Vol. 6, 1960

Haldane, Robert, *Epistle to the Romans* (Robert Carter & Brothers: New York, 1864)

Hodge, Charles, *Epistle to the Romans* (Eerdmans: Grand Rapids, 1964)

Hertz, J. H., *Soncino Edition of the Pentateuch & Haftorahs, The* (Soncino Press: New York, 1950)

Kittel, Gerhard, *Theological Dictionary of the New Testament* (Eerdmans: Grand Rapids, 1966)

Lange, J. P., *Epistle to the Romans* (Scribner and Sons: New York, 1871)

Liddell, Henry and Robert Scott, *Greek-English Lexicon* (Oxford Press: Oxford, 1961)

Liddon, Henry, *St. Paul's Epistle to the Romans* (Zondervan: Grand Rapids, 1961)

Luther, Martin, *Commentary on the Epistle to the Romans* (Zondervan: Grand Rapids, 1960)

Montefiore, E. G. and H. Lowe, *Rabbinic Anthology, A* (World: Cleveland, Ohio, n.d.)

Moulton, James H. and George Milligan, *Vocabulary of the Greek Testament, The* (Eerdmans: Grand Rapids, 1957)

Nestle, *Greek New Testament* (Ragster: England, 1952)

Newell, William R., *Romans Verse by Verse* (Moody Press: Chicago, 1941)

Newton, B. W., *Lectures on Romans* (C. M. Tuckey: England, 1918)

Norris, J. Frank, *Lectures on Romans*, n.d.

493

✓Robertson, A. T., *Word Pictures in the New Testament* (Broadman Press: Nashville, 1930)

Sanday, William and Arthur Headlam, *Romans: International Critical Commentary* (Scribner's: New York, 1898)

Scholtz, *Student Analytical Greek Testament, The* (Bagster & Sons, Ltd. Acquired by Macmillan Co., New York, n.d.)

  Septuagint Old Testament (Bagster, England, n.d.)

Spence, H. D. M. and J. S. Exell, *Pulpit Commentary, The* (Fleming Revell: New York, 1943)

Stenning, J. F., *Targum of Isaiah, The* (Oxford, The Clarendon Press: London, 1953)

Stifler, James, *Epistle to the Romans, The* (Fleming Revell: New York, 1960)

Thayer, Joseph H., *Greek-English Lexicon of the New Testament* (Zondervan: Grand Rapids, 1963)

Tischendorf, Constantine, *New Testament, The* (Pott & Amery, n.d.)

University of Chicago Press, *Greek-English Lexicon of the New Testament* (Zondervan: Grand Rapids, 1963)

Vincent, *Word Studies in the New Testament* (Eerdmans).

✓Wuest, Kenneth, *Romans in the Greek New Testament* (Eerdmans: Grand Rapids, 1958)

INDEX